PROOF *of* CONSPIRACY

ALSO BY SETH ABRAMSON

Proof of Collusion

PROOF *of* CONSPIRACY

How Trump's
International Collusion
Is Threatening
American Democracy

Seth Abramson

ST. MARTIN'S
PRESS
NEW YORK

First published in the United States by St. Martin's Press,
an imprint of St. Martin's Publishing Group

www.stmartins.com

Designed by Steven Seighman

The Library of Congress Cataloging-in-Publication Data is available upon request.

ISBN 978-1-250-25671-3 (hardcover)
ISBN 978-1-250-25672-0 (ebook)

Our books may be purchased in bulk for promotional, educational, or business use. Please
contact your local bookseller or the Macmillan Corporate and Premium Sales Department at
1-800-221-7945, extension 5442, or by email at MacmillanSpecialMarkets@macmillan.com.

First Edition: September 2019

10 9 8 7 6 5 4 3 2 1

For the nation

Contents

AUTHOR'S NOTE ON ENDNOTES, PREFATORY MATERIAL, AND NAMES

The 3,350 endnotes for *Proof of Conspiracy*, comprising 4,300 individual citations, run over 250 pages. For this reason—and to ensure that this key element of the text is both link-enabled and searchable—it has been published for free online rather than in the pages of this book. You can find it at www.read.macmillan.com/proofofconspiracynotes. The pages at this link are numbered in a manner consistent with the numbering they would have received had they appeared in the print edition of *Proof of Conspiracy*.

As this book is the sequel to *Proof of Collusion* (Simon & Schuster, 2018), the contents of that book should be regarded as prefatory material to the contents of this one. Except where clearly necessary, *Proof of Conspiracy* does not reiterate the information about the Trump-Russia investigation contained in *Proof of Collusion*.

Proof of Conspiracy discusses the activities of certain individuals with Arabic names. These names, and the others that appear throughout the text, are listed alphabetically in an index at the back of the book. Note that compound Arabic surnames that include a definite article as their prefix are maintained as such in this text. Thus, for instance, "Yousef al-Otaiba" is "al-Otaiba" throughout the work, rather than "Otaiba," despite conventions permitting either transliteration.

THE RED SEA CONSPIRACY AND THE GRAND BARGAIN

In late 2015, after Donald Trump has formally announced his candidacy for president, a geopolitical conspiracy emerges overseas whose key participants are the leaders of Russia, Israel, Saudi Arabia, the United Arab Emirates, Bahrain, and Egypt. These six men decide that Trump is the antidote to their ills: for Russia, U.S. sanctions; for Israel, the lack of Arab allies; for Saudi Arabia, the United Arab Emirates, Bahrain, and Egypt, perceived threats emanating from Iran. The conspirators commit themselves to doing whatever is necessary to ensure that Trump is elected. Trump's presidential campaign is aware of and benefits from this conspiracy both before and after the 2016 election.

On March 19, 2018, British journalist David Hearst, the former chief foreign leader writer for the *Guardian*, publishes the most important report of his career. Hearst, at one time the Moscow bureau chief at the *Guardian,* is now editor in chief of his own publishing venture, a London-based Middle East watchdog called the *Middle East Eye.* In the spring of 2018, he reports the existence of a years-long, continent-spanning conspiracy that will eventually envelop the president of the United States: the Red Sea Conspiracy.[1]

This book denominates the conspiracy Hearst uncovers as the "Red

Sea Conspiracy" for the simple reason that it is hatched on a yacht in the middle of the Red Sea, a seawater inlet of the Indian Ocean bordered by, among other countries, Saudi Arabia and Egypt.[2] One imagines that in his many years as a correspondent and commentator for the *Scotsman*, the *Huffington Post*, Al Jazeera (Qatar), *Al-Araby Al-Jadeed* (England), TRT World (Turkey), *Masr Al-Aan* (Egypt), and the *Guardian*, Hearst never thought he'd stumble on a story as far-reaching in its implications as the Red Sea Conspiracy.[3] But he did—and what he found could change the course of history.

This book chronicles the events around the globe that preceded and followed the fall 2015 origin of the conspiracy, with a special focus on how the conspiracy prompted Donald Trump and his aides, allies, and associates to covertly collude with six countries both before and after the 2016 presidential election: Russia, Saudi Arabia, the United Arab Emirates, Israel, Bahrain, and Egypt. Events that began on the Red Sea in 2015 now influence President Trump's foreign policy toward all of these countries, toward other countries not involved in the conspiracy such as Qatar and Iran, and, more broadly, toward Europe, Asia, and the Middle East.

The story of the Red Sea Conspiracy begins with a man named George Nader. As reported by Hearst in the *Middle East Eye*, toward the end of 2015 Nader—then an adviser to the crown prince of Abu Dhabi, Mohammed bin Zayed al-Nahyan (known as "MBZ")—convened, with his patron's permission, a summit of some of the Middle East's most powerful leaders.[4] Gathered on a boat in the Red Sea in the fall of 2015 were Mohammed bin Salman (known as "MBS"), deputy crown prince of Saudi Arabia, who would shortly become the heir apparent to the throne of the Saudi kingdom; MBZ himself, by 2015 the de facto ruler of the United Arab Emirates; Abdel Fattah el-Sisi, the president of Egypt; Prince Salman bin Hamad, the crown prince of Bahrain; and King Abdullah II of Jordan. Nader, the improbable maestro of these rulers' clandestine get-together, intended the plan he posed to the men to include the nation of Libya, but no representative from that nation attended the gathering.[5]

Of the leaders aboard the yacht, two—MBS and MBZ—are already close. According to a *New Yorker* interview with Richard A. Clarke, a counterterrorism adviser to Presidents Barack Obama and George W. Bush, MBS and MBZ "talk on the phone all day to each other."[6] The Red Sea meeting, though technically convened by Nader, is a means for MBZ to advance ambitions that he and MBS have designed together.[7]

The two Sunni Arab leaders' intention, Hearst records, is to remake the Middle East with the covert assistance of a highly placed American politician. They intend to do this by first renaming and reconstituting the membership of the six-member Gulf Cooperation Council (GCC)—which in 2015 comprises Saudi Arabia, the United Arab Emirates, Bahrain, Kuwait, Oman, and Qatar—while reorienting, too, its regional ambitions and global alliances.[8] The proposed GCC realignment would evict Kuwait, Oman, and Qatar from the council and replace these three countries with Egypt, Jordan, and Libya, thereby eliminating the entity's historical association with the Persian Gulf and remaking it as, instead, an alliance constituting "an elite regional group of six countries, which would supplant [the GCC and] . . . form the nucleus of [a coalition of] pro-U.S. and pro-Israeli states" in the Middle East.[9] According to two sources briefed on the 2015 Red Sea summit, "Nader said this group of states could become a force in the region 'that the United States government could depend on' to counter the influence of Turkey and Iran."[10]

Prior to 2015, Turkey and Saudi Arabia had intermittently enjoyed strong diplomatic ties, but by the second-to-last year of the Obama administration relations had soured considerably. As explained by Nader Habibi, a Brandeis University economist specializing in the Middle East, the Turkey–Saudi Arabia relationship "deteriorated in the '90s when the kingdom [Saudi Arabia] took Syria's side in several disputes with [Syria's] neighbor Turkey. These ups and downs in Saudi-Turkish relations were partly a result of Turkey's political instability, including several military coups in the '80s and '90s. Relations tended to improve when Islamist or civilian parties—which felt close cultural and religious links with Turkey's Muslim neighbors—were in power but worsened after the military deposed them."[11] This cycle continued unabated up until 2011, when, Habibi writes, "the Arab spring uprisings . . . led to the overthrow of governments in Tunisia, Egypt and Libya. As an advocate of political Islam, [Turkish president Recep Tayyip] Erdogan welcomed the revolutions and the new governments they yielded. The Saudi government, on the other hand, saw the revolts as destabilizing."[12] Erdogan therefore supported, while Saudi Arabia did not, Mohammed Morsi, the Muslim Brotherhood–linked politician who took power in Egypt in 2012.[13] So it is little surprise that, according to *Foreign Affairs* magazine, Saudi Arabia and Turkey were "bitter frenemies" by 2012.[14]

When a 2013 military coup ended Morsi's tenure as president, replacing him with el-Sisi, "Erdogan strongly condemned it [the coup] and gave the Muslim Brotherhood refuge in Turkey, while Saudi Arabia offered billions in financial aid to cement Egypt's new military rulers."[15] Saudi-Turkish relations immediately took a turn for the worse.

A similar reversal of historical trends—certain members of the Persian Gulf axis of Saudi Arabia, the UAE, and Bahrain supporting a military government and opposing an Islamist or civilian one—was seen in 2016 in Turkey, when a military coup sought to depose Erdogan; the Turks would subsequently accuse the Emiratis of sponsoring the attempted takeover.[16] The Emirates' alleged clandestine support for Erdogan's overthrow in 2016 had been preceded in 2014 by a Saudi- and Egyptian-led campaign to end Turkey's bid to become one of the nonpermanent members of the United Nations Security Council.[17] The evidence suggests, therefore, that by 2015 Saudi-Turkish, Egyptian-Turkish, and Emirati-Turkish relations were at a low point.

Following the Nader-orchestrated anti-Iran/anti-Turkey summit on the Red Sea, the six-nation Arab coalition Nader and his patron MBZ had originally imagined contracts. Libya, having not sent a representative to the Red Sea gathering, ceases to be a central part of its plan; and per the *Middle East Eye*, Jordan eventually "fell out dramatically with the group which had gathered on the yacht: Saudi Arabia decided that Amman did not go far enough in enforcing the [June 2017 Saudi] blockade against Qatar."[18] The Saudis were further angered by Jordan's refusal to vote in favor of Trump's December 2017 decision to move the U.S. embassy in Israel from Tel Aviv to Jerusalem; as Hearst writes in his exposé on the Red Sea Conspiracy, "The split between Saudi [Arabia] and Jordan widened further when Jordan voted against Trump's move to recognise Jerusalem as the capital of Israel, which threatens Jordan's role as custodian of the Holy Places in the city."[19]

Many months prior to the Red Sea summit, MBZ had begun advancing the political ambitions of his future co-conspirator MBS, "promoting Prince bin Salman in the Middle East and in Washington," according to the *New York Times*.[20] MBZ "has a history of personal antipathy toward [MBS's rival for the Saudi throne] Prince bin Nayef," the *Times* reports, and in April 2015, while meeting "a small delegation of top [Obama] White House officials . . . at his home in McLean, V[irginia] . . . the prince [MBZ] urged the Americans to develop a relationship with Prince bin Salman."[21] That Obama's then secretary of state, John Kerry, was unable to do so despite apparent good-faith efforts—leading MBS to issue a public rant against what he perceived to be American foreign policy's failures in the Middle East at the November 2015 G20 summit in Turkey—could not have been missed by MBZ.[22] By comparison, the *Times* will later note, during Trump's presidency "Mr. Trump has closely allied himself with the Emiratis, endorsing their strong support for the new heir to the throne in Saudi Arabia," MBS.[23]

As Nader is coordinating a new coalition of Sunni Arab nations on the Red Sea, and doing so alongside the future ruler of Saudi Arabia and the current ruler of the UAE, the Saudi government is publicly presenting a different face with respect to its regional ambitions. In December 2015, Saudi foreign minister Adel al-Jubeir announces a thirty-four-nation Islamic military alliance against terrorism, which—despite MBS's intention of kicking Qatar off the GCC—includes the long-standing American ally; Saudi Arabia, the UAE, Egypt, and Bahrain will be blockading Qatar by air, land, and sea within eighteen months (see chapter 7).[24] One sign that the Saudis' proposed anti-terrorism alliance, nominally the brainchild of MBS, is from its start pretextual is that after the list of nations involved in the coalition is announced, several of those included declare that they had had no idea of its existence; indeed, only four countries—the UAE, Bahrain, Qatar, and Kuwait—are able to immediately confirm that they have entered into a military alliance with the Saudis.[25]

As clandestine geopolitical conspiracies go, Nader's—or, more properly, MBZ's and MBS's—seemed, on its face, fairly benign. If the ambitions of these Arab leaders had been public, who in America would have objected to a seismic political and military realignment in the Middle East, if the result were to be a coalition of Arab nations willing to work cooperatively with both the United States and Israel? And could Israel be blamed for wanting to see a new coalition of Arab countries in the Middle East more committed to the Jewish nation's survival than any previous permutation of its neighbors had ever been? Indeed, in hindsight some part of the ambitious vision promoted by MBZ and MBS might have been admirable, broadly writ: along with Syria, Sudan, and North Korea, Iran has been a designated state sponsor of terrorism since 1984, so contending with its regional and occasionally global designs has long been a key element of American foreign policy.[26] Even so, systematized corruption—let alone a direct assault on American democracy—in the name of plausibly benign middle- or long-term goals has never been something most Americans will accept, so it is little surprise that, whatever his or his patrons' intentions may have been, by early 2018 Nader had become a "focus" of a federal investigation over "possible attempts by the Emiratis to buy political influence by directing money to support Mr. Trump during the presidential campaign."[27]

While the Saudis' and Emiratis' broad and deep hostility toward Iran in 2015 was well in line with years of pre-Obama foreign policy in the United States, the two countries' growing enmity toward both Qatar and Turkey was not. Qatar is home to the U.S. military's largest base in the Middle East, and, as the *Los Angeles Times* notes, "Since the start of the Cold War, Turkey has been one of the United States' top allies in a region [the Middle East] not known for pro-American sentiment."[28]

Yet even those who cherish Turkey's historical role as a U.S. ally would concede that, in recent years, the relationship between the two countries has become strained because of the other nation in the Middle East (besides Iran) the United States has designated as a state sponsor of terrorism: Syria.[29] Since the Syrian civil war began in 2011, Turkey has been aggrieved at America's support for Kurdish troops in and around the war-torn nation. In the early years of the civil war, the United States trained and equipped the Kurds while maintaining that it materially supported only those Kurdish forces "in areas east of the Euphrates River as well as Manbij [in northern Syria] against [the terrorist organization] Islamic State," considering any Kurdish forces in Afrin, a district in northwest Syria near Turkey, "a separate entity."[30] This policy was narrowly sustainable so long as the Islamic State remained a common enemy of the United States, Turkey, and Kurdish forces; once the Islamic State had been largely defeated in Syria, however, Kurdish-led troops formed a "border security force"—and America's and Turkey's interests diverged.[31]

In 2018, Turkey launched what it called Operation Olive Branch, an effort by Turkish troops and allied Syrian Arab militia to drive the Kurds from Afrin. As the *Times* notes, "Turkey's political leadership . . . touted the operation in Afrin as a war not just against Kurdish forces, but also against the United States."[32] Moreover, Turkish president Erdogan accused the United States of deliberately establishing a "terror corridor" in northern Syria by permitting Syrian Kurdish militia to operate there freely; the United States, for its part, considered these militiamen to be an "on-the-ground vanguard against [a resurgence of] the militant group Islamic State."[33]

America's relationship with Turkey was therefore, by 2018, at a "nadir," according to the *Times*, with Turkey "gripped by a patriotic frenzy" over the presence of armed Syrian Kurds in northwestern Syria and Erdogan calling "anyone in Turkey questioning the operation [to dislodge the Kurdish fighters] . . . a traitor."[34] Erdogan has said, of the prospect of protests in Turkey against Operation Olive Branch, "This is a national struggle. We would crush anybody who opposes this. There will be no compromises or tolerance on this issue."[35]

Meanwhile, another point of contention has arisen between Turkey and the United States: America's unwillingness to extradite to Turkey a Pennsylvania-dwelling cleric, Fethullah Gulen, who Erdogan claims was partially responsible for the failed mid-2016 military coup against his government. The question of Gulen's legal status became a flash point during the 2016 presidential election—and led to a federal criminal investigation against then candidate Donald Trump's top national security advisor, Michael Flynn.[36]

In January 2016, at the beginning of the Republican primary season, Donald Trump tells a crowd in Des Moines, "My whole life I've been greedy, greedy, greedy. I've grabbed all the money I could get. I'm so greedy."[37] The Iowans in the crowd pay close attention to the New York City businessman's words; so too, from afar, do royal observers in Saudi Arabia and the United Arab Emirates, who have known and taken advantage of Trump's greed for a long time—and who just a few months earlier had begun plotting, on a yacht in the Red Sea, how to turn Trump's greed into acquiescence to their geopolitical designs. MBS and MBZ know Trump will be of no mind to disclose any association they might covertly establish with him, any more than he would disclose his past financial ties to wealthy nationals from their respective countries. Indeed, in 2018 Trump will tweet—falsely—"For the record, I have no financial interests in Saudi Arabia . . . any suggestion that I have is just more FAKE NEWS."[38]

According to an opinion piece in the *Washington Post*, "If you're the Saudis, the nice thing about Trump is that he lacks any subtlety whatsoever, so you don't have to wonder how to approach him. He has said explicitly that the way to win his favor is to give him money. He has established means for you to do so—buying Trump properties and staying in Trump hotels."[39] Of course, once Trump becomes president any such publicly solicited largesse violates both his oath of office and the United States Constitution, a document that prohibits any president from accepting, as the *Post* observes, "'any present [or] Emolument . . . [from any] foreign State.' If a foreign country is putting money in the president's pocket on an ongoing basis, how in the world can we trust that the decisions he makes will be based on the best interests of the United States and not on his bank account?"[40]

The short answer is that in such a situation we would *not* be able to trust that U.S. foreign policy was in fact the product of American rather than foreign interests. The long answer—in Trump's case—is that if we trace the New York businessman's financial ties to the very nations that, in late 2015, decided to engage him in a clandestine conspiracy to fundamentally transform U.S. foreign policy, we quickly discover the difference between a president who works first and foremost for American interests and one who is, by his own confession, "greedy, greedy, greedy."

Trump's financial history with the nations of the Red Sea Conspiracy, as well as the two nations the conspirators seek to improve relations with, Israel and Russia, is long and illustrious. Trump has properties or other assets in two former Soviet republics, Saudi Arabia, UAE, Israel, and Egypt; he therefore maintains financial ties to three of the four nations involved in the conspiracy and one that stands to directly benefit from its successes.[41] While Trump's ongoing refusal to release his tax returns— despite promising to do so during the 2016 presidential campaign, then hiding behind the false excuse of an audit—makes it impossible to know the current status of his businesses in Israel or Egypt, Trump's ties to the other nations are clear.[42]

According to the *Washington Post*, "Trump's business relationships with the Saudi government—and rich Saudi business executives—go back to at least the 1990s."[43] CBS News calls Trump's ties to Saudi Arabia "long and deep," while noting that "he's often boasted about his business ties with the kingdom."[44] These ties include not just regular hotel and meeting-space bookings but much larger and more lucrative sales as well.[45] In 1987, Trump tells an interviewer, "I don't think anybody sells much more real estate than I do to . . . the Saudis. . . . They buy the most expensive apartments in the world, that I happen to build, and I know the people, and I like the people."[46] In 1991, as Trump faces close to a billion-dollar debt attributable to his failed casinos in Atlantic City, a Saudi royal, Prince Alwaleed bin Talal, purchases Trump's 281-foot yacht for $20 million, thereby helping save Trump from a potentially imminent bankruptcy filing.[47] Four years later, the same Saudi royal again saves Trump from bankruptcy by taking over Trump's 51 percent stake in New York's Plaza Hotel for $328 million—a financial transaction whose immediate result is that "Trump's creditors forg[i]ve $125 million of his debt."[48] The Associated Press reports that "in 2001, Trump sold the entire 45th floor of the Trump World Tower across from the United Nations in New York for $12 million, the biggest purchase in that building to that point. . . . The buyer: the Kingdom of Saudi Arabia."[49] And not long after Trump announces his presidential run in June 2015, he registers eight companies with "names tied to the country [Saudi Arabia]," according to the Associated Press, including several mentioning a major Saudi city, Jeddah.[50] The same day that he registers four of the companies—August 21, 2015—he tells a crowd at a rally in Alabama, "Saudi Arabia—and I get along great with all of them. They buy apartments from me. They spend $40 million, $50 million. Am I supposed to dislike them? I like them very much."[51] At another 2015 campaign rally Trump announces, "Saudi Arabia—I like the Saudis. They're very nice. I make a lot of money with them. They buy all sorts of my stuff. All kinds of toys from Trump. They pay me millions and hundreds of millions."[52] *Time* notes that "in 2016 business from the Saudis at the Trump hotel in Chicago helped offset losses there from reduced bookings."[53] While Trump's business ties to the United Arab Emirates are of more recent vintage, they are just as lucrative (see chapters 1, 2, and 9).

Yet by 2018, the year the possibility of Trump-Saudi collusion comes to be discussed by future committee leaders in the U.S. House of Representatives, Trump makes the following statements: "Saudi Arabia has nothing to do with me"; "I don't make deals with Saudi Arabia"; I don't have money from Saudi Arabia"; "I have nothing to do with Saudi Arabia"; and "I have no business whatsoever with Saudi Arabia. Couldn't care less."[54] Closer to the truth is a mid-2018 *New York Times* article reporting that Trump is "celebrated in the royal courts of Riyadh and Abu Dhabi as perhaps the best friend in the White House that their rulers have ever had."[55]

In 1980, a twenty-year-old college dropout by the name of George Nader founds an English-language magazine called *International Insight* in the basement of his Washington, D.C., apartment.[56] Nader, born in Batroun, Lebanon, but transplanted to the United States at the age of fifteen, has spoken English for less than five years, but has wanted to be a journalist since he was twelve.[57] The sixteen-page *International Insight*, with a circulation of 200 and an annual subscription cost of just $10, is produced by Nader and four assistants.[58]

After renaming the publication *Middle East Insight*, Nader is, by the late 1980s, featuring interviews with some of the top political figures in the Middle East.[59] In 1987, he meets Iran's Ayatollah Khomeini; his write-up of the event will be distributed by five hundred newspapers worldwide.[60] Nader's meeting with Khomeini also underscores his access to powerful figures in Afghanistan, Lebanon, and Egypt, as the event is attended by "leaders of the Afghan mujahedin, some senior officials of the Lebanese Shiite militia Hezbollah, and some Islamic fundamentalists from Egypt."[61] Nader will go on to interview other prominent figures in Middle Eastern and American politics, including President George H. W. Bush, President Bill Clinton (whom he interviews twice), former Iranian president Hashemi Rafsanjani, and Hezbollah secretary-general Hassan Nasrallah.[62] *Middle East Insight* eventually starts publishing policy forums, monographs, and roundtable discussions focused on hot-button topics from across the Middle East.[63]

Nader's professional successes in the 1980s are briefly interrupted when, in 1985, the twenty-five-year-old budding journalist faces a federal felony charge for transporting sexually explicit materials in foreign commerce—an offense colloquially known as "possession of child pornography"—in Washington, D.C.[64] The charges, involving the importation of magazines from the Netherlands depicting "pre- and post-pubescent boys engaged in a variety of sexual acts," are ultimately dismissed when the search warrant used to effectuate the search of Nader's home is invalidated.[65] During the case it is revealed that Nader "corresponded with several young boys and saved their letters," and that U.S. Customs inspectors also found in a package Nader had had delivered to his publication, in addition to the single obscene magazine over which he was charged, "two pictures . . . a film, four magazines, and an advertisement."[66] Nader denies all of the allegations.[67]

The mid-1980s sees Donald Trump, like Nader, run into some difficulties abroad that will later have repercussions for his life amid the world's political heavyweights. In 1987, Trump travels to Russia looking for real estate opportunities and finds none. He does, however, according to journalist Craig Unger—author of *House of Trump, House of Putin*—have an eventful trip nonetheless, with the Kremlin secretly collecting valuable blackmail material (known as *kompromat*) on the New York City real estate developer. According to Unger, whose information comes directly from former Russian general Oleg Kalugin, once the head of counterintelligence for the KGB, "Trump had lots of fun with lots of women" during his 1987 trip to Moscow, leading Kalugin to be "reasonably sure that the KGB had *kompromat* from that visit."[68]

During the 1990s, as Trump continues to pursue building opportunities in Russia, Nader's U.S.-based *Middle East Insight* becomes a bimonthly publication with a website, an internship program, and a circulation of nearly 10,000. It charges $100 for an annual subscription and comes to be considered, according to the *Daily Star* (Lebanon), as "one of the most authoritative publications on the Middle East" in the world.[69] In 1996, according to Israeli media outlet *Haaretz*, Nader "host[s] [Benjamin] Netanyahu [in Washington] shortly after his first election as prime minister," later "forg[ing] even closer ties with Netanyahu and his bureau [by] . . . serv[ing] as Ronald Lauder's assistant in the cosmetic tycoon's failed efforts to secure a peace deal between Netanyahu and Syria's president at the time, Hafez al-Assad. Netanyahu's advisers have acknowledged their contacts with Nader, who is said to have been especially close to Dore Gold, the prime minister's aide and former UN ambassador."[70]

The *Daily Star* will write in 2000 that a monograph published by *Middle East Insight* discussing disputed boundary lines in the Golan Heights not only was quoted in the *New York Times*, the *Washington Post*, and multiple Israeli newspapers but also was "used by the highest political officials involved in negotiations as the acceptable delineation of the [disputed boundary] line."[71] According to the Lebanese newspaper, and to Nader himself, *Middle East Insight* is distinguishable in the 2000s from other papers covering the Middle East by "present[ing] the public with pro-Arab and pro-American and pro-Jewish sides."[72] Nader tells the *Daily Star* in 2000 that his goal is to think about the Middle East "with fairness and from every angle possible. . . . To get the whole picture. . . . In the midst of the confusion of the '80s, the conflicts, the stress and bloodshed, there were too many polemics, too many dogmatic, heated, emotional parties running the publications [covering the Middle East] in the United States. We needed more balance, non-partisanism, an objective viewpoint."[73]

The result of Nader's even-handed ethos, however, is ultimately controversy for *Middle East Insight*. "Certain pro-Arabs," reports the *Daily Star*, "accuse [Nader] of spying and collaborating with 'the Zionist enemy' [Israel]."[74] The *New York Times* will later call *Middle East Insight* an "unusual Washington magazine" and note that Nader uses it as a "platform for Arab, Israeli and Iranian officials to express their views" to policymakers in Washington—making it as much a professional service for American politicians as a rhetorical vehicle for various influential foreigners.[75]

In 1991, just as *Middle East Insight* is gaining a significant reputation among D.C. politicos, the then thirty-one-year-old Nader pleads guilty to another federal charge of transporting sexually explicit materials in foreign commerce; he serves six months at a halfway house.[76] The child pornography had been found in his luggage at Washington's Dulles International Airport upon his return from a trip to Germany.[77] As the charge to which Nader pleads guilty carries a penalty of up to ten years in prison, being allowed to serve time in a halfway house is unusual; in 2018, *Politico* will reveal that Nader's lenient sentence was the result of an extraordinary arrangement between him and federal prosecutors.[78] "The court proceedings [in 1991] were far from typical," *Politico* writes. "While the charges were pending, Nader made at least five trips overseas with court permission: four to Beirut and one to Moscow. Prosecutors also agreed with the defense to put the entire case under seal 'due to the extremely sensitive nature of Mr. Nader's work in the Middle East,' court records show. Later filings make clear that the trips and delays in the case were due to Nader's involvement in negotiations to free U.S. hostages being held in Lebanon."[79] At the time, Nader's attorneys represented in filings to the court that "no one else" could do the negotiations in the Middle East that Nader was then doing, and that his work was therefore "essential" to America's interests.[80] Oddly, the federal prosecutors working on Nader's case told the court that the defendant's overseas work was even "opaque to the State Department and other officials."[81]

Nader's conviction and brief halfway house stint appear to have had no effect on the operation of his newspaper. Indeed, though prison records document that Nader completed a six-month stint in a Baltimore halfway house in June 1992, a video "aired on C-SPAN in March 1992 shows him [Nader] hosting a discussion in his capacity as editor" of *Middle East Insight*.[82]

As the 1990s wear on, high-profile D.C. politicians publicly express gratitude for the service Nader's work provides to the Washington political establishment. For instance, in 1996 Congressman Nick Rahall (D-WV) praises Nader on the floor of the House, lauding him as a "recognized expert" on the Middle East, noting that he has "remarkable access to key political and business leaders throughout the region," and praising *Middle East Insight* for publishing the viewpoints of powerful Egyptians (Hosni Mubarak), Israelis (Yitzhak Rabin), and Palestinians (Yasir Arafat).[83] A former top diplomat in the State Department who knew Nader in the 1990s, Frederic Hof—a specialist in Middle East geopolitics and affairs relating to Syria, Israel, and Lebanon particularly—will tell the *New York Times* in 2018, of his experiences with Nader during the Clinton administration, "He always struck me as a person who really thought he should be in the eye of the storm trying to make things happen" in the Middle East.[84] Nader's activities in the 1990s would seem to confirm Hof's observation, as according to the *Times* Nader had, by the end of the decade, "convinced the Clinton administration that he had valuable contacts in the Syrian government and took on a secretive role trying to broker a peace deal between Israel and Syria."[85] The newspaper notes that Nader had "contacts in both capitals [Damascus and Jerusalem]" who were sufficiently highly placed to "try to negotiate a truce" between the two nations.[86] Indeed, Nader is so well connected to government officials in Israel and several of its neighbors that Clinton's ambassador to Israel, Martin Indyk, will tell the *Times* that "in the 1990s, George was a very effective under-the-radar operator in the peace process" between Israel and several Muslim nations.[87] Indyk reports that Nader traveled to Syria with Lauder, the future president of the World Jewish Congress, "16 times" in 1998 alone to try to "advance an Israeli-Syrian peace agreement."[88] In 2001, Nader again proves his deep connections to the Israeli government by organizing an event whose featured guest is the prime minister of Israel at the time, Shimon Peres. The event is held at the home of Mark Penn, a former top adviser to President Bill Clinton. At least one congressman, Darrell Issa (R-CA), attends the event, as do a number of "Arab American businessmen."[89]

In June 2019, at a time when Nader is a cooperating witness in federal law enforcement's investigation of foreign influence on the 2016 presidential election—including possible payments by the Saudis and Emiratis to the Trump campaign—Nader will be arrested yet again on child pornography charges, this time on a federal arrest warrant issued by the Eastern District of Virginia; given Nader's status as a cooperating witness, the charges, which could imprison Nader for a minimum of fifteen and a maximum of forty years, strongly suggest that either he has breached his 2018 partial-immunity deal with the FBI or that the FBI has discovered new information about what Nader was doing in the United States and abroad in the run-up to Trump's victory.[90]

One of the major changes in global geopolitics during the 1990s involves Israel and another nation with whom Nader's professional career as a dealmaker will come to be entwined, the United Arab Emirates. A major thaw in relations between the UAE and Israel leads to Israel's agreement not to block an American sale of F-16 fighter jets to the Emiratis; that decision, in turn, leads the tiny Gulf nation to decide to engage with the Israelis directly (if discreetly) over the two countries' shared apprehension of what both perceive to be a growing Iranian threat.[91] Meanwhile, despite a long-standing Saudi-Emirati alliance, the Saudi-Israeli relationship remains virtually nonexistent. It will require a new ruler to arise in the kingdom for Riyadh to see, as the Emiratis increasingly do, the value in a semipublic military détente with the Israelis.[92] Whereas, toward the end of the Clinton administration, a senior Emirati official is heard by an American official conceding, "I can envision us being in the trenches with Israel fighting against Iran," as late as the first year of the Obama administration, Saudi king Abdullah bin Abdulaziz Al Saud tells President Obama, "We'll be the last ones [in the Middle East] to make peace with

[Israel]."[93] Both Emirati and U.S. officials must have seen, in 2008, that any Saudi-Israeli rapprochement would have to wait until the old guard within the House of Saud was gone. And by 2015, it would be.

Just like the word "collusion," "conspiracy" can be understood in both a lay sense and a legal sense. If your friends secretly agree to keep information from you about your spouse's marital infidelity, that's a conspiracy, but it's not illegal; by the same token, if six nations secretly agree to vote in a bloc on a given United Nations resolution, we might call that a conspiracy without also calling it a violation of international law. There is, of course, a U.S. criminal statute governing the legal—or, rather, illegal—sort of conspiracy, and it says, broadly, that if there's a meeting of the minds between two or more people to achieve an illegal purpose, and if a given member within that group of people executes an act in furtherance of that illegal purpose, that person is guilty of conspiracy whether or not the illegal purpose is ever achieved.[94] But as is evident from this broad legal definition, "conspiracy," even in the statutory sense, is a catchall term: there can be a conspiracy to bribe someone, or a conspiracy to commit fraud, or a conspiracy to commit computer crimes, or a conspiracy to solicit or receive illegal campaign contributions—essentially, anything one can do that is illegal can also be done in an inchoate form as part of a conspiracy to achieve that end alongside other people.

In this respect, "conspiracy" comes up in the context of the ongoing Trump-Russia scandal in the same way that the nonlegal term "collusion" does: both are things one can do without committing a crime, but also things that one can do *while* committing a crime. The main difference is that an illegal conspiracy is likely to be charged *as* a conspiracy, whereas non-conspiracy-related collusive behavior, when and where it is illegal, will be charged as something else—for instance, aiding and abetting, bribery, money laundering, or even, depending upon the underlying facts, obstruction of justice or witness tampering.

Broadly speaking, one engages in collusion when one acts purposefully in response to or in concert with the actions of another party, whether or not there is an underlying crime involved and whether or not there is an explicit agreement to work toward a common goal. Thus, if President Trump obstructs an investigation into Russian election interference in a way he knows will protect the Russian Federation from any repercussions for its illegal acts, and if the Kremlin responds by acting in a manner favorable to the Trump administration but contrary to U.S. law, both parties can see and appreciate the reactions their past, present, and future behaviors are provoking in the other party, and can see that those maneuvers are mutually beneficial, even if there is no unambiguous public agreement to proceed in that fashion. Collusive conduct at the level of the U.S. and foreign governments is a grave national security threat if one or more of the foreign nationals with whom U.S. government actors are colluding do not have America's best interests at heart—which, in the zero-sum game of global geopolitics, is often how the matter stands. To collude with a foreign nation is, definitionally, to act under its influence, and if the collusion is secret, the chances that one's self-justification is personal rather than patriotic are high.

In the case of the Trump-Russia scandal—not just that segment of it investigated by the special counsel, Robert Mueller, but the full scope of the scandal as it has come to encompass other entities and crimes besides those directly connected to Russian election interference in 2016—there is conspiracy to be found in both the lay and legal senses. The president's son-in-law, Jared Kushner, used an encrypted messaging app to conspire, throughout 2017 and 2018, with the Saudi crown prince, Mohammed bin Salman, in a way that altered permanently the geopolitics of the Middle East (see chapter 7); while these clandestine discussions were not in themselves illegal, they appear to have been coupled with the Trump campaign's acceptance of donations from Saudi and other foreign nationals during the 2016 campaign (see chapters 3, 5, and 7). Just so, while the Red Sea Conspiracy hatched in 2015 was not, at its birth, an illegal act—foreign nationals are entitled to passively root for one U.S. political candidate over another, and to form geopolitical alliances based on shared policy agendas—it became so when it blossomed into a course of covert pre-election assistance that included, per reporting, collusive behavior in both the lay and legal senses. And to the extent that this collusion continues today in the form of President Trump's historically idiosyncratic foreign policy in the Middle East—one that places the interests of the Saudis, Emiratis, Israelis, and even Russians ahead of those of Americans—it is criminal not because the president cannot form whatever foreign policy he wishes, but because he cannot form a foreign policy for which he has received compensation. Likewise, his agenda cannot induce continued crimes against America by foreign nationals or entities.

Just as I focused on two types of collusion in the prequel to this book, *Proof of Collusion*—both collusion in the lay sense and collusive behavior as we find it encoded in certain criminal statutes—in this book I consider both conspiratorial conduct of the geopolitical sort and also statutory conspiracies such as conspiracies to commit bribery or fraud, launder money, or obstruct justice.

Here, as in *Proof of Collusion*, I use the term "proof" in the sense it is commonly understood by laypeople: as evidence that helps establish the truth of a proposition. Proof exists, in a given situation, if there is evidence that helps establish something as true—whether or not the standard of proof required to reach a final conclusion is met. For instance, in a criminal prosecution, proof beyond a reasonable doubt is needed for conviction; in a counterintelligence investigation, proof by a preponderance of the evidence—or even less—may be sufficient cause to believe someone is acting under the influence of a foreign nation, and therefore is a potential national security threat. Used in this way, the term "proof" is equivalent to the legal phrase "probative evidence": that is, evidence that tends to point toward the truth of a proposition, whether or not it conclusively establishes it.

The backdrop for the conspiracies and collusive behavior described in this book is a geopolitical landscape in the Middle East markedly different than it was just twenty years ago. Today, Israel and many of its Arab neighbors—including and most particularly the Sunni nations Saudi Arabia, the United Arab Emirates, Bahrain, and Egypt—meet secretly on peaceful terms to share military technology and plot the destruction of their common enemy, Iran. Russia, a newly omnipresent superpower in

Middle Eastern politics, is increasingly seen by many of these nations as a viable economic and even military partner, in some instances more so than the United States is. The once all-encompassing Israeli-Palestinian conflict, while still on the minds of many in the Arab "street," has faded from view among certain leaders in the capital cities of Riyadh, Doha, Cairo, Manama, and Abu Dhabi. Many of the region's power brokers have come to believe that economic development and joint opposition to Iranian gambits in Syria, Yemen, Iraq, and elsewhere is more important to the future of the Middle East than the achievement of a hard-won two-state solution in the Israeli-occupied Palestinian territories—especially if pursuit of that ambition threatens a burgeoning Arab-Israeli alliance.

As fears about the continued viability of oil as a nation's chief export grow, the two most influential nations in the Persian Gulf, Saudi Arabia and the United Arab Emirates, increasingly lust not just for the expansion of their present dominant role on the global oil market but for nuclear power, possibly even nuclear weapons. More broadly, the internationalization of national interests—the way the future of a nation probably hinges more now on the relations between two or more other nations than was the case decades ago—is leading many Arab rulers to believe that only a historic détente between the United States and Russia can lead to economic prosperity and peace for many Middle Eastern countries. On the near side of that vision, however, looms a terrifying prospect: an all-out war between the United States, Israel, certain Sunni Arab nations, and Iran—a conflict that, especially if it draws into its maw such interested parties as Turkey and Russia or even China, could engulf the Earth in a third world war. Far preferable, the conspirators of the Red Sea Conspiracy concluded in 2015, would be a pre-election rapprochement between the GOP presidential candidate in 2016 and a Russian president whose divisive global agenda could be made to further the ambitions of several Arab states.

It is with all these stakes in mind that international onlookers watched the rise of Donald Trump in 2015. Trump was, as clearly to those abroad as to those in the United States, a man without set principles or dogma; he therefore was quickly adjudged to be a man whose sympathies, loyalties, and political agenda could be bought by any one or several of the nations that had already helped make him rich over the years. There has already been much discussion of how the Kremlin spotted early on the opportunities a Trump candidacy promised; simultaneously, however, the Saudis and Emiratis marked not just these myriad possibilities but the additional slate of possibilities opened up by the Kremlin's burgeoning interest in a political neophyte with malleable ethics. The same Arab nations that feared that President Obama's peaceful entreaties to Iran could be a preview of what a Hillary Clinton administration would bring therefore steeled their resolve to avoid that eventuality by whatever means possible.

The resulting plot to ensure—with the help of Donald Trump's vanity and boundless acquisitiveness—that a venal New York City businessman would be the next occupant of the Oval Office is the complex, globe-spanning subject matter of this book. The Red Sea Conspiracy, variously referred to by its participants and in media as the "grand bargain" or the "Middle East Marshall Plan," is in its basic contours relatively simple: the Saudis, Emiratis, Israelis, Bahrainis, and Egyptians, in conjunction with the Russians, aid Trump's election as the next U.S. president while encouraging him to drop all sanctions on the Russian Federation if and when he secures election. In compensation for this dramatic reversal of U.S. policy toward Russia—an about-face worth hundreds of billions of dollars to the Kremlin in recaptured post-sanctions revenue—the Russians will withdraw their support for Iran in Syria and elsewhere, thereby enabling the Red Sea conspirators to conclusively conquer their Iranian foes. The conspirators' post-bargain expectations are likewise easy to summarize: (1) the isolation of U.S. allies Turkey and Qatar, whose government-affiliated media organs have been unkind to the Saudis and their allies, and whose warm and comparatively uncomplicated relationships with America the Saudis and Emiratis particularly covet; (2) the receipt of American assistance in pushing back against Iranian aggression in the region, both indirectly (against alleged Iranian proxies in Syria and Yemen) and directly (in the form of aiding the Saudis and Emiratis in becoming nuclear powers capable of threatening Iran directly); (3) the receipt of a massive influx of out-of-region infrastructure and other investment from both the Americans and the Russians, with the aim of sidelining the Israeli-Palestinian debate in favor of a new focus on economic development across the Gulf region; (4) the establishment of a new pro-Israel and pro-American military alliance of Sunni Arab nations that will constitute one of the world's largest and most commanding fighting forces, to be overseen—in both its legal and illicit operations—by MBS and MBZ; (5) and the standing down of pro-democracy forces within and outside the U.S. government in the face of encroaching autocracy in Israel and certain of America's Arab allies— chiefly Saudi Arabia, the United Arab Emirates, and Egypt.

This grand bargain was to be overseen by MBZ, MBS, and Egypt's el-Sisi in coordination with both the Kremlin and Donald Trump. It is as audacious a plot as the world has seen in half a century, requiring years of continent-crossing communications, negotiations, and accommodations that must go unseen by major media until they are complete. It is a complex story drawing into its matrix of persons, places, and events nationals from at least a dozen countries, and it begins many years ago with the slowly converging exploits of three men: a pedophile, a mercenary, and a political flack.

CHAPTER 1

THE PEDOPHILE,
THE MERCENARY,
AND THE FLACK

As future Trump advisers George Nader, Erik Prince, and Elliott Broidy establish deep Israeli and Arab ties, Trump and his son-in-law, Jared Kushner, engage in a series of suspicious business transactions with foreign nationals, and Paul Manafort begins years of work for pro-Kremlin interests. The Kremlin's intense focus on connecting with Trump advisers during the 2016 election underscores foreign nationals' ongoing interest in pursuing relationships with Trump and those close to him both before and after his entrance into presidential politics.

In 2002, George Nader shutters *Middle East Insight* and "disappear[s]" from Washington.[1] A likely explanation for his disappearance is that in 2003 Nader receives a one-year prison sentence in the Czech Republic after he is convicted of ten counts of sexually abusing minors.[2] According to the *New York Times*, at some point thereafter Nader begins working for Vice President Dick Cheney.[3] He subsequently shows up in Iraq—shortly after the second American invasion of that country—having developed "close ties to national security officials in the Bush White House."[4] Nader's ties by this point extend well beyond the U.S. government, however. He is also now connected to the newly arrived private contractors who are working in Iraq post-invasion, most notably Blackwater USA, a "private security company" whose founder, future Trump national security adviser and Steve Bannon confidant Erik Prince, has hired him as a Middle East dealmaker.[5] Under oath during a 2010 deposition, Prince will claim—contradicting numerous American government officials who have worked with Nader over the years—that while in Prince's employ Nader was "unsuccessful" in making deals in the Middle East, "did not work directly" with either Prince or anyone in Blackwater despite having been hired by the company, and "pretty much worked on his own."[6]

Erik Prince will feature as a significant player in the many future interactions between Donald Trump, his inner circle of advisers and associates, and powerful Israelis, Saudis, Russians, and Emiratis. The Mueller Report will describe Prince as someone with "relationships with various individuals associated with the [2016] Trump Campaign, including Steve Bannon, Donald Trump Jr., and Roger Stone. . . . [He] sent unsolicited policy papers [to Trump campaign adviser and later CEO] Bannon on issues such as foreign policy, trade, and Russian election interference."[7] The report adds that after Election Day in 2016, Prince "frequently visited transition offices at Trump Tower, primarily to meet with Bannon but on occasion to meet Michael Flynn and others. Prince and Bannon would discuss, *inter alia*, foreign policy issues and Prince's recommendations regarding who should be appointed to fill key national security positions."[8] By the time of the presidential transition, Nader, by then an adviser to Mohammed bin Zayed, had "received assurances . . . that the incoming [Trump] Administration considered Prince a trusted associate."[9]

The Intercept, an online news organization, has referred to Prince as "America's most famous mercenary," but also, more important, as a man who has long been on an idiosyncratic personal mission: "He continues to dream of deploying his military services in the world's failed states," the digital media outlet writes, "and persists in hawking a crackpot scheme of privatizing the U.S. war in Afghanistan . . . [but] Prince has diversified his portfolio. No longer satisfied with contracting out former special forces operators to the State Department and Pentagon, Prince is now [in

2019] attempting to offer an entire supply chain of warfare and conflict. He wants to be able to skim a profitable cut from each stage of a hostile operation, whether it be overt or covert, foreign or domestic. His offerings range from the traditional mercenary toolkit, military hardware and manpower, to cell phone surveillance technology and malware, to psychological operations and social media manipulation in partnership with shadowy operations like James O'Keefe's Project Veritas."[10]

While Prince's present ambitions are grand—if chilling—*The Intercept* positions him, too, as a figure who poses a danger to international peace and stability as much because of his personality as his geopolitical designs. Prince is, the outlet reports, "a man desperately trying to avoid U.S. tax and weapons trafficking laws even as he offers military services, without a license, in no fewer than 15 countries around the world. Prince's former and current associates describe him as a visionary . . . who is nonetheless so shady and incompetent that he fails at almost every enterprise he attempts."[11] Prince's long string of failures appears to end at the dawn of the Trump era, however, as he finds in Trump and his aides, allies, and associates willing compatriots in some of his most audacious schemes.

In the late aughts, Prince's sudden resurgence on the global stage was still well in the future, however. At the time, he was reeling from September 2007 allegations that mercenaries in his employ had murdered seventeen Iraqis in Baghdad, a federal criminal investigation in which Prince had been, the *Nation* wrote in 2009, "implicated."[12] As Prince licked his wounds and considered his next moves, he was developing close ties to the Israeli government as well as to strongmen across the Middle East, with *Haaretz* reporting that Prince's "deep Israeli connections" came to include a long-standing business relationship with Ari Harow—former bureau chief and chief of staff to Israeli prime minister Benjamin Netanyahu— and another with Dorian Barak, Harow's onetime business partner.[13] By 2018, Harow will have been convicted of fraud and breach of trust and be working with Israeli prosecutors to testify against Netanyahu—who in 2019 becomes the first-ever sitting Israeli prime minister to face charges of bribery and breach of trust—but when Prince first entered Harow's milieu the latter was a well-connected businessman, and being linked to him put Prince in good stead in Israeli political circles.[14]

From 2012 on, Prince will hold an investment stake in a company co-managed by Harow and Barak, and by dint of his association with the two men he begins investing in Israeli security companies as well.[15] Barak also tries—it isn't known whether successfully or not—to get Prince to join billionaire Vincent Tchenguiz as a major investor in a new investment project: SCL Group, the parent company of the Trump campaign's data firm, Cambridge Analytica. Tchenguiz is known as well for being a close business associate of Dmitry Firtash, who is himself a business associate of 2016 Trump campaign manager Paul Manafort.[16] Tchenguiz is also an investor in Black Cube and Terrogence, two Israeli intelligence companies that will intersect consequentially with the Trump campaign, transition, and administration (see chapters 3, 4, and 8).[17] Black Cube, in particular, has ties to the Israeli government through many employees who are former members of the Israel Defense Forces (IDF), and its advertising "openly" features its "ties to Israeli spy agencies, including Mossad," according to the *New Yorker*.[18]

By 2018, Prince will be notorious in the United States for misleading Congress and the public on the subject of his activities in the Middle East—including a key January 2017 meeting in the Seychelles with a Kremlin agent that Nader successfully set up for Prince on behalf of MBZ and the Trump transition team (see chapter 6).[19]

Given his history of dealings with Nader, and Nader's history of dealings with men to whom Prince is also connected, the mercenary's mid-aughts account of Nader's incompetence in the midst of sensitive Middle Eastern negotiations seems to be at odds both with Prince's continued association with him and with an observation by a veteran State Department negotiator for the Middle East, Aaron David Miller, who will tell *Politico* in 2018 that Nader had "an absolutely amazing degree of contact with the people we [at the State Department] were talking to" in the Middle East.[20] *Al-Monitor*, an American media outlet covering the Middle East, says that at the time Prince claims Nader was ineffectual at making deals in the

Middle East, he was in fact "a deal broker in Iraq."[21] The outlet adds that "in Iraq in the mid-2000s, [Nader was] looking to translate his Rolodex of connections from his *Middle East Insight* days into work advising various Iraqi political clients, including some of Iraq's new Shiite political leaders, as well as Kurdish officials." According to Iraqi sources, Nader "helped arrange meetings for the 2005 visit to Washington of leading members of an Iraqi Shiite political party with close ties to Iran, the Supreme Council for the Islamic Revolution in Iraq."[22]

After his wide-ranging high-level work in Iraq, however, Nader falls off the grid again. Reached by CNN in 2018, the director of the Atlantic Council's Middle East center will call Nader a "man of mystery" whose name he hadn't heard mentioned by anyone in the field of Middle East studies for a dozen years, while another Middle East expert will express surprise "at finding out Nader was still alive" when contacted for comment about Nader's reemergence into the American news cycle.[23]

As Erik Prince is providing private security services in the Middle East during the early years of America's occupation of Iraq, another future Trump adviser, Elliott Broidy, is in the same place doing the same thing. In 2005, Broidy, described by the *New York Times* as a "Republican fund-raiser who is [also] a California-based investor with a strong interest in the Middle East," founds a private security company called Circinus, which, like Prince's Blackwater (later renamed Academi), "provides services to both United States agencies and foreign governments."[24] It is unclear whether Nader, who is working for Prince in the mid-aughts, crosses paths with Broidy at this point; what is certain is that the two men will be closely linked by the beginning of the Trump administration.

At approximately the same time Broidy is founding Circinus, he is also beginning what becomes a "long history" with onetime and future Israeli prime minister Benjamin Netanyahu, according to Israel's *Haaretz*. In 2003, the outlet writes, "then-Finance Minister Netanyahu took credit for convincing the New York State pension fund to invest $250 million in [the Broidy-led] Markstone [Capital Group]"—a firm whose success is later found to have been partly the result of bribes Broidy paid to the New York State comptroller.[25] Broidy will be convicted of a misdemeanor for these bribes in 2012.[26] Nader eventually establishes "long-standing connections" with Israel through Broidy, according to the *Middle East Eye*, including being "sent" by MBZ "during the [2016 U.S.] presidential elections" to "meet Israeli officials to discuss how the two states [UAE and Israel] can cooperate"—a course of negotiation that raises the question of whether Israeli officials were the first to point Nader in the direction of a key Israeli figure in the Trump campaign's orbit, Joel Zamel (see chapters 3 and 4).[27] The result of all these intertwining connections is that by the time of the 2016 election, three men who will be among Trump's foremost clandestine foreign policy advisers—Nader, Prince, and Broidy—all have longtime ties to the Israeli government and deep roots in Middle Eastern geopolitics.

Donald Trump spends the 2000s augmenting his own existing ties to the Middle East. In 2005, for instance, he attempts to partner with a billionaire from the United Arab Emirates, Hussain Sajwani, to build two massive Trump-branded towers in Dubai.[28] The project is ultimately unsuccessful.[29]

As the New York City businessman is building connections in Abu Dhabi, D.C. political consultant Paul Manafort is busy building connections in a former Soviet republic, Ukraine—a course of ingratiation and shilling that will lead directly to revelations, during the course of Robert Mueller's investigation into Russian election interference years hence, that not only implicate Donald Trump but also provide a window into how and why several foreign nations saw such promise in the 2016 Trump campaign.

Manafort begins his work as a flack in Ukraine by agreeing to consult for the Party of Regions, a pro-Russia political party funded in substantial part by Rinat Akhmetov, a Ukrainian tycoon who is one of the richest men in the country.[30] Manafort was working at the time for Akhmetov's System Capital Management (SCM).[31] During the Trump-Russia scandal following the 2016 presidential election, Manafort will be accused by special counsel Robert Mueller of secretly transmitting proprietary Trump campaign polling data to foreign nationals through a man "the FBI assesses to have ties to Russian intelligence," Konstantin Kilimnik, with the evidence suggesting that Manafort intended this information to ultimately be seen by, among others, Akhmetov "and another Ukrainian oligarch" (see chapter 4).[32]

Manafort's work for the Party of Regions—a political outfit "aligned with Moscow," according to CNN—begins in 2005 and ends in 2012, a seven-year period during which Manafort, who in 2016 will offer to work for Donald Trump for "free," earns $60 million for his services. Even after the Party of Regions payments cease, Manafort continues meeting with pro-Kremlin Ukrainian politicians, including a 2014 meeting with Viktor Medvedchuk—a man who will ultimately fall under U.S. sanctions for his role in the Russia-Ukraine conflict, and who is so close to Putin that the Russian president is his daughter's godfather—that takes place after Trump has made it known to GOP officials that he plans to run for president (see chapter 2).[33]

Most of Manafort's Party of Regions work comes in support of Ukrainian politician Viktor Yanukovych, a pro-Kremlin candidate for the presidency of Ukraine hobbled in significant part by the fact that he speaks fluent Russian but has "a hard time speaking Ukrainian."[34] A 2006 U.S. embassy cable describes Yanukovych as not only enjoying the backing of the Kremlin as Manafort tries to give him an "extreme makeover," but also as belonging to a political party that is "a haven . . . [for] mobsters."[35] A 2017 *Time* article will describe Yanukovych's mid-aughts political career as that of an "oafish and inarticulate" man with "rough manners and [a] criminal past," including past convictions for both violence and theft.[36] In the same article, the Party of Regions is described as "stained with blood" due to the abduction and beheading, organized by "some of Yanukovych's political patrons," of an investigative journalist, Georgiy Gongadze, who had been exposing high-level corruption in Ukraine.[37] When Manafort successfully orchestrates a Yanukovych victory in Ukraine's 2010 presidential election, "among the first official acts of [Yanukovych's] tenure [will be] to legally bar Ukraine from seeking NATO membership—a move that effectively granted Russia one of its core geopolitical demands."[38] Six years later, Manafort finds work with another presidential candidate, this time in the United States, whose candidacy is both supported by the Kremlin and marked by an intense hostility to NATO.

Another of Yanukovych's first acts as Ukrainian president is to jail his chief political opponent, former prime minister Yulia Tymoshenko, the "gold-braided heroine of the Orange Revolution"—a political movement that had successfully protested Yanukovych's elevation to the presidency back in 2004, partly on the grounds that the Kremlin had interfered in that election.[39] This, too, offers an echo of Manafort's subsequent work as a U.S. campaign adviser, with Donald Trump calling for the jailing of his own chief political opponent, Hillary Clinton, just five years after Yanukovych jails Tymoshenko, and winning higher office only after substantial Kremlin interference in his 2016 election as president. In the case of Yanukovych, writes Reuters, Putin "bankrolled" the Manafort-managed candidate during his bid to become Ukrainian prime minister in 2006, "sowed division" in Ukraine as part of his plan to back his desired candidate, was suspected of supporting an attack against his chosen candidate's opponent—Yanukovych's anti-Kremlin rival was "not-so-mysteriously poisoned," writes Reuters—and watched with satisfaction as Manafort "airbrushed" his favored candidate's "record of corruption, mismanagement, and alleged ties to Russia."[40]

Of Manafort's first presidential campaign of the 2010s—Trump's 2016 presidential campaign being his second—Reuters observes that "the [2010 Yanukovych] campaign came from Washington, but the money came from Moscow."[41] "There was no daylight between Yanukovych and Putin," the media outlet writes of the Manafort-run campaign, "and no daylight between Yanukovych and Manafort."[42] Indeed, as part of his "more than a decade of service to a Putin puppet," Manafort aided Yanukovych as the Ukrainian politician ensured that Ukraine was "allied with Russia," anti-NATO, and gave preferential economic treatment to Moscow—an agenda strikingly similar to the one Manafort's second candidate of the 2010s, Donald Trump, would propose in March 2016, in the midst of the Republican primaries.[43]

In 2006, Manafort signs a $10 million-a-year consulting and public relations contract with a man Reuters calls a "Putin crony," Oleg Deripaska, who not coincidentally had also been the man who originally connected Manafort to Akhmetov's Party of Regions.[44] In May 2019, U.S. Senator Ben Sasse (R-NE) will quote a Treasury Department document to describe Deripaska as "a designated [U.S.-sanctioned] individual. He possesses a Russian diplomatic passport. He regularly claims to represent the Russian government. He's an aluminum—and other metals—billionaire and he's been investigated by the U.S. government and by . . . our allies for money laundering. He's been accused of threatening the lives of his business rivals. He's been charged with illegal wire tapping [and] taking part in extortion and racketeering schemes. He's bribed government officials; he's ordered the murder of a businessman; and he has many links to Russian organized crime . . . he's a bad dude . . . a bottom-feeding scum-sucker and . . . he has absolutely no alignment with the interests of the U.S. people."[45] Deripaska is also, beginning in 2006 and extending into the 2010s, Paul Manafort's boss and the source of much of his annual income.

While the precise scope of the 2006 Manafort-Deripaska contract is unknown, just months earlier Manafort had pitched Deripaska a course of advocacy that would see Manafort working to "'greatly benefit the Putin government' by influencing politics, business dealings, and news coverage inside the United States" and abroad.[46]

Shortly after he begins working for Deripaska, Manafort purchases a $3.7 million condo in Trump Tower—Trump's home—using an LLC called John Hannah rather than a personal account, suggesting that the purpose behind the purchase of the condo may be business-related. John is Manafort's middle name, while Hannah is the middle name of Manafort's business partner at the time, Rick Davis; alternatively, John Hannah could refer to former Dick Cheney aide John Hannah, in which case the shell corporation's naming takes on a different and potentially more sinister cast (see chapters 4 and 6).[47] At the time that Manafort, now working for Putin ally Deripaska and, indirectly, Putin, moves into Trump Tower, the tower's owner is considering a run for the presidency in 2008, according to Fox News.[48] Per the cable network, by the end of the first week of 2006 Trump has "hinted" to the New York Post that "he may go for president in 2008" and has "strongly suggested he [is] interested in entering the national political arena in 2008," telling the *Post* that his decision not to run for governor of New York in 2006 "doesn't preclude me from doing something [political] in the future."[49] While Trump is coy about what this last comment means, "a political figure close to Trump" helpfully assists the *Post* in decoding the remark, telling the newspaper that "Donald is definitely interested in running for president in 2008, possibly as an independent candidate."[50]

As Manafort moves into Trump Tower on Deripaska's dime, he stands a good chance of coming into contact with the presidential-run-mulling Trump, as Manafort's consulting firm has by 2006 "represented Trump for years"—in fact, Trump was the firm's very first client after it was founded in 1980.[51] The *Atlantic* notes that from the moment Manafort moves to Trump Tower, he and Trump "occasionally see[ ] each other and ma[k]e small talk."[52] The magazine observes, too, that "while Manafort is alleged to have laundered cash [from Ukraine] for his own benefit, his long history of laundering reputations is what truly sets him apart. He helped persuade the American political elite to look past the atrocities and heists of kleptocrats and goons. He took figures who should have never been permitted influence in Washington and softened their image just enough to guide them past the moral barriers to entry. . . . Helping elect Donald Trump, in so many ways, represents the culmination of Paul Manafort's work. The president bears some likeness to the oligarchs Manafort long served."[53] In 2017, when a group of Manafort's friends secretly gather to strategize how to help Manafort escape allegations of collusion with a foreign government, one person contacted as part of the effort will note to the *Atlantic* that "there wasn't a lot to work with. And nobody could be sure that Paul didn't do it."[54]

By 2015, revenues from the course of work Manafort began in Ukraine in 2005 have "appeared to dry up," according to CNN—though around the time of his firing as Trump's campaign manager in August 2016 Manafort will tell his accountant that he still has $2.4 million coming to him in November 2016 "for work he did in Ukraine," suggesting that he was still in a business relationship with pro-Russia concerns while he was working atop the Trump campaign.[55] Indeed, the *New York Times* notes in mid-August

2016, as Manafort is leaving Trump's campaign amid recriminations over his past pro-Kremlin work, that "Ukrainian company records give no indication that Mr. Manafort has formally dissolved the local branch of his company, Davis Manafort International, directed by a longtime assistant, Konstantin V. Kilimnik."[56] Whether Manafort is in 2016 still business partners with Kilimnik—the man whom Trump deputy campaign manager Rick Gates calls a former Russian military intelligence officer, and whose co-workers in the 1990s at the Moscow office of the International Republican Institute called him simply "the guy from the GRU [Russian military intelligence]"— what is clear is that by 2015 Manafort's relationship with Deripaska, his and Kilimnik's old boss, has soured, with Manafort "deeply indebted" to the Putin crony.[57] Why Manafort is in debt is unclear. It could be because he has not adequately advocated for Putin's government in the United States under his contract with Deripaska, or because Deripaska at one point during his association with Manafort loaned the political consultant $10 million, or because Deripaska had unwisely "ploughed $18.9 million into a telecoms venture in Ukraine run by Manafort and his number two, Rick Gates," or because by early 2016 Manafort had somehow come to owe Deripaska "close to $20 million" for unknown reasons, or some combination of all of these. What is clear is that Manafort, in Deripaska's view, remains deeply in the red as the political flack lobbies for a job on the Trump campaign in early 2016.[58]

Soon after Manafort joins Trump's presidential campaign on March 28, 2016, Deripaska dispatches former GRU officer Victor Boyarkin to pressure Manafort to square his debts with the oligarch. "He owed us a lot of money," Boyarkin will tell *Time* in 2018, "and he was offering [in 2016] ways to pay it back. I came down on him hard."[59] Indeed, just two weeks after Manafort's hire (a hire that occurs once Manafort tells Trump friend Thomas Barrack that he "really needs to get to" Trump), Manafort emails "his old lieutenant" Kilimnik asking him how he can "use" his "media coverage" as Trump's campaign manager to "get whole" with Deripaska.[60] In the ensuing 120 days, Manafort meets face-to-face with Kilimnik at least twice, once on May 7 and again on August 2, not long after the Republican National Convention; offers "private briefings" on the Trump campaign to Deripaska; transmits proprietary Trump campaign polling data to Kilimnik with the aim of it reaching Deripaska, Manafort's old boss Akhmetov, and another Ukrainian oligarch, Serhiy Lyovochkin; and, as the campaign's overseer of the 2016 Republican convention in Cleveland, helps orchestrate a change in the Republican National Committee (RNC) platform regarding the provision of arms to anti-Kremlin Ukrainian rebels—a change that delights both the Kremlin and pro-Russia elements in Ukraine.[61] As to the last of these incidents, Kilimnik will tell associates in Europe just a few weeks after the convention that he played a role in the Republicans' unexpectedly pro-Kremlin platform decision in Cleveland.[62]

The key Trump campaign executor of Kilimnik's plan regarding the change to the GOP platform is J. D. Gordon, Republican senator Jeff Sessions's deputy on Trump's national security advisory committee—a body first conceived of by Jared Kushner and Dimitri Simes, the founder, president, and CEO of the Center for the National Interest (CNI), a conservative think tank that has consistently a pro-Kremlin viewpoint (see chapter 2). Both during and after the July 2016 convention in Cleveland, Gordon has substantial contacts with Russian nationals. According to the Mueller Report, on the third day of the convention, Gordon and Sessions both deliver speeches at the Global Partners in Diplomacy conference.[63] During Gordon's speech, which Russian ambassador Sergey Kislyak attends, Gordon argues "that the United States should have better relations with Russia."[64] The Mueller Report reveals that during Sessions's speech Kislyak may have asked a question of the Alabama senator, who has been, since being hired by the Trump campaign in early March, the GOP candidate's chief public-facing national security adviser.[65] Gordon speaks with Kislyak after the event to tell him that he "meant what he said in the speech about improving U.S.-Russia relations"; Sessions also speaks with Kislyak after the event and likewise discusses "U.S.-Russia relations" with the Russian ambassador.[66] At a reception following the event, Gordon has dinner with Kislyak, and they are joined by a fellow member of Trump's national security advisory committee, Carter Page.[67] Gordon and Kislyak speak for several minutes about U.S.-Russia relations, during which Gordon repeats to the Russian ambassador that "he meant what he said in his speech about improving U.S.-Russia relations."[68]

Nine days before Sessions, Gordon, and Page interact with Kislyak at the Global Partners in Diplomacy conference, Gordon participates in the Republican National Convention's committee hearings to debate amendments to the party platform. Prior to the hearings, Trump's policy director, John Mashburn—who will later testify to Congress that before the convention George Papadopoulos, another member of Trump's national security advisory committee, told him of the Kremlin having damaging information about Clinton—explicitly orders Gordon to "take a hands-off approach" to the hearings.[69] Gordon ignores Mashburn's directive and furiously objects to a platform amendment proposed by delegate Diana Denman; the amendment would "include[ ] provision of armed support for Ukraine" against pro-Kremlin forces as part of the GOP platform.[70] According to Mashburn's subsequent congressional testimony, Trump "had not taken a stance on the issue," and therefore Mashburn's directive to Gordon that "the Campaign should not intervene" was intended to hold during discussion of the party's stance toward the hostilities in Ukraine.[71] Echoing Mashburn, Matt Miller, a campaign staffer working with Gordon at the platform hearings, will later say that he "did not have any independent basis to believe that this language [Denman's proposed platform] contradicted Trump's views," and therefore he did not urge Gordon to get involved in a dispute with Denman, nor did he condone him doing so.[72]

Instead of remaining silent, however, Gordon—claiming to have heard Trump clearly articulate a position on Ukrainian rebels at a brief meeting in D.C. nearly four months earlier—feels "obliged to object to the proposed platform change and seek its dilution."[73] When his objection meets resistance from Denman and others, Gordon, according to Denman, picks up his phone, dials a number, and thereafter pretends, while arguing with Denman, to be on the phone with Trump campaign headquarters at Trump Tower in New York City—when in fact he appears to be getting his direction from a different source altogether, as he is actually on the phone with the office of his national security advisory committee supervisor, Jeff Sessions.[74] Gordon, who had apparently lied to Denman about being on the phone with "candidate Trump," will subsequently tell Mueller that not only Mashburn but Mashburn's colleague in Trump's policy shop, Rick

Dearborn, "supported" Gordon's position on the platform change—a claim Mashburn contradicts when he is confronted with it.[75]

The result of Gordon and Denman's bizarre exchange is that the latter's platform amendment proposal is defeated by, the evidence suggests, the machinations of Gordon and Sessions (the latter either directly or through a representative). Notably, Gordon and Sessions are the only two men involved in the platform dispute who are directly associated with Simes's and Kushner's national security advisory committee. Sessions in particular has, in the weeks leading up to the Republican National Convention, been meeting and speaking regularly with Simes and other members of Simes's think tank (see chapter 2). Sam Clovis, who hired some of the members of the national security advisory committee but is not one of its members, will later tell the special counsel's office that "he was surprised by the [platform] change" Gordon orchestrated. Mashburn will be even more forceful, insisting that Gordon—and presumably Sessions, if indeed it was he who green-lit Gordon's maneuvers in Cleveland—had "violated Mashburn's directive not to intervene" in platform disputes.[76]

After Gordon's July 11, 2016, actions at the Republican National Convention committee meetings, and his July 20 discussions with Kislyak at the Global Partners in Diplomacy conference, the Russian ambassador invites Gordon to his home.[77] Gordon tells Kislyak that he will have to take a "raincheck" because of bad press involving alleged connections between Russia and the Trump campaign. Before he can make good on his "raincheck," however, Gordon departs the presidential campaign for the Trump transition team.[78]

Having failed to set up a meeting with the number two national security adviser on Trump's national security advisory committee, Kislyak tries instead for the committee's chairman.[79] This time Kislyak is successful at setting up a meeting, scheduling a get-together with Sessions for September 8 in Sessions's office; September 8 is the day after Trump is slated to deliver, in Philadelphia, the second major foreign policy address of his campaign, and his first one post-convention.[80]

In Trump's September 7 speech, written, as was his April 27 foreign policy speech, with input from the man who created the committee of which Sessions is the chairman, Dimitri Simes (see chapter 2), Trump states the following about Russia: "Putin has no respect for President Obama or Hillary Clinton."[81] It is a sentiment he might easily have deduced from Kislyak's repeated private statements of support to his national security advisers in the weeks prior (see chapters 4 and 5).[82]

At Sessions's office the next day, Sessions and Kislyak discuss Iran, Syria, and Ukraine, and Kislyak once again informs a top Trump campaign representative—having consistently done so since Trump's first foreign policy speech in April—that the Kremlin is "receptive to the overtures Trump [has] laid out during his campaign."[83] Trump thereby receives feedback from pro-Kremlin sources immediately before and immediately after both his first and second major foreign policy addresses (see chapters 2 and 4). After the Sessions-Kislyak meeting on September 8, attended as well by two Sessions aides, Kislyak invites Sessions to come to his house alone to dine.[84] Sessions does not follow up on the invitation, however, as the Trump campaign—having recently asked Manafort to resign due to his ties to Ukraine and Russia—is just days away from asking two members of Sessions's committee, George Papadopoulos and Carter Page, to resign as well, and for the same reason.[85] While Sessions does not dine privately with Kislyak, his meeting with the Russian ambassador in his Senate office is itself a significant anomaly; though Sessions will later claim he met Kislyak only as a routine obligation of his role on the Senate Armed Services Committee, a CBS News poll taken of twenty of the committee's twenty-six members in March 2017 will reveal that not one of the twenty had met with Sergey Kislyak even once in 2016.[86]

Seventy-two hours before the Republican National Convention begins in Cleveland, another member of Sessions's team has contact with a Kremlin-linked Russian national. On July 15, 2016, Soviet-born U.S. businessman Sergei Millian—who will shortly "offer[ ] to serve as a go-between for a Belarusian author with ties to the Russian government and the Trump campaign"—contacts George Papadopoulos on LinkedIn.[87] Just as Maltese professor and Kremlin agent Joseph Mifsud had contacted Papadopoulos mere days after Sam Clovis hired Papadopoulos in March 2016 (see chapter 2), Millian's approach to Papadopoulos occurs shortly after the young Trump adviser has appeared on a conference panel with Clovis at the TAG Summit.[88] Millian tells Papadopoulos that he has "insider knowledge and direct access to the top hierarchy in Russian politics," and Papadopoulos agrees to meet him in New York City shortly after the convention.[89] The two men ultimately have two meetings in New York, on July 30 and August 1; after the second, Millian invites Papadopoulos to Moscow to attend a September energy conference.[90] Papadopoulos informs the campaign of his July 30 contact with Millian on the day it happens, as he does in other instances in which he has contact with a foreign national linked to the Kremlin—except, Papadopoulos will tell special counsel Robert Mueller, when Mifsud told him in April 2016 that the Kremlin had stolen Clinton emails—and is told on July 31 to hold off on further contacts with Millian because the press has begun connecting the Trump campaign with Russia far more than the campaign would like. Papadopoulos meets with Millian on August 1, anyway.[91]

On August 23, Millian sends a Facebook message to Papadopoulos— which Papadopoulos will insist to the special counsel's office he has no recollection of—telling him that he wants to "share with [him] a disruptive technology that might be instrumental in your political work for the campaign."[92] Papadopoulos meets Millian twice more after this offer of campaign assistance, once in November 2016 and once at Trump's inauguration in January 2017, apparently to discuss, among other things, a possible consulting partnership.[93] The partnership—Millian's idea—does not go forward.[94]

Less than six months after his fourth and final meeting with Millian, Papadopoulos will be approached in Tel Aviv by the founder of Terrogence, an Israeli business intelligence outfit dealing in digital marketing campaigns and intelligence services that could be considered "disruptive" technologies "instrumental" to those political campaigns willing to use them (see chapter 8). Millian is later revealed to be a key source—if an "unwitting" one—for much of the dossier compiled by former MI6 Russia desk chief Christopher Steele in 2016 and published in January 2017 by *BuzzFeed News*.[95]

Just as well-connected Israeli politicos and other key players in Middle Eastern politics have identified George Nader, Erik Prince, and Elliott Broidy as key U.S. political connections by the mid-aughts, so too have the Russians come to appreciate this same quality in Paul Manafort by the end of that decade. It is perhaps not surprising, then, that long after becoming Trump's de facto campaign manager, and just days before being officially named his campaign manager on June 20, Paul Manafort finds himself at a meeting in Trump Tower with a cadre of individuals sent to the campaign by the Kremlin.

Two days before this infamous June 2016 meeting—on June 7—Manafort attends what Trump attorney Rudy Giuliani will later call a "strategy" meeting; also at the meeting are Donald Trump Jr., Jared Kushner, Rick Gates, and at least one other (unnamed) person. The four (or five) Trump campaign advisers discuss how to approach the impending June 9 meeting with agents of the Kremlin, including a Russian attorney, Natalia Veselnitskaya, who has promised the campaign, through a British music promoter named Rob Goldstone, "very high level and sensitive information" that would "incriminate Hillary [Clinton]" and is "part of Russia and its government's support for Mr. Trump."[96]

According to two articles in *Business Insider*, one in 2017 and one in 2018, despite Trump Jr.'s 2017 testimony to Congress that he has "no recollection of documents being offered or left for us" by Veselnitskaya on June 9, in fact the Russian attorney "provide[s]" a "memo" to Trump Jr., Manafort, and Kushner on June 9.[97] The *New York Times* has since published the memo the Kremlin agent gave to Trump's son, son-in-law, and campaign manager at Trump's home in New York City. According to the arguments advanced by the five-page, highly detailed opposition research document, "the main sponsor[s]" of the Democratic Party and "both Obama election campaigns" committed serious federal felonies in order to raise a fortune that ended up, in part, in Obama's and the Democratic Party's coffers.[98] The *Times* reports that the memo is similar, indeed in many respects identical, to one the Kremlin had previously given to Rep. Dana Rohrabacher (R-CA) during an April 2016 trip the congressman made to Russia. Rohrabacher had gone to Moscow with his then-staffer Paul Behrends, a longtime close associate of Erik Prince; in Russia, Behrends and Rohrabacher met with Veselnitskaya, during which meeting she made the same pitch on U.S.-Russia sanctions to the congressman and Prince's associate that she would later make to the Trump campaign.[99]

The text of Veselnitskaya's memo offers some indication of what the Russian attorney may have actually said at the June 9 meeting, a matter that remains in some dispute. The Russian attorney's memo begins with two paragraphs on the Kremlin's complaints over U.S. sanctions, and proceeds to accuse Ziff Brothers Investments (headed by American brothers Dirk, Robert, and Daniel Ziff) of participating in an illegal stock-purchase scheme in Russia involving shares of Gazprom, Russia's state-owned natural gas company.[100] Perhaps not coincidentally, at the time Kremlin agent Veselnitskaya makes her accusation, the Trump campaign has two people formerly affiliated with Gazprom—Carter Page and Richard Burt—working on Trump's foreign policy agenda with respect to Russia (see chapter 2). The memo's outline of the Ziff brothers' alleged scheme recites relevant names and dates, identifies purported shell companies, quotes the astronomical dollar figures supposedly involved in the brothers' plot (at least $80 million), itemizes the federal statutes the Kremlin believes the brothers have violated, refers readers of the document to Rep. Rohrabacher for more information, and implicitly urges the Trump campaign to find out if the Ziff brothers have donated to Clinton as well as the Democratic National Committee (DNC) and both Obama's election and reelection campaigns—insisting that illegal foreign campaign donations to Clinton "cannot be ruled out."[101]

The memo given to Trump Jr., Manafort, and Jared Kushner is not, as Trump Jr. will subsequently say to Congress of Veselnitskaya's presentation, "vague" and "ambiguous," nor does it "ma[k]e no sense," nor is it devoid of "details or supporting information," nor does it lack "meaningful information."[102] Moreover, the Kremlin's opposition research document had been represented to Trump Jr. as coming from "the Crown prosecutor [sic] of Russia," a contention implying that the Kremlin had additional incriminating evidence in its possession, and that the Trump campaign had only received an evidentiary summary of a larger case file alleging suspicious donations to the Democratic National Committee and high-profile Democrats.[103] This latter fact will become significant just days after the June 9, 2016, meeting, when the Trump campaign, along with the rest of America, learns that the Kremlin has hacked the Democratic National Committee and is indeed in possession of stolen private documents regarding its operations and transactions (see chapter 4).

When it is released in redacted form in April 2019, the Mueller Report will reveal that, contrary to Trump Jr. and his father's mid-2017 contention that the Kremlin's chief purpose in meeting with Trump officials and advisers at Trump Tower in 2016 was to discuss U.S. citizens' adoptions of Russian children, the Russians' primary ambition had been as Rob Goldstone first represented it to Trump Jr.: to aid the Trump campaign with valuable opposition research about Clinton and the DNC, an action prohibited by U.S. law. Roman Beniaminov—an assistant to Azerbaijani-Russian pop singer Emin Agalarov, who helped set up the June 9 meeting with Trump Jr. on behalf of his father, Aras, and Yury Chaika, the prosecutor general of Russia—had before the meeting told Aras Agalarov employee Irakli "Ike" Kaveladze, an eventual meeting attendee, that "the purpose of the meeting was for Veselnitskaya to convey 'negative information on Hillary Clinton'" to the Trump campaign, an aim Kaveladze subsequently disclosed to the special counsel's office.[104] Kaveladze himself wrote in an email to his daughter after the meeting that the meeting was boring because it featured no "bad info on Hilary [sic]," an assessment that at once confirms that the Kremlin's opposition research stopped just short of implicating Clinton and implies that Kaveladze had gone to the meeting expecting derogatory information about the Democratic candidate to be the chief topic of conversation.[105] Beniaminov and Kaveladze's statements on the purpose of the Trump-Kremlin summit at Trump Tower thus mirror what Goldstone had told Trump Jr. in his initial email seeking the June meeting: "The Crown prosecutor of Russia met with his [Emin Agalarov's] father Aras this morning and in their meeting offered to provide the Trump campaign with some official documents and information that would incriminate Hillary and her dealings with Russia and would be very useful to your father. This is obviously very high level and sensitive information but is part of Russia and its government's support for Mr. Trump—helped along by Aras and Emin."[106]

The information the Kremlin presents to the Trump campaign is self-assured with respect to its allegations of illegal foreign financing of Barack Obama's two presidential campaigns, and self-assured with respect to its allegations of illegal foreign financing of the Democratic Party; it is speculative with respect to illegal foreign financing of the Clinton campaign and the Clinton Foundation. Even so, it gives the Trump campaign a possible line of attack in response to any future allegations that it is receiving illegal foreign campaign donations. It also augments the potentially damaging information about the Democratic Party that will be contained in the Kremlin's July and October leaks of hacked DNC emails. Moreover, it leaves only one piece missing in a potential allegation against Clinton herself—a missing piece Trump's opposition research team could locate simply by determining whether the Ziff brothers had donated to Clinton's campaign. That information was readily available to Trump staffers; indeed, it was merely a gestural gap in the information the Kremlin had provided to the campaign. A basic Google search conducted during the general election campaign would likely have revealed to Trump Jr., Manafort, or Kushner that the Ziff brothers' largest donation to a candidate for federal office in 2016 was indeed to Hillary Clinton.[107] Moreover, by June 2016 the Kremlin had represented to the Trump campaign, via a conversation between Joseph Mifsud and George Papadopoulos, that it was in possession of stolen Clinton emails, so the Trump campaign would have had, as of June 9, reason to suspect that any additional information on Clinton and the Ziff brothers held by the "Crown prosecutor of Russia" included incriminating emails written by Clinton herself. The campaign's pursuit of such Clinton emails—which would ultimately extend through the summer of 2016 (see chapter 5)—gave candidate Trump and his policy shop every incentive to extend and even augment the campaign's support for better relations with the Kremlin and an end to U.S. sanctions against Russia.

Both before and after his June 2016 meeting with Kremlin agents, Trump Jr. does all he can to conceal everything about the meeting from anyone but the very top brass on the Trump campaign.[108] In addition to, according to his own congressional testimony, hiding the meeting from his father until the *New York Times* uncovers it a year later, Trump Jr. also labels his email invite to Kushner and Manafort to attend the event "private and confidential"; falsely tells "senior campaign staff" days before June 9 that while an upcoming meeting is focused explicitly on "negative information" about Clinton, the source of the information is a "group from Kyrgyzstan"; "denie[s] meeting" any "officials from Russia" for the entirety of the presidential campaign and afterward, as subsequently noted by meeting participant Rob Goldstone in an email to Emin Agalarov; and declines to be voluntarily interviewed about the meeting by the special counsel's office.[109] According to an FBI interview with Trump's attorney Michael Cohen, Trump Jr.'s concealment of the meeting includes false testimony to Congress insisting that he never told his father of the meeting—as Cohen testifies under oath that he himself was in "Donald J. Trump's office on June 6 or 7 when Trump Jr. told his father that a meeting to obtain adverse information about Clinton was going forward. . . . From the tenor of the conversation, Cohen believed that Trump Jr. had previously discussed the meeting with his father."[110]

That the June 9 meeting is considered significant at the time is underscored by the fact that Trump's de facto (soon to be official) campaign manager, Manafort, takes notes throughout, and that Trump Jr., rather than shutting down the Kremlin agents once they proffer valuable but illegal campaign assistance, tells Veselnitskaya that his father "could revisit the [sanctions] issue" if he wins the presidential election—implicitly soliciting and encouraging a continuation of "Russia and its government's support for Mr. Trump," as previously spoken of by Goldstone.[111] So it is little surprise that the *New York Times* will report in May 2018 that, according to two individuals familiar with the campaign's multiple covert pre-election meetings with foreign nationals, "Trump campaign officials did not appear bothered by the idea of cooperation with foreigners."[112]

Less than a week after Kremlin agents represent to the Trump campaign that the Kremlin has evidence of illegal foreign campaign donations to the Democratic National Committee, "a cybersecurity firm and the DNC announce[ ] that Russian government hackers had infiltrated the DNC," according to the Mueller Report.[113] That the hack may have captured emails confirming the opposition research the Kremlin had already given Trump's campaign is not lost on at least one June 9 meeting participant, indeed the participant least interested in and knowledgeable about politics, by his own admission: Emin Agalarov's music industry manager, Rob Goldstone, who will tell multiple media outlets, "I know nothing about politics."[114] Goldstone nevertheless writes Emin "shortly after the DNC announcement" to make "comments connecting the DNC hacking announcement to the June 9 meeting"—an association almost certainly also made, as the Kremlin would have anticipated, by the experienced politicos working for the Trump campaign, especially the Kremlin's own longtime flack, Paul Manafort.[115]

With respect to Manafort's pre-election transmission of polling data to pro-Russian elements in Ukraine, the *New York Times* will note that at the time Trump's campaign manager secretly ordered proprietary campaign information transferred to Kremlin agents, "Russia was engaged in a full-fledged operation using social media, stolen emails and other tactics to boost Mr. Trump, attack Mrs. Clinton and play on divisive issues such as race and guns. Polling data could conceivably have helped Russia hone those messages and target audiences to help swing votes to Mr. Trump."[116] CNN will report in August 2017 that federal "investigators became more suspicious of Manafort when they turned up intercepted communications that U.S. intelligence agencies [had] collected among suspected Russian operatives, discussing their efforts to work with Manafort to coordinate information that could hurt Hillary Clinton's bid for the White House."[117] And in 2019 the Mueller Report will reveal that Manafort's order to Gates to share polling data with a man connected to Russian intelligence, Kilimnik, was a standing order, with Gates doing so "periodically . . . during the campaign."[118] As the report details, "Manafort instructed Rick Gates, his deputy on the Campaign and a longtime employee, to provide Kilimnik with updates on the Trump campaign—including internal polling data. . . . Manafort expected Kilimnik to share that information with others in Ukraine and with [Putin ally] Deripaska."[119]

When the special counsel's office approaches Deripaska deputy Victor Boyarkin to find out the extent of Manafort's "coordination" with pro-Russian elements—whether it be the Kremlin, Russian intelligence, Kremlin-linked oligarchs like Deripaska, or pro-Kremlin Ukrainian oligarchs like Rinat Akhmetov—Boyarkin tells the special counsel to "go dig a ditch."[120] Both Boyarkin and Deripaska will be, by 2018, under U.S. sanctions, the latter explicitly because he does not "separate [him]self from the [Russian] state," according to the U.S. Treasury Department. Meanwhile, Boyarkin's former employer, the GRU, will be found to be the very Russian intelligence agency that, the *Times* reminds its readers, "was engaged in a full-fledged operation . . . to boost Mr. Trump" during the 2016 election.[121] In an email to Manafort in mid-campaign, Kilimnik had called pleasing Boyarkin, and his boss Deripaska, his own and Manafort's "biggest interest."[122]

While Trump's degree of knowledge regarding Manafort's communications and coordination with a Russian oligarch and a former GRU agent during the campaign is unknown, this much is clear: Trump knew Manafort well when he hired him as his campaign manager. Manafort made his overseas work part of his job application to the Republican candidate in February 2016, and the State Department was immediately "alarmed" by Trump's hire of Manafort because of Manafort's "relationship to Russia"; in January 2018, NBC News reports that, in relation to the Mueller investigation, "Donald Trump is telling friends and aides in private that things are going great" in large part because "a key witness in the Russia probe, Paul Manafort, isn't going to 'flip' and sell him out."[123] What crime Trump may have committed involving Manafort as a co-conspirator that would allow Manafort to "flip and sell him out" goes unreported by NBC News, though it is known that Manafort met with Kilimnik to discuss the presidential campaign not only in May 2016 but also in early August 2016, doing so on this second occasion in the Grand Havana Room, a private club located at 666 Fifth Avenue—a building owned by Jared Kushner's family business, Kushner Companies, and located a fifth of a mile from Trump Tower (see chapter 5).[124] The meeting occurred soon after Kilimnik had met with Deripaska, with Kilimnik thereafter using Deripaska's plane to fly to the meeting with Manafort.[125] Manafort also met with Kilimnik in Madrid in either January or February 2017.[126] Kilimnik has called his pre- and post-election secret meetings with Trump's onetime campaign manager "very significant meetings," and special counsel Robert Mueller has since alleged, as has Gates, that Kilimnik had not just past but ongoing ties to Russian intelligence throughout the period he was meeting with Manafort.[127]

At the August 2, 2016, Manafort-Kilimnik meeting at the Grand Havana Room, Kilimnik conveys to Manafort a "message" from the Kremlin's onetime puppet president in Ukraine, Yanukovych. The message is a "peace plan" for Ukraine that Manafort later concedes to the special counsel's office was a "'backdoor' means for Russia to control eastern Ukraine."[128] According to the Mueller Report, Manafort and Kilimnik will again meet to discuss the plan, which also involves an end to U.S. sanctions on Russia, in December 2016, January 2017, February 2017, and spring 2018—with the most consequential meeting coming during the presidential transition, when Kilimnik tells Manafort, and Manafort thereafter communicates to the Trump transition team, that "all that is required to start the [Ukrainian crisis-resolving and sanctions-dropping] process is a very minor 'wink' (or slight push) from [Donald Trump]."[129] Whether Trump receives this message from Manafort is unclear; what is clear is that he shortly thereafter attempts to implement a plan constituting far more than just a "wink" or "push": immediately upon taking office, Trump sets into motion a sub rosa scheme to drop all sanctions on Russia—a scheme blocked by alarmed career officials in the State Department after a series of desperate backroom maneuvers.[130] Manafort will subsequently lie to the special counsel's office about his communications with both Kilimnik and the campaign regarding sanctions relief for the Kremlin. He will also take actions that keep the special counsel from "gain[ing] access to all of [his] electronic communications" during the relevant period.[131] A federal judge eventually finds by a preponderance of the evidence that, even while he was under a federal cooperation agreement and plea deal with the special counsel's office in 2018, Manafort "made multiple false statements to the FBI, the [special counsel's] Office, and the grand jury concerning his interactions and communications with Kilimnik." Notably, it is during this period that Trump—who, his attorneys claim, remains in a joint defense agreement with Manafort even after the latter's plea, meaning that the legal teams of the two men share both information and legal strategies— boasts to friends that he is safe from liability in the Mueller probe because Manafort will not "flip" on him.[132]

Trump's private statements about Paul Manafort's hold over his own legal future raise the specter that Trump had knowledge of his campaign manager's collusive mid-campaign interactions with a Russian intelligence agent, a knowledge that subsequently compels Trump to engage in, per legal analysts speaking to NBC News, acts that "could amount to obstruction of justice or witness tampering," such as floating a pardon in exchange for Manafort's silence.[133]

Manafort's initial lie to federal investigators about his involvement in negotiating a "peace plan" with a Kremlin agent sees him insisting that he discussed such a plan with Kilimnik only once, in August 2016. When prosecutors challenge his narrative, Manafort admits that he and the Russian intelligence agent discussed the plan at least three more times after August.[134] The judge in one of Manafort's two federal trials will ultimately say that Manafort's lies about the "peace plan" and Konstantin Kilimnik go to "the undisputed core of the . . . special counsel's investigation"—the question of Trump-Russia collusion.[135]

Manafort's nearly a decade of public relations work in Ukraine came to a halt in 2014, when a revolution against his and Putin's man in the country, Yanukovych, led to Yanukovych and his allies fleeing to Russia to seek Kremlin protection.[136] Putin's subsequent illegal annexation of Ukraine's Crimean peninsula was part of his pushback to this rebellion; his actions led to the very sanctions on Russia that Trump and Manafort would thereafter oppose throughout the 2016 primary and general election seasons.[137]

According to the *New York Times*, the approximately $12.7 million Manafort appears to have received from Yanukovych's Party of Regions before his and Yanukovych's simultaneous departure from Ukraine constituted "undisclosed cash payments . . . [that were] part of an illegal off-the-books system whose recipients also included election officials"—in other words, the monies listed as earmarked for Manafort, often hidden in offshore bank accounts, may well have been evidence of an election-interference scheme partly backed by the Kremlin.[138] Prosecutors in Ukraine now say that Manafort "must have realized the implications of his financial dealings" in that country preceding his purportedly "unpaid" work for Donald Trump.[139] Whether this explains Manafort's decision never to register as a foreign agent with the Department of Justice (DOJ) is unclear; regardless, Manafort's failure to register permitted him to keep the money he received from Putin ally Deripaska and Putin stooge Yanukovych hidden from U.S. authorities until it was uncovered by Robert Mueller in 2017. It also allowed him to be an undisclosed agent of pro-Kremlin forces for the entirety of the time he was working for Trump, a fact it would have been difficult for Trump not to know given his familiarity with Manafort's past political work.[140]

In 2006, the same year that Manafort moves into Trump Tower on a mission for Deripaska and Putin, the owner of the building—who has spent his career in real estate surfing on an ever-cresting wave of debt—suddenly shifts his philosophy on real estate development dramatically by putting up cash for most new projects. As the *Washington Post* explains, in 2006 Trump "began buying up land near Aberdeen [Scotland] . . . [for] $12.6 million. . . . [He] soon began to buy other properties in cash. . . . In 2008 and 2009, he paid $17.4 million in cash for two neighboring Beverly Hills homes. In 2009, Trump spent at least $6.7 million on two golf clubs. . . . In Charlottesville, he paid $16.2 million for a winery. . . . By 2011, Trump had spent at least $46 million on all-cash purchases" since 2006.[141] The *Post* notes that Trump's mysteriously accessible $46 million may have been attributable in part to a single transaction he completed in 2008: the sale of a Palm Beach mansion to a Russian oligarch, Dmitry Rybolovlev, who is close to a senior adviser to Vladimir Putin, Yuri Trutnev.[142] Trump had purchased the southern Florida estate for $41.4 million in 2004, and had sought to flip it immediately. After finding no takers for several years, in 2008 he was suddenly offered $95 million by Rybolovlev, an offer that at the time made the sale "the highest price paid for any single-family home" in the history of the United States. Trump's $53.6 million profit was enough to fund every one of his all-cash purchases between 2006 and 2011.[143]

When Rybolovlev makes his mysterious offer on Trump's unpopular Florida property in 2008, he calls it a "company investment," yet he eventually tears down all the buildings Trump has put up on the site. In March 2017, during special counsel Robert Mueller's investigation of Trump-Russia ties, Rybolovlev will suddenly change his story, claiming that, rather than a company investment, the purchase was for a "family trust."[144] These will be only two of Rybolovlev's shifting explanations for paying Trump well over twice what the New York City businessman had paid for a property Rybolovlev razed after its purchase; at other times the Russian billionaire will say the house was for "his children, or maybe an inheritance, or it might be used in connection with his daughter because she was an equestrian."[145] David Newman, a lawyer who reviewed the transaction as part of a team at the New York City law firm Sills, Cummis & Gross, will tell the *Palm Beach Post* in 2017 that despite the historic size of Rybolovlev's purchase, his team "never found any evidence Rybolovlev hired experts to weigh in on the property's condition as a residence—or its value as a teardown—before he bought the place."[146] How Trump came to Rybolovlev's attention in the first instance is unknown, though recent investigations suggest a connection to Trump's longtime, Kremlin-connected rainmaker, Felix Sater—a man who had by the time of the Trump-Rybolovlev sale spent years attracting Russian business clients to Trump properties.[147] Sater is a U.S. and Israeli citizen whose father, Mikhail, according to *Haaretz*, has been "named [by the FBI] as a lieutenant for Russian mafia kingpin [Semion] Mogilevich," the latter a man who has been called "the most dangerous mobster in the world."[148] Mogilevich is a former associate of

Boris Birshtein, a Russian oligarch who was once one of Donald Trump's partners in a major building project in Toronto.[149]

In 2007, the parents of a longtime Elliott Broidy associate, Lisa Korbatov, purchase a Rodeo Drive mansion for $10.5 million. A year later, Korbatov's parents sell the property for $10.3 million, taking a $200,000 loss, to "an Egyptian man with little money and a history of financial scams."[150] Six weeks later, this unlikely Egyptian purchaser of a Rodeo Drive mansion, Mokless Girgis, transfers the property to Donald Trump—for free.[151] When the bizarre transaction is caught and becomes the subject of a lawsuit, Girgis claims, as summarized by the Center for Investigative Reporting, that there was a "$10 million clerical error" and that he was never involved in the Rodeo Drive transaction at all.[152] He thereafter flees the country under threat of litigation from creditors.[153] In 2009, Trump sells for $9.5 million the property that Girgis had gifted to him—thereby making a profit of $9.5 million in under a year and with virtually no effort.

Just six months before the Korbatovs purchase the mansion on Rodeo Drive that will, in short order, move through Trump's hands, the New York City businessman incorporates two companies in Egypt that thereafter will remain (to all outward appearances) inactive: "Trump Marks Egypt Corp." and "Trump Marks Egypt LLC."[154] It would take access to Trump's tax returns to see what if any business Trump subsequently does with or through these companies; Trump has declined, however, to release his returns. As noted by the Center for American Progress, Trump "served as president, director, and chairman of Trump Marks Egypt Corp. and was listed as the president and a member of Trump Marks Egypt LLC. But because of Trump's continued insistence on hiding his tax returns and general evasiveness when it comes to his business dealings, it is unclear the purposes for which these companies were created and their future plans."[155]

The year 2007 also sees Jared Kushner, Trump's son-in-law, make the worst business decision of his career in real estate: the purchase of 666 Fifth Avenue in New York City for $1.8 billion, "the highest price [ever] paid at the time for a U.S. office tower," according to the *Washington Post*—which Kushner, then running his family's real estate firm, Kushner Companies, pays despite a general consensus in the New York City real estate market that the property is significantly overpriced.[156] The deal requires Kushner to put down $500 million in cash, and the company borrows the remaining $1.3 billion of the property's purchase price.[157] According to *The Intercept*, there are, at the time of Kushner's purchase of 666 Fifth Avenue, "clear signs that the price was too high and the debt was too much. The Kushners paid $1,200 a square foot, twice the previous per square foot record of $600, while records show that even with the building almost fully rented out, revenue only covered about two-thirds of the family's debt costs."[158]

After the 2008 financial crisis, 666 Fifth Avenue declines dramatically in value, "wiping out much of . . . [Kushner family's] initial investment."[159] Jared Kushner will spend the next decade struggling to keep the property from bringing the family business into deep financial distress, and 666 Fifth Avenue will come to be described in the press as "an extreme risk" and "severely underwater."[160] Kushner's desire to atone for the error of his 2007 purchase of the building will appear to drive his perspective on global geopolitics well into his term of service as a top adviser to Trump—a circumstance that in 2018 "raises questions about a possible conflict of interest" when he appears to support the punishment of the nation of Qatar via blockade just a month after Qatar's ministry of finance refuses to bail out Kushner Companies from its Fifth Avenue investment (see chapter 7).[161]

In the first months of the Obama administration, George Nader unsuccessfully tries to use his connections to the Syrian government to gain access to "senior members of President Barack Obama's foreign policy team," according to the *New York Times*. He is at the time already working with "former advisers to President George W. Bush" to advance various business deals; the details of these deals, including the names of their principals, are unknown.[162] While there are many thorny geopolitical quagmires across the Middle East in the months leading up to Obama taking office that Nader may have believed, based on his history in the region, he could aid the incoming Obama administration with, as of late 2008 the Saudis' or Emiratis' desire for American nuclear technology—whether for civilian or military uranium enrichment—is not one of them, as long-standing U.S. policy prevents the transfer of such technology to the Middle East, and indeed opposes any encouragement of such Saudi or Emirati ambitions. Nor do the Saudis or Emiratis expect any U.S. administration, with or without Nader's assistance, to act otherwise.

It is therefore unsurprising when, in the midst of the 2008 presidential campaign, the foreign minister of the United Arab Emirates, Sheikh Abdullah bin Zayed Al Nahyan, issues a public warning to nations across the Middle East at "a gathering of ministers and senior officials from the Middle East, North Africa, the subcontinent and the Group of Eight (G8) industrial nations" that "threats on the ground create a strong case for making the Middle East a region free of weapons of mass destruction. Any situation to the contrary would open the door for continuous conflicts and threaten regional and international peace and security."[163] The Emirates' concern about multinational nuclearization in the Middle East soon leads the UAE to endorse a draft resolution at the United Nations establishing the Middle East as a "nuclear weapon free zone."[164] The sheikh's admonition against the spread of nuclear weapons in the region, however, is a warning that the UAE and its closest ally, Saudi Arabia, will shortly ignore—as soon as they find an American politician willing to help them realize their long-dormant nuclear ambitions.

In 2009, mercenary company owner Elliott Broidy is convicted of a misdemeanor for paying $1 million in bribes to New York government officials; in exchange for these bribes, Broidy had secured $250 million in pension investments in a company he founded in Israel.[165] In Abu Dhabi, an American diplomat sends a cable to Washington observing that MBZ is building up a mercenary army to counter a nuclearized Iran: MBZ "sees the logic of war dominating the [Middle East] region," the cable says, "and this thinking explains his near-obsessive efforts to build up his armed forces."[166] That the Emirati military is small and "considered inexperienced" is a source of significant worry for MBZ.[167]

The man in charge of raising MBZ's mercenary army in 2010, working under the project title "Reflex Responses" or "R2," is Erik Prince—who is favored by MBZ not least because he is able to quickly congregate mercenary armies of non-Muslims, a critical skill set given that MBZ does not "believe Muslim soldiers could be trusted to kill other Muslims."[168] According to *The Intercept*, working on R2 gives Prince an opportunity he has long lusted for: "to own a piece of each part of the foreign conflict supply chain: planes, ships, vehicles, weapons, intelligence, men, and logistics. Reflex Responses gave him a blank check to do just that."[169] In running R2, Prince decides, as he has done with many of his prior companies, to create a shell corporation from which he can anonymously run his operation— the better to ensure, as *The Intercept* observes, that he can't be connected with any documents related to the project, has more freedom to engage in illicit self-dealing, and if need be can make the case, however implausibly, that his actions were not subject to U.S. laws like the State Department's International Traffic in Arms Regulations (ITAR).[170] Prince names R2's controlling shell corporation Assurance Management Consultants.[171] A former R2 colleague of Prince's will observe to *The Intercept* that "everything he [Prince] does, he skims. . . . He will run a contract through two companies and then dictate that those two companies have to subcontract out to another eight companies. What he doesn't disclose is that he owns all or part of those eight companies and will take 25 percent from each company. Then, he can use those same eight entities to make the money disappear."[172] Another former R2 employee will add that "there was a way to do it [run R2] legally and make lots of money, but Erik didn't care. When Erik wakes up in the morning, Erik does whatever he feels like doing. I always assumed that's how it is when your father is a billionaire."[173]

Between May 2009—when another billionaire, Donald Trump, sets up his Twitter account—and Barack Obama's 2012 reelection campaign against Mitt Romney (R-MA), Trump tweets at least nine times about Saudi Arabia, in each case criticizing either the Saudis' decisions regarding oil production or President Obama's alleged "bow" to the Saudi king during a trip to Riyadh; a running theme in his tweets is the false accusation that Obama has entered into a covert conspiracy with the Saudis in order to win reelection to the White House.[174] Indeed, Trump is conspicuously focused on the idea of a U.S. president gaining the White House partly through collusion with the Saudis, stating without evidence on April 4, 2012, that "Barack Obama made a deal with Saudi Arabia to pump the hell out of oil until after the election. Watch what happens to oil prices after the election (if he wins)—it won't be pretty."[175] Ninety days later he repeats the accusation on Twitter: "I believe Barack Obama made a deal with the Saudis to increase oil production until after the election. Then OPEC can have a field day."[176] Trump's theory of a clandestine Obama-Saudi conspiracy is substantially enlivened by the businessman's concurrent claim that the purpose of the conspiracy is, in part, a war with Iran that will make for good domestic politics for whichever American president starts it. "In order to get elected, Barack Obama will start a war with Iran," Trump tweets on November 29, 2011.[177]

While Trump's 2009, 2010, and 2011 tweets about Saudi Arabia and the White House are public libels against President Obama—just a few of the many Trump will author, online and off, in the run-up to his own presidential campaign—his words also betray a conviction that, if a U.S. presidential candidate can convince the royal family in Riyadh that doing so is in their best interest, secretly colluding with the Saudis is a possibility. Indeed, as the 2012 election nears, Trump's tweets about U.S.-Saudi collusion become even more melodramatic and oddly specific, with the then-businessman tweeting on October 11, 2012, again without evidence, that President Obama has collected "illegal donations" from the Saudis as an incumbent presidential candidate.[178] Several weeks later, on Election Day, Trump reiterates in a tweet what he imagines Obama's end of a collusive quid pro quo with the Saudis to be: the presidential candidate is permitting Saudi Arabia to get the better end of energy deals with the United States in exchange for an oil production schedule that keeps domestic oil prices low—a state of affairs that would be considered favorable to the U.S. political party then in power.[179] Trump's awareness, even if fanciful at the time it is expressed, of the benefits of covert pre-election collusion with Saudi Arabia will come to seem prescient in the years ahead, when Trump himself appears to engage in all of the behaviors he has falsely attributed to President Obama.

Shortly after Mitt Romney loses the 2012 presidential election, Trump makes the decision to run for president in 2016—revealing his plans to his close friend Roger Stone on January 1, 2013—and ceases tweeting conspiracy theories about Saudi Arabia's ties to powerful U.S. politicians.[180] He will not resume doing so for nearly a year. Thereafter, between October 2013 and October 2014, Trump's ten tweets about the Saudis abandon accusations of collusion in favor of Trump's long-standing policy complaint about the kingdom, which is that it does not pay enough for its own military defense.[181] Trump's focus in these ten tweets is on the presence of U.S. forces in Syria to fight ISIS, an effort Trump believes helps the Saudis more than their financial contribution to the effort would suggest.

As Trump nears the official announcement of his presidential candidacy, a shift in his tone toward Saudi Arabia is evident, with a number of his tweets being generally positive in tone beginning in January 2015. On January 29, 2015, for instance, Trump admonishes Michelle Obama for, in his view, not respecting Saudi culture enough to wear a headscarf in-country; "we have enuf [sic] enemies," he tweets.[182] Less than two months later, he warns that "Saudi Arabia is in big trouble" if the United States doesn't move away from Obama's Saudi policy—an expression of concern for the future of the Saudi people and their rulers that stands in contrast to his prior tweets on the subject.[183] Nevertheless, Trump continues to demand that the Saudis pay more for their own defense. The calls for this that he makes in 2015, however, are more insistent and oddly personal, suggesting that he is trying to appeal to a domestic electorate. In March 2015 he tweets that Saudi Arabia "must pay dearly" if it wants "our help and protection."[184] Just a few weeks later he tweets, "We are getting ready to protect Saudi Arabia against Iran and others. . . . How much are they going to pay us toward this protection."[185] And in his final tweet about Saudi Arabia before announcing his presidential candidacy, Trump declares on May 11, 2015, that a better leader than Obama would be able to get the Saudi king to meet with him, given the "billions of dollars" that "we spend . . . protecting Saudi Arabia."[186]

Throughout 2012, in the midst of Trump's criticism for Saudi Arabia on Twitter, a future Trump adviser, George Nader, spends much of his time developing closer ties with Russian interests. In the run-up to the Obama-Romney tilt, Nader begins developing "a substantial record of dealing with Russian elites," including "help[ing] broker a $4.2 billion arms deal between Russia and the Iraqi government."[187] Nader is so highly placed in both Russian and key Middle Eastern political circles that he not only acts as "an informal adviser to then-Iraqi Prime Minister Nouri Kamal al-Maliki" but actually "accompanie[s] him to Moscow" in October 2012 for the signing of the arms deal the Iraqis have agreed to with the Kremlin.[188] This alone establishes, as *Vox* will note in 2018, that beginning in 2012—at the very latest—"Nader was a power broker with real influence among Russian elites."[189] The Lebanese American businessman's close connection to prominent Kremlin agents will be of paramount relevance when he begins meeting regularly, and secretly, with top officials from the Trump campaign in the final months of the 2016 election (see chapter 5).

Nader's role in negotiating a Russia-Iraq arms deal is so central that it becomes controversial. In Moscow in August 2012, two months before al-Maliki signs the deal with Putin, Nader supersedes the authority of Iraqi defense minister Saadoun al-Dulaimi by—with al-Maliki's blessing—conducting negotiations with the Kremlin of which the Iraqi Defense Ministry is unaware.[190] Al-Maliki is so committed to using Nader as one of his top three negotiators in Moscow, rather than his own defense minister, that when former Russian energy minister Yuri Shafranik travels to Baghdad to ask al-Maliki directly with whom he should be negotiating in Moscow—at one point even offering the Iraqi prime minister "a direct communication line with Russian President Vladimir Putin to avoid confusion and leaks"—al-Maliki "welcome[s]" the entreaty but nevertheless shows up in Moscow two months later with Nader in tow as one of his chief negotiators.[191]

In 2012 Nader also attends the exclusive, invite-only St. Petersburg International Economic Forum, a meeting of the world's top economic and political power brokers that is "organized by senior officials in Putin's inner orbit."[192] The next year, the Russian Direct Investment Fund (RDIF), a Kremlin investment vehicle run through state-owned development bank Vnesheconombank and directed by a Putin lieutenant named Kirill Dmitriev, enters into a co-investment agreement with the UAE that will eventually lead to an infusion of $6 billion in Emirati cash to various Russian infrastructure projects; the agreement between the Kremlin and Abu Dhabi comes after a face-to-face meeting between Putin and MBZ.[193] By 2014, Nader has left his employ with Iraqi prime minister Nouri al-Maliki and is working as an adviser to MBZ, during which course of employment he becomes, according to the Mueller Report, a "close business associate" of Dmitriev, whom the report deems "closely associated" with Vladimir Putin. Though it is unknown whether Nader's prior access to top Kremlin officials led to him having direct involvement in the highly lucrative 2013 RDIF-UAE negotiations, what is certain is that once Nader becomes an adviser to the Emirati royal court he "return[s] to Russia frequently," according to the *New York Times*, and even "accompanie[s] [MBZ] . . . to Moscow on a number of those trips."[194] These contacts and trips make it "increasingly possible," writes *Vox*, that by the time Nader convenes a secret meeting aboard a yacht in the Red Sea in fall 2015 he has "contacts deep inside Putin's inner circle and could have acted as a messenger for key information about negotiations over how the U.S.-Russian relationship could be improved."[195] If indeed Nader is both a Kremlin intermediary and an Emirati agent as of fall 2015, the Red Sea Conspiracy must be seen as an agreement not only between the leaders of Saudi Arabia, the United Arab Emirates, Bahrain, and Egypt but involving Russia as well. Nader's confirmed ties to Benjamin Netanyahu must also be considered relevant in light of subsequent actions by individuals connected to the Israeli government that seem to import the consent of Netanyahu's office to any "grand bargain" agreed upon in late 2015 (see chapters 3, 4, and 8).

As Nader's star is rising in the Middle East and Russia, so too is that of Erik Prince, who by 2010 has moved to the United Arab Emirates amid widening legal difficulties for his private security company, Blackwater. In the UAE, Prince soon signs his $529 million deal with the Emirati royal family to build a "secret American-led mercenary army," specifically "an 800-member battalion of foreign troops," for the wealthy Arab nation.[196] R2, Prince's battalion of non-Emirati mercenaries, is a precursor to the assassination squads the UAE will have developed by 2015 (see chapter 3). In 2011, however, Prince's remit is to "conduct special operations missions inside and outside the country [UAE], defend oil pipelines and skyscrapers from terrorist attacks and put down internal revolts," and "be deployed if the Emirates face[ ] unrest in their crowded labor camps or [a]re challenged by pro-democracy protests like those sweeping the Arab world."[197] Prince is thus put in charge of a substantial percentage of the Emirates' military operations.

The mercenary's broadest mandate, however—and a significant basis for the $529 million the UAE is paying him—is to "blunt the regional aggression of Iran, the country's biggest foe."[198] That Prince's official brief should be this broad is indicative of a sea change in military logistics that arrives in the Middle East with the twenty-first century. According to the *New York Times*, in hiring Prince to develop a battalion of foreign soldiers on Emirati soil, "the Emiratis have begun a new era in the boom in wartime contracting that began after the Sept. 11, 2001, attacks. And by relying on a force largely created by Americans, they have introduced a volatile element in an already combustible region where the United States is widely viewed with suspicion."[199] An open question, however, is whether Prince's army—which includes American, Colombian, South African, British, and French guns-for-hire, among those of other nations—violates federal laws prohibiting U.S. citizens from training foreign soldiers without first securing a license from the State Department.[200] While it's unclear if Prince secures such a license in 2010, it is known that in the twelve years from its founding in 1997 to 2009, the company Prince formerly ran, Blackwater, paid $42 million in fines for illegally training foreign troops around the world.[201]

In keeping with MBZ's concerns about Muslim soldiers, Prince has, by 2010, established a strict "no Muslims" policy for his mercenary army, and is hoping, per the *New York Times*, to "build an empire in the desert, far from . . . trial lawyers, Congressional investigators and Justice Department officials."[202] One of the contracts he signs upon moving to the UAE, in addition to his $529 million contract with MBZ, is a multimillion-dollar contract to provide security "to protect a string of planned nuclear power plants," an arrangement that gives Prince a vested interest in the spread of nuclear power to nations in the Middle East currently prohibited from enriching uranium even for civilian use; it also suggests that by 2010 the Emirates is already transitioning away from its prior stance regarding the dangers of new uranium enrichment in the Middle East.[203] Prince also anticipates earning "billions more" than he will receive under these two contracts by "opening a giant complex where his company can train troops for other governments" besides the royal court in Abu Dhabi.[204] In the meantime, Prince hides his involvement in all of these ventures by refusing to sign any contracts personally and by asking his subordinates to refer to him by the code name "Kingfish."[205] Many of his dozens of American, European, and South African trainers don't even know that Prince is involved in their operations—as he rarely visits the compound he's built, in an effort to avoid being seen even by his own employees.[206] He also regularly changes the name of his company to avoid its operations being tracked, an approach he had also taken with his disgraced Blackwater outfit.[207]

ANNOTATIONS

How Trump came to Rybolovlev's attention in the first instance is unknown, though recent investigations suggest a connection to Trump's longtime, Kremlin-connected rainmaker, Felix Sater—a man who had by the time of the Trump-Rybolovlev sale spent years attracting Russian business clients to Trump properties.

In 2008, the year of the Trump-Rybolovlev real estate deal in Florida, Larisa Markus and Georgy Bedzhamov, co-owners of the Russian bank Vneshprombank, begin setting up shell companies with the assistance of a Russian accountant named Ilya Bykov.[208] According to the *Real Deal*, a widely respected New York City real estate trade publication, Markus and Bedzhamov will by late 2015 stand accused of using the shell companies they have set up (with Bykov's help) to launder money for Russian companies (including Russia's state-owned oil company, Rosneft) and prominent figures (including Russia's minister of defense and deputy prime minister).[209] The same month that Markus is arrested and Bedzhamov flees Russia to avoid arrest, Trump's business partner Sater partners with Bykov on a multimillion-dollar real estate deal in New York. Bykov is also, at the time of his partnership with Sater, an accountant for Aras Aglarov, Trump's business partner in a potential "Trump Tower Moscow" deal.

In May 2016, months after Sater's partnership with Aras Agalarov's accountant begins, Dmitry Rybolovlev intercedes to help Georgy Bedzhamov (who has been arrested in Monaco and is in prison there) make bail. Rybolovlev's efforts free Bedzhamov, and Monaco thereafter announces that it will not extradite him to Russia. Thus—and partly as a result of Rybolovlev's exertions—Bedzhamov may never have to answer questions about his dealings with Bykov, who by 2015 had come to be entangled with not just one but two of Trump's business partners.[210] Sater's intersection with Rybolovlev on the Bedzhamov-Bykov matter suggests a possible prior relationship between the two men that Sater could have translated into a real estate opportunity for Donald Trump.

In late 2018, Rybolovlev is arrested on corruption charges in Monaco on an unrelated matter, with France's *Le Monde* reporting that the Russian businessman "is at the heart of the investigation opened a year ago by the prosecutor general of Monaco into [alleged] acts of corruption, active and passive influence peddling, and complicity in these offenses."[211]

The Emirates' concern about multinational nuclearization in the Middle East soon leads the UAE to endorse a draft resolution at the United Nations establishing the Middle East as a "nuclear weapon free zone."

As of 2008, Israel is the only country in the Middle East not to have signed the Nuclear Non-Proliferation Treaty. The small Jewish state is widely presumed to have nuclear weapons, even as Iran and Syria are, by 2008, generally believed by the same observers to be engaged in nuclear weapons development. While the official position of the UAE in 2008 is that the "states [of the Middle East], including Iran," have a "right" to "develop peaceful nuclear energy programs," and in fact the Emiratis themselves have by that year "evaluat[ed] the potential of a UAE nuclear energy program," the conventional wisdom that even responsible nuclear energy exploration can soon lead to a nuclear weapons program will dominate the early 2010s.[212]

CHAPTER 2

THE IRAN NUCLEAR DEAL, THE CENTER FOR THE NATIONAL INTEREST, AND THE VALDAI DISCUSSION CLUB

2013 to 2014

Shortly after Trump decides to run for president, the Kremlin begins its covert election interference campaign. Tensions in the Middle East rise as Russia and a large alliance of Western nations sign a nuclear deal with Iran that both Israel and a Saudi-led Sunni axis in the Gulf strongly oppose. Two men with Kremlin ties who will have a profound effect on Trump's 2016 campaign, Dimitri Simes and Joseph Mifsud, make visits to a prestigious discussion venue in Moscow of which Vladimir Putin is the chief patron.

On January 1, 2013, Donald Trump tells one of his closest friends and advisers, Roger Stone, that he intends to run for president of the United States.[1] Shortly thereafter—knowing he will be a candidate but having not yet made it official—Trump records a video for distribution in Israel in which he enthusiastically endorses Benjamin Netanyahu for prime minister.[2] "[A] strong prime minister is a strong Israel," Trump says in the video. "And you [Israelis] truly have a great prime minister in Benjamin Netanyahu. There's nobody like him. He's a winner. He's highly respected. He's highly thought of by all. . . . So vote for Benjamin. Terrific guy. Terrific leader. Great for Israel."[3] Trump will later claim Netanyahu "personally solicited" his "help" in the form of "an ad or a statement," a claim the Israelis will deny.[4]

It is also in 2013 that Mohammed bin Zayed enters into a multibillion-dollar co-investment with Vnesheconombank's and Kirill Dmitriev's RDIF.[5] The co-investment, according to the *New York Times*, is "part of an effort [by the UAE] to build close relations to Russia." The immediate effect of the joint venture is that the UAE invests in a slew of major projects in Russia, including the building of roads, an airport, and several cancer treatment centers.[6]

Once the RDIF-UAE deal is signed, Dmitriev, considered by the Emiratis "a key conduit to the Russian government," becomes a regular visitor to Abu Dhabi, where Nader has begun advising MBZ.[7] By 2015, the Emirates' ambassador to Russia will be describing Dmitriev as a "messenger" who can transmit information directly to Putin.[8] Dmitriev also begins coordinating with the Israelis as his term as RDIF manager continues; by late 2017 or early 2018, the fund is "negotiating with Israeli government ministers on a $100 million project to open Israeli-run dairies in Russia."[9] The RDIF thereby becomes a crucial fulcrum in communications between Russia, Israel, and the Saudi-led axis of Sunni Arab nations plotting a new alliance.

In June 2013, a year after assuming the leadership of the Defense Intelligence Agency (DIA), future Trump national security advisor Lt. Gen. Michael Flynn asks his superiors whether he can travel to Russia to visit the headquarters of Russia's military intelligence unit, the GRU.[10] The GRU is, as the *New York Times* will report in January 2017, "the same agency that has since been implicated in interference in the 2016 presidential election."[11] In an August 2016 interview, Flynn will say of his 2013 visit to GRU headquarters, "I had a great trip. I was the first U.S. officer ever allowed inside the headquarters of the GRU. I was able to brief their entire staff. I gave them a leadership OPD [professional development class] and talked a lot about the way the world is unfolding."[12]

In March 2014, just weeks after Russia's invasion of the Crimean peninsula in Ukraine—an action that leads to punishing international sanctions
against Putin's regime—Flynn "pushe[s] to maintain a dialogue with Russian military intelligence . . . making plans to meet with Russian officials
[in late March 2014]."[13] As reported by the *New York Times*, however, "When
his [Flynn's] superiors found out about his plans, they ordered the meeting
canceled."[14] In October 2014, six months after Flynn is forced out of the
DIA, his former employer informs him via letter that he is prohibited from
receiving, without advance approval, any "consulting fees, gifts, travel expenses, honoraria, or salary from a foreign government unless congressional
consent is first obtained."[15]

Even as Flynn is exhibiting an unnatural fondness for the Russian military, and specifically Russian military intelligence, dramatic changes are
afoot within the military of another country in which Flynn will shortly
have a significant interest: Egypt. In July 2013, Egyptian minister of defense
and commander in chief of the Egyptian armed forces, Abdel Fattah el-Sisi,
leads a coup of the government of Egypt's "first freely elected president,"
Mohamed Morsi.[16] Within a few months, President Obama has halted military aid to Egypt—a decision that President Trump will reverse upon entering office—and between July 2013 and January 2017 "repeatedly criticize[s]
the Egyptian government's crackdown on political opponents."[17] According
to a September 2018 Al Jazeera story, human rights groups estimate that
el-Sisi's government detains forty thousand political prisoners in its first
sixty months of rule.[18] In light of these and other troubling developments
in Egypt, the Obama administration refuses, upon el-Sisi's ascension to
power, to participate in America's formerly biennial joint military exercises
with Egypt—and temporarily refuses, too, to return to Cairo several Apache
helicopters that the Egyptians had sent to America for maintenance.[19]

In November 2013, Donald Trump travels to Moscow for the Miss Universe
pageant. While there, he negotiates a lucrative deal for a Trump Tower
Moscow with several Kremlin agents, including the Kremlin's premier real
estate developer, the head of a state-owned bank, and the Kremlin official

in charge of building permits in Moscow—this last a Kremlin employee whom Putin has personally sent to the pageant in his stead. Social media posts tracking the event and discussing its aftermath, written by people who are with Trump's entourage in Moscow, indicate that Trump spends much of his time in Moscow discussing presidential politics.[20]

Within a few weeks of his return to the United States from Moscow, Trump is telling officials in the New York State Republican Party that he intends to run for president. For instance, in December 2013, at a meeting of New York state Republican officials at Trump Tower, Trump makes "it clear he want[s] to run for president," according to one attendee.[21] Trump will later confirm this, saying of his many meetings in Manhattan with Republican officials who wanted him to run for governor of New York that "even then, what I really wanted to do was run for president."[22] The GOP officials seeking to convince Trump to run for governor are so aware of Trump's ambitions in late 2013 that they even couch the governor's mansion in Albany as a springboard to a 2016 White House bid.[23] Among the state party officials in regular contact with Trump about his political ambitions is former president Richard Nixon's son-in-law Ed Cox, a veteran politico who will become instrumental in the early staffing of the 2016 Trump campaign's national security advisory committee—an intimate cadre of advisers under whose auspices most of the illicit Trump-Russia contacts eventually itemized by the Mueller Report occur (see chapter 4).

In March 2014, Trump finally ceases to hide what he has already indicated to his GOP allies in New York: that he plans to run for president of the United States. In the midst of his allies' ill-fated efforts to draft him to run for governor, Trump alerts his many Twitter followers that "[w]hile I won't be running for Governor of New York state, a race I would have won, I have much bigger plans in mind—stay tuned, will happen!"[24] According to witnesses close to Trump whom Fox Business will interview in 2018, by 2014 Trump is fully "committed" to running for president, despite him falsely tweeting in February 2018 that he could not have colluded with any "Russian group . . . formed in 2014" because he "didn't know" he was going to run for president until 2015.[25]

Trump's earlier-than-acknowledged public commitment to run for president is presaged by an event that occurs in January 2014: Trump's attorney Michael Cohen secretly pays an IT firm, RedFinch Solutions, to rig two online presidential polls in Trump's favor.[26] Trump will ultimately cheat the man he hired to cheat the two polls, one on the CNBC website and one on the *Drudge Report*; though Trump owes RedFinch $50,000 for fraudulently casting votes on his behalf in both polls, what Cohen gives the firm's owner as payment is "a blue Walmart bag containing between $12,000 and $13,000 and, randomly, a boxing glove that Mr. Cohen said had been worn by a Brazilian mixed-martial arts fighter."[27] In January 2019, Cohen will confirm that Trump—who spent much of 2016 and 2017 decrying alleged voter fraud in the United States—"knew he [Cohen] was trying to have the [CNBC and *Drudge Report*] polls rigged. 'What I did was at the direction of and for the sole benefit of [Mr. Trump],'" Cohen will say.[28]

At around the same time that Trump tweets about his national political ambitions, a strange saga begins at the London Academy of Diplomacy, a small outfit described by the *New York Times* as a "for-profit continuing education program."[29] In 2014 the academy is run by an obscure Maltese professor named Joseph Mifsud.[30]

That year, an attractive young Russian woman named Natalia Kutepova-Jamrom appears at Mifsud's financially faltering operation with what the *Times* calls "an improbably impressive résumé."[31] It is unclear why Kutepova-Jamrom, who is fluent in four languages, has worked in the Russian government as a "legislative aide," and thereafter worked for a state-owned newspaper in Russia, would want to apply for an internship at a nearly bankrupt for-profit academy in London—or indeed have anything at all to do with Mifsud, a man who has been described as a "snake-oil salesman" by a colleague.[32] What is clear, however, is that the mysterious twenty-four-year-old has connections at the highest level of the Russian government, and that after becoming professionally acquainted with Mifsud, she begins "introduc[ing] Mr. Mifsud to senior Russian officials"; even more startlingly, she gains him entry, in October 2014, to one of the most exclusive think tanks in Russia, the "prestigious" Valdai Discussion Club, which the *Times* reports is an "elite gathering of . . . academics that meets each year with Mr. Putin."[33] Mifsud is even given "a speaking slot" at Valdai during his very first appearance there; he uses the occasion to argue for the dissolution of U.S. sanctions against Russia over its annexation of Crimea earlier in 2014.[34]

It is quickly clear to at least one Valdai Discussion Club member that Mifsud does not belong there. His admittance to the group is "very, very strange," according to James Sherr, a Valdai member, and "might suggest he does have connections."[35] Indeed, by the time Mifsud appears at Valdai in October 2014, he has already begun his ascent to becoming "a popular pundit with state-run news outlets in Russia, praising the country and Mr. Putin."[36]

The 2014 Valdai meeting, at which Putin gives a lengthy address to the assembled 108 members of the club, is attended by another figure who, like Mifsud, is not just a club member but someone with "high-level Kremlin relationships" and a presence on state-run Russian media: future Trump campaign adviser Dimitri Simes.[37]

In December 2015, a former adviser to the Kremlin-owned natural-gas company Gazprom, Carter Page, asks Cox to help him get a job working for the Trump campaign.[38] On Cox's recommendation, Page is hired in January 2016 after Trump's national co-chair, Sam Clovis, does, he claims, no more than "a quick Google search" on him.[39] Just days after the Trump campaign brings Page aboard, its new hire sends an email to "senior Campaign officials" to tell them that, coincidentally, he has just "spent the past week in Europe" and has been "in discussions with some individuals with close ties to the Kremlin" who tell him they believe Trump can have a "game-changing effect . . . in bringing the end of the new Cold War"—and that, as a result of "discussions with these high level contacts," it is now possible that "a direct meeting in Moscow between Mr. Trump and Putin could be arranged."[40] Page adds at the close of his email that he opposes U.S. sanctions on Russia.[41] For all its energy, the email does not address how—or by whom—a Trump-Putin meeting can be orchestrated.

Fortunately, within days of Page's unusual email to senior Trump campaign staff, the campaign receives a job query from the very individual whose job on the campaign will ultimately be to set up exactly the sort of meeting Page has just proposed: George Papadopoulos.[42] Papadopoulos's broader campaign function, besides being one of Trump's first five national security hires, will be to keep the possibility of a Trump-Putin meeting on the campaign's radar at a time when the candidate himself has been told by his attorney Michael Cohen that—per the Kremlin-linked Felix Sater—meeting Putin can seal the $1 billion real estate deal Trump and Cohen have been secretly negotiating with the Kremlin for six months (see chapter 3).[43] Cohen has communicated not just to Trump but also to Trump campaign manager Corey Lewandowski that a trip by Trump to Moscow is critical to the project.[44]

Carter Page is an odd job candidate for the well-connected Cox—who claims to know Page from "business and political circles"—to endorse.[45] Clovis's "quick Google search" on Page fails to turn up what a standard pre-hire background check might well have uncovered, had either Clovis or Cox undertaken one: that just months before Cox provided him with an introduction to the Trump campaign, Page was wrapped up in criminal proceedings relating to the federal investigation of two Russian spies in the United States.[46] During the course of this investigation, federal law enforcement determined that Page gave two Kremlin agents nonpublic information about the U.S. energy sector; the Mueller Report notes that when questioned, "Page acknowledged that he understood that the individuals he had associated with were members of the Russian intelligence services," but said that he gave them nonpublic information anyway because, as he explained it to the special counsel's office, "the more immaterial nonpublic information I give [to Kremlin agents], the better for this country."[47] In fact, after Page delivered the material to the two Russian spies, he "spoke with a Russian government official at the United Nations General Assembly and identified himself so that the official would understand" that he had previously given information to Kremlin agents; his purpose in making this disclosure to a Russian official so soon after being informed by the FBI that he had been dealing with Russian spies, or for that matter his purpose in calling himself an "informal advisor to the staff of the Kremlin" in a letter to a publisher in 2013, will not be disclosed in the redacted Mueller Report.[48] How or why Page found himself once again in contact with Kremlin agents just days after being hired by Sam Clovis for the Trump campaign is unknown, though the same phenomenon occurs almost immediately after Clovis hires Papadopoulos in March and—yet again—almost immediately after Clovis appears on a conference panel with Papadopoulos in July. It is clear that the men to whom Clovis gives access to the Trump campaign's small national security shop very shortly thereafter are contacted by agents of the Kremlin (see chapter 4).

One of the senior Trump officials who receives Carter Page's January 2016 email about a Trump-Putin summit is Michael Glassner, the Trump campaign COO; Glassner is likewise the recipient of George Papadopoulos's job query, which he thereafter sends to Clovis via an intermediary, Joy Lutes.[49] At the time Papadopoulos sends his query to Glassner in early February, he is working for a company at which Valdai Discussion Club member Joseph Mifsud is a senior employee. Clovis ultimately hires Papadopoulos for the same committee for which he has already hired Page: Trump's national security advisory committee. The committee is the brainchild of two men, Jared Kushner and Valdai Discussion Club member Dimitri Simes (see chapter 3).[50]

Simes, the president and CEO of a pro-Kremlin conservative think tank, the Center for the National Interest (and a man Putin calls a "friend" at a Valdai Discussion Club event in 2013), will become active in the Trump campaign behind the scenes—indeed, the campaign's informal go-to adviser on Russia—just a few days after Papadopoulos is formally hired by Clovis in early March.[51] Within days of Simes becoming involved in advising the campaign, he and Jared Kushner agree that Trump must create a national security advisory committee of foreign policy experts.[52] By March 21, Trump has announced both Papadopoulos and Page as among the first five members of his national security advisory committee.[53]

Despite Dimitri Simes, Michael Flynn, and Erik Prince eventually becoming the Trump campaign's most trusted national security advisers—and the advisers with the most direct access to members of Trump's inner circle—none are ever publicly named to any Trump campaign national security or foreign policy advisory committee. Instead, they operate in the shadows, with their actions and advice not revealed to American voters until well after the 2016 election. As *Politico* will note of Simes in particular, "the Trump campaign never identified Simes as an adviser" despite his repeated contacts with senior campaign officials on the subject of Russia, with whom Simes laid out plans for a "new beginning" in several policy memos sent to Jeff

Sessions and Kushner.[54] That Simes is never acknowledged by the Trump campaign, but is mentioned in the Mueller Report 134 times, tells the complex story of a campaign looking to hide many of its most relied-upon foreign policy and national security assets from public view.[55] As *Politico* observes, "Trump made a point of publicly announcing a foreign policy advisory team in mid-2016, [but] his campaign never openly discussed Simes's quiet role."[56]

Even among "people who know Simes" there are some who consider him, per *Politico*, "at best a mysterious—and at worst alarming—player in Washington's foreign policy community . . . [a man] who cloaks his true agenda in Washington"; Simes's agenda is described by one former top Pentagon official, Michael Carpenter, as "completely pro-Kremlin."[57] Even a longtime friend of Simes's, Leslie Gelb, will acknowledge to *Politico* that there are many people in Washington who (in Gelb's opinion unfairly) suspect Simes of being "a secret Russian agent."[58] Whether Jared Kushner knew any of this when he recruited Simes as a Russia adviser for the Trump campaign in March 2019 is unclear; what is clear is that the concerns of the members of Washington's foreign policy establishment are not without basis. For instance, during the 2016 presidential campaign, not long before Simes began advising the Trump team in developing a pro-Kremlin foreign policy agenda, the CNI president was repeatedly asking a Russian alleged spymaster, Alexander Torshin, for help with a complex financial issue in Russia—a course of negotiation that could have put Simes deeply in debt to the Kremlin in advance of his work advising Kushner and, through Kushner, Trump.[59] According to private text messages Torshin sent to Kremlin operative Maria Butina months after Trump began running for president, Simes was "pressuring" and "appealing" to him to be his "helper" in dealing with the Russian Central Bank to resolve an issue involving tens of millions of dollars and a possible interruption of funding to the CNI.[60] Though Torshin at first rebuffed Simes—because of the "threat" Torshin believed helping Simes in the way Simes demanded posed to Torshin's "reputation"—once the CNI director became the Trump campaign's Russia whisperer six months later, one imagines the Kremlin coming to a very different conclusion. If it had previously been unclear to Torshin whether helping Simes was in his interest, after Simes's elevation to an informal advisory role within the Trump campaign it might have seemed to Torshin, as well as to his supervisors in Moscow, that any risk was worth the benefit of being on the right side of Simes's ledger of favors.

Certainly, the Kremlin had made this decision with respect to its handling of Simes by September 2018, when it decided to pay him roughly half a million dollars a year to work as a talk-show host for Kremlin-funded media—a Moscow-based job the Trump campaign's oft-relied upon Russia adviser still holds.[61] When Simes first entered into negotiations for this extremely profitable position within Russia's state apparatus is unknown; what is clear is that, as *Politico* reports, Simes "did use the opportunity [to advise the Trump campaign] to influence the campaign's posture toward Russia . . . [using] the brash billionaire [Trump] as a vehicle to drive the GOP toward his longtime project of improving U.S. relations with Moscow"—an ambition Simes was determined to pursue "despite Putin's ongoing election interference."[62]

There is already some evidence that Simes anticipated a quid pro quo from Torshin during the presidential campaign, as he aggressively pursued assistance from Russia's Central Bank via Torshin while "arrang[ing] meetings for Torshin with U.S. Treasury Department and Federal Reserve officials"—an indication that as Simes was facilitating Torshin's access to federal banking institutions, he might have thought it reasonable to expect Torshin to do the same for him with respect to banking institutions in the Russian Federation.[63] According to National Public Radio, both the Kremlin operative Butina and her handler Torshin had wanted access to top officials at the Treasury Department and Federal Reserve—access they received, with the help of CNI, in April 2015—to initiate an "unofficial channel of diplomacy," as Butina would later call it.[64] As for the role of Simes's CNI deputy Paul Saunders in setting up the meetings, Saunders will concede in May 2019 that CNI wanted to facilitate Kremlin contact with influential American officials because "we were about a year into U.S. sanctions on Russia following their annexation of Crimea, [so] we thought it would be interesting for Americans to hear from a Russian central bank official about the status of the Russian financial system" under the new sanctions regime.[65] Saunders's confession casts doubt on Simes's claim—

already belied by his actions in linking up the Trump campaign with Sergey Kislyak and Richard Burt (see chapter 3)—that neither he nor CNI ever sought to put anyone in the Trump campaign in touch with agents of the Russian government. This was, in fact, exactly the sort of interlocution his organization had already sought and achieved with respect to Torshin, Butina, and several U.S. government officials, including undersecretary of the treasury for international affairs Nathan Sheets and Federal Reserve vice chairman Stanley Fischer.[66] According to the NPR report, CNI had originally sought to get Torshin and Butina an audience with Federal Reserve chair Janet Yellen, settling for Fischer only when Yellen "passed on the meeting."[67] That the CNI donor Simes was ostensibly seeking Torshin's assistance on behalf of appears to have had no knowledge of Simes's efforts—"There's no evidence that [former AIG CEO Maurice "Hank"] Greenberg requested the outreach [to Torshin] or was even aware of it"— adds yet another troubling dimension to Simes's contacts with Torshin during the presidential campaign.[68] After Simes's clandestine lobbying of the Kremlin ostensibly on his behalf, Greenberg makes the decision to have his philanthropic foundation cut "much of its support" for CNI; its current level of aid is approximately 4 percent of what it was previously.[69] A Greenberg spokesman says the former executive is simply "scaling back his commitments to focus on his company and philanthropy"—the latter a category to which the foundation's donations to CNI appear to no longer belong, in Greenberg's view.[70]

Throughout the 2016 campaign, Simes will profoundly influence, from behind the scenes, the four most controversial components of candidate Trump's foreign policy agenda: his stances toward Putin, Russian election interference, the Kremlin's military adventures in Ukraine, and U.S. sanctions against Russia. From March through Election Day and beyond, Simes "provide[s] counsel . . . regarding Russia" to the campaign and transition, including, at a minimum, the following: helping, in April 2016, to "draft Trump's CNI-hosted foreign policy speech," in which "Trump called for an 'easing of tensions' with Russia"; "advising Trump on 'what to say about Russia'" during the summer of 2016; sending a policy memo with "several policy recommendations" to the head of Trump's national security advisory committee, Jeff Sessions, in June 2016; sending another "Russia policy memo" directly to Jared Kushner in August 2016; "pedd[ling] alleged compromising information to Jared Kushner on Bill and Hillary Clinton's ties to Russia" in mid-2016, including information that "the Russian government had tapes of Bill Clinton having phone sex with Monica Lewinsky"; setting up yet another meeting between Sessions and the Kremlin's ambassador to the United States, Kislyak, after the election; and "recommend[ing] for administration jobs" certain "longtime associates" during the presidential transition, including former Gazprom lobbyist and Russian Alfa Bank board member Richard Burt.[71] In his August 2016 memo to Kushner, Simes directly addresses Putin's top policy goal—the dissolution of the sanctions regime established by the U.S. government after Putin's illegal annexation of Crimea—by making "suggestions [to Trump] about how to handle Ukraine-related questions."[72] According to his colleagues at CNI, Simes believed his role on the Trump campaign to be a broad one, trying "to take Trump's intuitions [on Russia] and turn them into something coherent."[73] Russian American historian Yuri Felshtinsky, who co-wrote a book with Alexander Litvinenko—the London-dwelling Russian-intelligence defector the Kremlin assassinated using radioactive tea in 2006—has observed "the peculiarity of Simes's high-level Kremlin relationships and . . . his ability to address Putin directly at high-level public forums, like at the Valdai International Discussion Club," adding that, when it comes to the media's understanding of Simes's role in American and Russian politics, "we only know the tip of the iceberg."[74]

The Mueller Report calls Simes's CNI "a think tank with expertise in and connections to the Russian government" and explains that, in addition to the contacts with the Trump campaign already noted, Simes had "various other contacts" with the chairman of Trump's national security advisory committee, Jeff Sessions, during the 2016 campaign, even making Sessions a member of CNI's "board of directors . . . and advisory council."[75] The result of Sessions's acceptance of this position is that three close Trump advisers on Russia—Simes, Sessions, and Richard Burt, already a CNI board member at the time of Sessions's elevation—are part of "a think tank with . . . connections to the Russian government" even as they are advising Trump on Russia policy during the 2016 presidential campaign. Sessions goes on to have numerous contacts with Russian officials during the campaign, even as his friend Simes continues to be known for, per the Mueller Report, his "many contacts with current and former Russian government officials" and his center's "unparalleled access to Russian officials and politicians among Washington think tanks."[76]

If what is already known of Simes's advisory role on the Trump campaign is concerning, so too is the timing of his contacts with its senior staffers. Simes's first contact with Jared Kushner is on March 14, 2016, the day the Kremlin first makes contact with George Papadopoulos through Joseph Mifsud. Simes's second contact with Kushner comes on March 24, the day MBZ meets Putin in the Kremlin—the two men having just discussed "friendship and co-operation" between the UAE and Russia in a phone call eleven days earlier—and the day the Kremlin makes its second contact with Papadopoulos, with Mifsud this time introducing him, in London, to the mysterious "Olga Polonskaya," who presents herself as Vladimir Putin's "niece." Simes's third contact with Kushner comes on the day Trump's national security advisory committee meets for the first time, during which meeting Simes and Kushner speak of—apropos of the day's main event—Simes's advice, apparently already accepted by the campaign, that "the best way to handle foreign-policy issues for the Trump Campaign would be to organize an advisory group of experts to meet with candidate Trump"; seventy-two hours later, Simes's CNI publishes an article predicting, contrary to the conventional wisdom of the moment, that the Saudi royal family will "eventually soften its anti-Assad approach and diplomatically engage with Russia."[77] Simes also meets with Kushner on August 17, the same day Kushner's father-in-law has his first classified national security briefing—a briefing that warns the campaign about its possible infiltration by Kremlin agents.[78]

Three days after the DNC publicly announces, in mid-June 2016, that it has been hacked by the Russian government, Simes sends Sessions's deputy, J. D. Gordon, a memo urging the campaign to embrace "a new beginning with Russia." The memo references a recent Simes-Sessions meeting—whose timing with respect to the announcement of the DNC hack is unknown—

and proposes an initiative Trump would shortly adopt: the narrowing of his original national security advisory committee to a "'small and carefully selected group of experts' to assist Sessions with the Campaign."[79] Consistent with this advice, from mid-June 2016 onward the group advising Trump on national security and foreign policy issues is composed entirely of men who would thereafter have meetings with Russian nationals: Jeff Sessions, J. D. Gordon, Carter Page, George Papadopoulos, professor and political pundit Walid Phares, Michael Flynn, and Erik Prince.[80] There is no record of any other individuals—including any individuals originally appointed to Trump's national security advisory committee in March 2016—being involved in advising Trump on national security issues after Simes urges Trump to winnow down his team of national security advisers.

Simes, former Gazprom adviser Page, and Papadopoulos—along with CNI board member and former Gazprom lobbyist Richard Burt—help Trump adviser Stephen Miller shape, write, and edit Trump's first major foreign policy address in April 2016, even as CNI board member Jeff Sessions's chief of staff, Rick Dearborn, is organizing the Mayflower Hotel event at which Trump will deliver the speech.[81] Simes even offers input on the location of the speech, the logistics of the speech, and the roster of individuals who will be invited to the intimate pre-speech VIP reception—one of whom, Russian ambassador Sergey Kislyak, Simes invites to the speech personally.[82] At the VIP event, another brainchild of Kushner and Simes, Simes introduces Kislyak to Trump, and Kushner and Kislyak have a conversation during which the Kremlin representative tells Trump's son-in-law that "we [the Kremlin] like what your candidate is saying."[83] After Trump's speech at the Mayflower there is a private, unannounced luncheon attended by Simes, Kushner, and others, none of whose names are released to the press.[84]

Trump's Mayflower address, delivered on April 27, comes a day after Mifsud tells Papadopoulos that the Kremlin is willing to assist the Trump campaign by anonymously releasing damaging information about Hillary Clinton.[85] Papadopoulos is, at the time, part of the speechwriting team for the foreign policy speech Trump intends to give the next day. In the speech, Trump urges a détente in the form of a "deal" between the United States and Russia.[86] Papadopoulos tells investigators he does not recall telling candidate Trump about Mifsud's revelation before his speech at the Mayflower, but John Mashburn—who at the time is working alongside Rick Dearborn, the Mayflower event's organizer, in the campaign's policy shop— tells Congress that in fact he recalls receiving an email from Papadopoulos about the Kremlin having damaging information on Clinton and believes other senior Trump campaign officials received it as well.[87] Papadopoulos himself will "waver" on whether he remembers Sam Clovis (the man who hired him and originally assembled Trump's national security advisory committee, and who therefore would have been likely to receive any email Papadopoulos sent to Mashburn) getting angry at him for telling him about Mifsud's disclosure.[88] The day of Trump's Mayflower speech, Papadopoulos writes one of his "newfound Russian contacts," a colleague of Joseph Mifsud's named Ivan Timofeev, to say that the speech is the "signal" for Trump and Putin to meet.[89]

On May 23, four days after Trump names the longtime Kremlin-linked public relations man Paul Manafort his campaign chairman—he will elevate him again, to campaign manager, on June 20—Sessions attends Simes's and CNI's Distinguished Service Award dinner at the Four Seasons Hotel in Washington. CNI invites Sergey Kislyak to the event, and Simes's deputy Paul Saunders creates a seating plan that places him next to Sessions, though stories vary as to whether Kislyak appears at the dinner or not.[90] Simes's attempt to again facilitate direct discourse between the Trump campaign and the Kremlin would not have gone unnoticed by either party, however. Indeed, Simes will invite Sessions to two further dinners after May 23, both of which are also attended by Richard Burt, whom Simes later petitions Trump to name U.S. ambassador to Russia.[91] Burt, the former Russian Alfa Bank board member, is, in 2016, sufficiently known to the Kremlin that when Putin indicates to a man he has identified as one of his fifty most powerful and influential oligarchs, Petr Aven, that after the U.S. election Aven needs to contact the Trump transition team to protect Alfa Bank's assets in the event of a new round of sanctions from the Obama administration, it is to Burt that Aven turns (see chapter 6).[92]

After Kushner and Simes's conveniently timed March 2016 meetings, and the Mayflower Hotel event and foreign policy speech they coordinate, the two men have so many private meetings that the Mueller Report is unable to provide a date for each one, calling them simply "periodic" and indicating they include both "in-person meetings and phone conversations" that are often about directing the committee—Trump's national security advisory committee—that "Simes had proposed."[93] Simes's impossible-to-verify contention that he at one point told Kushner "it was bad optics for the Campaign to develop hidden Russian contacts" is belied by the fact that the campaign Simes was advising, which throughout its life span repeatedly took his advice on matters relating to Russia, had more hidden Russian contacts than any campaign for the presidency in U.S. history.[94] Simes's placement in the shadows of the Trump campaign policy shop obscures not only his level of access to the candidate's son-in-law but also his course of advising, as noted by the Mueller Report, on the two topics that were the subject of all the campaign's clandestine contacts with Kremlin agents: "what Mr. Trump may want to say about Russia" and "questions about Russia's invasion and annexation of Crimea"—that is, sanctions.[95]

Most troubling, in the timeline of Trump campaign–Simes connections, are Simes's attempts to peddle Russian *kompromat* to the campaign in advance of the first presidential debates.[96] In mid-August 2016, Simes writes and speaks to Kushner of "a well-documented story of highly questionable connections between Bill Clinton and the Russian government," claiming that the Kremlin is now "blackmailing" the Clintons.[97] While Simes will claim to the special counsel's office that his information on Bill Clinton originated from "U.S. intelligence sources," the former CIA operative named by Simes as his source has since confirmed that some of the information "was intercepted while the president [Bill Clinton] was traveling on Air Force One"—a clear indication that the provenance of the intelligence Simes urged the Trump campaign to use in 2016 was in fact Russian spycraft and *kompromat*.[98] Simes was so enthused about injecting this Russian-held blackmail material into the U.S. general election campaign that, according to Mueller's report, he even "provided the same information at a small group meeting of foreign policy experts that CNI organized for Sessions."[99] What is unclear is why Simes was discussing with his CIA source, in "2014 or 2015," what the *Washington Examiner* calls "a claim that Russians recorded President Bill

Clinton having phone sex with White House intern Monica Lewinsky";
while the Kremlin had already initiated its election-interference campaign
by 2014—a campaign that included the spreading of negative information
about the Clintons—it was not until mid-2015 that Trump joined the presidential race and not until spring 2016 that either Clinton or Trump had
clinched their respective parties' nominations.[100] That Simes was collecting
kompromat information on the Clintons as early as 2014 raises the question of
who if anyone had urged him to do so, and to whom he expected he would
ultimately transmit the information he was gathering.

After the 2016 election, Kushner relied on Simes to "identify which
Russian emissaries had political clout in Moscow," and was indeed so reliant on the CNI director that when he needed to confirm the name of the
Russian ambassador to the United States, he had his staff consult Simes
instead of Google.[101]

During the spring of 2014, as Trump is making his plans to run for president
public and the Kremlin is beginning its outreach to Papadopoulos's eventual
Kremlin conduit, Joseph Mifsud, the Internet Research Agency—a Kremlin-
linked disinformation project overseen by Yevgeny Prigozhin, known in
Russia as "Putin's chef"—begins to "hide its funding and activities" and
"consolidate [its] U.S. operations within a single general department, known
internally as the 'Translator' department," according to the Mueller Report.[102] These shifts signal a new stage in the Kremlin's upcoming election-
interference effort, and are followed in June 2014 by a clandestine visit to
the United States by four IRA employees.[103] Internal IRA documents will
not reflect the agency's pro-Trump position until February 2016, however,
with the operation purchasing its first anti-Clinton ads on social media
in March 2016 and its first pro-Trump ads in April 2016 (see chapter 4).[104]

In May 2014, Russia ramps up its nuclear infrastructure investments in
the Middle East, revealing its plans to build eight more nuclear reactors
in Bushehr, Iran, having signed its initial contract to build reactors for the
plant there in 1995 and then seeing the nuclear plant reach full reactor
capacity in August 2012.[105] The Kremlin's late-spring announcement comes

as Russia is one of six nations—with the United States, the United King-dom, France, Germany, and China—working with the European Union to seal a nuclear deal with Iran that will prohibit it from enriching uranium to build nuclear weapons. Under the terms of the Joint Comprehensive Plan of Action (known colloquially as the "Iran nuclear deal"), Iran will agree to process uranium ore to only 3.7 percent enrichment—90 percent being the minimum enrichment required for a nuclear weapon—for the next fifteen years, and to allow international inspectors into the country to confirm its compliance with this limitation. In exchange, the punishing international economic sanctions that had been leveled against Iran over its nuclear weapons program will be lifted.[106]

The Iran nuclear deal is vehemently opposed by Israel, whose "existen-tial fear of a nuclear-armed Iran," as the *Atlantic* terms it, causes Israeli prime minister Benjamin Netanyahu to say of the accord, just two weeks after it is signed, that it is a "stunning historic mistake" and "a very dan-gerous deal . . . [that] threatens all of us."[107] Meanwhile, Saudi officials, opining that the deal does not permanently end the Iranian nuclear threat, call it "extremely dangerous" and "unacceptable" and worry that the re-moval of sanctions will "allow Iran to fund proxy wars [in the Middle East] and extend its regional influence."[108] One result of the deal, according to a CBS News summary of the views of Tariq Al-Shammari, president of the Council of Gulf International Relations, is that "behind the scenes . . . Gulf Arab countries will work to try and keep Iran isolated politically and economically . . . [with] Saudi Arabia in particular . . . already mov[ing] to improve ties with Russia, which is a strong ally of Iran."[109]

In the Middle East, the *New York Times* has written, "many major players are closely allied with or supported by either Shiite Iran or Sunni Saudi Arabia, and any gain by one is often seen as a loss by the other."[110] This dynamic explains why the July 2015 Iran deal leads almost immediately to discussion of a "regional arms race," with the Saudis and their Emi-rati allies beginning to consider how they might match what they pre-sume will be increased Iranian uranium enrichment activity in the years ahead—despite the explicit terms of the nuclear deal Iran has signed.[111] The first step in this new nuclear standoff would be Saudi Arabia and its Sunni peers in the Gulf gaining the agreement of their Western allies to let them enrich uranium ore, and to do so at a higher level than previously thought appropriate for a country with no interest in weaponizing nuclear material. With this aim in mind, soon after the Iran deal is signed a "Saudi diplomat [says] his nation will look at embarking on a nuclear energy program so it can be closer to having nuclear weapons if Iran breaks the deal and weaponizes its [nuclear] program."[112]

Outside Saudi Arabia, attitudes toward the deal are mixed. The *Washington Post* will note that Qatar and Oman "have moved toward improved relations with Tehran" and therefore choose to register no public disapproval of the deal's terms; Turkey stands to "boost its oil imports from Iran" post-deal; and Iran's ally Syria calls the deal "a great victory" in a statement from President Bashar al-Assad.[113] All four of these nations will be left out of the historic geopolitical reorganization in the Middle East plotted by Saudi Arabia in late 2015. More unsettling to the Saudis, surely, is the ruler of its closest ally, the United Arab Emirates, Sheikh Khalifa bin Zayed al-Nahyan, publicly congratulating Iranian president Hassan Rouhani on the deal and saying that he hopes it will "contribute to strengthening regional security and stability."[114] Al-Nahyan's statement gives Saudi Arabia's Mohammed bin Salman additional grounds to seek an even closer alliance with MBZ, who occupies a separate and distinct matrix of power in the UAE.

As CBS News will note, none of the Sunni Arab nations in the Gulf are privately very enthusiastic about the deal, "worry[ing] that a deal gives Iran the means—through an economic windfall—and an implicit green light to push influence in the region."[115] Abdulkhaleq Abdullah, a professor of political science at United Arab Emirates University, tells CBS, "Deal or no deal, tension in the region is not going to go away. If Iran is bent on acting as a hegemon, as a regional power, I think we are in for some difficult times."[116] This lingering doubt over the repercussions of the Iran deal explains in part why, despite Sheikh Khalifa's words of congratulation to President Rouhani following the deal's signing, his younger brother, MBZ, will take a very different view of the accord in 2015 than the UAE's president. That by 2015 the UAE is enmeshed in another proxy war with Iran—this time fighting an army of allegedly Iran-sponsored Houthi rebels in Yemen—does far more to explain why the Emiratis' view of the Iran deal will soon change, however.

Though former secretary of state Hillary Clinton had left the U.S. State Department more than two years before the signing of the Iran nuclear deal, CNN will report in 2015 that "supporters, critics and experts agree: Clinton's fingerprints are all over the nuclear agreement."[117] It is all but certain that this fact is on the minds of MBS, MBZ, and el-Sisi as they meet on a yacht in the Red Sea in fall 2015 and make a decision about whom to support in the 2016 U.S. presidential election.

In June 2014, six months after Trump tells GOP officials in New York that he will be running for president, and seven months after discussing American foreign policy and presidential politics with his Russian business partners, the Agalarovs, in Moscow, the Trump Organization announces that it will purchase the Turnberry golf resort in Scotland from Leisurecorp—a unit of the Emirati government—for $48.5 million, an astounding $44.2 million less than the Emiratis had paid for the property just seventy-two months earlier.[118] Several weeks later, Trump travels to Turnberry to announce that he will pour approximately $130 million into the resort, just under three times its total purchase price.[119] Trump is, at the time, in the midst of building Trump Estates in the UAE, a development of more than a hundred "luxury villas" that will overlook a Trump-branded golf course to be named Trump International Golf Club Dubai.[120]

In less than forty-eight months, the new Trump-branded Turnberry property—Trump Turnberry—will lose $39 million despite Trump's $130 million in improvements (he will later claim $260 million, while his project manager will insist it was $181 million).[121] Nevertheless, by August 2018 Trump will announce that in addition to the $130 million (up to $260 million) he has already invested in his money-losing operation at Turnberry, he will now invest an additional $200 million in his other Trump-branded golf course in Scotland, Trump Aberdeen.[122] *Quartz* will call Trump's investments in golf properties in Scotland "a string of investments . . . that appear to make little business sense" and have consistently performed "terribly."[123] With Trump Aberdeen losing $9.2 million in its first six years of operation—2012 to 2018—and Trump Turnberry losing $39 million from 2014 to 2018, the *Atlantic* will note in August 2018 that the source of funds for Trump's planned improvements on these properties is a "mystery."[124]

Whereas, prior to 2006—around the time Felix Sater became Trump's fixer for real estate investments in Russia—the historically illiquid Trump denominated himself the "King of Debt," from that year on he inexplicably finds himself able to pay for all his projects, including his two Scottish golf courses, in cash.[125] The *Atlantic* reports that "onlookers have struggled to explain both this new [investment] model [for Trump] and Trump's Scottish projects." According to Adam Davidson of the *New Yorker*, Trump's purchase of Turnberry from the Emiratis is, from a business standpoint, "a bizarre, confounding move that raises questions about the central nature of his business during the years in which he prepared for and then executed his presidential campaign."[126] Davidson will observe, in a July 2018 report on Turnberry, that Trump's investment in the golf course "is so much bigger than his other recent projects that it would not be unreasonable to describe the Trump Organization as, at its core, a manager of a money-losing Scottish golf course that is kept afloat with funds from licensing fees and decades-old real-estate projects."[127]

Davidson's assessment—which includes the notation that, even at a staggering discount, the purchase of Turnberry from the Emiratis consumed "more than half of the [Trump Organization's] available cash"—is bolstered by the small amount of data publicly available on the Trump Organization's finances.[128] The *Wall Street Journal* finds that from January 2014 through June 2015, the pretax income for the entire Trump Organization was $160 million—an approximately $106 million annual income before taxes—yet during this period Trump was, by his own accounting, in the midst of a four-year, $260 million investment in Trump Turnberry and gearing up for an investment, in 2018, of $197 million at Trump Aberdeen.[129] All told, just these two investments—in a pair of golf courses in Scotland—add up to over 400 percent of the annual pretax revenue of the Trump Organization during the period assayed by the *Wall Street Journal.*

Incredibly, Trump's planned $197 million investment in Trump Aberdeen is just a down payment on a much larger investment: according to the *Atlantic,* in order to get permission to construct any additions at all to the Aberdeen property, Trump had to "promise [to] . . . spend $1.3 billion on two golf courses, a luxury hotel and hundreds of homes" on the site.[130] Even with that figure thereafter being dialed back to $971 million, there remains no explanation for how, absent massive loans, Trump could possibly afford the development he was planning in Aberdeen at the time of his inauguration in 2017.[131] Based on publicly available data, Trump should have been hundreds of millions of dollars short of being able to afford the announced project in Scotland, even if the Trump Organization were to pause all its other real estate investments and pending projects. It is little surprise, then, that the *New Yorker* concludes in 2018 that "it is hard to understand where all of the money spent on Turnberry came from."[132]

In May 2018, Eric Trump will insist to the *Washington Post* that the Trump Organization's odds-defying budgeting is the result of "incredible cash flow" from existing sources.[133] The *Post* will express some incredulity about the claim, noting Trump's "string of commercial bankruptcies" at the time the Trump Organization was spending lavishly in Scotland as well as "the Great Recession's hammering of the real estate industry."[134] And indeed Eric Trump's claim that the Trump Organization has used neither outside investment, borrowing, nor the selling off of assets to raise hundreds of millions of dollars not otherwise evident on its balance sheet is belied by a statement Eric subsequently makes to *Golf* magazine.[135] Trump's second son, "who runs the golf side of the Trump business" according to the *Atlantic,* is asked by *Golf* reporter James Dodson in 2013 how it is that, after the 2008 recession—when, per Dodson, no banks were "touch[ing] a golf course"—the Trumps managed to move hundreds of millions of dollars into a series of new golf course properties.[136] "Well, we don't rely on American banks," Eric tells Dodson. "We have all the funding we need out of Russia. . . . We've got some [Russian] guys that really, really love golf, and they're really invested in our programs. We just go there [for money] all the time."[137]

ANNOTATIONS

Internal IRA documents will not reflect the agency's pro-Trump position until February 2016, however, with the operation purchasing its first anti-Clinton ads on social media in March 2016 and its first pro-Trump ads in April 2016.

According to the Mueller Report, the IRA's activities will ultimately reach between 29 million and 126 million Americans via Facebook, across 80,000 posts and hundreds of thousands of followers of bogus IRA-run Facebook groups.[138] On Twitter, the IRA runs 3,814 accounts, which, all told, tweet 175,993 times in just the ten weeks before the 2016 election.[139] Approximately 1.4 million Americans are "in contact with" an IRA account on Twitter before the election, per the Mueller Report.[140] IRA tweets are retweeted or otherwise engaged with by many associates of and advisers to the Trump campaign, including Michael Flynn, Michael Flynn Jr., Donald Trump Jr., Kellyanne Conway, Roger Stone, Brad Parscale (now Trump's 2020 campaign manager), and a Fox News personality who advises Trump regularly on domestic policy issues behind the scenes, Sean Hannity.[141] "In total," the report states, "Trump campaign affiliates promoted dozens of tweets, posts, and other political content created by the IRA."[142]

The Mueller Report identifies an additional 50,258 Twitter accounts linked to the Kremlin—which combined send out more than a million tweets in the ten weeks before Election Day in 2016.[143]

Meanwhile, Saudi officials, opining that the deal does not permanently end the Iranian nuclear threat, call it "extremely dangerous" and "unacceptable" and worry that the removal of sanctions on Iran will "allow Iran to fund proxy wars [in the Middle East] and extend its regional influence."

The three proxy wars the Saudis and Emiratis are particularly concerned about include Iranian support for the regime of President Bashar al-Assad, who stands accused of war crimes in the Syrian civil war; alleged Iranian support for the Houthi rebels in Yemen fighting against a Saudi-Emirati coalition backed by the United States; and alleged passive Iranian support for Islamic State, as Iran "has extended its influence politically and militarily as the [Iraqi] government battles Islamic State extremists," according to the *Washington Post* in 2015.[144]

The *Wall Street Journal* found that from January 2014 through June 2015, the pretax income for the entire Trump Organization was $160 million—an approximately $106 million annual income before taxes.

As the *New Yorker* notes, "With that money, Trump had to pay for his business, his taxes (if he paid any), his personal life style, and that of his family. His Boeing 757 alone cost more than ten thousand dollars per hour of use, not to mention the dozens of staffers at his various properties, the clothes and food and jewelry of a status-conscious family, and countless other expenses that could easily eat up all of that income. There simply isn't enough money coming into Trump's known business to cover the massive outlay he spent on Turnberry."[145]

In 2014 Trump did more than buy Turnberry for $48.5 million, however. He also spent $29.2 million to buy yet another golf course, this one in Doonbeg, Ireland (ultimately named Trump International Golf Links & Hotel Ireland).[146] Between 2014 and 2018, the *Washington Post* reports, material improvements to the two properties notwithstanding, Trump had to drop another $164 million in cash just to keep Turnberry and Doonbeg open.[147] Doonbeg was priced at $16 million when it initially went on the market, according to the *Guardian*, suggesting that Trump may have overpaid for it by as much as $13.2 million.[148]

CHAPTER 3

THE YOUNG PRINCE, ISRAELI SPIES, THE NRA JUNKET, AND THE FLYNN INTEL GROUP

2015

As MBS ascends to power in Riyadh with the support and approval of MBZ, MBZ adviser Erik Prince insinuates himself into the Trump campaign. Meanwhile, Israeli business intelligence companies become involved with multiple GOP presidential campaigns. Trump's data firm, Cambridge Analytica, places itself at the center of a UAE-Israeli election-meddling scandal with Russian connections. The recently signed Iran nuclear deal and Trump's secret negotiations with the Kremlin over a proposed Trump Tower Moscow lend urgency to the actions of key players in several countries.

As 2015—the year the Iran nuclear deal becomes fully effective—begins, America's Arab allies in the Gulf are, with Israel, deeply concerned about whether the United States can be relied upon to help ensure security in the region as it once was. According to one senior Arab diplomat, "There is a determination among us now that if there are security issues, we have to take action [ourselves] and we will. We don't have to ask America's permission. We of course will collaborate with the U.S., but we won't wait for America to tell us what to do."[1] This new ethos of radical independence—

tinged as it is, at least in the American view, with the potential for recklessness by certain Sunni Arab states—will be a defining characteristic of 2015 in the Middle East. As CNN will note, the GCC (which in 2015 comprises Saudi Arabia, the UAE, Bahrain, Qatar, Kuwait, and Oman) is particularly emboldened by its divergence from the Obama administration's view of the wisdom of engaging with Iran.[2] Per CNN, "the Gulf states, along with Israel, worry that the deal with Tehran will pave the way for a nuclear bomb rather than prevent one, and unlock billions of dollars that Iran will use to wreak havoc in the region. That fear has forced the six [GCC] nations to overcome a host of internal differences, heal long-standing rifts and show a level of unity that has been lacking. It also has led the bloc to show less deference to the United States."[3] When representatives of the GCC nations travel to the White House and Camp David in May 2015 to meet with President Obama, their new unity will be on display; behind the scenes, the most powerful member of the bloc—Saudi Arabia—is ready to fundamentally change the composition of the GCC and significantly expand its already negative orientation toward engagement with Iran.

In January 2015, King Salman ascends to the throne of Saudi Arabia. Within sixty days, his twenty-nine-year-old son Mohammed bin Salman—a man with no military experience—is named minister of defense, deputy crown prince, and the head of Saudi Arabia's oil company, Saudi Aramco.[4] MBS immediately launches a war against Yemen to dislodge Houthi rebels, who have driven the Yemeni government into exile, from Sana'a, the Yemeni capital.[5] To the great consternation of his older cousins, MBS's war with Yemen is initiated without, as observed by the *New York Times* in October 2016, "full coordination across the security services"; indeed, as the kingdom's first strikes in Yemen are being carried out in March 2015, Prince Mutaib bin Abdullah, the head of the Saudi National Guard, not only hasn't been informed of the action but isn't even in the country.[6]

Shortly thereafter, in April 2015, King Salman names his nephew Mohammed bin Nayef as the crown prince and his successor, though he has already taken actions suggesting that his ultimate successor will be MBS. According to the *Times*, beginning in January 2015 "new powers . . .

flow[ ] to his [King Salman's] son [MBS], some of them undermining the authority of the crown prince [bin Nayef]. King Salman collapse[s] the crown prince's court into his own, giving Prince bin Salman control over access to the king. Prince bin Salman also hastily announce[s] the formation [in December 2015] of a military alliance of Islamic countries to fight terrorism," a plan that effectively freezes bin Nayef's Interior Ministry out of any meaningful role in the country's new counterterrorism agenda.[7] The *Times* notes that "Saudi Arabia is one of the world's few remaining absolute monarchies, which means that Prince bin Salman was given all of his powers by a vote of one: his own father."[8]

In its first year, MBS's war in Yemen—one of his most "concrete initiatives," notes the *Times*—"fail[s] to dislodge the Shiite Houthi rebels and their allies from the Yemeni capital . . . drive[s] much of Yemen toward famine and kill[s] thousands of civilians while costing the Saudi government tens of billions of dollars."[9] Shortly after the hostilities begin in March 2015, bin Salman disappears for an unexpected "vacation" in the Maldives, during which period even Ashton B. Carter, the U.S. secretary of defense, is unable to reach the young Saudi prince. The Maldives is an island nation in the Indian Ocean where, after several meetings in the Seychelles, future Trump adviser Erik Prince will reportedly meet with Russian and Emirati agents on Trump's behalf in early 2017 (see chapter 6).[10]

It is unknown whether Prince, or anyone else who will end up in the orbit of the Trump campaign, meets with the Saudi deputy crown prince (who is also the Saudi minister of defense) while MBS is "vacationing"—in the midst of a war he recently initiated—in the Maldives; there are indications this could have happened, however. At around the same time that bin Salman is mysteriously in the Maldives, allied intelligence agencies begin to intercept substantial chatter among Kremlin operatives discussing associates of Trump.[11] According to the *Wall Street Journal*, "the volume of the mentions of Trump associates by the Russians . . . have [European intelligence] officials asking one another, 'What's going on?'"[12] While there is, at present, no known direct association between bin Salman and Trump in spring 2015, it is clear that bin Salman's "brawny foreign policy" aligns with Trump's past statements about Saudi Arabia taking care of its own defense needs. MBS's plan, according to the *New York Times*, is to have the kingdom be "less reliant on Western powers like the United States for its security"—an echo of the policy position frequently articulated by Trump on Twitter.[13] Like Trump, bin Salman opposes any "thawing of America's relations with Iran," a euphemism for opposition to the Iran nuclear deal.[14] Andrew Bowen, a Saudi expert at the Wilson Center in Washington, D.C., will in 2016 associate bin Salman's belligerent policies with "a surge of Saudi nationalism," yet another mirroring of Trump's own political instincts.[15] MBS's "main message is that Saudi Arabia is a force to be reckoned with," according to another Middle East expert, Brian Katulis of Washington's Center for American Progress.[16]

Back in the United States, Paul Manafort spends the spring of 2015 in a clinic in Arizona, having suffered a "massive emotional breakdown," according to his daughter Andrea.[17] The onetime international operator calls his family daily with his voice "soaked in tears," according to the *Atlantic*, and intimates to his other daughter, Jessica, that "suicide [is] a possibility."[18] One of his chief stressors is what Andrea describes as a "tight cash flow state" resulting from his former patron Viktor Yanukovych having recently fled to Russia to escape execution at the hands of a nationwide revolution in Ukraine; whether Manafort is aware that the FBI has already begun investigating him for his work in Ukraine is unclear, but his daughters note that he suddenly seems unwilling or unable to access any of the offshore bank accounts that might have alleviated the serious financial strain he is experiencing.[19] He is also being hunted—quite literally—by Deripaska, to whom the United States has denied a visa due to what it believes to be his "ties to organized crime" and who, as Manafort would have been well aware, "won his fortune by prevailing in the so-called 'aluminum wars' of the 1990s, a corpse-filled struggle, one of the most violent of all the competitions for dominance in a post-Soviet industry."[20] The previous year one of Deripaska's attorneys had complained in open court that Manafort was on the run from Deripaska, saying of the former Yanukovych aide—and his business partner Rick Gates, who would soon end up as Trump's deputy campaign manager—that "it appears that Paul Manafort and Rick Gates have simply disappeared."[21]

Manafort's "disappearance" is short-lived, however. In February 2016, he surfaces at a business lunch with his old friend, longtime Trump confidant Thomas Barrack, telling the Lebanese American billionaire businessman and Colony Capital founder and executive chairman, "I really need to get to" Trump.[22] When Barrack helps him do just that—in March 2016 winning him a job, through a course of lobbying Trump, as Trump's "delegate counter"—the desperately cash-strapped Manafort, still owing millions of dollars to dangerous men overseas, nevertheless offers to work pro bono. As the *Atlantic* will note in early 2018, "When Paul Manafort officially joined the Trump campaign . . . he represented a danger not only to himself but to the political organization he would ultimately run. A lifetime of foreign adventures . . . evinced the character of a man . . . [with a] lifetime role as a corrupter of the American system. That he would be accused of helping a foreign power subvert American democracy is a fitting coda to his life's story."[23]

It is little surprise that Barrack has the influence with Trump to convince the GOP candidate to begin the process of replacing his campaign manager, Corey Lewandowski. As longtime Trump friend, adviser, and ally Roger Stone explains, "[Thomas Barrack] is the only person I know who the president speaks to as a peer. Barrack is to Trump as [Florida banker] Bebe Rebozo was to Nixon, which is the best friend."[24] But Barrack is also more than this to the extended Trump family: he is Jared Kushner's lender, holding $70 million of the debt owed by Kushner on the worst real estate investment of his career, 666 Fifth Avenue in New York City.[25] Barrack's late-2000s investment in Kushner helped save Ivanka's husband from bankruptcy, a circumstance that could have materially affected Trump's daughter as well.[26] The billionaire speaks Arabic, worked for Richard Nixon's personal lawyer—yet another Trump-circle confidant with Nixon ties, joining Roger Stone, Dimitri Simes, Ed Cox, CNI patron and Kushner acquaintance Henry Kissinger, and others—and made his fortune by networking with powerful Saudis and Emiratis, including an executive at the Saudi government-owned oil firm Saudi Aramco, the Emirati oil minister, a son of the Saudi kingdom's then ruler, and a host of other "Persian Gulf royals," to whom he became, according to the *Times*, a "concierge" who not only "look[ed] after their children on visits to the West" but also "vacation[ed] with them at his home in the south of France."[27] Barrack had even opened up a halal restaurant on the Sardinian coast specifically to cater to "Gulf royals who came by in their yachts."[28]

Barrack's skill at flattery, according to an account in the *Times*, has been directed most vigorously over the years at three targets: Donald Trump and the Saudi and Emirati royal families. During the presidential campaign, Barrack will tell the Emirates' ambassador to the United States, Yousef al-Otaiba, that if he works in conjunction with Barrack, they "can turn [Trump] to prudence. He needs a few really smart Arab minds to whom he can confer." Barrack adds that the Emirati ambassador is "at the top of that list."[29] Indeed, as Barrack predicts, the Emirates' agent, al-Otaiba, will become one of the Trump campaign's most important advisers—though also, like Dimitri Simes, one that the campaign never acknowledges, for reasons that will become clear over time (see chapters 4 and 6).

After announcing his candidacy for president of the United States on May 4, 2015, neurosurgeon Ben Carson, a Republican, begins forming a foreign policy team with a surprising number of experts on the nation of Israel— many of whom will move directly to the campaign of Donald Trump in the weeks before Carson officially suspends his flailing campaign in early March 2016.[30] One of the Israel experts who joins Carson's campaign as a foreign policy adviser is George Birnbaum, a longtime GOP operative who "has worked extensively as a campaign consultant for Israeli politicians and has developed a network of contacts with current and former Israeli security officials."[31] Another member of Carson's team with substantial Israeli security contacts—though not an adviser to Carson exclusively, as he is also advising Donald Trump at the time—is Michael Flynn. Flynn will tell the *Washington Post* in August 2016 that Carson is one of the Republican presidential candidates who "would ask me about national security, what's happening in the world, my thoughts on particular issues." Flynn confirms to the *Post* that he met directly with Carson, and that "if I saw something I thought was important I would share it with [Carson and several other GOP candidates]."[32]

Prior to joining the Carson campaign as an adviser, Flynn had been approached by an Israeli business intelligence company, Psy-Group, whose owner, Joel Zamel, sought to recruit him.[33] As the *Daily Beast* writes, "Zamel apparently wanted former national security adviser Michael Flynn to be a member of the firm's advisory board; Zamel spoke with him about it on multiple occasions about the time Flynn was forming his ill-fated Flynn Intel Group," a period between fall 2014 and summer 2015 that ended just weeks before Trump summoned Flynn to Trump Tower in August 2015 for the pair's first meeting.[34] Trump will later claim, falsely, that he did not know Flynn in 2015, though it was Trump who had his team call Flynn in 2015, and Trump who permitted his first meeting with Flynn to run for ninety minutes instead of the scheduled thirty minutes.[35]

The *Daily Beast* confirms that Flynn is extremely fond of Zamel in 2014 and 2015, having taken "a real shining" to him.[36] Flynn's Iranian American business partner at the Flynn Intel Group, Bijan Kian, who will later be indicted in the Eastern District of Virginia on "charges of trying to influence American politicians" on behalf of Turkey without registering as an agent of a foreign government, is responsible for introducing Flynn to Zamel.[37] Illegal lobbying on behalf of a foreign government is, according to CNN, a "rarely charged crime," suggesting that federal investigators may in 2018 be more interested in Kian's dealings with Flynn and Zamel during the 2016 general election than in Kian's role as an intermediary between Flynn and the Turkish government during the same period. The Flynn-Zamel relationship appears to be key to Trump campaign–Israeli collusion in the months before Election Day.[38]

In late summer 2016, after he has been serving as a top national security advisor to candidate Trump for a year, Flynn meets at the JW Marriott Essex House New York hotel "with top Turkish government ministers and discusse[s] removing a Muslim cleric [Fethullah Gulen] from the U.S. and taking him to Turkey."[39] The action discussed by the parties would violate the federal kidnapping statute, as it would be orchestrated to "get Gulen . . . to Turkey without going through the U.S. extradition legal process," according to the *Wall Street Journal*.[40] One of the attendees at the meeting, former CIA director James Woolsey, will summarize the plan under consideration at the time as "a covert step in the dead of night to whisk this guy away," and says the only reason he didn't speak up to decry the proposed federal felony was that Flynn and the Turkish officials never got around to discussing "actual tactics for removing Mr. Gulen from his U.S. home."[41]

Three weeks after the White House fires him in early 2017, Flynn's consulting firm, the Flynn Intel Group, will file with the Department of Justice as a foreign agent for Turkey. When this happens, press secretary Sean Spicer will tell the media that "Mr. Trump was unaware Mr. Flynn had been consulting on behalf of the Turkish government when he named him national security adviser," even though Congress had informed Vice President–elect Mike Pence (the head of Trump's presidential transition team) of this fact in a public letter in November 2016, and President Obama had, in a face-to-face post-election meeting with Trump in the Oval Office, strongly warned him against hiring Flynn.[42]

That the summer 2016 meeting Flynn attended in which the kidnapping of Gulen was discussed was a high-level event is demonstrated by the fact that the Turkish president's son-in-law and the country's energy minister both attended it. Also present at the meeting were both Turkish businessman Ekim Alptekin (see chapter 6) and Bijan Kian.[43] Woolsey, who by November 2016 is serving as a "senior adviser" to Trump's presidential transition team alongside Flynn and Kian, will later say that he was so concerned about the content of Flynn's mid-2016 conversation with Turkish agents that he informed the sitting vice president of the United States, Joe Biden, through an intermediary—an exchange that may offer yet another explanation, besides what President Obama called Flynn's "crazy ideas," for Obama's warning to Trump not to hire the former DIA chief.[44] According to *Politico*, in their meeting at the White House two days after Trump's election victory, Obama didn't just advise Trump against hiring Flynn but "forcefully told [him] to steer clear of Flynn," unambiguous advice from the nation's commander in chief (and Flynn's former boss) that Trump ignored for reasons that have never been explained.[45]

Kian is not merely a business partner of Flynn's at the Flynn Intel Group as the presidential transition begins in November 2016 but also, with Flynn, an incoming member of Trump's national security transition team; during the period from Election Day to Trump's inauguration, the Flynn Intel Group is shuttered.[46] As the *Washington Times* has noted, "[Kian's] Trump transition role offered influence in the selection of intelligence agency candidates and access to internal discussions of U.S. national security policy."[47] In a filing in his 2019 criminal case, Kian will appear to allege, through his attorneys, that Flynn secretly had contact with Kirill Dmitriev after the 2016 election and never disclosed the meeting to the Defense Intelligence Agency, the Defense Department, or any other federal agency—a possibility that would fundamentally change investigators' understanding of Dmitriev's meeting with George Nader and Trump adviser Erik Prince at a bar in the Seychelles in early 2017 (see chapter 6).[48] Dmitriev's denials of any such clandestine meeting with Flynn will lose much of their weight after the Putin lieutenant offers innocuous descriptions of his meeting with Prince that are subsequently contradicted by major-media reporting.[49]

That Flynn's connection to the Israeli Zamel—and Zamel's connection to Kian—extends into Trump's transition period is confirmed by the fact that Zamel met with Flynn, and possibly Kian, at least once during the presidential transition (see chapter 6).[50] Flynn had also, just two months after Ben Carson's presidential campaign closed down in spring 2016, joined the advisory board of a subsidiary of "hacking firm" NSO Group—"a secretive cyberweapons dealer founded by former Israeli intelligence officials"—and done consulting work for the private equity firm that controls NSO.[51] A year later, NSO will sell $55 million worth of cell phone–hacking technology to MBS's government; it is technology that becomes critical to MBS's Kushner-assisted crushing of domestic dissent in Saudi Arabia in late 2017 (see chapter 8). Flynn's involvement with NSO beginning in the midst of the 2016 presidential election—indeed, in the very month that his friend Zamel's Israeli "business intelligence" operation, Psy-Group, first contacts the Trump campaign seeking to conduct covert intelligence-gathering on its behalf—establishes a high-level connection between Trump's "shadow" national security team (including Simes, Prince, and Flynn) and Israeli government-associated spying outfits from May 2016 through Election Day and beyond. One of the two companies with which Flynn is most closely linked, NSO, deals in such sensitive technology that it must do so in conjunction with clearances from the Israeli Defense Ministry (see chapter 8).

Another Carson adviser with strong ties to Israel is an obscure Middle East energy analyst by the name of George Papadopoulos, who joins Carson's campaign in late 2015 as (according to Papadopoulos) the GOP candidate's "principal foreign policy adviser."[52] Lightly published and still largely unknown in his field, Papadopoulos boasts few international publications prior to joining the Carson campaign, though one is an essay he had written the year before in *Arutz Sheva*, a Zionist Israeli publication.[53] In the essay, entitled "A Southern Strategy in the Eastern Mediterranean," Papadopoulos argues for America to adopt a Middle East policy identical to the one that the leaders of Saudi Arabia and the UAE will ultimately push Trump to accept; it is a view of America and the Middle East that is virulently anti-Obama, anti-Turkey, anti-Iran, anti–Muslim Brotherhood, and pro-el-Sisi.[54] Papadopoulos's focus is on how to negotiate Russia's growing influence in the Middle East, with the young analyst noting that "Cyprus, Israel, Syria, and Egypt [are] seeking out greater ties with Russia to safeguard their national interests. . . . Russia's last-minute negotiated deal to remove chemical stockpiles from Syria without an attack . . . has now allowed Russia to achieve its desired objective of becoming essential to all seemingly intractable conflicts in the eastern Mediterranean from Tehran to Cairo."[55] Papadopoulos admiringly speaks of Russia's "leverage . . . increas[ing]" in the Middle East, and of the way that "Russia has politically outmaneuvered the U.S." under Obama.[56] He proposes that the United States augment its military partnerships with Cyprus, Israel, and Greece, the last of these an idea Papadopoulos will personally advance by meeting with Greece's defense minister Panos Kammenos—a known "Putin ally," according to *BuzzFeed News*—as a representative of the Trump campaign in May 2016.[57] According to one NATO military intelligence officer *BuzzFeed News* will speak to in spring 2018, the very ministry of defense Papadopoulos was advising Trump to partner with in 2016 "is considered [by NATO] to be compromised by Russian intelligence."[58] The day after Trump is inaugurated, Papadopoulos; Trump's new chief of staff, Reince Priebus; and one of the heads of the presidential transition, Steve Bannon, will meet with Kammenos at Washington's Hay-Adams Hotel.[59] Kammenos had by then already met with Priebus once in D.C., on the day before Trump's inauguration.[60]

Carson's chief foreign policy adviser on Israeli issues, however, is George Birnbaum, who, according to the *Times of Israel*, "served as chief of staff for [Israeli prime minister Benjamin] Netanyahu during his first term" and is the business partner of "Arthur Finkelstein, the GOP public relations guru . . . who also has advised Netanyahu."[61]

At some point during his ten-month candidacy for president, Carson and his team receive a "plan for voter manipulation in [general election] swing states" from an Israeli business intelligence company, Inspiration, which is "run by former Israeli Defense Force officers."[62] After Carson exits the presidential race in March 2016, he "personally present[s] Trump with Inspiration's plan," and thereafter Inspiration receives "enormous amounts of information" from a pro-Trump super PAC, information it uses to "compose strategies and slogans that would elevate Trump and 'float all kinds of things' about Hillary Clinton."[63] According to a major digital media outlet in Israel, Walla News, Inspiration is "managed by a former senior [IDF] intelligence official" from the Israeli government.[64] Located in a "mysterious building in central Israel" with "no sign or information on it," Inspiration is, per Walla, a company whose "website does not reveal anything about its founders or employees," but whose activities in 2016 and even before then are quite clear: Inspiration's "main activity in recent years has been working for the election of Donald Trump as president."[65] One Inspiration employee said that "the person who connected her to Trump [in 2016] was Ben Carson," adding that "Carson knew the company after working with a research body that worked for us."[66] That the "research body" referenced here may be either NSO (to which Flynn was linked in 2016) or Joel Zamel's Wikistrat or Psy-Group business intelligence firms (the latter of which Zamel sought to recruit Flynn to in 2014 or 2015) is underscored by the presence of not just Flynn but also George Birnbaum as an adviser to Carson's campaign. Birnbaum will, not long after Carson's campaign folds in March 2016, introduce Zamel to Rick Gates, Donald Trump's deputy campaign manager.[67]

Another former Inspiration employee tells Walla that Inspiration began "work[ing] for Trump's election . . . about three months before the 2016 election," placing the beginning of its involvement in the same month— August 2016—that Donald Trump Jr. responds approvingly to an offer of assistance from Zamel's firm after a meeting in Trump Tower, thereby providing more evidence that the Israeli "research body" Inspiration worked with to ensure Trump's election was Zamel's (see chapter 4).[68] Indeed, Inspiration will concede that it worked in August 2016 "in cooperation with another Israeli company in order to understand which voters are more likely or less likely to vote on election day . . . [and] trying to predict the behavior of the voters in . . . the swing states . . . [O]n the basis of this assessment, various [types of] content intended for different types of voters were prepared in a focused manner."[69] This description of Inspiration's research partner matches the sort of work done by Psy-Group, as well as a company closely linked to Psy-Group, Cambridge Analytica, which was Trump's data firm for the entirety of the 2016 general election season. While Inspiration will state publicly that its partner was not Israeli business intelligence firm Black Cube, it will not issue a similar statement with respect to either Psy-Group, Wikistrat, or NSO.[70] Inspiration's concurrent claim that it did not work with Cambridge Analytica is consistent with other evidence that when, prior to its dissolution in 2018, Cambridge Analytica worked with Israeli firms, as it has acknowledged doing, it did so through subcontractors rather than directly.[71] Even so, that Inspiration denies working with Cambridge Analytica in response to a question about working with Israeli business intelligence firms—which Cambridge Analytica is not—is curious.

In his June 16, 2015, speech at Trump Tower announcing his candidacy for president of the United States, Donald Trump declares, "I love the Saudis. Many are in this building."[72] He repeats his long-standing complaint, however, that the Saudis enjoy the benefit of military assistance from America without properly paying for the aid they receive. "If the right person asked them, they'd pay a fortune," Trump tells the assembled crowd, noting that the Saudis "have got nothing but money."[73] He does not explain in his speech how or why he is the "right person" to deal with the Saudi government regarding its domestic investments.

During his speech, Trump also makes a telling and unusual comment about the political situation inside Saudi Arabia that goes largely unnoticed at the time. Discussing the need for a new American leader who will deal differently with our traditional geopolitical competitors, Trump says of Saudi Arabia that it "is in big, big trouble. Now, thanks to fracking and other things, the oil is all over the place."[74] The comment—which implies that oil is now more plentiful in the United States and elsewhere due to advanced extraction techniques, and that Saudi Arabia's economy will therefore have to quickly evolve to accommodate this new reality—is one of the more informed observations Trump makes in his announcement address.[75] It is unclear what Trump would like to do as president to take advantage of Saudi Arabia's new vulnerability on energy issues, however. He avers that a new president can make decisions that force the Saudis to pay more money to the American government than they currently do, but he remains silent on how the Saudis' need to eventually transition away from oil can be exploited by a new U.S. foreign policy. It is an open question that the first major recruit to Trump's national security team, Michael Flynn, will shortly be able to assist him in answering—as Flynn by June 2015 is well aware that Saudi Arabia and its neighbor the United Arab Emirates are looking to move to nuclear power (see chapter 4).

Perhaps it is no surprise, then, that in his announcement speech the chief clue Trump provides with respect to his agenda on Middle Eastern energy issues is his somewhat opaque interest in nuclear energy. "Even our nuclear arsenal doesn't work," opines Trump, later adding, "We've got nuclear weapons that are obsolete."[76] Though the nuclear deal Obama has negotiated with the Iranians has by June 2015, per international inspectors, been successful at halting Iran's nuclear ambitions, Trump echoes on June 16 the strongly held belief of the Saudis, Emiratis, and Israelis that Obama's negotiations will not "stop Iran from getting nuclear weapons"—implying that some more dramatic action will have to be taken to ensure an Iranian nuclear weapon never tilts the balance of power in the Middle East against America's regional allies.[77]

Within three weeks of Trump's announcement of his candidacy, his friend Thomas Barrack—the billionaire real estate investor who has called Trump "one of [his] oldest friends"—is telling associates at a business lunch on the French Riviera that he believes Trump will become president of the United States.[78] At the time, Trump is facing off against at least sixteen Republicans who have declared their candidacies or else formed exploratory committees to consider a presidential run. Barrack's lunch mates consequently scoff at his prediction. In the months to come, however, Barrack will make Trump winning the 2016 presidential election his "obsession," according to Bloomberg, going so far as to "all but disappear[ ] from the company he'd founded in 1991 [Colony Capital] and built into one of the world's highest-profile real estate firms."[79] His commitment to a Trump election victory is so unwavering that Trump will eventually name Barrack, post-election, his inaugural committee chairman—even as Barrack also regularly volunteers his New York City office for "sensitive" meetings of the presidential transition team (PTT) to avoid tipping off the many media outlets assembled in the Trump Tower lobby as to whom the PTT is meeting.[80] Between his early support for Trump and his chairmanship of Trump's inauguration, Barrack will also "help[ ] install [Paul Manafort] as head of Trump's campaign," engage in regular "strategy calls" with Trump, and initiate contact between Trump's campaign and the United Arab Emirates (see chapter 4).[81]

During the same month Barrack is in the French Riviera discussing Trump's candidacy with wealthy friends, a very wealthy man and his son arrive in the French Riviera for a holiday: King Salman and MBS, joined by an entourage of more than a thousand aides, advisers, assistants, and hangers-on.[82] While in France, the young prince—who, as part of coming into his own as a royal power broker, has imposed draconian austerity measures on the Saudi government—spots and allegedly impulse-buys a 440-foot yacht owned by Yuri Shefler, a fugitive Russian vodka tycoon who is a longtime enemy of Vladimir Putin.[83] MBS purchases the yacht for approximately $550 million, demanding that the Russian oligarch vacate the boat—at least one media outlet will say "kicking [him] off" it—on the day of the purchase.[84] The power play is likely to please Putin, whom Shefler has "publicly battled for years" and began attacking in the press in 2014 for the Russian president's annexation of Crimea, opining at the time that "it's terrible when a country captures a neighbor's territory. I feel sorry for the Crimean people. . . . [T]here are no laws in Russia. There is only one law in Russia, and it's called 'Putin.' Only one justice, called 'Putin.'"[85]

As Thomas Barrack is becoming deeply invested in Trump's campaign, so too is another Republican billionaire: Erik Prince. Not long after Trump's June 2015 announcement of his presidential candidacy, Prince—a longtime employee of MBZ—begins secretly advising the Trump campaign on foreign policy, despite never being named to any of Trump's official foreign policy or national security teams and later telling Congress under oath that he had no role, official or unofficial, on the Trump campaign or Trump transition team. As to the latter claim, the truth, as Bloomberg will report in April 2017, is that Prince spent the transition period "providing advice to Trump's inner circle, including his top national security adviser, Michael Flynn."[86] Bloomberg explains Prince's assistance of the PTT by noting that "Trump was weakest in the area where the stakes were highest—foreign affairs. Among those his aides turned to was Prince."[87] Even so, it will be clear from the beginning of Prince's advising of the Trump campaign in 2015 that neither Trump, Prince, nor anyone on the Trump team wants Prince's involvement in the development of Trump's foreign policy to be discovered; it is for this reason, Bloomberg notes, that after Election Day Prince always "entered Trump Tower through the back, like others who wanted to avoid the media spotlight, and huddled with members of the president-elect's team to discuss intelligence and security issues."[88] The result: Prince, according to several sources familiar with his activities in November and December 2016, was "very much a presence" at Trump Tower during the post-election months.[89] Despite this, a Prince spokesman in London will issue a prepared statement in response to the Bloomberg report, declaring that "Erik had no role on the transition team"—a statement that is technically true, as Trump never gave the longtime mercenary any formal PTT role.[90] In his statement to Bloomberg, Prince also appears to accuse deep-state operatives in the intelligence community of illicitly monitoring his activities—an accusation that Trump will soon echo with respect to his own communications inside Trump Tower.[91]

Despite his public claims to the contrary, "over a two to three month period around the election," writes Bloomberg, Prince was himself telling "several people that . . . his role was significant."[92] As for the transition period in particular, "current and former U.S. officials" say that "while Prince refrained from playing a direct role in the Trump transition, his name surfaced so frequently in internal discussions that he seemed to function as an outside adviser whose opinions were valued on a range of issues."[93]

Bloomberg reports that the topics on which Erik Prince secretly advised the president-elect included, among others, terrorism, counterintelligence, and potential government appointees.[94] While Prince's meetings with the PTT usually began with Prince entering Trump Tower through its private back entrance, on occasion they occurred elsewhere; Bloomberg details one meeting between Prince and two PTT members on the Acela Express train from New York City to Washington.[95] This "meeting" was attended by both Kellyanne Conway, Trump's third and final campaign manager, and Kevin Harrington, a future member of Trump's National Security Council.[96] One of Bloomberg's sources, a person close to Prince, tells the media outlet that "the discussions [Prince had with the campaign] were intended to remain private."[97]

Prince was also in contact with Trump and his inner circle prior to the transition, however, and not just at various social-cum-political events attended by both Trump and Prince, such as Robert Mercer's "Heroes and Villains" party or Trump's election-night victory party.[98] Despite telling Congress under oath that he "played no official or, really, unofficial role" on the Trump campaign, Prince also concedes that he donated to Trump, attended multiple Trump fundraisers (including some Trump attended), and, most importantly, wrote policy papers "on different foreign policy positions and . . . kicked them up into the adviser-sphere on what should be done on Middle Eastern or African counterterrorism issues."[99] Given that Prince had, in the early 2010s, all but run the United Arab Emirates' military operations, and that his boss MBZ had participated in George Nader's secret fall 2015 summit on the Red Sea—indeed, to put a finer point on it, that MBZ did business with Erik Prince via a $529 million contract to "help bring in foreign fighters [to the UAE] to help assemble an internal paramilitary force capable of carrying out secret operations and protecting Emirati installations"—Prince's admission that he advised Trump on "Middle Eastern counterterrorism issues" prior to Election Day means that he was simultaneously a counterterrorism adviser to the UAE and to Donald Trump during the 2016 presidential election.[100] This suggests that Trump and his inner circle had more pre-election interlocutors connected to members of the Red Sea Conspiracy than just Nader and Emirati ambassador Yousef al-Otaiba; Prince had access to Trump through his top advisers—including, according to Prince's concession to Congress, Bannon and Flynn—for the whole of the presidential campaign.[101]

In March 2015, the Obama administration declines to enforce its "ambitious" conditions on the release of military aid to Egypt, sending several weapons systems to el-Sisi in Cairo after pleas from "Egypt's regional allies—Israel, Saudi Arabia, and the United Arab Emirates," all of whom have "lobbied hard" against the hold.[102]

The following month, Donald Trump apparently has contact with alleged Kremlin spymaster Alexander Torshin at the annual NRA conference in Nashville. According to *Business Insider,* "Torshin tweeted in November 2015 that he knew 'D. Trump (through NRA)' . . . [and] later added that he saw Trump in Nashville, Tennessee in April 2015"; just eight weeks after the event in Nashville, Torshin's protégé, Kremlin operative Maria Butina, will pose as a reporter at FreedomFest in Las Vegas in order to invite Trump to issue a televised public statement on Russian sanctions.[103] The Russian woman's unusual question to Trump—on an issue surely of limited interest to most U.S. voters—gives Trump an opportunity to declare in a televised public forum his categorical opposition to Russian sanctions. Within a month of his declaration, Trump will be contacted for an interview by a Russian digital media outlet run by former Duma member Konstantin Rykov, who has just registered two pro-Trump websites in Russia: Trump2016.ru and DonaldTrump2016.ru.[104] Rykov, the founder of Moscow's first and largest "dark web" brothel, is a friend of Artem Klyushin, who had been a part of Trump's Moscow entourage during the 2013 Miss Universe pageant—an event during which *kompromat* of Trump with Russian prostitutes was allegedly acquired by the Agalarov family.[105]

At an Alabama campaign rally on August 21, 2015, a few weeks after FreedomFest, Trump says of the Saudis, "I get along great with all of them. They buy apartments from me, they spend $40 million, $50 million, am I supposed to dislike them? I like them very much."[106] Nevertheless, Trump complains that the Saudi government "makes $1 billion a day [from oil revenues] . . . [but] we get nothing" in compensation for the military protection the U.S. military offers the kingdom.[107] Trump's statements will cause the *Washington Post* to write that "everything in foreign policy is personal with [Trump] . . . and he likes the Saudis. And why does he like them so much? Because they pay him."[108] Calling "appalling" Trump's statement about liking wealthy Saudis—including Saudi royals—because they're customers of his, the *Post* notes that Trump's confession of venality is difficult to process even when heard several times: "Here you have a candidate for president of the United States saying that he is favorably disposed toward a foreign country *because they have given him millions of dollars*, and all but promising to shape American foreign policy in their favor for that very reason."[109]

Only a few weeks after Trump implies that his foreign policy toward Saudi Arabia is influenced in part by his receipt of significant revenues from Saudi royals and other wealthy Saudis, MBS breaches international protocol to publicly embarrass President Obama during a press conference. At a September 2015 meeting in D.C. between President Obama, King Salman, and MBS, the young prince "delivers a soliloquy about the failures of American foreign policy" while sitting before the American president—an action considered a transgression under the conventions of international diplomacy because it is done in public.[110] According to the *Middle East Eye*, within a matter of weeks of seeking to embarrass President Obama in this way, MBS is on a yacht in the Red Sea plotting with other

Middle East leaders on how to strike a bargain with the man they hope will be Obama's Republican successor.[111]

At around the same time that MBS, MBZ, and el-Sisi are meeting on the Red Sea—and during the same period that Trump's primary national security advisor, Michael Flynn, is working directly with the Saudis on what he calls a Middle East Marshall Plan to counter ISIS and Iran (see chapters 4 and 5)—Trump makes a startling statement at a campaign stop.[112] On November 12, 2015, at a community college theater in Fort Dodge, Iowa, Trump tells the assembled crowd, "I know more about ISIS than the [active-duty U.S.] generals do. Believe me."[113] Trump also tells the crowd that he has a plan for defeating ISIS—but that it's a secret.[114] No one in the crowd could know that Trump's top national security adviser at the time indeed had such a plan, let alone that it had been developed with direct input from the Saudis. Trump's seeming willingness to listen to input from foreign agents over U.S. intelligence will be confirmed in February 2019, when it is revealed that in mid-2017 Trump told his intelligence briefers that on the question of whether North Korea's chairman, Kim Jong-Un, had just tested a new intercontinental ballistic missile that could reach the United States, "I believe Putin." The president of the Russian Federation was at the time was telling Trump, contrary to what the U.S. president was hearing from his own intelligence community, that no such launch had occurred.[115] By July 2017, however, the Trump administration will have conceded that the launch did in fact take place.[116]

Just a matter of weeks after he meets with Nader, MBZ, and el-Sisi on the Red Sea, MBS announces, on December 14, 2015, a new "Saudi-led Islamic alliance to fight terrorism . . . and train, equip, and provide forces if necessary for the fight against Islamic State militants."[117] One of the men most likely to be intrigued by MBS's new anti–Islamic State alliance is Michael Flynn, who sources in the American intelligence community will tell the *New York Times* in June 2017 was "willing [in 2015 and 2016] to be used by Russia if he could advance his views on forging a united front to battle the Islamic State."[118] A united front to battle the Islamic State is exactly what MBS is offering by mid-December 2015, and his proposed alliance will indeed require Russian assistance—as the Russians are already fighting the Islamic State in Syria, just as MBS's Saudi-led coalition is hoping to do.

On December 2, less than two weeks before MBS's announcement, Flynn and his son meet with Russian ambassador Kislyak at his home in Washington.[119] According to emails later reviewed by the House Intelligence Committee, not only is the meeting set up by the Flynns rather than Kislyak, but Flynn Jr. contacts the Russian embassy following the meeting to describe the encounter as "very productive."[120] In May 2017, Reuters will report that, according to six "current and former U.S. officials," "before the election, Kislyak's undisclosed discussions with . . . Flynn focused on fighting terrorism and improving U.S.-Russian economic relations," which the news outlet takes to mean an adjustment of the sanctions regime leveled on the Kremlin after Putin's annexation of Crimea in March 2014.[121] Prior to the Reuters report, it had not been known that Flynn secretly met with the Kremlin's top agent in the United States during the presidential campaign, and, moreover, at a time when he was Trump's top national security advisor.

Reuters makes a further revelation, however, that is even more surprising: that Flynn's December 2015 face-to-face contact with Kislyak was not his only pre-election conversation with the Russian ambassador. As part of its reporting that in 2016 "there were at least 18 undisclosed calls and emails between Trump associates and Kremlin-linked people in the seven months before the November 8 presidential election, including six calls with Kislyak," Reuters will note that two U.S. officials "familiar with those 18 contacts said Flynn . . . [was] among the Trump associates who spoke to the ambassador by telephone."[122] The report will also indicate that Jared Kushner spoke to Kislyak via telephone—and failed to report it—sometime between April 2016 and Election Day, with the exact date of the call unknown. According to Reuters, it is "not clear whether Kushner engaged with Kislyak on his own or with other Trump aides," nor whether the call occurred before or after the nation learned, in mid-2016, that the Kremlin was behind the hacking of the DNC and the Clinton campaign.[123]

Flynn's pre-election contacts with Kislyak involved even more than phone calls and a meeting at the Russian ambassador's personal residence, however. In December 2018, a major investigative report by *Mother Jones* will reveal that in the months leading up to Election Day, Michael Flynn told close associates that he was having a series of clandestine contacts with Kislyak—contacts that apparently included not just phone calls but also texts and in-person contacts.[124] The nature and timing of these contacts creates the appearance of Flynn "try[ing] to strike a 'grand bargain' with Moscow as it attacked the 2016 election," writes *Mother Jones*—a particularly troubling prospect given that Flynn was present with Trump at the August 17, 2016, classified intelligence briefing at which Trump was thoroughly briefed on the scope of the Kremlin's illegal election interference (see chapter 5).

The extent to which the "grand bargain" Flynn is discussing with the Russians in the weeks before the 2016 election is the same as the bargain discussed by MBS, MBZ, and el-Sisi on the Red Sea a year earlier is unknown—but there are compelling indications that the two are in fact one and the same. Per *Mother Jones*, one of the Flynn associates who speaks with Flynn about his pre-election contacts with Kislyak reports that "Flynn discussed with Kislyak a grand bargain in which Moscow would cooperate with the Trump administration to resolve the Syrian conflict and Washington would end or ease up on the sanctions imposed on Russia for its annexation of Crimea and military intervention in Ukraine."[125] A second Flynn associate tells *Mother Jones* that "Flynn said he had been talking to Kislyak about Syria, Iran, and other foreign policy matters that Russia and the United States could tackle together were Trump to be elected."[126] A third associate of Flynn's speaks of identical subject matter being discussed by Flynn and Kislyak, without specifying the timing of the discussion: the "associate recalls that shortly after the election, Flynn told him he had been in contact with Kislyak about Syria," writes *Mother Jones*.[127] The Mueller Report will indicate, with respect to Flynn's pattern of behavior in 2016, that his known telephonic negotiations with Kislyak in December 2016 only occurred after repeated check-ins with the campaign to be certain he was authorized to say what he planned to say.[128] Whether Flynn followed a different protocol with respect to any pre-election negotiations he had with Kislyak is unknown.

The December 2018 report by *Mother Jones*, written by David Corn, author of *Russian Roulette: The Inside Story of Putin's War on America and the Election of Donald Trump*, implicitly makes the case that—if Flynn indeed had the contacts he claims, and if he indeed sought approval for his pre-election Russia contacts just as he did for all his post-election ones—the Trump campaign committed the federal crime of "aiding and abetting" Russian election crimes after the fact, as it offered the Russian Federation policy inducements after it learned, via the briefing Trump and Flynn received in August 2017, that the Kremlin was committing crimes against the United States.[129] Aiding and abetting a crime that has already been committed or is in the midst of commission is an act that falls under a different federal statute, with different statutory elements, than a before-the-fact "conspiracy"—the statutory offense investigated by special counsel Robert Mueller with respect to the Trump campaign and two Russian government entities, the Internet Research Agency and Russian military intelligence (GRU).[130] As Corn writes for *Mother Jones*, if "Flynn held clandestine meetings or communications with Kislyak during the 2016 general election, it would mean Trump's chief national security aide was secretly interacting with the representative of a foreign power as that government was mounting information and cyber warfare against the United States. Such an interaction could signal to the Vladimir Putin regime that Trump didn't mind the Kremlin's interference in the election and would be willing to work with Moscow despite its efforts to subvert the U.S. election."[131] Moreover, writes Corn, "If Flynn held such conversations with the Russian ambassador, this could have bolstered the Kremlin's preference for Trump . . . especially if there was any talk of a sanctions-for-Syria deal."[132] Such actions could therefore be considered "inducement" under the federal aiding and abetting statute (18 U.S.C § 2), with their immediate and foreseeable effect being that the Kremlin would continue to commit computer crimes against the United States.[133]

Eight days after Michael Flynn and his son meet with Sergey Kislyak at his D.C. home in December 2015, and just four days prior to MBS's announcement of a counterterrorism alliance almost certainly requiring Russian cooperation, Flynn—who is in contact with the Saudis on foreign policy issues (see chapter 5)—receives $45,000 from RT, the Kremlin-financed news network, to attend and speak at a gala event in Moscow; at the event, which his son also attends, Flynn dines with Vladimir Putin.[134] As NBC News will note, Flynn was "already advising" Trump at the time of both his face-to-face meeting with Kislyak in D.C. and his face-to-face meeting with Putin in Moscow, and was almost certainly brought to Moscow because of that role. "It is not coincidence that Flynn was placed next to President Putin [at the RT gala]," former U.S. ambassador to Russia Michael McFaul tells NBC in April 2017. "Flynn was considered a close Trump adviser. Why else would they want him there?"[135] Whether Flynn and Putin discuss in more detail the secret counterterrorism plan Trump had hinted at in Iowa four weeks earlier—a plan the evidence suggests was Flynn's—is unknown.

While in Moscow, Flynn "trie[s] repeatedly to meet officers at the C.I.A.'s station in Moscow—housed inside the American Embassy—to press for closer ties with Russia's spies."[136] The CIA declines to have anyone meet with him, however.[137]

In his address to an audience of influential Muscovites at the RT gala, Flynn offers a plan for the Middle East consistent with the contours of the Red Sea Conspiracy that George Nader had (with the assistance of MBS, MBZ, and el-Sisi) orchestrated just weeks earlier. In Flynn's own words, "I basically told the audience that Russia should get Iran to back out of the proxy wars that Iran is running so we [can] stabilize the Middle East. That was my whole purpose for going."[138] The plan for "stabilizing the Middle East" Flynn presents in Moscow in December 2015 will mirror the so-called Middle East Marshall Plan Flynn supports a year later as Trump's designated national security advisor (see chapter 7).[139] The plan calls for "Trump and Russian President Vladimir Putin ... [to] cooperate on a project that would boost Middle East economies" by "ending Ukraine's opposition to lifting sanctions on Russia by giving a Ukrainian company a $45 billion contract to provide turbine generators for [nuclear] reactors to be built in Saudi Arabia and other Mideast nations. The contract to state-owned Turboatom, and loans to Ukraine from Gulf Arab states, would 'require Ukraine to support lifting United States and European Union sanctions on Russia.'"[140]

That Flynn in December 2015 would have wanted to relay to Sergey Kislyak in D.C. and Vladimir Putin in Moscow the same Middle East Marshall Plan that he was then supporting and would still be supporting in November 2016 is nearly certain. The reason: Flynn was working in secret for an American company called ACU Strategic Partners on a closely related plan from summer 2015 through at least June 2016—and indeed, other documents will suggest, until he was fired as Trump's national security advisor in February 2017.[141]

In summer 2015, Flynn had taken a trip to Saudi Arabia to "talk about nuclear power plants"; shortly thereafter, "the Saudis made a $100 billion deal with the Russian state nuclear corporation, Rosatom, to build 16 nuclear power units."[142] Documents subsequently produced confirm, according to McClatchy DC, that Flynn made his trip to Saudi Arabia "on behalf of a U.S./Russia business plan to build nuclear reactors."[143] According to *Newsweek* and McClatchy, Flynn's summer 2015 trip was part of a "joint venture . . . involv[ing] U.S. companies, a Russian state-sponsored company, and Saudi financing, and was geared towards providing nuclear power to the Arab world."[144] One indication that Flynn sees the complications inherent in attempting to broker such a transnational deal is that he fails to disclose this trip to Saudi Arabia when he seeks a new federal security clearance in late 2016.[145] Moreover, he fails to properly disclose a second, October 2015 trip to Saudi Arabia that is part of the same joint venture. In hiding the details of this second trip from federal authorities, he makes up the name of the hotel he allegedly stayed at, and obscures his business interests in Saudi Arabia under the false claim that he was in the kingdom "for six days to speak at a conference."[146] He also fails to disclose the identity of the "friend" who traveled with him to Saudi Arabia and the company that paid for his trip.[147] It is a federal crime punishable by up to five years in prison per offense to "knowingly falsify or conceal a material fact" on a federal security clearance application.[148]

Flynn makes at least two additional trips for ACU during the summer of 2015: one trip to Egypt and one to Israel, both in June.[149] The *Washington Post* confirms that these trips are related to the same joint venture as Flynn's trip to Saudi Arabia, that being ACU's "hope[ ] to build more than two dozen nuclear plants in [the Middle East], in partnership with Russian interests."[150] As with his trip to Saudi Arabia, Flynn will fail to disclose these Middle Eastern business trips: federal law requires that all such trips be disclosed in security clearance paperwork.[151] It is unclear why Flynn would want to hide his efforts to connect the United States, Russia, Saudi Arabia, Egypt, and Israel just a matter of weeks before becoming an adviser to the Trump campaign in August 2015, though it is noteworthy that within a month of Flynn's return from his trips to Saudi Arabia, Egypt, and Israel Trump publicly announces his opposition to sanctions on Russia—a prerequisite for broader cooperation between the very countries Flynn was at the time secretly working with.[152] That Maria Butina (the Russian "journalist" whose question at the FreedomFest conference in Las Vegas in July 2015 allows Trump to express his opposition to U.S. sanctions on Russia) is indicted as an unregistered Kremlin agent three years later further complicates all of these events.[153]

Shortly after ACU's managing director, Alex Copson, hires Flynn in April 2015, Flynn begins linking ACU's multinational nuclear power deal to American national security, "warning publicly," according to the *Washington Post*, "that America's national security would be at risk if the United States allowed Russia and other countries to spearhead nuclear energy projects in the Middle East"—though his odd solution to the problem is to partner with Russia, rather than to supplant it as the major player in the Middle East energy market or else flatly oppose any nuclearization of the Middle East altogether.[154] In Israel in June 2015, Flynn "assure[s] Israeli officials that ACU's plan [to contract Ukrainians to build nuclear reactors in the Middle East as part of a deal that would end Russian sanctions] could prevent Israel's enemies from obtaining material for nuclear weapons"—an apparent reference to Iran, which just weeks later will announce the "nuclear deal" with the Obama administration aimed at curtailing its nuclear weapons program.[155] The rhetorical link Flynn seeks to establish between his 2015 and 2016 private consulting arrangements and America's national security offers significant intelligence on what Flynn might have discussed with Trump when the two men first met at Trump Tower, at Trump's invitation, in August 2015—and what Trump may have been referring to when he said in Iowa that November, "I know more about ISIS than the [active-duty U.S.] generals do."

As *Lawfare* has observed, "In order for [the ACU] deal to go through, Flynn would have to convince the Trump administration to 'rip up' the sanctions imposed by the Obama administration on Russia for their interference in the U.S. election," so it is little surprise that by December 2017, as the digital media outlet notes, "a whistleblower has come forward with information suggesting that Flynn's true motive to soften these sanctions wasn't to ease tensions with Russia, but to further the financial interests of those selling these reactors."[156] Just as significant, Flynn's advocacy with ACU for a nuclear deal involving Russian entities, and later for a similar deal—with another company, IP3—involving Chinese entities, poses a clear national security threat as, per the report in *Lawfare*, while "U.S. civilian nuclear technology sales require significant national security provisions . . . Russian and Chinese technology agreements do not."[157] Specifically, deals involving American nuclear technology require what is called a "123 agreement," an Atomic Energy Act–derived standard that precludes American materials and technology from being developed into nuclear weapons when sold to a foreign power.[158]

To the extent the "consortium" idea Flynn was advocating around the globe in 2015 and 2016 opened the door to sales of U.S. nuclear materials and technology without a 123 agreement—and to the extent Flynn was simultaneously opposing the Obama administration's Iran nuclear deal, which was provably curtailing Iran's nuclear program—the retired lieutenant general's foreign policy agenda has made more likely a nuclear confrontation in the Middle East in the medium term.[159] In a September 2015 interview with the *New York Observer*, whose owner and publisher at the time was Jared Kushner, Flynn laid out his idiosyncratic plan for nuclear weapons in the Middle East: "Open the entire region to nuclear energy to neutralize Iran from starting a nuclear weapons arm[s] race in the region. Have other nations outside the region, such as Russia or the U.S., conduct the advanced levels of the nuclear in and out fuel cycle processing required to create a nuclear energy program."[160] That Flynn was ambivalent about whether the United States or Russia should oversee the accelerated nuclearization of the world's most volatile region could not have come as anything but a shock to the U.S. Defense Department and Department of Energy when Flynn first aired the view in mid-2015, which may offer an additional explanation for why President Obama advised President-elect Trump to keep Flynn out of the White House in the forty-eight hours after the 2016 election.[161]

Trump had not spent the 2016 general election backing denuclearization in the Middle East and around the world, however; instead, he had argued that the United States must "renovate and modernize" its nuclear arsenal, at one point even advocating for precisely the view of a nuclearized Middle East Flynn had been advancing both in the media and behind closed doors: that Saudi Arabia should have not just nuclear energy but nuclear weapons.[162] As early as a CNN town hall event in March 2016, Trump indicates that Saudi Arabia could "absolutely" be in line for nuclear weapons, with two proffered justifications: first, that the United States would otherwise be paying for Saudi Arabia's defense, and second, that Saudi Arabia's acquisition of nuclear weapons "is going to happen anyway. It's going to happen anyway. It's only a question of time."[163] The first of these two justifications for arming the Saudis with nuclear weapons calls to mind Trump's repeated claims on Twitter that Saudi Arabia does not pay enough for its own defense; these complaints, along with his statement on CNN, may well have served as a signal to the Saudis—and their allies— that as president Trump would get out of their way if they ever sought to begin arming themselves in "self-defense."

Flynn's 2015 and 2016 policy prescriptions for Saudi Arabian energy and nuclear weapons development would not merely impact Riyadh, however. *Lawfare* explains that, "in 2009, the United Arab Emirates voluntarily included a legally binding provision to its 123 agreement to never acquire or develop enrichment and reprocessing technology. The agreement also bound the U.S. to impose those same conditions in future agreements on other countries in the region, or if not, to lift them on the UAE."[164] MBZ therefore knows, in 2015, that any decision the U.S. government makes on nuclear energy in Saudi Arabia—including a decision to allow or even encourage Saudi Arabia to pursue nuclear weapons—applies to the UAE as well. Moreover, Egypt, another member of the Red Sea Conspiracy, has a clause identical to the Emiratis' in its own nuclear agreements with the United States.[165]

As Vladimir Putin is hosting Michael Flynn in Moscow on December 10, 2015, the Kremlin is also playing host to other individuals central to Trump's campaign: top officials at the National Rifle Association (NRA) who make a trip to the Russian capital, from December 8 through December 13, that is jointly orchestrated by the organization and U.S.-dwelling Kremlin operative Maria Butina.[166] In Moscow, the NRA officials and some of their most prominent U.S. supporters—a travel group that includes former NRA president David Keene, future NRA president Pete Brownell, NRA fundraiser Joe Gregory, NRA "benefactor" Arnold Goldschlager, and high-profile Trump surrogate David Clarke—meet with Kremlin officials. The NRA pays for the group's travel expenses and for the gifts they present to their Kremlin hosts.[167] Keene in particular is interested in securing a "private interview" with Putin.[168]

According to the *Daily Beast*, Maria Butina's boyfriend, GOP operative Paul Erickson—who will later be indicted for wire fraud and money laundering—exchanges emails with certain of the NRA travelers prior to their Moscow trip. The emails reveal that the officials "believed they were meeting with Kremlin power players who could influence the country's president."[169] The reason officials at the NRA would want to "influence" Putin is likewise revealed in Erickson's emails: the GOP operative's plan, apparently embraced by the NRA brass with whom he spoke, was to "creat[e] a way for the Kremlin to connect with a future Republican president."[170] Because U.S. presidents ordinarily can call other world leaders at will, the implication in the Erickson-NRA effort is that the channel they wish to create to the Kremlin is a covert back channel—an ambition that carries with it the desire to hide GOP-Kremlin contacts from the American public, U.S. media, the U.S. intelligence community, or all three. Indeed, Erickson will represent in his emails to the NRA officials—possibly on intelligence received, at least in part, from his Russian girlfriend—that "Russia believes that high-level contacts with the NRA might be the best means of neutral introduction to . . . the next American President."[171] Erickson underscores that the officials' Moscow trip therefore has "enormous diplomatic consequences."[172] He adds that the Kremlin's interest is only in communicating via back channel with a Republican president, and that nothing he has said to NRA representatives applies if the next U.S. president is a Democrat.[173]

Among the Kremlin officials the NRA delegation meets in Moscow are Sergey Lavrov, the Russian foreign minister—whose ministry will make contact with the Trump campaign using Ivan Timofeev and Joseph Mifsud as cutouts just ninety days later—deputy prime minister Dmitry Rogozin, and Dimitri Simes's Russian Central Bank contact (and its deputy governor) Alexander Torshin, who will later be accused by federal prosecutors, as an unnamed and unindicted co-conspirator, of being Maria Butina's handler in the United States.[174] Many of those the NRA officials meet with, including Rogozin and Torshin, will later be sanctioned by the United States as punishment for the Kremlin's election hacking and interference during the 2016 presidential campaign.[175] As for the NRA, it will ultimately contribute at least $30 million toward Trump's election, a sum still being investigated by both media and federal law enforcement as possibly having been illegally commingled with "Russian money."[176]

More of Trump's lucrative but clandestine connections to the NRA will surface in 2019, when the *Daily Beast* reveals that "the Trump 2020 campaign is reportedly using a shell company to buy ads in coordination with the National Rifle Association, using the same potentially illegal techniques as the 2016 campaign."[177]

On April 7, 2015—eight months before he hosts NRA officials in Moscow—Torshin, along with Butina, is introduced by Simes to Federal Reserve

vice chairman Nathan Sheets and treasury undersecretary for interna-
tional affairs Stanley Fischer.[178] Not long after these meetings between two
Kremlin agents and two of America's top public financial institutions, the
Kremlin makes its first contact with a unit of the Treasury Department,
the Office of Terrorist Financing and Financial Crimes, to propose what
it calls the "ISIL Project": an information-sharing agreement between the
Kremlin and the United States focused on "financial institutions in the
Middle East suspected of supporting ISIS."[179] Incredibly, officials within
the Treasury Department agree to the Kremlin's proposed project using "a
Gmail backchannel with the Russian government"—a channel that thereafter will be used by Kremlin agents not to track ISIS but to "press[ ]
their American counterparts for private financial documents on at least
two dozen dissidents, academics, private investigators, and American citizens . . . [including] sensitive documents on Dirk, Edward, and Daniel Ziff,
billionaire investors who had run afoul of the Kremlin."[180] That the Kremlin is seeking information on the Ziff brothers months before it releases
a summary of its principal conclusions on the subject to the Trump campaign only underscores how seriously the Kremlin takes this research. Indeed, U.S. intelligence officials have since said that the Russian outreach
to the Obama administration's Treasury Department in 2015 was by 2016
almost certainly an espionage operation directly orchestrated by Russian
intelligence.[182] The Treasury Department has "refused to tell *BuzzFeed News*
why its officials were communicating with unofficial Gmail accounts at
the same time that Russia was sending the suspicious requests, or to say
whether it eventually turned over any documents [to the Kremlin] in response."[183] The Kremlin's 2015 espionage, and the Treasury Department's
silence over what it ultimately disclosed to the Russians, does suggest that
by the time Kremlin agents arrived at Trump Tower on June 9, 2016, they
knew or had good reason to suspect that the individuals on whom they
would be providing the Trump campaign so much information, the Ziff
brothers, were indeed Clinton donors.

In February 2015, two months before he sets up a meeting between
Torshin and Butina and Treasury and Federal Reserve personnel Fischer
and Sheets—and just over a year before he becomes a key Trump campaign

national security and foreign policy adviser—Dimitri Simes, along with the Russian-born publisher of the Center for the National Interest's in-house publication, the *National Interest*, travel to Moscow to meet personally with Vladimir Putin.[184] While it is unknown what Simes, his publisher, and Putin discuss in Moscow, that it may well have involved Donald Trump is underscored by the fact that, in the same month Trump announces his presidential run, Simes publishes an article by Butina stating that "certain U.S. politicians and Russians share many common interests," an article that at the time appears to apply only to one GOP candidate: a New York City businessman with a surprisingly sunny view of both the Russian Federation and its president.[185]

When the Mueller Report reveals, in April 2019, that Simes acted as perhaps the Trump campaign's most indispensable adviser on Russia, it will give many Americans an opportunity to learn about the Soviet-born think tank director and his Center for the National Interest for the first time. Simes's center was founded by former president Richard Nixon as the Nixon Center in 1994; Nixon personally installed Simes as the president and chief executive of the conservative think tank that year.[186] In 2011, the center changed its name to the Center for the National Interest, but the Nixon family remains closely involved in the think tank, with Julie Nixon Eisenhower—whose brother-in-law is Ed Cox, the New York state GOP chairman who introduced Carter Page to Trump's campaign—sitting on CNI's board along with Simes, his fellow Trump adviser Richard Burt, and (by spring 2016) Jeff Sessions, head of Trump's Simes-concocted national security advisory committee.[187]

Simes's decades at the Nixon Center/Center for the National Interest apparently also include contact with Putin ally Oleg Deripaska, the onetime Manafort boss who infamously said, "I don't separate myself from the [Russian] state."[188] In 2005, when Deripaska, as part of his push to transform Western perceptions of Putin's regime, approached Paul Manafort for this task, he also reportedly sought out Simes and the Nixon Center; in 1972, President Nixon had famously worked toward a long-term détente with the Soviet Union at a conference in Moscow—a conference also attended by Ed Cox and the honorary chairman of CNI during the 2016 presidential campaign, Henry Kissinger, who helps facilitate the first meeting between Kushner and Simes in March 2016.[189] Simes, described in 2005 in *Kommersant*—Russia's largest business daily—as "close to Vladimir Putin," meets with Deripaska in 2005 at a time when, according to both the *Moscow Times* and *Kommersant*, the oligarch was considering whether to "bankroll a new think tank in Washington to focus on Russian issues," with "Moscow hop[ing] for a 'well-disposed' approach . . . [to] Russian present-day life."[190] Deripaska's—and Putin's—evident hope in 2005 was that any resulting think tank would aspire to have the same effect as the public relations campaign for which Deripaska had just begun paying Paul Manafort. According to the Mueller Report, "A [Manafort & Davis Consulting] memorandum describing work that Manafort performed for Deripaska in 2005 regarding the post-Soviet republics referenced the need to brief the Kremlin and the benefits that the work could confer on 'the Putin Government.'"[191]

According to *Kommersant*, the Kremlin's proposed new think tank was the "brainchild of [Kremlin political consultant] Gleb Pavlovsky and Dimitri Simes"—and Pavlovsky, for his part, was interested in working with Deripaska.[192] Simes, while approvingly citing as "background" for such a project the then developing plans for an English-language version of the state-owned RT (plans that called for, per Simes, "a 24-hour, English news channel funded by the Kremlin"), nevertheless expressed uncertainty about whether a Deripaska-funded think tank would be received as credible by the D.C. political establishment. That Simes was willing to discuss a new pro-Kremlin think tank with Kremlin agents in 2005 is clear, however: as the *Moscow Times* would report at the time, citing Deripaska by name as a potential funder of the project, "Plans are in the works to set up a Washington-based think tank that would be funded with Russian money and combat the U.S. perception of Russia 'as a bad pupil,' Kremlin-connected consultant Gleb Pavlovsky said Monday."[193] It is telling that Simes's co-ideator in envisioning this prospective pro-Kremlin think tank (indeed, a man the Nixon Center actually contracted with for this purpose) was a "Kremlin-connected consultant" whom Simes's think tank had "paid for . . . [along with] several other Russian political analysts to visit Washington in November [2005] for a research project."[194] Given

Simes's and Pavlovsky's "closeness" with Putin at the time, Simes could have had no illusions about Pavlovsky—a man *Vanity Fair* has since called a "Kremlin political consultant and manipulator."[195] Pavlovsky has even bragged publicly about working with Putin in Russia on a "strategy" to get "everyone . . . thinking the way we want[ ] them to."[196]

Whether or not the Kremlin's imagined institute ever progressed beyond the ideation stage, that Deripaska was associated in international media as a possible patron for a pro-Kremlin Simes-Pavlovsky think tank project at the very same time the Russian oligarch was acting as Manafort's patron for a pro-Kremlin public relations project is deeply troubling. Manafort would go on, a little over a decade later, to be Donald Trump's campaign manager, even as Simes would, at the same point in Trump's campaign— March 2016—appear in Trump's orbit as the GOP candidate's top behind-the-scenes adviser on Russia; moreover, Manafort is the Trump campaign official who "enlisted" CNI board member Richard Burt to "join Trump's campaign and help[ ] draft his [foreign policy] speech" at the Mayflower Hotel in April 2016.[197] While it is unclear whether Simes ever developed, like Manafort, a long-term relationship with Deripaska, he clearly stayed in touch with Pavlovsky after 2005, inviting him to a conference hosted by CNI in 2008.[198]

In 2013, less than sixty days before Trump was to arrive in Moscow for the Miss Universe pageant—an event during which Trump himself said he expected to meet with Putin, a meeting that he had been promised by his Russian business partner—Simes "graced the stage alongside Putin [in Russia] at the Valdai International Discussion Club, a conference . . . frequented almost exclusively by Putin apologists. At Valdai, Putin referred to Simes as his 'American friend and colleague,'" and Simes, for his part, said he "fully support[ed]" Putin's "tough stance" on the Syrian civil war.[199]

Within a few weeks of returning to the United States from his 2013 visit to Moscow, Trump is talking to New York state GOP politicos about his political ambitions. Chief among Trump's advisers on his possible run for governor of New York is Ed Cox, connected to the board of Simes's CNI through his sister-in-law and from having worked alongside honorary

CNI chairman Kissinger; Cox will, oddly, become the first person in the New York State Republican Party to voice to his peers that he does not believe the governorship is the job Trump really wants.[200] In March 2014, Cox meets with Trump at Mar-a-Lago to discuss the businessman's political future; while the content of their conversation is unknown, within days of Cox leaving Mar-a-Lago Trump announces on Twitter that he has "much bigger [political] plans in mind" than the governorship of New York, and that readers should "stay tuned" because his new political plans "will happen."[201] It is Trump's first public indication that he will eventually declare his candidacy for the 2016 GOP presidential nomination. Trump communications adviser Michael Caputo will later say that, when Trump was deciding between the New York governor's race or a run for the presidency, the man whose actions most clearly forced Trump down the latter path was the CNI-connected Ed Cox.[202]

Twenty-one months after his consequential meeting with Trump at Mar-a-Lago, Cox is responsible for Carter Page being the first hire for what eventually becomes (at Simes's urging) Trump's national security advisory committee.[203] At the time Cox recommends Page, the energy consultant is less than a year removed from admitting to federal agents that he transferred nonpublic information about the U.S. energy sector to two men he knew were Russian spies. Page, like Cox, also has an evident connection to Simes's center: like CNI board member Richard Burt, Page has for years been involved with Russia's state-owned gas company, Gazprom.[204] Page and Burt end up not merely as Trump campaign Russia advisers but as two of the key writers and editors—along with Stephen Miller, George Papadopoulos, and Simes—of Trump's Russia policy.[205] While Page's path to involvement in the Trump campaign runs through Ed Cox, Burt's path, per *Politico*, runs through Manafort.[206] The monthslong formalizing and public dissemination of Trump's pro-Kremlin foreign policy that begins in March 2016 is therefore a joint effort of Simes, Kushner, and Manafort, with Burt and a small number of individuals on the national security committee Simes and Kushner conceived of in mid-March acting as executors of the policy: Sessions, Gordon, Page, and Papadopoulos.

When one of Simes's key Kremlin contacts in the United States, Maria

Butina, is arrested in Virginia in August 2018, the reaction of the Trump campaign's trusted Russia adviser is telling.[207] Within a matter of days, Simes, a man the *Washington Post* calls "the Washington expert most well connected in Moscow and whose organization [CNI] provides a unique link between the two cities' elite," leaves the United States for Moscow—and a job running a political talk show on a Kremlin-owned television network for a mid-six-figure salary.[208] The sudden disappearance of the "native Russian" (as Bloomberg describes him) from the day-to-day operations of the Center for the National Interest catches his assistants and employees entirely unaware; per the *Washington Post*, "Many organization employees were shocked when, in mid-2018 . . . Simes decided to take a job co-hosting a prime-time news and analysis show on Channel 1, a major Russian television network that is majority-owned by the Russian government. The new job suddenly focused a spotlight on Simes's ties to Moscow."[209] The Kremlin-funded, Moscow-based television program Simes now co-hosts is called *Bolshaya Igra* (The Great Game), a reference to the high-stakes, decades-long diplomatic cat-and-mouse game that the Russian Empire played with the West in the nineteenth century, with Russia's ambition throughout being the establishment of an even larger empire than it already had—and the frustration of the British Empire's similar designs.[210] Numerous media outlets around the world, including the *Washington Post*, begin writing stories shortly after Simes's show premieres in September 2018 indicating that Russia is, under Putin, "back in the 'Great Game'"—but this time with the United States as its chief adversary.[211] That Trump's chief campaign adviser on Russia now runs the television edition of the Kremlin's "Great Game" on behalf of Vladimir Putin can give no comfort to those who fear that Simes's advice to the Trump campaign was given implicitly or explicitly at the Kremlin's bidding. Indeed, the sight of Simes and his co-host Vyacheslav Nikonov, the grandson of Stalin's foreign minister, chatting with Kremlin officials like Sergey Lavrov—the man the Steele dossier alleges coordinated Russian election interference in 2016, and to whom Trump boasted about firing FBI director James Comey over the Russia investigation in 2017—is surely unsettling to many.[212]

Lavrov's appearance on Simes's Kremlin-run talk show isn't the first time the two men have sat down together since Trump's election, however. In late February 2017, almost immediately after Trump finally fires his national security advisor, Michael Flynn, Simes travels to Russia to meet with Lavrov.[213] The two men discuss the ongoing Russia investigation being conducted by the FBI, including the danger that Russian ambassador Sergey Kislyak will be caught up in it. Simes is well aware that Kislyak will be named in the investigation, as he has facilitated the Kremlin agent's contacts with the Trump campaign in the past.[214] Within 120 days of the Simes-Lavrov meeting in Russia, Kislyak will be recalled to Moscow by Putin, putting him beyond the reach of special counsel Mueller.[215]

In December 2015, Michael Flynn dines in Moscow with Putin, Putin's spokesman and "de facto national security adviser" Dmitry Peskov, and Sergey Ivanov, Putin's chief of staff—two of whom (Putin and Ivanov) are under U.S. sanctions at the time. All three Russians are men who, just a few weeks later, Trump's attorney Michael Cohen will consider central to closing a Trump Tower Moscow deal.[216] According to emails released to and summarized by international media, in January 2016 Cohen emails Peskov "to request a meeting either with Russian President Vladimir Putin's then-chief of staff Sergey Ivanov or Peskov himself"; in a telephone response, Peskov's office invites Cohen to attend the St. Petersburg economic forum in June 2016, an event at which Felix Sater (Cohen's conduit to the Kremlin) says the Trump attorney may be able to meet, via Peskov's introduction, Putin himself.[217]

Part of Sater and Cohen's plan to secure a Trump Tower Moscow deal is to offer Putin a $50 million penthouse to entice him to approve the development—as his approval is essential to the Trump Organization proceeding with the deal with Russian businessman Andrey Rozov.[218] As Sater tells Cohen across two November 3, 2015, emails, if Trump can close the Trump Tower Moscow deal after a meeting with Putin, Putin will be more likely to support his presidential candidacy, a premise that takes on a sinister cast in light of Sater's proven access to Kremlin officials and the illegal hacking and propaganda campaigns the Kremlin has, by late

2015, already initiated. As Sater explains it to Cohen in November, if "Putin gets on stage with Donald for a ribbon-cutting for Trump [Tower] Moscow," Trump will be proving—not to American voters but to Putin— that, unlike Hillary Clinton, Trump "doesn't stare down, he negotiates."[219] Sater adds that, as to the 2016 presidential campaign and the ongoing U.S.-Russia diplomacy that will necessarily succeed it, "Putin only wants to deal with a pragmatic leader." As Sater, presumably searching for additional euphemisms for the dropping of sanctions on Russia, summarizes the philosophy that he believes both Putin and Trump share, "Business, politics, whatever . . . it all is the same for someone who knows how to deal."[220] In the United States, the sort of juxtaposition of business and politics Sater describes is often chargeable as bribery under 18 U.S.C. § 201; bribery is also one of the two enumerated impeachable offenses in the U.S. Constitution.[221]

Sater has an additional reason to urge Trump to please Putin, however: there are early indications that, due to the intended height of the tower Trump intends to build with Rozov, direct approval from the Russian government is actually needed as a matter of Russian law.[222] This, as well as Sater's proposed commingling of personal profit and presidential politics, may explain in part why Sater tells Cohen that the Trump-Kremlin negotiations over the Trump-Rozov tower are "very sensitive" and are being conducted, through Sater, with "Putin[']s very very close people."[223] In one October 2015 email Sater is even more direct with Cohen, writing that "we need . . . Putin on board."[224] As for Trump's views on the matter, the GOP presidential candidate expresses during his presidential campaign the same degree of comfort as Sater with the fusion of moneymaking and policymaking, telling his lawyer Cohen at one point that his candidacy is an "infomercial" for the Trump Organization with respect to potential new business clients—including, as by then would have been clear to both Trump and Cohen, Russian nationals.[225]

After telling media in October 2017 that "he received [Cohen's January 2016] email but did not reply . . . [and does] not remember any discussions about Cohen attending the St. Petersburg economic forum," Kremlin press secretary Dmitry Peskov will, in November 2018—once Cohen has pled guilty to federal crimes and admitted the truth of his contacts with the Kremlin—reveal that his office at the Kremlin "told [Cohen and the Trump Organization] that . . . if they want to invest in Russia we will be happy to see them at [the] St. Petersburg [International] Economic Forum" in mid-June 2016, an invite-only event.[226]

November 2018 is also the month that the Department of Justice announces that "Russian trolls are interfering online with the [2018] midterm" elections, further undercutting Trump's statement from a few months earlier—made while standing beside Putin himself in Helsinki, Finland— that "I don't see why it would be Russia" interfering in U.S. elections. It is a statement Trump will try to walk back shortly thereafter, following significant outcry in U.S. media, by contending that what he meant to say was, "I don't see why it *wouldn't* be Russia."[227] A Senate report published before the 2018 midterms will declare that, prior to those elections, "Kremlin-linked trolls consistently push[ed] narratives supportive of President Donald Trump and critical of impeachment talk."[228]

When the Mueller Report on Russian election interference and allegations of obstruction of justice against Trump is released to the public, with redactions, in April 2019, Americans will learn much more about Cohen's 2015 and 2016 efforts to help Trump build a Trump-branded tower in Moscow. The report will reveal not only that Cohen did "provide updates directly to Trump throughout 2015 and 2016" but that their conversations about the project "were not off-hand . . . because the project had the potential to be so lucrative."[229] It will also reveal that, according to Trump attorney Rudy Giuliani, discussions between Trump, Cohen, and the Kremlin about a Trump Tower Moscow "went on throughout 2016 . . . the president can remember having conversations with him [Cohen] about it. . . . The president also remembers . . . could be [the conversations went] up to as far as October, November [2016]."[230] At another point in the report Giuliani is quoted as saying that, according to what Trump told him, discussions of Trump Tower Moscow were "going on from the day I announced [in June 2015] to the day I won [in November 2016]."[231] On November 29, 2018, when pressed on whether it was appropriate for him to be negotiating a business deal with the Kremlin while running for president on a pro-

Russia foreign policy and claiming to have no involvement with Russia at all, Trump tells members of the media, "It doesn't matter because I was allowed to do whatever I wanted during the campaign."[232]

It is consistent with this mantra—one Trump only reveals post-election—that on November 2, 2015, the candidate secretly signs a letter of intent to build a Trump Tower Moscow that he believes will require Kremlin approval, even though he is in the midst of a presidential campaign in which the formulation of and basis for his foreign policy, particularly with respect to Russia, has already become a topic of public discussion.

Within ten days of Trump signing the letter of intent with prospective Russian business partner Andrey Rozov, Ivanka Trump receives an email from Lana Erchova, the wife of the Russian energy minister's former press secretary, Dmitry Klokov.[233] At the time Ivanka receives the email, Klokov is working for the Russian government as director of external communications for the state-owned "Federal Grid Company of Unified Energy System [sic]."[234] Klokov offers his "assistance" to the Trump campaign through his wife's email to Ivanka, who forwards the email to Cohen, who thereafter has multiple contacts with Klokov about helping the Trump campaign achieve "synergy on a government level" with the Russian Federation through a meeting in Russia between Trump and Putin.[235] Rather than rebuffing the offer of a face-to-face meeting with the Russian president for then-candidate Trump, Cohen discusses with Klokov his desire to do "site surveys" for the Trump Tower Moscow project and to speak to "local developers" in Moscow, adding that he would like to meet with Klokov on Trump's behalf, or have Trump himself travel to Moscow as part of an "official" visit (a visit pursuant to a formal invitation from the Kremlin).[236] Klokov's insistence that the visit "has to be informal" suggests that he understands that what Trump's attorney is suggesting is both politically and diplomatically improper.[237]

In his several interactions with Cohen, Klokov is coy about the entangling of business and politics, at one point insisting that he must "separate their negotiations over a possible meeting between Trump and [Putin] from any existing business track," even as at another point in the conversation he emphasizes to Cohen that a Trump-Putin summit would be publicized in such a way as to have a "phenomenal" impact on the "business dimension" of Trump's interest in the Russian president, and that Putin's prospective support for Trump would have, as the Mueller Report quotes Klokov, "significant ramifications for the 'level of projects [Trump can do in Russia] and their capacity.'"[238] Klokov's message is clear: if Trump can please Putin and earn his support, Putin can ensure that Trump enjoys nearly boundless business opportunities in Russia. While Klokov may be correct in telling Trump's lawyer that there is "no bigger warranty in any [Russian building] project than the consent of the person of interest"— Klokov's euphemistic appellation for Putin—in America's legal and political systems affairs of state are conducted differently, a fact neither Cohen nor Klokov acknowledges in their negotiations despite the involvement, in the deal they are discussing, of a candidate for the U.S. presidency.[239]

That the Cohen-Klokov discussion is part of a Kremlin effort to bribe Trump is made clear by a subsequent email from Erchova to the special counsel's office, in which the Russian national confirms that her then husband (they have since divorced) was offering Trump "cooperation . . . on behalf of . . . Russian officials."[240] She adds that these "officials" wanted, among other things, to offer Trump "land in Crimea" alongside the benefit of an "unofficial" meeting with Putin.[241]

Less than two months after declining to pursue Klokov's offer, Cohen decides to contact the Kremlin directly to win its support for Trump Tower Moscow.[242] His "ask" of the Kremlin ultimately goes beyond "support," however; he tells a Kremlin agent from the office of Kremlin press secretary Dmitry Peskov, Elena Poliakova, that he wants the Kremlin to help Trump with "securing land to build the project and with financing," according to the Mueller Report.[243] Poliakova promises to follow up on the Trump Organization's request. Within twenty-four hours, the Kremlin has gotten in touch with its intermediary to Trump's business, Sater, who thereafter tells Cohen that he has the necessary permission to arrange for, as the Mueller Report will describe it, "an invitation . . . signed by Andrey Ryabinskiy of the company MHJ" for Cohen to travel to "Moscow for a working visit" about the "prospects of development and the construction business in Russia," "the various land plots available suited for construction of this enormous Tower," and "the opportunity to co-ordinate a follow up visit to Moscow by Mr. Donald Trump."[244] Though the invitation Sater secures will be signed by an agent of MHJ, Sater explains, the actual host of Trump's trip to Moscow would be VTB, one of the largest state-owned banks in Russia and—at the time of its prospective invitation to Cohen—an entity subject to the very sanctions the Kremlin wants Trump to eliminate if he wins election in November 2016.[245] Sater explains that VTB is merely being used as a front for the Kremlin, however, as VTB is allowed to discuss financing for a Trump Tower Moscow but "politically neither Putin's office nor [the Russian] Ministry of Foreign Affairs cannot [sic] issue [an] invite, so they are inviting [you] commercially/business."[246] Most startlingly, Sater tells Cohen that not only will VTB CEO Andrey Kostin be present at Cohen's meetings in Moscow, but so too will Putin himself.[247] The presence of Kostin at the meetings, Sater explains, is to make each meeting plausibly "a business meeting not political."[248] Cohen's plans to travel to Moscow to meet Kostin and Putin get as far as Cohen sending his passport to Sater and acquiring Trump's passport from Trump's personal secretary.[249] Cohen tells Sater that Trump will travel to Moscow "once he becomes the nominee[,] after the convention."[250]

On May 5, 2016, just as Trump is clinching the GOP nomination for president, Sater informs Cohen that the Kremlin's press secretary, Peskov, wants to personally invite Cohen to be his "guest" at the St. Petersburg economic forum from June 16 to June 19. According to Sater, Peskov "wants to meet there with you and possibly introduce you to either Putin or [Russian Prime Minister Dmitry] Medvedev . . . the entire business class of Russia will be there as well. He [Peskov] said anything you want to discuss including dates and subjects are on the table to discuss."[251] By early June, Sater is telling Cohen there is a "very strong chance" that he will meet Putin in St. Petersburg.[252] On June 14—the day it is revealed that Russian government hackers have penetrated the DNC and stolen materials from the committee—Cohen informs Sater he will not be traveling to St. Petersburg after all.[253] Cohen will subsequently tell the special counsel's office that his only reason for declining Peskov's personal invitation to attend the St. Petersburg economic forum was that he suddenly decided, on June 14, that "Russian officials were not actually . . . interested in meeting with him"—a view strongly contradicted by the whole of the Kremlin's corre-spondence with him through Sater.[254] Cohen appears to offer the special counsel's office no additional information about his decision.

Whether known to Cohen in June 2016 or not, a deputy prime minister of the Russian Federation, Sergei Prikhodko, had in December 2015 in-vited Trump himself to the St. Petersburg forum, shortly after Flynn dined with Putin in Moscow.[255] A February 2018 report will link Prikhodko to Oleg Deripaska, alleging—with both audio, video, and photographic evidence—that Deripaska has been bribing Prikhodko, and that among the topics the two men have discussed during their clandestine meetings is Russian election interference.[256] Deripaska's then girlfriend, Nastya Rybka, will claim to have sixteen hours of audio recordings establishing Deri-paska's involvement with Russian election meddling; Rybka is arrested in Moscow and held by local police until she agrees to relinquish the tapes in her possession to Deripaska.[257] A viral video released in January 2019 shows Rybka's arrest at an airport in Moscow; the young woman is uncer-emoniously dragged through the airport by unidentified law enforcement officers just before she is about to speak to a bank of reporters about her evidence of Deripaska's alleged involvement in Kremlin crimes.[258]

Rhona Graff, Trump's personal secretary, declines Prikhodko's Decem-ber 2015 invitation in January 2016. Prikhodko repeats his offer in March 2016, just seventy-two hours after Trump national security adviser George Papadopoulos makes his first contact with the Kremlin—a conversation with Joseph Mifsud he immediately reports to the campaign.[259] On the same day Graff is preparing Trump's second letter of declination to Prikhodko, a New York–based investment banker, Robert Foresman, emails Graff to say that a presidential aide at the Kremlin has asked him to reach out to Trump personally to convince him to come to St. Petersburg.[260] In his entreaty to Trump, Foresman brags of his "personal and professional expertise in Russia and Ukraine . . . [and] his work in setting up an early 'private channel' between Vladimir Putin and former U.S. President George W. Bush."[261] Foresman insists to Graff that he is asking for Trump's attendance at the St. Petersburg economic forum following an "approach . . . from senior Kremlin officials" on the subject.[262] Foresman also tells Graff he has things he needs to discuss with Trump that he cannot discuss over "unsecure email."[263] It is unknown whether Trump's demurrals regarding the St. Petersburg forum stem from his belief, at the time, that Cohen would be attending in his stead.

Just a few weeks after MBS announces his new anti-terrorism alliance in December 2015, Trump's attitude toward Saudi Arabia on Twitter undergoes an about-face. Whereas previously Trump had falsely accused the Saudis of secretly and illegally colluding with candidate Obama during the run-up to the 2012 presidential election, and had seemingly approached U.S.-Saudi relations as an opportunity for America to increase its revenue from overseas military and peacekeeping operations, on January 3, 2016, Trump for the first time accuses Obama of being *hostile* to Saudi interests—implicitly positioning himself as the pro-Saudi alternative in American politics. "Iran, with all of the money and all else given to them by Obama, has wanted a way to take over Saudi Arabia & their oil. THEY JUST FOUND IT!" tweets Trump, referring to the rollback of certain international sanctions against Iran pursuant to its compliance with the Joint Comprehensive Plan of Action.[264]

The sanctions rollback required under the Iran nuclear deal unfreezes about $100 billion in Iranian funds then held by the United States, which the Obama administration thereafter returns to Iran; according to CNBC, "Tehran will only have access to roughly $55 billion because much of that money will go toward repaying loans and other long-term commitments. The rest will likely be used to address Iran's ailing oil operations and other infrastructure that went without maintenance for years."[265] According to a summary of remarks by Secretary of State John Kerry published by CNBC, while Iran, post-deal, will likely continue to support groups the United States considers terrorist organizations, "support for such groups has never made a difference in the power structure in the region . . . [as] Saudi Arabia alone spends much more than Iran per year on defense."[266] Iranian and Saudi defense spending "is so incredibly disproportionate," says Kerry, "that I believe that working with our Gulf state partners . . . we have the ability to guarantee that they will be secure, that we will stand by them."[267] Trump's tweet about the deal imagines instead that

Saudi Arabia is gravely threatened by the sudden influx of funds Iran will receive subsequent to confirming that it is not enriching uranium beyond the exceedingly low level (3.67 percent) permitted by the nuclear deal it has signed.[268] Uranium must be enriched to over 90 percent to be weaponized, according to a May 2019 BBC report on the deal.[269]

Trump's tweet—and his outspoken opposition to the deal negotiated by Kerry—comes less than twenty-four hours after Kerry has issued a rare rebuke to the Saudi royal family following its execution on January 2, 2016, of forty-seven people, including most notably a dissident Shiite cleric, Nimr al-Nimr, who, per CNN, "had repeatedly spoken out against the government and the Saudi royal family."[270] Amnesty International calls the mass executions "appalling," the European Union expresses "serious concerns regarding freedom of expression [in Saudi Arabia] and the respect of basic civil and political rights," the UN secretary-general calls the killings "deeply dismay[ing]," and the U.S. State Department says it is "particularly concerned" about Saudi actions "exacerbating sectarian tensions" in the kingdom. But Trump's tweet implies that were Obama to be replaced by someone with his own inclinations, it would help protect both Saudi Arabia and its oil reserves.[271] CNN, recounting al-Nimr's arrest, imprisonment, prosecution, and execution, will quote a 2011 interview al-Nimr gave to the BBC in which he advocated nonviolence in opposing the Saudi government, preferring "the roar of the word against authorities rather than weapons. The weapon of the word is stronger than bullets, because authorities will profit from a battle of weapons," he says.[272]

According to *BuzzFeed News*, by December 29, 2015, American mercenaries employed by private U.S. companies are working with the United Arab Emirates to assassinate enemies of the Emirati royal family.[273] The digital media outlet reports on a December 29 operation its reporter Aram Roston calls "the first operation in a startling for-profit venture. For months in war-torn Yemen, some of America's most highly trained soldiers [will work] on a mercenary mission of murky legality to kill prominent clerics and Islamist political figures."[274] While it is unknown whether the mercenary company run for MBZ by Trump shadow national security adviser Erik Prince supplies mercenaries for this December operation, or whether the "anti-terrorism" alliance announced by MBS days earlier corresponds in part to this clandestine assassination agenda promoted by the crown prince of Abu Dhabi, it is clear that the operation occurs simultaneously with another event of dubious legality: the discussion Michael Flynn participates in regarding the possible kidnapping, rendition, and prosecution for treason of Turkish cleric and prominent Erdogan critic Fethullah Gulen.[275]

The December 2015 operation chronicled by *BuzzFeed News* is executed by Spear Operations Group, an American company founded by Abraham Golan, a Hungarian Israeli contractor who, coincidentally like the cleric Gulen, lives in the Pittsburgh area.[276] In speaking with *BuzzFeed News*, Golan concedes his company "ran" a "targeted assassination program" sanctioned by both the UAE and the coalition fighting alongside the Emiratis in Yemen—a coalition including nine countries, of which the two chief participants besides the UAE (and the only other countries with troops on the ground) are Saudi Arabia and Sudan.[277] Golan's statement about the multinational nature of the Emiratis' assassination squad increases significantly the odds that MBS's "anti-terrorism alliance"—which few of its member nations even knew they had joined—is the same entity as the project established by MBZ, which itself may enjoy significant overlap with Erik Prince's Emirates-based Reflex Responses unit. Just so, all three of these entities may be connected to Saudi Arabia's Rapid Intervention Group (RIG), which MBS creates to carry out his own extrajudicial killings and kidnappings (see chapter 6).

Abraham Golan tells *BuzzFeed News* in October 2018 that from December 2015—the very month MBS created his "anti-terrorism alliance"—onward, his mercenaries were "responsible for a number of the [Saudi-Emirati-Yemeni] war's high-profile assassinations."[278] He argues that the Trump administration should institute an assassination program modeled on that executed by Saudi Arabia and the UAE, adding, "Maybe I'm a monster. Maybe I should be in jail. Maybe I'm a bad guy. But I'm right."[279] *BuzzFeed News* will call Golan's program part of a larger trend in contemporary warfare (indeed, one being strongly advocated for by Trump adviser Erik Prince at the time):

"War has become increasingly privatized, with many nations outsourcing most military support services to private contractors."[280]

Given Prince's communication with—at a minimum—Trump advisers Flynn and Bannon on national security matters during the 2016 presidential campaign, even more striking in Roston's reporting for *BuzzFeed News* is his assessment of whether anyone in America knew about the Emiratis' targeted assassination program in 2015: "Experts said it is almost inconceivable that the United States would not have known that the UAE— whose military the United States has trained and armed at virtually every level—had hired an American company staffed by American veterans to conduct an assassination program in a war it closely monitors."[281] Roston adds, chillingly, that "a former CIA official who has worked in the UAE initially told *BuzzFeed News* that there was no way that Americans would be allowed to participate in such a program. But after checking, he called back: 'There were guys that were basically doing what you said.' He was astonished, he said, by what he learned.... The mercenaries, he said, were 'almost like a murder squad.'"[282]

Golan's particular squad has been contracted to do its wetwork by Mohammed Dahlan, a former security chief for the Palestinian Authority who by 2015 has been exiled to the United Arab Emirates.[283] According to former CIA officials, Golan is "ruthless" and "calculating" and is "the kind of guy you hire" when you need someone to do "crazy shit."[284] As for Dahlan, he lost his senior position in the Palestinian Authority in 2007, when he was accused of secretly conspiring with both Americans and Israelis.[285] After fleeing to the UAE, he became a "key adviser" to MBZ and, per a former CIA officer who knows him well, a "pit bull" for the Emiratis.[286] In 2013, Dahlan destabilized the Palestinian Authority and delighted Benjamin Netanyahu by suing Mahmoud Abbas, the president of the Palestinian Authority, for "corruption [and] intimidation," and doing so using an "Israeli law firm"; the same year, he assisted el-Sisi in coming to power in Egypt by orchestrating the delivery of messages and financing from MBZ and MBS to el-Sisi's collaborators in the Egyptian military.[287] In 2014, Dahlan, now cemented as an ally of both MBZ and el-Sisi, entered "talks" with Netanyahu to formally become Abbas's chief political rival in the Palestinian territories and a prearranged "peace partner" for Netanyahu.[288] That same year, he also "act[ed] as a proxy for the United States and Israel" in the Middle East, according to the *Middle East Eye*, which noted at the time that, on MBZ's behalf, Dahlan invested in the Serbian arms trade in a way that allowed him to distribute weapons across the Middle East to advance not just Emirati but American and Israeli interests, which were threatened at the time by the prospect of Turkish encroachment into the Balkans.[289] Dahlan's connections in the Israeli government are said to reside in the Israeli intelligence community—precisely where those of Trump national security advisers Prince and Flynn do.[290] That Mohammed Dahlan ends up in exile in the UAE in 2015 points toward the long-standing but sub rosa synergy between Israeli and Emirati military interests that will later become public.

Dahlan spends 2015 "raising money in Gulf countries" and lobbying el-Sisi to open the Gaza-Sinai border in preparation for his return to Gazan politics, with his hope, according to reports, being to right the mistakes of Palestinian leaders past—most notably, in Dahlan's view, Yasser Arafat's rejection of a 2000 Clinton-backed peace plan that would have given Palestinians "statehood in more than 90 percent of the West Bank and Gaza Strip."[291] In 2016, Dahlan is accused of helping to funnel money into Turkey to fund the July 2016 military coup there, another effort of which Netanyahu—who has publicly said he considers Erdogan a dangerous anti-Semite—is likely to have been supportive, and which Egypt and the UAE are, at the time, widely suspected of bankrolling.[292] During the fallout from the coup's failure, Dahlan flees from the UAE to his other safe harbor, Egypt.[293] Meanwhile, there is again talk in July 2016 of the UAE, Egypt, and Jordan—the last of these one of the original Red Sea conspirators, but one that leaves the conspiracy well after mid-2016—secretly plotting to install Dahlan in Abbas's place to facilitate a new round of peace talks with Netanyahu's government.[294] MBZ is said to be the plan's chief architect.[295]

Erik Prince eventually becomes more than just an adviser to the Trump campaign: Prince gives Trump's campaign at least $100,000 through a political action committee run by billionaire hedge fund manager Robert Mercer, who is also the primary funder for both Steve Bannon's longtime media outlet Breitbart and Trump's general-election data firm, Cambridge Analytica.[296] Prince later becomes connected to Mercer's post–Cambridge Analytica data company, Emerdata, when the deputy chairman of Prince's Frontier Services Group, Johnson Chun Shun Ko, is named to its board.[297] Other Emerdata board members include Mercer's daughters Rebekah and Jennifer (the former a Trump transition team official), while Emerdata directors include Julian Wheatland (chairman of Cambridge Analytica's parent firm SCL Group), Alexander Tayler (Cambridge Analytica's chief data officer), the aforementioned Ko, and Cambridge Analytica's former CEO, Alexander Nix—who in 2018 is suspended from his job "following revelations that it [Cambridge Analytica] misused millions of Facebook users' information, plus incriminating undercover recordings which show the executives boasting of their ability to manipulate elections and even blackmail political opponents."[298]

All told, Prince gives Trump a quarter of a million dollars in the less than 120 days between the Republican National Convention and Election Day, spreading his giving across direct donations to Trump's campaign, the national Republican Party, and Mercer's super PAC.[299] More broadly, the *Washington Post* reports that "Prince and his family were major GOP donors in 2016. The Center for Responsive Politics reported that the family gave more than $10 million to GOP candidates and super PACs, including about $2.7 million from his [Prince's] sister, [Trump secretary of education Betsy] DeVos, and her husband."[300]

The direct and indirect involvement of Prince, Bannon, Mercer, Kushner, and other top Trump aides, allies, and family members with the British company SCL Group—and, more important, its subsidiary Cambridge Analytica—is deeply troubling, given what is now known about Cambridge Analytica as reported in American and British media from 2017 and 2018. According to the *New York Times*, in 2015 and 2016 Cambridge Analytica, incorporated in 2013 by GOP mega-donor Mercer and future Trump campaign CEO Bannon, "harvested private information from the Facebook profiles of more than 50 million users without their permission . . . one of the largest data leaks in the social network's history. The breach allowed the company to exploit the private social media activity of a huge swath of the American electorate."[301] Christopher Wylie, a Cambridge Analytica co-founder and subsequently its chief whistleblower, will eventually tell the *Times* that for Cambridge Analytica, "Rules don't matter. . . . For them, this is a war, and it's all fair. They want to fight a culture war in America. . . . Cambridge Analytica was supposed to be the arsenal of weapons to fight that culture war."[302] Indeed, there is no evidence that Cambridge Analytica has divested itself of the "psychographic" voter data it improperly compiled in 2015 and 2016, with the *Times* reporting that as of March 2018 the company "still possesses most or all of the trove" of data it took from Facebook prior to the 2016 presidential election.[303]

The data that Cambridge Analytica took from American voters in 2015 and 2016 was in the first instance "harvested" by an "outside researcher," who purportedly was collecting it for "academic purposes."[304] Facebook has called the actions of this researcher, a Russian American named Aleksandr Kogan, a "scam" and a "fraud"; as of 2018, however, it could not conclusively confirm for its users that either Kogan or Cambridge Analytica had deleted the data in their possession.[305] Inquiries in 2017 and 2018 will reveal that Nix, who was the CEO of Cambridge Analytica during its tenure as the Trump campaign's data firm, not only lied repeatedly about having or using any data from Facebook—including offering false testimony at a British parliamentary hearing on the subject in early 2018— but lied about ordering the data deleted once Cambridge Analytica finally acknowledged possessing it.[306] England's information commissioner is now investigating whether Cambridge Analytica "illegally acquired and used" the information it was employing for modeling purposes during the 2016 election.[307]

The scope of Cambridge Analytica's work for the Trump campaign is still being investigated—as is its connection to the Russian Federation. According to the *Times*, many "Cambridge Analytica employees . . . worked for the Trump team"; the company's "British affiliate [SCL Group] claims to have worked in Russia"; shortly before the 2016 election, Michael Flynn took on an advisory role with SCL Group, a fact he did not reveal publicly until an August 2017 financial filing; and in October 2017 Kremlin cutout Julian Assange revealed that Alexander Nix himself "reached out to him during the [presidential] campaign in hopes of obtaining private emails belonging to Mr. Trump's Democratic opponent, Hillary Clinton"—a revelation that, along with Flynn's secretive work for SCL Group, puts SCL Group and its offshoot Cambridge Analytica squarely in the midst of the Trump campaign's repeated attempts to secure Clinton's stolen emails from Russian sources throughout the summer of 2016.[308]

Cambridge Analytica begins its work for the Trump campaign in June 2016 as the result of a decision made by Jared Kushner; Kushner's decision is opposed by outgoing campaign manager Corey Lewandowski—it is unknown if his opposition is in part responsible for his exit—as well as incoming campaign manager Paul Manafort, who has his own reasons for wanting internal campaign data to remain within his own sphere (and that of his handpicked pollster, Tony Fabrizio) rather than anyone else's, particularly that of a company co-founded by Steve Bannon (see chapter 4).[309] That Lewandowski leaves the campaign just as Cambridge Analytica joins it, and that Manafort's departure from the campaign on August 17, 2016, is immediately followed by Bannon's ascension to the role of campaign CEO, underscores the central position the data firm has during the 2016 general election.

The *New York Times* reports that in co-founding Cambridge Analytica in January 2013, Christopher Wylie's ambition was to use "inherent psychological traits to affect voters' behavior"; in funding Cambridge Analytica, Mercer's hope was to become "a kingmaker in Republican politics"; and in steering Cambridge Analytica first toward Texas senator Ted Cruz's GOP primary campaign and ultimately into Trump's general election campaign, Bannon aimed to "shift America's culture and rewire its politics" through "personality profiling."[310]

In 2014, after the Psychometrics Centre at Cambridge University had refused to work with Wylie and his team, a professor at the university, Kogan, agreed to do so, beginning his work in June, three months after

Trump's "soft" announcement of his presidential candidacy on Twitter.[311] Kogan in short order authored an app that represented to end users that any personal data it harvested would be used exclusively for academic purposes; in reality, copies of everything were being transmitted to Bannon, Mercer, Wylie, and Nix.[312] Yet the situation was far worse than even this for most social media users caught up in the scheme, as only 270,000 users actually consented—by participating in a survey with substantial fine print—to have their data harvested at all, even as Kogan was providing more than 50 million raw profiles to Cambridge Analytica (30 million of which were robust enough to produce psychographic voter profiles).[313]

In transmitting the profiles, Kogan tells Bannon and his team that the profiles he has created have predictive qualities: they reveal whether a given voter is open, conscientious, extroverted, agreeable, neurotic, satisfied, intelligent, fair-minded, male or female, old or young, and conservative or liberal. They can even offer information on a voter's job, religion, hobbies, major at university, and belief in astrology.[314]

Impressed with Kogan's 2014 work, Mercer and Bannon, who had formed the American company Cambridge Analytica as an offshoot of the British firm SCL Group in late 2013, form SCL USA (later renamed Cambridge Analytica UK) at the beginning of 2015; the duo's two transatlantic incorporations appear to be a byzantine effort to either honor or subvert U.S. election laws—which one being a subject of ongoing investigation. Of the original Cambridge Analytica the *New York Times* will report, "the firm was effectively a shell . . . any contracts won by Cambridge, originally incorporated in Delaware, would be serviced by London-based SCL [Group] and overseen by Mr. Nix, a British citizen who held dual appointments at Cambridge Analytica and SCL. Most SCL employees and contractors were Canadian, like Mr. Wylie, or European."[315] The business model the *Times* describes is a problem—potentially a serious violation of federal law—as months earlier, in July 2014, "an American election lawyer advising the company, Laurence Levy, warned that the [Cambridge Analytica–SCL Group] arrangement could violate laws limiting the involvement of foreign nationals in American elections."[316] According to the *Times*, by the time of the 2016 general election, Cambridge Analytica had—its 2015 incorporation of SCL USA/

Cambridge Analytica UK notwithstanding—made few substantive changes to its employment model, "hir[ing] more Americans to work on the races that year" even as it remained the case that "most of its data scientists were citizens of the United Kingdom or other European countries."[317] These foreign nationals "performed a variety of services," reports the *Times*, including "designing target audiences for digital ads and fund-raising appeals, modeling voter turnout, buying $5 million in television ads, and determining where Mr. Trump should travel to best drum up support."[318] In a U.S. presidential election Trump wins in the nation's Electoral College by only 80,000 popular votes, there is no way to know whether his presumptively illegal use of foreign nationals in his campaign data operation is what puts his campaign over the top; what is known is that Trump's digital director and liaison to Cambridge Analytica in 2016, Brad Parscale, is now the campaign manager for Trump's 2020 reelection effort.[319]

As for how effective Cambridge Analytica was in assisting the Trump effort in 2016, Nix has declared, as the *Times* summarizes, that its work "helped shape Mr. Trump's strategy."[320] While others have disputed Nix's account, suggesting that Facebook had plugged any holes in its data leakage by the end of the summer of 2016 and that the Trump campaign ultimately used "legacy data" from Ted Cruz's primary effort, neither circumstance renders Cambridge Analytica's data any more legally obtained than it was when harvested for Republican usage in late 2015.[321]

In June 2018, investigative reporters Carole Cadwalladr and Stephanie Kirchgaessner, writing for the *Guardian*, will reveal that immediately after Trump's inauguration, Cambridge Analytica director Brittany Kaiser visited Julian Assange in the Ecuadorean embassy in London to discuss the election. The two reporters also discover that Kaiser had previously claimed to friends that she "channeled cryptocurrency payments and donations to WikiLeaks."[322] Coupled with the additional revelation that Nix's July 2016 outreach to Assange included, too, an offer to "index and disseminate" WikiLeaks' stolen Democratic materials, news of Kaiser's WikiLeaks payments startles on both sides of the Atlantic.[323] In March 2019, Cambridge Analytica will stand accused in a British court of "trying to liquidate the company before a full investigation into the company [can] be held" and of having compiled "up to 87 million clandestinely harvested Facebook profiles to create a state of the art voter database that helped Trump win election in 2016."[324] The company itself has claimed to have "4,000 data points on some 230 million Americans."[325]

In December 2018, the *Daily Beast* will report that "a trove of digital artifacts from Trump's [2016] social-media campaign . . . provides the first hard evidence that Team Trump made continuous use of audience lists created by Cambridge Analytica to target a portion of its 'dark ads' on Facebook. The ads were deployed from July 2016 through the end of the election—and beyond, to the inauguration in January 2017."[326] By the end of 2018, Channel 4 in the United Kingdom will have run an undercover sting operation on Alexander Nix that reveals him "boasting about his company's work for Trump and effectively claiming credit for the *Apprentice* star's election victory. Cambridge Analytica, Nix says, 'did all the research, all the data, all the analytics, all the targeting, we ran all the digital campaign, the television campaign, and our data informed all the strategy' for Trump's presidential campaign."[327] Nix adds that he met Trump personally "many times."[328] Nix's claims are bolstered by statements made by Trump's 2016 digital director, Parscale, immediately after the election, when he tells associates, according to CNN, that "Cambridge [Analytica] provided a much-needed infusion of data staff for a bare-bones campaign."[329] Parscale tells one questioner during a 2016 Google forum that "Cambridge [Analytica] actually provided a full-time employee that could sit next to me all day" to help process data.[330] While the Trump campaign also uses RNC data during the campaign to target voters, Parscale has conceded that there were some purposes—for instance, the development of supplemental data to daily tracking polls—for which Cambridge Analytica's work was essential to the campaign.[331] The contradictions between Nix's and Parscale's claims about the involvement of Cambridge Analytica in the 2016 election have never been resolved.

News of Nix's boasts, his discussion with Channel 4 of clandestine and illicit methods for assisting Cambridge Analytica clients, and the Cambridge Analytica–fueled "dark ads" used by the Trump campaign sits uneasily beside the declaration by a "senior Trump official" in October

2016 that the campaign was then secretly running "three voter suppression efforts" through its digital operation—efforts targeting liberals, young women, and black voters. These efforts reportedly occurred at a time when "as much as 45 percent of Trump's campaign budget in a given month" was being devoted to "digital outreach and research," according to *Fortune*.[332] A 2018 Bloomberg article on this chilling claim by a senior Trump official is titled "Russia's Voter Suppression Operation Echoed Trump Campaign Tactics."[333] Evidence recently unearthed by the *New Yorker* also reveals that Cambridge Analytica played a much larger—but still secretive—role in the Brexit vote in the United Kingdom than was previously appreciated, and that Steve Bannon was entwined with that effort as well.[334] The exposé discloses that Bannon "was in the loop on discussions taking place at the time between his company [Cambridge Analytica] and the leaders of Leave .EU, a far-right nationalist organization."[335]

In view of the foregoing, a pressing question remains: Did the Russians gain access to any of Trump's data firm's psychographic data in the course of their own 2016 efforts to target American voters? The answer appears to be yes. Christopher Wylie has said publicly that "when I was at Cambridge Analytica, the company hired known Russian agents, had data researchers in St. Petersburg, tested U.S. voters' opinions on Putin's leadership, and hired hackers from Russia—all while Bannon was in charge."[336] Kogan, Cambridge Analytica's "academic" researcher, has since been revealed as an employee of Russia's Kremlin-owned St. Petersburg State University as well as Cambridge University in the United Kingdom; his work at the Russian institution included not only a teaching position but "grants for research into the social media network," according to the *Guardian*.[337] In 2014, the *Guardian* found that a few months before Cambridge Analytica was founded, its British parent company, SCL Group, gave a "presentation" of its work on "micro-targeting individuals on social media during elections" to Russian energy firm Lukoil, an entity "with links to the Kremlin."[338] SCL Group documents shown to Lukoil in 2014, as the Internet Research Agency's propaganda campaign in the United States was just ramping up, included "posters and videos apparently aimed at alarming or demoralizing voters, including warnings of violence and fraud."[339] Nor were the SCL presentations low-level affairs, as the materials were shared with Lukoil's CEO, a "former Soviet oil minister who has said the strategic aims of Lukoil are closely aligned with those of Russia."[340]

Cambridge Analytica has troubling intersections with Israeli business intelligence firms, as well. While Joel Zamel's Psy-Group was doing work for Ben Carson's ill-fated presidential campaign in late 2015, so too was Cambridge Analytica, according to CNN.[341] More important, however, on December 14, 2016, five weeks after the 2016 election, Psy-Group and Cambridge Analytica were reunited when the two announced a partnership to "provide intelligence and social-media services . . . to an array of clients."[342] This joint effort was apparently connected to Trump's election victory, with the *Wall Street Journal* reporting that "the partnership was intended in part to help win government contracts—something that Cambridge [Analytica] and its parent company, SCL Group, were aggressively seeking to do as their allies in the Trump administration took power."[343]

But Psy-Group had also sought business with Trump prior to his election, with Zamel pitching Donald Trump Jr. directly at Trump Tower on August 3, 2016, by "extoll[ing] his company's ability to give an edge to a political campaign," according to the *New York Times*, which notes that Zamel and Psy-Group had by the August 2016 meeting "already drawn up a multimillion-dollar proposal for a social media manipulation effort to help elect Mr. Trump."[344] Several aspects of this meeting raise serious questions about possible connections and overlap between Cambridge Analytica and Psy-Group: that Zamel's pitch came just a few weeks after the campaign had hired Cambridge Analytica as its data firm; that Cambridge Analytica had been accused in 2015, by seven individuals with "close knowledge" of a Cambridge Analytica election campaign in Nigeria that year, of "work[ing] with people they [the seven individuals] believed were Israeli computer hackers"; that in the weeks leading up to the 2016 election Michael Flynn, who had been actively (if apparently unsuccessfully) recruited by Psy-Group, took on an advisory role with SCL Group; that by the end of 2016 Psy-Group and Cambridge Analytica would announce a formal partnership; and that in 2018 both Cambridge Analytica and Psy-Group would declare bankruptcy within seventy-two hours of each other—at a time when both outfits were under investigation by special counsel Robert Mueller.[345]

Most troubling, however, is that on August 3, 2016—just a few weeks after Cambridge Analytica came aboard the Trump campaign—Donald Trump Jr., according to the *New York Times*, "responded approvingly" to a proposal from Psy-Group that was on its face redundant with the work already being done (and that would continue to be done) by Cambridge Analytica.[346] Apropos of this confusion, the *Times* notes that "the details of who commissioned it [the August 2016 Psy-Group proposal] remain in dispute."[347] What is clear is that during Channel 4's undercover investigation into Alexander Nix and Mark Turnbull, two top executives at Cambridge Analytica, Turnbull tells two reporters posing as prospective Cambridge Analytica clients that his firm does "intelligence gathering" using "specialist organizations that do that kind of work" and with whom Cambridge Analytica has "relationships and partnerships"—a description that perfectly fits Psy-Group, a business intelligence outfit.[348] Turnbull says to Channel 4 on camera that these "specialist organizations" allow Cambridge Analytica clients to learn their opponents' "secrets" and "tactics."[349] In another Channel 4 video, Turnbull speaks of his firm offering, as part of its suite of services, the involvement of "various intelligence-gathering operations that operate very discreetly to find [political opponents'] information"—he accepts the term "dirt" when it is offered to him by the undercover reporters, and he himself adds the phrase "skeletons in the closet."[350] What Turnbull describes is identical to the services Psy-Group pitches to the Trump campaign with respect to Hillary Clinton. Tellingly, Turnbull tells Channel 4 that when Cambridge Analytica is engaged in intelligence-gathering activities, sometimes the firm "contract[s]" with "a different entity" with "a different name," so that "no record [of the intelligence-gathering operation] exists with our name attached to it at all."[351] Nix, for his part, discusses with the reporters the use of "honey traps" (ruses involving sexual seduction and blackmail) to target and destroy selected politicians.[352] He says further that Cambridge Analytica is "used to operating through different vehicles, in the shadows."[353]

According to the *Wall Street Journal*, "One person familiar with the work of both firms [Cambridge Analytica and Psy-Group] said Mr. Nix in the [Channel 4] video appeared to be referring to Psy-Group, which does work that tracks closely with Mr. Nix's description."[354] The *Journal* notes that, per its sources, Psy-Group was as of 2016 known for using honey traps on clients' political opponents.[355] The reporting by the *Journal* seems to be conclusively confirmed by Nix's most candid comment on the question: the Cambridge Analytica CEO at one point tells Channel 4's undercover reporters that "we use Israeli companies," among other entities, as they are "very effective in intelligence gathering."[356]

The initial outreaches from the Trump campaign to Cambridge Analytica and to Psy-Group both occur in spring 2016. According to reporting by the *Times of Israel* and the *Daily Beast*, three Trump campaign members—Rick Gates and two unnamed "members of Trump's inner circle"—solicit Psy-Group in April 2016 to create "secretive proposals for the Trump campaign" that will involve not only mass disinformation operations but also "collecting opposition research on Clinton and ten of her associates" using both open-source methods and unnamed "complementary intelligence activities."[357] After Gates allegedly "reject[s]" the resulting proposals—in June, around the time the campaign decides to use Cambridge Analytica's services—Psy-Group's Zamel nevertheless is given the opportunity to pitch directly to Trump's son Don: a development, partially coordinated by Erik Prince, that throws into doubt whether Gates's response to Zamel was in fact a rejection or merely a referral up the chain of command. Certainly, the campaign had previously used Trump Jr.—a trusted member of the Trump family, but also outside the campaign's infrastructure—to vet potentially explosive campaign gambits, such as the receipt of Clinton "dirt" from Natalia Veselnitskaya in June 2016.

The proposals Gates sees in late spring 2016 are so top-secret within and outside the Trump campaign that they use code words for the two major-party candidates: "Lion" (Trump) and "Forest" (Clinton).[358] Zamel's initially "rejected" proposal would have cost more than $3 million, a hefty price tag partially explained by the fact that, at the time, it included a primary-related pre–Republican National Convention targeting of Ted Cruz (denominated "Bear" in Zamel's proposal).[359] Notably, immediately after the 2016 election George Nader, MBZ's adviser, pays Zamel $2 million, an amount roughly commensurate with Zamel having provided only the general-election work he pitched to Gates in spring 2016.[360] Indeed, the *New Yorker* reports that certain of Psy-Group's services were available for as little as six figures; "one company document reported that Psy-Group's influence services cost, on average, just $350,000."[361] That Zamel did not conduct any GOP primary work for the Trump campaign is confirmed by the fact that, per the *New York Times*, he didn't receive any approving signal from Trump's campaign until he met with Trump Jr. in August 2016, several weeks after the RNC in Cleveland.

In estimating the cost of the services Zamel might have provided the Trump campaign, the *Guardian* offers a report establishing that $2 million—the exact amount Nader pays Zamel immediately after the 2016 election—was Cambridge Analytica's total fee for the complex, large-scale, last-minute general-election campaign it had been hired to conduct in Nigeria in 2015.[362] During its campaign in Nigeria, Cambridge Analytica represented to its client that its intelligence-gathering partners for the project actually worked for Israeli intelligence; some of the firm's own staff, speaking months later to the *Guardian*, said they were surprised to learn that Israelis working on the project, whether governmental or nongovernmental, were in possession of a large trove of hacked materials from Nigerian servers.[363]

Tellingly, the period in which Gates first fields proposals from Psy-Group is the same period during which Cambridge Analytica is pitching some—though perhaps, in retrospect, not all—of its services to the Trump campaign.[364] The possibility that the Emiratis used George Nader to pay for the illicit components of the media package Cambridge Analytica provided to the Trump campaign—and that this arrangement was sealed at Trump Tower on August 3, 2016, with representatives of Trump, Psy-Group, and the UAE all present—is never addressed in the Mueller Report, which notes that it has omitted counterintelligence information in favor of providing it directly to the counterintelligence division of the FBI.[365]

Nader and Zamel have since 2016 provided contradictory accounts regarding the $2 million post-election payment the former made to the latter, suggesting that one of the two—or both—is not telling the truth about their relationship.[366] Just so, while the *New York Times* reports that Trump Jr. in August 2016 "responded approvingly" to Psy-Group's proposal, Trump's son, through his current attorney, has claimed that he "was not interested." Here again, one of two sources is evidently not telling the truth.[367]

Significant to unpacking both of these mysteries—that of Nader's payment to Zamel and that of Don Jr.'s disposition toward Zamel's proposal—might be the following: that Psy-Group's attorney (up until the firm's dissolution and his own departure for a new job) was Marc Mukasey, a longtime law partner of future Trump attorney Rudy Giuliani and also, more important, the longtime attorney for Donald Trump Sr., Donald Trump Jr., Ivanka Trump, and Eric Trump.[368] In a similar vein, the presence of the UAE-dwelling, UAE-advising Erik Prince at the August 2016 Trump Tower meeting, coupled with the May 2018 revelation by the *Wall Street Journal* that Zamel not only had been "making contacts" in the UAE since 2014 but had begun working for MBZ via his company Wikistrat, significantly increases the odds of Trump-UAE-Zamel coordination.[369] Tellingly, Zamel's work with MBZ began around the same time Trump first made his presidential ambitions public in 2014.

Campaign donations to the Trump campaign by the UAE would be illegal under 52 U.S.C. § 30121, as would any efforts by the Israeli government to direct toward the Trump campaign clandestine Israeli intelligence services that might have assisted Trump in securing victory against Hillary Clinton.[370] The *Times of Israel* reports that Psy-Group does much foreign intelligence work that is "known to the Israeli government . . . specifically the Ministry of Strategic Affairs," even though the work is not paid for by the government.[371] The *Times* reports, moreover, that Rick Gates "first heard about Psy-Group from . . . George Birnbaum"—Israeli president Benjamin Netanyahu's longtime chief of staff.[372] Birnbaum did much more than passively direct Trump's deputy campaign manager to Zamel and Psy-Group, however, as he "introduce[s]" Gates to Psy-Group at a meeting at the Mandarin Oriental hotel in Washington in March 2016 that Birnbaum himself attends.[373] Birnbaum will later say that he believed Psy-Group was a good fit for the Trump campaign, which he calls "interested" in Psy-Group's offerings, because the Israeli business intelligence outfit had "the technology to achieve what they [the Trump campaign] were looking for."[374] Whether Birnbaum would have dared insert himself into an American presidential election, particularly through the intermediary of an Israeli company whose work was known to be followed by the Israeli Ministry of Strategic Affairs, without first consulting with the Israeli leader for whom he had worked for so long, Benjamin Netanyahu, is unclear. What is clear, however, is that Netanyahu is a longtime Trump ally who is personal friends with Jared Kushner and his family. According to the *New Yorker*, Netanyahu has had "a long friendship with Charles Kushner, the father of Ivanka Trump's husband, Jared Kushner. In recent years, the Kushners, Orthodox Jews who made their fortune in the real-estate business and hold conservative views on Israel, have donated large sums of money to Israeli causes and charities, including tens of thousands of dollars to a yeshiva in the Beit El settlement, in the West Bank. When Netanyahu visited the Kushners at their home in New Jersey, he sometimes stayed overnight and slept in Jared's bedroom, while Jared was relegated to the basement."[375] Meanwhile, Netanyahu has known Trump for so long that Ron Dermer, Israel's ambassador to the United States, recalls "accompanying Netanyahu to Trump Tower, in New York, in the early aughts for a meeting with Donald Trump."[376] As for Psy-Group itself, the *Wall Street Journal* notes that several individuals closely linked to the company are "veteran Israeli intelligence officials."[377]

Of equal significance to the question of Zamel's and Nader's connection to the Trump campaign is the matter of the two consultants' employers. Not only do Zamel and Nader share an employer in MBZ, with Nader acting as an "adviser" and Zamel, according to the *New York Times*, as a "consultant," but Zamel, like Nader, has also worked closely with individuals closely linked to the Russian government. Per the *Times*, Zamel has previously worked for "oligarchs linked to Mr. Putin, including Oleg V. Deripaska and Dmitry Rybolovlev, who hired the firm for online campaigns against their business rivals."[378] The Zamel-Deripaska link is particularly intriguing given the Mueller Report's finding that Paul Manafort was secretly sending polling data and strategy updates to Deripaska through Konstantin Kilimnik during the presidential campaign, and given additional claims by Nastya Rybka that the oligarch was involved in Russian

election interference. As for Rybolovlev, besides being involved in a mysterious business transaction with Trump in 2008 that netted Trump tens of
millions of dollars more than the value of the property he was selling, he
has also faced allegations, based on flight data, that he twice secretly met
Trump on airport tarmacs in the last days of the 2016 general election.[379]
That MBS, with the assistance of MBZ, publicly transferred hundreds of
millions of dollars to Rybolovlev in 2017 through a bizarre international
art auction is also a source of significant concern (see chapter 8). As for
Nader, the New York Times notes that the Lebanese American businessman "visited Moscow at least twice during the presidential campaign as a
confidential emissary from [MBZ]" even as he was, in the United States,
meeting "often" with Kushner, Flynn, and Bannon "in the hectic final
weeks of the [2016] campaign."[380] In view of the foregoing, it is not difficult
to imagine both Nader and Zamel having a strong grasp of the Kremlin's interests, intentions, and efforts with respect to the 2016 presidential
election at the time they met with Donald Trump Jr. in Trump Tower in
August 2016.

That Zamel has previously worked for both a man known to be a
business associate of Donald Trump and another man accused of being
involved in Russia's 2016 election interference raises another troubling—if
remote—possibility that may be addressed in any ongoing FBI counterintelligence investigation into Trump's election victory. In its undercover exposé of Cambridge Analytica and the exploits of its CEO, Alexander Nix,
England's Channel 4 captures Nix revealing that a favored Cambridge
Analytica tactic, executed through one of its "vehicles" rather than itself,
is to send an operative to a politician and "offer them a deal that's too
good to be true and make sure that that's video recorded. These sorts of
tactics are very effective—instantly having video evidence of corruption. . . .
We'll have a wealthy developer come in—somebody posing as a wealthy
developer—they will offer a large amount of money to the candidate, to
finance his campaign, in exchange for land, for instance, we'll have the
whole thing recorded on cameras."[381] Nix also discusses using "very beau-
tiful Ukrainian girls" to catch a politician in an indelicate position on
camera.[382] Apropos of Nix's reference to Ukraine, and in the process of

providing a specific example of how Cambridge Analytica can and does work with outside outfits, Nix's deputy Mark Turnbull tells Channel 4's undercover reporters, "We've just used a different organization to run a very, very successful project in a, um . . . Eastern European country . . . where they did a really—no one even knew they were there. They were just ghosted in, did the work, ghosted out, and produced really, really good material. So we have experience in doing this."[383] In light of Trump's acknowledgment that his Moscow hotel room in late 2013 was audio and video bugged, and representations by Giorgi Rtskhiladze, a Soviet-born U.S. citizen who is a mutual business associate of both Trump and Aras Agalarov, to Trump's attorney Michael Cohen that "videos" of Trump were indeed produced during that trip (see chapter 5), the possibility remains that Cambridge Analytica's intelligence-gathering capabilities might have been used not only against Clinton but also to create—or, alternatively, to confirm or deny the existence of—compromising video or audio of Trump himself.[384] Moreover, Nix's reference to his subcontractors, some of which are Israeli business intelligence outfits, offering their politician marks "a deal that's too good to be true" calls to mind Lana Erchova's claim that Russian officials wanted to offer Trump "land in Crimea among other things."[385] Joel Zamel's long-standing business relationships with Russian oligarchs connected to both Trump and Kremlin election interference would therefore have made either Psy-Group or Wikistrat valuable adjuncts in any effort by the Kremlin to entrap Trump or, far more likely, efforts by the Trump campaign to determine whether or not the Kremlin indeed had *kompromat* involving the GOP candidate.

As for George Nader's many foreign connections—and his willingness to use them during the 2016 presidential campaign—the *New York Times* reports that, beginning in May 2016, while Zamel was working on social media and intelligence-gathering proposals for the Trump campaign, Nader "began making inquiries on behalf of the Emirati prince [MBZ] about possible ways to directly support Mr. Trump, according to three people with whom Mr. Nader discussed his efforts."[386] While the special counsel's observations or conclusions as to non-Russian foreign aid flowing to the Trump campaign during the 2016 general election fall outside the scope of his April 2019 report, the *New York Times* notes that there are indeed "indication[s] that countries other than Russia may have offered assistance to the Trump campaign in the months before the presidential election," adding that these "interactions are a focus of the investigation by Robert S. Mueller III" and that Mueller has "questioned numerous witnesses in Washington, New York, Atlanta, Tel Aviv and elsewhere about what foreign help may have been pledged or accepted, and about whether any such assistance was coordinated with Russia, according to witnesses and others with knowledge of the interviews."[387] The *Times* adds that according to two people familiar with the Trump campaign's pre-election meetings with Saudi and Emirati emissaries, "the Trump campaign officials [who met with the emissaries] did not appear bothered by the idea of cooperation with foreigners."[388]

According to the Mueller Report, any such information on multinational collusion gathered by the special counsel's office would have been considered, in the words of the report, "foreign intelligence information relevant to the FBI's broader national security mission" and would have been "identif[ied] and convey[ed]" to the FBI rather than being included in Volume 1 of the report.[389] For the purposes of detailing counterintelligence evidence, therefore, and especially evidence involving foreign governments other than Russia's, the special counsel underscores that the report is merely a "summary"—missing not only redacted counterintelligence material and any counterintelligence material considered outside the narrow scope of the inquiry but also any material deemed unnecessary for the purposes of the summary.[390] While the size of the special counsel's underlying investigative case file is unknown, the *Times* proposes that "Mr. Mueller probably collected and generated hundreds of thousands if not millions of pages of paper during his investigation," and the report itself notes that the special counsel's office "issued more than 2,800 subpoenas . . . executed nearly 500 search-and-seizure warrants; obtained more than 230 orders for communication records . . . obtained almost 50 orders authorizing use of pen registers; made 13 requests to foreign governments pursuant to Mutual Legal Assistance Treaties; and interviewed approximately 500 witnesses, including almost 80 before a grand jury."[391]

While the Mueller Report is silent on when Joel Zamel first encountered George Nader and MBZ, and how any of these three men came into the orbit of the Trump campaign, in advance of any future counterintelligence report derived from Mueller's and more than a dozen other ongoing FBI investigations, reporting from across the world fills in many of the gaps in public knowledge on these topics.[392] According to the *Wall Street Journal*, Zamel "began making contacts in the UAE" in 2014, so quickly "becoming close to the national security adviser [of the UAE]" that he was able to sign up the royal government in Abu Dhabi as one of his company Wikistrat's "major clients."[393] Wikistrat, like Psy-Group an Israeli business intelligence outfit, did work for MBZ that included conducting "war-games scenarios for the government of the UAE," though many Wikistrat employees at the time say that the identity of their client was hidden from even them—a fact underscoring the level of secrecy with which MBZ operates out-of-country.[394] That "there are no known publicly available pictures of [Zamel]," according to the *Daily Beast*, points toward Zamel's own penchant for secrecy.[395]

It is while Zamel is working with the UAE that he launches Psy-Group, which quickly expands its operations into America and the United Kingdom.[396] Psy-Group's marketing materials lean heavily on the firm's association with the Israeli military, inasmuch as they emphasize that the Israeli company was "founded and is managed by an experienced group of former high-ranking officers from elite units of some of the world's most renowned intelligence agencies. [Psy-Group] has a proven track record in information gathering, analysis, research, special intelligence operations and technology in the physical and cyber domains."[397] Tellingly, Psy-Group appears to begin its operations in the weeks and months immediately after the fall 2015 meeting MBZ attended with MBS and el-Sisi on a yacht in the Red Sea, at which meeting the three Arab leaders agreed to work to elect Donald Trump as U.S. president. Certainly, Wikistrat and Psy-Group's corporate histories confirm that Zamel was at least a "consultant" to MBZ at the time of the meeting; notably, part of the Red Sea Conspiracy's underlying scheme was to bring several Sunni Arab Gulf states more closely in league with Israel, particularly the Israeli military.[398]

As Zamel is winding down Wikistrat in 2015—the firm goes up for sale in 2016—ostensibly because he wishes to spend more time on Psy-Group, Wikistrat completes a major new war-game simulation.[399] By 2015, war-game simulations (that is, simulations of how a business intelligence company can intervene in an election) have made up the bulk of Wikistrat's work for UAE, though it is unclear if the unusually large simulation Wikistrat works on in 2015, so close in time to its closure, was commissioned by the UAE, one of Zamel's Kremlin-connected past employers, both UAE and Russian oligarchs in tandem, or some other client.[400] What is known, according to the *Daily Beast*, is that just "days after Donald Trump rode down an escalator at Trump Tower [in mid-June 2015] and announced he'd run for president, a little-known consulting firm with links to Israeli intelligence [Wikistrat] started gaming out how a foreign government could meddle in the U.S. political process. Internal communications, which the *Daily Beast* reviewed, show that the firm conducted an analysis of how illicit efforts might shape American politics. Months later, the Trump campaign reviewed a pitch from a company [Psy-Group] owned by that firm's founder—a pitch to carry out similar efforts."[401]

This major investigative report in the *Daily Beast*, conducted in late 2018 and early 2019, strongly points toward MBZ having commissioned Zamel to generate Wikistrat's 2015 war-game simulations, as the "similar" pitch Zamel made to Trump Jr. in August 2016 was made alongside George Nader—one of MBZ's top advisers—and Erik Prince, the man running the Emirates' mercenary army. Moreover, as the *Daily Beast* observes, at the time Zamel first pitched his plan to the Trump campaign—in April 2016, to Rick Gates—it "echoed . . . the real election interference already underway by the Kremlin," an observation that becomes more troubling when added to the fact of MBZ adviser George Nader's repeated trips to Moscow during the presidential election and his substantial past engagements with top officials in the Russian government.[402]

Zamel incorporated Psy-Group in Israel in December 2014.[403] According to the *Daily Beast*, as the head of Psy-Group "Zamel took part in at least two meetings in Washington in 2016 and 2017. And his staff at Psy-Group made several connections about their social media manipulation plan with individuals who represented themselves as close to the Trump team." More explicitly, "former employees of [Psy-Group] . . . said part of the plan [for the Trump campaign] was carried out."[404] Peter Marino, a Wikistrat employee who worked on Zamel's election-interference war-game in 2015, notes the similarity of his work to what actually occurred during the 2016 election: "At the time we were discussing the subject of cyber-interference in democratic processes, it seemed and felt like just another idle intellectual exercise and scenario planning project for political scientists. . . . But retrospectively, it feels a bit too on-the-nose not to be disturbing."[405] Another Wikistrat analyst who spoke to the *Daily Beast* analogized the Israeli firm's style of work to that of the Internet Research Agency, pointing to a 2015 summary of Wikistrat's suite of services that echoed IRA techniques at a time, the digital media outlet notes, "after the St. Petersburg–based Internet Research Agency had begun its U.S. election interference, but well before the American public knew about it."[406] A third 2015 Wikistrat employee was even more direct, referencing Zamel's work with Nader, and Nader's subsequent attendance at a UAE-Russia summit with Erik Prince in January 2017, and adding, "The problem is when you combine that [information] with the fact of all the other allegations against Mr. Zamel, including the allegations that he received payment from George Nader, that Psy-Group was allegedly involved with a social media manipulation campaign first during the primary and then during the general [election in the United States]—you combine all of that with the fact that at another company he owns, Wikistrat, his analysts came up with a scenario that's eerily similar to what wound up happening [with Russian election interference] . . . it is very concerning."[407]

When one considers that Joel Zamel began working with the UAE just as the Emirati government was initiating a massive cyberhacking initiative called Project Raven, the level of concern required by Zamel's 2015 and 2016 actions deepens. As one Project Raven employee will put it to Reuters, "I am working for a foreign intelligence agency who is targeting U.S. persons. I am officially the bad kind of spy."[408] A recent *New York Times* report reveals that, whether this practice is connected to Project Raven or not, the UAE "use[s] Israeli phone-hacking technology to spy on political and regional rivals as well as members of the media," noting that at least one Israeli company, NSO, directly "participat[es] in the cyberattacks"—an observation suggesting that NSO and Zamel's Psy-Group, the two Israeli business intelligence companies with which Michael Flynn has been linked, simultaneously were working with the Emirati government on related projects in 2014.[409] The *Times of Israel* adds to this report by reminding its readers that for the UAE to access certain Israeli technologies from an Israeli intelligence company in the first instance, the company must "receive the express permission of Israeli's Defense Ministry"—raising the question of whether Wikistrat or Psy-Group ever sought or received express permission from the Israeli Defense Ministry or the Israeli Ministry of Strategic Affairs to do business with the Emirati government, especially if that work could have influenced the 2016 U.S. presidential election.[410] Moreover, since the Saudis have been using NSO's Israeli Defense Ministry–approved Pegasus 3 hacking software since 2013, if any Wikistrat or Psy-Group work with the UAE in 2014 or thereafter used Pegasus as part of a Saudi-UAE joint venture, it would lay at the doorstep of the Israeli government a good deal of the responsibility for any illegal intrusion into America's electoral processes that may have resulted.[411]

Given that Pegasus has been called "one of the most sophisticated pieces of cyberespionage software" ever created, it is difficult to imagine the UAE declining to use it in conjunction with any business it did with Zamel, especially if Nader's entreaty to Trump Jr. in August 2016 indeed imported that the Saudis and Emiratis were working together to advance Trump's cause. The *Times of Israel* confirms that the UAE has used Pegasus to "spy on foreign government officials" many times in the past, including during the period of the U.S. election—and confirms, too, that Pegasus has been used to spy on North American officials, for instance in Mexico—leaving only the question of whether any U.S. political figures were targeted by the Emiratis, the Saudis, or any of their Israeli contractors.[412] As to this question, it must be noted that in November 2018 ex-CIA contractor and NSA whistleblower Edward Snowden alleged that Pegasus had been used by Saudi Arabia and the UAE to track *Washington Post* journalist Jamal

Khashoggi—an allegation that NSO has denied.[413] The *Times of Israel* confirms, however, that NSO's Pegasus technology had been sold to the Saudis by the time Riyadh was using the surveillance tools available to the royal family to track, ensnare, and ultimately assassinate Khashoggi (see chapter 9).[414] As for whether Psy-Group was in 2015 and 2016 willing to work in the United States, the answer is yes. The *New Yorker* reports, for instance, that in 2016 and 2017 Psy-Group "mounted a campaign [Project Butterfly] on behalf of wealthy Jewish-American donors to embarrass and intimidate activists on American college campuses who support a movement to put economic pressure on Israel because of its treatment of the Palestinians."[415] Per the *New Yorker*, Project Butterfly demonstrated Psy-Group's closeness to the Israeli government: one of the operators involved in the project was Ram Ben-Barak, who not only was one of Psy-Group's "biggest hired guns" but, after serving as a deputy director for Israeli intelligence agency Mossad through 2014, was promoted to director general of Israel's Ministry of Strategic Affairs.[416] Another adviser for Psy-Group during Project Butterfly was Yaakov Amidror, "a former national-security adviser to Prime Minister Benjamin Netanyahu."[417] And the outside counsel Psy-Group worked with during the project had "advised five Israeli Prime Ministers, including Netanyahu," the *New Yorker* reports.[418]

There were also other, less visible connections between Psy-Group and the Trump campaign during the 2016 election cycle. For example, one of Psy-Group's twenty-nine employees was Eitan Charnoff, who simultaneously worked for Zamel during the presidential election and directed iVote Israel, a "right-leaning" entity focused on helping Americans in Israel vote in presidential elections; Charnoff's operation has been accused of "intentionally suppressing votes" and maintaining "ties to the Republican Party" despite its formal nonpartisan status.[419] According to the *Jerusalem Post*, Psy-Group employee Charnoff's outfit "was perceived," at its 2012 founding, "as having a true aim of unseating Barack Obama in the 2012 presidential election."[420] Even Charnoff admits that many observers perceive the "purpose of the organization" to be "to get Republicans [in Israel] registered [to vote]" in U.S. presidential elections.[421]

With the revelation of the existence of UAE's Project Raven, the question of whether the Emiratis have used the technology at their disposal to track American targets has been answered in the affirmative.[422] According to Reuters, Project Raven is a massive UAE cyberintelligence operation that began running in 2009 with the Israeli cyber tool Karma, limited American oversight, and virtually no ethical or legal strictures in place; it did not accrue FBI Counterintelligence Division attention until 2016, during the presidential election.[423] Three former Project Raven operatives report that, after years without FBI oversight, the FBI suddenly wanted to know, as the presidential campaign progressed, "Had they been asked to spy on Americans?"[424] This sudden FBI interest in the Emiratis' hacking activities in the United States, after seven years of only modest CIA oversight, seems plausibly related to activities happening stateside at the time—including the possibly Emirati-sponsored approach to the Trump campaign by an Israeli cyberespionage company.[425] Indeed, the answer to the FBI's query about the UAE targeting American citizens inside the United States in 2016, the Reuters investigative report into Project Raven confirms, was yes.[426]

What is less clear is whether Trump himself was aware of Joel Zamel's and George Nader's actions during the 2016 presidential campaign. According to *Haaretz*, shortly after dropping out of the presidential race in early March 2016, Republican Ben Carson "personally presented Trump with [Israeli business intelligence firm] Inspiration's plan for [general election] voter manipulation in swing states."[427] *Haaretz* further reports that Inspiration subsequently received "enormous amounts" of information from a pro-Trump super PAC, "which it then used to compose strategies and slogans that would elevate Trump and 'float all kinds of things' about Hillary Clinton."[428]

It is widely suspected that Israeli business intelligence firms do at times work with one another. Ongoing legal litigation initiated by Canadian hedge fund West Face Capital has accused, for instance, Zamel's Psy-Group of "conspiring" with one of its apparent competitors in the Israeli business intelligence market, Black Cube, "to provide reporters, news agencies (including the *National Post*, Bloomberg News and the Associated Press) . . . with edited, distorted or otherwise falsified recordings and/or transcripts of meetings between operatives of Black Cube and its targets, including current and former employees. According to the complaint, Psy-Group . . . worked in tandem with Black Cube, publishing defamatory articles and social media posts about West Face and using sophisticated masking techniques to hide their tracks."[429] Inspiration, the company Carson pitched directly to Trump, has been accused of working "in cooperation with another Israeli company in order to understand which voters are more likely or less likely to vote on election day"—a description that fits the public-facing, Cambridge Analytica–run segment of the work the Trump campaign contracted for, possibly along with complementary "dark" intelligence work by Psy-Group, during the presidential election.[430] An additional possibility raised by some Psy-Group employees in speaking with the *Daily Beast* is that Zamel "developed his own separate operation," apart from but still connected to Psy-Group, during the 2016 presidential campaign—but because of Zamel's predilection for secrecy, it was impossible for them to know for sure.[431]

ANNOTATIONS

MBS launches a war against Yemen to dislodge Houthi rebels, who have driven the Yemeni government into exile, from Sana'a, the Yemeni capital.

The Shiite Houthi movement began in the early 1990s as a "theological movement" that "preached tolerance and peace," according to Ahmed Addaghashi, a Houthi expert and professor at Sana'a University.[432] Officially known as Ansar Allah (Partisans of God), the Houthis, per Addaghashi, are a discrete religious group with a "stronghold in the northern province of Saada" but "originally held a considerably broad-minded educational and cultural vision . . . [that] fell into internal strife between two lines; the first called for more openness, while the second urged sticking to the traditional legacy of the Shia sect."[433] The movement's first leader, Hussein Bader Addian al-Houthi, favored the former approach, but the Houthis nevertheless took up arms—in self-defense, they insisted—when their first major conflict with the Yemeni government began in 2004.[434] The issue at the time was whether the Houthis would be permitted to protest in mosques; when al-Houthi refused to order his followers to stop the practice, the government sought his arrest, leading quickly to outbreaks of violence.[435] It was therefore little surprise when, in 2011, the Houthis were among the many anti-government factions that rebelled against then-president Ali Abdullah Saleh.[436] Equally unsurprising was the movement's resistance to the subdivision plan intended to end the 2011 conflict. The plan, which would have reestablished Yemen as a six-region federal state, would have put the Houthi stronghold of Saada into the region most directly controlled by Saleh (the Sana'a region).[437] While the Houthis did not demand or even propose complete independence from the government in Sana'a, they did seek "regional autonomy" under the new federal system, according to Al Jazeera.[438]

By August 2014, the Houthi movement had gained so much popularity in Yemen that it was in a position to credibly demand that the existing Yemeni government in Sana'a disband.[439] Al Jazeera reports that, "Among other demands, Houthi leader Abdulmalek al-Houthi requested that fuel subsidies, which had been cut significantly in late July [2014], be reinstated. If the government failed to meet an ultimatum, he said, 'other steps' would be taken. The Houthis also demanded a more representative form of government that would reflect the seats allocated to political groups and independent activists during Yemen's 10-month National Dialogue Conference, which mapped out the political future of Yemen after its 2011 uprising."[440] Thereafter, the rebels "raided key government institutions in the capital" and "pushed into other provinces, taking over the strategic port city of Hodeida on the Red Sea."[441] This, despite Yemeni president Abd-Rabbu Mansour Hadi having previously "called for a dialogue with the Houthis, inviting the group to join a 'unity government' . . . [and] sign[ing] a peace deal brokered by the UN envoy to Yemen, Jamal Benomar."[442] According to Al Jazeera, the rebels did not ultimately comply with the deal.[443]

In October 2015, Hadi named Yemen's envoy to the United States, Khaled Bahah, as the nation's new prime minister, a pick that seemed to have bipartisan (both government and Houthi) support. This concurrence lasted only until January 2016, however, when the Houthis objected to a first draft of the country's new constitution, which proposed dividing the country into six regions. The Houthis demanded Hadi abandon his plan for subdivision, and when he refused, they stormed his palace, pressured him to appoint their allies to key positions in government, placed him and two of his ministers under house arrest, and ultimately, in February 2016, forced him to resign. A temporary five-person council was installed in his place. Hadi subsequently fled to Aden and declared himself the rightful Yemeni president. Within a few weeks, the Saudis had given shelter to Hadi in Riyadh and a Saudi-led military coalition had begun bombing Yemen.

It is little surprise that Barrack has the influence with Trump to convince the GOP candidate to begin the process of replacing his campaign manager, Corey Lewandowski. As longtime Trump friend, adviser, and ally Roger Stone explains, "Thomas Barrack is the only person I know who the president speaks to as a peer. Barrack is to Trump as [Florida banker] Bebe Rebozo was to Nixon, which is the best friend."

Barrack and Trump are not just friends—they are also business associates. "I've been a financial partner of his on many things that he's done, [and] he's been a partner of mine on many things I've done," Barrack tells Bloomberg TV on June 1, 2016.[445] In his interview with Bloomberg, Barrack repeatedly assures his interviewer, "I'm not political." He adds that "I spend half my time in the Middle East."[446]

When Trump is elected, Barrack refuses all proffered roles in the Trump administration—including ambassador to Mexico and secretary of the treasury—angling instead for "special envoy for Middle East economic development," a role that would put him at the center of hundreds of billions of dollars in Middle East commerce.[447] He is unable to secure the posting he wants, however.[448] Later events suggest that Barrack's long-standing ties to Qatar may have put him at odds with both Kushner's private ambitions as a businessman and his public ambitions as an amateur diplomat. By the time of Trump's May 2017 visit to Riyadh, Kushner has become close to MBS—and MBS is just weeks away from initiating an air, land, and sea blockade on Qatar. Moreover, in November 2017 MBS arrests and detains for three months Barrack's former Saudi investing partner, Prince Alwaleed bin Talal. According to *The Intercept*, bin Talal may have been on a list of MBS's enemies that MBS claims was given to him by Kushner in October 2017 (see chapter 8).[449]

Given bin Talal's long-standing business relationship with Barrack, one of Trump's closest friends, a call bin Talal makes just days prior to his arrest and detention in November 2017—after the first wave of MBS-ordered arrests and detentions in October 2017—will in 2018 draw significant media attention. Shortly before MBS's agents place him under arrest, bin Talal calls *Washington Post* journalist Jamal Khashoggi, a U.S. resident, to "praise MBS" and his "vision" and to invite Khashoggi "to come back to the Kingdom and be part of [that vision]."[450] Khashoggi "resist[s] [the] pressure from Riyadh" and does not return to Saudi Arabia.[451]

After Trump names Barrack the chairman of his inaugural committee instead of special Middle East envoy, Bloomberg quotes two sources who say they heard Barrack unhappily compare his transition role to that of a "wedding planner."[452]

After announcing his candidacy for president of the United States on May 4, 2015, neurosurgeon Ben Carson, a Republican, begins forming a foreign policy team with a surprising number of experts on the nation of Israel—many of whom will move directly to the campaign of Donald Trump in the weeks before Carson officially suspends his flailing campaign in early March 2016.

Like several of his campaign aides, Ben Carson will end up on Trump's transition team in November 2016.[453] Trump thereafter successfully nominates him to be secretary of housing and urban development.

Another member of Carson's team with substantial Israeli security contacts—though not an adviser to Carson exclusively, as he is also advising Donald Trump at the time—is Michael Flynn.

Flynn—whose foreign policy views, according to the *New York Times*, were in 2015 undergirded by a devout belief that America "needed to cultivate Russia as an ally in the fight [against terrorism]"—spent that year and the next receiving money from entities connected to three foreign countries: Israel (via a cyberweapons firm specializing in cell phone hacking), Turkey (via work for GreenZone Systems Inc., a firm run by an Iranian American businessman simultaneously working as an agent of the Turkish government), and Russia (via contracts with or appearances for Kaspersky Lab—"a Russian research firm that works to uncover Western government spyware, and whose founder has long been suspected of having ties to Russian intelligence services"—Volga Dnepr Airlines, and RT, the "Kremlin-financed news network").[454] For his efforts, Flynn earns in 2016, while acting as Trump's top national security advisor, between $1.37 million and $1.47 million.[455] Another company for which Flynn does consulting work, Brainwave Science, had previously seen one of its board members—and its principal investor—get "convicted [in the 1990s] of trying to sell stolen biotech material to the Russian KGB espionage agency."[456] The company's chief scientist warned Flynn against working with Brainwave, in part due to the company being "the target of a federal investigation . . . [about which he] declined to provide further details" to the *New York Times*, but Flynn ignored him.[457] "I'm a capitalist at heart," Flynn tells the *Times* in October 2016.[458]

Prior to joining the Carson campaign as an adviser, Flynn had been approached by an Israeli business intelligence company, Psy-Group, whose owner, Joel Zamel, sought to recruit him.

The *Daily Beast*, writing of Zamel's other business intelligence company, Wikistrat, notes that "the vast majority of Wikistrat's clients [are] foreign governments . . . [and] the company work [is] not just limited to analysis. It also engage[s] in intelligence collection."[459] Zamel, who considers himself "the Mark Zuckerberg of the national-security world," per the *Daily Beast*, "exploits 'in country . . . informants' as sources."[460] Indeed, the digital media outlet confirms that prior to its closure 74 percent of Wikistrat's revenue came from partnerships with governments, not private individuals, and that while Zamel unsuccessfully sought to recruit Flynn to his operations, he did successfully recruit another former DIA director, David Shedd.[461] James Kadtke, a former senior analyst for Wikistrat, says that while the company was still extant that there was "more to this company than meets the eye. '[When I interviewed] it was clear to me that both of these guys [the two Wikistrat executives with whom he interviewed] had intelligence backgrounds, [and were] intelligence professionals, not academics or analysts. They were using their experts for tacit information going on in various parts of the world. I got the impression they were doing things outside of Wikistrat. It seemed mysterious.'"[462] As the *Daily Beast* summarizes, "Wikistrat appeared [to Kadtke] to be more about intelligence collection than anything else."[463] When asked about covert intelligence collection, another Wikistrat employee confirms that, indeed, Zamel "could have done this."[464] A third Wikistrat employee tells the *Daily Beast*, "I felt like I had no real visibility into what the company was really doing. [Zamel] was very secretive, everything was highly compartmentalized. . . . It was clear that he kept the entire company in the dark. Even [company executives] didn't have the whole picture. I suspected he was involved in other stuff simply because a man without secrets doesn't need to be secretive. If he had nothing to hide, he would've been much more open. I thought he was involved in other operations [outside the company]."[465]

The chances that Zamel was in fact an Israeli government agent while ostensibly working in the Israeli private sector in the intelligence business are increased by the fact that, as one of his employees confirms to the *Daily Beast*, Zamel would not allow himself to be photographed, and would never allow even Wikistrat employees to go anywhere near his phone or laptop.[466] Evidence of Zamel having unusual government connections includes the fact that, as the *Daily Beast* recounts, "one of his connections was the former head of the Israeli intelligence directorate, Amos Yadlin"; his COO was a "former counterterrorism officer for Israeli intelligence"; and his director of analytic community and chief security officer, Shay Hershkovitz, was previously a "major in an elite Israeli intelligence-analysis unit."[467] Whether or not Zamel was himself an Israeli agent, the question remains whether he would have been willing to work on behalf of a U.S. presidential campaign without informing any of his contacts in Israeli intelligence—men and women who might well have considered information-sharing under such circumstances obligatory rather than optional.

At some point during his ten-month candidacy for president, Carson and his team receive a "plan for voter manipulation in [general election] swing states" from an Israeli business intelligence company, Inspiration, which is "run by former Israeli Defense Force officers." After Carson exits the presidential race in March 2016, he "personally present[s] Trump with Inspiration's plan."

Inspiration is run by Col. Ronen Cohen, "the head of the terror division in the Research Division of [Israeli] Military Intelligence [and] the deputy head of the Research Division . . . [who also served as an] intelligence officer of the [Israeli] Central Command."[468] Cohen had retired from serving with Israel's military intelligence units approximately thirty-six months before Trump formally announced his presidential run, and less than twelve months before Trump made the decision to run shortly after Election Day in 2012.[469]

On November 12, 2015, at a community college theater in Fort Dodge, Iowa, Trump tells the assembled crowd, "I know more about ISIS than the [active-duty U.S.] generals do. Believe me." Trump also tells the crowd that he has a plan for defeating ISIS—but that it's a secret.

At the time Trump says this, his top foreign policy and national security adviser, Flynn, has just returned from Saudi Arabia, where he has pitched (on behalf of ACS) a Middle East Marshall Plan that addresses the ISIS threat directly and in a way the Saudis approve of—one emphasizing hostility toward Iran and friendliness toward Russia rather than the reverse, which is, in the Saudi view, what the Obama administration has thus far been offering. Whether Flynn's views on the subject are on Trump's mind in Fort Dodge are unclear; what is clear, especially in coverage of the event by the *Washington Post*, is that something un-explained is perturbing Trump on November 12. *BuzzFeed News* reports that it was around this time that Dmitry Klokov was promising Trump—unrealistically, it turns out—a face-to-face meeting with Vladimir Putin to expedite his effort to build a Trump Tower Moscow with Russian oligarch Andrey Rozov; Trump had just signed a letter of intent to build the tower with Rozov (a letter of intent that even his organization's lead attorney, Alan Garten, appeared not to know about) two weeks before the event in Iowa.[470]

According to coverage of the Fort Dodge rally in the *Post*, Trump arrived to the November 12 event forty minutes late with his voice "hoarse, his hair mussed, his tone defensive. He promised to take questions from the audience but instead launched into a 95-minute-long rant that at times sounded like the monologue of a man grappling with why he is running for president . . . Even for a candidate full of surprises, the speech was sur-prising. . . . He uttered the word 'crap' at least three times, and promised to 'bomb the shit' out of oil fields benefiting terrorists. He signed a book for a guy in the audience and then tossed it back at him with a flip: 'Here you go, baby. I love you.'"[471]

In January 2019 the *New York Times* will report, after Trump has launched a public assault against his director of national intelligence, Dan Coats, his CIA director, Gina Haspel, and other top intelligence agents, "While it is unusual for a president to pick a fight with his intelligence chiefs, this is not the first time for Mr. Trump. After the 2016 election and before he took office in 2017, Mr. Trump was publicly skeptical of intelligence conclusions that Russia interfered in the 2016 presidential election, and he mocked intelligence agencies for their role in the lead-up to the Iraq war. Mr. Trump also contradicted last year's global threat assessment from senior intelligence officials, whom he had appointed to his administration. While his top intelligence officials warned [in 2018] about Russia's continuing efforts to conduct influence operations, Mr. Trump continued to dismiss any notion that Russia had interfered in American elections."[472]

Trump's willingness to listen to input from foreign agents over U.S. intelligence will be confirmed in February 2019, when it is revealed that in mid-2017 Trump told his intelligence briefers that on the question of whether North Korea's chairman, Kim Jong-Un, had just tested a new intercontinental ballistic missile that could reach the United States, "I believe Putin."

Early 2019 will see Trump publicly disregard the assessments of his intelligence chiefs as to nearly every major geopolitical hotspot, including the influence of Iran in the Middle East, the war in Afghanistan, the nuclear threat posed by North Korea, and the current battle-readiness of ISIS forces. When director of national intelligence Dan Coats, CIA director Gina Haspel, and other top intelligence officials disagree with Trump's opinions of these topics in testimony before Congress, Trump will announce on Twitter that his own government's foremost intelligence experts are "passive and naive" on Iran—an opinion that happens to be shared by his allies in Saudi Arabia and the UAE—and likewise "wrong" on the other topics they spoke of. "They need to go back to school," he will say.[473] At no point during or after his diatribe does Trump reveal which intelligence sources he trusts, or offer any hint of where he has been getting his intelligence since he began his presidential run in mid-2015.

Moreover, [Flynn] fails to properly disclose a second, October 2015 trip to Saudi Arabia that is part of the same joint venture. In hiding the details of this second trip from federal authorities, he makes up the name of the hotel he allegedly stayed at, and obscures his business interests in Saudi Arabia under

the false claim that he was in the kingdom "for six days to speak at a conference." He also fails to disclose the identity of the "friend" who traveled with him to Saudi Arabia and the company that paid for his trip.

According to the *Washington Post*, Flynn's "friend" appears to have been ACU Strategic Partners' senior scientist, Thomas Cochran, which would explain why Flynn wouldn't have wanted to disclose the name to the federal government—it would have raised questions about Flynn's ties to ACU and his need for (as the *Post* terms Cochran) an "expert on nuclear nonproliferation issues" during his travels in Egypt and Israel.[474] The *Post* reports in November 2017 that ACU paid for Flynn's Israel and Egypt trips and wrote him a $25,000 check for "the loss of income and business opportunities" that ACU claimed—in a letter to the House Oversight Committee—the trips represented.[475] Despite Flynn's claim of being a proud capitalist, he for some reason never cashes the check that ACU gives him.[476]

Roston adds, chillingly, that "a former CIA official who has worked in the UAE initially told *BuzzFeed News* that there was no way that Americans would be allowed to participate in such a program. But after checking, he called back: 'There were guys that were basically doing what you said.' He was astonished, he said, by what he learned. . . . The mercenaries, he said, were 'almost like a murder squad.'"

In an eerie echo of the October 2018 assassination of *Washington Post* journalist Jamal Khashoggi, killed because of his opposition to MBS (see chapter 9), Spear Operations Group mercenary Isaac Gilmore concedes that on occasion "there is the possibility that the target [the UAE asked his team to kill]" was not a valid target but just someone "MBZ doesn't like."[477]

Between 2009 and 2018, the United States government approves at least $27 billion in arms sales and defense services to the United Arab

Emirates, according to a 2018 *BuzzFeed News* article.[478] But "the UAE is hardly alone in using defense contractors," the digital media outlet writes. "In fact, it is the US that helped pioneer the worldwide move toward privatizing the military. The Pentagon pays companies to carry out many traditional functions, from feeding soldiers to maintaining weapons to guarding convoys. The US draws the line at combat; it does not hire mercenaries to carry out attacks or engage directly in warfare."[479] Even so, Pentagon protocols implicitly facilitate freelancing by U.S. veterans; according to a high-level Navy SEAL officer who speaks to *BuzzFeed News,* "If the soldiers [who wish to work as for-profit mercenaries abroad] are not on active duty . . . they are not obligated to report what they're doing."[480] Because, as of 2018, the pay scale for in-demand, well-trained military veterans on security details begins at $500 a day, whereas Abraham Golan is in 2015 offering $830 a day—or $25,000 per month—to members of his murder squads, it may be easier for some veterans to put aside their qualms and sign on to legally dubious work details abroad.[481] Nevertheless, Golan business associate and former Navy SEAL Isaac Gilmore tells *BuzzFeed News* that "a lot" of the elite American ex-soldiers Golan approaches about working in Yemen turn him down.[482]

During the December 2015 operation in Yemen that is the subject of the *BuzzFeed News* investigative report on Golan and his crew, Gilmore admits to a reporter that he didn't know which of his twenty-three UAE-identified Yemeni targets were politicians, which were religious figures, and which were alleged terrorists.[483] The deck of playing cards from which Gilmore is working, supplied to him and his peers on Golan's squad by an Emirati military officer, gives no information about why the targeted individual is designated for assassination.[484]

With respect to U.S. policy on the use of manned wetwork operations overseas, it is clear from recent American political history that the Saudis and Emiratis would have every reason to support a Republican presidential candidate over a Democratic one. Whereas, as *BuzzFeed News* notes in 2018, "under President George W. Bush . . . the CIA developed covert assassination capabilities" that went beyond drone strikes, "President Barack

Obama halted the agency's secret assassination program" while ramping up the use of drones.[485] As the Saudis and Emiratis lack the drone capabilities of the United States, the more acceptable targeted assassinations conducted by mercenaries are to a given U.S. presidential administration, the easier it is, presumably, for the Saudis and Emiratis to recruit former U.S. special forces personnel either experienced in such actions or willing to engage in them despite a lack of experience.[486] *BuzzFeed News* notes that "President Donald Trump has further loosened the rules for drone strikes" compared to those established under President Obama, underscoring that Trump's attitude toward the killing of foreign nationals in targeted strikes is more permissive than his predecessor's.[487]

According to Elisabeth Kendall, an expert on Yemen who works at Oxford, those individuals on Abraham Golan's hit list who are members of the Al-Islah political party in Yemen work through the political process, not—like al-Qaeda or other terrorist groups in the region—through violence.[488] This commitment to the political process led Al-Islah to receive more than 20 percent of the vote in Yemen in the most recent (2018) elections.[489] Asked about the distinction between killing unarmed Al-Islah politicians and armed terrorists, Golan tells *BuzzFeed News* that to him, the divide between the two groups is "a purely intellectual dichotomy."[490]

Al-Islah is a Sunni Islamist party whose chief political rival in Yemen is the Houthis. Al-Islah accuses the Houthis of being an Iranian proxy, while the Houthis contend that during the 2011 Yemeni uprising that led to the overthrow of then-president Ali Abdullah Saleh, Al-Islah waged aggressive military campaigns against the northern Saada province that had long served as the Houthis' stronghold in Yemen.[491] Even as now exiled Yemeni president Abd-Rabbu Mansour Hadi accuses Iran of arming the Houthis, the Houthis accuse Al-Islah of inciting nonsectarian Yemenis to fight them, even encouraging government military regiments to engage them in armed conflict.[492] The Houthis deny receiving any assistance from Iran, and indeed for a time in 2012 and 2013 it appeared that Hadi would successfully keep government forces from undue entanglements in local struggles between the Houths and Al-Islah.[493] This effort broke down, however, during a 2013 National Dialogue Conference intended to resolve the political, sectarian, and military chasms left by the 2011 uprising.[494] The Houthis, who held 35 of 565 seats at the conference—just over 6 percent—rejected efforts to gerrymander their Saada stronghold into the Sana'a (capital) region.[495]

CHAPTER 4

THE EMIRATI AMBASSADOR, THE MAYFLOWER HOTEL, AND PROJECT ROME

January 2016 to July 2016

As voting begins in the 2016 GOP primaries, a flurry of secret meetings occurs that will culminate in the Red Sea conspirators getting to the very doorstep of Trump Tower. Thomas Barrack secretly communicates with the Emirati ambassador; the Emirati ambassador secretly communicates with Jared Kushner; Michael Flynn works with the Saudis, Egyptians, and Israelis; and George Nader—already in contact with MBS, MBZ, and the Kremlin—cooperates with Israeli businessman Joel Zamel in a plan to assist the Trump campaign using foreign money, receiving the assistance of a top aide from Benjamin Netanyahu's office in doing so. Throughout, those working in Trump's national security advisory committee—a group conceived of by Putin "friend" Dimitri Simes—shape Trump's first major foreign policy speech, scheduled for the Mayflower Hotel on April 27, 2016, and do their best to make high-level Kremlin connections.

In the year Donald Trump wins the U.S. presidency, MBZ meets with Putin on multiple occasions, each time "urg[ing] the Russian leader to work more closely with the Emirates and Saudi Arabia—an effort to isolate Iran."[1] In the final weeks of the year, MBZ will meet secretly with Trump's top three aides at Trump Tower in New York City to plan an overseas meeting with envoys from Putin and Trump; as the *Washington Post* notes in April 2017, MBZ "wanted to be helpful to both leaders [Trump and Putin], who had talked about working more closely together, a policy objective long advocated by the crown prince. The UAE, which sees Iran as one of its main enemies, also shared the Trump team's interest in finding ways to drive a wedge between Moscow and Tehran."[2] MBZ's chief goal with respect to Donald Trump in 2016 is therefore to "establish[ ] an unofficial backchannel between Trump and Putin"—an ambition he ultimately achieves through a year's worth of behind-the-scenes contacts, via several intermediaries, with the Trump campaign and the Trump transition team.[3]

By the first week of March 2016, the Trump campaign has hired Carter Page and George Papadopoulos as the first two members of what will become, by the end of the month, Trump's national security advisory committee. The committee is run by Jeff Sessions, with the assistance of J. D. Gordon in its day-to-day operations. In the second week of March, a Kremlin agent, Joseph Mifsud, makes contact with George Papadopoulos in Rome, the Russian government's third known contact of the campaign season with a Trump national security adviser—the first two having been Michael Flynn's meetings with Sergey Kislyak and Putin himself in D.C. and Moscow, respectively, in December 2015.[4] During the same week the Kremlin is making contact with Papadopoulos through Mifsud, Russian military intelligence, the GRU, sends ninety "spearphishing" emails to accounts at HillaryClinton.com.[5] The day after Papadopoulos and Mifsud meet, the GRU begins "targeting Google email accounts used by Clinton Campaign employees" for the first time, as well as "a smaller number of dnc.org email accounts."[6] These intrusions will result in the theft of tens of thousands of Democratic emails.[7]

As Trump is recruiting the final members of his national security advisory committee in the latter half of March, WikiLeaks releases "a searchable archive of approximately 30,000 Clinton emails that had been obtained through FOIA [Freedom of Information Act] litigation," the IRA begins running its first anti-Clinton ads on social media, and the GRU begins hacking the email accounts of Clinton campaign employees and volunteers.[8] An internal WikiLeaks email reveals that the purpose of its new Clinton archive is to reveal Clinton's "plotting" at the State Department, "annoy" the Democratic presidential candidate and her campaign, and turn WikiLeaks into "a resource/player" in the presidential election, as the organization believes publishing Clinton's emails will "encourage people to send us even more important leaks."[9]

In April, as CNI board members Dimitri Simes and Richard Burt, along with two members of Trump's new Simes-proposed advisory committee, Papadopoulos and Page, are preparing the GOP candidate's first major foreign policy address—an address that proposes a "deal" with Russia to resolve any ongoing disputes with the United States—both the IRA and GRU move to the next phase of their operations: the IRA begins publishing pro-Trump ads on social media, and the GRU begins a systematic hack of the Democratic National Committee.[10] During this same time frame, the GRU successfully gains access to the Democratic Congressional Campaign Committee (DCCC) network; it will ultimately obtain unrestricted access to twenty-nine DCCC computers.[11] The GRU will also, over time, start targeting, as recounted by the Mueller Report, "individuals and entities involved in the administration of the [U.S.] elections. Victims include[ ] U.S. state and local entities, such as state boards of elections, secretaries of state, and county governments, as well as individuals who worked for those entities . . . [and] private technology firms responsible for manufacturing and administrating election-related software and hardware, such as voter registration software and electronic polling stations."[12]

The special counsel's office declines to "investigate further" the GRU's attacks on America's electoral infrastructure, citing the existence of an ongoing probe by the Department of Homeland Security.[13] However, one week after the release of the Mueller Report in April 2019, it will be revealed that secretary of homeland security Kirstjen Nielsen has been told not to even mention Russian election interference in front of President Trump because the topic angers him—a bizarre prohibition that makes development of a coherent federal strategy to combat the recurrence of such election interference all but impossible.[14] In May 2019, the *Washington Post* reports that, contrary to years of federal government denials, the GRU was in fact able to access "voter information files" in at least two U.S. counties in 2016, both in Florida; when one of the two counties is identified by *Politico* as Washington County, neither county officials nor the FBI is willing to release additional information about the hacks to the public.[15] Whether the GRU successfully gained access to sensitive voter information in other "battleground" states—information that could, if altered, affect U.S. voters' ability to cast a ballot for president—remains unknown.

In the seventy-two hours in April 2016 before the Trump campaign announces Trump's upcoming major foreign policy address—an address substantially written and edited by four men with Kremlin connections—the GRU begins "planning the release[ ]" of "documents stolen from the Clinton Campaign and its supporters," going so far as to anonymously register one of the websites it will ultimately use to leak these stolen materials, DCLeaks.com.[16] The Mueller Report will eventually conclude that DCLeaks.com is "operated by the same or a closely related group of people" at the GRU as another entity the Kremlin uses to release stolen documents to the American public, the "Guccifer 2.0 persona."[17] Roger Stone, the Trump adviser and friend who is also a longtime business partner of Paul Manafort, will ultimately make direct contact with Guccifer 2.0.[18]

The first meeting of Trump's national security advisory committee occurs on March 31 at the Trump International Hotel in D.C. The youngest member of the all-male group is energy consultant George Papadopoulos, who was among the first five selected for the committee and is the only one of its twelve members personally vouched for by Trump, who tells the media that Papadopoulos is "an excellent guy."[19] Papadopoulos is just two weeks removed from making his first contact with Kremlin agents, a fact he relays via email to key national security advisers within the Trump campaign a week before the committee's March 31 meeting.[20]

During the meeting Papadopoulos will, as he later recounts to CNN, "look[ ] at candidate Trump directly in his eyes" and say, of the possibility of a secret pre-election summit between Trump and Putin, "I can do this for you, if it's in your interest, and if it's in the campaign's interest."[21]

The reaction to his offer to act as a Trump-Russia "intermediary," per Papadopoulos, is positive: "The collective energy in the room seemed to be interested," he will tell CNN's Jake Tapper in 2018.[22] According to Papadopoulos, Trump himself "gave him a sort of a nod ... he was thinking," and Jeff Sessions, the chairman of the national security advisory committee, was "actually enthusiastic about a meeting between the candidate and President Putin" and said "this is a good idea."[23] Sessions will in 2017 tell Congress, under oath, that he had "pushed back" against Papadopoulos's proposal, while his top aide, J. D. Gordon, will tell media that Sessions "strongly opposed Papadopoulos' proposal and said no one [on the Committee] should speak of it again."[24] Meanwhile, three other meeting attendees will tell the special counsel that Papadopoulos's account is in fact the correct one.[25]

In the weeks leading up to Trump's April 27 speech at the Mayflower Hotel, Thomas Barrack is in conversation with MBZ through an intermediary.[26] According to the *New York Times*, Barrack has "depended on [Persian Gulf princes] for decades as investors and buyers" in his real estate ventures.[27] *Fast Company* adds that Barrack's "real estate business has profited handsomely from Emirate deals."[28] It is for both business and personal reasons, therefore, that in spring 2016 Barrack becomes concerned about the reception Trump is receiving among powerful figures in the Middle East. Just four months or so on from the development of the Red Sea Conspiracy, MBZ expresses to Barrack through the Emirati ambassador to the United States, Yousef al-Otaiba, that "confusion about your friend Donald Trump is very high," adding that Trump "has many people extremely worried" because of his call for a travel ban impacting certain Arab nations.[29] Despite MBZ's trepidation, the Emirati prince knows, as presumably does his emissary al-Otaiba, that a select group of Sunni Arab leaders has lately chosen Donald Trump to be their future American partner in realigning the balance of power in the Middle East.

Barrack, seeking to reassure al-Otaiba—a man he considers a "longtime friend"—as well as MBZ, emails the former on April 26, the day before Trump's Mayflower speech, to assure him that, like Barrack himself, "[Trump] also has joint ventures in the UAE!"[30] Barrack thus appears to assure members of the Emirati government that Trump will not develop a foreign policy disadvantageous to them because it would hurt his business interests in the Emirates. It is likely, in any case, that MBZ and al-Otaiba are overstating their concerns about Trump, as al-Otaiba already has connections to individuals inside Trumpworld: in 2010, he was the man who introduced Erik Prince to MBZ, at a time when Prince was unsuccessfully—due to DOJ restrictions imposed upon him after "a series of . . . arms trafficking violations"—trying to sell the UAE a modified crop duster capable of carrying top-of-the-line surveillance equipment and laser-guided missiles.[31] According to *The Intercept,* Prince soon thereafter joined MBZ's "inner sanctum" of trusted "foreign policy and military advisers."[32]

As Barrack is wooing the Emiratis on Trump's behalf in the early spring of 2016, he is also engaged in an identical effort with respect to the Emiratis' allies in Saudi Arabia. As the *New York Times* will report, not only was Barrack "a top fund-raiser and trusted gatekeeper" for Trump during the campaign but he "opened communications with the Emiratis and the Saudis."[33] Barrack's effort to ingratiate Trump with both MBS and MBZ—at least a month and a half before Trump has even clinched the GOP nomination—eventually poses new problems for Barrack, who has had a long relationship with Hamad bin Jassim bin Jaber Al Thani (known as "HBJ"), the man who led Saudi and Emirati rival Qatar between 2007 and 2013 and who also managed the Qatar Investment Authority during that period.[34] While Barrack has had relationships with Saudi princes dating back to the 1970s, none have been with anyone close to MBS, and by spring 2016 Barrack's closeness to several prominent Qataris has become a significant mark against him in Riyadh.[35] His April 2016 email exchange with al-Otaiba is another opportunity, then, to connect Trump with MBZ, and thereby with MBS, the latter of whom is about to announce Vision 2030, a major initiative concerning the future economic and political development of Saudi Arabia.

On April 25, 2016, just two days before Donald Trump's Mayflower speech, MBS's Vision 2030 is formally announced. It is an initiative MBS personally has been developing for many months.[36] If successful, the plan will fundamentally transform Saudi Arabia, most notably by transitioning its economy away from oil and toward other energy sources—including nuclear energy.[37] Bin Salman's concern for the future of Saudi oil revenues is well founded; while Saudi Arabia ia a low-cost oil producer with many years of oil reserves, the possibility that demand for oil will drop in the coming decades means that transitioning the Saudi economy to new forms of energy and energy production is mission-critical for the future of the kingdom.[38]

The next day, April 26, the Trump campaign receives, according to the Mueller Report, "indications from the Russian government that it could assist the Campaign through the anonymous release of information damaging to Democratic presidential candidate Hillary Clinton."[39] Papadopoulos is the Trump campaign representative who gathers this intelligence from Kremlin agent and Valdai Discussion Club member Joseph Mifsud.[40] Besides Mifsud's connections to an organization whose highest-profile patron is Vladimir Putin, among the Maltese professor's "contacts" in April 2016, per the Mueller Report, is a "one-time employee of the [Internet Research Agency]" and a digital account "linked to an employee of the Russian Ministry of Defense"—an account that "had overlapping contacts with a group of Russian military-controlled Facebook accounts." The Russian military accounts linked to Mifsud's defense ministry contact "included accounts used to promote the DCLeaks releases in the course of the GRU's hack-and-release operations."[41]

Papadopoulos's first contact with Mifsud, the substance of which he in short order communicates to senior officials on the Trump campaign, is met with approval, with Trump campaign national co-chair Sam Clovis telling Papadopoulos that his mid-March 2016 correspondence with a Kremlin agent on the subject of a Trump-Putin summit has been "most informative" and is "great work."[42] That Papadopoulos's March 31 update to Trump's national security advisory committee finds Trump "interested . . . and receptive to the idea of a meeting with Putin" is confirmed by J. D. Gordon, the committee's director of day-to-day operations, even as he disagrees with Papadopoulos about Sessions's reaction to the proposal.[43]

By the time of Papadopoulos's late March report to Trump, the GOP candidate has long since learned from his attorney Michael Cohen that a face-to-face meeting with Vladimir Putin is the critical missing piece in his plan to build a Trump-branded tower in Moscow that could net him more than $1 billion—approximately a quarter of his reported total net worth at the time.[44] Papadopoulos, speaking in 2017 to the special counsel's office after his arrest for making false statements to federal law enforcement, insists to the special counsel that his outreach to the Kremlin was also pleasing to Sessions—Gordon's demurral notwithstanding—and that Sessions was "supportive of his efforts to arrange a [Trump-Putin] meeting."[45]

Papadopoulos's conversations with Kremlin agents—including not just Mifsud but Ministry of Foreign Affairs–linked think tank director Ivan Timofeev and a woman, "Olga Polonskaya," pretending to be Putin's niece—appear to quickly go beyond the question of a Trump-Putin summit, however, with "Polonskaya's" text messages to Papadopoulos referencing "initiatives between our two countries" and Papadopoulos's own plans to "engage with the Russian Federation" over a longer period of time.[46] According to the special counsel's office, among the topics Mifsud and Papadopoulos discuss during their "extensive communications over a period of months" are "cybersecurity," "hacking," and "foreign policy issues"—the last of these indicating that Papadopoulos was discussing foreign policy with a known Kremlin agent even as he was helping to edit Trump's first foreign policy address in April 2016.[47] Throughout his interactions with Mifsud, the Mueller Report observes, "Papadopoulos understood Mifsud to have substantial connections to high-level Russian government officials."[48]

Mifsud's April 26 revelation that the Kremlin possessed "dirt" on Clinton in the form of "thousands of Clinton emails"—and was willing to actively "assist the Campaign through the anonymous release of information that would be damaging to Hillary Clinton"—came immediately upon Mifsud's return to London from a meeting of the Valdai Discussion Club, a meeting that Trump campaign Russia adviser and Mifsud's fellow Valdai Discussion Club member Dimitri Simes presumably did not attend in person, given his concurrent responsibility for helping edit as well as host Trump's April 27 speech at the Mayflower Hotel.[49]

Despite Papadopoulos's demonstrated habit of immediately reporting his contacts with Kremlin agents to his supervisors at the Trump campaign—and the fact that just ten days after receiving Mifsud's shocking news, he shared it with a man he had just met, Australian diplomat Alexander Downer (as well as, three weeks after that, yet another man he had just met, Greek foreign minister Nikos Kotzias)—Papadopoulos will tell the special counsel that he does not think he ever gave to anyone on the Trump campaign the most valuable piece of information he would acquire in his eight months of working for the GOP presidential candidate.[50]

Papadopoulos was emailing with senior campaign officials during the seventy-two-hour period in which he received his top-shelf intelligence from Mifsud, including an April 25 email to Trump domestic policy adviser Stephen Miller on the Kremlin's "open invitation by Putin for Mr. Trump to meet him when he is ready" (an email that included some suggested logistics for the meeting) and a second message to Miller on April 27—the day after his conversation with Mifsud—in which he told the Trump domestic policy adviser about "interesting messages coming in from Moscow."[51] Papadopoulos also sent an April 27 email to Trump's campaign manager at the time, Corey Lewandowski, on the subject of a Trump-Putin summit.[52] Indeed, according to the Mueller Report, Papadopoulos would spend all of April, May, June, July, August, and September 2016 regularly emailing senior Trump campaign staff—including Miller, Lewandowski, Clovis, Manafort, Phares, and others—about the prospect of a Trump-Putin meeting, at one point forwarding to the campaign's top brass an email from Timofeev, his contact affiliated with the Russian foreign ministry.[53] By August, Papadopoulos is telling the campaign that he has received backchannel summit requests from "multiple foreign governments" besides Russia; by September, he is proposing to the campaign that, he, Phares, and Clovis meet with Kremlin agents in London in secret, "without the official backing of the Campaign"—a plan he admits in his private notes involves "a lot of risk."[54] It is unclear if Papadopoulos knows that by the summer of 2016 several other members of the national security advisory committee, including Sessions, Gordon, and Page, have met with Russian ambassador Sergey Kislyak, or that Jared Kushner and Dimitri Simes have been in regular communication, with Simes having better confirmed access to the Kremlin than Mifsud, Timofeev, or the mysterious woman calling herself "Olga Polonskaya." Nevertheless, Sam Clovis in mid-August

"encourage[s]" Papadopoulos and Phares "to make the trips" to meet secretly with Kremlin officials in London.[55]

There are many reasons, therefore, to doubt Papadopoulos's claim that
he withheld from the Trump campaign—for any length of time—the critical intelligence he received from Mifsud on April 26, 2016. Indeed, the
Mueller Report will in April 2019 cast some doubt on Papadopoulos's
contention, noting that the Trump adviser "remembered an incident in
which Clovis had been upset after hearing Papadopoulos tell [him] that
Papadopoulos thought 'they [the Kremlin] have her emails.'"[56] While Papadopoulos subsequently "waver[s]" in his recollection of this incident, its
chief component—that Papadopoulos shared what he knew with top Trump
campaign officials—is confirmed by John Mashburn, the Trump campaign's policy director, who worked closely throughout the campaign with
Sessions's chief of staff, Rick Dearborn, the senior Trump official who was
orchestrating the Mayflower Hotel event at which a speech Papadopoulos
had helped edit would be read by Trump.[57] Given Papadopoulos's certain
role and Mashburn's apparent one in the April 27 event at the Mayflower,
as well as Papadopoulos's later insistence to Mifsud that Trump's Mayflower speech was the "signal [for Trump and Putin] to meet," one might
expect Papadopoulos to not only tell the campaign about Mifsud's intelligence as soon as he received it but directly inform one of the campaign
officials coordinating the Mayflower event.[58] Indeed, this is exactly what
Mashburn will tell the Senate Judiciary Committee in March 2018, according to the *New York Times*: that he remembered an email "alerting the
Trump campaign that Russia had damaging information about Hillary
Clinton" coming "from George Papadopoulos, a foreign policy adviser to
the campaign who was approached by a Russian agent, sometime before
the party conventions and well before WikiLeaks began publishing [on July
22] messages stolen in hackings from Democrats."[59]

If on April 26 or April 27 Papadopoulos sent an email about Mifsud
to Clovis, who had hired him, and to Mashburn, who was helping run
an event laying out Trump's Russia policy that Papadopoulos considered
of paramount importance, this would fit the time parameters Mashburn
gave Congress. According to the *Times*, the senators and staff before whom

Mashburn was testifying believed him to be "telling the truth," and when they "gave him an opportunity to change his story, he stuck to his testimony."[60] Nor was Mashburn's testimony fainthearted; he "repeatedly" told the committee that he "recalled receiving a message with some detail about Russian information on Mrs. Clinton, and that other campaign officials almost certainly would have been copied on the memo."[61] Mashburn was not asked to name the other campaign officials, and did not recall the date of the message.[62] However, at the time of Trump's first foreign policy speech, Mashburn had just joined the Trump campaign, after which he immediately began "working closely with Rick Dearborn," the man who coordinated the Mayflower event.[63] Mashburn told the Senate that "he recalled replying to Mr. Papadopoulos to instruct him to raise the issue with someone else" and that he "might have forwarded the email to Mr. Dearborn."[64]

Mashburn's congressional testimony is so explosive that it results in a bipartisan letter from the Senate Judiciary Committee to the Trump campaign, according to a *New York Times* report in May 2018; the letter is "the first joint request by the two sides [of the Senate Judiciary Committee] in months."[65] Partial confirmation for the possibility Papadopoulos emailed Mashburn and other campaign staff about Mifsud's revelation on the day before (or the day of) Trump's Mayflower speech comes from the discovery, among Mashburn's emails, of a June 2016 email in which he discusses with Dearborn and J. D. Gordon receiving correspondence from Papadopoulos about work he did for the campaign just days after the Mayflower event.[66] The Mueller Report concludes its analysis of whether Papadopoulos revealed Mifsud's intelligence to the campaign by noting that the several campaign officials who could not recall such a message from Papadopoulos exhibited "varying degrees of certainty" in their testimony.[67] Though Senate investigators ultimately do not find the email to which Mashburn refers in his testimony, the absence of the email in Trump campaign members' digital archives is consistent with a troubling trend noted at several points by the investigators from the special counsel's office who wrote the Mueller Report: that "some of the individuals we interviewed or whose conduct we investigated—including some associated with the Trump Campaign—

deleted relevant communications" (see chapter 11).[68] The evidence compiled in the report will strongly suggest that many of these deletions and much of Trump officials' reliance on encrypted communications were intended to evade future document requests by Congress or other federal investigators. For instance, both Steve Bannon and Erik Prince will claim to have no knowledge of why their phones were missing all text messages from prior to March 2017, a period during which the two men are known to have engaged in illicit meetings with foreign nationals and to have exchanged, per phone records acquired by the special counsel's office, dozens of text messages.[69] The absence of Papadopoulos's email to Mashburn and other Trump campaign officials in campaign members' digital materials is therefore not probative from an investigative standpoint—meaning that it cannot be used to draw a conclusion about whether Papadopoulos lied to federal investigators (again) regarding his conduct while working for the Trump campaign.

Two days before Trump's speech at the Mayflower Hotel, and a day before Mifsud communicates to Papadopoulos that the Kremlin has thousands of stolen Clinton emails, Trump writes a note to his Russian business associate Aras Agalarov, who had in late February, according to the Mueller Report, "expressed interest in Trump's campaign, passed on 'congratulations' for Trump's primary victories," and issued an "offer" to Trump of both his own "support and that of many of his important Russian friends and colleagues[,] especially with reference to U.S./Russian relations."[70]

Not long after Trump speaks at the Mayflower and MBS rolls out his Vision 2030 plan, Barrack successfully orchestrates a meeting between Jared Kushner and Emirati ambassador al-Otaiba, having written al-Otaiba to confide that Kushner "agrees with our agenda."[71] Once contact is made between Trump's son-in-law and the Emirati ambassador, Kushner expresses to both Barrack and al-Otaiba—and, through al-Otaiba, to MBZ—that he is "receptive to an alliance among Gulf countries, the United States, and Israel," thereby providing the Red Sea conspirators with a strong indication that Trump and his team embrace their geopolitical agenda.[72] By June 1, Barrack is confidently telling Bloomberg TV that "the United Arab Emirates and Saudi Arabia and Israel—in my opinion—

will align as allies very quickly here."[73] Barrack calls the two Sunni Arab nations and Israel "the best allies to America," and says that the United States "should reward our energy-producing Middle East partners who are helping us stamp out terrorism abroad."[74] Asked what he expects Trump's foreign policy to be in the Middle East, Barrack says that instead of a "travel ban" keeping Muslims from the United States, he thinks Trump would, as president, "find a way to make a deal that lessens the impact and starts solving this problem [of terrorism]."[75] The *New York Times* reports that almost immediately after Kushner and al-Otaiba meet for the first time, the Emirati ambassador "position[s] himself as an informal adviser on [the Middle East] to Mr. Kushner"—a breach of diplomatic protocol for the ambassador, whose role in the midst of a U.S. election, by tradition, would be to avoid even attending partisan political events, let alone assuming the role of an "adviser" to one of the nation's two competing presidential campaigns.[76] Indeed, al-Otaiba's actions during the general election likely involve repeated solicitations for Kushner to violate the Logan Act, 18 U.S.C. § 953, a federal criminal statute that regulates U.S. citizens' ability to discuss policy issues with foreign diplomats "with intent to influence the measures or conduct of any foreign government or of any officer or agent thereof, in relation to any disputes or controversies with the United States."[77]

Al-Otaiba becomes much more than simply a protocol-breaching policy adviser to Jared Kushner, however. In the same way Trump aides such as George Papadopoulos work behind the scenes to set up a meeting between Trump and Putin during the campaign—the sort of summit that must be handled delicately because of its potential inappropriateness, per diplomatic norms—by June 2016 al-Otaiba is trying to "arrange meetings between [Saudi deputy crown prince Mohammed bin Salman] and the Trump campaign" with Barrack's assistance, which likewise could become inappropriate if they involve any substantive discussion of changes to U.S. foreign policy under a prospective Trump administration.[78] Little is known of al-Otaiba's clandestine machinations in early summer 2016, except that they appear to culminate in an August 3, 2016, meeting at Trump Tower between MBZ's emissary George Nader, MBZ adviser Erik Prince, MBZ consultant Joel Zamel, Trump policy adviser Stephen Miller, and Trump's son

Don Jr. (see chapter 5). A second result is undoubtedly a meeting at Trump Tower in December 2016 between MBZ and Kushner—at which meeting MBZ "recommend[s] Prince Mohammed of Saudi Arabia as a promising young leader," according to a person familiar with the meeting who speaks to the *New York Times*.[79] Though present reporting does not indicate that Trump attended Kushner's meeting with MBZ, this is consistent with a trend observable within both the Trump campaign and Trump transition: not acknowledging any meetings Trump may have attended, even when, as with the December 2016 Kushner-MBZ meeting, Trump was available to meet—was possibly even in the building where the meeting occurred as it happened—and MBZ's ambassador al-Otaiba had been working for six months to connect MBZ to Trump's inner circle. Indeed, it is difficult to imagine a de facto head of state with such long-standing (if mediated) ties to the Trump campaign breaching international diplomatic protocol to enter the United States secretly, traveling to Trump Tower, and then being denied access to the president-elect.

Just four days before Barrack's June 1 interview with Bloomberg TV about Trump's prospective foreign policy with respect to Saudi Arabia, the United Arab Emirates, and Israel, the Trump campaign sends the preeminent Israel expert on its national security advisory committee, George Papadopoulos, to Greece. Papadopoulos's visit coincides with a visit to the city by Vladimir Putin, and both Papadopoulos and Putin meet with the same government official while in Athens, Greek defense minister Panos Kammenos—in both instances discussing the subject of U.S. sanctions on Russia.[80]

Between Papadopoulos's two visits to Greece in May 2016, one in early May and one in late May, one of Papadopoulos's chief supervisors, Sam Clovis, the man who hired Papadopoulos to the campaign in March, receives a message from a relative of Trump Organization attorney Jason Greenblatt.[81] Greenblatt is Trump's future special envoy to the Middle East; his relative is writing Clovis to try to arrange a Trump-Putin summit through Berel Lazar, a Russian rabbi who is a "very close confidante of Putin."[82] Greenblatt, Greenblatt's relative, and Lazar ultimately convene at Trump Tower in the summer of 2016 for a meeting—though whom they meet with at Trump Tower is unknown, and their reason for selecting Clovis as their campaign contact for a secret Trump-Putin summit is unclear.[83] Lazar will later claim that, despite being put forward as a critical conduit for future Trump-Putin communications and despite having met with one of the Republican presidential candidate's top attorneys, he subsequently kept from Putin any information about his meeting at Trump Tower.[84] It is shortly after this initial outreach by Lazar that the Trump campaign's chief Israeli expert, Papadopoulos, travels to Athens with Clovis's permission while Putin is already in the city—the Russian president's only trip to an EU country during the 2016 presidential campaign, and to precisely the sort of "neutral city" Papadopoulos had previously told his campaign superiors the Kremlin preferred to use for covert meetings.[85]

On May 26, 2016, Trump officially clinches the GOP nomination. Two weeks later, he returns to his old line of attack regarding Saudi Arabia: that the Saudis are willing to collude illegally with an American politician if they believe that politician is willing to act in their interest as president. In June 2016 he accuses Saudi Arabia of giving "vast amounts of money to the Clinton Foundation"—money, Trump says, that Clinton must return because Saudi Arabia "want[s] women as slaves and to kill gays."[86] Trump follows this tweet with a demand that "Crooked Hillary" "call on Saudi Arabia and other countries to stop funding hate. I am calling on her to immediately return the $25 million she got from them for the Clinton Foundation!"[87] These are the last two tweets mentioning Saudi Arabia that Trump will publish before Election Day, and indeed the last substantive tweet referencing the kingdom he will issue before visiting Riyadh in May 2017 as president. Post-June events involving Trump and Saudi intermediaries do much to explain the notoriously vociferous tweeter's five-month pre-election silence on Twitter regarding the oil-rich Arab nation—a period of quiescence that is out of keeping with Trump's long-established pattern on the social media platform.

In May 2016, the same month Trump clinches the Republican nomination and his new "de facto campaign manager" Paul Manafort orders deputy campaign manager Rick Gates to share internal Trump campaign polling data with Russian intelligence, Manafort convinces Trump to hire Tony Fabrizio as the campaign's chief pollster.[88] Manafort had begun "advocating Fabrizio's hiring soon after he joined Trump's campaign in March," despite having himself only been hired by Trump as a "delegate counter."[89] The long relationship between Manafort and Fabrizio is sufficiently close—or sufficiently fraught—that it will be revealed in March 2019 that Fabrizio is secretly funneling substantial sums (at least $125,000) into Manafort's legal defense against a bevy of federal criminal charges.[90] CNBC notes that "the path taken by this $125,000 also highlights the ways that Manafort took advantage of the Trump campaign's underdeveloped leadership structure to install his allies in top positions across the Trump political landscape."[91]

Fabrizio is a longtime friend and neighbor of Roger Stone's, as well as a former business associate of both Manafort and new Trump deputy campaign manager Rick Gates. Fabrizio has known Stone for thirty-eight years and has known Manafort for at least twenty-seven years, working with Manafort and his deputy Gates in assisting pro-Kremlin Ukrainian politicians between 2011 and 2012.[92] According to the Mueller Report, "Gates said [to the special counsel's office] that Manafort's instruction [to send polling data to Kilimnik] included sending internal polling data prepared for the Trump campaign by pollster Tony Fabrizio. Fabrizio had worked with Manafort for years and was brought into the campaign by Manafort."[93] The report will capture July and August 2016 emails from Kilimnik to associates and journalists in the United States in which the Russian spy boasts of having seen "internal [campaign] polling" and having special insight into the "status of the Trump campaign" and "Trump's prospects for victory"—all critical pieces of data for the Kremlin in assessing and evolving its election-interference strategy in the summer of 2016.[94] Kilimnik is boasting of having unique access to the Trump campaign just a matter of days after an early July email from Manafort promising Kilimnik and/or Deripaska "private briefings" on the campaign if they want them.[95] Manafort will concede to the special counsel's office that at the time he made the offer to Kilimnik and Deripaska he expected the latter to "use" him post-election "to advance whatever interests Deripaska had in the United States"—interests that Deripaska has himself identified as co-extensive with those of the Kremlin.[96] Manafort concedes, too, that he did "brief[ ] Kilimnik on the Trump Campaign," and that he knew the content of his briefings would get back to "individuals in Ukraine and elsewhere"—the "elsewhere" almost certainly a reference to Moscow, given Deripaska's publicly stated allegiance to the Kremlin's agenda.[97]

The data Manafort communicates to Russian intelligence includes not just proprietary internal campaign polling data but "discussion of 'battleground' states, which Manafort identifies to Kilimnik as Michigan, Wisconsin, Pennsylvania, and Minnesota."[98] Only one of these states—Michigan—had previously (in 2014) been identified by the Internet Research Agency as a key state for its pre-election domestic reconnaissance, with the IRA's scouting activity in the United States in that year being focused on presumed battleground states Nevada, New Mexico, and Colorado, as well as larger, non-battleground states like California, Illinois, Texas, and New York.[99] By the fall of 2016, the chief foci of IRA activity will be two of the four states Manafort commended to the Kremlin, Michigan and Wisconsin, with CNN reporting in October 2017 that the Kremlin's illicit maneuvers in these two states "appeared [to be] highly sophisticated in their targeting of key demographic groups in areas of the states that turned out to be pivotal."[100] The IRA will also be found to have launched "a series of pro-Trump rallies across both Florida and Pennsylvania in the months leading up the election," thereby reaching one of the other two states that Manafort had previously indicated to Russian intelligence would be a key election battleground.[101] Manafort will subsequently lie to the special counsel's office about whether he discussed "battleground states" with Kremlin agents in August 2016 or at any other time.[102]

Because Tony Fabrizio, upon his hire by the Trump campaign in May 2016, becomes Trump's chief pollster, "it [is] his job to share polling information with Trump's campaign manager," Manafort.[103] The polling firm Fabrizio most closely liaises with during his work on Trump's campaign, National Research, is responsible during the 2016 campaign for putting polls in the field in—among several other battlegrounds—Michigan and

Wisconsin, two of the three states "where both the Trump campaign and Russia's Internet Research Agency focused their efforts."[104] The *New Yorker* will note that one reason Russia would have wanted Fabrizio's polling data from Manafort is that the data "potentially offered demographic targets for Russia's [pre-election] bots and propaganda."[105]

The Fabrizio polling data Manafort and Gates—both of whom will later be indicted by Robert Mueller—transmit to the Kremlin is seventy-five pages of "relevant," "very detailed," "very complex" information that is the "most recent" available internally within the Trump campaign.[106] Indeed, it is so advanced that Manafort's lawyer will, after Manafort is indicted, tell a federal court that he cannot himself understand it.[107] For Kilimnik's part, he will send at least six emails (believed to be to Manafort and Gates, though the emails are redacted in court filings) regarding the data.[108] Additional court filings suggest that the data Manafort and Gates give Kilimnik may have come from the very end of the Republican primary season, a fact that leaves open the possibility that some of the polling data Manafort has Gates transmit in the final months of the 2016 campaign is from Cambridge Analytica; according to the BBC, in working with the Trump campaign during the general election, Cambridge Analytica largely used "legacy data models" and primary-campaign hard data—that is, information it had gathered while working on behalf of Texas senator Ted Cruz.[109] Adam Geller, the founder and CEO of National Research, which collected Fabrizio's data for not just Michigan and Wisconsin but also battleground states Missouri and Iowa, now says that "I honestly have no idea what was . . . shared with the Russians."[110] Broadly, however, it is known that Fabrizio's internal polling data, by Fabrizio's admission after the election, micro-targeted and micro-analyzed American voters not just by state but by race, income level, voting habits, and their opinion of America's sociocultural trajectory. Fabrizio also assessed voters' susceptibility to the sort of racialized appeals on immigration and other hot-button issues that both the Trump campaign and the Internet Research Agency would later exploit in seeking election-clinching victories for Trump in Michigan, Wisconsin, and Pennsylvania.[111]

Fabrizio is not a solo operator upon his hire by his longtime associates Manafort and Gates in May 2016. In fact, he works for Arthur J. Finkelstein and Associates, a consultancy run by controversial right-wing political consultants Arthur Finkelstein and George Birnbaum.[112] Apart from having advised both Richard Nixon and Ronald Reagan, Finkelstein is famous for having been the "secret campaign manager" behind Benjamin Netanyahu's historically narrow election as prime minister of Israel in 1996, a campaign that made Finkelstein a "star," according to *BuzzFeed News*.[113] Two years later, Finkelstein hired Birnbaum to work with him for Netanyahu's Likud party, and ten years after that, in 2008, Finkelstein and Birnbaum were loaned by their client Netanyahu to an aspiring Hungarian politician, Viktor Orban—a man who, after becoming Hungary's prime minister in 2010, will in July 2016 breach diplomatic convention by endorsing Donald Trump for president.[114] As of 2018, one of Orban's top political advisers is another Trump ally: Steve Bannon, CEO of Trump's presidential campaign.[115]

By 2016, Finkelstein and Birnbaum are famous for their years of work for Orban, whose 2010 election as Hungarian prime minister—his second stint in the role—was considered an "electoral masterpiece . . . with implications around the world."[116] One implication of Finkelstein and Birnbaum's actions is Orban's construction of an anti-Semitic alternate reality inside Hungary's cloistered political sphere, one in which George Soros—a wealthy Hungarian-born Jew with few ongoing ties to Hungary—is positioned as the nation's foremost bogeyman. Finkelstein and Birnbaum's demonization of Soros not only bolsters Orban's political standing in Hungary but "please[s] his Russian neighbors," as "Putin was afraid of the so-called 'color revolutions' [popular uprisings] like the one in Ukraine, and the Arab Spring, and had begun attacking Soros and his support for liberal causes" as a domestic distraction.[117] By 2016, Finkelstein and Birnbaum have made Orban's 2018 reelection campaign almost entirely about certain Hungarians' implicitly anti-Semitic fear of the octogenarian Soros; as *The Intercept* will note, Orban was thus convinced by two Jewish men, Finkelstein and Birnbaum, to "focus[ ] his entire re-election campaign on the imaginary threat [to Hungary] posed by Soros."[118] Per *BuzzFeed News,* "Orban's campaign against Soros never actually used the word Jew, but it was often implicit. Orban told his people they would have to fight against an 'enemy' who was 'different,' who didn't have a 'home.' It was common to see anti-Semitic graffiti on 'Stop Soros' ads—voters knew what they were being told."[119] Incredibly, "even [Israeli prime minister Benjamin] Netanyahu's son Yair posted an anti-Semitic meme in 2017 showing Soros and reptilians controlling the world."[120]

During the same forty-eight-hour period in March 2016 in which Donald Trump meets with his national security advisory committee for the first time, Paul Manafort and Rick Gates pitch Trump on bringing aboard Fabrizio—an employee of Finkelstein and Birnbaum—and Gates meets with Birnbaum in Washington.[121] The two men discuss whether Birnbaum, with his "close ties to current and former Israeli government officials," can link up the Trump campaign with Psy-Group.[122] Gates "request[s] proposals [from Psy-Group's Joel Zamel] to create fake online identities, to use social media manipulation and to gather intelligence to help defeat . . . Clinton, according to interviews and copies of the proposals."[123] According to the *New York Times*, "the documents show that a senior Trump aide [Trump's deputy campaign manager] saw the promise of a [digital] disruption effort to swing voters in Mr. Trump's favor."[124] Because it is Birnbaum, the "senior aide" to Netanyahu who had previously co-managed one of the Israeli prime minister's campaigns—and who the *Times of Israel* notes has "closely worked with a wide range of Israeli politicians over the years"—who makes the Gates-Zamel introduction, Gates and Birnbaum's late March 2016 meeting bears many of the hallmarks of an attempt by a foreign power to tamper in the 2016 election through a trusted intermediary.[125] Indeed, the chief identification the *Times of Israel* gives to Finkelstein and Birnbaum is as "longtime" Netanyahu advisers.[126]

The possibility that Israeli prime minister Benjamin Netanyahu sought to tamper with America's 2016 presidential election is a grave one, requiring some consideration not only of whether it was within his power but in the character of the man to do so. Apropos of this inquiry, in 2018 Israeli police will recommend not just once or twice but three times that Netanyahu face criminal charges for "taking bribes, fraud, and breach of trust," allegations that ultimately do lead to Netanyahu becoming the first sitting Israeli prime minister to face criminal charges (see chapter 10).[127] The first allegation against Netanyahu involves him secretly colluding with a foreign billionaire (Australian entrepreneur James Packer) to advance his own interests; the second allegation submits that Netanyahu attempted to secretly collude with top Trump donor Sheldon Adelson in an effort to manipulate media coverage; and the third allegation, like the second, involves an attempt at clandestine collusion with a telecommunications and media conglomerate.[128] Consequently, while Netanyahu has not to date been linked with his former top aide's attempt to—possibly illegally—connect an Israeli company specializing in telecommunications and media strategy with the Trump campaign, neither can it be said that such an act of collusion would lie outside Netanyahu's reputed sphere of activity.

As for whether interference by Zamel and Psy-Group in the 2016 election offers some additional evidence of involvement by the Israeli government, worth noting is a *New York Times* report confirming that Psy-Group is indeed "staffed by former Israeli intelligence operatives."[129] The *Daily Beast* and the *Times of Israel* have both reported that not just Gates but two members of "Trump's inner circle" reached out to Psy-Group looking for election assistance; the names of these top-level Trump aides are at present unknown.[130] What is known is that Zamel was so determined to get to Trump he "even asked Newt Gingrich, the former House Speaker, to offer Zamel's services to Jared Kushner, Trump's son-in-law."[131] Gingrich was at the time a member of Psy-Group's advisory board, as was Elliott Abrams, a man Trump has since named as his special envoy "to oversee U.S. policy toward Venezuela," per the *New Yorker*.[132] Gingrich forwarded Zamel's May 2016 email to Jared Kushner; as already noted, Kushner's family is close to Netanyahu, and it is Kushner who ultimately decides, over objections from both Corey Lewandowski and Paul Manafort, to hire Cambridge Analytica—a decision that may well have meant, too, hiring an Israeli business intelligence firm run by Zamel.[133] Zamel, for his part, admired "Trump's vocal support for Israel and his hardline views on

Iran," according to the *New Yorker*, saying in his email to Gingrich that ended up in Kushner's in-box that Psy-Group could "provide the Trump campaign with powerful tools that would use social media to advance Trump's chances. Zamel suggested a meeting in Washington to discuss the matter further."[134] Kushner thereafter discussed the idea with Brad Parscale, then Trump's digital campaign director; subsequently, Rick Gates requested that Zamel send additional proposals to the campaign, which the Israeli business intelligence expert did in June.[135]

In June 2016, the same month Zamel sends three full-length social-media disinformation campaign proposals to the Trump team, the Israeli businessman meets with MBZ adviser George Nader—whom he has known for years, having been introduced by former Dick Cheney aide John Hannah—at the very economic forum in St. Petersburg that Felix Sater had been trying to get Michael Cohen to attend, and that Deripaska associate (and Russian deputy prime minister) Sergei Prikhodko had invited Trump to attend on two separate occasions. In St. Petersburg, Zamel tells Nader that he is "trying to raise money for a social-media campaign in support of Trump"—an entreaty strongly suggesting that the Trump campaign was willing to use Zamel's work, but not to pay for it directly, and that Zamel had reason to believe Nader's patron MBZ, for whom Zamel was already a consultant, would be willing to secretly do so.[136] And indeed, according to the *New Yorker*, Zamel ultimately does ask Nader for "Nader's Gulf contacts . . . [to] contribut[e] financially."[137]

According to the *Times of Israel*, one of the three campaigns Psy-Group proposes to the Trump team in June 2016 in response to contact with multiple top campaign advisers suggests "us[ing] fake online profiles to bombard [targets] with messages" that appear to come from American voters and decry Trump opponents' "ulterior motives or hidden plans." Meanwhile, a second proposal solicited by the Trump campaign would use an identical strategy to "target female minorities . . . in swing states to push them toward Trump and away from Clinton."[138] A third proposal "sketche[s] out a monthslong plan to help Mr. Trump by using social media to help expose or amplify division among rival campaigns and factions"—an idea that dovetails with the Kremlin's effort to suppress Democratic turnout in

November 2016 by exacerbating divisions between supporters of Hillary Clinton, Bernie Sanders, and Jill Stein.[139] These proposals, submitted formally to the Trump campaign in the spring and summer of 2016 under the code name Project Rome, are thus substantively indistinguishable from the interference the Kremlin was orchestrating during the general election.

That Psy-Group knows the activities it proposes to Gates and two other top Trump aides will have to be covert is confirmed by its proposals using code words for Trump and Clinton and discussing the need for "intelligence activities"—which the proposals explicitly contrast with "open source methods"—for the plans to come off properly.[140] One plan even discusses using "clandestine means to build 'intelligence dossiers' on Clinton," a strategy that mirrors the one the Trump campaign will accuse the Clinton campaign of using once the Steele dossier, which outlines serious allegations of Trump-Russia collusion, is published in January 2017 by *BuzzFeed News*.[141] That Psy-Group knows its proposals are illegal appears to be confirmed by a subsequent *Times of Israel* investigation, which finds that Psy-Group "was reportedly told by an American law firm that its activities would be illegal if non-Americans were involved."[142] The top brass at Psy-Group, including Zamel himself, are all foreign nationals; moreover, the *Times of Israel* will note that in at least one other sphere—anti-BDS (boycott-divest-sanction Israel) campaigns—Psy-Group is working covertly overseas in a way that is "known to the Israeli government, and specifically the Ministry of Strategic Affairs."[143]

According to an investigative report by the *Daily Beast*, Rick Gates and the two unnamed aides in Trump's "inner circle" who solicit digital campaign ideas from Psy-Group are "very, very interested" in Zamel's proposals, despite the campaign's future protestations to the contrary.[144] These protestations, which also insist that the campaign never used Psy-Group's services, will be challenged by several "former employees" of Psy-Group who "dispute[ ] [the] claim" that "the firm never went forward with its plan to help the [Trump] campaign."[145]

Zamel strategically compartmentalizes his offer to collude with the Trump campaign in a way that makes it more difficult for his employees to see who their client is. Some "former Psy-Group employees who spoke with the *Daily Beast* said they only interacted with [George] Birnbaum, whom they were introduced to by an intermediary, and did not have contact with Gates."[146] The possibility that a longtime aide to Benjamin Netanyahu represented himself as Psy-Group's client to block Psy-Group employees from identifying the Trump campaign as the end user of their work product is deeply troubling. Yet other Psy-Group employees report having direct contact with the Trump campaign, including several who tell the *Daily Beast* that they had contact with two unnamed Trump aides rather than Gates. These employees do tell the *Daily Beast*, however, that the members of Trump's inner circle they met "were introduced to [them] by 'brokers,' including Birnbaum . . . [the] employees said that they could not reveal the names [of the Trump aides], citing non-disclosure agreements"; it is unclear whether it was Psy-Group or the Trump campaign that asked them to sign nondisclosure agreements—though either is possible, given that the Trump campaign has become infamous for its aggressive use of such legal instruments during the 2016 general election.[147] One former Psy-Group employee offers this explanation for the divergent stories coming from Psy-Group employees about whether the organization executed a media disinformation campaign for Trump: "Joel [Zamel] is a very secretive guy, he holds all his cards very close to the chest. It's very possible he was running some sort of side operation that used Psy resources but didn't include the staff."[148]

According to the *Times of Israel*, one thing that is clear is that the "several secretive proposals" that Zamel—in conjunction with Psy-Group or otherwise—created for Gates's and others' review were created "at the behest of" Gates.[149] Moreover, the *Times* reports that the proposals Zamel offered to the Trump campaign in spring 2016 were the same ones he later offered to Donald Trump Jr. in August, suggesting that Gates's response to Zamel's initial approach, whatever it was, either encouraged or did not deter Zamel from taking his offer to the Trumps directly. In May 2018, a whistleblower from the Trump campaign's data firm, Cambridge Analytica, tells Congress that he knows of "relationships that Cambridge had had with former members of Israel's security forces," opening the possibility that whether or not Rick Gates, Donald Trump Jr., or the two unnamed aides in Trump's "inner circle" partnered with Zamel or men like Zamel, they may well have referred such people—and their plans for domestic disinformation operations—to the campaign's data firm.[150]

According to a startling October 2018 report by the *Daily Beast*, it wasn't just Gates, Trump Jr., and two members of Trump's circle who heard Zamel's pitch. While it will remain unclear if the candidate himself ever met with Zamel face-to-face pre-election, according to the *Daily Beast*, Trump "heard Zamel's plan."[151] Contradicting the campaign's claim that Zamel never worked with it pre-election, the *Daily Beast* will report that, indeed, "Trump's team drew in Zamel . . . during the campaign."[152]

As a company run by ex-Israeli military officers is approaching members of the Trump campaign in the United States, the campaign's nominal Israel expert, Papadopoulos, is making his two unusual, campaign-approved trips to Greece. During the first, in early May, he meets with a Greek journalist from Kathimerini and acts like "a second-rate actor in a political thriller," according to the journalist, Alexis Papachelas, who says Papadopoulos "lowered his voice so as not to be overhead . . . [and] dropped hints of major contacts, mainly in Israel."[153] Papachelas concludes that Papadopoulos has been "assigned" a "job" by the Trump campaign but might be "too green or too flippant" to carry it out successfully.[154] According to the *Washington Post*, which quotes Adonis Georgiadis, a leading Greek politician, when Papadopoulos came to Greece in May 2016 he was "totally unknown. But then [Greek defense minister Panos] Kammenos took him by the hand and promoted him everywhere."[155] The *Post* describes Kammenos as "a pro-Russian Greek nationalist who brag[s] often of his insider Moscow connections . . . and pushed for an end to sanctions imposed on Russia [by the United States and others]."[156] Georgiadis calls Kammenos "one of the strongest Putin supporters in Greece."[157] Curiously, Kammenos was in D.C., attending the annual American Israel Public Affairs Committee (AIPAC) conference, on the day Trump convened his national security advisory committee for the first time at the Trump International Hotel— the event at which Papadopoulos revealed to Trump that he had been tasked by the Kremlin to act as an "intermediary" in setting up a secret Trump-Putin summit.[158] It is unclear if Papadopoulos met Kammenos in Washington in late March 2016, though Kammenos's extraordinary commitment to introducing Papadopoulos to powerful figures in Athens five weeks later suggests it is possible.

By the time Papadopoulos returns to Greece in late May 2016—a trip that occurs while Vladimir Putin is also in Athens—he is, according to the *Post*, "quietly holding meetings across town and confiding in hushed tones that he [is] there [in Athens] on a sensitive mission on behalf of his boss, Donald Trump."[159] The nature of the mission, at least in part, is, according to Papachelas's interview with Papadopoulos at the time, to "secretly plan[ ] a pre-election trip by Trump to Greece and Israel, which he [Papadopoulos] saw taking place that July."[160] Whether the campaign's decision to have Papadopoulos travel to Greece while Putin is there is indeed connected to a "secret plan" to have Trump visit Greece and Israel in July is unclear; however, Papadopoulos had just weeks earlier told Trump that the Kremlin wanted him to set up a Trump-Putin summit, preferably in a neutral city—and being in Athens while Putin's entourage was there would afford him an excellent opportunity to try to do so.[161]

The day before Putin's scheduled meeting in Athens with the Greek foreign minister, Nikos Kotzias, Papadopoulos meets with Kotzias and tells him he knows the Kremlin possesses "thousands" of Hillary Clinton's emails.[162] He does so immediately after—and in response to—Kotzias saying to Papadopoulos that "where you are sitting right now, tomorrow Putin will be sitting there."[163] In an interview he will give to CNN in September 2018, Papadopoulos will say that at the time it was "his impression" that "the Russians [were] trying to hire [him] to be a source for them."[164] As to whether, by May 2016, Papadopoulos had already told the Trump campaign about the Kremlin's possession of the Clinton emails, Papadopoulos will cryptically tell CNN, "At this time, I don't remember." When CNN's Jake Tapper reminds him of Trump aide John Mashburn's congressional testimony that he received an email from Papadopoulos informing the campaign of the Kremlin's crimes, Papadopoulos comments, "I don't think that proof has been provided."[165] Pressed by Tapper as to whether he might have told anyone on the Trump campaign about the Clinton emails—in the same way he had told the Greek foreign minister in May 2016, despite having just met him and not being in his employ—Papadopoulos will finally answer, "I might have," adding that he "can't guarantee" he didn't.[166] Papadopoulos also will concede to Tapper that it's "possible" he told the Australian ambassador during a meeting in London just a few weeks before he traveled to Greece that "the Russians might use material that they have on Hillary Clinton."[167]

It is just a week after Papadopoulos's meeting with Kotzias that Trump's son Don Jr. receives—via Rob Goldstone—a message from the son of one of Trump's Russian business partners stating that the Kremlin has "documents and information that would incriminate Hillary."[168]

In mid-June 2016, WikiLeaks announces that it has "emails relating to Hillary Clinton which are pending publication," and the Democratic National Committee announces that it has just discovered it was hacked in April by the Russian government, a hack later determined to have been conducted by Russia's military intelligence unit, the GRU.[169] The same week as the DNC announcement, the GRU begins disseminating the materials it stole.[170] As for the emails the GRU stole from the Clinton campaign's employees and volunteers in March, many of these will indeed ultimately be released by WikiLeaks in October 2016.[171] In mid-June, however, the Trump campaign erroneously believes that these materials will be coming out in late June or early July, having heard from Roger Stone that WikiLeaks will shortly be releasing materials damaging to Clinton.[172] WikiLeaks ultimately publishes stolen DNC emails in July, leading to Trump being "generally frustrated that the Clinton emails had not been found" or, if found, not yet released.[173] Meanwhile, Manafort "press[es] excitement" about WikiLeaks' July release and asks to be "kept apprised" of any new information about future releases.[174] The Mueller Report will broadly conclude that "the Trump Campaign showed interest in WikiLeaks' releases of hacked materials throughout the summer and fall of 2016."[175] According to the report, by late summer the campaign "was planning a press strategy, a communications campaign, and messaging based on the possible release of Clinton emails by WikiLeaks," with Trump somehow having a separate channel of information about WikiLeaks besides Manafort (whose conduit was Gates) as evidenced by Trump telling Gates, upon the completion of a phone call from an unknown party, that "more releases of damaging information would be coming" from WikiLeaks—an organization that Trump's first CIA director and eventual secretary of state, Mike Pompeo, subsequently labels, after Trump is elected, a "hostile non-state intelligence service often abetted by State actors like Russia."[176]

In late June 2016, Michael Flynn ends his consulting work with ACU Strategic Partners—work intended to bring together the governments of the United States, Russia, Saudi Arabia, Egypt, and Israel—and begins consulting for an affiliated group, IP3/IronBridge, which is run by a former ACU adviser.[177] By August 2016, IP3/IronBridge, in conjunction with Flynn, has produced a PowerPoint presentation for MBS's father called "A Presentation to His Majesty King Salman bin Abdul Aziz."[178] That the IP3/IronBridge presentation—which, as with ACU's work, focuses on multinational deals to build nuclear power plants in the Middle East—is intended to propose a new alliance between Saudi Arabia and the United States is confirmed by the presence, in the PowerPoint slides, of official Saudi and American seals next to each other. As Flynn is by now widely known to be a top Trump adviser, the implication in the presentation cannot be missed: a Trump presidency means the possibility of a multibillion-dollar U.S.-Saudi alliance on nuclear energy. IP3/IronBridge produces the PowerPoint presentation during the same month that an emissary from the Saudi and Emirati governments, George Nader, is meeting with Trump Jr. at Trump Tower to offer the kingdom's assistance in electing Trump Sr. president.[179]

IP3 officials will tell media in November 2017 that they never hired Flynn as an adviser and never paid him any money; their claims are contradicted, however, by Flynn himself, who reported on "various financial disclosure forms," according to the *Washington Post*, that he had acted as a "consultant," "board member," and "advisor" to IP3.[180] Given the numerous high-profile omissions from Flynn's federal forms, the likelihood that he disclosed his role with IP3 merely out of "an abundance of caution," as the company subsequently asserts, is remote.

Yet there is more direct evidence that Flynn remains closely involved with IP3 after June 2016. During the presidential transition, Flynn will tell Thomas Barrack that he should meet with IP3.[181] Given that Flynn had previously worked on a "Middle East Marshall Plan" with ACU, it is telling that in November 2017 the *Washington Post* will report that—while Barrack was working on Trump's transition team with Flynn—he became "interested in developing a Middle East 'Marshall Plan' to provide aid to poor regions of the Persian Gulf as a way to combat terrorism" (see chapter 5).[182] The *Post* notes that "both the ACU and IP3 proposals . . . would require numerous governmental approvals to proceed," underscoring the significance of key members of Trump's presidential transition team working on Middle East plans of this scope and complexity.[183]

On June 9, 2016, Donald Trump Jr., Paul Manafort, and Jared Kushner attend a meeting at Trump Tower at which they have been promised they will receive incriminating information about Hillary Clinton from agents of the Russian government. Among the Russian attendees at the meeting is Ike Kaveladze, a high-level employee for Aras Agalarov's Crocus Group, which the Mueller Report notes "holds substantial Russian government contracts."[184] Trump Jr. and Kaveladze are already intimately acquainted, as according to the Mueller Report Trump Jr. was the "primary negotiator" for the Trump Organization and Kaveladze the primary negotiator for the Crocus Group when Donald Trump and Aras Agalarov were planning to build a Trump Tower Moscow in 2013 and 2014.[185] The principals to that deal, Trump and Agalarov, had ultimately signed a letter of intent in January or February 2014, under the terms of which Trump would receive 3.5 percent of all sales related to the multibillion-dollar project.[186] The Trumps and Agalarovs were in contact about the project both before and after Trump's "soft" announcement of his national political ambitions in March 2014, with Ivanka traveling to Moscow to visit the site in February 2014 and discussions between the two parties on "'design standards' and other architectural elements" lasting well into the summer of 2014.[187]

According to the *New York Times*, in June 2016 Thomas Barrack and Ambassador al-Otaiba hatch a plot to "arrange a secret meeting between Paul Manafort"—who has just officially become Trump's campaign manager, after doing the job unofficially for two months—and MBS.[188] It is the perfect time for an introduction, the men reason, as Trump has just recently clinched the Republican nomination for president. Barrack, having gotten his friend Manafort his job with Trump, is now positioning Manafort as Trump's intermediary to the Saudis; indeed, the *Times* notes that in an email to al-Otaiba, Barrack presents "a Manafort meeting as a prelude to an [MBS] meeting with Mr. Trump."[189] Barrack writes to al-Otaiba on June 21, "I would like to align in Donald's mind the connection between the UAE and Saudi Arabia which we have already started with Jared."[190] Barrack feels urgency in connecting MBS and Trump because MBS has already secretly reached out to Trump for a meeting through Blackstone, a private equity company with whom Barrack's own private equity firm competes—raising the possibility that Blackstone, not Barrack, will get credit for establishing a pre-general-election relationship between the Republicans' designated presidential candidate and the Saudi crown prince.[191]

Blackstone is a particularly troubling MBS-Kushner interlocutor because the firm loans Kushner Companies $400 million between 2013 and mid-2017, when it receives a $20 billion investment from MBS just days after Trump (now president) and Jared Kushner negotiate what they say is a $350 billion arms deal with the Saudis.[192] The MBS-Blackstone deal implies that MBS is shoring up one of Kushner's most critical financial pipelines as a reward for steering the United States and the Saudi kingdom toward what Trump calls the biggest military equipment order in the two nations' diplomatic history.[193] The MBS-Kushner-Blackstone connection is made even more problematic by the presence of Blackstone's co-founder and chief executive officer, Stephen Schwarzman—who is also the head of Trump's business advisory council—in Riyadh with Kushner and the president.[194] As Bloomberg will later report, "The Saudi promise to invest in Blackstone's fund drove the firm's stock up more than 8 percent."[195]

In speaking to al-Otaiba about his friend Manafort, Barrack says Trump's campaign manager is "totally programmed" on the present and future need for Trump to appreciate "the closeness and alignment of the UAE," and he calls Manafort a "friend of [MBZ] and the UAE."[196] Though Barrack arranges a secret MBS-Manafort meeting for June 24, at a location designed to "avoid the news media," Manafort cancels at the last minute due to a scheduling conflict. Nevertheless, Manafort offers MBS two deliverables over the next three weeks: first, a private campaign "clarification" that "modulate[s]" Trump's "Muslim ban" proposal (likely a promise that the kingdom will not be affected by the policy), and second, and more important, the removal of a platform plank at the Republican National Convention that would have, as Barrack put it to the Emiratis, "embarrass[ed]" Saudi Arabia by un-redacting certain pages of the federal government's 9/11 report that pertain to the Saudis.[197] Manafort's ability to compel significant Republican platform changes to please foreign nationals on short notice underscores his involvement—much touted by his former employee Kilimnik overseas—in the even more controversial RNC platform change regarding the provision of lethal weaponry to anti-Kremlin Ukrainian rebels.

With Barrack having supplied the Emiratis with direct access to the Trump campaign through Kushner beginning in spring 2016, and with Manafort having delivered to the Saudis at least two pro-Saudi policy shifts in early summer, the question remained: What would the Trump campaign receive in return? Barrack communicates to al-Otaiba post-election his sense of anticipation for "the things that we will have to do together . . . together being the operative word," and al-Otaiba replies, "Let's do them together," to which Barrack immediately assents. But what value did the Saudis and Emiratis offer the Trump campaign before it achieved victory on Election Day, if not payment for Psy-Group's intelligence-gathering and disinformation services?[198] A similar question must be asked with respect to what the Israelis expected would happen after Trump's election as president.

Regarding the Israelis, one possible answer comes a few weeks after Trump calls Jerusalem "the eternal capital of the Jewish people" in
a March 2016 speech to AIPAC—the same month his campaign begins
seeking aid from Israeli company Psy-Group. That May, Trump discusses
moving the U.S. embassy in Israel to Jerusalem with billionaire Sheldon
Adelson, a Jewish mega-donor with a long history of donating to the GOP
and such substantial connections to Benjamin Netanyahu that former Israeli prime minister Ehud Olmert had once opined that Netanyahu "works
for" Adelson.[199] By mid-August 2016, Trump, according to Adelson, has
made an ironclad promise to the Republican donor that he will indeed
move the embassy.[200] In May 2018, Trump does as he has promised and
makes the controversial move, a decision quickly hailed by Netanyahu as
"a great day for the people of Israel."[201] Lauding Trump for being "bold,"
the Israeli prime minister also thanks Trump for his "leadership and
friendship."[202]

On July 15, 2016, the Turkish military attempts a coup of President Erdogan's government. The coup is unsuccessful; nevertheless, it has profound
consequences for the region. According to Al Jazeera, "certain Arab governments and their operatives were openly supportive of the coup plotters
and even offered logistical support to FETO, the armed organisation led
by the US-based Turkish national Fethullah Gulen that orchestrated the
failed coup." While Gulen will immediately deny any involvement in the
coup attempt, Al Jazeera's accusation that state actors have played a role
in the event reverberates.[203] Specifically, the Qatari media outlet identifies
Egypt as "the most vocal supporter" of the failed rebellion, in large part
because Egyptian president el-Sisi offered asylum to Gulen in the event
he was forced to leave his permanent residence in the United States.[204]
Al Jazeera also identifies the UAE—like Egypt, a nation participating in
the Red Sea Conspiracy—as a supporter of the coup, partly because MBZ
adviser Mohammed Dahlan broadcasts an interview with Gulen on a
television station he owns and partly because "emails leaked from the
personal account of Abu Dhabi's ambassador to Washington, Yousef al

Otaiba, reveal[ ] that . . . [he] was in close contact with senior officials from the Foundation for Defense of Democracies (FDD), a US-based think-tank primarily financed by the pro-Israel businessman Sheldon Adelson. An exchange between the UAE ambassador and John Hannah, a senior counsellor at the foundation, provided valuable insights into Abu Dhabi's relationship with the coup plotters in Turkey."[205] The *New York Times* has noted that Adelson "enjoys a direct line to [Trump]"; the *Jerusalem Post* reports that Adelson "pledged . . . to fund [Trump's] path to [Election Day] victory" in spring 2016, subsequently donated $25 million to Trump's campaign, and went "all in on the Republican nominee" a week before Election Day with a pledge of up to $25 million more; and the *Guardian* calls Adelson "the casino mogul driving Trump's Middle East policy."[206] The *Daily Beast* reports that John Hannah, who would end up on Trump's transition team just 120 days after the coup attempt in Turkey, subsequently found himself "in Mueller's sights" as part of a "lesser-known side" of the ongoing federal investigation of the Trump campaign, "one that deals with Israeli, Emirati, and Saudi influence in the 2016 presidential elections. Hannah is one of the individuals who sits at the center of that nexus."[207] It is unknown whether Hannah is now a subject of one of the fourteen ongoing federal criminal investigations using evidence compiled by the special counsel's office.[208]

While Sheldon Adelson's influence with Trump is well established by the time of the July 15, 2016, coup attempt in Turkey, Hannah's role in developing Trump's pro-Saudi, pro-Emirati, and pro-Israeli foreign policy will not be disclosed until after Election Day. In late 2018, the *Daily Beast* will report that during the 2016 campaign Hannah had interactions with both George Nader and Joel Zamel, and that these interactions continued into the transition period, when Nader, Zamel, and Hannah "met with a top Saudi general . . . to discuss plans to undermine and overthrow the government of Iran."[209] Per the digital media outlet, Hannah had known Zamel prior to 2016, and introduced Nader to him in 2016, either at the June 2016 St. Petersburg economic forum in Russia or before then—but certainly before Nader and Zamel attended an August 3, 2016, meeting together at Trump Tower.[210] The outlet reports that in 2016 Hannah is "close with Nader and Zamel," and even is listed on the website of Wiki-strat, Zamel's pre-Psy-Group business intelligence firm, as a member of the company's advisory council.[211] As the *Daily Beast* will note, "One of Zamel's companies, Wikistrat, was well-connected in Washington and had built up a base of high-level American military and intelligence officials to serve . . . as consultants to the firm."[212]

The Nader-Hannah relationship predates 2016 as well, with Nader hav-ing worked with Hannah on Iraq policy as far back as the second George W. Bush administration, when Nader was working for Erik Prince in the mid-aughts.[213] Former acting CIA director John McLaughlin, considering how the Hannah-Nader-Zamel nexus could come under scrutiny by Robert Mueller, will say in 2018 that "Mueller might be opening another front here. His mandate is to examine Russian collusion, but there's the clause in his mandate that's very open-ended—to the effect of, 'and any associated matters.' It could be a separate line of inquiry about efforts to influence the election by foreigners."[214] Significant to Mueller's inquiry, certainly, and to any federal prosecutor to whom the special counsel referred any line of inquiry involving Hannah and Nader, would be the fact that, as noted by the *Daily Beast,* in 2016 Nader was "developing his relationship with . . . senior Saudi officials, which included Mohammed Bin Salman, the de-facto leader of the kingdom. Throughout 2016 and 2017, Nader met with the two Gulf leaders and developed strategy on how to work with the Trump campaign."[215] This observation must be coupled with one offered by *Vox* in April 2018: that George Nader's "extensive personal ties to Russia" include the fact that he has "traveled to Russia, done business with Russia, and developed relationships with Russian President Vladimir Putin's inner circle at least as far back as 2012."[216] It is therefore little surprise that, as the *Daily Beast* reports, "Mueller has questioned Zamel about his role pitching top campaign officials on an influence operation to help Trump win the election—which could have broken federal election laws."[217]

On July 30, 2016, a senior Justice Department attorney, Bruce Ohr, meets with longtime friend and former MI6 Russia desk chief Christopher Steele.[218] Steele tells Ohr that, according to his Russian sources, the Kremlin's intelligence apparatus believes that it has Donald Trump "over a barrel"—meaning that the just-nominated GOP presidential candidate has been compromised by blackmail material in the Russian Federation's possession.[219] At the same meeting, Steele tells Ohr that Trump national security adviser Carter Page is lying about his contacts with Kremlin officials during a conference earlier that month; Page says that he met no Kremlin officials in Moscow, but Steele's Russian sources say that he did in fact do so.[220] Steele's sources will turn out to be correct, as it is revealed in the Mueller Report in April 2019 that Page met with both Russian deputy prime minister Arkady Dvorkovich and Andrey Baranov—a senior aide to Rosneft CEO and top Putin ally Igor Sechin—and then tried to hide these two meetings from U.S. media.[221] At the time of the Ohr-Steele meeting, Steele is considered "a reliable FBI informant who [has] delivered credible and actionable intelligence" in past contacts with federal law enforcement.[222]

Page's trip to Moscow in early July 2016 is, the Mueller Report will reveal, a significant event for the Kremlin and its agents. Officials at the New Economic School (NES) in Moscow, which hosts a lecture by Page during his trip, will later tell the special counsel that their "interest in inviting Page to speak at NES was based entirely on his status as a Trump Campaign advisor who served as the candidate's Russia expert," even though the Trump campaign will later claim Page's travel was unrelated to the campaign.[223] Prior to Page's arrival, several Kremlin officials and associates will be made aware of Page's impending lecture, including Maria Zakharova, the director of the Information and Press Department within the Russian Ministry of Foreign Affairs, and Dmitry Peskov, the Kremlin's press secretary.[224] Peskov declines to invite Page to the Kremlin itself, but within twenty-four hours of Page's arrival in Moscow, he is introduced to Russian deputy prime minister Arkady Dvorkovich during the event at the NES.[225] The deputy prime minister informs Page—just as the Russian ambassador to the United States, Sergey Kislyak, has done repeatedly during the same period in meetings with other Trump officials—that the Kremlin wants to "work[ ] together in the future."[226] Page's Moscow meeting with

Baranov, the head of investor relations at Russia's state-owned oil company, leads to the two men discussing "non-public information," per the Mueller Report, including information about Rosneft CEO Igor Sechin, who is both a former KGB agent and one of Putin's top lieutenants—a "hard man" that British media outlet the *Guardian* calls "one of the most powerful figures of the Putin era."[227]

When the Steele dossier, much derided by Trump allies, is published by *BuzzFeed News* in January 2017, it will correctly recount the details of both Page's private meeting with the Russian deputy prime minister and his private meeting with Rosneft's director of investor relations, the latter of which appears to have included discussion of a pending sale of Rosneft stock (a cut of which sale, Steele's dossier alleges, is offered to Trump via Page).[228] After his covert meetings with Dvorkovich and Baranov, Page excitedly emails the Trump campaign, promising several officials "a readout soon regarding some incredible insights and outreach I've received from a few Russian legislators and senior members of the Presidential Administration here."[229] The next day, Page emails Sam Clovis—one of the men who hired him, but not a member of the national security advisory committee he serves on—to tell him the details of his meetings with both Dvorkovich and Baranov, including the former's "strong support for Mr. Trump and a desire to work together toward devising better solutions in response to the vast range of current international problems." Page adds, significantly, that Dvorkovich's view is "widely held at all levels of [the Russian] government."[230]

Despite the volume of details it compiles about Page's July 2016 trip to Moscow, the Mueller Report will conclude that it did not receive the full truth from Page, noting that, as far as "who Page may have met or communicated with in Moscow," his "activities . . . were not fully explained."[231] Though J. D. Gordon, Page's peer on the Trump campaign's national security advisory committee, will not disclose to the special counsel any interactions between Page and Sergey Kislyak at the Republican National Convention following Page's return from Moscow, Page will after the convention tell campaign officials that he did indeed speak with Kislyak in Cleveland and that the ambassador was "very worried about candidate Clinton's world views."[232]

The special counsel's office will note that some part of the information it was unable to obtain about Page's activities in Moscow may have been reported by Yahoo News in September 2016, when the digital media outlet reveals, as summarized by the Mueller Report, that "U.S. intelligence officials [are] investigating whether . . . [Page] opened private communications with senior Russian officials to discuss U.S. sanctions policy under a possible Trump Administration."[233] If Page indeed did so, and at candidate Trump's direction or with his knowledge, Trump's request for Russian hackers to attack Clinton's email servers on July 27, 2016—less than three weeks after Page returns from Moscow—would likely be regarded as a federal felony under the aiding and abetting statute, 18 U.S.C. § 2.[234] As to whether this occurred, the special counsel's office cannot say—in substantial part because of evidence and testimony withheld from it by members of the Trump campaign.

When Page returns to Moscow in December 2016, it is months after the Trump campaign says it has severed ties with him. While there, however, Page will "give individuals in Russia the impression that he [has] maintained his connections to President-Elect Trump."[235] Indeed, on December 8, 2016, Kremlin agent Konstantin Kilimnik will write to Manafort to say that "Carter Page is in Moscow today, sending messages he is authorized to talk to Russia on behalf of [Donald Trump] on a range of issues of mutual interest, including Ukraine."[236] During his second 2016 trip to Moscow, Page again meets with Andrey Baranov of Rosneft, and again discusses with him Putin lieutenant Igor Sechin; Page also dines with Russian deputy prime minister Arkady Dvorkovich, the same Kremlin official he had met with in July.[237] According to the Mueller Report, Page and Dvorkovich discuss "connecting" the Kremlin with Trump's presidential transition team so that the two parties can discuss future "cooperation."[238]

In 2016 and 2017, the U.S. Foreign Intelligence Surveillance Court will four times find probable cause to believe that Page is an agent of the Kremlin.[239]

ANNOTATIONS

Fabrizio is not a solo operator upon his hire by his longtime associates Manafort and Gates in May 2016. In fact, he works for Arthur J. Finkelstein and Associates, a consultancy run by controversial right-wing political consultants Arthur Finkelstein and George Birnbaum.

Finkelstein is the developer of a concept in elections called "rejectionist voting": the idea that to win elections a politician should "demonize the enemy so much that even the laziest of voters would want to get out and vote, just to reject them."[240] Finkelstein for years advises his politician clients "not to talk about themselves, but instead to focus their campaigning on destroying their opponents," even if it means polling prospective voters to see if they might cast an anti-Semitic vote against a Jewish candidate—as Finkelstein did in the 1980s.[241] *BuzzFeed News* implies that Finkelstein, who died in 2017, may well have originated the phrase "Make America Great Again," as the slogan appeared in a 1980 Reagan commercial while Finkelstein was a high-ranking member of Reagan's marketing team.[242] Finkelstein also worked directly for Trump in the mid-2000s, just a few years before the businessman trademarked the slogan "Make America Great Again" in November 2012.[243] Trump's 2012 registration of his future presidential campaign slogan offers corroborating evidence for the claim made by a top consultant of his at the time, Sam Nunberg, that Trump decided to run for president while watching the returns from the 2012 presidential election, having hired Nunberg (and Nunberg's business associate Roger Stone) in 2010 "when he was thinking of running for president [in 2012]."[244] At the very latest, Trump made his final decision to run for president on New Year's Day in 2013, according to Stone, his longtime friend and adviser.

Orban was convinced by the Jewish Finkelstein and Birnbaum to "focus[ ] his entire re-election campaign on the imaginary threat [to Hungary] posed by Soros."

Not only Putin but Trump as well picks up on the Finkelstein/Birnbaum-developed plan to make Soros an international pariah in the interest of electing populist, often bigoted right-wing politicians—or protecting autocrats from political fallout for their policies. As *BuzzFeed News* recounts, "Putin referred dismissively to Soros during a press conference with Trump in Helsinki. Trump even claimed that the demonstrations against Supreme Court candidate Brett Kavanaugh were sponsored by Soros."[246]

As *BuzzFeed News* and many other news outlets have reported, in October 2018 a self-proclaimed Trump supporter sent a parcel bomb to Soros. Less than a week later, media reported that a man who killed eleven Jews in a Pittsburgh synagogue "saw himself as part of a fight against a Jewish conspiracy, which he believed was funding mass migration, and talked about the caravan and Soros on social media."[247] By joining Putin and Orban in demonizing Soros, a Holocaust survivor, Trump has arguably contributed to an international political environment in which the eighty-eight-year-old Hungarian American—who has no direct involvement in any political party—has repeatedly been falsely cast, usually in anti-Semitic terms, as a "puppet master secretly plotting to seize control" of various countries.[248]

As for whether interference by Zamel and Psy-Group in the 2016 election offers some additional evidence of involvement by the Israeli government, worth noting is a *New York Times* report confirming that Psy-Group is indeed "staffed by former Israeli intelligence operatives."

Many Israeli business intelligence firms identical to Psy-Group in their mission and the constitution of their employee base—former Israeli intelligence agents—are active outside Israel in covert activities. Black Cube, for instance, has been accused of attempting to interfere in elections in Hungary in support of Netanyahu's friend and ally Viktor Orban.[249] This interference involved secretly recording friends and allies of George Soros.[250] Black Cube was accused of similar spying activities against the Obama administration during the period in which the administration was working to reach a nuclear deal with Iran.[251] International accusations that Black Cube was connected to the Trump campaign and transition were apparently ubiquitous enough in 2018 that the company had to issue a statement insisting that it "has no relation whatsoever to the Trump administration, to Trump aides, to anyone close to the administration, or to the Iran nuclear deal. Anyone who claims otherwise is misleading their readers and viewers."[252]

CHAPTER 5

THE GRAND HAVANA ROOM, THE TRUMP-NADER MEETING, AND THE MIDDLE EAST MARSHALL PLAN

August 2016 to November 2016

As Trump's campaign manager, Paul Manafort, makes a last-ditch effort to offer value to his former Kremlin-connected bosses via his work on the Trump campaign before being forced to resign, Trump's son has a fateful meeting at Trump Tower with two foreign nationals that brings one of them, George Nader, into the campaign's inner circle. Meanwhile, a cadre of enterprising Trump advisers is working in parallel to Manafort's anti-sanctions efforts, joining their cause to those of the Red Sea conspirators in an all-encompassing geopolitical plan for the Middle East that will make them rich if Trump ends sanctions on Russia. In the midst of these plots, Trump and Flynn receive a classified security briefing that puts an end to any questions about Putin's intentions.

On August 17, 2016, Trump, Flynn, and Trump's transition chief at the time, Chris Christie, receive at the FBI field office in New York City the GOP candidate's first classified national security briefing from U.S. intelligence agents. During the meeting, NBC News will later report, Trump is "personally briefed on Russia's role in the [spring 2016] hacks by U.S.

officials."[1] NBC notes, quoting "a senior U.S. intelligence official," that during the briefing "the Russian government's attempts to interfere in the 2016 election . . . [were] discussed extensively" with Trump, and that after the briefing Trump had "all the information . . . need[ed] to be crystal clear" on the Kremlin's responsibility for attacks on the Democratic National Committee and the Clinton campaign.[2] Specifically, Trump was shown "classified materials . . . [establishing] 'direct links' between Vladimir Putin's government and the recent hacks and e-mail leaks."[3] According to Fox News, the hours-long briefing also lays out, more broadly, "threats to the United States and other security issues." The night of the briefing, Trump is asked if he trusts the intelligence he's just received; he responds, "Not so much from the people that have been doing it for our country."[4]

Whatever Trump's views on trusting U.S. intelligence services versus foreign intelligence services, or advice from his own national security advisers versus advice from his designated intelligence briefers, Trump's August 17 briefing activates a legal trigger under 18 U.S.C. § 2, the federal aiding and abetting statute, as post-briefing Trump has what the law considers "foreknowledge" of the legal elements of Russia's computer crimes.[5] This means that Trump cannot, at any time after August 17, "knowingly" engage in any act, verbal or physical, that would "induce" either the continuation of Russian crimes against the United States or any new crimes that are both related to their predecessors and foreseeable to Trump following the briefing.[6] Trump's legally discernible "foreknowledge" is, shortly after August 17, augmented by a second classified intelligence briefing at which he—and possibly, again, Flynn and Christie, as the "candidate is allowed to choose two people to bring with them to the briefing"—"receive[s] additional briefings on the Russian hack."[7]

The degree of specificity in Trump's first two classified national security briefings is significant. According to CNN, during the first of these briefings Trump is "personally warned . . . that foreign adversaries—including Russia—would likely attempt to infiltrate his team or gather intelligence about his campaign."[8] Moreover, not only does Trump have Russia's election interference activities explained to him in detail, but his briefers also explain to him "potential activities by China"—meaning that Trump's briefing distinguishes between Russian and Chinese threats with respect to both Trump's own campaign and attacks on the nation's elections infrastructure.[9] Finally, according to CNN law enforcement analyst Josh Campbell, formerly a supervisory special agent for the national security and criminal divisions of the FBI, at his two late-summer briefings Trump would have been "told to reach out to the FBI if they [he or anyone on his team] sensed anything suspicious."[10]

Despite these warnings and requests regarding Kremlin attempts to "infiltrate" his campaign—an infiltration Trump knew had already occurred on several fronts, including, for instance, in his aide George Papadopoulos's confession to being a Kremlin "intermediary" on March 31, 2016—there is no evidence that Trump passed any information to the U.S. intelligence community about what he and his campaign had already observed firsthand. Under the circumstances, his answers to any FBI queries on this score may have constituted an abetting of Russian crimes as well as an offense under 18 U.S.C § 1001, which prohibits making false statements to federal law enforcement officers.[11]

Despite Trump passing a legal watershed on August 17, after his classified briefings he does the following: (1) professes, at two 2016 presidential debates, to have no knowledge of whether Russia has attacked or is attacking the United States; (2) falsely declares, in May 2018, that "the FBI never warned his campaign that Russians might try to infiltrate his team"; and (3) continues to deny, well into 2017, Russian involvement in election interference. Trump's recalcitrance stands in the face of a July 26, 2016, *New York Times* article reporting that U.S. intelligence agencies "now have 'high confidence' that the Russian government was behind the theft of emails and documents from the Democratic National Committee"; Trump's August 17 briefing and its follow-up; an October 7 public statement by U.S. intelligence officials confirming that "Russia's senior-most officials . . . directed the recent compromises of e-mails from US persons and institutions"; a December 10 report that "U.S. intelligence agencies had 'concluded that Russia interfered in . . . [the] presidential election to boost Donald Trump's bid for the White House"; and a January 6, 2017, classified briefing that unfolded for Trump the entirety of the intelligence community's evidence against the Kremlin's hackers and propagandists.[12] Moreover, as the Mueller Report will note, six weeks before the July 26 *New York Times* article revealing the U.S. intelligence community's "high confidence" assessment on Russian election hacking, the "cybersecurity firm that had conducted in-house analysis for the Democratic National Committee posted a [public] announcement that Russian government hackers had infiltrated the DNC's computer and obtained access to documents."[13]

That the summer 2016 public warnings from the media, Democratic cybersecurity experts, and U.S. law enforcement about Russian election interference—as well as the substance of the private warnings Trump received in August and thereafter—reached the Trump campaign's national security advisory committee is suggested by the actions of the members of that team. On August 8, the number two official on the committee, J. D. Gordon, "decline[s] an invitation to Russian ambassador Sergey Kislyak's residence because the timing [is] 'not optimal' in view of media reports about Russian interference."[14] On August 19, Trump's campaign manager is asked to resign, ostensibly because of "media coverage scrutinizing his ties to a pro-Russian political party in Ukraine and links to Russian business," and a few weeks later the campaign "terminate[s] [Carter] Page's association with the Campaign" on the basis of his "connections to Russia."[15] On September 8, after the chairman of Trump's national security advisory committee, Jeff Sessions, has met with Russian ambassador Sergey Kislyak, Sessions declines Kislyak's invitation to dine with him at his home, on the advice of his legislative director, Sandra Luff, who tells him that he must be careful because Kislyak is an "old school KGB guy."[16] These and other similar incidents—for instance, Papadopoulos's temporary dismissal from the campaign after he gives an interview to a Russian media outlet, Interfax, in September—demonstrate that the Trump campaign broadly writ was aware of the threat posed by Russia and its agents in August and September 2016.

The Trump campaign's intermittent avoidance of visible conflicts of interest involving the Russian Federation occurs despite Trump having announced at a press conference on July 27—the day after the *New York Times* published the intelligence community's "high confidence" assessment of Kremlin involvement in the hacking of U.S. persons and entities—that he would "be looking at" the lifting of sanctions on Russia, a statement he makes while, in the same address, inviting Russian hackers to steal Hillary Clinton's emails.[17] The latter comment, a request to the Kremlin made concurrently with the inducement of possible sanctions relief, will lead "within five hours" to "a Russian intelligence service . . . targeting email accounts associated with Hillary Clinton for possible hacks," according to the Mueller Report.[18] Shortly after the press conference, during which Trump says "I have nothing to do with Russia" five times, his attorney Michael Cohen confronts him with the fact that these statements about his non-involvement with Russia are untrue—to which Trump replies that his Trump Tower Moscow plans have not yet gone to final contract. "Why mention it if it is not a deal?" he says to Cohen.[19] This late July 2016 comment to Cohen bears the additional significance of confirming that Trump believes his Trump Tower Moscow deal with Rozov to be an active negotiation, despite Cohen not having spoken about it with Kremlin officials since June.[20]

Despite the New York Times reporting in August 2016 that Trump asked Manafort to leave the campaign on August 19 because he felt the veteran politico was "low energy," and Eric Trump telling the Times that his father "just didn't want to have the distraction [of Manafort's Ukrainian ties] looming over the campaign," in fact Trump continues to be advised by Manafort long after his campaign manager "resigns."[21] According to the Mueller Report, "Despite his resignation, Manafort continued to offer advice to various Campaign officials through the November election . . . [including] Kushner, Bannon, and candidate Trump."[22] Manafort even advises the campaign, through an email in late October to Jared Kushner, on how it should handle a topic—WikiLeaks—by then intertwined with the very issues the campaign said it had separated itself from Manafort to avoid.[23]

Almost immediately after he departs the campaign on August 19, Manafort goes on a mysterious cruise in the waters off Greece with Thomas Barrack and "five friends from [Barrack's] company, Colony NorthStar."[24] According to the New York Times, the cruise is now part of a federal investigation in New York into whether "anyone from Qatar or other Middle

Eastern countries . . . contributed money, perhaps using American inter-mediaries," to either the Trump campaign, pro-Trump super PACs illegally coordinating with the Trump campaign, or Trump's post-election inaugural fund.[25] One of the men Manafort and Barrack meet with during their cruise is Hamad bin Jassim bin Jaber Al Thani, a former Qatari prime minister and, up until thirty-six months before the cruise, the director of Qatar's $230 billion sovereign wealth fund.[26] HBJ is, in August 2016, "a highly influential member of the [Qatari] governing royal family" and "one of the world's richest men."[27] Federal investigators are also looking into, apparently as part of the same sequence of events, possible illicit connections between Barrack and Rashid Al Malik, "an associate of Mr. Barrack's who heads a private investment firm in the United Arab Emirates . . . [and is] close to a key figure in the UAE's government"—though the *New York Times* report on this line of inquiry does not reveal whether the "key figure" referenced is MBZ or not.[28]

The Mueller Report notes that, after the election, Manafort travels to "the Middle East" to discuss, for a fee, "what a Trump presidency would entail."[29] The report also details a transition-period meeting between Manafort and former Russian embassy employee Georgiy Oganov—a meeting arranged by Kilimnik and Deripaska deputy Victor Boyarkin at a time when Manafort is still in touch with Trump campaign officials—focused on "Ukraine and Russia," "global politics," and "recreating [the] old friendship" between Manafort and Deripaska.[30] Three days after his meeting with the former Russian embassy staffer, Manafort emails Trump's number two national security official, K. T. McFarland, to tell her that he has "some important information" that he needs to convey to her.[31] That same week, Manafort had met in Virginia with Kilimnik and Ukrainian oligarch Serhiy Lyovochkin to again discuss the pro-Kremlin "peace plan," and its accompanying sanctions relief, that he had already discussed with Kilimnik both before and after his departure from the Trump campaign.[32] At the time of the Manafort-Kilimnik-Lyovochkin meeting, Manafort is still close enough to Trump's inner circle that the Russian-intelligence-linked Kilimnik believes Manafort might be named Trump's "'special representative' . . . [to] manage [the] process" of ending Russian sanctions and delivering eastern Ukraine to Putin. At another point during the transition, Manafort proves his continued influence with Trump's inner circle by writing Jared Kushner to tell him to find a position in the incoming administration for Manafort's banker. "On it!" Kushner replies to him in short order.[33]

One reason Manafort's August 2016 cruise with Barrack continues to be a subject of interest to federal investigators is that they suspect he may have met with Kilimnik during this trip as well, according to *Business Insider*.[34] Just as important, the cruise is seen as having possible links to a pro-Trump super PAC, Rebuilding America Now, that Manafort set up in mid-2016 at Trump's request. The super PAC was run by two men, Laurance Gay and Ken McKay, who had just weeks before taking over Rebuilding America Now been working for the Trump campaign—even though federal law requires a "120 day cooling-off period before a campaign staffer can play a role in a super PAC supporting that campaign."[35] The Campaign Legal Center, a nonpartisan, nonprofit D.C. organization focused on "holding candidates and government officials accountable regardless of political affiliation," observes that the cooling-off period mandated by federal law is intended to ensure that "a [campaign] staffer can't take a campaign's strategic plans to a super PAC and execute them with unlimited funds." The center also alleges that "at several points during the 2016 cycle, Rebuilding America Now appeared to cross legal lines prohibiting coordination with the Trump campaign. But it nonetheless raised $23 million in the 2016 cycle, and was one of the top super PACs supporting Trump's 2016 election."[36]

Two outstanding questions are whether any money flowed to Rebuilding America Now from foreign sources and whether any monies from Rebuilding America Now ended up in Manafort's pocket—the latter being one of many ways pro-Trump forces could have helped ensure Manafort's silence about campaign activities after he was separated from the campaign. Of particular interest to federal investigators, according to *Vox*, is a limited liability corporation Manafort created the very day he left the Trump campaign, just before his cruise with Barrack: Summerbreeze LLC.[37] *Vox* reports that shortly after the Manafort-Barrack cruise, Summerbreeze received a $3.5 million loan from Spruce Capital, an investment firm backed by Soviet-born businessman Alexander Rovt, a Trump donor and one of the authors of the "peace deal" Manafort began negotiating with Kremlin agents in early August and continued negotiating through early 2018; these negotiations were apparently on the Trump campaign's—and then the Trump transition team's, and then the Trump administration's—behalf, given that they occurred both during and after an eight-month period following Manafort's resignation from the campaign that he was in periodic contact with Trump himself (see chapter 8).[38]

Summerbreeze will mysteriously receive, during the presidential transition, $16 million more in loans from Federal Savings Bank of Chicago, whose CEO, Steve Calk, was a Trump economic adviser in August 2016 and reportedly was seeking an administration job—with Manafort's help—after the election.[39] Both Manafort and Spruce took actions to try to hide their transaction from federal officials, according to the *New York Daily News*.[40] Several questions remain open: whether Manafort was given millions in loans either to buy his silence or to buy his influence with the Trump team, whether he was being paid to engage in clandestine sanctions negotiations with Kremlin agents in a way that induced the Kremlin to continue committing crimes against the United States pre-election, and whether, as the *New York Times* reports, "people from Middle Eastern nations—including Qatar, Saudi Arabia, and the United Arab Emirates—used straw donors to disguise their donations" to Trump's inaugural fund, Rebuilding America Now, or, for that matter, Manafort's personal bank account.[41] Investigators reportedly are looking at, among many other unusual intersections, Al Malik's attendance at an expensive, difficult-to-access, Barrack-hosted inaugural dinner in D.C. in January 2017; during the same dinner, Kushner's Emirati adviser, Yousef al-Otaiba, was seated with K. T. McFarland, Jeff Sessions, Sheldon Adelson, and Israel's ambassador to the United States, Ron Dermer.[42]

August 2, 2016, is the day that Manafort, Trump's then-campaign manager, enters into a course of clandestine negotiations with the Kremlin on the topic of sanctions relief that will extend into 2018.[43] The day before, Trump had seemed to make reference to the "grand bargain" envisioned by

MBS and MBZ in speaking to a crowd in Columbus, Ohio: "It would be really nice if we got along with Russia and others that we don't get along with right now. And wouldn't it be nice if we teamed up with Russia and others, including surrounding [Middle Eastern] states . . . and we knocked the hell out of ISIS and got rid of these people?"[44] Manafort's meeting with Gates and Kilimnik the next day is the beginning of just such a team-up: the three men congregate at the Grand Havana Room in New York City, a private club known to be future Trump attorney Rudy Giuliani's "favorite New York City hangout spot."[45] The building in which the Grand Havana Room is located is 666 Fifth Avenue—the desperately underwater property purchased by Kushner in 2007 and now owned, to its great detriment, by Kushner Companies.[46]

By 2018, all three of the men who meet at the Grand Havana Room on August 2, 2016, will be under federal indictment for having committed crimes while working on behalf of a pro-Kremlin politician in Ukraine.[47] Kilimnik, per Gates "a former Russian intelligence officer with the GRU," had just days earlier met with Russian oligarch (and his, Manafort's, and Gates's former boss) Oleg Deripaska.[48] Kilimnik had also, days earlier, flown from Kiev to Moscow to meet with longtime Kremlin stooge and former Ukrainian president Viktor Yanukovych, the pro-Kremlin politician in whose employ all three of the men who meet at the Grand Havana Room committed federal crimes.[49]

While future federal legal filings on the Grand Havana Room meeting will be heavily redacted, a review of these court submissions reveals that "prosecutors believe Manafort lied about refusing something that Kilimnik offered at the meeting," and also lied about the "peace plan"—one of the chief subjects of discussion in the meeting—never being discussed again by Manafort and Kilimnik after August 2.[50] Concerned that the fact of their meeting will be detected, Manafort, Gates, and Kilimnik "[take] the precaution . . . of leaving [the Grand Havana Room] separately."[51]

The U.S. State Department describes Deripaska as "among the two or three oligarchs Putin turns to on a regular basis" and "a more-or-less permanent fixture on Putin's trips abroad," while for his part, Deripaska has famously said that he doesn't "separate [himself] from the state"; in his words, "I have no other interests."[52] In 2016, Deripaska and Kilimnik were willing and able to meet openly; now that Kilimnik's "former" unit, the GRU, has been formally accused of "waging 'information warfare' against U.S. politics using social media and email hacking," Kilimnik and his family have left their home in Ukraine to live "in a gated community in Khimki, the same Moscow suburb that houses the GRU unit accused by [special counsel] Mueller in an 11-count indictment in July [2018] of spearheading the hacking of Democratic emails in 2016."[53]

The August 2, 2016, Manafort-Gates-Kilimnik summit is months in the making. According to the *Guardian*, "right after Manafort joined the Trump campaign in March 2016, he and Kilimnik began emailing and brainstorming about avenues to . . . improve ties with" the Kremlin-linked Deripaska.[54] In May 2016, Kilimnik had visited the United States to see Manafort, though it's unknown whether the two men discussed sanctions relief.[55] Sometime after his hire by Trump but before mid-June 2016, Manafort—along with Rick Gates—had begun electronically transferring internal campaign polling data to Kilimnik, data that had been, according to the *New York Times*, "developed by a private polling firm" whose work product was nonpublic.[56] In July 2016, Manafort had emailed Kilimnik to tell him to offer Deripaska, on Manafort's behalf, "private briefings" on the internal workings of Trump's campaign.[57] And after their sanctions negotiations on August 2, 2016, the two men would discuss the topic again via email in December 2016; in person in January 2017; in February 2017 (possibly in person, according to a redacted special counsel filing); "in Madrid" sometime "in early 2017"; and again in the winter of 2018.[58] The volume of these discussions, as well as Manafort's willingness to lie about them at the risk of losing his cooperation deal with the federal government—an event that ultimately comes to pass—underscores both their significance to the Trump-Russia investigation and their deep entanglement with the upper echelon of Trump's presidential campaign, possibly including Trump himself.[59]

On August 3, 2016, George Nader—as *Vox* notes, a man "so close to the Kremlin that he's taken a photo with Putin"—arrives at Trump Tower for a meeting with Trump's son Don, Joel Zamel, Stephen Miller, and Erik Prince.[60] The meeting is arranged by Prince.[61] Zamel has recently asked Nader, at the St. Petersburg economic forum in Russia, to fund Psy-Group's work for the Trump campaign; at the meeting at Trump Tower, Nader says the Emiratis and Saudis are willing to assist Trump in winning his election—a statement that seems to presume, given that Zamel is one of the meeting attendees, that Nader, on behalf of MBZ and MBS, has accepted Zamel's request for the Saudis and Emiratis to fund his initiative on the Trump campaign's behalf. Prince has known Nader as a geopolitical power broker for more than a decade, and indeed worked with him in Iraq at a time Nader was negotiating with the Kremlin on the Iraqis' behalf; he therefore likely knows, as *Vox* observes, that Nader's "extensive personal ties to Russia" include the fact that he has "traveled to Russia, done business with Russia, and developed relationships with Russian President Vladimir Putin's inner circle."[62] Nader's network of associations with the Russian government, adds *Vox*, "raises questions of whether he could have benefited financially from helping establish more harmonious ties between the US and Russia. And it raises the possibility that he could've acted as an informal broker on behalf of Russia during those meetings [before and after the election] or provided expert counsel on how to get in touch with the Kremlin."[63] The *New York Times* notes that "Mr. Nader's visits to Russia and the work Mr. Zamel's companies did for the Russians have both been a subject of interest" to federal investigators.[64]

Nader presents himself to Donald Trump Jr. as far more than a potential Russia adviser, however, given that he brings Zamel with him to the meeting—a man who has done substantial work in the past not merely for Russian oligarchs generally, but for at least one (Deripaska) who self-identifies as a Kremlin agent. In October 2018, the *Daily Beast* will note that special counsel Robert Mueller questioned Zamel about his attendance at this August 2016 meeting, as the overtures Zamel makes to the Trump campaign at Trump Tower on August 3 "could have broken federal election laws."[65] *Haaretz* reports that, aside from any general-election plot Nader may have presented to Trump Jr. on August 3, the "secret plan" Nader pitched to Trump's son on that date to "destabilize the Iranian regime

[is] an objective now being pursued, despite their denials, by both Israel and the United States."[66] That the "plan" Nader presents to Trump Jr. is the Red Sea conspirators' "grand bargain" is suggested by the fact that its ultimate ambition—as is the case with the grand bargain—is to weaken Iran and degrade its ability to threaten its neighbors directly or through proxies.

At the August 2016 Trump Tower meeting Nader is acting, per the *New York Times*, as an "intermediary for Saudi Arabia's crown prince, Mohammed bin Salman," and as "a political adviser to the de facto ruler of the United Arab Emirates," MBZ, meaning that based on his established international connections he is in a position to act as an agent or interlocutor for at least three nations—Saudi Arabia, the UAE, and Russia—in addition to having a long history of ties to the Israeli government.[67]

As the meeting occurs, Trump International Golf Club Dubai, in the UAE, is under construction and just six months from its grand opening. The *New York Times* will report in 2018 that the Trump Organization's massive golf club project "needs permits from the UAE"—a government controlled by Nader's boss, MBZ—"to function."[68] In August 2016, while his father is on the campaign trail, Trump Jr. is the Trump Organization representative in charge of the Trump International Golf Club Dubai project, and will attend its grand opening personally in February 2017.[69] CNN notes that "the Dubai-based property developer [for Trump International Golf Club Dubai] stood by Trump even in the wake of comments Trump made about banning Muslims from entering the United States." Notably, despite two Emiratis having participated in the September 11, 2001, terrorist attacks in New York City—and foreign terror being the primary stated basis for President Trump's eventual designation of seven countries as subject to a travel ban—the United Arab Emirates will not be included on the Trump administration's 2017 travel ban list.[70] Citizens of the seven nations subjected to the ban, unlike the UAE, "have not carried out any deadly terrorist attacks in the United States," per *Politifact*.[71]

According to the *Atlantic*, federal law enforcement's interest in Nader's meetings with Trump aides and associates focuses on "whether the United Arab Emirates funneled money into Trump's campaign"—not merely his transition, administration, or future Trump Organization projects—"in re-turn for political influence."[72] The magazine's reporting appears to confirm that the pre-election collusive assistance Nader offered Trump Jr. in Au-gust 2016 on behalf of the United Arab Emirates and Saudi Arabia, and possibly either Israel or Russia or both, was indeed monetary. The *Atlantic* also confirms, citing a "person with knowledge of their [the Nader-MBZ] relationship," that Nader was acting as "the crown prince's 'messenger'" during the 2016 presidential campaign.[73]

That Nader's August 3 attempt to work his way into Trump's inner circle goes well is an understatement. As *New York* magazine reports, "The [August 3] meeting clearly got Nader into Trumpworld. He went on to frequently meet with members of Trump's inner circle [during the general election campaign], including son-in-law Jared Kushner, national security advisor Michael Flynn, and Trump campaign chairman Steve Bannon. His relationship with these top officials . . . intensified in the final weeks of the election."[74] According to the *New York Times*, federal investigators will come to worry that in the final months of the 2016 presidential campaign Nader was doing more than just seeking to give top Trump campaign offi-cials advice; per the *Times*, after his May 2017 appointment Robert Mueller "pressed witnesses for information about any possible attempts by the Emi-ratis to buy political influence by directing money to support Mr. Trump during the presidential campaign."[75] Indeed, between his August 3 meeting with Trump Jr. and Election Day, and then on into the transition period, Nader is "embraced as an ally" by the Trump campaign.[76] Nader's longtime connection to Zamel, and Zamel's repeated meetings with Rick Gates in spring 2016, leaves open the possibility that Nader had, like Zamel, met with Gates first, prior to August 2016, in order to gain access to the Trump family. Consistent with this possibility is the fact that in May 2019, Gates, by now a cooperating federal witness, sees his sentencing hearing delayed for a sixth time because he is still working on "ongoing investigations"—with one of these investigations, per the *Daily Beast*, being a federal probe of "possible Middle Eastern election influence."[77]

Whereas Nader's offer to the Trump campaign, according to the *New York Times*, is a broad one—he tells Trump's son that "the princes who le[a]d

Saudi Arabia and the United Arab Emirates [are] eager to help his father win election as president"—Zamel's possibly related offer is more tightly focused, involving "an influence operation to help Trump win the election."[78] Both offers appear to be illegal, however.

On August 19, Paul Manafort resigns as Trump's campaign manager, though the move is a cosmetic one only. As the *New Yorker* will later report, "FBI wiretaps show that Manafort continued his association with Trump long after he resigned. Manafort was also in touch with his business partner," Rick Gates, who after Manafort resigns remains on the campaign but "transition[s] to become [campaign] liaison with the Republican National Committee," according to NBC News; post-inauguration, Gates will come to be regarded as a "White House insider."[79]

As the Trump campaign's RNC liaison, Gates will come into regular contact with Elliott Broidy, vice chairman of the Trump Victory Committee, a joint endeavor of the Trump campaign and the RNC. Gates's association with Broidy will continue well past Election Day and Trump's inauguration, with the two men being linked in a scheme to get Broidy defense contracts in Romania and in the financing of a film whose producers will be accused of defrauding investors.[80]

In May 2017, *Politico* will reveal that after his firing Manafort not only stays in touch with the campaign, and later the presidential transition team, but even advises Trump staffers—and Trump himself—on how to navigate the FBI's investigation into Trump-Russia ties.[81] As the digital media outlet writes in an article entitled "Manafort Advised Trump Team on Russia Scandal," Manafort "remained in contact with the president and his aides" even after the FBI's Russia probe began, "brief[ing]" Trump and his team on details of his own ties to Russian interests. Per *Politico*, these Trump-Manafort conversations include discussion of Ukraine as well as Manafort's many conversations with Konstantin Kilimnik, which had focused on sanctions relief and a pro-Kremlin Ukrainian "peace deal."[82] Trump will later tell federal investigators, under penalty of a federal indictment for making false statements to law enforcement, that he "do[es] not remember Mr. Manafort communicating to me any particular positions Ukraine or Russia would want the United States to support."[83] As to whether Trump's statement to the special counsel's office is true, only he and Manafort would know. In January 2018, Trump will tell friends privately that he believes he can escape legal liability in the special counsel's Russia investigation because "he's decided that a key witness in the Russia probe, Paul Manafort, isn't going to 'flip' and sell him out."[84]

Among the many topics on which Manafort will advise Trump administration officials is how Trump and his team can best "distract [public] attention from the parallel FBI and congressional Russia probes."[85] But even in the approximately ninety days between his resignation in August 2016 and Election Day, Manafort "continue[s] discussing campaign strategy with people on the campaign," according to *Politico*, among them Jared Kushner, and will in many respects maintain his previous campaign duties by staying in "regular contact with key state directors" within the Trump campaign operation.[86] Three Manafort associates will confirm to *Politico* that after Trump's inauguration Manafort spoke directly to the president on a number of occasions, a practice that appeared to end only in March or April 2017.[87] According to one of these sources, Manafort spends his post-inauguration calls with Trump offering "political input" just as an adviser would.[88] By 2017, Trump has known Manafort for twenty-nine years, and Manafort has lived in the same building as Trump for eleven years; as noted earlier, Manafort moved into Trump Tower the same year he began working for Oleg Deripaska, and immediately after signing "a $10 million [deal] with Deripaska . . . to 'influence politics, business dealings and news coverage inside the United States, Europe and former Soviet republics to benefit President Vladimir Putin's government."[89] On the evidence of his post-resignation activities, Manafort continued serving that function into 2017 and beyond—though the means of his compensation, if any, is a matter of dispute.

The Trump campaign's clandestine summer 2016 efforts to secure the Clinton emails allegedly stolen by the Russians continue after Manafort's departure—despite the fact that if the campaign were to receive the emails, it would be not only receiving stolen property but potentially aiding and abetting the computer crimes that led to the theft of the emails in the first instance. Alongside separate efforts to secure Clinton's emails executed by Trump national security adviser Joseph Schmitz—a man once caught running a Saudi-financed scheme to sell Russian weapons in Syria—and longtime Trump friend and adviser Roger Stone, another effort, led by a GOP operative named Peter W. Smith, had begun in June 2016 and involved searching the "dark web" for Clinton's emails.[90]

In late July, his public comments on the matter notwithstanding, Trump had privately broached the sort of effort Smith had been involved in for weeks, "ask[ing] individuals affiliated with his Campaign to find the deleted Clinton emails," according to the Mueller Report.[91] The report indicates that in July and August 2016 Trump issued this order to his staff "repeatedly," and that the order led directly to his chief national security advisor, Flynn, contacting at least three individuals outside the campaign who had already started looking for the emails—including Smith.[92] Smith had by then been periodically in contact with a former Senate staffer, Barbara Ledeen—wife of Michael Ledeen, another shadow Trump national security adviser—who had written to Smith of eagerly seeking "classified" emails "purloined by our enemies," even if doing so meant dealing, through intermediaries, with "various foreign services."[93] Barbara Ledeen believed the effort to acquire stolen Clinton emails would be worth the risk of unsavory contacts with America's enemies if the intelligence services of (among others) the Russians had "reassemble[d] the [Clinton] server's email content" after stealing it and would be willing to provide even one stolen email to either her or Smith—a development that, notwithstanding it constituting the receipt of stolen classified material from a foreign intelligence service, would be "catastrophic to the Clinton campaign," in Ledeen's view.[94]

Smith had ultimately declined to work with Ledeen, but only because, in his estimation, her "initiative was not viable at th[e] time."[95] After Trump's order to Flynn, however, Smith changes his mind; just as Trump's July 27 request for additional Russian hacks against U.S. targets leads immediately to additional Russian hacks against U.S. targets, Trump's order that his staffers seek Clinton's stolen emails leads, through Flynn, to Smith intensifying his effort to find Clinton's emails. Beginning in July 2016, Smith takes all the necessary steps to do so: he establishes a limited-liability corporation, KLS Research LLC, for the purposes of funding a massive, monthslong hunt for the emails; he raises tens of thousands of dollars from Republican donors to fund his work, including assisting in directing money from Trump adviser Erik Prince toward Ledeen's ongoing efforts; he tells friends and associates his efforts are "coordinated" with the Trump campaign; and he ultimately reveals to those assisting him, and to those seeking to fund his work, that he is planning to meet with, as summarized by the Mueller Report, "hackers with 'ties and affiliations to Russia' who ha[ve] access to the [Clinton] emails."[96]

During the weekend of August 27, 2016, Smith meets with "several groups of hackers" at a suburban Washington hotel, only two of which (out of five) he identifies as Russian; he is just eleven days from producing documentation claiming that his efforts to find Clinton's emails are known to top Trump advisers Mike Flynn, Steve Bannon, Sam Clovis, and Kellyanne Conway—all of whom, per Smith, he is "coordinat[ing] [with] to the extent permitted as an independent expenditure."[97] According to the *Wall Street Journal*, Smith's Washington meetings occur at a time when he "and his associates" say they are "in touch with several groups of hackers, including two from Russia" who they believe are "tied to the Moscow government."[98] The *Journal* notes also that during this period "reports from intelligence agencies . . . tell of Russian hackers discussing how to get emails from Mrs. Clinton's server and transmit them to Mr. Flynn via an intermediary."[99] Whether Smith was meant by the Kremlin or its agents to be the Russian Federation's chosen intermediary with Flynn is unknown, though it is clear, according to the *Journal*, that by the tail end of his monthslong, Trump-campaign-"coordinated" search for Clinton's emails, Smith had raised $100,000 from Republican donors for his illicit efforts.[100]

Smith, called by the *Wall Street Journal* "a veteran political operative with access to wealthy donors and deep connections in Republican politics," spends months on his "single-minded quest to find incriminating information about Mrs. Clinton," continuing "even after government officials warn[ ] of Russian involvement in U.S. politics."[101] After he meets with two groups of Russian hackers on August 28, he sends Trump campaign national co-chair Sam Clovis and others an encrypted email that says he is "just finishing two days of sensitive meetings here in DC with involved groups to poke and probe" on "Secretary Clinton's unsecured private email server."[102] He tells Trump's national co-chair that he has determined Clinton's home email server was "hacked with ease by both State-related players . . . and private mercenaries," and that the stolen emails will be released by one or more of several "parties with varying interests . . . ahead of the election."[103] While it is unknown who else besides Clovis receives Smith's August 28 email—or who, more broadly, Smith is in contact with about his efforts besides Flynn and Clovis—Smith has, by late August, already represented to donors that his "coordination" with the Trump campaign also involves not just Bannon (the Trump campaign CEO) and Conway (Trump's post-Manafort campaign manager), but also Jerome Corsi, a friend of Trump adviser Roger Stone who will ultimately enter into a joint defense agreement with Trump.[104] The special counsel's office confirms that Smith's efforts to find Clinton's emails had begun before Trump ordered Flynn to find them, and that Smith, while in contact with multiple members of the Trump campaign, came up with his own game plan for achieving the results Trump wanted—meaning that, in the view of the Mueller Report, technically the campaign had neither "initiated" nor "directed" Smith's efforts, even if the evidence suggests that Trump's repeated directives to his staff materially encouraged and advanced those efforts.[105]

Smith does receive direct assistance in his efforts from Trump adviser Erik Prince, however, as Prince "provide[s] funding to hire a tech adviser to ascertain the authenticity of . . . emails" Barbara Ledeen brings to Smith's attention in September 2016.[106] Prince's expert determines that the emails are fakes, but this does not deter Prince from falsely telling an interviewer from Steve Bannon's Breitbart media outlet two months later that local law enforcement in New York City has found "those 650,000 emails" from Clinton's email server, and that the emails contain, per Prince's false account, "State Department emails . . . [and] a lot of other really damning criminal information, including money laundering, including the fact that Hillary went to this sex island with convicted pedophile Jeffrey Epstein . . . [and] Bill Clinton went there more than 20 times . . . [while] Hillary Clinton went there at least six times. The amount of garbage that they found in these emails, of criminal activity by Hillary, by her immediate circle, and even by other Democratic members of Congress was so disgusting they gave it to the FBI and they said, 'We're going to go public with this if you don't reopen the investigation and you don't do the right thing with timely indictments.'"[107] Everything Prince says to his interviewer is untrue; what is unknown is whether Prince has taken his information from the fake emails provided to him by Russian hackers through Ledeen and Smith. An investigative report by *Rolling Stone* in November 2017 will reveal that Russian sources were indeed behind much of the disinformation Prince spread on Breitbart pre-election.[108] Nor is Prince's pre-election promotion of Russian disinformation exclusive to him within the Trump campaign and Trump's circle of advisers; Prince's Russian disinformation-laced interview with Breitbart will be retweeted on Twitter by Michael Flynn, and its substance tweeted out by Donald Trump Jr.[109]

Throughout Smith's search for Clinton's emails, the veteran GOP operative acts with great secrecy, suggesting that he is aware his endeavors run the risk of violating federal law. He uses a fake name ("Robert Tyler"); raises money under the false pretense that it is going toward a scholarship fund for Russian students; uses "draft" emails to communicate with his co-conspirators over a shared server; and utilizes both encrypted email and multiple telephone numbers.[110] A longtime friend and confidant of Smith's, Thomas Lipscomb, says that across several phone calls with Smith the octogenarian political operative dropped "big names" whom he said he was "calling for help"—a roster of significant personalities that Lipscomb confirms included Michael Flynn, who had by then been ordered by Trump to pursue the issue.[111] Smith's claim to have spoken with Flynn by telephone will be partially substantiated by later reporting noting that Flynn and Smith had "established" a "working relationship" apart from the Clinton email issue by November 2015 at the latest, with the *Journal* quoting a friend of Smith's as saying that the relationship was a "business relationship."[112] Smith even "told associates . . . that he was using the retired general's connections to help him on the email project."[113] More troublingly, a friend of Smith's, John Szobocsan, will claim that he and Smith spoke to Flynn "the day he [Flynn] left for his [December 2015] trip to Moscow."[114] In a July 2017 interview with the *Wall Street Journal*, Smith will imply that Flynn was indeed "aware of his efforts."[115]

Emails and documents associated with Smith's research—an encompassing and sophisticated effort that swept into its net "technical experts, lawyers, and a private investigator in Europe who spoke Russian," as well as "two controversial alt-right activists . . . journalist-turned-entrepreneur Charles Johnson and his former business partner Pax Dickinson"—identify Flynn Intel Group and Michael Flynn's son Michael Flynn Jr. as "allies in the operation."[116] Whatever the Trump campaign may have believed about Smith's efforts, the Mueller Report casts some doubt on whether Smith indeed met with Russian hackers, though it does not issue the same caveat with respect to Barbara Ledeen, with whom Smith coordinated and whose connection to Trump's national security advisory corps, via her husband, is far more direct than Smith's. The *Guardian* describes Ledeen as a "friend" of Flynn's and her husband, Michael—a Trump national security adviser alongside Flynn during the transition, and like Flynn associate Bud McFarlane, an infamous figure from the Iran-Contra scandal—as a "confidant" of the retired general who also co-authored a book with him in 2016. These connections suggest that Flynn may have been aware of Barbara Ledeen's outreach to foreign hackers (whether Russian state actors or, as Peter W. Smith would later discuss, non-Russian "private mercenaries") as early as the beginning of her efforts in 2015—prior to Flynn and Flynn Jr.'s trip to see Sergey Kislyak in Washington and Flynn's dinner in Moscow with Putin, and as Flynn was being recruited by the Israeli cyberespionage mercenaries of Psy-Group.[117]

As for Smith's representations that he had contact with Clovis, Conway, and Bannon, *Politico* will report that Jonathan Safron, a former Smith assistant, said that Smith "spoke to him of knowing Clovis, who was a well-known conservative activist . . . before becoming co-chairman of Trump's campaign, and that he had seen Smith email Clovis about matters unrelated to Clinton's emails."[118] Smith's connection to Bannon, if any, is unknown, though one of his key partners in searching for Clinton's emails, Charles Johnson, was a former reporter for Breitbart, and Smith's emails reveal that he had previously been in touch with Matt Boyle, the Washington bureau chief for the digital media outlet (for which Bannon was executive chairman until leaving to be CEO of the Trump campaign).[119] Johnson's statement to *Politico* on whether Smith knew Bannon, a man Johnson concedes Smith very much wanted to meet, is oddly equivocal: "I sort of demurred on some of that," he says when asked if he facilitated contacts between the two men.[120] Johnson does put out a call to a "hidden oppo network" of right-wing researchers to help Smith, and later notes that "the magnitude of what [Smith] was trying to do was kind of impressive. He had people running around Europe, people talking to Guccifer [2.0, a digital persona operated by Russian military intelligence]."[121] As for Conway, Trump's fall 2016 campaign manager will tell the *Journal* that she had indeed spoken to Smith at certain points in the past but did not do so during the presidential campaign.[122] (In January 2017, Conway will infamously coin the phrase "alternative facts" in explaining the Trump administration's statements on the size of the new president's inaugural crowd; Dictionary.com defines "alternative facts" as "falsehoods, untruths, [or] delusions," while *USA Today* explains Conway's coinage as meaning "arguments used to support claims that do not conform to objective reality. Traditionally known as false or misleading claims; also, lies.")[123]

In May 2017, Peter W. Smith dies under suspicious circumstances, just days after disclosing his clandestine, "coordinated" efforts to acquire Clinton's emails to the *Wall Street Journal*.[124] The note Smith leaves behind in a Minnesota hotel room, reading in part "NO FOUL PLAY WHATSOEVER," will cause consternation to journalists because of statements made thereafter by retired Wall Street financier Charles Ortel, a friend of Smith's who says "he spoke with Mr. Smith on the phone in the hours before his death about a new project to brief the Obama Foundation on and warn its leaders against the mistakes they believed were made by the Clinton Foundation. According to Mr. Ortel, Mr. Smith sounded excited, and he began brainstorming who to contact and how to proceed."[125] Hours

later, Smith was dead by what was officially ruled a "suicide."[126] The ruling, which hinges in part on supposed evidence of Smith having long
planned his own death—for instance, the fact that he "left a carefully prepared file of documents, including a statement . . . in which he said he was
in ill health and a life insurance policy was expiring"—will be contradicted
by Ortel's insistence that just hours before his death Smith was "excited"
about an upcoming project.[127]

In October 2018, the *Wall Street Journal* will report that not only was
Smith excited and optimistic about a new venture mere hours before
his "suicide," but that he had also, just weeks earlier, according to statements he made to multiple friends, "finally obtained the missing [Clinton]
emails"—an "all-consuming" mission, his friends said, which, by the time
of his death in July 2017, he had been working on for over a year.[128] Just
ten days before his death Smith detailed his efforts for the *Journal*, seemingly willing to endure the inevitable publicity that would follow.[129] Indeed,
Smith was so energized by his hunt for Clinton's emails that even well
after the presidential election, in December 2016, he was emailing Ortel
an update on what he called the "Clinton Email Reconnaissance Initiative," revealing that his "team" had come across "multiple individuals"
who had stolen Clinton emails in the fall of 2016.[130] He told these friends
that he had advised such individuals to send the emails to WikiLeaks
for release; Smith had, in the past, "claimed ties with" Julian Assange's
organization.[131] Asked whether it had ever had any contact with Smith,
WikiLeaks, "citing a policy of not disclosing its sources," "decline[s] to
say," per *Politico*.[132] Smith's optimism about future opportunities extended
far enough into 2017 that following Trump's inauguration the veteran
GOP operative was in contact not only with Flynn but also with defense
secretary Jim Mattis, looking for "a possible way into [the] cybersecurity
[industry] to involve Lt. Gen. Mike Flynn."[133] The *Journal* notes that "other
emails that Mr. Flynn is copied on"—the newspaper does not note their
dates but says it has seen them—"show Mr. Smith either communicating
directly with high-level Trump administration officials and allies or discussing such connections."[134]

Longtime Trump friend and adviser Roger Stone also spends the period from June 2016 through Election Day trying to get access to Clinton's stolen emails through clandestine means—or, failing that, to get sufficient information about when the Kremlin will leak the emails that he can pass this information on to the GOP candidate himself. Trump and Stone have known each other for decades, with Stone intermittently doing consulting work for Trump. During these courses of consultation, the terms of their association are clear: Trump is the boss and Stone the subordinate. In 2000, for instance, Stone assisted Trump in preventing Native American casinos from coming to New York, as Trump believed the new gambling facilities would threaten his own gambling operations in Atlantic City. Trump's campaign required Stone to engage in a bevy of the former Nixon aide's self-described "dirty tricks"; when Stone was later deposed in the perhaps inevitable civil lawsuit, he "admitted under oath that everything he did with this [anti-casino] campaign was approved by Trump."[135] As Stone's longtime business partner Paul Manafort will put it in the documentary film *Get Me Roger Stone*, "Roger's relationship with Trump has been so interconnected that it's hard to define what's Roger and what's Donald."[136] In his answers to questions from the special counsel's office, Trump will state, under penalty of a federal indictment for making false statements to law enforcement, "I spoke by telephone to Roger Stone from time to time during the [2016 presidential] campaign. I have no recollection of the specifics of any conversations I had with Mr. Stone between June 1, 2016 and November 8, 2016."[137]

The part of Trump's statement to the special counsel's office on Roger Stone that is readily confirmable is that during the 2016 primary and general election campaigns, Stone and Trump were indeed in regular contact—even after Stone ceased holding any official position in the Trump campaign in August 2015.[138] In a 2018 court document, Robert Mueller will refer to Stone, as summarized by the *Washington Post*, as "someone understood to be in regular contact with senior Trump campaign officials [in 2016], 'including with then-candidate Donald J. Trump.'"[139] The *Post* recounts that "the calls [to Stone from Trump] almost always came deep into the night. Caller ID labeled them 'unknown,' but Roger Stone said he knew to pick up quickly during those harried months of the 2016 presidential campaign.

There would be a good chance that the voice on the other end of the line would belong to his decades-long friend—the restless, insomniac candidate Donald Trump—dialing from a blocked phone number."[140] Stone's candor in acknowledging that Trump uses a blocked phone number contrasts with that of Trump's son Don, who will tell the Senate Judiciary Committee in September 2017, under penalty (like his father months hence) of a federal indictment for lying to Congress, that though he speaks to his father often, he has no idea if Trump Sr.'s calls show up on his phone as originating from a blocked number.[141] The issue of whether candidate Trump used a blocked number during the 2016 campaign will become significant during the course of the special counsel's investigation, given that, in the midst of Trump Jr.'s telephone discussions with Emin Agalarov about the June 2016 meeting at Trump Tower—a meeting that involved multiple Kremlin agents—Trump's son on at least two occasions makes calls to or receives calls from blocked numbers.[142]

Stone's account of speaking regularly to Trump Sr. during his presidential run is supported by phone and contact logs given to Mueller by the Trump Organization, which show "multiple calls between the then-candidate and Stone in 2016," though the newspaper adds that "the records are not a complete log of their contacts—Stone [says] . . . Trump at times called him from other people's homes."[143] In November 2016, Stone reveals that the two men have been speaking once a week for some time; according to the incomplete records turned over by Trump to the special counsel, "they spoke from 'time to time' during 2016. . . . A handful of calls were lengthy."[144] Since entering the White House, Trump has often lied to his advisers about whether he speaks to Stone, telling many of them that "he no longer talks to Stone" even though "people close to [him]" tell the *Post* that he does, in fact, "occasionally talk[ ] to him."[145] Why Trump wants or needs his staff to believe he does not speak to his close friend and adviser is unclear; while investigators do not know what was said in any Trump-Stone phone calls, Trump has supplied written answers to federal investigators claiming that he never spoke with Stone about WikiLeaks releasing harmful information on Clinton or the Democrats.[146]

What is clear is that in the final months of the presidential campaign, Stone does in fact have information related to WikiLeaks to relay to Trump if he so chooses. On August 2, 2016, a friend of Stone's, Jerome Corsi, calls him to tell him that "WikiLeaks [is] planning a major release of 'very damaging' material [to Clinton]."[147] Less than twenty-four hours later, Stone calls Trump; he has since claimed that not only did he not tell Trump that "very damaging" information about Clinton was about to be released, but he never broached the subject of WikiLeaks with his longtime friend at all—despite Trump having just days earlier told his staff that he wanted as much information about any stolen Clinton emails as possible.[148]

The backstory to the August 2 Stone-Corsi call is a telling one. On July 25, 2016, Stone heard from a Fox News reporter that WikiLeaks was planning "a massive dump of Clinton emails relating to the Clinton Foundation in September."[149] Stone immediately wrote Corsi to issue an order to him: "Get to [Assange] [a]t Ecuadoran Embassy in London and get the pending [WikiLeaks] emails . . . they deal with the [Clinton] Foundation, allegedly."[150] While Corsi will subsequently tell federal investigators that he did nothing with Stone's request, it will ultimately be found, and Corsi will eventually admit, that he forwarded Stone's urgent request—which may or may not have been a by-product of Trump's contemporaneous and equally urgent request on the same subject—to a Trump adviser in London, Ted Malloch.[151] Corsi demanded that Malloch "put [him] in touch with Assange," simultaneously "suggest[ing] that individuals in the 'orbit' of U.K. politician Nigel Farage might be able to contact Assange" and asking Malloch "if [he] knew" those individuals.[152]

It is eight days after Corsi writes Malloch that he writes Stone back to inform him that "WikiLeaks possesse[s] information that would be damaging to Hillary Clinton's campaign and plan[s] to release it in October."[153] He will later tell the special counsel's office that he is "convinced that his efforts had caused WikiLeaks to release the emails [of Clinton campaign chairman John Podesta] when they did."[154] Whether or not this is correct, Mueller will in fact subsequently investigate Malloch over his "frequent appearances on RT, which U.S. intelligence authorities have called Russia's principal propaganda arm"; per the *Guardian*, the "Special Counsel's alleged focus on RT is important because the Russian news channel also has a close relationship with WikiLeaks founder Julian Assange."[155] The British media outlet reports that court filings in the United States, as well as visitor logs at the Ecuadoran embassy in London, where Assange lived for years until his arrest in April 2019, "show that RT staff met and interviewed Assange on the same day—August 2, 2016—that Roger Stone, the self-described 'dirty trickster' and longtime Trump associate who had previously bragged about having special access to WikiLeaks, was passed information about Assange's plans."[156]

While the *Guardian* calls Malloch an "unpaid adviser" to Trump's 2016 campaign, Malloch himself will write, in a January 2017 book, that he has known Trump for decades and has given to several charities to which Trump is linked.[157] As for whether Malloch indeed knows Assange, the evidence suggests that he had previously told Stone and Corsi that he knew the WikiLeaks founder, with Malloch making the claim during a late February or early March 2016 dinner with the two men in New York City.[158] The *Guardian* notes that Malloch was, during the campaign, a vocal advocate on RT and elsewhere for "friendlier U.S.-Russia relations" and predicted that Trump would, if elected, "soften U.S. economic restrictions on Moscow."[159] During a February 2017 RT appearance—even as Stone's business associate Manafort was working on getting sanctions lifted through a Russia-Ukraine "peace deal"—Malloch said, "If those sanctions were removed, would not the world be a better place?"[160]

On October 7, 2016, the day the now-infamous *Access Hollywood* tape of Trump confessing to being a serial sexual assailant was released, WikiLeaks released the first of thirty-three tranches of emails authored by Clinton campaign chairman John Podesta—an action that had the effect of bumping the *Access Hollywood* tape from the top of certain newscasts in the days ahead.[161] But for the partial distraction of the WikiLeaks release, the Trump campaign might have ended on October 10, with then Speaker of the House Paul Ryan (R-WI) telling congressional Republicans in a "rare" all-members conference call that "they could abandon Trump" and no longer needed to "remain loyal to the party's [presidential] candidate due to the deeply disturbing tape of Trump's 2005 comments."[162]

Six days before the October 7 WikiLeaks release, comedian and radio host Randy Credico had written Roger Stone a text message that read, "Hillary's campaign will die this week."[163] Indeed, despite the *Access Hollywood* tape, NBC News will note that it was the WikiLeaks releases in October 2016 that "alter[ed] the trajectory of the presidential race."[164] Between October 7 and November 7, WikiLeaks will release all thirty-three tranches of Podesta emails, and the organization's work will be cited by Trump in campaign speeches at least 137 times.[165]

Nevertheless, the revelation of the sexually explicit *Access Hollywood* tape will augment the already significant anxiety within the Trump campaign about the potential for information regarding Trump's personal conduct to be released pre-election.[166] Ten days before the election, on October 30, Trump receives a significant scare in this respect. Giorgi Rtskhiladze, a Soviet-born U.S. citizen who is a mutual business associate of both Trump and Aras Agalarov, texts Trump's attorney Michael Cohen to assure him that he has "stopped [the] flow of tapes from Russia."[167] Rtskhiladze will tell the special counsel that his reference to multiple Russia-produced videos of interest to the Trump campaign involves "compromising tapes of Trump rumored to be held by persons associated with [Aras Agalarov's] Russian real estate conglomerate Crocus Group," a family and company whose last contact with Trump in Russia was in 2013 during the Crocus Group–hosted Miss Universe pageant.[168] Rtskhiladze has himself been in business with Trump since 2011 on projects in the former Soviet republics of Georgia and Kazakhstan.[169] More recently, he has been in contact with Cohen to discuss the Trump Tower Moscow proposal Cohen was, in the fall of 2015, negotiating—with the aid of his friend Felix Sater—with both Rozov and the Kremlin. Rtskhiladze was also working with Cohen on the possibility of a Trump-Putin summit in New York City, telling another business associate via email that he wanted to help Trump land a project that "would definitely receive . . . worldwide attention."[170] Rtskhiladze then assisted Cohen in drafting a communication to the mayor of Moscow—whom Rtskhiladze called the "second guy in Russia [after Putin]"—whose support for the Trump-Rozov tower Rtskhiladze told Cohen was essential. In one of Rtskhiladze's other fall 2015 emails to Cohen, the businessman seemed to echo what the Kremlin-connected Sater had been saying to Cohen for many weeks: that from the perspective of the Russian government, a Trump Tower Moscow would stand as a monument to the (in the United States, largely illegal) juxtaposition of personal profit and national policymaking, a "symbol of stronger economic, business, and cultural relationships between New York and Moscow and therefore the United States and the Russian Federation."[171]

Less than ninety days after Rtskhiladze texts Cohen about compromising "videos" in the possession of Trump's Russian business partners the Agalarovs, the BBC will report that, according to "active duty CIA officers dealing with the [Trump-Russia counterintelligence investigation] case file," the Kremlin is in possession of compromising "audio and video" tapes of Trump from both his 2013 stay at the Ritz Moscow as a guest of the Crocus Group and from another date in St. Petersburg; according to the officers, there is "more than one tape," from "more than one date," involving "more than one place," and the tapes are "of a sexual nature."[172] That Trump knew the Kremlin or its cutouts were claiming to have such tapes in the days before the 2016 election—at a time he was promoting a foreign policy that greatly pleased Putin—is confirmed by Cohen, who will tell the special counsel's office that he "spoke to Trump about the issue [before Election Day] after receiving the texts from Rtskhiladze."[173] In the months after the January 2017 BBC report on Kremlin *kompromat*, various British media outlets will reveal several independent witnesses, including witnesses from both the Ritz Moscow and the Trump Organization, who step forward to confirm individual elements of the BBC report and the version of the report contained in Christopher Steele's dossier of raw intelligence on Trump's Russian activities.[174]

After the November 2016 election, Jerome Corsi attempts to scrub his computer of his emails to Stone, deleting all his email correspondence from prior to October 11—a move that mirrors the apparent destruction by Steve Bannon and Erik Prince of all the texts on their phones that predate March 2017.[175] During the period of time covered by Corsi's digital expurgation, Stone contacted Corsi seeking to have him falsely state, in a public forum, that Randy Credico, not Corsi himself, was Stone's "intermediary" with WikiLeaks.[176] In addition to eventually acquiring all Corsi's saved and deleted digital evidence, the special counsel's office also uncovers information suggesting that Stone made private statements in the fall of 2016 about the timing of WikiLeaks releases to Steve Bannon, who was at the time the chief executive officer of Trump's campaign.[177] According to the *Washington Post*, federal investigators have asked Bannon about "private comments [Stone made] that matched his public declarations of having knowledge of WikiLeaks' plans."[178] It is unclear why (or if) Stone would make such comments to Bannon but not to Trump himself.

In late 2018, after Mueller shows Corsi a draft of a statement of offense (a document attendant to a federal indictment) that he intends to file against him for lying to federal investigators, Corsi will reveal he has secretly been in a "joint defense agreement" with Donald Trump's legal team for months—for what reason is unknown—and that the deal "was intended to be kept from public view."[179] The *New York Times* will report that "Corsi's dealings with Mr. Mueller's prosecutors have caused alarm among the president's legal team . . . [because] prosecutors claimed [in Corsi's draft statement of offense] that Mr. Corsi understood that Mr. Stone was 'in regular contact with senior members of the Trump campaign, including with then-candidate Donald J. Trump' when he asked Mr. Corsi in late July 2016 to 'get to' Julian Assange, the founder of WikiLeaks."[180] Despite being in a long-standing joint defense agreement with Corsi—an agreement implying that, insofar as Trump and Corsi are subjects and even targets of various lines of inquiry in the Russia investigation, the two men's legal interests are aligned—Trump says in November 2018, "I don't know Corsi."[181]

The revelation of a secret legal arrangement between Trump and Corsi follows a pattern of covert contacts, by Trump and his legal team, with witnesses in the Russia investigation, with the *New York Times* revealing in November 2018 that Trump's attorneys were also secretly in an information-sharing arrangement with Manafort's attorneys from the moment Manafort began cooperating with federal investigators—at which point Trump surrogates began publicly musing about the possibility of pardoning Manafort, even as Trump tweeted repeatedly about the value of loyalty.[182] Privately, according to the Mueller Report, the president was "ask[ing] his lawyers for advice on the possibility of a pardon for Manafort and other aides," even as "Manafort remained in a joint defense agreement with the President following Manafort's guilty plea and agreement to cooperate, and . . . Manafort's attorneys regularly briefed the President's lawyers on the topics discussed and the information Manafort had provided in interviews with the Special Counsel's Office."[183] After Manafort's bail was revoked, the report notes, "the President's personal lawyer, Rudolph Giuliani, gave a series of interviews in which he raised the possibility of a pardon for Manafort."[184] Other covert contacts with federal witnesses by Trump and his legal team include Trump contacting Michael Flynn in April 2017 and telling him to "stay strong"; a November 2017 phone call to Flynn by Trump's attorney John Dowd, a call that, according to the special counsel's office, "could have affected both [Flynn's] willingness to cooperate [with federal prosecutors] and the completeness of that cooperation"; and an allegation by former Trump attorney Michael Cohen that one of his successors in that role, Jay Sekulow, "reviewed, shaped, and edited" Cohen's false testimony to Congress beforehand, an allegation Sekulow has since denied.[185]

As for the secret—and highly irregular—post-conviction Trump-Manafort joint defense agreement, federal prosecutors will allege that Manafort was lying to them repeatedly and systematically for the entirety of the period he was in his information-sharing arrangement with the president and his lawyers, giving federal law enforcement no information of lasting value while reporting back to Trump's legal team the areas of inquiry the special counsel was pursuing.[186] The Mueller Report will conclude of Trump's behavior as Manafort's cases unfolded in Virginia and D.C. that "the President and his personal counsel made repeated statements suggesting that a pardon was a possibility for Manafort, while also making it clear that the President did not want Manafort to 'flip' and cooperate with the government."[187] The report notes one particular incident in which Trump's legal team announced that "individuals involved in the

Special Counsel's investigation could receive a pardon 'if in fact the president and his advisors . . . come to the conclusion that [the individual has] been treated unfairly"—thereby using a term, "unfair," that Trump had within the preceding forty-eight hours publicly used to describe the treatment Manafort had faced from the special counsel.[188] Yet even as Trump is repeatedly tweeting about and speaking in interviews of fairness—at one point saying, "I do want to see people [like Manafort] treated fairly. That's what it's all about"—he is privately, according to the Mueller Report, expressing a very different concern, "discuss[ing] with aides whether and in what way Manafort might be cooperating with the Special Counsel's investigation, and whether Manafort knew any information that would be harmful to [him]"; Trump attorney John Dowd's November 2017 phone call to Flynn's counsel expresses the very same anxiety, with Dowd telling Flynn attorney Robert Kelner in a voicemail, "If . . . there's information [that Flynn has] that implicates the president, then we've got a national security issue . . . we got to deal with, not only for the president, but for the country. So . . . then, you know, we need some kind of heads up. Just for the sake of . . . protecting all our interests, if we can . . . remember what we've always said about the president and his feelings toward Flynn and, that still remains."[189] The Mueller Report also reveals that less than ninety days after Manafort and Gates were charged with federal felonies, "Manafort told Gates that he had talked to the President's personal counsel and they were 'going to take care of us.' Manafort told Gates it was stupid to plead [guilty], saying that he had been in touch with the President's personal counsel and repeating that they should 'sit tight' and 'we'll be taken care of.'"[190] Implicit and explicit pardon promises from Trump and his legal team to known federal witnesses aside, the special counsel's report will also observe that "some evidence supports a conclusion that the President sought . . . to influence the [Manafort] jury."[191] Jury tampering is a federal crime under 18 U.S.C. § 1504.[192]

The Mueller Report also reveals that, in an episode reminiscent of Trump and his legal team's handling of Manafort's two federal cases, Michael Cohen "understood based on . . . conversations with the President's personal counsel that as long as he stayed on message" about his 2015 and 2016 contacts with Russian businessmen and government officials on Trump's behalf, "he would be taken care of by the President, either through a pardon or through the [Russia] investigation being shut down."[193] The "message" Cohen was supposed to hold fast to—a falsity—was that his contacts with the Kremlin and its agents over a multibillion-dollar Trump real estate deal in Moscow stopped before Americans began voting, and that Trump knew little to nothing about either the Trump Tower Moscow project Cohen was working on or Cohen's extensive contacts with Kremlin officials while seeking to secure land and financing for the project.

In late August 2016, Roger Stone, having already been in communication with Jerome Corsi about WikiLeaks, reaches out to another friend of his, Randy Credico, asking him to get "information about WikiLeaks." For a long time thereafter, Stone will claim that Credico was "his main source of information about Assange's plans"—a claim contradicted by subsequent revelations about Stone's contact with Corsi.[194] As for Corsi, who not only discussed WikiLeaks with Stone but, per the Mueller Report, had "multiple Face Time discussions about WikiLeaks" with Ted Malloch, beginning in 2018 he will claim that he was merely bluffing with Stone, and that all of his statements of fact to him about WikiLeaks were merely blind guesses.[195] To confuse matters further, at least two witnesses before special counsel Mueller's grand jury in D.C. will testify that "Credico acknowledged in conversations [with them] being the source of material for Stone's [public] statements and tweets about WikiLeaks."[196]

In 2018, Mueller indicts Roger Stone for three crimes: obstruction of justice, witness tampering, and making false statements to federal law enforcement.[197] A subsequent court filing by Stone's attorneys will reveal that federal law enforcement at various points strongly considered filing additional felony charges against the longtime Trump friend and adviser, including accessory after the fact, misprision of a felony (failure to report a felony), conspiracy, unauthorized access of a protected computer, wire fraud, attempt and conspiracy to commit wire fraud, and illegal solicitation of foreign campaign donations.[198] As for the three federal indictments ultimately brought, the special counsel office's court filings will include allegations that Stone directly "communicated with WikiLeaks" and, moreover, with Guccifer 2.0, the digital persona constructed and run by Russian military intelligence during the 2016 presidential campaign.[199] The special counsel's office will further allege that in advance of WikiLeaks' first dump of stolen Democratic emails during the campaign—which came on July 22, 2016—Stone told "'senior Trump campaign officials' between June and July 2016 that WikiLeaks possessed stolen emails that could damage the Clinton candidacy."[200] According to the Stone indictment, "A senior Trump campaign official was directed to contact Stone about any additional releases and what other damaging information [WikiLeaks] had regarding the Clinton campaign."[201] Because few people on the Trump campaign besides the candidate himself would have had the authority to "direct a senior Trump campaign official," media outlets have speculated that the individual who issued such a directive during the presidential campaign was Donald Trump.[202]

In September 2016, an unnamed Trump campaign official schedules a meeting between George Papadopoulos, Michael Flynn, Jeff Sessions, and Greek foreign minister Nikos Kotzias—a meeting that is, according to Papadopoulos, a surprise, given that Kotzias is the man he told in late May 2016 about the Kremlin being in possession of Clinton's stolen emails; Kotzias had been slated to meet face-to-face with Putin the next day.[203] Papadopoulos takes his invitation to join Kotzias, Flynn, and Sessions—just a few weeks after Flynn attended Trump's first classified security briefing and was fully briefed on Russian efforts to cyber-attack the United States—as a sign that the Trump campaign has in fact been "informed of what [he] told the Greek foreign minister" in May, and that the campaign therefore knows for certain, as of September 2016, that the Kremlin says it possesses stolen Clinton emails.[204]

On September 20, just a few weeks after Donald Trump Jr. has, as reported in the *New York Times*, responded approvingly to an offer of collusive pre-election assistance from two of the Red Sea conspirators, MBS and

MBZ, Trump Sr. meets the third key member of the plot, Egyptian president Abdel Fattah el-Sisi, for the first time.[205] In a breach of protocol, el-Sisi appears to offer an endorsement of Trump's candidacy for president after his meeting with him, telling CNN that he has "no doubt" Trump would make a "strong leader."[206] While el-Sisi meets with the Democrats' presidential candidate, Hillary Clinton, the same week, the meeting with Clinton is businesslike, whereas the meeting with Trump, according to *Politico*, is "striking in how much praise the Republican heaped on Egypt"; moreover, whereas el-Sisi compliments Trump by adjudging him a "strong leader," his assessment of Clinton is a backhanded compliment that actually serves as a further endorsement of the political neophyte Trump: "Political parties in the United States would not allow candidates to reach that level [of being a party's presidential nominee] unless they are qualified to lead a country the size of the United States of America."[207] When Trump and el-Sisi meet, the Egyptian president appears confident that Trump will not, in fact, institute a temporary ban on Muslim visitors from certain nations to the United States, noting that "during election campaigns many statements are made and many things are said . . . governing [the United States] would be something different. And will be subject to many factors."[208] It is unclear whether el-Sisi is unconcerned about any ban on travel from certain Middle Eastern countries being instituted, or simply that he is certain that any ban Trump institutes will not affect the country he leads.

The same day as the meeting between Trump and el-Sisi, Trump Jr. begins to have "direct electronic communications with WikiLeaks," according to the Mueller Report.[209] If Trump Jr. has received any information about the Russian threat to the 2016 election from either of Trump's first two security briefings—information held not only by Trump but also by Michael Flynn and Chris Christie—the presidential candidate's son is required under the federal law against aiding and abetting to take no action that might induce further crimes by the Russian government's non-state cutout, WikiLeaks. Arguably, Trump Jr. is already in this position on the basis of public statements made by the U.S. intelligence community and a DNC-hired cybersecurity firm regarding Russia's election-related hacking. What Trump Jr. does on September 20 and September 21, however, is agree to access a password-protected anti-Trump website with a password sent to him by WikiLeaks; confirm to the campaign via email that he follows WikiLeaks on Twitter; respond to a "direct message" from WikiLeaks on Twitter; email "a variety of senior campaign staff" information he received as a result of his direct message from WikiLeaks; and tell WikiLeaks via Twitter direct message that he will "ask around" in response to its request for "comments" on the website to which it had just directed him.[210] Less than two weeks later, Trump Jr. receives and replies to another query from WikiLeaks and adds one of his own: "What's behind this Wednesday leak I keep reading about?"[211] Then, on October 14, two days after WikiLeaks sends Trump Jr. a private message thanking him and his father for "talking about our publications" and asking Trump to tweet out a specific link, Trump Jr. tweets the WikiLeaks-specified link himself.[212]

On September 30, Interfax, a Russian news agency, publishes an interview with George Papadopoulos that Trump's youngest national security adviser was given explicit permission to participate in by Bryan Lanza, Trump's deputy communications director.[213] Though weeks earlier it had been publicly revealed that Russia was suspected of being involved with the dissemination of stolen Democratic documents through WikiLeaks, Papadopoulos forwards the Interfax interview to his Kremlin contact, Joseph Mifsud.[214] In the interview, Papadopoulos had touted Trump's "willingness to usher in a new chapter in U.S.-Russia ties" and opined that "[U.S.] sanctions [against Russia] have done little more than to turn Russia towards China as a primary market for Russian goods, services and energy. It is not in the interest of the West to align China and Russia in a geopolitical alliance that can have unpredictable consequences for U.S. interests in the South China Sea, Eastern Mediterranean, and Middle East."[215] Papadopoulos's statement to Russian media echoes his statements to Israeli researchers during his campaign-approved trip to Israel in April 2016, when he told the Israelis that Putin was "a responsible actor and potential partner."[216] Nevertheless, the campaign temporarily "dismisses" Papadopoulos after the Interfax interview is publicly reported, as it has, in the view of the campaign, "generated adverse publicity."[217]

In Israel in fall 2016, Israeli prime minister Benjamin Netanyahu is looking forward to the end of the Obama presidency. Netanyahu has said to his aides that Obama has "no special feeling" for Israel and is dangerously foolish for wanting to "foster a kind of balance of power between Saudi Arabia and Iran."[218] Netanyahu's belief is that Saudi Arabia must always hold the upper hand over Iran for the Jewish state to maintain its security. As for the Obama administration, by fall 2016 it has long since ceased to believe that Netanyahu earnestly wants a peace deal with the Palestinians; President Obama believes Netanyahu has deceived him and other U.S. politicians with an only illusory commitment to peace. As early as 2012, the mistrust between Obama's team and Netanyahu's had been such that Obama suspected the Israeli prime minister of secretly backing Mitt Romney's presidential bid and hoping, moreover, to goad the United States into a military conflict with Iran.[219] Obama's fears about Netanyahu with respect to the 2012 election will appear prescient, given Netanyahu's clandestine positioning vis-à-vis the 2016 Trump campaign and his hawkish posture toward Iran from 2017 onward (see chapter 10).

In October 2016, discussions within the Israeli government on Obama's last days in office focus on the possibility that the outgoing U.S. president will try to "punish" Israel at the United Nations for building new settlements in contested areas at such a pace and in such a volume that it makes it appear as though Netanyahu is deliberately digging the Israeli-Palestinian peace process an early grave.[220] There is confidence within the Netanyahu administration that a President Trump would take no such step, and yet no confidence at all that a President Clinton would do anything but quickly seek a UN resolution condemning new Israeli settlements. As the New Yorker will report in June 2018, prior to the 2016 presidential election Netanyahu was "confident that Trump would look out for his interests and share his opposition to Obama's policies [in the Middle East]. Even before Trump entered the White House, Israeli officials talked about having more influence and a freer hand than ever before."[221] Netanyahu has already decided what he will do with this "freer hand," too; during the Obama administration the Israeli prime minister has developed a "grand strategy for transforming the direction of Middle Eastern politics. His overarching ambition [is] . . . to form a coalition with Saudi Arabia and the United Arab Emirates to combat Iran."[222] Netanyahu's plan dovetails with the "grand bargain" imagined by Michael Flynn and Thomas Barrack, contemplated in great detail by the Red Sea conspirators, and hinted at in Trump's public speeches.

In midsummer 2016, per Bloomberg, Dustin Stockton, a writer for Breitbart, sponsors a "10-week [media] blitz aimed at convincing black voters in key states to support the Republican real estate mogul [Trump], or simply sit out the election."[223] Steve Bannon's level of involvement in the Breitbart writer's campaign is unknown, but in May 2018 a former employee of Trump's data firm—Bannon's Cambridge Analytica—will tell a Senate committee "that Bannon tried to use [Cambridge Analytica] to suppress the black vote in key states."[224] The similarity between this Bannon-led effort and Stockton's Breitbart-led effort will prompt Bloomberg to call Stockton "an employee at Bannon's former news site [who] worked as an off-the-books political operative in the service of a similar goal" as the man who had been—until quite recently—his boss.[225]

At former Bannon employee Stockton's direction, a man named Bruce Carter founds Trump for Urban Communities (TUC), an organization that, according to Bloomberg, "never disclose[s] its spending to the Federal Election Commission—a possible violation of election law."[226] Carter will say that in founding Trump for Urban Communities, "he believed he was working for the [Trump] campaign" and that the campaign was therefore reporting all spending by TUC in accordance with federal law.[227]

Lawrence Noble, former general counsel at the Federal Election Commission (FEC) for both Republican and Democratic administrations, will tell Bloomberg in 2018 that, legally speaking, there are "real problems" with TUC, if its operations were as described by Carter.[228] As Bloomberg summarizes, "The operation suggest[s] possible coordination between Trump's campaign and [Carter's] nominally independent effort. If there was coordination, election law dictates that any contributions to groups such as [TUC] must fall within individual limits: no more than $2,700 for a candidate."[229] Bloomberg will note that one supporter of TUC alone "far exceeded that cap, giving about $100,000" to the organization.[230] Noble, now director and general counsel at the nonpartisan Campaign Legal Center, says, "I would think this is more than enough evidence for the FEC to open an investigation."[231]

Stockton will tell Bloomberg that "Trump performed particularly well in the areas [TUC] targeted," noting that in Pennsylvania—one of the three states that determined the outcome of the 2016 election, with Trump beating Clinton by 44,000 votes out of 6.2 million cast (0.7 percent)—"Clinton won about 35,000 fewer votes [in Philadelphia] than Obama did in 2012, and that drop was primarily in majority-black wards."[232] "Those ballots alone," Bloomberg notes, "could have cut Trump's victory margin in Pennsylvania by more than half."[233] Stockton, who now admits his operation was "telling people not to vote," says "Trump vastly outperformed the projection models [for African American voters] in the twelve areas Bruce [Carter] was targeting" in three battleground states: Pennsylvania, Florida, and North Carolina, all of which are states Trump won on Election Day in 2016.[234] For his part, Carter now says that Breitbart was "aggressive" in pursuing him, a "courtship" that consisted, in substantial part, of Breitbart staffer Stockton "mak[ing] him aware of some of the research that Breitbart was pushing at the time," which in Stockton's case largely comprised articles detailing WikiLeaks' October 2016 data-dumps.[235]

Breitbart's recruitment of Carter occurred while Bannon was an executive there, and once Bannon became the Trump campaign's chief executive officer on August 17, 2016, it included promises that Carter would be able to "engage with Bannon" directly.[236] Emails uncovered by Bloomberg in 2018 will reveal that, following this promise by Stockton to Carter, TUC directly coordinated with Bannon and other Trump campaign officials as to funding, strategic planning, and market identification and targeting.[237] A TUC staffer created a TUC Twitter account in September 2016, but thereafter it was accessed by multiple parties Carter cannot identify; it appears that some of the tweets made by these unknown parties "highlight[ed] the rolling WikiLeaks dumps of stolen Democratic campaign emails" as well as the work of "right-wing provocateurs" like Mike Cernovich—a Twitter personality who spent much of the 2016 general election tweeting about "Pizzagate," a conspiracy theory later tied to Russian sources by *Rolling Stone*.[238]

By early October, Carter and TUC are requesting additional funds directly from the Trump campaign—specifically, $160,000 from Steve Bannon.[239] Bannon puts Carter in touch with two men then deeply involved in a national social media manipulation campaign paid for directly by the Trump campaign: former Navy SEAL Jon Iadonisi and Dallas-based venture capitalist Darren Blanton (see chapter 6).[240] Iadonisi is a business partner of Trump's top national security advisor, Mike Flynn—indeed, the two men are, at the time, sharing an office—with Iadonisi simultaneously working with Flynn on a secret lobbying campaign for Turkey as well as a social media manipulation campaign for Trump. Blanton is a future Trump transition adviser who is paid $200,000 during the presidential transition period for social media manipulation work a company of his did during the campaign.[241] According to Carter, when he meets Iadonisi and Blanton for the first time in Dallas, hoping to receive a six-figure investment in TUC from them, they are accompanied by "an Army veteran who ran a Blackwater-like company that provided paramilitary services" who remains unidentified.[242] Blanton promises to help TUC raise money and proceeds to do so; Iadonisi—still Flynn's business partner and one of the Trump campaign's social media operatives—also offers to directly assist TUC.[243] It is unclear whether it is associates of Flynn, Iadonisi, Blanton, or the unidentified veteran who later tweet out WikiLeaks- and Pizzagate-related content from TUC's Twitter account.

While Carter's description of the "Army veteran" matches that of Trump adviser Erik Prince, Prince can be excluded as the third participant in the Carter-Iadonisi-Blanton meeting—but only because Blanton introduced Carter to both Michael Flynn and Erik Prince on October 19, 2016, within two weeks of Carter first meeting the Dallas businessman.[244] On the same day, Flynn, Prince, and Blanton introduce Carter to Rebekah Mercer, the owner of Trump's data firm, Cambridge Analytica.[245] In the ensuing week, Alexandra Preate—a spokeswoman for Bannon, Breitbart, and Mercer—drafts a press release hyping Carter and TUC.[246] At the end of that weeklong period, on October 26, Trump announces, in what he calls a "major policy speech" in North Carolina, a "new deal for Black America."[247] The next day, *BuzzFeed News* reports that, according to a Trump campaign aide, the Trump campaign is self-admittedly running "three major voter suppression operations" in the lead-up to Election Day, and that one of these efforts is targeting black voters.[248]

Just days after the election, everyone associated with the Trump campaign who had been in contact with Bruce Carter cuts ties with him, with Blanton in a terse email citing, as justification for the move, a past criminal conviction that Carter had done nothing to hide and that would have shown up in any background check conducted on him by the Trump campaign pre-election.[249]

In late October 2016, Thomas Barrack writes an op-ed for *Fortune* that details what the longtime Trump adviser believes the next president—which he long ago predicted would be Trump—should do in the Middle East. In his editorial, Barrack insists that "the United States should make a radical, historic shift in its outreach towards the Arab world. . . . America should forge alliances with a new generation of Arab leaders. . . . [T]he US should take the lead in establishing a 21st century 'Marshall Plan' of economic aid" to the Middle East.[250] While attempting to maintain his existing relationships in the region with words of praise for America's long-standing ally Qatar, Barrack writes also of the hope he finds in "the rise of a new generation in government," mentioning both Saudi Arabia and the UAE as countries with "brilliant young leaders . . . crafting forward-looking policies to effectively forge a new Middle East. American foreign policy must persuade these bold visionaries. . . . These leaders need and deserve active, engaged US support," writes Barrack.[251] Strikingly, Barrack writes of precisely the realignment of interests that began on a yacht in the Red Sea in late 2015, noting that the threat from Iran and Iranian militias "may create what has been a previously unthinkable alliance between our Gulf Cooperation Council partners and Israel."[252] The only error Barrack makes in his assessment, perhaps born of his historical ties to Qatar, is believing that that country will also be part of this new alliance with Israel.[253] Barrack does, however, include Egypt—a Red Sea conspirator but not a GCC member—in his proposed pro-Israel alliance of GCC nations, identifying Turkey (a foe of the Red Sea conspirators but not a Gulf nation) as a prospective enemy of such an alliance.[254] Barrack notes, too, the threat posed by a "renewed Russian push" in the region.[255] However, he blames "the chill in US-Russia relations"—a euphemism for the Obama administration's ongoing sanctions against Russia—for emboldening Putin in his support of Iran, implying that a U.S.-Russia détente, presumably brought about by the curtailing of sanctions, would have the opposite effect.[256] This is precisely the theory behind the "grand bargain" the Red Sea conspirators have sought with Trump and the Kremlin. Moreover, much of Barrack's lengthy editorial is a panegyric to Saudi Arabia, with the Trump friend, adviser, and confidant lauding the Saudis as "reliable defenders of the West's diverse interests in the region . . . [and] America's principal ally in the Middle East for more than seventy years."[257]

All told, two obligatory references to his old business partners the Qataris notwithstanding, Barrack's editorial is a summary of the bargain Trump's campaign has at times implicitly and at times explicitly sought with the Saudis, Emiratis, Israelis, and Russians for many months. Barrack insists that "the only solution [in the Middle East] is one that works with Russia and not against them," and even advises the very Syria policy Trump will announce two years post-inauguration—that "Bashar Assad may well be our only hope in fighting the various terrorist factions that are attempting to form an ISIS state [in Syria]."[258] Barrack therefore submits that the United States should shift its Syria policy away from regime change and American "boots on the ground"—a tactic Barrack deems "impractical and ineffective"—and toward a political solution to the Syria crisis, an outcome also favored by the Kremlin.[259] Given Barrack's level of access to Trump and his regular employment as a Trump intermediary with Middle Eastern interests, as well as his ongoing behind-the-scenes dialogues with both Jared Kushner and the Emirati ambassador, Yousef al-Otaiba, the window Barrack's *Fortune* article offers into the campaign's thinking on the "grand bargain" in October 2016 is highly revealing.

Barrack's insistence that the next president must "draw [up] a comprehensive solution similar to the Marshall Plan" echoes a "concept" drawn up by the very company, ACU Strategic Partners, that Michael Flynn was advising in 2016.[260] Under the ACU plan endorsed by Flynn, Trump and Putin would sign a Middle East Marshall Plan whose ambition would be identical to the Marshall Plan proposed by Barrack: increased economic development in U.S.-allied Arab nations in the Middle East. Barrack's echoing of the ACU/Flynn plan for the Middle East is no accident, however, as it will be revealed in November 2017 that throughout this period of the 2016 presidential campaign Flynn and Barrack are involved in "an intense and secretive lobbying push," along with Rick Gates and others, to provide nuclear technology to MBS.[261] Indeed, Flynn and Barrack are the two ringleaders of the effort. Because the plan the two top Trump advisers are championing requires that Trump drop sanctions on Russia, it is little surprise when, at the direction of a "senior transition official"—who communicates with Flynn through his deputy K. T. McFarland—the retired general and future Trump national security advisor tells Russian ambassador Sergey Kislyak on December 29, 2016, that if Russia will hold off on retaliating for the sanctions just imposed upon it by President Obama (sanctions imposed for the Kremlin's pro-Trump interference during the 2016 election), Trump will review the entire U.S.-Russia sanctions regime post-inauguration.[262] Kislyak eventually agrees, informing Flynn in a subsequent phone call that the Kremlin will stand down and not retaliate for the new sanctions.[263]

The next day, December 30, Trump tweets to the nation, "Great move on delay (by V. Putin)—I always knew he was very smart!"[264] Trump makes no mention of any negotiations between his transition team and the Kremlin urging such a "delay," though the Mueller Report will intimate that Trump was told, just after the new sanctions were announced, that his top national security advisor, Flynn, would imminently be speaking with the Russian ambassador.[265]

Minutes after Trump's tweet praising Putin, the Russian embassy in D.C. retweets it.[266] The Kremlin's positive response to Trump's tweet is apparently both well informed and well warranted, as at the time, it will later be reported, Trump either is developing or has already developed a plan to drop all sanctions against Russia—a move that would make possible the Barrack-Flynn nuclear reactor deal as well as obviate the need for any sanctions retaliation by the Kremlin.[267] Tom Malinowski, a former State Department official, will tell *Business Insider*—crucially, at a time when he does not know that Trump's intended dropping of sanctions on Russia would have paved the way for a clandestine "nuclear deal" with Russia and Saudi Arabia—that if indeed Trump had dropped sanctions on Russia at the beginning of his presidency, it would have given the Russians "exactly what they wanted in exchange for absolutely nothing."[268] Malinowski is one of several State Department officials whose actions in early February 2017 block Trump's secret sanctions plan from being enacted.[269]

Just eleven minutes after Trump takes the oath of office in D.C. on January 20, his new national security advisor, Mike Flynn, texts Alex Copson, the managing partner of ACU Strategic Partners, to tell him that ACU's "nuclear reactor project" is "good to go."[270] That night, Copson will tell someone with whom he's attending an inaugural event that he is having "the best day of [his] life" because "his company's effort to create a U.S.-Russia energy partnership in the Middle East . . . includ[ing] more than two dozen nuclear plants in the region, [is] moving forward."[271] Copson tells this individual—who will eventually become a government whistleblower working with federal law enforcement—that Trump is going to "rip up" all the sanctions against Russia that the Obama administration had imposed.[272] In so doing, Copson confirms that the Saudi, Emirati, and Egyptian nuclear deals Trump's top advisers have been working on are, in fact, one and the same with Trump's plan to drop all sanctions on Russia—the very plan that forms the impetus for the Russians' election interference on Trump's behalf. Moreover, these two plans are both key to the larger and more ambitious geopolitical plot developed by the Red Sea conspirators, which can most easily be executed if Iran remains the Middle East's chief bogeyman. Rejecting Obama's Iran nuclear deal is, as is evident by the time of Trump's inauguration, the clearest path to ensuring that Iran remains a clear and present danger to U.S. allies in the region.

According to the *Washington Post,* Copson's boast about Trump "ripping up" U.S. sanctions against Russia comes directly from Michael Flynn, who has told Copson that removing all sanctions on Russia is exactly what Trump will do post-inauguration. Copson explains to the future whistleblower with whom he is speaking at Trump's inauguration that "this is the start of something I have been working on for years. . . . Mike [Flynn] has been putting everything in place for us"—a comment that suggests Flynn's course of foreign policy advising on the Trump campaign may well have been part of "putting everything in place" for a grand bargain on nuclear materials and technology involving Russia, Saudi Arabia, the UAE, and Arab allies of the Saudis and Emiratis.[273] Indeed, when the whistleblower speaking with Copson informs Congress of the ACU-Copson-Flynn plot regarding Russian sanctions, Representative Elijah Cummings (D-MD), chairman of the House Oversight and Government Reform Committee, will say of the account that it constitutes a "credible allegation . . . [that] Michael Flynn sought to manipulate the course of international nuclear policy for the financial gain of his former business partners."[274] That Flynn and those partners planned on enriching and otherwise benefiting Trump's most reliable foreign allies through a redirection of U.S. foreign policy—including allies who had offered Trump collusive assistance pre-election—closes the circle on a broader multinational bargain. As Copson tells the whistleblower at Trump's inauguration, "This is going to make a lot of very wealthy people."[275]

One of the Russian companies necessary to Copson's and Flynn's plan is OMZ OAO, which is at the time under sanctions by the United States.[276] This explains, in part, why Copson says to the whistleblower that the sanctions placed on Russia for its illegal annexation of Crimea in 2014, and the further sanctions placed on Russia for interfering in the 2016 presidential election to assist Trump in gaining the Oval Office, "fucked everything up in my nuclear deal."[277]

That the "nuclear deal" Copson references is synchronous with the Red Sea Conspiracy in its essential elements will be underscored by a September 2017 letter Rep. Cummings sends to Robert Mueller as well as to Flynn and Copson, decrying, as summarized by *Business Insider*, Flynn's failure to "disclose a trip he took to Egypt and Israel in 2015 to pursue 'a joint U.S.-Russian, Saudi-financed program to build nuclear reactors in the Arab world,'" including the UAE.[278] Cummings's letter about Flynn's activities in 2015 thereby cites, explicitly or implicitly, six of the seven countries (all but Bahrain) intimately involved in George Nader's 2015 scheme for the remaking of the Middle East: the United States, Russia, Israel, Egypt, the United Arab Emirates, and Saudi Arabia. Indeed, Reuters describes ACU's "ready-to-go" nuclear consortium as including Israeli interests as well as Russian ones, and mentions, too, a Ukrainian interest that ACU planned to convince on the matter of dropping Russian sanctions by giving it "a $45 billion contract to provide turbine generators for reactors to be built in Saudi Arabia and other Mideast nations."[279] The Ukrainian money—effectively a bribe to facilitate sanctions relief for Russia—is therefore scheduled to come, Copson writes in a November 2016 email, from "Gulf Arab states."[280] That Thomas Barrack is one of the people who stands to become wealthy from the "grand bargain," and is a substantial creditor of at least one member of the Trump family as of Trump's inauguration, explains, too, one of the many ways the Trumps might have expected to benefit financially from Flynn's Middle East Marshall Plan. That other members of the consortium standing to benefit from the plan include Trump deputy campaign manager Rick Gates and Bud McFarlane—K. T. McFarland's mentor, a close associate of Trump national security adviser Michael Ledeen during the Iran-Contra scandal, a VIP attendee at Trump's April 2016 Mayflower speech, and a visitor to Trump Tower during the presidential transition period—underscores just how long work on this multinational deal has been ongoing.[281]

On January 28, 2017, two days after acting attorney general Sally Yates warns White House counsel Don McGahn that the nation's national security advisor, Mike Flynn, is susceptible to Russian blackmail and is therefore compromised—and one day after Yates gives that warning to McGahn a second time, face-to-face—Flynn receives an email from Bud McFarlane, who is at the time a member of the U.S. Energy Security Council.[282] The email, which is sent also to McFarlane's protégé (and Flynn's deputy) K. T. McFarland, includes two documents: first, a "cover memo," to be given to the president of the United States, intended to "launch the Marshall Plan for the Middle East" by formally outlining the "origins, geopolitical necessity, benefits—to the United States and host countries—[and] structure" of the plan and by naming Thomas Barrack chief executor of the plan on Trump's behalf; and second, a memo "for the president to sign" ordering cabinet members to give Barrack any resources he needs.[283] McFarlane notes that both Barrack and "our team"—meaning the team at post-ACU/post-IP3 entities SCP Partners, Iron Bridge Cybersecurity, and Iron Net Cybersecurity, all of whom are copied on the email—are on board with the content of the memos.[284]

Flynn, now a government employee, continues work on this private-company-proposed plan by "instructing his staff to rework [the] memo" sent to him by Copson "into policy for Trump to sign."[285] Flynn manifests no doubt that once the document is formatted correctly Trump will sign it. In the process of transitioning McFarlane's work product into a policy agenda, Flynn and his staff strip any mention of ACU from the proposal and focus primarily on how the plan will see the United States "working with Russia on a nuclear reactor project."[286] Less than a month earlier, one of the people now working on turning the memo into a policy Trump and the Russians can agree to, K. T. McFarland, had highlighted in an email to a fellow Trump transition team official that Trump must avoid a "tit-for-tat escalation" on Russia sanctions.[287] The same email underscored that the Russians had "just thrown [the] U.S.A. election to [Trump]"—a phrasing that summarizes Mc-Farland's view of the debt owed to the Kremlin by the new president.[288]

McFarland's advisory role in Flynn's late December contacts with Russian ambassador Sergey Kislyak over the question of U.S. sanctions is believed to have been directed by someone higher up in the transition; as *Business Insider* will note, quoting a former national security adviser to Vice President Joe Biden, "incoming Deputy National Security Advisors don't order their incoming boss [Flynn] what to do . . . unless they were instructed to do so by someone higher in the chain of command."[289] A former National Security Council spokesman who speaks to *Business Insider* will agree, telling the digital media outlet that McFarland "wasn't calling the shots, and certainly not giving her own orders to her putative boss."[290] The list of those who outranked Flynn on national security issues during the presidential transition period was short indeed; similarly, the circle of those within the PTT who understood the interconnected nature of the Middle East Marshall Plan and the Russian sanctions issue was small, though McFarland was herself a member. At one point during the transition she writes future Trump homeland security adviser Thomas Bossert to remind him that "Russia is key that unlocks door [sic]."[291] Bossert forwards McFarland's email to four people, one of whom is Mike Flynn and another of whom is Steve Bannon.[292] In the days following Flynn's ouster, Trump will be so concerned about alienating McFarland that when his first pick to replace Flynn as national security advisor, Vice Admiral Robert Harward, says that he will only take the job if he can replace McFarland, Trump withdraws the job offer.[293]

According to the *New Yorker*, just days before the 2016 presidential election, MBZ, "during a private meeting . . . float[s] to a longtime American interlocutor what sounded, at the time, like an unlikely grand bargain. The Emirati leader told the American that Vladimir Putin, the Russian President, might be interested in resolving the conflict in Syria in exchange for the lifting of sanctions imposed in response to Russia's actions in Ukraine."[294] The magazine notes that not only the UAE but Israel and Saudi Arabia backed the plan, and at various points they had "encouraged their American counterparts to consider ending the Ukraine-related sanctions in return for Putin's help in removing Iranian forces from Syria."[295]

Almost immediately after Trump's election, "a delegation of Saudis close to [MBS] visits the United States . . . and [brings] back a report [to MBS] identifying Jared Kushner as a crucial focal point in the courtship of the new administration."[296] The Saudis' secret report on Kushner notes his "scant knowledge about [the Middle East], a transactional mindset and an intense focus on reaching a deal with the Palestinians that [meets] Israel's demands."[297] Almost immediately, even though Trump is still only the president-elect and cannot legally negotiate U.S. foreign policy, MBS reacts to this report on Kushner by "offering [to Trump] to help resolve the dispute between Israel and the Palestinians . . . and offer[ing] hundreds of billions of dollars in deals to buy American weapons and invest in American infrastructure."[298] Moreover, MBS has his agents in D.C. invite Trump to come to Riyadh for his first foreign trip as president.[299] The Saudi delegation to Kushner is extremely high-level, including Musaad al-Aiban, "a cabinet minister involved in economic planning and national security," and Khaled al-Falih, "minister of energy and chairman of the state oil company."[300]

In a portion of its notes on Kushner leaked to the Lebanese newspaper *Al Akhbar*, MBS's November 2016 delegation to the president-elect and Kushner reports that "[Trump's] inner circle is predominantly deal makers who lack familiarity with political customs and deep institutions, and they support Jared Kushner."[301] According to the *New York Times*, another section of the Saudi delegates' report makes "special note of what it characterized as Mr. Kushner's ignorance of Saudi Arabia."[302] MBS's team underscores Kushner's unfamiliarity with the history of Saudi terrorism—for instance, the fact that nearly all of the 9/11 hijackers were Saudi citizens. MBS's agents plan to remedy this knowledge deficit to Kushner's "satisfaction" by "explain[ing]" to him what they describe as "their international leadership in fighting Islamist extremism."[303] The Saudis also propose an "intelligence and data [exchange] to help the [incoming] American administration carry out its strategy of investigating those requesting residency" in the United States—a proposal relevant to what will become Trump's travel ban two months later (a ban that will, in the event, be crafted to leave Saudi travel to the United States unaffected).[304]

Two additional November 2016 Saudi proposals to Kushner will end up becoming active agenda items early on in the Trump presidency: the first, "a joint center to fight the ideology of extremism and terrorism," will be inaugurated when Trump travels to Riyadh in May 2017 as part of his first foreign trip, and the second, "an Arab NATO" (see chapter 9), is presented to Kushner as "an Islamic military coalition of tens of thousands of troops" effectively under Trump's command—available for mobilization, the Saudis tell Kushner, "when the president-elect wishes to deploy them."[305] The idea of the Saudis deploying their coalition forces (including the Emiratis) under circumstances and in locations of Trump and Kushner's choosing emerges around the same time the Saudis join Trump and Egyptian president el-Sisi in inaugurating the Global Center for Combatting Extremist Ideology in Riyadh in May 2017, with the Saudis leading a coalition of Arab nations to blockade Qatar shortly thereafter.[306] The Saudis also promise Kushner $350 billion or more in new orders of American military equipment and other investments in the American economy over the next ten years.[307] These promises, favorably received in U.S. media at the time, will turn out to be hollow: by the end of 2018—nearly two years into Trump's presidency—the Saudis will have produced none of the $350 billion promised, and will have announced only $70 billion in future deals and investments. As for Saudi support for Kushner's Middle East peace push, the *Times* will report in December 2018 that King Salman "has appeared to resist Mr. Kushner's Middle East peace plans as well."[308] Yet despite this lack of investment in America or accordance with Kushner's policy agenda, the Trump-Saudi and Kushner-Saudi relationships will only grow over time, suggesting that the Saudis are pleasing their new allies in D.C. in other, perhaps less public ways.

MBS uses the notes his team brings back to Riyadh in November 2016 almost immediately, as just a few weeks later his close Emirati ally MBZ travels secretly to the United States—without informing the Obama administration of his travel, as required by international protocol—to meet with Kushner, George Nader, Steve Bannon, Mike Flynn, and Yousef al-Otaiba in Trump Tower, ostensibly, the *New York Times* reports, to talk about "the Israeli-Palestinian peace process." In fact, a good deal of MBZ's discussion with Kushner is about how "promising [a] young leader" MBS is—a course of persuasion that will help define Kushner's actions in the months to come.[309] As with almost every other high-level meeting that occurs in Trump's home during either the presidential campaign or the presidential transition period, there will be no public indication afterward of Trump having attended the meeting or even having any knowledge of it. In answering questions from the special counsel's office in 2018, Trump will deny having any knowledge of any pre-election meetings his advisers may have had with foreign nationals at which any form of assistance to him or his campaign was offered, telling the special counsel, "I have no recollection of being told during the campaign that any foreign government or foreign leader had provided, wished to provide, or offered to provide tangible support to my campaign."[310]

The December transition team meeting with MBZ at Trump Tower, set up in part by hedge fund manager Rick Gerson—a man *Vanity Fair* will call Jared Kushner's "BFF" (best friend forever)—is followed by a text message from Gerson to MBZ saying, "I promise you this will be the start of a special and historic relationship."[311] On January 19, the eve of Trump's inauguration, Gerson will again write MBZ, detailing a conversation he had with Kushner in New York City before the president-elect's son-in-law left for Washington for good and telling MBZ, "You have a true friend in the White House."[312]

ANNOTATIONS

Kilimnik, per Gates "a former Russian intelligence officer with the GRU," had just days earlier met with Russian oligarch (and his, Manafort's, and Gates's former boss) Oleg Deripaska.

It is not only Gates who says this about Kilimnik. According to Ken Vogel of the *New York Times*, the FBI has assessed that Kilimnik has "a relationship with Russian intelligence." This assessment is first revealed during a court hearing involving the special counsel's team in February 2019.[313] At the time, Andrew Weissmann, an attorney for the special counsel's office, says that the team's "larger view of what we think is going on, and what we think the motive here is [for Manafort coordinating with Kilimnik]"—something that goes "very much to the heart of what the Special Counsel is investigating"—is closely connected to the August 2, 2016, Manafort-Gates-Kilimnik meeting.[314]

The *New York Times* will underscore the significance of the August 2, 2016, meeting as well, in addition to its many follow-up meetings, by noting in a January 2019 article that "for Russia, trying to influence the incoming Trump administration's policy on Ukraine was of paramount importance. The economic sanctions imposed after Russia annexed Crimea damaged the Russian economy, and various emissaries have tried to convince [Trump] administration officials to broker a resolution to a long-running guerrilla war between Russia and Ukraine."[315]

Sometime after his hire by Trump but before mid-June 2016, Manafort—along with Rick Gates—had begun electronically transferring internal campaign polling data to Kilimnik, data that had been, according to the *New York Times*, "developed by a private polling firm" whose work product was nonpublic.

In the first ten months of his presidential campaign, not only does Trump decry pollsters, but indeed he has no polling operation of his own. By Election Day, Trump will have five polling firms on staff, all of which were engaged after Trump hired Manafort in late March 2016.[316]

On August 19, Paul Manafort resigns as Trump's campaign manager, though the move is a cosmetic one only.

Once Manafort becomes a target of the special counsel office's investigation, Trump and his aides move to obscure the importance of Trump's former campaign manager to the president's 2016 campaign. In 2017, Trump's White House press secretary, Sean Spicer, falsely describes Manafort as a man "who played a very limited role for a very limited amount of time."[317] An unnamed former Trump campaign worker falsely tells *Politico*, "We didn't really have that much interaction with Paul. He wasn't part of the core campaign team."[318] The same anonymous campaign worker will also falsely say that Manafort "didn't have a relationship" with Trump before March 2016.[319] In fact, as *Politico* will note in May 2017, "Manafort's lobbying firm worked for Trump in the 1980s and 1990s fighting the expansion of Indian casinos that could compete with his Atlantic City gambling business, and trying to change the flight path of planes that Trump said disturbed guests at his newly purchased Mar-a-Lago club in Florida."[320] Trump is Manafort's first-ever client as a political consultant with Black, Manafort & Stone, the consultancy Manafort founded in 1980 with Roger Stone and Charles R. Black Jr.[321]

Politico reports that after his March 2016 hire by Trump, Manafort "quickly exerted his influence over the entire campaign, which was headquartered at Manhattan's Trump Tower." Manafort had owned an apartment there since 2006, the first full year in which Felix Sater worked under an exclusive deal with the Trump Organization to help Trump build a tower in Moscow.[322] Bloomberg and *Washington Monthly* have noted that 2006 was also the year Sater and his Bayrock Group assisted Trump in signing one of the biggest deals of his career, Trump SoHo, several of whose funders "hailed from the former Soviet Union" and had "reported ties to the Kremlin;" many had also "faced allegations of corrupt and criminal behavior, ranging from money laundering to smuggling to involvement in a prostitution ring."[323]

As to the extent of Manafort's engagement with Trump following his late March 2016 hire, in early April 2016 Manafort's daughter texts her sister that "Dad and Trump are literally living in the same building and mom says they go up and down all day long hanging and plotting together."[324] She adds that her father and Trump are "perfect allies."[325] While Manafort will not officially gain "complete control" over Trump's campaign until June 2016, by mid-April 2016 he has so sidelined Trump's campaign manager, Corey Lewandowski, as the authority behind Trump's operation that NBC News reports that Manafort is Trump's "de facto campaign manager" and Lewandowski no more than a "body man and scheduler."[326]

In January 2018, Trump will tell friends privately that he believes he can escape legal liability in the special counsel's Russia investigation because "he's decided that a key witness

in the Russia probe, Paul Manafort, isn't going to 'flip' and sell him out."

The NBC News report in which these private conversations are disclosed contains another, equally shocking revelation: that "Trump is even talking to friends about the possibility of asking Attorney General Jeff Sessions to consider prosecuting Mueller and his team."[327] The report doesn't indicate what charges Trump wants the Department of Justice to bring against the man investigating him and his aides, allies, and associates, but it confirms, with a Trump adviser as a source, that Trump's aim in such a prosecution would be to make it impossible for Mueller to "run the federal grand jury" in the Russia investigation because he would be busy defending himself against criminal allegations.[328]

In midsummer 2016, per Bloomberg, Dustin Stockton, a writer for Breitbart, sponsors a "10-week [media] blitz aimed at convincing black voters in key states to support the Republican real estate mogul [Trump], or simply sit out the election."

Stockton spends October 2016 as Breitbart's primary interlocutor for WikiLeaks, at least six times writing stories for the formerly Bannon-led digital media outlet that are simply vehicles for the dissemination of DNC and other documents the Kremlin has stolen.[329]

CHAPTER 6

CSMARC, THE INCOGNITO PRINCE, THE SEYCHELLES, AND THE CHAIRMAN'S DINNER

November 2016 to January 2017

The presidential transition period is a time of secret meetings involving Trump agents, Emiratis, Russians, Israelis, and Saudis. These secret meetings occur at Trump Tower, in the Seychelles, at Trump inaugural events, and elsewhere. During the transition there are substantial revelations about ties between the Trump campaign and Israeli, Russian, and Saudi entities, including former Israeli intelligence officers, businessmen from Russia, and Saudi and Emirati death squad leaders. A clandestine Trump-Putin back channel—one focused on sealing a "grand bargain" in the Middle East—is conclusively established.

In 2016 and 2017—both before Donald Trump is elected president and after—anti-money-laundering specialists at his longtime bank, Germany's Deutsche Bank, "recommend[ ] that multiple transactions involving legal entities controlled by Donald J. Trump and his son-in-law, Jared Kushner, be reported to a federal financial-crimes watchdog."[1] According to a May 2019 investigative report in the *New York Times*, the transactions by Trump and Kushner "set off alerts in a computer system designed to detect illicit activity" and result in the internal production at Deutsche Bank of "suspicious activity reports" that the bank's money-laundering experts believe need to be sent to the U.S. Treasury Department immediately.[2] The financial transactions Deutsche Bank flags are of the sort that might threaten Trump's candidacy for president if disclosed in the middle of an election cycle in which it is known, by June 2016, that Russian nationals are systematically attacking America's election infrastructure in a way intended to benefit Trump—and in which Trump has repeatedly declared that neither he nor, to the best of his knowledge, anyone in his campaign has financial ties to Russia.[3]

What Deutsche Bank has discovered in Trump's and Kushner's financial dealings are "transactions . . . involv[ing] money flowing back and forth with overseas entities or individuals, which bank employees considered suspicious . . . [and] a series of transactions involving the real estate company of Mr. Kushner . . . [in which] money had moved from Kushner Companies to Russian individuals."[4]

The money-laundering specialist who flags the Trump and Kushner transactions for her superiors at Deutsche Bank, Tammy McFadden, will be terminated in 2018 after "rais[ing] concerns about the bank's practices" with respect to potential acts of money laundering. McFadden will raise her concerns at a time when "Deutsche Bank . . . had been caught laundering billions of dollars for Russians" and federal regulators had ordered it "to toughen its scrutiny of potentially illegal transactions."[5] In 2016, however, when McFadden provides the first "suspicious activity report" to her superiors regarding Trump and Kushner—two men Deutsche Bank has, over the years, lent "billions of dollars to," according to the *New York Times*—bank executives bury the report. The suspicious transactions, potentially indicative of money laundering, thereafter continue into 2017.

On April 15, 2019, just days before the release of the redacted Mueller Report, congressional Democrats issue a subpoena to Deutsche Bank demanding Trump's banking records.[6] Trump and his legal team move quickly to try to block the subpoena, though initial indications are that this effort is unlikely to be successful—with Trump failing to block the subpoena at the case's first hearing, before U.S. District Court Judge Edgardo Ramos in late May 2019.[7]

At 2:40 a.m. on the morning of November 9, 2016, Democrat Hillary Clinton calls Republican Donald Trump to concede the 2016 presidential election.[8] Within twenty minutes, Vladimir Putin has had an emissary contact Trump to set up a phone call with the Kremlin.[9] Putin's emissary is Sergey Kuznetsov, an official from the Russian embassy in Washington.[10] The message from Putin that Kuznetsov sends to Trump via email, after Kuznetsov's phone connection—according to Hope Hicks—is too faint for the White House to make out what the Kremlin agent is saying when he calls at 3:00 a.m., is that Putin "look[s] forward to working with [Trump] on leading Russian-American relations out of crisis."[11] Hicks forwards the message from Putin to Kushner, who immediately contacts his longtime adviser on all matters Russia-related, Putin "friend" Dimitri Simes.[12] According to Kushner, his main purpose in writing Simes is to find out the name of the Russian ambassador, though this information is readily available by typing "Russian ambassador" into a Google search.[13]

A few hours later, in the late morning of November 9, Russian Direct Investment Fund (RDIF) director Kirill Dmitriev—who, according to the Mueller Report, has been "kept abreast" throughout the general election of George Nader's "efforts" to "develop[ ] contacts" with the Trump campaign—contacts Nader and asks him to "introduce him to Trump transition officials."[14] Robert Mueller will find, during the course of his investigation into Trump-Russia ties, that Dmitriev "report[s] directly to Putin and frequently refer[s] to Putin as his 'boss,'" a revelation that means George Nader has been in touch with a top Putin lieutenant during the same span of time pre-election that he is regularly meeting with top Trump campaign officials (see chapter 5).[15] Indeed, Mueller finds that Dmitriev told Nader pre-election, as the Lebanese American businessman was having regular contacts with the Trump campaign, of "his and the government of Russia's preference . . . for candidate Trump to win."[16] Nevertheless, in his written responses to the special counsel's office, President Trump will state that he has "no recollection of being told during the campaign that Vladimir Putin or the Russian government 'supported' my candidacy."[17]

Someone—possibly Nader, as the redacted Mueller Report implies but does not say—writes to Dmitriev on November 9, the day after Election Day, to observe that "Putin has won."[18] One indication that this declaration of a Kremlin victory following America's 2016 presidential election came from Nader is Mueller's description of the closeness of the Nader-Dmitriev relationship: "RDIF has co-invested in various projects with UAE sovereign wealth funds," the Mueller Report finds. "Dmitriev regularly interacted with Nader, a senior adviser to UAE Crown Prince Mohammed bin Zayed, in connection with RDIF's dealings with the UAE. Putin wanted Dmitriev to be in charge of both the financial and political relationship between Russia and the Gulf states."[19] Indeed, the report observes that "Nader considered Dmitriev to be Putin's interlocutor in the Gulf region, and would relay Dmitriev's views directly to [MBZ] . . . [and] Dmitriev and Nader had previously [pre-election] discussed Nader introducing him to the contacts he had made within the Trump Campaign."[20] Dmitriev's specific task, in making these contacts with Trump officials, is likewise revealed by the special counsel's report: "Dmitriev told [Kushner friend Rick] Gerson that he had been tasked by Putin to develop and execute a reconciliation plan between the United States and Russia."[21]

Dmitriev's task is of sufficient importance that only hours after Trump becomes America's president-elect, Dmitriev is asking Nader to set up a meeting between him and "the 'key people' in the incoming Administration," whom Dmitriev says he must speak to "as soon as possible" to "start rebuilding the [U.S.-Russia] relationship."[22] Dmitriev thereafter asks for, and receives almost immediately, Putin's personal permission to travel to the United States for the purpose he has just laid out to Nader. According to the Mueller Report, Dmitriev is, upon landing in New York City late in the day on November 9, "particularly focused [on meeting with] Kushner and Trump Jr."—perhaps because of Nader's past interactions with the two men.[23]

Seventy-two hours after Trump's victory, Kremlin operative Maria Butina contacts her handler, Alexander Torshin, regarding the presidential transition team's plans for a secretary of state nominee.[24] Butina has had re-peated contacts during the presidential campaign with Dimitri Simes and J. D. Gordon—the latter the day-to-day director of the national security advisory committee that was Simes's brainchild—while Torshin has had repeated contacts with Simes and at least one substantive contact with Donald Trump Jr. at a National Rifle Association event, and he says he "know[s]" Trump Sr. through the NRA.[25] Butina contacts Torshin because the Trump campaign has already revealed to her whom it is considering picking for secretary of state—one of the most important cabinet decisions President-elect Trump will make—and Butina tells Torshin that "our [the Kremlin's] opinion will be taken into consideration" when it comes time to make a final selection. Torshin has by this time repeatedly been called "President Putin's emissary" in the United States by both American and British media.[26] It is unclear whether Butina is told of the Trump cam-paign's plans for the State Department before or after Election Day, and whether it is Dimitri Simes, Butina's boyfriend, Paul Erickson, or someone else who passes this intelligence to her; Trump has long been planning to unilaterally drop sanctions on Russia via his secretary of state, though he keeps this plan secret pre-election—notwithstanding telling Butina her-self, at FreedomFest in Las Vegas in July 2015, that he'd like to see the sanctions removed.[27] Federal prosecutors, after convicting Butina of being an unregistered agent of the Russian Federation, will tell a federal judge in April 2019 that her work in the United States, including substantial contacts with top Republican officials and operatives and even Trump himself, "provided the Russian Federation with information that skilled intelligence officers can exploit for years and that may cause significant damage to the United States."[28]

Six days after Trump's election victory, he speaks with Putin by tele-phone. During the call Trump "agree[s] to work to improve [U.S.-Russia] ties," according to the Associated Press.[29]

A week after Election Day, Kislyak emails Kushner about setting up a meeting with him, and Kushner immediately checks in with Dimi-tri Simes to make sure that Kislyak is the "right guy" in the Kremlin's administrative superstructure for him to be taking a meeting with post-election.[30] On November 30, Kushner and Flynn meet with Kislyak at Trump Tower to express to the Kremlin agent "a desire on the part of the incoming Administration to start afresh with U.S.-Russian relations"—a fresh start that could occur only if the incoming administration drops all sanctions on the Russian Federation, as all three men are aware from past interactions between the Trump campaign and Kislyak.[31] Kushner and Flynn also discuss with Putin's designated representative "U.S. policy toward Syria" and the possibility of the Russian military communicating directly with the Presidential Transition Team (PTT) via a secure line untraceable by U.S. intelligence. When Kushner suggests that the PTT could secretly communicate with Russian generals via a secure facility at the Russian embassy, Kislyak adjudges the idea a step too far—and indeed, former CIA director John McLaughlin will tell MSNBC in May 2017 that Kushner's plan would have constituted espionage under federal law.[32]

As the transition wears on, the PTT will diversify its cadre of Russia advisers beyond Simes, adding to it Robert Foresman, the banker who in March 2016 had acted as a Kremlin conduit to the campaign (see chapter 3).[33] In December 2016, Flynn and his deputy K. T. McFarland ask Foresman for his advice on whether Kislyak is the right conduit for the PTT to use to communicate with the Kremlin during the transition period; Foresman retrieves an answer for Flynn and McFarland by checking with "a source he [Foresman] believed to be close to Putin," an act of interlocution that occurs without Flynn's direct request but nevertheless underscores the ease with which Trump's national security team is able to access the Kremlin post-election.[34]

By December 6, a week after Kushner and Flynn's meeting with Kislyak, Kislyak has set up for Kushner a meeting with a man who has a "direct line to Putin"—Sergey Gorkov, the head of a Russian state-owned bank, Vnesheconombank (VEB), who was a senior manager at another state-owned Russian bank, Sberbank, at the time (November 2013) it agreed to finance the Trump Tower Moscow project Trump and Aras Agalarov negotiated in Moscow.[35] Gorkov, according to the *Washington Post*, is also "a graduate of the Federal Counter-Intelligence Academy, which prepares students for service in [Russian] foreign intelligence or the Federal Security Service (FSB), the successor agency to the KGB."[36] According to the Mueller Report, Gorkov had talked to Foresman "just before Gorkov left for New York to meet Kushner . . . [and] told him [he] was traveling [with others] to New York to discuss post-election issues with U.S. financial institutions, that their trip was sanctioned by Putin, and that they would be reporting back to Putin upon their return."[37] For his part, Kushner will claim to the special counsel's office that he didn't even Google Gorkov before meeting him, despite Kislyak having indicated that Gorkov would be Kushner's direct line to Putin.[38]

Kushner's honesty on the subject of his meeting with Gorkov will be further placed in doubt by his readout of the event. While Kushner will tell federal investigators that the meeting was purely "diplomatic"—Kislyak having ostensibly set up the meeting in response to Kushner saying he wanted a conduit to Putin—Gorkov will say his meeting with Kushner occurred, as summarized by the Mueller Report, "in Kushner's capacity as CEO of Kushner Companies, for the purpose of discussing business, rather than as part of a diplomatic effort."[39]

A potential second meeting between Kushner and Gorkov in February 2017 will be scuttled by the unfolding Flynn scandal.[40]

With U.S. media coverage of Russian election interference steadily increasing in December 2016, the Kremlin changes tack midmonth and switches its strategy for securing new clandestine meetings with the PTT from using known Kremlin agents to using individuals already working as Trump advisers. After Putin has intimated to oligarch Petr Aven that he wants Aven to use his Alfa Bank contacts to set up a conduit to the Trump transition, especially on the "prospect of forthcoming U.S. economic sanctions," Aven "instruct[s] [Trump adviser] Richard Burt to make contact with the incoming Trump Administration."[41] Even as Aven is pursuing Putin's desires in this regard, Dimitri Simes is turning to Burt for the same purpose.[42] Simes's and Putin's lines of engagement with the PTT in late December 2016 and early January 2017 are so synchronous that, according to the Mueller Report, Burt "decide[s] to approach CNI president Dimitri Simes for help facilitating Aven's request" even as Simes is "lobbying the

Trump Transition Team, on Burt's behalf, to appoint Burt U.S. ambassador to Russia."[43] Simes appears to dissemble with the special counsel's office regarding his contacts with Burt, however. Whereas Burt tells Mueller's team that Simes "agreed to discuss [using Burt as a Trump-Kremlin conduit] again after the New Year [January 1, 2017]," Simes says that "he did not want CNI to have any involvement or apparent involvement in facilitating any [Trump-Kremlin] connection."[44] Burt underscores Simes's attentiveness to the idea of a Trump-Kremlin conduit when he reveals to the special counsel that Simes had already done the necessary work in his interactions with the Trump campaign to determine that there was a clear "interest" in establishing such a "communications channel."[45]

The day after Trump's election victory, a Saudi journalist living in the United States, Jamal Khashoggi, criticizes Trump's Middle East policy at a think tank event in Washington. Within days, MBS has "banned [Khashoggi] from writing in newspapers, making television appearances, and attending conferences" in Saudi Arabia, forcing the journalist to seek work abroad.[46]

Khashoggi's criticism of Trump—calling his agenda for the Middle East "contradictory"—is relatively mild, and yet it touches on a major paradox at the heart of MBS's plan for cooperation with Trump: inasmuch as the Red Sea Conspiracy requires that America please Russia by various means, and inasmuch as the United States withdrawing troops from Syria would have that effect but also strengthen Iran's hand, Trump will be granting a major victory to both Russia and its ally Iran if he effectuates MBS's grand plan for the destruction of Iranian power by changing U.S. policy in Syria.[47] In calling this plan—Trump's and, in effect, MBS's—"contradictory," Khashoggi gives the lie to the broader Trump-MBS agenda. As the article that gets Khashoggi banned from practicing journalism in Saudi Arabia argues, "Mr. Trump has been vocally anti-Iran, [but] he has hinted he will support President Bashar al-Assad in Syria's civil war, a move which will ultimately bolster Iran."[48] The observation is true as a matter of geopolitics, but is also potentially damning for MBS, as it is he who idiosyncratically believes that appeasing Russia—and therefore risking, concurrently, the aiding of Iran—is a wise course for his nation. Khashoggi's argument at the think tank event in D.C. that it would be exceedingly difficult for Trump to "ally more closely with Russia" while supporting Sunni Arab states like Saudi Arabia in their efforts to stabilize the Middle East is self-evidently true, based simply on the present status of in- and out-of-region military alliances. It is only the counterintuitive and still-secret tenets of the Red Sea Conspiracy that alter the equation. MBS cannot allow Khashoggi's narrative to discredit, explicitly or implicitly, the counternarrative that he, MBZ, and el-Sisi are planning to pursue. And so it is that MBS ends, in an instant, the long journalistic career of Jamal Khashoggi, a man who had previously been a columnist for *Al Hayat* for five years and an editor in chief at several Saudi newspapers, including the *Arab Times* and *Al-Watan*.[49]

As Khashoggi's journalistic career in Saudi Arabia ends, a new organization arises in the kingdom: a paramilitary unit that U.S. officials will come to call the Saudi Rapid Intervention Group (RIG), which functions as an intensification of the secret military unit already constituted within MBS's Center for Studies and Media Affairs at the Royal Court (CSMARC). The CSMARC unit, run by MBS aide Saud al-Qahtani, was founded in 2015, at MBS's direction, to kidnap Saudi citizens abroad and bring them back to Riyadh for detention (see chapter 9).[50] Whereas the CSMARC unit's efforts have focused on kidnapping and extraction, the RIG mandate is broader, and includes the "surveillance, kidnapping, detention and torture" of Saudis around the world.[51] American intelligence believes there to be personnel overlap between RIG and CSMARC, as Saud al-Qahtani runs both and uses Maher Abdulaziz Mutreb as his deputy for both. Another top RIG operative named by the *New York Times* is Thaar Ghaleb al-Harbi, "a member of the royal guard who was promoted in 2017 for valor during an attack on a palace of [MBS's]."[52]

What is unclear is whether there is also personnel or operational overlap between RIG, CSMARC, and the "Islamic military coalition of tens of thousands of troops" that would be available to Trump "when the president-elect wishes to deploy them"—a third ostensibly "counterterrorist" force, which the Saudis promise to Kushner in New York City in November 2016 (see chapter 5).[53]

From 2017 onward, RIG will be involved in at least a dozen operations around the world.[54] In one instance reported by the *New York Times*, a RIG detainee and torture victim, Eman al-Nafjan, a "university lecturer in linguistics who wrote a blog about women in Saudi Arabia," tries to kill herself after prolonged "psychological torture" at RIG's hands.[55] Torture is illegal under Saudi law, notes the *Times*, but U.S. intelligence has information suggesting that women detained by MBS, including al-Nafjan, "were frequently . . . [subjected to] interrogation, which included beatings, electric shocks, waterboarding and threats of rape and murder."[56] One victim's sister writes in an op-ed for the *Times* that al-Qahtani "threatened to kill her [sister] and throw her body into the sewage system."[57] Illegal RIG kidnappings and extractions are known to have occurred in, at a minimum, Jordan, Morocco, Kuwait, UAE, and Turkey.[58]

As MBS increases the Saudi government's illegal renditions around the world, and also its chargeless detentions at home, so too does he increase the kingdom's financial investments abroad—particularly in the United States, with an emphasis on the administration of Donald Trump.[59] In 2016, Saudi Arabia spent $10 million lobbying the Obama administration; in 2017, it spends $27 million lobbying Trump.[60] According to *Time*, "The Saudi government saw an opening for improved relations with Trump's presidency, and immediately began investing—both monetarily and diplomatically."[61] Ben Freeman, founder and director of the Foreign Influence Transparency Initiative at the Center for International Policy, says that "with Trump I think [the Saudis] saw the opportunity for a . . . reset in U.S-Saudi relations, and really for Trump they had someone who was already pretty biased to their point of view. He had these personal business connections that I think the Saudis were pretty prepared to capitalize on."[62] Evidence in support of Freeman's conclusion includes Saudi-funded lobbyists reserving five hundred rooms at Trump's D.C. hotel, at a cost of well over a quarter of a million dollars, in the weeks before and after Trump's inauguration.[63]

Shortly after Trump's election, George Nader pays Joel Zamel $2 million. According to the *New York Times*, there are "conflicting accounts" of the reason for the payment.[64] The special counsel's office is concerned enough that the $2 million may be a foreign payment for services illegally rendered for the Trump campaign during the election that Mueller subpoenas Zamel's Cyprus banking records and begins interviewing Psy-Group employees.[65] Bloomberg reports that almost immediately thereafter, in February 2018, "Psy-Group CEO Royi Burstien informed employees in Tel Aviv that the company was closing down. Burstien is a former commander of an Israeli psychological warfare unit."[66]

Nader's claim that he paid Zamel for a presentation on how Trump scored an electoral victory is, in a narrow way, true: according to the *New Yorker*, "Shortly after the election Zamel bragged to Nader that he had conducted a secret campaign that had been influential in Trump's victory. Zamel agreed to brief Nader on how the operation had worked."[67] What is unknown is whether Nader, as an agent of the UAE, was asking to see evidence of actions he had no forewarning of or was entitled to a detailed presentation by Zamel because it was MBZ who had paid for Zamel's work product in the first instance. The *New Yorker* describes the December 2016 Nader-Zamel meeting—followed hard upon by meetings between Nader, Zamel, Flynn, Bannon, and the Saudis' spy chief (see chapter 8)—as "Zamel show[ing] Nader several analytical reports, including one that described the role of avatars, bots, fake news, and unattributed websites in assisting Trump. Zamel told Nader, 'Here's the work that we did to help get Trump elected,' according to [a] Nader representative. Nader paid Zamel more than two million dollars, but never received copies of the reports, that person said."[68] If indeed Zamel did the work for the Trump campaign that he claimed, it would have violated U.S. law, which prohibits campaign donations from foreign nationals; federal law therefore offers a compelling reason for Zamel to have resisted distributing documentary evidence of his illicit efforts.

A Psy-Group employee who speaks to the *New Yorker* appears to confirm that the company did work for Trump, saying of Psy-Group's disinformation techniques and the post-election "increase" in "interest in Psy-Group's services"—as expressed by what the company was hearing from prospective clients in 2017—"The Trump campaign won this way. If the fucking President is doing it, why not us?"[69] This increased interest in Psy-Group sees its founder, Burstien, giving presentations on Psy-Group's capabilities all around Washington. Per the *New Yorker*, "As part of [his] presentation, Burstien point[s] out that Russian operatives had been caught meddling in the United States; Psy-Group, he [tells] clients, was 'more careful.'"[70]

The *Washington Post* reports that by the first day of the transition period, Trump and his team have already outlined "a very specific policy position" on how to approach the Russia-Iran axis—and their position is identical to that of MBZ and his Red Sea co-conspirators.[71] As the *Post* reports, the Trump transition and presidential administration "and the UAE appear to share a similar preoccupation with Iran. . . . Trump advisers were focused throughout the transition period on exploring ways to get Moscow to break ranks with Tehran."[72] According to a former intelligence official who met with Trump transition officials, "Separating Russia from Iran was a common theme [in their conversations]. It didn't seem very well thought out. It seemed a little premature. . . . [T]hey hadn't even taken the reins and explored with experts in the U.S. government the pros and cons of that approach."[73]

The second day after Trump's election finds multiple Russian officials communicating to the media that "the Russian government . . . maintained contacts with Trump's 'immediate entourage' during the campaign."[74] Russian deputy foreign minister Sergey Ryabkov speaks at slightly more length on the issue, telling a journalist, "I cannot say that all [of Trump's entourage], but a number of them maintained contacts with Russian representatives. . . . I don't say that all of them, but a whole array of them supported contacts with Russian representatives."[75]

The Trump transition team responds to the Kremlin's confession with a grave misstatement that at once misleads the media and the public on the existence of Trump-Russia, Trump-Saudi, and Trump-Emirati contacts: the transition team's press secretary, Hope Hicks, tells U.S. media,

"We are not aware of any campaign representatives that were in touch with any foreign entities before yesterday [November 9], when Mr. Trump spoke with many world leaders."[76] Hicks would later reveal to the special counsel's office that she spoke to none of Trump's foreign policy advisers or national security advisers before representing that no one on Trump's campaign communicated with foreign nationals; instead, she spoke only to domestic policy advisers, including Kellyanne Conway, Jason Miller, and Stephen Miller—the last of whom, despite being a domestic policy adviser, was in fact present at Trump Tower on August 3, 2016, when Donald Trump Jr. met with Joel Zamel, an Israeli citizen.[77] Hicks will tell the special counsel that she may have spoken to Bannon and Kushner as well—two men whose campaign briefs spanned both domestic and foreign policy—but she could not be sure.[78]

That Trump and his transition team immediately evince a policy agenda with respect to Russia and Iran identical to that of the UAE without consulting domestic foreign policy experts is telling. Former U.S. ambassador Michael McFaul, who speaks to the Trump transition team during the transition period, comes away with the impression that the team doesn't realize how much Putin will have to be offered to curtail his support for Iran. "When I would hear [their plans]," McFaul will say in spring 2017, "I would think, 'Yeah, that's great for you guys, but why would Putin ever do that?' There is no interest in Russia ever doing that. They have a long relationship with Iran. They're allied with Iran in fighting in Syria. They sell weapons to Iran. Iran is an important strategic partner for Russia in the Middle East."[79] It is unclear if the transition team reveals to McFaul its pre-election plan to eliminate all U.S. sanctions on Russia in compensation for its abandonment of Iran, a move that would end a punishing regime of financial restrictions on the country that has "shaved off," per the Council on Foreign Relations, 1 percent to 1.5 percent of Russia's economic output and could, in the long term, have an even more significant impact—as it is keeping the Kremlin from fully exploring the Arctic for oil.[80] Just a single potential drilling partnership that the Kremlin has had to forgo because of sanctions, an agreement with Exxon, could alone have brought in revenues of up to $500 billion, according to a Kremlin estimate.[81]

Whether it is revealed to McFaul or not, according to a June 2017 *News-*

week article Trump and his team have, in fact, developed a secret plan to end all sanctions on Russia immediately upon entering office—a plot foiled only when career civil servants in the State Department successfully move to block it.[82] Dan Fried, the State Department's coordinator for sanctions policy through February 2017, will tell Yahoo News that in the first few weeks of Trump's presidency "he got several 'panicky' calls from U.S. officials. They asked: 'Please, my God, can't you stop this?'"[83]

Career government officials are right to be panicked. According to *Newsweek*, Trump's plan calls for ending all sanctions on Russia over its 2014 annexation of Crimea, ending all sanctions on Russia over its interference with the 2016 presidential election, and returning Russian diplomatic compounds in the United States that were seized following the election.[84] According to Tom Malinowski, the assistant secretary of state for democracy through Trump's inauguration, Trump's plan—per those who spoke with his transition team—"would have been a win-win for Moscow."[85] Malinowski further will say, in speaking with Yahoo News, "that he heard the administration was working on a 'grand bargain' with Russia."[86] Certainly, if the Russians had caught wind, at any time before Election Day in 2016, of Trump's plan to trade sanctions relief for Russia's abandonment of Iran in Syria—for instance, during any of Flynn's contacts with Kislyak, Kushner's contacts with Simes or Barrack's contacts with al-Otaiba—it would have supplied a strong motive for the Kremlin to illicitly support Trump's candidacy for president.

Among those hired for the presidential transition team is Iranian American businessman Bijan Kian, the longtime business partner of Trump's top national security advisor, Mike Flynn. The two men co-founded the Flynn Intel Group in 2014.[87] In December 2018, Kian will be indicted by special counsel Robert Mueller for secretly being an agent of the Turkish government at the time he joined the presidential transition team's national security staff.[88]

In June 2017, three months after Kian and Flynn have finally registered as 2016 Turkish agents—but long before Kian's 2018 indictment—a Trump administration official will insist, as summarized by the *Washington Times*, that "Kian's records did not show his foreign work for Flynn Intel or that he planned to file with the government as an agent for his work for a foreign interest. 'He did not indicate that to us in his transition documents. We would have no reason to know.'"[89] These mid-2017 claims will be cast into doubt, however, by a May 2017 *New York Times* story revealing that "Flynn told President Trump's transition team weeks before the [January 2017] inauguration that he was under federal investigation for secretly working as a paid lobbyist for Turkey during the [2016] campaign."[90] Given that Flynn engaged in this work with his business partner Kian, as part of a company that he and Kian jointly operated, and that in fact Kian had been the one who introduced Flynn to the Turkish client they worked for, the chances Flynn revealed his foreign lobbying for Turkey to Trump transition officials while keeping them in the dark about—and avoiding questions about—Kian, his fellow transition team member, would appear to be small.[91]

The identity of Flynn and Kian's Turkish client helps to explain how Kian, and thereafter Flynn, first encountered Israeli business intelligence expert Joel Zamel—which perhaps explains, in turn, why it is so important for the Trump administration to deny knowledge of Flynn's dealings with Kian. In 2016, Flynn and Kian were working secretly on behalf of Ekim Alptekin, a Turkish businessman who not only hired the Flynn Intel Group in 2016 but actually employed Kian at "one of his Turkish companies at the same time [Kian] was working for Flynn Intel."[92] Flynn and Kian had apparently known Alptekin for some time, as they both "attended galas put on by the Nowruz Commission, a nonprofit run by Kian . . . [for which] Alptekin was named a board director" in 2011; moreover, "Kian and Alptekin had an existing business relationship when Flynn Intel began its foreign work . . . [as] Kian had been vice chairman of [Alptekin's] Istanbul-based aviation company, EA Havacilik, since November 2011 . . . [and] Alptekin said he and Kian regularly strategized" on business matters.[93] Evidently, a key part of Alptekin and Kian's strategy was ensuring that no one knew they were working with the Flynn Intel Group: Kian told a journalist whom he'd asked to produce a pro-Turkey documentary, "We don't want anyone to know the Flynn Intel Group has anything to do with this."[94]

Despite the Trump transition team's later claims that it didn't know about Kian's foreign lobbying—but was, per reports, aware of Flynn's lobbying efforts by January 4, 2017, at the very latest—Alptekin will say that Kian was the "main one" he dealt with when he was closely working with the Flynn Intel Group in the final ninety days of the 2016 general election. The date Flynn and Kian began working with Alptekin matches, almost to the day, the date Joel Zamel offered his services to the Trump campaign.[95] Meanwhile, the Trump transition team's claims that it didn't know Flynn was working for the Turks until January 2017 will be severely undercut with the revelation that Congress informed transition chief and Vice President–elect Mike Pence of this critical national security information, and did so in writing, on November 18, 2016.[96] No action was taken by the Trump transition with respect to Flynn's security clearance in November 2016, December 2016, or January 2017, however.

As of 2016, Alptekin is, legally speaking, an agent of the Turkish government, as he is "a member of a foreign trade board managed by the country's economic ministry."[97] His longtime employee, consultant, and business associate Kian had, during his years of work for the Export-Import Bank pre-2011, spent much of his time "meeting officials in Russia, Saudi Arabia, the United Arab Emirates and other nations, according to State Department cables."[98] The $530,000 Kian and Flynn received for working for Alptekin from August through November 2016 was paid by two entities: the Alptekin-owned Inovo BV, a Dutch consulting company, and (curiously, given that all the work Flynn and Kian did for Alptekin was ostensibly on behalf of the Turkish government) Ratio Oil Exploration, an Israeli natural gas company.[99] About half ($270,000) of the $530,000 Alptekin paid Flynn and Kian is unaccounted for in Flynn's transition-period federal paperwork seeking a security clearance, and Alptekin now says "he does not know where the money went."[100] In December 2018, Alptekin is indicted alongside Kian for illegally lobbying on Turkey's behalf, with Flynn scheduled to testify for the federal government as its star witness.[101]

An addendum to Flynn's security clearance paperwork will subsequently reveal that Alptekin's Inovo was in fact, in working with Flynn and Kian, "represent[ing] a private sector company in Israel that sought to export natural gas to Turkey."[102] In 2017 Alptekin will sometimes deny ever working for Ratio while at other times admitting it, even as Ratio denies having any relationship with him.[103] Ratio's denials will eventually be proven, in late 2017, to be a lie, as *BuzzFeed News* will acquire "numerous documents, emails, photographs and bank statements showing a business relationship [between the Israeli company and Alptekin]."[104]

The documents *BuzzFeed News* uncovers reveal that the secretive Alptekin-Ratio relationship—which eventually becomes a Flynn-Kian-Alptekin-Ratio relationship—began on April 13, 2016, just nine days after Trump national security adviser George Papadopoulos appeared with Alptekin on a panel at a conference in Israel.[105] Papadopoulos had been sent to Israel by the Trump campaign twenty-four hours after revealing to Trump, Sessions, and the rest of Trump's national security advisory committee that he was acting as an "intermediary" for the Kremlin.[106] Papadopoulos's trip to Israel to be on a panel with Alptekin also occurred just three weeks after he met Maltese professor Joseph Mifsud, a Kremlin agent, in Italy; Mifsud and Alptekin were both, during that period of time, members of a relatively small international organization called the European Council on Foreign Relations.[107]

Papadopoulos's wife will "unequivocally" tell National Public Radio in early 2018 that "everything [her husband] did during the campaign was authorized by the top levels of the campaign," including his foreign trips.[108] It remains unclear why Alptekin originally represented his work with Flynn and Kian as involving only the building of a public case against exiled Turkish cleric Fethullah Gulen, rather than any oil-and-gas analyses for the Israeli company Ratio Oil, and why Alptekin subsequently lied to media about whether any Israeli monies had been used to pay the co-founders of the Flynn Intel Group.[109] While it is known that Papadopoulos communicated with Flynn during the period both men worked as national security advisers on Donald Trump's presidential campaign, it is unknown how closely they interacted while both working as national security advisers on Ben Carson's relatively small campaign—or whether

Flynn had any role in Trump's mysterious hiring of Papadopoulos in March 2016, just weeks before Papadopoulos met Flynn's future client Alptekin.[110]

One clue about the missing $270,000 from the contract Flynn signed in August 2016 with Alptekin and an Israeli oil company—a contract signed at the same time Israeli Joel Zamel made a pitch at Trump Tower to create a social media manipulation campaign for Donald Trump for the final ninety days of the 2016 election—may come in the form of work Flynn business associate Jon Iadonisi did for Flynn during the same period Zamel was pitching to the Trump campaign. Iadonisi's work for Flynn ostensibly related to Flynn's efforts on behalf of the Turkish government; at the same time, however, Iadonisi was running an "under-the-radar project" for the Trump campaign now described as a "social-media project that involved video-content creative and 'millennial engagement.'"[111]

The Trump campaign didn't pay Iadonisi for his work at the time he did it, or even disclose the work Iadonisi was doing in campaign finance reports, as required by law (this despite Trump boasting in 1999 that "nobody knows more than me about campaign finance"). Instead, a month after the election the Trump campaign paid $200,000 to "Colt Ventures, a Dallas-based venture-capital firm that is an investor in VizSense, a social-media company co-founded by Iadonisi."[112] Michael Glassner, executive director of the Trump campaign committee, "declined to comment on why the payment went to a venture-capital firm and whether campaign officials were aware of the firm's connection to VizSense and Iadonisi."[113] In May 2017, the *Washington Post* will report that the founder of Colt Ventures, Dallas investor Darren Blanton, "served as an adviser to Trump's transition . . . [and] met frequently with Trump strategist Stephen K. Bannon at Trump Tower during the campaign. . . . Colt also sent a report to Bannon about work done for the campaign."[114]

As the co-founder of VizSense, Iadonisi—a former Navy SEAL who has done work with the CIA—was offering VizSense clients, in 2016, the means to "weaponize your brand's influence" through "military-grade influencer marketing and intelligence services."[115] In a 2015 interview, Iadonisi said that VizSense "helps clients track online video performance and identify which social-media users drive the most traffic." He compared VizSense's technology with the capacity of Al Qaeda fighters who "were really good at making viral videos" that "catalyze" the opinions of those who see them.[116]

Throughout the 2016 campaign, the Flynn Intel Group and Iadonisi's VizSense shared an office in Alexandria, Virginia. Flynn's rental agreement for the space was with White Canvas Group, another Iadonisi-founded and -owned operation.[117] According to the Justice Department, Iadonisi's White Canvas was working with the Flynn Intel Group on the Gulen project while Iadonisi's VizSense was working with the Trump campaign on its "under-the-radar" social media manipulation operation.[118] The chief executive of White Canvas, Tim Newberry, was simultaneously the chief executive of Flynn Intel Group Cyber (FIG Cyber), a subsidiary of Flynn's company.[119] Missing Israeli monies paid to the Flynn Intel Group were therefore well positioned to end up in a VizSense social media manipulation campaign seemingly identical in its contours to the project being proposed (at the very same time) by Israeli social media guru Joel Zamel.[120]

That Iadonisi served in Iraq with Michael Flynn and shared an office with him, and that Zamel had previously sought to recruit Iadonisi's officemate Flynn to work with Psy-Group, increases substantially the odds of an Iadonisi-Zamel connection or even partnership—especially given their common military experience and common interest in social media disinformation campaigns.[121] Indeed, in describing itself as "deliver[ing] military-grade influencer marketing and intelligence services," Iadonisi's company VizSense offers up a corporate description also answered to by Psy-Group.[122] According to the *Washington Post*, Flynn's contract with Inovo describes Iadonisi, without name attribution, as "the head of Flynn Intel Group's Special Operations Cyber Force" and a "former top security and intelligence official"—a description that may just as easily be applied to Zamel.[123]

In December 2016, during the presidential transition, Israel's ambassador to the United States, Ron Dermer, calls Jared Kushner. One of Prime Minister Netanyahu's former speechwriters had introduced Kushner to Dermer nine months earlier, in March 2016. During the December

Dermer-Kushner call, Dermer tries to induce Kushner to violate the federal Logan Act (18 U.S.C. § 953) by asking to negotiate U.S. foreign policy with President-elect Trump—who is still a month from taking office—through his son-in-law.[124] Specifically, Dermer asks Kushner "for the transition team's help in blunting the work [at the United Nations] of the sitting President."[125] "Work" here refers to the Obama administration's open-minded stance toward an Egyptian resolution at the United Nations criticizing Israel for its aggressive settlement policy under Netanyahu. Underscoring the comity between the Trump campaign and both the Israelis and the Egyptians, as well as Israel's surprisingly strong influence on decision-makers in Cairo, Egypt quickly withdraws its resolution "under pressure from Netanyahu and Trump"—despite the fact that it is illegal for either the president-elect or any member of his transition team to seek to negotiate U.S. foreign policy with a foreign power.[126] When four other United Nations Security Council members revive Egypt's resolution, Trump's team again, despite the clear prohibitions of the federal Logan Act, directly negotiates foreign policy before the administration of which they're a part has assumed power in Washington. Kushner orders Mike Flynn to contact the Russians for their help in defeating the resolution, which Flynn immediately does.[127] He will later be charged with a federal crime for lying about this and other phone calls to Russian ambassador Sergey Kislyak in the last ten days of December.[128]

As Netanyahu's agent is apparently orchestrating violations of 18 U.S.C. § 953, Netanyahu takes yet another step considered by American intelligence veterans to be a "breach of protocol": he sends Yossi Cohen, the head of Israel's intelligence agency, Mossad, to meet with Trump's top national security advisor, Flynn, about the threat Iran poses in the Middle East. Cohen's charge is to "insure that the two governments [are] closely aligned in their approach [to Iran]."[129]

Meanwhile, Trump foreign policy adviser George Papadopoulos, who has in prior publications strongly advocated for America to more robustly align its military with those of Israel and Greece, is in Piraeus, a city near Athens, meeting with Greek defense minister Panos Kammenos.[130] Papadopoulos had previously met with Kammenos during a late May 2016 trip to Athens—the same weekend that Kammenos met with Vladimir Putin in the Greek capital.[131] The May Kammenos-Papadopoulos meeting occurred just three weeks after Papadopoulos learned from his Kremlin-agent contact, Maltese professor Joseph Mifsud, that the Kremlin had stolen thousands of Hillary Clinton's emails.[132]

Kammenos is a "Putin ally" whose defense department is deemed by NATO intelligence to be "compromised by Russian intelligence," and whose Athens-based Institute for Geopolitical Studies is in an active "memorandum of understanding" with the Russian Institute for Strategic Studies, a unit of the office of Vladimir Putin that is a "think tank managed by Russia's foreign intelligence services."[133]

After his December 2016 dinner with Kammenos, Papadopoulos emails Steve Bannon and Michael Flynn a report on the meeting, suggesting that not only does the meeting have implications for the campaign's national security agenda, but also that it requires a briefing directly to a shadow national security shop (Flynn's) residing outside the campaign committee on which Papadopoulos had served.[134] In his email to Bannon and Flynn, Papadopoulos informs the two men that Greece wants to sign a "government-to-government agreement with the United States for all rights to all energy fields offshore, [offering a] strategic foothold in the Mediterranean and Balkans."[135] European Union security officials will regard the Papadopoulos-Kammenos meeting as "alarming," deeming it a mistake for the Trump transition to "allow[ ] a representative to meet with him"; Kammenos's "close ties to the Russians," in the words of one Greek official, likely explain this alarm inside the European intelligence community.[136] One central European counterintelligence official will tell *BuzzFeed News* that if, as Papadopoulos has claimed, the Trump transition knew in advance of the itinerary for Papadopoulos's trip to Greece, "they knew [Trump] officials were meeting with a [ministry of defense] in Athens that has a big black mark next to it due to Russian infiltration."[137] "Kammenos has never been shy about his affection for Russian President Vladimir Putin," writes *BuzzFeed News,* "often bragging to associates and even the public of his close connections to Putin."[138] Since becoming the Greek defense minister in 2015, Kammenos has not only advocated for Greek-Russian military partnerships but announced that Greece is "prepared to act as a go-between" between Russia and Western countries, suggesting a possible explanation for the Trump campaign's eagerness to have Papadopoulos meet with him.[139]

Between December 2015 and July 2016—a period of time that encompasses Papadopoulos's April 2016 trip to Israel, two May 2016 trips to Greece, and several March and April 2016 meetings in London with Joseph Mifsud—seven intelligence agencies in countries allied with the United States (the United Kingdom, France, Germany, the Netherlands, Australia, Estonia, and Poland) had contacted the United States intelligence community to report "suspicious 'interactions' between figures connected to Trump and known or suspected Russian agents," as well as intercepted "conversations in which Russians were discussing contacts with Trump associates . . . [including] people close to Trump meeting with Russians in Britain, the Netherlands and in other countries."[140] It is unknown whether Papadopoulos's early 2016 meetings in Israel, Greece, and England are among the interactions reported to American intelligence agencies between late 2015 and summer 2016, but the level of counterintelligence chatter provoked by Papadopoulos's December 2016 trip to Athens suggests it is likely.

As the *Washington Post* will write in April 2017, November and December 2016 are marked, for Trump's presidential transition team, by "separate private discussions in New York involving high-ranking representatives of Trump with both Moscow and the [United Arab] Emirates."[141] These meetings include Flynn and Kushner meeting with Kislyak on November 30; Kushner meeting with Gorkov on December 13; and Flynn, Kushner, and Bannon meeting with an officially incognito MBZ in mid- to late December.[142] Of the last meeting, during which MBZ expresses the view that "Iran [is] the problem, not Israel," Bannon will later say to Emirati ambassador al-Otaiba, "That was one of the most eye-opening meetings I've ever had."[143] Of what he calls Kushner's "Middle East Initiative," Bannon will say, "Jared and I were at war on a number of other topics, but not this."[144]

It is on December 21, 2016, just days after MBZ meets with senior members of the PTT, that MBZ's Red Sea co-conspirator Abdel Fattah el-Sisi, the autocratic president of Egypt, submits his UN resolution demanding that Israel "cease settlement activities in Palestinian territory."[145] The alacrity with which Kushner, Flynn, and "multiple members of the Transition Team" join Trump himself in "communicat[ing] with foreign government officials" to "rally support to delay the vote or defeat the resolution" is telling.[146] That Flynn is tasked with calling Kislyak, with whom he has had numerous prior communications, is unsurprising; it is the speed with which Trump is able to convince Red Sea conspirator el-Sisi to postpone a vote on his resolution that is particularly revealing—and, even now, mysterious.[147]

On December 29, new sanctions on Russia imposed by the Obama administration as punishment for Russian election interference go into effect.[148] Once again, senior transition officials—including Flynn, Bannon, Priebus, and McFarland—immediately become involved in clandestine negotiations with a foreign power, this time with the Kremlin over refraining from any retaliatory actions against the United States. Flynn, who had received a text from Kislyak on December 28, ultimately calls the Russian ambassador on December 29 after McFarland "exchang[es] emails with multiple PTT members and advisors about the impact the sanctions would have on the incoming Administration."[149] McFarland discusses the issue directly with Bannon and Priebus, telling each that Flynn shortly plans on speaking to Kislyak about the sanctions issue—even as all four Trump advisers, per their subsequent claims to the special counsel's office, inexplicably keep any information about their plans to negotiate sanctions with the Kremlin from the president-elect.[150]

Before contacting Kislyak, Flynn speaks with McFarland about the upcoming call, and receives advice on what he should say, through McFarland, from other unnamed PTT members. He also has a twenty-minute conversation with Trump national security adviser and former Bud McFarlane associate Michael Ledeen—the husband of Barbara Ledeen, the Flynn friend who spent late fall of 2015 and all of 2016 trying to secure stolen Clinton emails from Russian hackers.[151] It is unclear if Michael Ledeen, like his wife, made contact with Russian nationals during the 2016 campaign.

After speaking with Ledeen and McFarland, Flynn calls the Russian ambassador to "discuss[ ] multiple topics . . . including the sanctions, scheduling a video teleconference between President-Elect Trump and Putin, an upcoming terrorism conference, and Russia's views about the Middle East."[152] After discussing all these matters—including, Flynn's topic selection suggests, the "grand bargain"—with Kislyak, and after Kislyak has taken the PTT's request to forgo retaliation over new sanctions back to the Kremlin, the Russian Federation agrees not to retaliate against the United States.[153] The Mueller Report will, in April 2019, confirm that "multiple Transition Team members were aware that Flynn was speaking with Kislyak that day," adding that on the day of the Flynn-Kislyak call McFarland also gave a briefing to Trump himself—during which Trump expressed a clear preference for no new sanctions being put on the Kremlin, as he was, he said, using sanctions as "leverage" with Putin for an unspecified purpose.[154]

While he is absent from Mar-a-Lago during the late December 2016 Flynn-Kislyak sanctions negotiations, Jared Kushner has had plenty of contacts with the Russians over the course of the month. Kushner's December 13 meeting with Vnesheconombank chief executive Gorkov—a bank known for "advancing the strategic interests of Russian President Vladimir Putin and for its role in a past U.S. espionage case," according to the *Washington Post*—raises red flags for the special counsel's office due to the parties' divergent explanations for its purpose and content.[155] Gorkov, who speaks Arabic, contends the meeting "was held as part of a new business strategy and was conducted with Kushner in his role as the head of his family's real estate business," while the White House says "the meeting was unrelated to business and was one of many diplomatic encounters" Kushner was holding ahead of the inauguration."[156]

Sometime in December, George Nader, Jared Kushner, Steve Bannon, Michael Flynn, and MBZ—and possibly others—meet secretly at Trump

Tower.[157] As with every other pre-election and transition meeting at Trump Tower between members of the Trump campaign or PTT and foreign nationals, the participants will give no indication of whether Trump had knowledge of the meeting before, during, or after its occurrence—despite it happening in the building in which he works and lives.[158]

On January 3, 2017, Nader meets twice with Erik Prince to discuss Putin's emissary Dmitriev, with whom Nader has been in touch throughout the general election campaign.[159] Based on his years of familiarity with Prince and his months of pre-election contacts with the Trump campaign, Nader considers Prince to be in Trump's "inner circle," and moreover someone who "wield[s] influence," is "trusted," and is "well connected" within that circle. Therefore, Nader decides, Prince is a good person for Dmitriev to meet as the latter man tries to execute Putin's plan to negotiate sanctions relief with members of the PTT.[160] On January 4, Nader sends Prince a series of documents regarding Dmitriev that Prince opens almost immediately from a location inside Trump Tower. During the same three-hour period Prince is at Trump Tower reading the documents Nader has sent him about Putin's emissary, Prince speaks with former Trump campaign manager Kellyanne Conway, future Trump commerce secretary Wilbur Ross, future Trump treasury secretary Steve Mnuchin, and Bannon, the former Trump campaign CEO.[161] Within seventy-two hours—even before Nader has informed Dmitriev that Prince has agreed to meet with him—Prince has booked a ticket to the Seychelles for a January 11 meeting with the RDIF director.[162] According to Nader, the decision to have Prince meet Dmitriev was made by Bannon; Prince, however, will tell the special counsel's office that he cannot recall if Bannon knew of his trip to the Seychelles in advance—one of dozens of Prince statements to Congress and the special counsel that contradicts statements made by other witnesses, including witnesses under cooperation agreements with federal law enforcement that guarantee swift legal punishment for any deceit.[163] Notwithstanding Prince's repeated misstatements, he will eventually concede to the special counsel's office that "it was fair for Nader to think that [he] would pass information on to the Transition Team."[164] Bannon, however, will make no such concession to the special counsel, claiming that he had no knowledge of Prince's trip in advance despite Mueller's cooperating witness Nader saying otherwise.[165]

On January 11, Prince meets with Dmitriev twice in the Seychelles: once for thirty to forty-five minutes with Nader in Nader's villa on the island, and once for a briefer meeting with Nader and the Russian at a restaurant inside the Four Seasons Hotel.[166] During the first meeting, Dmitriev seeks to "outlin[e] a strategic roadmap for both countries [the United States and Russia] to follow" in restarting their relationship. During the second meeting, Prince, despite the clear restrictions imposed upon the negotiation of U.S. foreign policy by private citizens, negotiates U.S. foreign policy toward Libya with the Kremlin agent, informing him that Libya is "off the table" for Russian intervention because "the United States"—an entity for whom Prince does not speak—"could not accept any Russian involvement in Libya because it would make the situation there much worse."[167] It will later be revealed by the *Washington Post* that Trump ally MBS has been secretly involving himself in Libya, "egg[ing] on and materially support[ing]" a Libyan warlord (and accused war criminal) named Khalifa Hifter; this may explain why Trump's emissary in the Seychelles, Prince, does not want either Russia or any of its allies, particularly Iran, becoming involved in the troubled North African nation.[168] As Libya was originally envisioned as the sixth member of the Red Sea Conspiracy (along with Saudi Arabia, the UAE, Egypt, Bahrain, and Jordan), it is also possible MBS's designs on the war-torn country significantly precede Hifter's rise to prominence.[169]

Upon his return from the Seychelles, Prince gives Bannon a full briefing on his meetings with Dmitriev—though here again, Bannon will subsequently contradict both Nader and Prince, telling the special counsel that he "never discussed with Prince anything regarding Dmitriev, RDIF, or any meetings with Russian individuals or people associated with Putin."[170] The special counsel is unable to confirm Bannon's account, or Prince's, because they have apparently erased all their text messages from prior to March 2017. Both men will claim to the special counsel that their phones automatically deleted the messages—in both their cases, from the exact same time frame—against their wishes.[171] The Mueller Report will

286 | SETH ABRAMSON

note, however, that "provider records indicate that [Prince] and Bannon exchanged dozens of messages" prior to March 2017.[172]

That two top Trump campaign national security advisers both delete their text messages to avoid having them discovered by federal law enforcement raises the specter that other national security advisers—including those, such as George Papadopoulos, accused of lying to investigators—may likewise have deleted critical messages from their phones or email accounts in an effort to prevent or forestall their discovery. Indeed, as noted earlier, the Mueller Report will opine about the deletion of "relevant communications" preventing the special counsel from being able to "corroborate witness statements . . . or fully question witnesses about statements that appeared inconsistent with other known facts."[173] This caveat from the special counsel's office calls to mind Papadopoulos's oddly stilted statement to CNN about the spring 2016 email Trump policy director John Mashburn claimed Papadopoulos had sent him revealing the Kremlin's theft of Hillary Clinton's emails: "I don't think that proof has been provided."[174]

Both the Emiratis and Israeli-government-linked Israelis are heavily engaged with the PTT in December 2016 and January 2017. The Emiratis' national security adviser introduces Dmitriev to a friend of Jared Kushner's, Rick Gerson, though whether this particular connection was known at the time to Kushner or Emirati ambassador Yousef al-Otaiba, who were in contact throughout the general election, is unclear.[175] However, Gerson, like al-Otaiba, has been in touch with Kushner throughout the campaign, and is indeed the man partially responsible for MBZ's diplomacy-busting secret trip to New York City to meet with the PTT.[176] Gerson meets with Dmitriev in early December 2016, during the same period that Kushner is meeting with Kislyak and Gorkov, and promises Putin's agent that he will "ask Kushner and Michael Flynn who the 'key person or people' [are] on the topics of [U.S.] reconciliation with Russia, joint security concerns, and economic matters"—the last of these a probable euphemism for sanctions, the subject of the "task" Putin has personally assigned Dmitriev.[177] On the same day that Dmitriev is deciding whether to meet Prince in the Seychelles—January 9, 2017—Dmitriev speaks with Gerson about Kushner, raising the possibility that Gerson communicates to Dmitriev on this date that Kushner is aware of and supports Nader's proposed Seychelles (Dmitriev-Prince) summit.[178]

An even more telling indication that Kushner is aware, through Gerson, of the Dmitriev-Prince meeting scheduled for January 11 in the Seychelles is that when Dmitriev arrives in the Seychelles, Gerson is also there. Gerson, whom *Vanity Fair* describes as Kushner's best friend, therefore not only sets up the secret December 2016 summit between the Trump PTT and MBZ in New York City that Nader attends, and not only meets with Dmitriev in December, but also appears at the series of Seychelles meetings with MBZ and Dmitriev that Nader schedules following MBZ's highly irregular appearance at Trump Tower.[179] While Prince and Dmitriev are in the Seychelles, Gerson meets with not just MBZ—who in turn meets with Nader, Prince, and Dmitriev—but also with Nader.[180] As for Nader, he not only meets in the Seychelles with Prince, Dmitriev, Gerson, and MBZ, but also with Emirates-dwelling assassination squad coordinator Mohammad Dahlan and the chief of Emirati intelligence (the latter of whom is likely the same person—though the Mueller Report is not clear on this point—as the "Emirati national security adviser" who introduced Gerson to Dmitriev).[181]

Given that Dmitriev's RDIF has, on its advisory board, a Kushner friend named Leon Black, whose Apollo Global Management will be one of two entities (with Brookfield Property Partners) to bail out Kushner's ailing business just a few months into the Trump presidency (see chapters 9 and 10), it can be said that during two days in mid-January 2017 the Seychelles is teeming with Russians, Emiratis, and Trump advisers who can both connect Kushner to a leading Red Sea conspirator (MBZ) and also assist him in saving his floundering real estate company. Nevertheless, Kushner will tell federal law enforcement that when Gerson returns from the Seychelles and gives him a detailed multipage plan for U.S.-Russian reconciliation that he has negotiated with Dmitriev, Kushner had at that point "not heard of Dmitriev" at all.[182]

The Gerson-Dmitriev plan presented to Kushner on January 18, just two days before Trump's inauguration, calls for a five-point détente between the United States and Russia: (1) the two countries will jointly fight terrorism in the Middle East; (2) the two countries will jointly battle the spread of weapons of mass destruction; (3) the two countries will jointly develop "win-win" economic and investment initiatives, likely a euphemism for immediate sanctions relief for Russia; (4) the two countries will "maintain[ ] an honest, open, and continual dialogue regarding issues of disagreement," likely a euphemism for the establishment and maintenance of a permanent White House–Kremlin back channel of the sort Kushner had been searching for since Election Day; and (5) the two countries will "ensur[e] proper communication and trust from 'key people' from each country"—a likely reference to the creation of a back channel that cannot be overseen or interfered with by the U.S. intelligence community, a problem discussed by Kushner and Kislyak face-to-face in late November 2016.[183]

A Gerson spokesman will say in May 2018 that Gerson was in the Seychelles at the same time as Prince, Nader, Dmitriev, and MBZ—and meeting with at least the latter three of these people, just as they were all meeting with one another—as part of a "vacation" he was taking unrelated to Prince or Prince's meetings on the island, which Gerson's spokesman will say Gerson "knew nothing about."[184] Two U.S. officials briefed about the Senate Select Committee on Intelligence's subsequent investigative interest in Gerson will tell NBC News through an intermediary, however, that members of the select committee have by mid-2018 "inferred that Gerson was there [the Seychelles] because of his connection to Kushner" and that "UAE officials [in the Seychelles] considered Gerson to be 'Kushner's guy.'"[185] Gerson's spokesman, while denying that Gerson is under federal investigation, will decline to say whether Gerson has ever been "personally contacted by Mueller."[186]

Joel Zamel will, like his longtime acquaintance George Nader, repeatedly make contact with members of Trump's transition team. According to the *Daily Beast*, in January 2017 "Zamel . . . led conversations with Trump transition officials about his company helping [to] assist other Middle Eastern players, such as Saudi Arabia, with regime change in Iran."[187] These Zamel-led conversations occur just before Prince leaves for the Seychelles, and involve not only Michael Flynn, Steve Bannon, and George Nader but also a Saudi general dispatched from Riyadh by MBS.[188] The general, Ahmed al-Assiri, is the chief of Saudi intelligence—and will be accused, in twenty-one months, of helping to orchestrate the murder of *Washington Post* journalist

Jamal Khashoggi.[189] The topic the five men discuss is the very topic Trump had been talking about regularly on campaign stops in the fall of 2015, when Mike Flynn began acting as his chief foreign policy adviser: countering America's adversaries in the Middle East.[190] According to the *Daily Beast*, Flynn's meetings with Saudi intelligence in January 2017 are "attended and brokered" by Nader.[191] Former CIA acting director John McLaughlin will tell the *Daily Beast* in October 2018 that meetings like the transition-period Flynn-Bannon-Nader-Zamel-Assiri meeting would be considered "very unusual" in the intelligence community. "It's concerning to me as a former intelligence official," McLaughlin will say, "because of the fact that it smacks of covert action planning, which is the most sensitive thing the U.S. government does and is so uniquely the province of the sitting president."[192]

Flynn meets with al-Assiri more than a year after the Saudi intelligence chief, working in conjunction with MBS's "right-hand man" Saud al-Qahtani, has developed a military unit within CSMARC whose job is to "engage[ ] in the kidnapping—sometimes overseas—and detention and harsh interrogation of Saudis whom the monarchy perceives as a threat. The interrogations [lead] to repeated physical harm to the detainees," according to the *Wall Street Journal*.[193] In 2018 a CIA assessment will conclude that, since 2015, CSMARC's military arm has been used by MBS "to target his opponents domestically and abroad, sometimes violently."[194] The *New York Times* reports that "numerous Washington lobbying and public affairs firms . . . assist [CSMARC]" in "promoting a positive story about the [Saudi-]Yemen war in Washington," suggesting that the center's public-facing civilian activities are not wholly outside Beltway political discourse.[195]

While it is unknown whether al-Assiri and Flynn discuss CSMARC during the presidential transition, their discussion of counterterrorism operations in the Middle East dovetails with CSMARC's ostensible charge, and both MBS and the Trump administration will identify Qatar as a state sponsor of terrorism—an about-face in U.S. policy—within a few months of Trump being inaugurated. When MBS orders a *Washington Post* journalist kidnapped and assassinated by CSMARC in 2018 (see chapter 9), his explanation to Trump's son-in-law will be that it was a "counterterrorism" operation. MBS's use of "counterterrorism" as a euphemism for illegal rendition increases the likelihood that Flynn was introduced to CSMARC, at least conceptually, during the presidential transition period.

At the January 2017 transition meeting between Zamel, Nader, Flynn, Bannon, and al-Assiri, the five men also discuss regime change in Iran. Communications relating to the meeting since leaked to the media "show that participants in the meetings discussed a multi-pronged strategy for eroding, and eventually ending, the current Iranian regime—including economic, information, and military tactics for weakening the Tehran government."[196] MBS adviser al-Assiri "hobnobs in New York with Michael Flynn and other members of the transition team" not long after these same Trump advisers have done so with MBZ. Given that Zamel, Nader, Flynn, Bannon, and al-Assiri discuss not just "economic . . . and military tactics for weakening the Tehran government" but also "information tactics," Zamel's presence at the meetings make sense, as such tactics are his specialty—and what he had offered to the Trump campaign at Trump Tower in August 2016.[197] The *Daily Beast* notes that Zamel's presence at such a high-level meeting underscores that he "remained close to the Trump team throughout the election and into the transition," observing that he was able to do so because of an "easy in": "he had been introduced to Nader"—whom the digital media outlet calls "closely connected with the Trump campaign"—"years earlier by John Hannah, a former aide to Dick Cheney now working as a senior counsel at the Foundation for Defense of Democracies, a right-leaning think tank known for its anti-Iran work."[198] Hannah later ended up on the advisory council of Wikistrat, one of Zamel's two "business intelligence companies."[199] It is as the former head of Wikistrat and current head of Psy-Group that Zamel presents, at his January 2017 meetings with members of the Trump transition, a plan the *Daily Beast* calls as "audacious" as his August 2016 plan to win the presidential election for Trump: a "bound presentation full of tactics to undercut [Iran's] government."[200] If indeed Nader and the Israeli Zamel have known one another for "years," it means the men were associates in fall 2015, when Nader convened a meeting of Sunni Arab leaders on a yacht in the Red Sea to discuss a conspiracy in which Israel was to play a part.

Nader's role at the January 2017 meetings with Flynn, Bannon, Zamel, and al-Assiri, according to the *Daily Beast,* is possibly linked to the "economic sabotage against Iran" that he will pitch directly not just to members of the administration over the first weeks and months of the Trump presidency but also to "Saudi [and] UAE officials."[201] The outlet notes that these meetings cover the same topic as the Kushner-Flynn-Bannon-MBZ New York City meeting of just a few weeks earlier: Iran policy.[202] By meeting with al-Assiri, Trump transition team members Bannon and Flynn are as good as meeting with MBS himself, as the *Daily Beast* reports that "sources familiar with the Saudi footprint in Washington describe[ ] Assiri as one of MBS's closest allies and most trusted confidants."[203]

In the first week of January 2017, several American intelligence agencies issue a joint report "accusing Russia of intervening clandestinely during the 2016 election to help Trump win the White House."[204] Meanwhile, the FBI is already investigating Flynn's December phone calls to Kislyak; these communications become public knowledge on January 12, the second day of meetings in the Seychelles—meetings whose scheduling and conduct are apparently unaffected by a public report accusing Russia of secretly aiding Trump's election chances.[205]

That George Nader "uses his connections to Russia" to set up and attend the meetings in the Seychelles underscores that when he gathered together MBS, MBZ, el-Sisi, and others on a yacht in the Red Sea in fall 2015 he may well have been doing so mindful of his ability to access and to some degree represent the interests of top Kremlin officials. It also suggests that he may have played this same role in meeting with Trump Jr. and Stephen Miller at Trump Tower in August 2016 alongside Joel Zamel, who had previously worked for Kremlin-linked oligarchs—and that in the Seychelles Nader may once again have been acting in the interests of the Kremlin.[206] According to the *Washington Post*, Nader will tell Robert Mueller that the purpose of the Seychelles meetings was to have "a representative of the Trump transition . . . meet with an emissary from Moscow to discuss future relations between the countries . . . [and] establish a back-channel line of communication between Moscow and the incoming administration."[207] Prince will under oath contradict Nader, telling the House Permanent Select Committee on Intelligence, as detailed by CNN, that the meetings in the Seychelles were "not part of an effort to set up a Russian backchannel with the Trump administration."[208] Prince will further contradict the Seychelles meetings' organizer by saying that he was not acting as a Trump representative in attending any of the events on the island.[209] Prince will tell Congress that he didn't know who Dmitriev was before meeting him, and that he only Googled him seconds before he met him so he would be able to recognize his face. He will also tell Congress that he would have done more research on the RDIF director and Kremlin agent before meeting him to discuss geopolitics—including urgent matters touching on U.S.-Russia relations—but "data roaming is expensive when you're overseas."[210] According to publicly available information, Prince is a billionaire worth a reported $2.4 billion.[211]

When the Mueller Report is released in April 2019, it will confirm Nader's narrative, rather than Prince's, in all particulars. Contemporaneous reporting from media in the United States will reach the same conclusion. According to *The Intercept,* when Prince arrived in the Seychelles his long-time friend and business partner MBZ told the Emiratis gathered at the Four Seasons Hotel that Erik was "his guy" and that the UAE "owed Erik a favor."[212] The digital media outlet adds that, from MBZ's perspective, "Trump's public infatuation with Putin and his apparent eagerness to improve relations with Russia gave the UAE a chance to play dealmaker [between Trump and Russia] and diminish Iran's position in the Middle East, starting with the war in Syria."[213] MBZ putting a Trump adviser, Prince, together with one of Putin's top lieutenants, Dmitriev, was therefore both making good on a favor owed to Prince and robustly advancing the interests of the UAE. As *The Intercept* summarizes, the Mueller Report establishes "that the meeting was a pre-arranged attempt to establish a backchannel between Russia and the incoming Trump administration and has led House Intelligence Committee chair Adam Schiff to make a criminal referral to the Justice Department for perjury [by Erik Prince]."[214]

The order of events in the Seychelles is first a meeting between Nader, Prince, and MBZ—a meeting that is also attended by Hamad al Mazrouei, the head of the Emirates' chief intelligence service, and Mohammad Dahlan, who is "fluent in Russian and . . . a conduit from the UAE to Putin's

Kremlin"—and then the first of two meetings between Prince, Nader, and Dmitriev, the last of whom has "close ties to Putin" that have put him atop the RDIF.[215] The RDIF has, within the preceding nine months, become wholly Kremlin-owned, after previously being controlled by VEB, the Kremlin-owned bank whose CEO Jared Kushner had just met privately with a few weeks earlier.[216] As *Vox* notes, such "off-the-grid" meetings are "a key focal point for the Trump-Russia investigation . . . [and] could offer answers about any potential deals or informal understandings between Trump and Russia right before [Trump] took office."[217] MBZ is represented at those Seychelles meetings he does not personally attend by Nader, who according to the *New York Times* is in the second meeting, between himself, Prince, and Dmitriev, "represent[ing] the crown prince in the three-way conversation."[218] The *Washington Post* will go further, reporting in April 2017 that MBZ, rather than Nader, was in fact the original animating force behind the U.S.-Russia meetings in the Seychelles: "The United Arab Emirates arranged a secret meeting in January [2017] between Blackwater founder Erik Prince and a Russian close to President Vladimir Putin as part of an apparent effort to establish a back-channel line of communication between Moscow and President-elect Donald Trump, according to U.S., European and Arab officials."[219] The *Post* adds that "Emirati officials believed Mr. Prince was speaking for the Trump transition team" and "Dmitriev represented Mr. Putin, according to several people familiar with the meeting. Mr. Nader, who grew close later to several advisers in the Trump White House, had once worked as a consultant to [Prince's former company] Blackwater, a private security firm now known as Academi. Mr. Nader introduced his former employer [Prince] to the Russian [Dmitriev]."[220]

In fully disentangling the complex web of alliances, courses of representation, and prior histories of the many players in the Seychelles meetings, the *Post* concludes that the purpose of the meetings, finally, was the furtherance of a bargain in which Trump would drop sanctions on Russia in exchange for the Kremlin limiting its assistance to Iran in the Middle East. As described by the *Post*, "UAE agreed to broker the meeting in part to explore whether Russia could be persuaded to curtail its relationship with Iran, including in Syria, a Trump administration objective that would be likely to require major concessions to Moscow on U.S. sanctions."[221] The meeting thus casts Erik Prince in the same role he had served in for the entirety of the 2016 presidential campaign: at once an adviser to Donald Trump and to the UAE on counterterrorism issues in the Middle East. In pursuit of this dual role at the fulcrum of the Red Sea Conspiracy, reports the *Post*, Prince "presented himself as an unofficial envoy for Trump to high-ranking Emiratis involved in setting up his [January 2017] meeting with the Putin confidant [Dmitriev]."[222]

Reporting from the *New Yorker* underscores that the idea of a multi-national bargain in the Middle East was not a mere post-election trial balloon. According to the magazine, "shortly before the November, 2016, election, Mohammed bin Zayed, the crown prince of Abu Dhabi, floated to a longtime American interlocutor what sounded, at the time, like an un-likely grand bargain. The Emirati leader told the American that Vladimir Putin, the Russian President, might be interested in resolving the conflict in Syria in exchange for the lifting of sanctions imposed in response to Russia's actions in Ukraine."[223] The *New Yorker* adds that "three countries that enjoyed unparalleled influence with the incoming Administration— Israel, Saudi Arabia, and the UAE—privately embraced the goal."[224] Two of these nations (Saudi Arabia and the UAE) will have already begun their détente with Russia by 2017, "making billions of dollars in investments in Russia and convening high-level meetings in Moscow, Abu Dhabi, [and] Riyadh" prior to the meetings in the Seychelles.[225]

What this timeline suggests is that the Kremlin may have always in-tended to bargain with the United States on sanctions, via Saudi Arabia and the United Arab Emirates, even as it was attacking America's electoral infrastructure. It may not have been, in fact, a latecomer to the notion of a grand bargain in the Middle East, but rather a major player in the con-spiracy from the start. Indeed, the *New Yorker* notes that MBZ's pre-election proposal for a grand bargain as easily could have come "from Putin him-self or one of his confidants" as the Emirati crown prince, given the depth of the Emiratis' contacts with the Russians, in many instances through George Nader, prior to Election Day in 2016.[226]

While the Israeli government's pre-election stance toward a Trump-Russia bargain was more opaque, especially given Psy-Group's status as a plausibly deniable cutout for Netanyahu's office, as soon as Trump's election victory is announced, per the *New Yorker*, "the Israeli government [is] encouraging the incoming Trump Administration to cooperate more closely with Putin"; by May 2019, Netanyahu has publicly announced that he "proposed to Trump and Putin to form a U.S.-Russia-Israel trilateral committee that will meet in Jerusalem to discuss the security situation in the Middle East," a proposal he notes is "unprecedented" and which, he adds, both Trump and Putin have already accepted.[227] It is unknown whether the deal Netanyahu hopes to broker in 2019 is the same one that, per the *New Yorker*, he'd been seeking immediately after Trump's election; that deal, as described to a former U.S. official by an "Israeli cabinet minister with close ties to Netanyahu," involved Trump "trading Ukraine [U.S.-Russia sanctions] for Syria."[228]

That Erik Prince got his pre-Seychelles marching orders from participants in the highly unusual December 2016 meeting at Trump Tower—the meeting between Bannon, Kushner, Flynn, Nader, and MBZ—is underscored by an April 2017 *Washington Post* report revealing that "following the New York meeting between the Emiratis and Trump aides, [MBZ] was approached by Prince, who said he was authorized to act as an unofficial surrogate for the president-elect. . . . He wanted [MBZ] to set up a meeting with a Putin associate."[229] This may explain why Prince bought his ticket to the Seychelles before Nader had even asked Dmitriev to meet him there: Prince, on authority granted to him by someone in Trump's inner circle, had already spoken to MBZ about a secret Trump-Russia summit in the Seychelles and was, like Nader, thereafter acting as an agent for both MBZ and the PTT. As the *Washington Post* will report, "Current and former U.S. officials who have worked closely with [MBZ] . . . say it would be out of character for him to arrange the January 11 [Prince-Dmitriev] meeting without getting a green light in advance from top aides to Trump and Putin, if not the leaders themselves."[230] MBZ's contacts with Putin are well established; less clearly understood is whether, as posited by the *Post*, MBZ may have gotten his green light from Kushner or even Trump himself when he visited Trump Tower in December 2016—with the latter possibility seeming to presuppose a protocol-busting meeting with the president-elect that would perhaps have required, in MBZ's view, that he enter the United States in secret. In this telling of events, the two days of Seychelles meetings were nothing less than a Trump-Putin summit, arranged by the principals themselves and conducted by their most trusted agents.[231] Of Prince the *Post* will write, "Prince would probably have been seen as too controversial to serve in any official capacity in the Trump transition or administration. But his ties to Trump advisers, experience with clandestine work and relationship with the royal leaders of the Emirates—where he moved in 2010 amid mounting legal problems for his American business—would have positioned him as an ideal go-between."[232] MBZ therefore had every reason to believe, the *Post* observes, that Prince "had the blessing of the new administration to act as its unofficial representative."[233]

Speaking on behalf of the Trump administration in April 2017, White House press secretary Sean Spicer will say that "we are not aware of any meetings [in the Seychelles]."[234]

When Prince testifies under oath before Congress about his meetings in the Seychelles, he fails to mention the presence on the island of either al Mazrouei or Dahlan, stating only that MBZ had "some of his brothers" and an "entourage" with him; he will also claim that he and Dmitriev only met one-on-one at a hotel bar as a fortuitous encounter suggested by an Emirati whose name Prince could not recall.[235] Lying to Congress is a federal crime chargeable as perjury (18 U.S.C. § 1621) or making false statements (18 U.S.C. § 1001) depending upon whether the witness was placed under oath pre-testimony; each count of perjury or making false statements carries a maximum penalty of five years in prison.[236]

The *Daily Mail* calls al Mazrouei "one of the Arab world's top spies" and Dahlan "a shadowy conduit [from MBZ] to Putin's Kremlin."[237] That Prince lives in the UAE underscores that there was no need for MBZ, the de facto ruler of that country, to summon him to the Seychelles—unless it was to keep any meeting that occurred under MBZ's direction a secret. Just so, MBZ's meeting with Bannon, Kushner, and Nader in Trump Tower a month earlier had been a secret when it easily could have been arranged as part of an official state visit or, at a minimum, a declared visit with prior notification to the U.S. State Department. MBZ's secrecy in the Seychelles is in keeping with that of the company he keeps there, however; according to a "source close to bin Zayed . . . Hamad [al Mazrouei] supervises all these things. Those guys supervise major secret operations."[238] The *Daily Mail* notes that al Mazrouei is not just the Emiratis' chief intelligence officer but "bin Zayed's right-hand man . . . giving him access to the country's advanced surveillance technology. Sources say he is at the center of an Emirati plan to exert influence on both western democracies and [the UAE's] neighboring Gulf states."[239] Al Mazrouei has allegedly, in the past, "threaten[ed] to release naked photos of Kuwaiti politicians in an attempt to influence the country's parliamentary elections" and "threatened to release fabricated sex tapes of [a Qatari] news anchor."[240] Dahlan, a "security adviser" to MBZ, began working for bin Zayed in 2011 as "an informal UAE emissary to the Kremlin, helping coordinate the UAE's military action to cooperate with Russian interests . . . [and] going on secret missions [and] meeting at the Kremlin on behalf of MBZ."[241]

According to an Emirati source close to MBZ, after the Prince-Dmitriev meeting in the Seychelles "Dahlan [meets] with Erik Prince and the Russians several times in the Maldives," a separate island archipelago off the eastern coast of Africa.[242] Prince says nothing of any such meeting to Congress when he testifies before the House Permanent Select Committee on Intelligence in late 2017. The *Washington Post* reports that, whether or not there were in fact follow-up meetings after the first set of Trump-Russia meetings in the Seychelles, "the Seychelles meeting [between Prince and Dmitriev] was deemed productive by the UAE and Russia."[243] That the principals—including Putin—who appear to have orchestrated the Seychelles summit should be pleased over its outcome when the description of it provided by its participants is relatively anodyne should be cause for some concern. Indeed, it is clear the American public has little of the information it needs to have about what really happened on the island, from an answer on whether Rick Gerson was really there on "vacation" to an explanation for Prince having done his utmost to avoid discussing Mohammed Dahlan and Hamad al Mazrouei.

As NBC News notes, "Mueller's interest in Gerson is another sign that he is examining connections between the UAE and Trump associates. Counterintelligence investigators have been scrutinizing UAE influence in the Trump campaign since before Mueller was appointed as special counsel, and the probe has continued in coordination with Mueller's team."[244] That the findings of this counterintelligence probe are not included in the Mueller Report means that they remain, as of summer 2019, known only to certain members of the U.S. intelligence community.

On January 11, *BuzzFeed News* publishes the so-called Steele dossier, a thirty-five-page collation of raw intelligence compiled by Christopher Steele, the former Moscow desk chief for the United Kingdom's foreign intelligence service (MI6).[245] The headline for the article containing a link to the dossier declares that Trump has "deep ties" to Russia; Trump responds to the report and the dossier with what will later be revealed as five substantial lies: (1) "I have no dealings with Russia"; (2) "I have no deals that could happen in Russia"; (3) "we [the Trump Organization] have stayed away [from deals in Russia]; (4) "I . . . don't want to [do deals in Russia]"; and (5) "I think that [deals in Russia] would be a conflict."[246]

On January 18, two days before Trump's inauguration, Jared Kushner submits his SF-86 security clearance form to the FBI.[247] Kushner's initial submission is later found to have well over a hundred errors and omissions, including at least a hundred foreign contacts that Kushner failed to declare, contrary to law. Submitting false information on an SF-86 is a federal crime punishable by up to five years in prison.[248] Kushner is forced to update his SF-86 form three times to fix his many errors and omissions—and even after his third resubmission, he leaves off key meetings with foreign nationals, including the highly controversial June 2016 Trump Tower meeting in which he meets with Kremlin agents alongside Trump Jr. and Manafort.[249] Charles Phalen, director of the National Background Investigations Bureau, a division of the Office of Personnel Management, will later tell Congress that in his entire professional career he has never seen as many errors and omissions on an SF-86 form as he saw on Kushner's.[250] Kushner will submit the fourth update of his SF-86 five months into the Trump presidency, on June 21, 2017, this time including the June 2016 Trump Tower meeting—which is by then just two and a half weeks from being revealed in a *New York Times* article.[251]

Career national security officials ultimately deny Kushner's application for a permanent security clearance over fears that he is, at the time of the denial, susceptible to "foreign influence," as well as due to unanswered concerns relating to his "personal conduct and . . . business interests."[252] Kushner's security clearance application is one of at least twenty-five Trump administration applications denied by career national security officials over concerns about "foreign influence"—all of which denials will be overruled by a Trump political appointee.[253] Some Trump staffers will even receive access to classified information in the face of articulable, documented concerns about "drug use and criminal conduct."[254]

Despite all the problems with his permanent security clearance application, Kushner will request to see classified materials "more . . . than almost every other White House official" once a Trump political appointee has—at Trump's direction—overruled the denial of his application.[255]

On January 20, Trump is inaugurated as the forty-fifth president of the United States.

As chairman of Trump's inaugural committee, Thomas Barrack raises a record $106.7 million.[256] His employees at Colony Capital notice, simultaneously, "a pickup in Israeli interest" in Barrack's business ventures.[257] Special counsel Robert Mueller will in 2018 investigate donations to the committee Barrack ran, indicting Paul Manafort associate Sam Patten for "helping a Ukrainian oligarch disguise a $50,000 contribution" to the committee. The oligarch is described as a "pro-Russian" figure by the *New York Times*.[258] Despite the amount of money Barrack raises for Trump's inauguration being double the previous record for a presidential inauguration, Trump ultimately puts on one-quarter the number of inaugural events as George W. Bush's second inaugural committee.[259]

Trump's inaugural week is overseen by WIS Media Partners, a company run by Stephanie Winston Wolkoff, a member of Melania Trump's "inner circle" who is also known to be a "diligent enforcer" for the First Lady.[260] According to *Vanity Fair*, in the lead-up to Trump's inaugural week Wolkoff works "in close proximity to the Trump family and inaugural chair Tom Barrack."[261] Nearly a quarter of the $107 million raised by Barrack ($26 million) goes to Wolkoff's company, even as a much larger sum—$40 million—ultimately can't be accounted for at all.[262]

Nearly $24 million of the $26 million paid to Wolkoff's WIS Media Partners goes not to Wolkoff but to an entity tied to another person close to the Trumps, television producer Mark Burnett. Per *Vanity Fair*, the bulk of the WIS Media Partners payment ended up in the coffers of Inaugural Productions, "an independent organization run by individuals formerly associated with television producer Mark Burnett, which was responsible for staging several [inaugural] events."[263] The magazine writes that "Burnett . . . wanted to keep his involvement [in the inaugural events] private," a fact made troubling not only by the size of the payments made to entities connected to him but by allegations in the month before Election Day 2016 that Burnett was in possession of—and was protecting from release—hours of audiotapes of NBC's *The Apprentice* in which Trump makes comments about women and African Americans that would have spelled doom for his candidacy for president.[264]

During the transition, Burnett asks Barrack to sit down with Robert Foresman, the American banker with, as ABC News reports, "established ties inside the Kremlin."[265] If hired for the job he is seeking with the Trump administration, Foresman would be in a position to act as an interlocutor between Trump and the Kremlin.[266] Barrack is scheduled to meet with Foresman on a day during the transition period when he is also set to meet with Trump and Kushner; the meeting never occurs, and it is unknown whether Barrack discusses Foresman—who "lived for years in Moscow, where he led a $3 billion Russian investment fund" and maintained "connections to Russian President Vladimir Putin's inner circle"—in his meetings with Trump and Kushner.[267] Shortly thereafter, however, Foresman is granted an audience with Michael Flynn.[268] Foresman also meets with Sergey Gorkov, the Russian banker and Putin ally, around the same time that Kushner does.[269] Foresman now refuses to answer questions from congressional investigators about his contact with Gorkov.[270] In a civil deposition, however, Foresman has admitted to knowing Igor Sechin extremely well; Sechin is the Putin aide and "former" Russian intelligence officer who was running Rosneft, the Kremlin-owned oil company, in December 2016, at which point it sold off a large stake to the Qatar Investment Authority (a deal discussed in Steele's dossier).[271]

In February 2018, when the White House unceremoniously terminates Wolkoff's ongoing work for the First Lady, the administration will put out to the press that the basis for the termination is "displeasure from the Trumps" over the payment of $26 million to Wolkoff's firm—a payment both Melania and Donald Trump will claim no knowledge of, with White House press secretary Sarah Huckabee Sanders saying that "the president was focused on the transition during that time [pre-inauguration], and not on any of the planning for the inauguration."[272] Subsequent reporting will show exactly the opposite, however, with Bloomberg revealing that Trump was so "actively" involved in even intimate details of various inaugural events that he "fussed over tablecloths" and the booking of individual entertainers, with Barrack "frequently" calling Trump so he could voice his opinion on such matters.[273] According to statements Barrack makes to his aides during the transition, Trump specifically "wanted to know everything about the inauguration's finances."[274] By 2019, the inaugural finances Trump was so minutely tracking will be under federal investigation by the Southern District of New York, the New Jersey attorney general's office, the D.C. attorney general's office, and the House Judiciary Committee—the last of which will seek, as part of its inquiry, "campaign and transition . . . communications 'regarding Russia, the United Arab Emirates, Qatar, or Saudi Arabia.'"[275]

Congressional interest in intersections between the inaugural committee and the presidential transition is understandable, given that, as Bloomberg notes, "Barrack planned much of the inauguration . . . [but] was also a key player in the transition effort taking place . . . at Trump Tower. His dual role allowed him to keep Trump apprised of the inaugural committee's efforts, according to people familiar with their conversations."[276]

A link between the campaign and the inaugural committee is likewise established when Barrack selects Rick Gates, Trump's deputy campaign manager and later RNC liaison, as the inaugural committee's deputy.[277] Interestingly—given Gates's pre-RNC solicitation of a proposal by Joel Zamel for a general election marketing campaign—Bloomberg will note that Trump's relationship with Gates had taken a turn for the worse after Trump got upset about "how more than $700,000 for a direct mail contract had been allocated [by Gates] . . . while [Paul] Manafort and Gates were overseeing plans for the Republican convention."[278] Whatever Gates had done with a $700,000 set-aside for campaign marketing at a time he was secretly soliciting marketing proposals from an Israeli business intelligence firm, Trump is allegedly concerned enough about it that he tells Barrack to fire Gates shortly after Election Day, an order Barrack declines to execute.[279] In fact, Barrack, who by 2018 is himself being investigated by the Southern District of New York—after Gates becomes a cooperating federal witness—does the opposite of firing Gates: not only does he keep Gates on as his deputy, but he pays him $100,000 for just seventy days of work, the equivalent of a $525,000 annual salary.[280] If Trump is indeed paying close attention to his inaugural budget during the transition period, Barrack's significant payment to Gates after Trump had ordered his firing is one that Trump might have been expected to notice.

One of the most high-profile events of Barrack's tenure as inaugural chair is his Chairman's Dinner, an event he orchestrates with Gates that is held the week of the inauguration and features attendance by Trump himself and a "swarm" of "foreign diplomats."[281] According to Bloomberg, Barrack will make use of the "network of connections" he and Gates establish between Trump and representatives of "foreign governments" to "pursue deals arising from Trump's promised $1 trillion infrastructure push."[282] While the identities of the foreign nationals Barrack and Gates target for involvement in their sub rosa lobbying of the president are unknown, Bloomberg notes that this kind of lobbying effort "was considered viable within Colony [Barrack's firm] until at least April 2017, according to two people familiar with the plans. That month, Gates dined at an upscale Washington restaurant with Treasury Secretary Steven Mnuchin,

Barrack and seven Middle Eastern ambassadors."[283] The guest list at that April 14 dinner in a private room at Fiola Mare in Georgetown included, along with Barrack, Gates, and Mnuchin—the last of whom met with Colony executives at least three times in the 120 days post-inauguration—the ambassadors of Saudi Arabia, the United Arab Emirates, Bahrain, Jordan, Oman, Kuwait, and Qatar.[284]

According to an eight-page document Gates writes that summarizes Colony's plans to capitalize on connections made between Trump and associates of Barrack during the Chairman's Dinner, the dinner put Gates and Barrack in a position to "build a bridge to where government and business intersect globally . . . to strategically cultivate domestic and international relationships while avoiding any appearance of lobbying."[285] Bloomberg notes that by the time of the Chairman's Dinner, Barrack has "develop[ed] extensive ties with Trump and investors across the globe. He [has] nurtured special relationships with the Qatari sovereign wealth fund [the Qatar Investment Authority] and other Middle Eastern investors."[286]

Events such as the Chairman's Dinner—and missing funds such as the $40 million unaccounted for in a budget Trump was closely monitoring—will eventually lead to questions not just about the business opportunities Barrack and Gates sought to spin out of their inaugural roles but about donations made to the inaugural fund itself. Federal prosecutors will investigate how it came to pass that "several wealthy Russians and Ukrainians attended the inauguration," given "questions about how they gained access [to the events]."[287] In August 2018, Sam Patten, an associate of Gates's former boss, Paul Manafort, will plead guilty to using a straw buyer to help a pro-Kremlin Ukrainian oligarch, Serhiy Lyovochkin, attend the inauguration, a plan Patten executed through a firm he jointly ran with Konstantin Kilimnik.[288] According to the New York Times, Lyovochkin "was one of a clutch of oligarchs who paid Mr. Manafort more than $60 million [between 2007 and 2014] to promote pro-Russian political forces in Ukraine."[289] In his own future federal criminal proceedings, Gates will acknowledge the "possibility" that he on multiple occasions used "sham invoices" to the inauguration committee to receive reimbursement for unapproved expenses, including "personal expenses."[290] Vanity Fair adds that during the inaugural planning "Gates approached a couple individuals working on the inauguration and asked if they would be willing to be paid directly for their work by a donor, rather than by the inaugural committee"—a highly irregular arrangement that would in theory have allowed Gates to submit sham invoices for these services to hide donations from parties not eligible to give to the inaugural fund.[291]

Even as numerous media outlets will note the utility of Manafort to federal prosecutors as a cooperating witness, the same will be said of Patten, who in addition to his business relationship with Kilimnik has counted among his business associates Rinat Akhmetshin, "a Russian-born Washington lobbyist who attended the June 2016 Trump Tower meeting at which Kremlin-linked insiders had promised to provide the Trump campaign with damaging information about Mrs. Clinton." Patten is also connected to Trump's data firm Cambridge Analytica, a company with which he had a "yearslong business relationship" that saw him acting as a "consultant for election campaigns."[292] Patten's involvement in aiding foreign contributions to Trump's inaugural fund will come into even greater relief when it is revealed in February 2019 that his business partner Kilimnik not only came to D.C. for Trump's inauguration but met secretly with Patten's former business associate Paul Manafort while there—specifically to discuss a Russia-Ukraine "peace plan" that would lead to the end of sanctions on Russia.[293]

In June 2018, ABC News will report that "several billionaires with deep ties to Russia attended exclusive, invitation-only receptions during Donald Trump's inauguration festivities . . . and were given unprecedented access to Trump's inner circle."[294] ABC will add that "at least one oligarch was ushered into Statuary Hall in the U.S. Capitol for the traditional Inaugural Day luncheon," an event so exclusive it is typically "out of reach to donors and even most rank-and-file members of Congress."[295] Event attendees include the Russian Viktor Vekselberg, who sat with Michael Cohen at a candlelight dinner for inaugural donors of $1 million or more; the Soviet-born Leonard Blavatnik, the majority shareholder of Amedia, the largest television production company in Russia; the Russian-born entrepreneur Alexander Shustorovich, who has "a background in nuclear energy" and previously had a donation of his returned by the Republican National Committee "because of his past ties to the Russian government"; the Soviet-born Alexander Mashkevitch, a mining magnate whose Eurasian Natural Resources Corporation has done significant business with the Oleg Deripaska–controlled Russian aluminum company Rusal; and Russian ambassador Sergey Kislyak.[296]

ABC News will also note one significant British and one significant American guest on the list of attendees to the inauguration's most exclusive events. The Brit is Cambridge Analytica CEO Alexander Nix, who will, fourteen months after Trump's inauguration, resign his position after an undercover investigation catches him bragging about engaging in illicit election-tampering schemes; the American is Steve Wynn, who will in short order be named the Republican National Committee's finance chair by Trump—along with Michael Cohen and Elliott Broidy as deputy co-chairs—a position Wynn later must abdicate amid a "swarm of sexual misconduct allegations."[297] Broidy will also step down from his position, in his case due to revelations that he has been making secret "hush" payments to a Playboy Playmate. Cohen, likewise, will step down from his RNC finance position once he begins facing investigations of his own finances.[298]

The ABC News list of notable attendees of major Trump inaugural events adds to a list compiled by the *Washington Post* that includes Alexey Repik, a Russian pharmaceutical executive who has in the past been asked by Russian media about "rumors that he had ties to the FSB" (the successor to the KGB); Natalia Veselnitskaya, the self-described Kremlin "informant" who, at Donald Trump Jr.'s invitation, peddled dirt on Hillary Clinton at Trump Tower in June 2016; Rinat Akhmetshin, linked by his own colleagues to Soviet intelligence, who likewise attended the June 2016 Trump Tower meeting; Maria Butina, later convicted of being an unregistered Kremlin agent; Alexander Torshin, believed to be Butina's handler, and an unindicted co-conspirator in her federal charging documents; and Boris Titov, a politician "running for president of Russia with the Kremlin's blessing.[299] Veselnitskaya will later be indicted for obstruction of justice by the Southern District of New York, in part for lying about her relationship to the Kremlin.[300]

According to the *Post*, the full guest list for Trump's most selective inaugural events "caught the attention of counterintelligence officials at the FBI, according to former U.S. officials . . . because some of the figures had surfaced in the agency's investigation of the Trump campaign's ties to Russia."[301] ABC News will subsequently report that federal law enforcement is also investigating "inaugural donations tied to the UAE, Saudi Arabia, and Qatar."[302] In 2019, NBC News will report that fourteen "major contributors" to Trump's inaugural fund—donating more than $350,000 on average—received nominations to be U.S. ambassadors.[303]

On the payout side of the inaugural ledger, *Vanity Fair* will reveal that $1.5 million was paid to Trump's International Hotel in D.C. to house Gates and more than a dozen inaugural staffers, and that the hotel provided the inaugural committee with a surprisingly high cost estimate for pre-inaugural events.[304] More troublingly, the magazine reports that—despite claims that Trump and Gates had had a falling-out and that Trump wanted Barrack to fire Gates—Gates's position in fact gave him a "high access level . . . security pass within Trump Tower" and that his "closeness with the Trump family" was readily apparent.[305] Gates was, in particular, in "constant communication" with Trump's adult children, "frequently work[ing] out of Donald Trump Jr.'s office [in Trump Tower]" despite the offices for the inaugural committee being across the street from the Trump-owned building.[306] Per *Vanity Fair*, as the presidential transition period wore on, Wolkoff increasingly was "left out of meetings" she was supposed to be invited to regarding the inaugural committee's finances, and found that time and time again she "could not justify the [budget] numbers coming in," as it seemed the inaugural committee was repeatedly being suspiciously overcharged by certain vendors.[307]

According to *Vanity Fair*, Wolkoff's gravest concern regarding inauguration spending focuses on Barrack's Chairman's Dinner, which received an inordinate amount of money and attention, according to the chief inaugural planner.[308] Perhaps most telling is the revelation of a draft guest list for the event, which includes a number of named individuals—among them Michael Flynn, Elliott Broidy, Michael Cohen, Rick Gates, Steve Mnuchin, K. T. McFarland, Mitch McConnell, Kevin McCarthy, Mike

Pence, Reince Priebus, Wilbur Ross, Rex Tillerson, Kellyanne Conway, Steve Bannon, Franklin Haney (see chapter 9), and the Emirati ambassador to the United States, Yousef al-Otaiba—but also seven unnamed Saudi "foreign ministers," one unnamed foreign minister from Qatar, and one unnamed foreign minister from the United Arab Emirates.[309] *Vanity Fair* notes that the Saudis, the Qatari, and the Emirati were the only dinner guests whose names were not revealed.[310]

Now that the inaugural committee is the subject of, as described by ProPublica, a "wide-ranging federal criminal investigation," assessments of the players involved—and the laws potentially broken—are becoming public. ProPublica observes that inaugural money being paid to Trump's D.C. hotel, and Ivanka Trump being involved in the negotiations for those payments, could violate federal tax laws; it notes, too, that the Trumps' inaugural planners were so set on using Trump's hotel for inaugural events that they pushed the hotel's management to cancel a prayer breakfast to make space for an event Trump then billed to the inaugural fund.[311] In February 2019, the Southern District of New York will announce that it is investigating possible mail fraud, wire fraud, money laundering, false statements, election fraud, and conspiracy to defraud the United States in conjunction with Trump's inauguration, issuing subpoenas seeking "all information related to inaugural donors, vendors, contractors, bank accounts of the inaugural committee and any information related to foreign contributors to the committee," according to the *Washington Post*, which further notes that "only U.S. citizens and legal residents can legally donate to a committee established to finance presidential inaugural festivities."[312] According to the *New York Times*, the subpoenas are intended not just to determine if "any foreigners illegally donated to the committee" but also to discover "whether committee staff members knew that such donations were illegal, asking for documents laying out legal requirements for donations."[313]

Two recipients of inauguration-related subpoenas are Los Angeles venture capitalist Imaad Zuberi and Avenue Ventures, a firm Zuberi is affiliated with; by January 13, 2019, Avenue Ventures had donated a total of $1 million to the inaugural committee and the host committee for the 2016 Republican National Convention.[314] Over the same period, Zuberi himself gave nearly $500,000 to Trump's reelection committee and to the Republican National Committee.[315] At issue in the ongoing investigation of Zuberi is likely one of two possibilities: that Zuberi was used as a straw donor for illegal foreign donations to Trump by Qataris, Emiratis, or Saudis, or that the Trump transition team guided new business in the Middle East to Zuberi's operation in exchange for his donations to inaugural, 2020 Trump campaign, Republican National Convention, and Republican National Committee funds.

Zuberi went to Trump Tower in December 2016 in the company of Michael Flynn, on the same day Flynn was meeting with the Qatari foreign minister and Steve Bannon. While Zuberi also met with the Qatari foreign minister that day, he claims now that his discussions with Flynn and the Qatari all came during a walk to Trump Tower from another location—and then in an elevator at Trump Tower—but not in Trump's transition offices.[316] The next day, however, following a meeting between the Qatari foreign minister and transition officials, Zuberi meets with him again, almost immediately thereafter flying to Saudi Arabia and the United Arab Emirates on unknown business.[317] Zuberi's attorney will tell the *Times* that Zuberi merely "bumped into Mr. Flynn at Trump Tower and asked to take a selfie," and that while he did also have discussions about possibly doing business with both Michael Cohen and Elliott Broidy, these discussions were "brief."[318] The *Times* notes that Zuberi was at a "dinner for foreign diplomats in Washington" associated with the inauguration—a dinner that matches the description of Thomas Barrack's Chairman's Dinner—where he sat with, among others, Howard Lorber, the man whom Donald Trump Jr. called as soon as he found out in June 2016 that the Kremlin would be delivering opposition research on Hillary Clinton to Trump Tower. Zuberi and Lorber also sat with a diplomat from Bahrain. According to the *Times*, "executives who do business in the Persian Gulf and a person close to Mr. Zuberi said his firm had done business or sought investments in several gulf kingdoms, including Qatar, Saudi Arabia, the United Arab Emirates and Bahrain."[319]

Another entity subjected to a subpoena relating to inaugural giving is Stripe, a tech firm among whose backers is Thrive, an investment company run by Jared Kushner's brother, Josh Kushner.[320]

In December 2018, the *New York Times* will reveal that federal prosecutors in the Southern District of New York (Manhattan) and Eastern District of New York (Brooklyn) investigating Trump's inaugural fund and a pro-Trump super PAC are focusing "on whether people from Middle Eastern nations—including Qatar, Saudi Arabia and the United Arab Emirates—used straw donors to disguise their donations to the two funds." According to the newspaper, the federal investigation "underscores the growing scope of criminal inquiries that pose a threat to Mr. Trump's presidency."[321] The super PAC under investigation is Rebuilding America Now, the fund for which Thomas Barrack began raising money in mid-2016— when, according to the *Times*, "Mr. Trump's presidential campaign was short of cash" in substantial part because, "while Mr. Trump insisted that he could finance his own campaign, he refused to dig too deeply into his own pockets."[322] Barrack tells federal investigators in December 2017 that Paul Manafort, Trump's campaign manager in mid-2016 and the man who encouraged him to create Rebuilding America Now, "seemed to view the political committee as an arm of the campaign, despite laws meant to prevent such coordination," creating the possibility that Trump's broken promise to self-finance his presidential campaign directly led to fundraising efforts that ran afoul of federal law.[323] Moreover, given that the super PAC was created less than three weeks after the Saudis and Emiratis told Trump Jr. that they wanted to aid the Trump campaign, any donations to Rebuilding America Now by Saudis or Emiratis, or straw donors representing Saudis or Emiratis, could constitute illicit pre-election collusion between Trump's campaign and a foreign power—especially if the campaign treated the super PAC as an adjunct, not an independent entity.

Rebuilding America Now ultimately raises $23 million, "making it one of the important sources of funds for advertisements, polls and other political expenditures on Trump's behalf."[324] The *Times* notes that shortly after Manafort was fired from the Trump campaign in August 2016, he and Barrack took a cruise during which the two men met with Hamad bin Jassim bin Jaber Al Thani, who until 2013 had been the director of the Qatar Investment Authority (see chapter 4); the cruise is reportedly of interest to the investigators probing Rebuilding America Now.[325]

Per an accounting conducted by the *Times*, there are now at least a dozen federal investigations into "President Trump or his family business or a cadre of his advisers and associates" that did not end when Robert Mueller's investigation ended in March 2019, though these investigations "grew out of his work, all but ensuring that a legal threat will continue to loom over the Trump presidency" even after the April 2019 publication of a redacted version of the Mueller Report.[326] The *Times* describes these dozen investigations as far broader in scope than the special counsel's work, and notes that Trump is so concerned about the course of these probes that in late 2018 he "privately asked the former acting attorney general, Matthew G. Whitaker, if someone he [Trump] viewed as loyal could be put in charge of the investigations."[327] According to John S. Martin Jr., a retired federal judge and the former United States attorney in the Southern District of New York, "The important thing to remember is that almost everything Donald Trump did was in the Southern District of New York. He ran his business in the Southern District. He ran his campaign from the Southern District. He came home to New York every night."[328] In addition to the numerous Southern District investigations produced by Mueller's work, the *Times* notes that Mueller-related investigations continue, at a minimum, in the Eastern District of New York, the U.S. Attorney's Office in D.C., the Eastern District of Virginia, Main Justice ("which continues to investigate the business and political dealings of Elliott Broidy"), and the Central District of California.[329]

In January 2019, Robert Mueller announces that, nearly a year after former Trump deputy campaign manager Rick Gates began cooperating with federal prosecutors, he is still cooperating on "several ongoing investigations" other than the special counsel's investigation.[330] In March 2019, the *Guardian* reports that "Donald Trump's inauguration received tens of thousands of dollars from shell companies that masked the involvement of a foreign contributor or others with foreign ties," with $25,000 of these payments attributable to Elon Lebouvich, an Israeli businessman active in New York City real estate who bought inauguration tickets for himself and a companion he would not name when contacted by the British media outlet.[331] In May 2019, Gates's sentencing hearing will be delayed for the sixth time, in part, the *Daily Beast* reports, because he is participating in an ongoing probe of "possible Middle Eastern election influence."[332]

As officials at the State Department are successfully preventing Trump from executing his plan to drop all sanctions on Russia as one of his first acts as president, he moves forward on a second proposal that delights two other countries with whom his campaign has had highly suspicious interactions pre-election: Saudi Arabia and the United Arab Emirates.[333] On January 27, Trump issues a ban on all travel to the United States from three nations with substantial blocs of citizens then hostile to the Saudis and Emiratis—Iran, Syria, and Yemen—with an additional ban on travel from Sudan, whose government is in 2017 in conflict with Riyadh and Abu Dhabi but will, by 2018, have reached a détente with each.[334] Libya, which was originally expected to be part of the Red Sea Conspiracy in late 2015 but did not send a representative to the landmark meeting with MBS, MBZ, el-Sisi, and George Nader, also makes Trump's list.[335]

The travel ban is written by Stephen Miller, who had met with Nader and the president's son Don Jr. at Trump Tower in August 2016 to discuss MBS's and MBZ's support for the Trump campaign and their desire to assist it—regardless of the legality of doing so—prior to Election Day.[336] While many will criticize the Trump-Miller travel ban, claiming that it is targeting Muslims rather than terrorists, in fact the relatively small number of Muslim countries selected by Trump and Miller, and the lack of any connection between these countries and domestic terrorism in the United States, underscores that the intent of the order is something else entirely.[337] As the *Atlantic* notes, "nationals of the seven countries that Trump banned killed exactly zero people in terrorist attacks on U.S. soil between 1975 and 2015"; meanwhile, Trump "ignored the country that produced the vast majority of the 9/11 hijackers. Fifteen of the nineteen hijackers on September 11, 2001, were Saudi Arabians, yet Saudi Arabia was not on Trump's list."[338] Three of the four remaining 9/11 hijackers were from either the United Arab Emirates or Egypt—two other nations involved in the Red Sea Conspiracy and not on the travel ban list.[339]

ANNOTATIONS

Among those hired for the presidential transition team is Iranian American businessman Bijan Kian, the longtime business partner of Trump's top national security advisor, Mike Flynn.

Though an Iranian American, Kian shares Flynn's animus for the Iranian regime. Moreover, in addition to "shar[ing] Flynn's strong public opposition to Iran's theocratic government," Kian, the *Washington Times* writes in June 2017, has "a common interest [with Flynn] in the development of secure communications systems."[340] Throughout the 2016 campaign, Flynn and Kian are both on the board of GreenZone Systems Inc., a technology firm that Kian runs until April 2017.[341] GreenZone Systems, before being acquired by SAIFE, was a "leading supplier of secure mobile voice and data communications solutions," providing organizations with software that ensures their devices are "cloaked and hidden from discovery."[342] GreenZone's software also allows organizations to "create secure communities of interest that . . . [could] securely share data over the Internet to reduce third party [detection]."[343] The press release for SAIFE's acquisition of GreenZone Systems notes that the latter's products are largely used by militaries.[344]

Despite being—in a manner foreseeable to the Trump transition team—a foreign agent whose specialization is encrypted communications for military operations, Kian joins Trump's transition as deputy lead to the Office of the Director of National Intelligence, in which role he offers "policy input, strategic guidance and operational counsel to prepare candidates for the director of national intelligence, the CIA and other top officials."[345]

According to the *Washington Times*, Kian helps with the job search that results in Mike Pompeo being tapped by Trump as his CIA director.[346] Pompeo will later become Trump's secretary of state, a position from which, alongside Trump national security advisor John Bolton, he will, according to *USA Today*, "pick[ ] a fight with Iran that could lead America into war"; Pompeo replaces Rex Tillerson, who, according to an August 2018 article in

The Intercept, was not just fired at the insistence of the Emiratis and Saudis but specifically because his actions had prevented—in the summer of 2017—a full-scale ground invasion of Qatar by Saudi Arabia and the UAE.[347]

Kammenos is a "Putin ally" whose defense department is deemed by NATO intelligence to be "compromised by Russian intelligence," and whose Athens-based Institute for Geopolitical Studies is in an active "memorandum of understanding" with the Russian Institute for Strategic Studies, a unit of the office of Vladimir Putin that is a "think tank managed by Russia's foreign intelligence services."

Kammenos met a very different response from the Obama administration when he traveled to Washington in 2015. Both Secretary of Defense Ash Carter and Deputy Secretary of Defense Robert Work canceled their meetings with Kammenos at the last minute. According to *BuzzFeed News*, "Greek media tied the snub to Kammenos's very public support of a military-to-military relationship between his country and Russia."[348] Kammenos was permitted to meet, instead, with Undersecretary of Defense for Policy Christine Wormuth, but according to a former Pentagon official, "the sit-down soon became a testy back-and-forth."[349] The reason for the hostility was quite possibly the reason, too, for Papadopoulos's visit, the following year, to Kammenos: Russian sanctions. According to *BuzzFeed News*, "Wormuth tried to convince Kammenos to back another round of sanctions on Russia, and he refused, calling Russia 'an ally and friend, with whom we are related to with indissoluble bonds.'"[350] In an interview with Greek journalists upon his return to Athens, Kammenos reported that he was "asked to support the prolongation of the [Russian] sanctions, particularly in connection with Crimea. I explained the Ukrainian issue was very sensitive for Greece, as some 300,000 Greeks live in Mariupol [a city in southeastern Ukraine] and its neighborhood, and they feel safe next to the [Russian] Orthodox Church."[351]

CHAPTER 7

THE GANG OF SIX, WHATSAPP, AND THE QATAR BLOCKADE

February 2017 to June 2017

As Kushner and MBS become fast friends, MBS and MBZ use various intermediaries to profoundly alter U.S. foreign policy to their benefit—particularly a group of six Trump aides and advisers with substantial ties to Russia and Israel as well as Saudi Arabia and the United Arab Emirates. Meanwhile, Kushner and Trump prioritize their own business interests ahead of even the basic diplomatic and administrative processes of the new Trump administration, abandoning a longtime American ally, rewarding war crimes, and encouraging destabilizing regional aggressions even as Trump feels the pressures of a newly reinvigorated Russia investigation.

During the week of Trump's inauguration, George Nader and Trump Victory Committee vice chairman Elliott Broidy meet for the first time.[1] By February 2017, Nader and Broidy have become "fast friends" and begun "exchanging emails about potential contracts for [Broidy's private security company] Circinus with both the UAE and Saudi Arabia, and also about Saudi and Emirati objectives in Washington, such as persuading the United States government to take action against the Muslim Brotherhood or put pressure on its regional ally, Qatar."[2] Nader soon arranges a meeting between Broidy and MBZ, whereafter Broidy signs contracts with the

UAE worth "several hundred million dollars"—ostensibly for services to be rendered by Broidy's mercenary company.[3]

That "Saudi and Emirati objectives in Washington" include lobbying the U.S. government to "take action against the Muslim Brotherhood" is in alignment with a major concern of Egyptian president and Red Sea conspirator Abdel Fattah el-Sisi, as is an ancillary effort—cheered by both Nader and Broidy in their emails to each other—to block former United States ambassador to Cairo and then assistant secretary of state for Near Eastern affairs Anne Patterson from getting a job at the Pentagon.[4] According to the *New York Times*, MBZ, MBS, el-Sisi, Nader, and Broidy all consider Patterson "too sympathetic" to one of el-Sisi's chief enemies, deposed and imprisoned Egyptian president and Muslim Brotherhood member Mohamed Morsi; on June 17, 2019, the democratically elected president will die mysteriously of a "heart attack" in an Egyptian court just days, according to the *Middle East Eye*, after the el-Sisi administration gives the incarcerated politician an ultimatum—disband the Muslim Brotherhood or face dire consequences—that Morsi refuses.[5]

From the time of their first meeting onward, writes the *New York Times*, Broidy and Nader "work[ ] to sway the Trump administration on behalf of the United Arab Emirates and Saudi Arabia at a time when Mr. Broidy [is] seeking contracts worth hundreds of millions of dollars from the two countries."[6] Broidy and Nader even jointly lobby the White House on an issue important to the Malaysians and Chinese when they discover the possibility of Emirati kickbacks in doing so. They consistently find an amenable bargaining partner in the president—who must quickly see that MBZ and MBS have found, in UAE adviser Nader and GOP mega-donor Broidy, their preferred conduits for continuing their pre-election relationship with Trump and his staffers.[7]

As he is lobbying the Trump administration on behalf of Saudi Arabia and the UAE, one of Broidy's side projects sees him seeking "billions" in oil, gas, and mining assets in Angola while helping Angolan politicians gain access to both Republicans in Congress and members of the Trump administration.[8] Broidy is aided in this effort by Lisa Korbatov—the same Trump associate whose parents in 2007 sold "small-time scam artist" Mokless Girgis a mansion under suspicious circumstances, with the final stages of the transaction accruing to Trump's benefit in an effortless $9.5 million profit in just twelve months.[9] Korbatov's arrangement with Broidy's private security firm in the Angola affair promises her a 3 percent finder's fee of any security contract Broidy's security company, Circinus, signs.[10] While wooing the Angolans, Broidy scores multiple tickets to Trump's inauguration and entices his clients with possible meetings with President Trump, Vice President Pence, and defense secretary Jim Mattis, the last of whom has been an "unpaid adviser" to MBZ in the past.[11]

On April 3, 2017, at a time it would have been clear to both Trump and his top aides that Broidy had been acting as an agent of MBZ and MBS, Trump names the former Trump Victory Committee vice chairman (and presidential inaugural committee vice chairman) the new national deputy finance chairman of the Republican National Committee.[12] Trump's decision significantly increases the ability of Saudi Arabia and the United Arab Emirates to access top GOP officials.

By May 2019, a series of scandals involving Broidy—already a convict from a 2009 federal charge of "rewarding official misconduct"—leads the Republican Party to scrub its webpage announcing Broidy's appointment as one of its top finance officials.[13] In 2018, Al Jazeera writes critically of Broidy's "history of bribery and pro-Israel advocacy," and indeed it is in 2018 that the media outlet publishes allegations that Broidy has secretly worked as an unregistered agent for a Russian principal since June 12, 2014, when he took on a multimillion-dollar lobbying contract with VTB, a Russian bank eventually subjected to U.S. sanctions; Al Jazeera's allegations include publication of the purported consultancy agreement between Broidy and VTB.[14] Of the six countries in the "expanded" Red Sea Conspiracy—including Russia and Israel as well as Saudi Arabia, the UAE, Bahrain, and Egypt—Broidy's lobbying history shows him working at various points on behalf of foreign nationals or entities from four of these.

As part of Broidy's 2014 contract with VTB, he commits to offer the Russian bank "political advocacy" in Washington, among other services such as well-informed "investment advice."[15] Al Jazeera reports that Broidy's lobbying on behalf of Russia is, in many respects, a Russia-UAE joint venture, with Broidy's payment for his VTB work coming from a UAE-headquartered company whose chief shareholder, Yuri Soloviev, worked for Deutsche Bank from 2002 to 2008 and is a powerful enough figure in the world of Russian finance that he appears on an investment forum panel beside Vladimir Putin in Moscow in October 2017.[16] That Broidy's boss Soloviev should have high-level Kremlin connections is no surprise; in 2010, when Soloviev is the chief executive of VTB Capital, the *New York Times* notes that the venture capital firm is "supported in part by the Russian government."[17] In 2011, *Financial News* reports, regarding Soloviev's work with VTB Capital, that "Soloviev has not . . . had to rely solely on his deal-making talents. Vladimir Putin, the Russian prime minister, [has] put his weight behind the firm from its launch—and business from state-run companies played a substantial role in VTB Capital's rapid rise."[18] The Putin-linked Soloviev is still paying Elliott Broidy for "political advocacy" and "investment advice" as the Trump administration begins on January 20, 2017.[19]

Both Broidy and Nader enjoy ready access to the White House in the early days of the Trump presidency. According to the *New York Times*, in the first weeks of the new administration Nader makes "frequent trips to the White House . . . meeting with Stephen K. Bannon and Jared Kushner to discuss American policy toward the Persian Gulf States . . . By some accounts, it was Mr. Bannon who pushed for [Nader] to gain access to White House policymakers. Others said Mr. Kushner backed him."[20]

On January 26, acting attorney general Sally Yates goes to the White House to inform White House counsel Don McGahn that the nation's national security advisor, Michael Flynn, has been compromised by a foreign power by virtue of having lied to federal investigators about December 2016 negotiations he held with the Kremlin over U.S. sanctions.[21] The next day, McGahn calls Yates back to the White House to ask her "why the Justice Department would be concerned whether one White House official [Flynn] lied to another [Vice President Pence]" about the content of a phone call, a line of questioning that requires the acting attorney general to—as she later tells Congress—underscore to McGahn that "it is a matter of some urgency" when the president's national security advisor is "compromised with respect to the Russians."[22] McGahn gives little indication of why the White House is inclined to defend Flynn from any repercussions for his actions, instead asking Yates to provide the White House with all the evidence it has compiled against the nation's top national security official.[23]

On January 27, the same day that Yates reconfirms for McGahn that Flynn has committed a serious federal offense involving the Russians, and just forty-eight hours before Trump is due to speak with Saudi Arabia's King Salman (MBS's father) on the phone, one of Flynn's top aides, Derek Harvey, meets in the White House with the co-founder of IP3, Bud McFarlane, and a number of backers of IP3's plan for U.S.-Saudi-Russian cooperation on nuclear power.[24] Harvey, who in the first week of Trump's presidency had told a future congressional whistleblower that "Flynn [has] already decided to adopt IP3's nuclear plan and develop 'dozens of nuclear power plants' [in Saudi Arabia]," ends his meeting with McFarlane—who had met with Michael Flynn at Trump Tower on December 5—by "direct[ing] NSC [National Security Council] staff to add information about IP3's 'plan for 40 nuclear power plants' to the briefing package for Trump's call with King Salman."[25] When Harvey is told that such a plan would be illegal unless Saudi Arabia finally agrees to a "123 agreement" with the United States, the Flynn aide "ignore[s] these warnings," insisting "that the decision to transfer nuclear technology to Saudi Arabia [has] already been made."[26] Harvey does not clarify who has been the final arbiter in this decision—Flynn, the president, or someone else—and his statements cause so much alarm in the White House that "NSC staffers, ethics counsel and lawyers alert[ ] the top NSC legal adviser, John Eisenberg." On January 30, "Eisenberg instruct[s] the NSC staffers to stop all work on the [IP3] plan."[27]

The same day that Eisenberg moves to block the advance of the nuclear power component of Flynn's Middle East Marshall Plan on legal and national security grounds, and just twenty-four hours removed from Trump's first-ever call with Saudi Arabia's King Salman, the president announces a high-profile firing: Sally Yates.[28]

Following the dismissal of the acting attorney general, Michael Flynn sees no change in his employment status, and indeed even retains his top-secret security clearance until public pressure on the White House forces its revocation more than two weeks later.[29] Harvey, who retains his job after Flynn is finally forced out of the White House on February 14, will continue speaking regularly with the disgraced national security advisor until at least March 2, saying during a White House meeting on that date, "I speak with Michael Flynn every night."[30] By this point it has long been national news that Flynn is, as the *Washington Post* reported on February 14, "vulnerable to blackmail by Moscow."[31]

By mid-March, Flynn's deputy K. T. McFarland, who has also kept her job despite her involvement in Flynn's clandestine December 2016 sanctions negotiations, will tell White House staff that it is Trump who has approved Flynn and McFarlane's Saudi plan and, moreover, put Thomas Barrack in charge of it.[32] Harvey shortly thereafter calls Barrack and Gates—the latter by then working for Barrack as a consultant—to get the IP3 plan into a position for "Kushner to present it to the president for approval."[33] A few weeks later, in April, despite knowing that Flynn is under federal criminal investigation for a series of events involving both him and his transition team, Trump contacts Flynn to tell him to "stay strong."[34]

Derek Harvey will, like Flynn, eventually be let go—though not until July 2017, after which he goes to work for former Trump transition official Devin Nunes on the House Permanent Select Committee on Intelligence, a committee whose Republican members, in particular Nunes, will by early 2018 have received criticism for secretly collaborating with the White House to block the Russia investigation, including any investigation of Flynn's dismissal.[35] By the time Harvey leaves the White House, the IP3 plan is opposed, on legal and national security grounds, by both "White House lawyers and National Security Council officials," according to the *Washington Post*, but is pushed forward anyway by Trump, Kushner, and Barrack (see chapter 10).[36]

The day after Flynn's firing, Trump makes an unusual comment to his friend and former transition chief Chris Christie at a private meeting attended also by Jared Kushner. Christie and Flynn had been the only members of Trump's team to join him at his first classified national security briefing on August 17, 2016—the briefing that conclusively established for the Trump campaign brass that the Kremlin was seeking to infiltrate the campaign and interfere in the 2016 presidential election. At a lunch meeting with Christie and Kushner on February 15, 2017, Trump tells Christie that the "Russia thing is all over now, because I fired Flynn," and explains that he "fired Flynn" because Flynn "met" with "the Russians"—a narrative that contradicts his public insistence that Flynn was fired for lying about a phone call to Vice President Mike Pence.[37]

Though it is known that Flynn did indeed meet with Sergey Kislyak during the campaign, it is not clear which meeting—or negotiation—held between Flynn and Kremlin agents during the primary season or general election Trump deems to have been a danger to him. What the Mueller Report details, however, is that Trump's chief of staff, Reince Priebus, believed the president was afraid of "Flynn saying bad things about him" after he was fired; that Trump's counsel John Dowd anxiously contacted Flynn's counsel to ask him if he had transmitted any "information that implicates the President" to federal law enforcement; and that Flynn's deputy K. T. McFarland—who worked closely with Flynn during the transition, on Russia policy in particular—could not make any representation one way or another about whether Trump had ordered Flynn's contacts with Russian nationals before or after Election Day.[38] Nevertheless, Trump "sought to have [her] . . . draft an internal letter stating that the President had not directed Flynn to discuss sanctions with Kislyak."[39]

As recounted in the Mueller Report, during a press conference after Flynn's firing Trump declares, oddly, that "it certainly would have been okay with me if [Flynn] did [discuss sanctions] with Kislyak. I would have directed him to do it if I thought he wasn't doing it."[40] Trump thereby suggests that he knew Flynn was negotiating sanctions with the Kremlin, even though he had never told him to do so nor told anyone else to tell him to do so. This sentiment is a problematic one, given that Flynn's sanctions negotiations in December 2016 appear to have been a federal crime under the Logan Act—one for which the retired general escaped prosecution in part because the act is rarely enforced. As for any sanctions negotiations that may have occurred between Flynn's (and Trump's and Christie's) August 17, 2016, classified briefing on Russian election interference and Election Day, Trump may well have feared, as intimated by

Dowd's calls to Flynn's counsel, that these could be considered a federal felony (aiding and abetting, 18 U.S.C. § 2) if Trump knew about them at the time.[41] Fears regarding the aiding and abetting statute could thus explain Trump's insistence to Christie that "the problem" with Flynn—which in Trump's view created a "Russia thing" he had to deal with—was that "Flynn met with the Russians."[42] As for McFarland's claim that she couldn't definitively state whether or not Trump had directed Flynn to speak to the Russians before or after the election, on this point the Mueller Report notes that Trump had sufficient knowledge of such meetings and/or conversations that when "Flynn listed [for Trump during the week of February 6] the specific dates on which he remembered speaking with Kislyak . . . the President corrected one of the dates he listed."[43]

The Mueller Report will also reveal, though not resolve, another mystery: the fact that, prior to any public revelation of Flynn's December 2016 contacts with Kislyak, Trump was so "unhappy" and "upset" with his top national security advisor that "he would not look at him during intelligence briefings," a circumstance Hope Hicks said was caused by Trump thinking Flynn had shown "bad judgment" in the past.[44] While the report offers Flynn's "tweets" as one possible basis for Trump's ire, given Trump's own controversial tweeting habits a more plausible explanation is that Trump's leading adviser on national security issues had in fact kept his boss apprised of his ongoing contacts with the Russians during and after the campaign—as well as his contacts with other foreign nationals—and that those contacts, or simply being told of them, had angered Trump.[45] Certainly, the report confirms that after Flynn's contacts with the Russians became public knowledge, Trump was angry, per Reince Priebus, with "the reporting on Flynn's conversations with Kislyak" rather than with the conversations themselves, and that Trump used Priebus to tell Flynn he needed to "kill the story."[46] Trump's "kill" directive led to Flynn's deputy McFarland "providing false information" about Flynn's actions to the *Washington Post*—a course of deceit that had the effect of covering up Flynn's apparent violation of the Logan Act and contributing to McFarland subsequently being denied an ambassadorship by Congress.[47]

While the Mueller Report will fail to establish with high confidence whether Trump knew beforehand of Flynn's December 2016 sanctions negotiations with Kislyak, it does provide some evidence that the Flynn-Kislyak contacts were persistent and that Trump may have had knowledge of them. Prior to the December Flynn-Kislyak calls, the report observes, "the FBI had opened [before 2016] an investigation of Flynn based on his relationship with the Russian government. Flynn's contacts with Kislyak [in 2015 and 2016] became a key component of that investigation"—a statement that suggests Flynn may have had contacts with the Russian ambassador after his December 2015 visit to Kislyak's home but before December 2016.[48] In December 2016, Flynn's deputy McFarland, according to Reince Priebus, had told Trump and others gathered at a meeting at Mar-a-Lago that there were means available for the transition team to "cool[ ] down" and "not escalate[ ]" the U.S.-Russia tensions caused by the Obama administration's imposition of new sanctions in response to Russian election interference.[49] McFarland herself told the special counsel's office that at the end of that meeting "someone may have mentioned to the President-Elect that Flynn was speaking to the Russian ambassador that evening."[50] And according to Flynn's statements to the special counsel—statements made while he was in a cooperation agreement with the government—four days later, on January 3, 2017, Flynn "saw the President-Elect in person and thought they discussed the Russian reaction to the sanctions."[51] The picture therefore painted by the report, in total, is of a politician kept reasonably well informed by his top aides of their most important political and diplomatic maneuvers.

Less than ninety-six hours after Flynn's February 14 firing—an event that for a moment seems to leave in limbo IP3's U.S.-Saudi-Russian nuclear deal, and therefore, due to its arrangement with the United States, the United Arab Emirates' nuclear ambitions as well—Trump's sons, Don and Eric, travel to the UAE with the assistance of more than $16,000 in taxpayer funds for security.[52] The trip is ostensibly for the opening of Trump International Golf Course Dubai, though while there Don "praise[s] the development of the UAE," saying that "to see the incredible vision Sheikh

Mohammed [MBZ] has been able to put forward for this country is truly awe-inspiring. As a developer . . . it is truly incredible to be part of that vision."[53] It is unknown if either or both of the brothers meet with any members of the Emirati royal family, including MBZ, during their trip, or with any of MBZ's Saudi allies, but what is known is that as Trump's two eldest sons travel to the United Arab Emirates, the most powerful man in that country is just weeks removed from entering the United States in secret to meet with Jared Kushner and only a few months away from using his intermediaries George Nader and Elliott Broidy to try to set up a "private," off-the-grid meeting with Don and Eric's father. Moreover, Don and Eric visit the UAE as construction has just begun on yet another Trump-branded golf course in the country MBZ rules, Trump World Golf Club Dubai.[54]

Meanwhile, in the United States, Thomas Barrack begins paying Rick Gates—Barrack's deputy on the inaugural committee—$20,000 a month for post-inaugural "consulting on legislative and regulatory matters."[55] Barrack does this despite having, as a longtime friend of the new president, direct access to Trump and, consequently, top Republican legislators and regulators. Barrack's payments to Gates do not appear to have been intended to aid Barrack in accessing the president; indeed, as the *New York Times* notes, after becoming the subject of multiple federal investigations Gates maintains access to top Trump advisers only "because he was seen as having the blessing of Mr. Barrack, a close friend and business associate of Mr. Trump's."[56] As Barrack is paying Gates, Barrack is himself lobbying Trump to have his first trip overseas as president be to Saudi Arabia, a course of persuasion that will ultimately achieve its desired result.[57]

In March 2017, Broidy, who worked with Gates on the Trump Victory Campaign before the election, and worked also with Barrack on Trump's inaugural committee finance team during the transition, begins paying Gates $25,000 a month for "advis[ing] Mr. Broidy on how to pursue both a contract for his [private security] business and appointments for associates and provid[ing] insight into the new administration's foreign policy plans."[58] As these two major Trump fundraisers and inaugural committee officials, Barrack and Broidy, are both paying Gates exorbitant amounts to lobby an administration they already have ready access to, Gates is under investigation by the FBI in a case that could ultimately—if Gates agrees to cooperate with the FBI—lead to significant legal liability for Barrack, Broidy, and perhaps even the president himself.

As Barrack and Broidy continue making unusual payments to Gates, they continue, too, lobbying Trump on various issues involving the Middle East. Noting the irregularities in these arrangements, CNBC will observe that Barrack's and Broidy's payments to Gates "raise[ ] questions of why the two men . . . each of whom ha[s] close ties to the Republican Party and, in Barrack's case, to the president himself, [a]re paying a lobbyist like Gates for guidance on how to deal with the new administration."[59] According to the *Wall Street Journal*, post-inauguration Broidy "often [meets] with the president at the White House and at Mr. Trump's Florida resort, Mar-a-Lago," further muddying the question of whether and why the venture capitalist and mercenary company owner needs Gates's assistance in connecting with Trump.[60]

The payments made by Broidy to Gates are made to Gates's Konik Madison Group LLC, which also bills the Trump campaign for $37,000 in "strategic consulting fees" in the weeks leading up to the 2016 election.[61] Prior to transitioning from being Trump's deputy campaign manager to his RNC liaison upon Paul Manafort's departure from the campaign in August 2016, Gates's two primary contributions to Trump's 2016 presidential run had been, apparently, to field proposals from an Israeli business intelligence company connected to Michael Flynn (proposals geared toward executing a clandestine social media disinformation campaign on Trump's behalf) and to regularly send proprietary internal polling data to Russian intelligence during the general election.[62] Gates is also, by the transition period if not before, part of a secret lobbying consortium, with Flynn and Barrack, seeking to convince Trump to give the Saudis (and thus the Emiratis) nuclear technology.[63]

While Broidy is paying Gates seemingly extraneous consulting fees, MBS arrives in the United States for a March 20 meeting at the White

House.[64] In the weeks preceding the meeting, George Nader had begun proposing a plan to "Saudi, UAE, and American officials . . . to carry out economic sabotage against Iran."[65] Shortly after the Trump-MBS summit, Nader travels to Riyadh to meet with "senior Saudi military and intelligence officials" to continue the pitch for his sabotage plan, having become convinced that "economic warfare [is] the key to the overthrow of the government in Tehran."[66] By the time Trump and Kushner travel to Riyadh in May, Nader has already "tried to persuade Mr. Kushner to endorse the [economic sabotage plan] to Crown Prince Mohammed in person."[67] While Nader is pitching his ideas to Kushner in April or early May, he is also "in discussions with [Erik] Prince . . . about a plan to get the Saudis to pay $2 billion to set up a private army to combat Iranian proxy forces in Yemen."[68]

By spring 2017, therefore, the chief elements of a new anti-Iran foreign policy in the United States have been actively developed between just six men—Flynn, Barrack, Gates, Prince, Nader, and Broidy—on a for-profit basis: (1) weaponized uranium for Saudi Arabia and the UAE; (2) economic sabotage of the Iranian economy; (3) counterterrorist mercenaries deployed throughout the Middle East, with a green light to assassinate opponents of MBZ and MBS; and (4) coordination with pro-Kremlin officials to maintain U.S.-Russian relations and ensure at least tacit Kremlin approval of American efforts to weaken Iran, Russia's most important ally in the Middle East. Four of the men in this "gang of six"—Flynn, Prince, Nader, and Broidy—also have significant ties to another key enemy of the Iranian regime, Israel. Throughout the lobbying efforts of these six men, the primary foreign beneficiaries of their work are two foreign leaders, MBS and MBZ, who, through George Nader, had offered the Trump campaign illicit pre-election assistance at a meeting at Trump Tower on August 3, 2016—an offer Trump's son responded to approvingly, per the *New York Times*.[69] Also present at that meeting was a man, Joel Zamel, brought to the attention of the Trump campaign by a top aide from the office of Israeli prime minister Benjamin Netanyahu.

As part of these covert lobbying campaigns—in Washington, Moscow, and several capitals in the Middle East—Prince and Nader travel to Riyadh in March 2017 to pitch directly to top Saudi government officials their $2 billion anti-Iran "private army."[70] During the meeting that ensues, "top Saudi intelligence officials close to" MBS ask the men "about using private [military] companies [like the ones Nader and Prince are proposing] to assassinate Iranian enemies of the [Saudi] kingdom."[71] One of the Saudi intelligence officials behind this query is Major General Ahmed al-Assiri, the same Saudi intelligence chief who had met with Trump's then-national security advisor, Michael Flynn, during the presidential transition—and who will, in 2018, be accused of helping orchestrate the assassination of a non-Iranian MBS enemy, *Washington Post* journalist Jamal Khashoggi.[72]

According to the *Times*, the army Nader and Prince envision is one comprising primarily "intelligence operatives." It is telling, then, that an intelligence operative by March 2017 well known to both the Trumps and Trump aides, Israeli business intelligence expert Joel Zamel, joins Nader and Prince at their meetings in Riyadh.[73] The *Times* notes that, while technically an independent operator, Zamel has "deep ties to [Israel's] intelligence and security agencies."[74]

By the time Nader, Prince, and Zamel make their presentation to al-Assiri, they have already pitched it to both MBS and Trump—suggesting that the meetings in Riyadh are focused on further development of the proposal rather than on an initial acceptance of it.[75] Nader's original plan had been to conduct economic espionage against Iran, however; it is al-Assiri who asks Nader, Prince, and Zamel whether they can also conduct "kinetics"—a euphemism for targeted assassinations.[76] According to the *Times*, in response to al-Assiri's query Nader refers the Saudis to "a London-based company run by former British special operations troops."[77] By 2018, media reports on both sides of the Atlantic will reveal that the UAE has been hiring former U.S. soldiers to conduct "kinetics" throughout the Middle East, with stories on this subject appearing in the *Daily Beast*, *BuzzFeed News*, the *Middle East Monitor*, National Public Radio, and elsewhere.[78] Given that some of the other foreign mercenary units the UAE puts into the field at the same time—predominantly Colombian in their derivation—had previously been trained by Erik Prince, Prince's presence alongside Nader and Zamel as the Emiratis plot military as well as intelligence maneuvers to combat Iranian proxies across the Middle East is telling.[79]

As for the economic-espionage-oriented plan Nader, Prince, and Zamel pitch in Riyadh in March 2017, it "dates to the beginning of 2016," according to the *New York Times*, "when [the three men] started discussing an ambitious campaign of economic warfare against Iran similar to one waged by Israel and the United States during the past decade aimed at coercing Iran to end its nuclear program."[80] The timing of the plan's development suggests that at some point during the 2016 campaign all three progenitors of the scheme were advising the Trump campaign and that Nader began working with Zamel and Trump adviser Prince not long after his fall 2015 meeting on the Red Sea with MBZ, MBS, and el-Sisi. The contours of the Nader-Prince-Zamel proposal suggest that Zamel's role in it has been particularly key, with the *New York Times* reporting that the proposal prominently features "revealing [the] hidden global assets" of enemies; "creating fake social media accounts . . . to foment unrest"; secretly "financing . . . opposition groups"; and "publicizing accusations, real or fictitious, against . . . senior officials to turn them against one another."[81] Indeed, from its description in the *Times*, this appears to be a plan similar to the one Zamel suggested to Trump Jr. during the 2016 presidential election—with the target, in the latter case, being an unsuspecting American electorate.[82] Reports indicate, indeed, that after the election "Mr. Nader and Mr. Zamel traveled to New York to sell both Trump transition officials and Saudi generals" on their plan, though now, as to its social media elements, applied to Iran rather than America.[83] The plan is considered "so provocative and potentially destabilizing" that when Nader, Prince, and Zamel suggest it to al-Assiri in New York City during the presidential transition at a meeting atop the Mandarin Oriental hotel, al-Assiri says he would have to "get the approval of the incoming Trump administration before Saudi Arabia paid for the campaign."[84] That Nader, Prince, and Zamel's plan required green-lighting by Trump, who had not yet assumed the authority to negotiate U.S. foreign policy, suggests that the plan had indeed been devised as a new, covert U.S.-Saudi policy initiative; just so, the willingness of the Saudis in December 2016 to secretly pay for a social media disinformation campaign devised by Joel Zamel—but only if they are asked to do so by Trump—calls to mind the possibility that this same process may have played out in August 2016 with respect to the social media disinformation scheme then being offered by Zamel to the Trump campaign.

The approval from "the incoming Trump administration" sought by al-Assiri is ultimately given, it appears, by Michael Flynn, at a subsequent meeting with the Saudi general during the transition. The result is that the Trump administration, prior to assuming power, has already secretly approved a plan to have a foreign government commit acts of espionage against a nation (Iran) with which the United States is in a state of détente.[85] Under the plan, the Saudis would spend money, with explicit approval from Trump's team, on a military initiative that would undercut the foreign policy of the existing U.S. government, then run by President Obama.

Just days before MBS is set to make his first visit to Washington to meet with the new president, Trump receives terrible news: FBI director James Comey informs the congressional "Gang of Eight"—which includes the chairs and ranking minority members of the Senate and House intelligence committees—that its counterintelligence investigation into Russian election interference has identified "4-5 [American] targets" whose actions require substantial additional investigation by the U.S. intelligence community, and could compel criminal prosecution.[86] A week later, the Republican chair of the Senate Intelligence Committee, Richard Burr (R-NC), briefs the White House counsel's office on what was said in the classified briefing.[87] Burr appears to inform the office that the four individuals under investigation by the FBI's counterintelligence division are Flynn, Manafort, Page, and Papadopoulos; a redaction in the Mueller Report indicates that there may have been a fifth individual as well.[88]

Trump's reaction appears to be a dramatic one. Three days after Comey's Gang of Eight briefing, but four days before Burr briefs the White House counsel, Trump is suddenly in a "panic" and a state of "chaos," according to contemporaneous notes taken by Annie Donaldson, White House counsel Don McGahn's chief of staff; Donaldson records that "all things related to Russia" must immediately be put in "binders" for Trump's review.[89] That Trump's reaction is borne in substantial part by the White House counsel's office suggests that Burr's briefing of the office four days later may well have been the result of Trump's White House meltdown. Indeed, the Mueller Report implies this is the case, noting that "the week after Comey's briefing, the White House Counsel's Office was in contact with SSCI Chairman Senator Richard Burr about the Russia investigations and appears to have received information about the status of the FBI investigation."[90]

Donaldson's March 16, 2017, notes indicate that Burr's briefing of the White House counsel's office took place on that day, and that, per Burr, Manafort was not being investigated for his activities on the Trump presidential campaign—suggesting it is more likely that Trump's dramatic reaction was to the news of one or more of the other three men being under investigation for their contacts with Russian nationals. The timing of the briefing, just a month after Flynn's firing and during a period in which both Trump and his attorneys would contact Flynn worriedly, strongly argues for Trump's chief concern being his former national security advisor, of whom Donaldson's March 16 notes say that the "DOJ [is] looking for phone records."[91] Donaldson's notation for Page ("$ game") may also have caused Trump concern, given Page's representations in Moscow in December 2016 that he was there to discuss, as Trump's incognito representative, the sale of a substantial percentage of Russia's state-owned oil company, Rosneft, among other things (see chapter 4).[92] By comparison, Annie Donaldson's note regarding George Papadopoulos merely says, "Greek guy."[93]

Of the four targets Burr reveals to the White House, all but Page are eventually indicted for federal felonies; the status of any federal investigation of Page is currently unknown. Burr's disclosure of classified intelligence to the White House is not entirely surprising, as he had served as one of Trump's national security advisers during the presidential campaign, and had told North Carolina voters in 2016 that there was "no separation" between him and Trump.[94] As for Trump's panic at learning the names of the FBI's targets, the Mueller Report implies it was as notable as any moment of anxiety Trump exhibited during the Russia investigation, on par with his reaction, just days earlier, to Attorney General Jeff Sessions's decision to recuse himself from the Russia probe—an event Steve Bannon recalled made the president "as mad as [he] had ever seen him," with Trump "scream[ing] at [Don] McGahn about how weak Sessions was."[95] Trump's reaction to Sessions's recusal was so destabilizing in the West Wing that an internal White House counsel's office note recorded, at the time, that the office thereafter had "serious concerns about obstruction." Given the office's history, its concern was most likely centered on the president's urgent directives to the office to speak with Sessions about the Russia probe.[96] One of Trump's many concerns about Sessions's recusal, according to the Mueller Report, was that it made the attorney general "look guilty" for "omitting details [about his contacts with Russian nationals] in his confirmation hearing."[97] What the president believed Sessions could look (or be) guilty of was unclear.

MBS's March 2017 trip to D.C. begins a long and mutually profitable friendship between Kushner and MBS that makes Nader's efforts to convince Kushner—and through him, Trump—to back MBS's plans a fait accompli. According to the *Washington Post*, though Kushner and MBS had met briefly prior to March (and Kushner had already met with MBS's Emirati ally MBZ), it was in the spring of 2017 that "a bond developed between the two men."[98] The *Post* notes that at least one of their shared interests involved Israel, as both men had been tasked by their fathers to address the Israeli-Palestinian conflict, and both, as would shortly become clear, had taken a view of the conflict considerably favorable to the Israelis: Kushner as part of a long-standing commitment to Israel, and MBS as part of his commitment, since at least the 2015 Red Sea summit, to building a new pro-Israel Arab security alliance.

Between MBS's March trip to Washington and Trump's May trip to Riyadh, Kushner and MBS, per the *Post*, "consult[ ] with one another frequently," and indeed it is Kushner who "successfully pushe[s] the president to make Saudi Arabia his first foreign visit . . . against objections from other senior administration officials," including secretary of state Rex Tillerson.[99] At one point Tillerson even tells Trump's son-in-law that "his advice to [Trump] to endorse Saudi Arabia's aggressive diplomatic and strategic campaign against Qatar, an important American ally, 'had endangered the United States.'"[100]

At another point, Tillerson "heard 'chatter' between Kushner" and MBS "belittling" him," an intriguing revelation given that agents of MBS and MBZ would later work behind the scenes to get Tillerson fired (see chapter 8).[101]

Kushner's relationship with MBS in short order comes to "unsettle [ ] national security and intelligence officials," according to the *Washington Post*, as Kushner is "relying on personal relationships instead of standard government channels" and in a way that generates "particular wariness about Kushner's embrace of" MBS.[102] According to a 2018 *Vanity Fair* article, during spring 2017, Tillerson says of Kushner's relationship with MBS, "The kid's a rookie. He doesn't know the region."[103] Another former West Wing official will tell *Vanity Fair* that "there were many confrontations between Tillerson and Jared where Tillerson was . . . angry that Jared was in contact with MBS. I remember in a couple of instances, Tillerson would confront Jared about directly talking to MBS."[104]

According to a Saudi government statement, the close relationship between Kushner and MBS is explained by the fact that "President Trump has given Mr. Kushner the important task of overseeing the peace process, and this has been the primary subject of discussion between Mr. Kushner and His Royal Highness the Crown Prince."[105] Unsaid in the statement is that MBS's plan for remaking Middle East geopolitics through a new Arab security alliance with him at its head has, from the start, been positioned as a means of achieving "peace"—but does so by risking a bloody, possibly nuclear war between a Saudi-led Sunni coalition and Iranian Shiites. Every Kushner-MBS phone call and meeting on the subject of "peace" is, for the latter, necessarily a conversation about the contours of the Red Sea Conspiracy and its need for an American partner. As the *Post* will note, "Some intelligence and national security officials worry that [MBS's] argument about how to resolve conflict in the Middle East—that his country is the chief hope for peace and Iran is the root of all strife—is too simplistic. They fear his appeal has gained traction with White House officials who have little experience with the region's politics."[106]

While he is in Washington in March 2017 with Trump, Kushner, a sizable Saudi delegation, and several Emirati allies, MBS's agents begin injecting into polite Washington discourse the idea of a grand bargain involving Saudi Arabia, the UAE, Israel, and Russia. According to the *New Yorker,* "the idea was raised . . . by Adel al-Jubeir, the foreign minister of Saudi Arabia, and Abdullah bin Zayed, the foreign minister of the U.A.E., during a private March 2017 dinner that included several other guests. 'Their message was "Why don't we lift the Ukrainian sanctions on Russia in exchange for getting the Russians to push Iran out of Syria,"' an attendee recalled the foreign ministers saying. . . . The dinner attendee . . . [said], 'It wasn't a trial balloon. They were trying to socialize the idea.'"[107]

As MBS's D.C. entourage is spreading his idiosyncratic diplomatic ideations in public settings, Kushner is taking his relationship with the Saudi crown prince into increasingly private realms—particularly with respect to the duo's preferred modes of communication. Beginning in March 2017, Kushner periodically broaches new topics with MBS without informing anyone else in the federal government; as the *Washington Post* will note in a March 2018 article, at one point "White House Chief of Staff John F. Kelly asked a question in an intelligence briefing about a sensitive policy matter related to Saudi Arabia in preparation for the crown prince's [March 2018] visit. In response, intelligence briefers told him that virtually all of the conversations that U.S. officials had with the Saudis on the matter had been between Kushner and Mohammed."[108] The *Post* adds that "Kushner and his staff have often arranged private conversations with the Saudi crown prince and other senior leaders in foreign countries that were not always coordinated with national security or diplomatic officials, according to multiple officials familiar with his activities."[109] Nor is this lack of coordination merely accidental or the product of Kushner's limited diplomatic experience: the *Post* writes that Kushner is quite self-consciously "wary of letting others in the [intelligence] agencies [and state and defense departments] know what he [is] doing for fear opponents would make his plans public."[110] This is an observation with troubling implications, inasmuch as it suggests that whatever Kushner is doing behind closed doors, he believes any career government officials who discover it are likely to soon thereafter become whistleblowers or adversaries.

Even more troublingly, the increasingly frequent conversations between Kushner and MBS are not just private but unreviewable, as they mostly occur, according to *The Intercept,* via WhatsApp, a secure messaging application.[111] It is these WhatsApp conversations that will cause fear in the White House that "the Saudis [a]re playing [Kushner]," according to a former White House official.[112] Despite crowing to friends that "Jared's gotten the Arabs on his side," Trump will claim to have no knowledge whatsoever of Kushner using WhatsApp to contact MBS.[113]

While Kushner's attorney's spokesman, Peter Mirijanian, will contend that Kushner's use of a secure messaging application complies with the Presidential Records Act, it seems unlikely that Kushner's attorney himself believes this—given that since the WhatsApp conversations were revealed, according to *The Intercept*, "Kushner's attorneys have . . . told him not to use the app for official business."[114] It is unknown whether Kushner has, by summer 2019, heeded his attorneys' advice.

Throughout 2017, Kushner's means of communicating with MBS is an abiding issue in the Trump administration, with *The Intercept* noting that "Kushner's unconventional communications with regional leaders excluded diplomats during the summer of 2017, when Saudi Arabia and the UAE initiated an economic blockade aimed at weakening their Gulf neighbor Qatar. Tillerson's attempts to mediate the crisis were quickly undercut by Trump and Kushner, who supported the blockade. Three State Department officials told *The Intercept* that Tillerson was largely in the dark about Kushner's communications with MBS during that period."[115] Tillerson, the nation's top diplomat, will tell State Department colleagues during the Qatar blockade that trying to talk sense into MBZ in the midst of the international crisis created by his precipitousness was "'pointless' given that Kushner was already in close and direct contact with him."[116]

While Tillerson is in the dark about what Kushner and MBS are secretly discussing via WhatsApp in the first half of 2017, subsequent reports will reveal that it is almost certainly the topic foremost on MBS's mind at the time: taking control of Saudi Arabia by deposing Mohammed bin Nayef, the Saudi prince next in line for the kingdom's throne.[117] According to the *New York Times*, the Kushner-MBS conversations in February 2017 are believed to have been about MBS's ascension to the Saudi throne, as it was during this period that Kushner began "inquiring [around the White House] about the Saudi royal succession process and whether the United

States could influence it, raising fears among senior officials that he sought to help Prince Mohammed, who was not yet the crown prince, vault ahead in the line for the throne . . . American diplomats and intelligence officers feared that the Trump administration might be seen as playing favorites in the delicate internal politics of the Saudi royal family."[118] By March, just a few weeks into Trump's presidency, Kushner has not only orchestrated a White House visit for MBS but has arranged, in a violation of protocol, for MBS to be treated as a head of state though he is not even next in line for the Saudi throne.[119] It is during this period that Kushner first reveals to senior White House officials that he has been speaking privately with MBS, something that should have been impossible under the national security protocols long in place in the federal government.[120]

Even as Kushner is in regular contact with one Red Sea conspirator, he is also routinely in touch with a key emissary for a second, MBZ. According to the *New York Times*, the Emirati ambassador, Yousef al-Otaiba, whom Kushner has been advised by since May 2016, writes Trump friend Thomas Barrack in spring 2017 to tell him that he is "in constant contact with Jared and that has been extremely helpful."[121]

In Washington in March 2017, MBS meets with Kushner and Trump in the Oval Office to "discuss[ ] opportunities for U.S. companies to invest in Saudi Arabia."[122] A readout of the meeting between the three men makes reference to "a new United States-Saudi program . . . in energy, industry, infrastructure, and technology potentially worth more than $200 billion in direct and indirect investments within the next four years."[123] The supposed "program" is so unknown to the nation's foreign policy and national security apparatus at the time Trump and Kushner discuss it with MBS that a House Oversight Committee report will later quote one senior government official saying to a staffer at the National Security Council, "What the hell is going on?"[124]

In June, Kushner's new friend MBS summons bin Nayef to the royal palace in Mecca and "[holds] him against his will" until he agrees to abdicate his claim to the Saudi throne.[125] The process of convincing bin Nayef to give up his birthright takes all night; the full slate of methods employed by MBS's agents is unknown, though the *Times* reports that all bin Nayef's means of communication were taken from him and the fact that he is both a diabetic and still hampered physically by the aftereffects of a 2009 assassination attempt was used against him in cruel fashion as the night wore on.[126] According to the *New Yorker*, one element of the persuasion employed by MBS's agents was making bin Nayef stand up for hours, a form of torture for the injured prince that would have, given his conditions, "caused excruciating pain."[127]

The question of why Kushner would go to such extraordinary lengths to get as close to MBS and MBZ as possible—bypassing national security protocols to engage in clandestine communications, deliberately sidelining career diplomats and even the secretary of state, offending a king-in-waiting by treating his inferior like a head of state, and using an Emirati ambassador as an adviser during a presidential campaign—goes unanswered until the Saudi blockade of Qatar in summer 2017, an event that also may explain the timing of MBS's move against bin Nayef in June. According to the *New York Times*, "One American official and one adviser to a Saudi royal said Mohammed bin Nayef opposed the embargo on Qatar, a stand that probably accelerated his ouster."[128] Bin Nayef's recalcitrance about his country taking an aggressive, even warlike posture toward a key U.S. ally may also explain, incredibly, Kushner's support for MBS—as MBS's summer blockade of the tiny Gulf nation leads indirectly, as will become clear in the coming months, to more than $1 billion in desperately needed new loans for Kushner Companies.[129] It is a windfall that likely would have been impossible with bin Nayef on the Saudi throne.

After bin Nayef swears allegiance to MBS on video, he is sent back to his palace in Jeddah on the Red Sea, where he is immediately placed under house arrest.[130] Within days, writes the *New York Times*, CIA officials are briefing Trump "on their concern that the ouster of Mohammed bin Nayef and the possible removal of General Huwairini [one of bin Nayef's top security chiefs] could hamper intelligence sharing" with the United States.[131] Because of his direct communications with MBS, Kushner likely has far less concern on this score than the rest of the federal government.

Since June 2017, "indications have emerged that Mohammed bin Sal-man plotted the ouster" of bin Nayef over a period of time, raising the possibility that—given Kushner's intense interest in the process of succes-sion in Saudi Arabia in early spring 2017—some part of his conversations with MBS were about the young prince's political ambitions and perhaps even his intentions.[132] The overnight shift from a bin Nayef power center in Saudi Arabia to an MBS power center "spread[s] concern among coun-terterrorism officials in the United States, who saw their most trusted Saudi contacts disappear" almost immediately—even as Kushner's top Saudi contact has just become, instantaneously, the most powerful man in the kingdom.[133] The shift in power in Riyadh quickly becomes a shift in power in Washington, D.C., too.

As Saudi Arabia's succession crisis unfolds in a flurry of activity in mid-2017, Americans are unaware that the president's son-in-law has sidelined the National Security Council with respect to certain foreign policy and national security crises in the Middle East, with the top Middle East ad-viser to the NSC, U.S. Army Col. Michael Bell, "complain[ing] . . . that he was out of the loop on the Gulf crisis and the Arab-Israeli conflict . . . [as] Kushner frequently micromanaged those subjects through direct inter-action with regional leaders, without offering [NSC representatives] any worthwhile readout on their interactions."[134] As Kushner's chief contacts in the Middle East by mid-2017 are MBS, MBZ's ambassador al-Otaiba, Nader, and Netanyahu (the last of these "long a friend of the Kushners," according to the *Jerusalem Post*), the effect of Kushner's bureaucratic mach-inations in the first few months of the Trump presidency is to put two Red Sea conspirators and their plot's chief beneficiary in the Middle East, Israel, atop America's foreign policy apparatus—with both the State De-partment and the National Security Council deliberately marginalized.[135]

Between MBS's March 2017 trip to D.C. and Trump's May 2017 trip to Riyadh—a period of mere weeks—an important event occurs that will have a significant bearing on the fortunes of the nation of Qatar from 2017 through 2019. In April 2017, Charles Kushner, a convicted felon and Jared

Kushner's father, meets with Qatari finance minister Ali Al Emadi to beg him to assist Kushner Companies in refinancing its disastrous investment in 666 Fifth Avenue in New York.[136] The elder Kushner knows that the property is twenty-one months from seeing its full $1.2 billion interest-only mortgage coming due, and knows further that there is no equity in the office (as opposed to retail) section of the building—the only part of the property the Kushners still own.[137] As *The Intercept* notes, "The family's initial $500 million investment, once heralded as an example of Jared's emergence as a brash real estate star, has for now been effectively wiped out. A massive refinancing and construction of a new tower that dramatically increases the building's value is one way to try to get out of that hole."[138] Getting the Kushners "out of the hole" at 666 Fifth Avenue has, by spring 2017, become a matter of great emergency for both Charles and Jared, as the family is also, at the same time, seeking $250 million to pay off debt connected to a Jersey City apartment building, and must, moreover, pay CIT Group $140 million by September 2017.[139]

Charles Kushner's April 2017 entreaty to the Qataris is at least the fourth time the country has been pitched to by a Kushner since Trump announced his presidential run, with Jared and his father meeting directly with Qatari investor and Thomas Barrack friend Sheikh Hamad bin Jassim bin Jaber Al Thani at least twice in 2015 and 2016 and Charles Kushner meeting by himself with HBJ in early 2017.[140] While the early 2017 Kushner-HBJ talks briefly seem promising, by April 2017 they have fallen apart entirely, thus necessitating Charles Kushner's urgent meeting with Al Emadi. According to the *Washington Post*, the Kushners' desperation during this period will be noted immediately by one foreign player in particular: the United Arab Emirates. The *Post* reports in early 2018 that "officials from the UAE identified Kushner as early as the spring of 2017 as particularly manipulable because of his family's search for investors in their real estate company"—a finding that may explain the Emiratis' seeming confidence that Kushner would support their eventual blockade (alongside Saudi Arabia) of Qatar.[141]

During the thirty-minute meeting between Charles Kushner and Al Emadi at the St. Regis Hotel in New York in April 2017, the Qatari refuses to invest in the Kushners' "critically distressed asset," which had become, according to *The Intercept*, "essentially worthless."[142] The next day, a second meeting between the two takes place, this time at the property itself—coincidentally, the same building where, eight months earlier, Paul Manafort and Konstantin Kilimnik had met to discuss a U.S.-Russia "peace deal."[143] As Thomas Barrack will tell the *Washington Post* in 2018, the Kushners' 2017 negotiations with the Qataris—which Barrack will confess he tried to help broker—were "crushed" by Kushner entering the White House, as it "just about completely chilled the market, and [potential investors] just said, 'No way—can't be associated with any appearances of conflict of interest.'"[144] Barrack's comments underscore that when Charles Kushner's efforts with Al Emadi fall through in April 2017, the Kushners realized it would take a dramatic development for foreign investors like the Qataris to overcome their fear of Jared Kushner's conflicts of interest—not at all the reception Trump's son-in-law had expected to find for his business proposals when he moved to Washington.

Just a few weeks later, on June 5, four of the five Red Sea conspirators— Saudi Arabia, the UAE, Bahrain, and Egypt—cut all diplomatic ties with Qatar, a nation the first three of these four countries are at the time serving alongside in the Gulf Cooperation Council.[145] Jordan refuses to join the Saudi-led action, causing it to be dropped from the conspirators' plans for a new GCC.[146]

In addition to ending diplomatic outreach to Qatar, the four members of the Saudi-led axis also close their airspace to Qatari aircraft; declare that "foreign airlines [will] have to seek permission for overflights to and from Qatar"; block Qatar's only land border (with Saudi Arabia); "ban from docking at many ports" any "ships flying the Qatari flag or those serving Qatar"; and issue a thirteen-item list of demands on Qatar that include some expected items ("curb diplomatic ties with Iran"), some speculative ones ("stop all funding for individuals or organizations designated as terrorists"), and some that are overbroad or overreaching ("end interference in other sovereign countries' internal affairs," "pay reparations and compensation for loss of life caused by [Qatari] policies," and "shut down Al Jazeera").[147] The blockade immediately has a significant effect on Qatar, as 40 percent of the nation's food arrives via its land border with Saudi Arabia.[148]

As the Qatari crisis deepens—a troubling development in the United States, given that Qatar hosts the largest U.S. military installation in the region—Kushner, whose dad has just twice been denied a business-saving loan by an investor linked to the Qatari government, will not only "provide[ ] critical support" to Qatar's enemies, reports *The Intercept*, but "undermine" attempts by Secretary of State Tillerson to end the conflict.[149] The Qataris will be so convinced that Kushner's actions constitute a reprisal for their former prime minister (HBJ) deciding not to bail out the Kushners financially that in January 2018 "Qatari government officials visiting the U.S. '[will] consider[ ] turning over to [special counsel Robert] Mueller what they believe is evidence of efforts by their country's Persian Gulf neighbors in coordination with Kushner to hurt their country.'"[150] Qatari officials ultimately decide not to cooperate with Mueller, however, fearing reprisals from the Trump family, including President Trump himself.

The result of Kushner's actions will be, according to *The Intercept*, to "push[ ] Qatar, home to the Middle East's largest U.S. military base, closer to Turkey and Iran."[151] As the digital media outlet will note in the midst of the blockade, upon news that the seemingly doomed early 2017 Kushner-HBJ deal to rescue 666 Fifth Avenue is in fact now said to be—quite suddenly—merely "on hold", "If the [Kushner-HBJ] deal is not entirely dead, that means Jared Kushner is on the one hand pushing to use the power of American diplomacy to pummel a small nation, while on the other his firm is hoping to extract an extraordinary amount of capital from there for a failing investment. If, however, the deal is entirely dead, the pummeling may be seen as intimidating to other investors on the end of a Kushner Companies pitch."[152]

A second major event in the period between Trump's March 2017 and May 2017 meetings with MBS is that the president names Elliott Broidy the deputy finance chair of the Republican National Committee.[153] Broidy will act as an intermediary for MBS's policy agenda in the months ahead, receiving significant payment from MBS emissary George Nader for his work. It is during this period, in which MBS's man Broidy is at the RNC, Kushner is having WhatsApp conversations with MBS, and Nader is meeting regularly at the White House with Bannon, Kushner, and others, that Trump makes the decision—over the objection of his secretary of state, Rex Tillerson—to break with historical precedent and travel to Saudi Arabia rather than Canada or Mexico for his first overseas trip as president.[154]

A third key development in the spring of 2017, though it occurs unbeknownst to anyone outside the U.S. intelligence community, is that Trump's May 2017 firing of James Comey—coupled with Trump's claim, to both NBC News and two Kremlin officials he ushers into the Oval Office after he has done the deed, that it was done to stall or eliminate the Russia investigation—leads the FBI to open up a counterintelligence probe into whether Trump "is working on behalf of Russia."[155]

Trump's agreement to go to Riyadh in May 2017, just months into his presidency, does not come without a price tag attached.[156] According to the *Washington Post*, Trump "tell[s] Kushner they would go [to Riyadh first] if the Saudis promised to make U.S. weapons purchases and increase counterterrorism efforts."[157] The Saudis agree to Trump's demands, though the $110 billion in immediate American arms purchases King Salman announces after Trump arrives in Riyadh—which Trump will "boast" was the product of his decision to travel to Saudi Arabia before visiting any of America's closer allies—had in fact "been on the books for more than a year," meaning well before the 2016 presidential election. And by 2018 officials would acknowledge that "most of the deals [had] not progressed since Trump's visit."[158]

Trump's quid pro quo with MBS is suspicious for another reason, however: the dollar amount attached to the first phase of Trump's $350 billion arms-for-attention shakedown, $110 billion, will be almost exactly the amount that the Saudi government recoups—$106 billion—as the result of a fall 2017 domestic "purge" of wealthy Saudi dissidents and MBS enemies that appears to have benefited from Trump and Kushner's direct assistance (see chapter 8).[159] The Saudis estimate that an additional $13 billion in "settlements" with MBS's enemies will come to the royal family by the end of 2018.[160]

In April 2017, secretary of state Rex Tillerson suddenly announces that—contrary to the plan Trump and his transition team had established pre-inauguration—the United States will not lift sanctions on Russia until the Kremlin has withdrawn its armed forces from the Crimean peninsula.[161] It is unknown whether President Trump concurs with Tillerson's declaration; the *New York Times* will observe that "Trump at times . . . appear[s] to side with the Arab monarchies [Saudi Arabia and the United Arab Emirates] against his own cabinet secretaries. . . . Also in concert with the Saudis and Emiratis, Mr. Trump . . . take[s] a far more hawkish stance toward Iran than . . . his cabinet."[162] Indeed, as late as May 2017, even Republican senators are so convinced that Trump still plans to end sanctions on Russia—Tillerson's statement on the matter notwithstanding—that a bipartisan bill supported by Senator John McCain (R-AZ) is advanced that would wrest control of all Russian sanctions away from the executive branch.[163] McCain may be pushing the bill because he has heard the same news that, per *Newsweek*, journalists and diplomats are hearing at the time: "In its early days, the Trump administration sought to strike a [sanctions] deal with Russia by seeking cooperation against the Islamic State militant group in Syria in return . . . [a plan that] came in the form of a 'tasking' order at the Bureau of European and Eurasian Affairs within the State Department. The order asked officials to draw up a list of options, including sanctions relief and the return of . . . seized [diplomatic] buildings in Maryland and New York."[164]

That Russia is aware of at least the outline of Trump's plan by December 2016—at the very latest—is evident from intercepts of Flynn's phone calls with Russian ambassador Kislyak that month. In the calls, observes *Newsweek*, "Flynn reportedly indicate[s] to Kislyak . . . that Russia could expect a review of the [Crimea and post-election] sanctions under the Trump

administration."[165] Whether this is merely a reiteration of something Flynn
has already told Kislyak pre-election, perhaps in one of the Flynn-Kislyak
meetings Trump tells Chris Christie he fired Flynn over, is unclear. Certainly, it is known that Flynn and his son visited Ambassador Kislyak
at his private D.C. residence on December 2, 2015—nearly a year before
Election Day—and flew to Moscow for dinner with Vladimir Putin at an
RT gala just eight days later.[166] Little is known of the meeting at the ambassador's house in late 2015 other than that Flynn was advising Trump
on foreign policy and national security at the time, had been doing so for
approximately four months and visited Kislyak as a "courtesy call . . . prior
to his trip" to Moscow to deliver an address on "Middle East issues"; it is
Flynn or his son who asked Kislyak for the meeting; and Flynn's son later
called the meeting "very productive."[167] As for any Flynn-Kislyak meetings
between December 2015 and Election Day, in December 2018 *Mother Jones*
will report that in the months leading up to Election Day, Flynn told several
people he was having in-person as well as telephone contact with Kislyak.[168]

In searching for other root causes of the Saudi-Emirati axis's blockade of
Qatar, the *New York Times* will note the possible influence of George Nader
on a high-profile event hosted by the Hudson Institute in early 2017. The
think tank organizes a conference that "feature[s] heavy criticism of Qatar
and the Muslim Brotherhood"; according to the *Times*, a $2.7 million pay-
ment Nader made to Broidy appears to have helped pay for the conference,
a violation of Hudson Institute policies (which prohibit donations from
foreign governments that are not democracies) if Nader was being used as
an MBZ intermediary to pay Broidy.[169] According to the Hudson Institute,
Broidy represented to them, in offering to pay for the conference, that none
of the money he was using to fund the event had come from a foreign
government.[170] Broidy also falsely represented to the Hudson Institute that
at the time of his donation he had no business contracts in the Middle
East.[171] Per the *Times*, both Nader and Broidy used foreign corporations
under their control—Nader an Emirati one, Broidy a Canadian one—to
facilitate the funding for the conference.[172]

Nader meets "several times with senior administration officials in the White House during Mr. Trump's first weeks in office."[173] Among those he meets with are Steve Bannon, Jared Kushner, and several other "White House policymakers," according to the *New York Times*. It is unknown whether he meets with Trump himself.[174] In these meetings, Nader offers advice "on American policy toward the Persian Gulf states in advance of Mr. Trump's trip to Saudi Arabia in May 2017."[175] Reporting on these meetings, Axios will call Nader a "mysterious" and "little-known" Bannon associate "who boasts of his well-placed connections in the Middle East"; the digital media outlet adds that Nader "regularly" visits Bannon in his White House office once Trump is inaugurated.[176] Axios will also report, somewhat cryptically, that something about Nader—it is not clear what, or how it is discovered—unsettles Kushner as he begins looking more deeply into the Lebanese American businessman's background; one possibility is Nader's history of pedophilia (see Introduction).[177] Others whom Axios asks about Nader will draw a blank. According to reporter Jonathan Swan, "A number of well-connected and experienced Middle East hands in Washington told me they'd never heard of Nader. I could only find a few people who have met him. Nobody was quite clear about what he does for a living."[178]

In 2017, Saudi lobbyists will spend more than a quarter of a million dollars reserving rooms at a single Trump property: the Trump International Hotel in D.C.[179] The Saudis' commitment to Trump reflects his commitment to them; as Voice of America will note, "Saudi Arabia is an unprecedented destination for an initial overseas visit by any U.S. president, but the oil-rich nation, which has deep, long-standing energy and defense ties to the United States, was not named in the travel bans" announced by Trump on January 27, 2017.[180]

Kushner accompanies his father-in-law to Riyadh, as does secretary of state Rex Tillerson, about whom MBZ has begun complaining to the White House, through Elliott Broidy, by May 2017—and whose dismissal Broidy will consequently demand from Trump in a face-to-face meeting 120 days later. In the private conversation the two men have in October

2017, as Broidy reports in an email to Nader immediately thereafter, "President Trump asked me about the job Rex was doing. I responded that he was performing poorly and should be relieved but only at a good time, politically."[181] Broidy's opposition to Tillerson is based in part on him being, in the view of the Emiratis, "insufficiently hostile to Qatar"—one of the nations whose representatives Trump meets with in May 2017 in Riyadh, when the Saudi-Emirati axis's blockade of the country is still a few weeks away.[182] Reportedly, Tillerson single-handedly prevented a full-scale invasion of Qatar by Saudi Arabia and the UAE in the summer of 2017 (see chapter 6).

At the time of the Trump-Qatari meeting in Riyadh, Qatar is still a member in good standing of the Gulf Cooperation Council alongside Saudi Arabia, the United Arab Emirates, Kuwait, Oman, and Bahrain. The agreement reached on a yacht in the Red Sea in late 2015 had called for the "replace[ment] of the GCC and Arab League" by swapping out Qatar, Kuwait, and Oman in the former council with Egypt, Jordan, and Libya.[183] However, given that Libya "was not represented" on the yacht and Jordan "[falls] out dramatically with the group . . . [when] Saudi Arabia decide[s] that it did not go far enough in enforcing the blockade against Qatar," the Saudis and Emiratis are in fact, by mid-2017, simply planning on replacing Qatar, Kuwait, and Oman in the GCC with Egypt, while retaining Bahrain.[184]

MBS, Nader, and Broidy likely oppose Tillerson for another reason as well: his hostility to the ever-increasing role Jared Kushner is playing in Middle East geopolitics, particularly with respect to Saudi Arabia. *The Intercept* will later report that during this period, "senior U.S. government officials . . . [are] worried about Kushner's handling of sensitive foreign policy issues given his lack of diplomatic experience. They have also raised concerns about the possibility that foreign officials might try to influence him through business deals with his family's real estate empire."[185] According to the *Washington Post*, two of these "senior U.S. government officials" are secretary of state Rex Tillerson and national security advisor H. R. McMaster, who very "early" in the Trump administration "expressed . . . concern that Kushner was freelancing U.S. foreign policy."[186] The *Post* reports that at one point Tillerson angrily asked his staff, in reference to Kushner, "Who is secretary of state here?"[187] That Kushner had been involved in meetings with Nader, MBS's emissary, to discuss Middle East policy, and that Nader was involved in Broidy's attempts to secure Tillerson's dismissal in conversations with Trump, underscores that Tillerson's eventual firing is at least partly the product of systematic coordination by Kushner and his allies, MBS included. That Kushner—and his wife, Ivanka Trump—hold this sort of authority in the White House will be often written of in the months ahead, including in a *Politico* report on Trump's search for a new chief of staff after John Kelly leaves that concludes, "any potential hire must . . . win the approval of Jared Kushner and Ivanka Trump. Trump's son-in-law and daughter, who are also White House advisers, want a political ally in the chief of staff job, and they are using their unrivaled influence to ensure they get one."[188] Of the Kushner-Tillerson relationship, *Business Insider* will write that "former Secretary of State Rex Tillerson reportedly believe[s] President Donald Trump's son-in-law, Jared Kushner, stoked rumors of his impending ouster."[189] Shortly before he is fired, Tillerson gives an interview with the *New Yorker* in which he acknowledges that one person in the administration in particular wants to see him gone. "'I know who it is," he says. "I know who it is. And they know I know." The magazine adds, "Tillerson was reportedly referring to Trump's son-in-law and adviser Jared Kushner."[190]

In December 2018, CNBC will report that Tillerson felt Trump repeatedly "encouraged him to break the law" while the former Exxon CEO was secretary of state, a statement that presages the Mueller Report's subsequent revelation that Don McGahn believed Trump had asked him to do "crazy shit" and that Reince Priebus once referred to a directive Trump gave him as legally "all wrong."[191]

Trump's commitment to the four nations in a prospective reimagined GCC—Saudi Arabia, the UAE, Bahrain, and Egypt—is underscored by his actions in Riyadh in May 2017. The only bilateral meeting Trump holds during his stay in the kingdom is with the Saudi king, King Salman, who awards Trump "the kingdom's highest civilian honor" during their meeting. Trump attends a multilateral meeting with three current GCC members—Qatar, Kuwait, and Bahrain—as well as Egypt, but thereafter he only accepts an invitation to visit Egypt, saying, "We will absolutely be putting that on the list very soon. . . . [There are] some very important talks going on with Egypt." Of the fourth Saudi-and-Emirati-approved GCC nation, Bahrain, Trump not only says in a press conference in Riyadh that "there won't be strain [between the United States and Bahrain] with this administration" but also agrees to "go ahead with the multibillion-dollar sale of military jets and related equipment" to Bahrain, a sale that had been "held up during the Obama administration by human rights concerns."[192]

But Trump saves the biggest gift of his Riyadh trip for the Saudis, signing a ten-year, $350 billion arms deal with the kingdom that is the largest arms deal in American history.[193] The deal is "partially negotiated" by Kushner, who even makes a call to American military equipment company Lockheed Martin to personally ask it to lower the cost of a missile defense system for the Saudis.[194] The $110 billion first phase of the sale, which will in 2018 be threatened by the Saudi government's assassination of *Washington Post* journalist Jamal Khashoggi (see chapter 9), includes "Abrams tanks, combat ships, missile defense systems, radar, and communications and cybersecurity technology."[195] Trump signs the deal even though "Riyadh is expected to use at least some of the weapons in its military intervention in Yemen's civil war, where the Saudi-led coalition has been accused of war crimes"; this complication leads human rights organizations to warn the White House that "the deal risks making the United States complicit" in the Saudis' and Emiratis' crimes.[196] For Saudi Arabia's part, it rewards Trump's largesse by announcing, upon his arrival in Riyadh, $55 billion in new business deals with American companies in the energy and chemical sectors.[197]

While Trump vaguely suggests the possibility of selling arms to Qatar while meeting with the Qatari emir in Riyadh, it shortly becomes clear that the agreements Trump has made in Saudi Arabia are of a different character altogether. Just two weeks after he leaves Riyadh, the Saudi axis's blockade of Qatar begins.[198] After the country is cut off, the demands made by MBS and his Sunni Arab allies aim to fundamentally remake geopolitics in the Middle East by denying Iran, Turkey, and the elements opposing el-Sisi in Egypt access to the resources they have supposedly been receiving from Qatar. The axis's voluminous list of demands include an insistence that Qatar immediately "close the Iranian diplomatic missions in Qatar," "cut off military and intelligence cooperation with Iran," "halt military cooperation with Turkey inside Qatar," "shut down [a] Turkish military base currently under construction [in Qatar], "declare [the Muslim Brotherhood] a terror group as per the list announced by Saudi Arabia, Bahrain, UAE and Egypt, and concur with all future updates of this list," "shut down . . . all news outlets directly and indirectly funded by Qatar," "cease contact with the political opposition in Saudi Arabia, the UAE, Egypt, and Bahrain," "pay reparations" to Saudi Arabia and its allies in an amount to be determined, and "align Qatar's military, political, social and economic policies with the other Gulf and Arab countries . . . per [a prior] agreement reached with Saudi Arabia."[199] In short, MBS demands that Qatar cede most of its sovereignty to him and his co-conspirators, with the Qataris' journalistic, military, diplomatic, geopolitical, cultural, and economic decisions being brought forcefully into line by expansive edicts from Riyadh. This illustrates the conclusions of a 2017 Associated Press article republished in top Israeli media outlet *Haaretz*, which observes that "governments across the [Middle East] region routinely cite terrorism as justification to clamp down on political opposition and rights activists. Some groups Qatar has backed—such as the Muslim Brotherhood—are seen by many as a legitimate political force. Others, including some hardline Sunni rebel factions in Syria, are not that different ideologically from groups that Saudi Arabia backs there."[200] That the United States has not historically shared MBS and his allies' professed concerns about Qatar is underscored by the fact that America "continues to sell Qatar billions in weapons," the two media outlets note.[201] Their finding that Qatari money has at times "indirectly" supported Islamist militant groups—as a result of chaos on the ground in sectarian conflicts in the region—echoes a similar finding in February 2019 by CNN, which reports that both MBS and MBZ have permitted American weapons sold to them by the Trump administration to "ma[k]e their way into the hands of Iranian-backed rebels battling the [Saudi-Emirati] coalition . . . exposing some of America's sensitive military technology to Tehran and potentially endangering the lives of U.S. troops."[202]

The Associated Press and *Haaretz* regard some of the demands by the Saudi-led axis as nonsensical. For instance, "Saudi Arabia has . . . accused Qatar of backing Iranian-allied rebels in Yemen, known as Houthis. However, Qatar was a member of a Saudi-led coalition bombing the Houthis in Yemen. Experts say there is no evidence to support the [Saudi] claims."[203]

Nevertheless, not only does Trump immediately voice his support of MBS's blockade, but he "appear[s] to take credit" for it, per the *Guardian*, tweeting, "During my recent trip to the Middle East I stated that there can no longer be funding of Radical Ideology. Leaders pointed to Qatar—look! So good to see the Saudi Arabia visit with the King and 50 countries already paying off. They said they would take a hard line on funding extremism and all reference was pointing to Qatar. Perhaps this will be the beginning of the end to horror of terrorism!"[204] According to the *Guardian*, "The president's remarks on Tuesday will come as a shock to Qatar," as the Gulf nation "regarded itself as an ally of the United States and is home to 10,000 U.S. troops, and will delight Saudi Arabia, which until recently had been fighting off claims in Washington that Riyadh was the chief sponsor of terrorism."[205] The British media outlet notes that Trump's position "runs counter to the tone of other administration officials calling for compromise and reconciliation," including Rex Tillerson, who immediately after the blockade began "called for calm."[206]

In its coverage of the blockade, the *Guardian* reports that one reason Trump's position shocks even officials in his own administration is that Qatar "spent more than $1 billion building [the U.S. base there] and [it] has been used to stage attacks against ISIS in Syria and Iraq."[207]

Qatar's response to the blockade is to suggest that its enemies have conspired to create a "rift with the United States and its allies."[208] As the *Guardian* reports at the time, Qatar "feels it is the victim of an orchestrated and well-planned operation designed to end its independent foreign policy."[209] Even more troubling is a CNN report revealing that American officials believe it is Russia that has orchestrated the blockade crisis by using hackers to plant fake news on the Qataris' state-run television channel.[210] Per the CNN report, "intelligence gathered by the U.S. security agencies indicates that Russian hackers were behind the intrusion first reported by the Qatari government two weeks ago . . . The alleged involvement of Russian hackers intensifies concerns by U.S. intelligence and law enforcement agencies that Russia continues to try some of the same cyber-hacking measures on U.S. allies that intelligence agencies believe it used to meddle in the 2016 elections."[211] The alleged Russian hack appears calibrated to provide cover for Saudi Arabia and the UAE in their decision to blockade Qatar, with a May 23 news report from the Qatar News Agency "attribut[ing] false remarks to [Qatar's] ruler that appeared friendly to Iran and Israel . . . and question[ing] whether President Donald Trump would last in office."[212] The hack, which Qatari foreign minister Sheikh Mohammed bin Abdulrahman al-Thani will say has been "confirmed" and "proved" by the FBI as a "planting of fake news," is therefore equally offensive to Saudi Arabia and the UAE (because of its indication of a positive turn in Qatari-Iranian relations) and Trump himself (because of its indication of a negative turn in Qatari-Trump relations).[213]

An open question is whether the Saudis' and Emiratis' credulous response to a Qatari news report many in the U.S. government deemed inauthentic was strategic. Certainly, the Saudi-led blockade is conveniently coincident with tweets from Trump shifting the focus of accusations of terror financing in the Middle East from Saudi Arabia to Qatar.[214] That Trump, the Saudis, and the Emiratis are overstating their case with respect to Qatar's support for international terrorism is only emphasized when the U.S. State Department issues a statement—mere hours after Trump's pro-blockade tweets—saying that Qatar has "made progress on stemming the funding of terrorists."[215] The statement contradicts Trump's remarks even as, per CNN, his words include "criticism of Qatar that mirrors that of the Saudis" and fail to mention at all the possible hacking of the Qatar News Agency.[216] Saudi Arabia's announcement that its blockade is "partly in reaction" to an incident that U.S. media considers a possible "false news report" is telling: by ignoring the findings of the FBI and the concerns of American media outlets, and focusing instead on the words of support tweeted out by Trump, Saudi Arabia is emboldened into a course of action for which it otherwise might have had little support outside the region.[217]

The Qataris will tell U.S. media that the Saudis' posture toward Qatar changed suddenly and unexpectedly as soon as Trump and Kushner met with King Salman. A "high-level Qatari source" tells *The Intercept* that "the Emir [of Qatar] was in Jeddah [Saudi Arabia] before the [Trump-Salman] summit, had a meeting with King Salman. King Salman did not bring up any subject about differences with Qatar. After the summit, the Saudis and the Emirates, they thought, after signing all these [military] contracts [with Trump], they can have the upper hand in the region and they don't want any country not to be in the same line."[218] Certainly, the chief complaint about Qatar the Saudis declare after their king's summit with Trump—that Qatar, a chief U.S. ally in the region, is in fact secretly a major state sponsor of terrorism—is of the sort that, if valid, normally would have been communicated first through diplomatic channels to the Qatari government prior to the summit and only then made public.

Less than a month after Trump departs Saudi Arabia, he will falsely declare that Qatar has "historically been a funder of terrorism at a very high level."[219] Secretary of State Tillerson tells several peers, in response, that Trump's unsupported claim about Qatar's financing of terrorism "had been written by UAE Ambassador Yousef al-Otaiba and delivered to Trump by Jared Kushner."[220] At a fundraiser shortly after leaving Riyadh, Trump will so align himself with Saudi Arabia and the UAE that he will abandon America's long-standing alliance with Qatar and associate himself instead with the aggressors arrayed against the tiny Gulf country. "We're having a dispute with Qatar," he tells a roomful of Republican donors in late June, adding, "I prefer that they don't fund terrorism."[221]

Trump's sudden abandonment of the Qataris, inasmuch as it emboldens the Saudis and Emiratis and prolongs their blockade of Qatar, operates as a crushing financial punishment for the Qataris refusing—even if only temporarily—to bail out his son-in-law. According to a source in the region quoted by *The Intercept,* "Had the Qataris known where things were heading diplomatically" they would have immediately and "happily ponied up the money [to Jared Kushner], even knowing that it was a losing invest-ment. 'It would have been much cheaper,' he [the source] said."[222]

As Trump is in Saudi Arabia in May 2017, his friend Thomas Barrack is finalizing a deal to buy One California Plaza in Los Angeles. At a time when Barrack holds exactly $70 million of Jared Kushner's debt, Barrack receives exactly $70 million in investments for his hoped-for purchase of the Plaza from two separate sources: MBZ and "an Israeli insurance company."[223]

Just weeks earlier, Kushner's family business had received a $30 mil-lion investment from Menora Mivtachim, an Israeli insurance company—possibly, though the full details of Barrack's One California Plaza pur-chase are unknown, the same unnamed Israeli insurance company that helped give Barrack $70 million while Trump was in Saudi Arabia.[224] According to the New York Times, "Menora, which is also Israel's largest manager of pension funds, has done numerous other real estate deals, including several in the United States."[225] Despite the coincidence of Bar-rack holding $70 million in Kushner debt and then receiving $70 mil-lion from an Israeli insurance company that may well have been simultaneously doing business with Kushner as well—all while Kushner was in the Middle East negotiating Iran policy with the Saudis, to the great interest of the Israeli government—Kushner's attorney Abbe Lowell will tell the Times that "connecting any of [Kushner's] well-publicized trips to the Middle East to anything to do with Kushner Companies or its busi-nesses is nonsensical."[226]

In early 2018, a major Washington Post report will identify the UAE and Israel as two of four countries that, per U.S. intelligence intercepts, "have privately discussed ways they can manipulate Jared Kushner," specifically "by taking advantage of his complex business arrangements [and] financial difficulties," as well as his "lack of foreign policy experience."[227]

During the same period in which Kushner receives $30 million from

Menora, he has already received $200 million in real estate purchases and investments from Beny Steinmetz and his family; Steinmetz, an Israeli, is in May 2017 "the subject of a United States Justice Department bribery investigation."[228] By May 2017 Kushner also has four outstanding loans from Israel's largest bank, Bank Hapoalim, which at the time is "the subject of a Justice Department investigation over allegations that it helped wealthy Americans evade taxes."[229] The possibility that these financial transactions could represent a conflict of interest for Kushner—given that, just months earlier, he had directed Flynn, irrespective of the federal Logan Act, to negotiate with several countries on the subject of a UN resolution affecting Israel—will cause one ethics expert who speaks to the *Times* to opine that Kushner's standard on government corruption appears to be "some version of, 'It's a conflict when I think it's a conflict, and I'll make that judgment myself.'"[230]

The same month Trump and Kushner travel to Riyadh, Egypt takes a major step toward realization of the Red Sea conspirators' goal of improving relations with Russia in hope of softening its support for Iran, Turkey, and the regime of Syrian president Bashar al-Assad: it announces a deal with Moscow that will see Russian firms building Egypt's first nuclear power plant.[231] According to the *Washington Post*, "The arrangement was supported by Russian President Vladimir Putin."[232] While Flynn's ambition, when he traveled to Egypt in 2015, had been to convince Egypt not to partner bilaterally with Russia but to participate instead in a broader Middle East Marshall Plan, such two-party arrangements as the Egypt-Russia nuclear deal became a fait accompli when the ongoing Trump-Russia scandal prevented Trump from executing his original plan to drop all sanctions on Russia—a prerequisite to Flynn's expansive proposal. As *Newsweek* reports just weeks after the Egypt-Russia accord, "Trump's administration moved quickly to try to lift economic sanctions on Russia and other punishments former President Barack Obama had put in place just as soon as it took office in January [2017]. 'There was serious consideration by the White House to unilaterally rescind the sanctions,' according to Dan Fried, who retired in February [2017] as Coordinator for Sanctions Policy at the State Department."[233] But because Trump's plan—which had not been shared with career officials at the State Department—resulted in numerous calls from State to Fried asking him to block the initiative, Fried soon began lobbying Congress to codify the Russian sanctions, thereby protecting them from presidential interference.[234]

The Egypt-Russia deal for a nuclear plant in Dabaa, Egypt, is not Russia's first foray into building nuclear plants in the Middle East. In March 2015 it had signed a $10 billion deal with Jordan to build that nation's first-ever nuclear power plant, and nine months earlier, in June 2014, it had agreed to build two such plants in Iran—precisely the sort of Russia-Iran coordination the Red Sea Conspiracy had been conceived, in late 2015, to disrupt.[235]

On May 17, eight days after firing FBI director James Comey, Trump learns that the acting attorney general, Rod Rosenstein, has just appointed a special counsel to investigate Russian interference in the 2016 presidential election. Trump's director of strategic communications, Hope Hicks, will eventually tell the special counsel's office that on the day of the special counsel's appointment Trump was "extremely upset," indeed so upset that in the entirety of her time working for him "she had only seen the President like that one other time, when the *Access Hollywood* tape came out during the campaign."[236] According to Hicks, on the day of Robert Mueller's appointment Trump called the assignment of a special counsel to investigate his and his campaign's ties to Russia "the worst thing that ever happened to me" and actually "slumped back in his chair" when he heard the news.[237] "Oh my God," Hicks reports Trump saying. "This is terrible. This is the end of my Presidency. I'm fucked."[238]

CHAPTER 8

TEL AVIV, THE PURGE, THE CHAIRMAN, AND THE SPY ARMY

July 2017 to December 2017

In the first year of Trump's presidency, MBS and MBZ not only erect direct conduits to Trump but see him execute both their grandest and most minute policy demands—from personnel changes to policy initiatives, from passing them classified intelligence to continuing to seek ways to bring to fruition MBZ's "grand bargain" for the Middle East. Hundreds of millions of dollars in suspicious transnational transactions, coupled with a spate of suspicious meetings involving Kremlin agents, Israeli spies, Saudi torturers, Emirati mercenaries, and two "princes" (Kushner and MBS) help confirm that U.S. foreign policy is for sale and the federal government less transparent than ever—an impression only solidified when a Trump adviser plots to develop two secret international "armies" under Trump's control.

On July 18, 2017, special counsel Robert Mueller, just two months into his appointment, establishes probable cause before a federal court that a personal attorney of the president of the United States is an unregistered foreign agent.[1] While the special counsel's successful application for a search warrant doesn't state which foreign nation he believes Michael Cohen to be a foreign agent of, one likely candidate is Russia, for in January 2017, Cohen had acted as a courier for a Russia-Ukraine "peace deal" that "had the backing of Russians close to the Kremlin."[2] A *Mother Jones* investigation will reveal that in fact the deal Cohen brought to the White House was not only backed by Kremlin-linked oligarchs but had been approved by the Kremlin itself—even initiated by it, inasmuch as it was "senior aides to Putin [who] encouraged him [the deal's author] to push the plan" by trying to get it to Trump.[3]

The so-called peace deal is an agreement to have the new American president drop the sanctions levied in response to Russia's illegal annexation of the Crimean peninsula in Ukraine in early 2014. By the time Cohen acts as a courier for the deal and is asked to pass it along to the White House, however, it has grown to encompass all outstanding U.S. sanctions on Russia—including those imposed on the Russian Federation in December 2016 to punish the Kremlin's pro-Trump interference in the 2016 presidential election.[4]

In explaining the process by which a Kremlin-approved treaty was "given to a Trump associate for delivery to the administration," McClatchy reveals that the deal's first draft, involving only Crimea-related sanctions on Russia, was written in February 2016, the month Trump became the prohibitive favorite in the Republican primaries. Three men authored the plan: Andrii Artemenko, a former member of the Ukrainian parliament; Alexander Rovt, a Ukrainian American billionaire who made his fortune in the fertilizer business in the former Soviet Union; and former Republican congressman Curt Weldon, who the *Atlantic* will report has "ties to the Trump campaign . . . as well as to powerful figures in Russia and Ukraine," including Viktor Vekselberg—a Russian oligarch who both attended Trump's inauguration and allegedly funded, through a company called Columbus Nova, the effort by Artemenko, Rovt, and Weldon to get the Kremlin-approved sanctions deal to Trump via Cohen.[5]

Weldon had previously been investigated by the FBI for political corruption relating to his ties to the "Russian-managed Itera International Energy Corporation, one of the world's largest oil and gas firms."[6] The allegation that Weldon had illegally acted on behalf of a Russian oil and gas company did not lead to criminal charges but "tarnished" Weldon's reputation, per the *Philadelphia Inquirer*.[7]

Like Weldon, Rovt has business ties to a Soviet-born oligarch—in his case Dmytro Firtash, to whom Rovt "sold most of his foreign fertilizer assets in 2007." Firtash was "a chief financier of ex-president Viktor Yanukovych's pro-Russian political party [in Ukraine] before Yanukovych was ousted in 2014 and fled to Moscow. That party paid millions of dollars to yet another key figure in the Trump-Russia investigation, Paul Manafort, who was a top Yanukovych adviser before he became Trump's campaign chairman."[8] Firtash is often accused, notes the *Daily Beast*, of being a "Moscow [Kremlin] front" because his work in the Russian gas industry eventually resulted in him being in business with the Russian government; indeed, his "thick business ties with the Kremlin" include "a 50-50 partnership with Russia's state-backed Gazprom to sell gas in Ukraine."[9]

Just as Artemenko and Weldon present as credible cutouts for Vekselberg, Rovt presents as a credible front man for Firtash. According to Bloomberg, "Through much of 2017, as the nascent Trump administration navigated controversies of its own making, Vekselberg was giving Russian officials and fellow businessmen vague yet certain assurances about his influence in the White House, according to six people who interacted with him at the time. He'd attended Trump's swearing-in ceremony in Washington as a guest of [his American cousin and Columbus Nova founder Andrew] Intrater, who'd donated $250,000 to the inaugural committee, and come back with a newfound sense of clout, they said."[10] After being interviewed by Robert Mueller in March 2018, both Vekselberg and another noted "aluminum baron," Oleg Deripaska, will be subjected to new sanctions, which by the end of 2018 have cost Vekselberg (in total) over $2 billion of his $16.4 billion fortune.[11] The oligarch's financial impetus to want sanctions removed is therefore profound as he helps coordinate the transmission of the Artemenko-Rovt-Weldon deal to Cohen and, thereafter, the White House.

In late December 2018, it will be revealed that Len Blavatnik, "a longtime business associate of Russian oligarchs Oleg Deripaska and Viktor Vekselberg," had in 2015 suddenly amended his political donation habits, which for years had been bipartisan. As soon as Trump announces his candidacy, Blavatnik begins giving almost exclusively to Republicans, including "$3.5 million to Senate Majority Leader Mitch McConnell's PAC from 2015 to 2017" and a "hefty sum" to staunch Trump ally Senator Lindsey Graham (R-SC).[12] Trump will also enjoy Blavatnik's largesse directly, with the Soviet-born billionaire donating $1 million to Trump's inauguration.[13]

The story of how, as the *Atlantic* will put it, "a foreign national sought to influence the president through one of his closest advisers" begins during the presidential transition period, when Cohen and Vekselberg meet on January 9 to "discuss[ ] U.S.-Russia relations."[14] Just days later, shortly after Trump's inauguration, Columbus Nova, Intrater's New York City investment management firm—one of whose biggest clients is the Vekselberg-owned company Renova Group—begins paying Cohen a consulting retainer (monthly payments of $83,333) that will total over $500,000 in seven months.[15] Vekselberg's cousin Andrew Intrater is not only the founder of Columbus Nova, but also its president.[16]

Cohen is thereafter introduced to Artemenko by Felix Sater, who had spent 2015 and 2016 secretly working on a Trump Tower Moscow deal with the Kremlin, Andrey Rozov, Cohen, and Trump. Trump's Russian real estate "fixer" is therefore, over the period from September 2015 to February 2017, assisting Trump with both a multibillion-dollar property transaction and with a clandestine agreement on U.S. foreign policy—with both deals involving Trump and the Kremlin as consequential principals.[17] Any connection between the two deals, such as each using Sater as a Trump- and Kremlin-connected intermediary, raises the prospect of a quid pro quo and therefore a federal charge of bribery; bribery is an impeachable offense under the U.S. Constitution.

The Kremlin-backed Artemenko-Rovt-Weldon-Vekselberg sanctions agreement Cohen ultimately ferries to the White House—with national security advisor Mike Flynn as its initial intended recipient—is fairly simple in its contours, and operates as a Putin-supported alternative to the Red Sea Conspiracy; the latter is a plan that likewise would lead to the ending of all U.S. sanctions on Russia, but potentially at a much higher long-term cost to the Kremlin via the loss of its alliance with Iran. By comparison, as summarized by McClatchy, the Artemenko-Rovt-Weldon-Vekselberg simply says that Trump will "lift[ ] sanctions on Moscow if the

Kremlin withdraw[s] Russian forces from Eastern Ukraine," though it would also "permit[ ] Russia to keep Crimea, which it annexed in 2014."[18] As deals go, it is squarely, even exclusively, to the benefit of the Kremlin, as under international law Putin's armed forces are illegally in Eastern Ukraine; the deal is thus more properly seen as thin diplomatic cover for the unilateral ending of all U.S. sanctions on Russia, without any of the illusory (or merely transitory) benefits to the United States of the plan supported by MBS, MBZ, el-Sisi, and the "gang of six" (Flynn, Barrack, Gates, Prince, Nader, and Broidy).

Mueller's July 2017 search warrant for Cohen's emails—and the Southern District of New York's April 2018 warrants for Cohen's home and office, as well as a hotel room used by the president's attorney—therefore present a clear danger to President Trump, as Cohen's communications can establish not only his and Sater's secret real estate dealings on Trump's behalf in 2015 and 2016 but also the fact that he and his friend Sater were lobbying Trump on U.S. foreign policy both before and after his inauguration.[19]

In February 2019, the House Judiciary Committee will say it has evidence that Trump asked acting attorney general Matthew Whitaker whether the Department of Justice could reinstall the recused Geoff Berman—a former law partner of Trump attorney Rudy Giuliani—as overseer of the Southern District of New York's probe into Cohen.[20] This new evidence will cause the Judiciary Committee to open an investigation into whether Whitaker committed perjury before Congress, as he had told the Judiciary Committee in sworn testimony that "at no time has the White House asked, nor have I promised, any promises or commitments concerning the special counsel's investigation or any other investigation."[21] According to the New York Times, after Whitaker told Trump that Berman could not "unrecuse" himself following his recusal from the Cohen case, "the president soon soured on Mr. Whitaker . . . and complained about his inability to pull levers at the Justice Department that could make the president's many legal problems go away."[22] The Times will also report that Whitaker had "privately told associates that part of his role at the Justice Department was to 'jump on a grenade' for the president."[23]

CNN will report on additional problematic interactions between Trump and the DOJ over the various ongoing Cohen investigations. In one incident detailed by CNN, Trump "vented to his acting attorney general [Whitaker]" about the Cohen investigation, "angered by federal prosecutors who referenced the President's actions in crimes his former lawyer . . . pleaded guilty to."[24] Per CNN, the president was "frustrated . . . that prosecutors Matt Whitaker oversees filed charges that made Trump look bad . . . [and] lashed out" at the acting attorney general.[25] In another incident, just a week later, Trump "again voiced his anger at Whitaker after prosecutors in Manhattan officially implicated the President in a hush-money scheme to buy the silence of women around the 2016 campaign . . . Trump pressed Whitaker on why more wasn't being done to control prosecutors in New York."[26] The cable news network will conclude that "the episodes offer a glimpse into the unsettling dynamic of a sitting president talking to his attorney general about investigations he's potentially implicated in"—a status that applies to all of the various federal investigations into Michael Cohen's business and political activities, from the probe of Cohen's pre-election hush money payments to Stormy Daniels to any pending federal probe of his involvement with the Artemenko-Rovt-Weldon-Vekselberg "peace deal" in early 2017.[27] Trump's conversations with Whitaker are seen as particularly troubling, as Whitaker had become acting attorney general only when Trump fired the recused Jeff Sessions—after months of public complaints that Sessions was not protecting him from federal investigations—and upon Whitaker's elevation to acting attorney general, he was told by a senior DOJ ethics official that, like Sessions, he should recuse himself out of an "abundance of caution."[28] Yet Whitaker refused to do so.[29]

Whitaker, previously a Sessions deputy, was said prior to his promotion to have "a close relationship with Mr. Trump, and had been described," writes the *New York Times*, "as the White House's eyes and ears inside the Justice Department."[30] The *Times* adds that "Whitaker had also sharply criticized the Russia investigation while he was a legal analyst on CNN . . . [and] worked on the [2014 Iowa state treasurer campaign] of Sam Clovis, who is a witness in the Mueller investigation" as well as having been national co-chair of Trump's 2016 presidential campaign.[31] In December 2018, Whitaker will be observed by media getting aboard Marine One with Jared Kushner in D.C., the sort of impromptu meeting between an attorney general and an interested party to a federal criminal investigation that Trump had long railed about when the parties in question were attorney general Loretta Lynch and former president Bill Clinton—though of course the former president was not as closely linked to the investigation of his wife's email practices as Kushner is, by December 2018, to the Russia investigation.[32] While at the DOJ as Sessions's deputy, Whitaker, according to *Vox*, "in his conversations with the president, presented himself as a vigorous supporter of Trump's position and 'committed to extract as much as he could from the Justice Department on the president's behalf.'"[33] At one point the future acting attorney general went so far as to "let it be known [in the White House] that he was on a team, and it was the president's team."[34] *Vox* will add that "during this period, Whitaker frequently spoke by phone with both Trump and Chief of Staff John Kelly. . . . On many of those calls, nobody else was on the phone except for the president and Whitaker . . . As one senior law enforcement official told [*Vox*], 'Nobody else knew what was said on those calls except what Whitaker decided to tell others, and if he did, whether he was telling the truth. Who ever heard of a president barely speaking to his attorney general but on the phone constantly with a staff-level person?"[35] When he is asked by the media how well he knows Whitaker upon elevating him to acting attorney general, Trump will say, "I don't know Whitaker."[36]

Other attempts by Trump to interfere with federal investigations of Michael Cohen include the following: evidence that Trump directed Cohen to lie publicly and to Congress about the details of his ongoing negotiations for a Trump Tower Moscow during the general election (information *BuzzFeed News* will report it gained from "interviews with multiple witnesses from the Trump Organization and internal company emails, text messages, and a cache of other documents"); evidence that Cohen was in "regular contact" with Trump's legal team while writing and editing his false statement to Congress about the Trump Tower Moscow deal, including evidence his statement was reviewed and edited by at least one Trump attorney, Jay Sekulow; evidence that "lawyers who claimed to be associates of Rudy Giuliani" contacted Cohen two weeks after his home, office, and hotel room were raided in 2018 to "convince Cohen to remain loyal to Trump" by staying in a "joint defense agreement" with the president; evidence that in April 2018, "an attorney who said he was speaking with President Donald Trump's lawyer Rudy Giuliani reassured Michael Cohen . . . that Cohen could 'sleep well tonight' because he had 'friends in high places'"; evidence that the president was aware, at a minimum after the fact, that one of his top House allies, Rep. Matt Gaetz (R-FL), had threatened Cohen with exposure of an extramarital affair the night before his public congressional testimony ("I was happy to do it for you," Gaetz told Trump during a subsequent telephone call); and evidence that Trump may have directly (face-to-face) or indirectly (through his attorneys) floated the possibility of a pardon for Cohen prior to him signing a cooperation deal with federal prosecutors, including evidence that Giuliani "left open the possibility [of a pardon]" in his conversations with Cohen's legal team.[37]

Trump lawyer Rudy Giuliani will falsely claim Trump never signed a letter of intent to build a Trump Tower Moscow with Andrey Rozov in the fall of 2015 just days before CNN anchor Chris Cuomo produces the signed document live on-air.[38] When his deceit is caught out, Giuliani responds by arguing that Trump signing a multibillion-dollar deal to build a tower in Moscow with financing from a Kremlin-owned bank during the 2016 election—at a time he was telling American voters he had no association of any kind with the Russians—is "meaningless."[39] In October 2018, ProPublica will reveal that Giuliani "has often traveled to Russia or other former Soviet states as guests of powerful players there. And since Trump was elected, [Giuliani] appears to have stepped up the frequency of those trips."[40] Giuliani's odd overseas meeting partners include an Armenian businessman whose construction firm once helped reconstruct the Kremlin and a Russian cybersecurity expert currently on the U.S. sanctions list with whom Giuliani appeared on a conference panel; the company that "claims credit for organizing the trips," TriGlobal Strategic Ventures, includes among its board members a former Russian government minister.[41] In December 2018, Giuliani—still working for Trump—travels to Bahrain, one of the nations involved in the Red Sea Conspiracy, to make an in-person pitch for a "lucrative security consulting contract with the [Bahraini] government."[42]

According to the *Jerusalem Post*, a Chabad house in Long Island—Chabad being an Orthodox Jewish Hasidic movement—was a key location both in the Cohen-Sater axis that led to Trump's secret negotiation of a Kremlin-connected Moscow real estate deal during the presidential campaign and in pro-Kremlin Ukrainians' efforts to gain access to Trump through Cohen. Per the Israeli media outlet, which is working in part from a BBC report, "Individuals who attended the Chabad of Port Washington allegedly facilitated contact between Ukrainian President Petro Poroshenko and U.S. President Donald Trump by connecting loyalists of Poroshenko with Michael Cohen."[43] A politician who has called Putin his chief political "opponent," Poroshenko allegedly "sought an audience with Trump and directed confidantes to orchestrate it . . . using the Chabad house as a channel to reach Cohen and, through him, the president.[44] While not itself illegal, this outreach will by 2019 become what the *Jerusalem Post* calls a "fulcrum" in federal investigations into Trump's foreign contacts because, according to a BBC report, "Cohen was paid $400,000 to connect Poroshenko's aides with the White House, where the Ukrainian leader succeeded in meeting with Trump in June. Cohen did not register as a foreign agent representing Ukrainian or Russian interests, as is mandated by U.S. law."[45] The *Post* mentions "Russian interests" because of the popular belief that the Trump-Poroshenko meeting led to an easing of Ukrainian investigations of Paul Manafort's pro-Kremlin work in Ukraine, the revelation of which could have been embarrassing or even directly damaging to Trump; the possibility of his eventual extradition to Ukraine could also have persuaded Manafort to cooperate with the special counsel's office more fully than he previously had. Yet "shortly after the June [Poroshenko] meeting with Trump," writes the *Post*, "Ukraine's anti-corruption agency dropped its investigation into Trump's former campaign manager, Paul Manafort . . . [a] top target in the Mueller probe."[46] The *Post* adds that the Long Island Chabad whose members allegedly facilitated the Trump-Poroshenko meeting was also accused by *Politico* in April 2017 of "connecting Trump and Putin's oligarchs"—specifically Lev Leviev and Roman Abramovich, who *Politico* reported "used the Chabad network as their base" to act as Putin's "envoys" to Trump.[47] Not only was Leviev longtime friends with the late Tamir Sapir, a development partner and investor for the Trump SoHo project, but also, per the *Post*, close enough to Trump himself that the two men had met in 2008—two years after Trump SoHo opened—to "discuss Moscow real estate opportunities"; this meeting suggests that the Putin envoy and "confidante" (also Chabad's "top donor") had, on Putin's behalf, been priming Trump for future Moscow investments in the twenty-four months before the New York businessman began seriously considering a run for president in 2012. Notably, ABC News has called Michael Cohen "the man behind Donald Trump's possible 2012 presidential campaign."[48]

Trump's tweets in support of Saudi Arabia in June 2017 echo his tweets praising the kingdom the month before, during his visit to Riyadh. In great contrast to his angry pre-visit tweets castigating NATO and America's European allies, his tweets while in Saudi Arabia reflect his enthusiasm for both the visit and his hosts: "Great to be in Riyadh, Saudi Arabia. Looking forward to the afternoon and evening ahead," he tweets on May 20, and then, shortly after he leaves Saudi Arabia, "Israel, Saudi Arabia, and the Middle East were great. Trying hard for PEACE. Doing well."; according to 2019 testimony by former secretary of state Rex Tillerson before the House Foreign Affairs Committee, the first of these two tweets was sent the same day that Jared Kushner and Steve Bannon secretly met with MBS and MBZ in Riyadh, at which clandestine gathering Bannon and Kushner were told of the Saudi and Emirati plan to blockade Qatar.[49] Whereas American presidents have traditionally referred to "peace" in the Middle East in the context of the Israeli-Palestinian conflict, Trump appears to be referring instead to the chief subject of his discussions with Saudi Arabia's King Salman and the leaders of other Muslim countries in Riyadh: "[America's] differences with Iran . . . and how to crack down on Islamic militancy." Significantly, Trump treats "Islamic militancy" no differently whether it is a direct action by the Iranians or actions taken by an alleged Iranian proxy with perhaps only distant or unconfirmed links to Tehran.[50] That Trump is not looking for "peace" with Iran through diplomacy—in stark contrast to the Obama administration's approach, typified by the Iran nuclear deal—is underscored by the fact that the key event Trump attends in Riyadh is a "regional summit focusing on combatting extremism" to which no Iranian officials are invited; as late as June 2019 Trump will still be saying, of possible diplomacy with Iran, "I personally feel that it is too soon to even think about making a deal."[51]

According to Bob Woodward's *Fear*, in April 2017 Trump tells one of his attorneys, John Dowd, that Egyptian president Abdel Fattah el-Sisi is a "fucking killer" who is "worried about this [Mueller] investigation" because he anticipates needing to ask Trump for a "favor" in the future.[52] Just a few weeks earlier, Trump had invited the autocrat to visit the White House— something his predecessor, Barack Obama, had steadfastly refused to do— and called him a "fantastic guy."[53] Trump also "pledged close cooperation" with the Egyptian leader and stated in a press conference, "I just want to let everybody know, in case there was any doubt, that we are very much behind President Sisi. He's done a fantastic job."[54] By 2018, el-Sisi will be celebrating his "reelection" in a vote in which he "earns" 97 percent of the vote; Trump will immediately call el-Sisi to offer his "sincere congratulations" for the statistically improbable win.[55]

According to an April 2018 article in the *Washington Post*, el-Sisi's re-election is internationally deemed a "sham," and Trump's highly vocal approval of it is widely seen as "another signal of the Trump administration's stated goal to improve relations with Egypt" after el-Sisi's deposing of its democratically elected government. Trump's congratulatory message "comes shortly after Trump faced widespread pushback for congratulating another foreign leader, Russian President Vladimir Putin, who similarly won a race that was broadly criticized as neither free nor fair."[56]

In his first White House meeting with el-Sisi, Trump confirms that he considers his administration to be in a "strategic partnership" with the Egyptian strongman's, a reversal of U.S. policy toward el-Sisi and an acknowledgment of Trump's ongoing coordination with a Red Sea conspirator.[57] Tellingly, Trump says during his joint appearance with el-Sisi that the autocrat is "someone that's been very close to me from the first time I met him . . . [we] met during the campaign, at that point there were two of us . . . it was a very long—it was supposed to be just a quick, brief meeting, and we were with each other for a long period of time. We agree on so many things . . . I just want to say to you, Mr. President, that you have a great friend and ally . . . in me."[58]

In fact, Trump is not telling the truth when he says that he met el-Sisi alone in September 2016.[59] At least three men besides Trump and el-Sisi were present at the meeting—two of whom, George Papadopoulos and Michael Flynn, will subsequently be indicted for, and convicted of, a federal felony by the special counsel's office. The fifth participant in Trump's meeting with el-Sisi, Jeff Sessions, will also be investigated by federal law enforcement for lying about his contacts with foreign nationals, in Sessions's case under oath and before Congress.[60]

Two of the (at least) five men present when Trump meets el-Sisi, Flynn and Papadopoulos, had also worked on the Carson campaign in late 2015, a time when that campaign was using an Israeli business intelligence firm, Inspiration, for its voter targeting operation.[61] Flynn, by late 2015, had taken "a real shining" to—and been recruited by—Joel Zamel, head of two other Israeli business intelligence firms, Wikistrat and Psy-Group.[62] Given that Zamel would, in August 2016, make a proposal at Trump Tower alongside George Nader, one of the architects, with el-Sisi, of the Red Sea Conspiracy, there is some reason to suspect an association between either Flynn's or Papadopoulos's ties to individuals in Israel and the warm reception Trump receives from el-Sisi and vice versa. Indeed, a man Papadopoulos meets in Tel Aviv in June 2017, Arabic-fluent Israeli businessman Charles Tawil—whom Papadopoulos will accuse of working for the Israeli government—will tell media, in response to Papadopoulos's allegation, that the young energy consultant first came to his attention following his arrangement of the mid-presidential campaign meeting between Trump and el-Sisi in September 2016.[63]

When Papadopoulos meets Tawil for the first time in Israel in June 2017, just a few months into Trump's presidency, Tawil gives the former

Trump national security adviser $10,000 in cash for unspecified reasons.[64] Tawil denies Papadopoulos's claims that he was or is an Israeli spy, but acknowledges that in June 2017 he did indeed give a large sum of money to Papadopoulos; he contends, however, that Papadopoulos was "desperate" to be in a partnership with him at the time.[65] In the same November 2018 interview with the *Times of Israel* in which Tawil denies Papadopoulos's allegations that he is a spy for the Israeli government, Tawil admits that he is on friendly terms with a top agent of the Emirati government, minister of tolerance Sheikh Nahayan Mabarak Al Nahayan.[66]

Papadopoulos's meeting with Tawil in 2017 is not, of course, his first meeting with Israeli nationals during his period of service for Donald Trump or afterward. In early April 2016, just a month after his hire by Sam Clovis, Papadopoulos was sent by the campaign to speak to research associates at the Begin-Sadat Center for Strategic Studies at Bar-Ilan University in Tel Aviv.[67] During the same trip, Papadopoulos spoke to unnamed Israeli diplomats to "discuss Trump's foreign-policy priorities" and was on a panel at the Hadera Energy Conference in Tel Aviv with Eli Groner, a top aide in Israeli prime minister Benjamin Netanyahu's office.[68] Indeed, Papadopoulos will have so many contacts with Israeli nationals during the 2016 presidential campaign, during the presidential transition, and after Trump's 2017 inauguration that in August 2017 the special counsel's office seeks and receives from the Department of Justice the authority to investigate Papadopoulos as a possible Israeli agent.[69] According to Papadopoulos's wife, Simona Mangiante, the special counsel's office went so far as to, in its conversations with Papadopoulos, "threaten[ ] to charge him with being an Israeli agent."[70] Papadopoulos's significant Israeli ties, like Flynn's, suggest the probability that one or both men communicated pre-election not just to agents of Red Sea conspirators like el-Sisi but to individuals associated with the Israeli government such as Groner that the Trump campaign was on board with what the Emiratis and Saudis considered a "grand bargain"; both men were well positioned, too, to report back to the Trump campaign that the Israelis were similarly inclined to participate in the proposed geopolitical arrangement. Apropos of many Trump campaign aides and associates having close Israeli ties, just days after Trump meets with el-Sisi alongside Papadopoulos and Flynn, the GOP candidate has another consequential meeting with a key figure in the Red Sea Conspiracy, this one at Trump Tower—where he meets with Kushner, Bannon, Israeli ambassador Ron Dermer, and Benjamin Netanyahu himself.[71]

By the time of his September 25, 2016, meeting with Trump, Trump's son-in-law, and Bannon, Netanyahu has had a "long friendship" with Kushner's father, convicted felon Charles Kushner, sometimes staying at the Kushners' home when visiting the United States.[72] As for the Israeli ambassador, Dermer had first met Trump at Trump Tower alongside Netanyahu in the early aughts, and first met Kushner in March 2016, thereafter "working closely" with him and remaining "in close touch" with him "throughout the campaign and the transition"—meaning that from March onward, Kushner was being regularly advised behind the scenes by an Israeli (Dermer), an Emirati (al-Otaiba), and a Soviet-born "friend" of Vladimir Putin (Simes), with none of these men ever being acknowledged by the Trump campaign as key advisers.[73] Notably, the *New Yorker* reports that the Israeli and Emirati ambassadors were in communication pre-election about the shared interests of their two nations with respect to the Trump campaign and, later, the Trump administration; indeed, the magazine reveals that, "toward the end of Obama's second term"—a period of time that includes both the hatching of the Red Sea Conspiracy in late 2015 and Papadopoulos's secretive efforts in May 2016 to schedule mid-campaign trips to Greece and Israel by Trump—"U.S. intelligence agencies learned of phone calls between senior U.A.E. and Israeli officials, including calls between a senior Emirati leader and Netanyahu. Then U.S. intelligence agencies picked up on a secret meeting between senior U.A.E. and Israeli leaders in Cyprus. U.S. officials suspect that Netanyahu attended the meeting, which centered on countering Obama's Iran deal."[74] As for Steve Bannon, who is Papadopoulos's interlocutor with Trump in setting up the el-Sisi meeting—and who attends the September 25 Trump-Netanyahu meeting—he becomes so close to Ron Dermer during the presidential campaign and presidential transition that he will on several occasions, according to the *New Yorker*, call Dermer "my wingman."[75]

By September 2016, Netanyahu has developed, per the *New Yorker*, a "grand strategy for transforming the direction of Middle Eastern politics" that he believes only a President Trump can help him execute.[76] The plan: "form a coalition with Saudi Arabia and the United Arab Emirates to combat Iran" while sidelining, perhaps permanently, the debate over the Palestinian territories.[77] At Trump Tower on September 25, Netanyahu "press[es] his strategic agenda," something he does not do when he meets with Clinton the same week, pitching her instead on a plan that focuses on "improving the lives of the Palestinians" in exchange for Arab states "taking steps toward" recognizing Israel—this being a trade-off far more solicitous of the Palestinians than anything Netanyahu's "grand strategy" in fact envisions.[78]

Netanyahu and Dermer's "well articulated" strategy for "an alliance between Israel and the Gulf states," discussed in detail with Trump, Kushner, and Bannon at Trump Tower months before Election Day, "blow[s] away" Bannon, who will later recount that it "dovetailed exactly with our [the Trump campaign's] thinking." Another Trump campaign adviser will tell the *New Yorker* that "the germ of the idea" of a grand Israeli-Arab alliance "started in that room . . . on September 25, 2016, in Trump's penthouse."[79] Because the exact timing of the secret meeting in Cyprus Netanyahu holds with Emirati leadership toward the end of President Obama's second term is unknown, it is unclear whether Netanyahu meets with Trump having recently spoken with Abu Dhabi—perhaps even MBZ—about countering Iran, or whether it is Netanyahu's meeting at Trump Tower that provides Netanyahu with sufficient intelligence on Trump's intentions that the Israeli prime minister is then able to discuss with the Emiratis the candidate's amenability to a "grand bargain."

On June 21, 2017, Saudi crown prince Mohammed bin Salman becomes the heir apparent to the throne of his father's kingdom, having just deposed his cousin Mohammed bin Nayef.[80] The same month, an Israeli business intelligence company that "specializes in cyber espionage tools," NSO Group, enters into a $55 million agreement with the Saudi government to give the Saudis Pegasus 3—proprietary software that will allow MBS and his father to "hack their citizens' cell phones, and to listen to calls as well as conversations that take place near the phones."[81] While the NSO deal with Riyadh draws significant public attention, a November 2018 *Times of Israel* report will disclose that throughout 2017 "Israeli cyber spying companies [meet] several times with Saudi figures at European locations to talk about the sale of various [intelligence] technologies"—suggesting a new era of Israeli-Saudi coordination has begun, one that in short order will have substantial repercussions across the globe.[82] That MBS intends to use such technology to destroy domestic opposition to his regime is evidenced by the fact that "in one [NSO-Saudi] meeting, Israeli representatives refused a Saudi request to identify the user behind an anti-regime Twitter account as a way of showing the ability of their technology"—though NSO officials did agree to "demonstrate[ ] how [Pegasus 3] could take control of a brand-new iPhone [if] it was provided the phone's number."[83]

While the identities of the NSO and Saudi negotiators are unknown, the *Times of Israel* will note that one of the people involved in helping the Saudis acquire Pegasus 3 was "an Israeli businessman dealing in defense-related technologies who operates through Cyprus . . . and [who] flew NSO founder Shalev Hulio to a location in the Gulf for three days of meetings in June 2017."[84] According to the *New York Times*, two lawsuits brought against NSO in August 2018 will accuse the company of "actively participating in illegal spying," in one case involving spying conducted by the UAE.[85] This is a particularly explosive charge given that, as the *Times of Israel* notes, "to sell Pegasus to the UAE [or Saudi Arabia] the company would have had to receive the express permission of the [Israeli] Defense Ministry, as such software is considered a weapon."[86] If the lawsuits against NSO are successful, they may therefore establish that the Israeli government (as well as the "Israeli businessman dealing in defense-related technologies who operates through Cyprus") is assisting the UAE—and likely Saudi Arabia—in conducting illegal international spycraft.

The same month NSO sells Pegasus 3 to the Saudis, another—or perhaps the same—UAE-connected "Israeli businessman dealing in defense-related technologies who operates through Cyprus," Charles Tawil, meets with George Papadopoulos.[87] According to Papadopoulos, on June 8, 2017, Tawil, who identifies himself as a "pro-Trump citizen," introduces him to Shai Arbel, co-founder of Israeli cyberintelligence company Terrogence, at the Crowne Plaza Tel Aviv City Center Hotel.[88] As reported by the

New Yorker, Psy-Group, Joel Zamel's Israeli business intelligence outfit (see chapters 3 and 4), "emerged more directly from Terrogence" than did other spin-offs of the Israeli business intelligence pioneer, though the company's first-in-its-field status means that not only Psy-Group but NSO is an heir to its inheritance. Per the *New Yorker*, "In 2008, [Terrogence co-founder Gadi] Aviran hired an Israel Defense Forces intelligence officer named Royi Burstien to be the vice-president of business development. . . . Burstien urged Aviran to consider using [online] avatars in more aggressive ways, and on behalf of a wider range of commercial clients. Aviran was wary. After less than a year at Terrogence, Burstien returned to Israel's military intelligence, and joined an élite unit that specialized in PsyOps, or psychological operations . . . . [in 2014], Burstien founded Psy-Group."[89]

Though Burstien is Psy-Group's founder, Joel Zamel is its owner, via a Cyprus-based company called IOCO Limited.[90] Zamel bases his company in Cyprus to make it easier for Arab states—which often eschew being seen doing business with an Israeli company—to become his clients.[91] Psy-Group's early work in 2016, which involves "mak[ing] money by investigating jihadi networks," according to the *New Yorker*, is modeled on the business plan of Terrogence.[92]

Also present at the June 2017 Terrogence-Papadopoulos meeting are several unnamed "founders of an Arabic language digital marketing company" and, according to Papadopoulos, multiple "ex-Israeli intelligence people," raising the possibility that Papadopoulos is, as he will later say he suspects, meeting with representatives of foreign governments who are incognito. Another possibility is that he is meeting with representatives from Israeli business intelligence firms—and perhaps their clients—other than Terrogence.[93] Papadopoulos will later say that the purpose of his meeting with Tawil, Terrogence co-founder Arbel, several Arab businessmen, and former Israeli intelligence officers with unclear affiliations was for the mysterious Israeli veterans to "pitch[ ] a social media manipulation operation . . . [that was] basically what they [the FBI] were accusing the Russians of doing regarding social media" during the 2016 presidential election."[94]

Papadopoulos is, at the time, so startled by the similarities between the Israeli and Russian interference operations presented to him (a similarity that in retrospect underscores the similarity between the work Zamel did for the Trump campaign and the crimes the Kremlin committed to aid the Trump campaign) that he begins to fear he will be "framed" for a crime if he agrees to go into business with the Israelis.[95] Tawil, in a subsequent interview with the *Times of Israel*, will say that the meeting involved a "social media marketing company aiming to do business in the Arab world."[96] He does not explain how or why the Israeli veterans' proposed social media manipulation campaign came to be nearly identical, in Papadopoulos's accounting of events, to the Russian election interference operation organized by the Internet Research Agency. Nor does Tawil explain why he ultimately—according to Papadopoulos—asks for the $10,000 he gave Papadopoulos in Tel Aviv back, sending the former Trump staffer "an email [on September 9, 2018] threatening to sue him and saying Papadopoulos should act like they never met."[97] Papadopoulos will later say that Mueller and federal investigators put "tremendous scrutiny on my ties to Israel, to the point where I had apparently a formal charge of acting as an agent of Israel . . . by the time I had my first interview with the FBI, they led me to believe that they knew about certain meetings I was having, who I knew in the Israeli government domestically and abroad."[98]

Papadopoulos does not return the $10,000 as Tawil requests; instead, he will relinquish it to federal law enforcement as part of his plea in his federal criminal case, even as he maintains that he does not understand why it was given to him—or explain why he agreed to take it—in the first instance.[99] One of the founders of the "Arabic language digital marketing company" Papadopoulos had met with in June 2017, when later contacted by the *Times of Israel*, will claim to not recall having ever attended a meeting of the sort Papadopoulos describes.[100] Tawil will later provide the *Times of Israel* with a cell phone text as evidence that—despite Papadopoulos's claims that Tawil "terrified" him at the meeting and gave him $10,000 only to "frame" him—the two men were still in cordial digital contact at least as late as July 7, 2017, a month after their meeting in Tel Aviv.[101] In the text Tawil discloses to the media, Papadopoulos confirms that he wants to be involved in unspecified "deals" with Tawil that would see the onetime Trump national security adviser working "with" Tawil for a monthly retainer.[102]

Whatever "deals" Tawil and Papadopoulos are working on in the summer of 2017, they clearly attract attention at the very highest levels of the Israeli government. After Papadopoulos's meeting with Terrogence's co-founder, "ex-Israeli intelligence people," Tawil, and an "Arab language digital marketing company" on June 8—as well as the exchange of $10,000 for no purpose either Papadopoulos or Tawil is willing to admit—"someone in the Israeli Prime Minister's Office invite[s] Papadopoulos to come to Thessaloniki, Greece, where Benjamin Netanyahu [is] arriving for an energy and security summit with the Greek and Cypriot presidents."[103] An entry from Tawil's calendar for the week of the Terrogence-Papadopoulos meeting and the Netanyahu visit to Thessaloniki reads "Crisis with George." "Something happened in Athens," Tawil tells the *Times*.[104]

In retrospect, it is unclear why an Israeli business intelligence firm like Terrogence would be interested in an obscure energy consultant like George Papadopoulos, let alone for the Israeli government to invite Papadopoulos to an event that its prime minister was attending—unless the Israelis believed or had been given reason to believe that Papadopoulos was still representing Trump's interests long after he had officially left Trump's employ. In fairness, Trump aides continuing to work with Trump "post-employment" is an identifiable pattern with the New York City businessman; Roger Stone, Paul Manafort, Carter Page, Rick Gates, and others in Trump's inner circle all continue to advise and assist Trump long after they have been (variously) fired, forced to resign, or in some other way separated from Trump's public-facing activities. Just so, $10,000 does not change hands in a Tel Aviv hotel room without purpose or explanation, nor does an Israeli businessman dealing in defense-related technologies tell someone to act like they have never met before unless some sort of "crisis"—as Tawil terms it—has indeed occurred. While it cannot be said that Papadopoulos, Tawil, or any of those involved in the June 2017 Tel Aviv meeting have fully relayed to U.S. or Israeli media what occurred there, two conclusions seem reasonable: as of mid-2017, the Israelis believed Papadopoulos still had ties to Trump's political team, and Papadopoulos at one point agreed to establish a new connection in Israel but thereafter pulled back.

As to what sort of interactions with the Israelis Papadopoulos embraces in Tel Aviv but thereafter seeks to divest from, an event that occurs eighteen days after the Papadopoulos-Terrogence meeting offers a possible clue. On that day, Papadopoulos emails Tawil to set up a meeting between Tawil, himself, and the directors of the London Centre of International Law Practice (LCILP)—the employers of Papadopoulos's Kremlin-agent contact, Joseph Mifsud. LCILP is, per its website, an entity that provides "specialized training, technical assistance, and advice to government ministries [and] embassies."[105] That Papadopoulos seeks to connect his former employers at the anodyne-seeming LCILP with someone he will later say he suspects is an Israeli intelligence agent suggests that he believes— perhaps even believed when he took a job with the LCILP in February 2016—that both his unexpected hire by the Trump campaign in March 2016 and the sudden appearance of Joseph Mifsud in his professional milieu that same month were causally related to LCILP being a front for international spycraft. Indeed, the rapid succession of events that begins with Papadopoulos's hire by the LCILP and ends with him meeting Mifsud—two events that bookend Papadopoulos suddenly getting hired by a political campaign he has wanted to work for since mid-2015—imply that the LCILP is not what it would at first appear: merely a subsidiary of "EN Education," a "global education consultancy."[106]

Papadopoulos's email to Tawil in late June 2017 does nothing to quell such concerns. The unemployed former Trump national security adviser tells Tawil that meeting with Mifsud's bosses will open up "avenues of tremendous opportunity" that will be partly based on his and Tawil's "various contacts in Saudi [Arabia] and Washington" and the fact that "the Trump administration has signed a $350 billion arms agreement with Saudi [Arabia]."[107] That Papadopoulos insists to Tawil that "we can be involved" in the aftermath of the Trump-Saudi arms deal—the largest arms deal in U.S. history—underscores the sort of connection Papadopoulos believes he still has to the Trump administration in the summer of 2017, as well as the connection he perceives the LCILP to maintain with the government of either Saudi Arabia, Russia, Israel, the United States, or some combination of these four.[108]

Papadopoulos's linkage of Trump and Kushner's arms deal with Israeli intelligence is rather more straightforward. Just a few days after Trump and Kushner leave Riyadh and MBS deposes his cousin bin Nayef, MBS invests $20 billion in Blackstone, one of Kushner Companies' largest creditors; the investment firm has loaned Kushner and his family $400 million over a four-year period from 2013 to 2017.[109] Almost immediately after MBS invests billions in Blackstone, it is revealed that Blackstone is in "advanced talks" to buy 40 percent of NSO Group—the maker of the Pegasus 3 cyberhacking technology—for $400 million, the exact amount the Kushners owe Blackstone.[110]

All of Papadopoulos's interactions in Tel Aviv—cryptic in their totality, but evidently involving the Saudis and Israeli intelligence technology—occur in the days leading up to MBS's investment in Blackstone and Blackstone's investment in NSO. A fact that may or may not be related to this is that Trump attorney Rudy Giuliani is in Israel for reasons he says have to do with his interest in "cybersecurity" at the same time Papadopoulos and Tawil are interacting in Tel Aviv on that very subject and Papadopoulos is receiving a request to join Netanyahu at a conference in Greece.[111] Giuliani had previously been named an "unofficial adviser on cybersecurity" to President-elect Trump during the transition period, in which role he met face-to-face with Netanyahu in Israel in January 2017 and "delivered a personal message from Trump to the prime minister"; according to the *Times of Israel*, Giuliani and Netanyahu "have been friends for 25 years."[112]

That Israeli businessman Joel Zamel's digital marketing and intelligence-gathering business is based in Cyprus, and that Zamel has done extensive work with the Emiratis on anti-Iran social media campaigns; that Israeli businessman Charles Tawil's business is also based in Cyprus, and that Tawil has also had extensive contact with the Emiratis and is, like Zamel, focused on new social media campaigns in the Middle East; and that Israeli prime minister Benjamin Netanyahu has sometime in the months prior to Trump's January 2017 inauguration been in secret talks in Cyprus with the Emiratis over plans to counter Iran all suggest another possibility behind Netanyahu's strange invitation of Papadopoulos to a meeting involving the presidents of Greece and Cyprus: that the

Israelis, Emiratis, Trump administration, or all three are trying to use Trump's onetime Israel expert as a go-between in a post-election plot to target Iran with a digital psy-ops campaign. Certainly, the shifting stories (or silence) from all those involved in Papadopoulos's mid-2017 meetings in Israel and Greece—Papadopoulos, Tawil, Arbel, the Arab businessmen and former Israeli intelligence officers who meet with Papadopoulos in a Tel Aviv hotel room, and even Netanyahu himself—suggest geopolitical intrigue well beyond what Papadopoulos has thus far revealed to federal law enforcement.

Just days after his email to Tawil about the "tremendous opportunity" offered to him and Tawil by the Trump-Saudi arms deal, Papadopoulos is arrested by the FBI at Dulles International Airport, in part due to suspicions that he has been acting, in both Israel and Greece, as an unregistered agent of the Israeli government.[113] According to a summary of June 2018 remarks to the press by Papadopoulos's wife, Simona Mangiante, "Special Counsel Robert Mueller last summer [summer 2017] threatened to charge George . . . with acting as an unregistered agent of Israel."[114] Per Mangiante, whatever the special counsel's office thought of Papadopoulos's meetings in Israel and Greece in June and July of 2017—and of what he said in each meeting and to whom—it believed, strikingly, that following its review of the evidence and relevant counterintelligence data, it had sufficient basis to charge Papadopoulos as an Israeli agent based exclusively on his actions "while he was serving as an energy consultant before he joined the Trump campaign [in March 2016]."[115]

Subsequent media reports on Papadopoulos's connections to Israel will reveal a new piece of information that explains much of the special counsel's and Papadopoulos's own actions: as of the day in mid-2017 that Papadopoulos was asked by the Israeli prime minister's office to come immediately to Thessaloniki, Greece, Papadopoulos had, for at least two years, been in semi-regular contact with Eli Groner, "a top aide to Israeli Prime Minister Benjamin Netanyahu"; this suggests that Papadopoulos's appearance "alongside" Groner at the Hadera Energy Conference in Tel Aviv in April 2016—while he was a Trump adviser and, moreover, on a Trump campaign-approved trip—may not have been mere coincidence.[116]

That Papadopoulos, one of the most active members of the Trump campaign's twelve-man national security advisory committee, had direct access to the Israeli prime minister's office for the entirety of his employment by Trump—March 2016 to January 2017, though he had first approached the campaign about a job in mid-2015, when he first met Netanyahu's aide Groner, itself a troubling concurrence—casts a new light on the efforts of at least one Israeli business intelligence firm, Psy-Group, to try to assist Trump's team through a social media manipulation campaign in the final three months of the 2016 presidential election. That Psy-Group was introduced to the Trump campaign by George Birnbaum, a man who, like Groner, was a Netanyahu aide; that Papadopoulos's June 2017 meeting in Tel Aviv was with former Israeli soldiers "pitching a social media manipulation operation"; and that unofficial Trump cybersecurity adviser Giuliani was in Israel that month working on cybersecurity issues suggests that Papadopoulos may not have been entirely aloof from efforts to link the Israeli government and Trump in 2015, 2016, and 2017—especially as two of Joel Zamel's Trump campaign contacts during the period he was pitching Rick Gates in spring 2016 remain "unnamed" and Papadopoulos's 2017 Israeli contact Charles Tawil has said, for his part, "I support Trump . . . I like the fact that Trump is president. I wanted him to be president."[117]

Papadopoulos will tell the *Times of Israel* in 2018 that the work Tawil wanted him to do was "not . . . legitimate," but that he cannot say more because the details are "incredibly sensitive."[118] He will be more forthcoming with *Rolling Stone*, however, calling Tawil an agent for Mossad and saying that the money Tawil offered him was not for consulting work but to "keep [his] engagements"—the implication being that either the Israeli man believed Papadopoulos had been working for the Israelis and needed to continue doing so, or, alternatively or in addition, that Tawil (and possibly Terrogence) wanted Papadopoulos to maintain what they perceived to be his ongoing relationship with Donald Trump's national security team.[119]

If indeed Tawil works for Mossad, as Papadopoulos speculates, it would also be the case that the Israeli government's understanding of Papadopoulos's ongoing links to the Trump administration is based not on guesswork but intelligence. Tellingly, Papadopoulos's wife Simona has insisted to ABC News that Papadopoulos was merely the "first domino" to fall in the special counsel's and related federal investigations, implying that the information Papadopoulos gave to Mueller will eventually lead to further federal indictments or probes.[120] "This is much more complicated than Watergate," Papadopoulos himself will tell *Rolling Stone*. "We are talking about foreign governments, intelligence, various countries, decoys, hacking, honey pots . . . and, of course, one of the most-watched presidential campaigns of history. I am . . . in the middle of it."[121] Of the LCILP, whose directors Papadopoulos wanted to introduce to a man he says is a Mossad agent, Papadopoulos now says it is a "hotbed with potential spies and all this craziness."[122] This "hotbed with potential spies" is also where Papadopoulos met his wife, Simona, who began working for the LCILP in September 2016, as Papadopoulos was working for the Trump campaign; according to Mangiante, Mueller's team "suspected she may have been a Russian spy" tasked with seducing Papadopoulos.[123]

Tawil now says that the relationship he sought with Papadopoulos was merely a "consulting business . . . for the petroleum industry," and that Israeli "independent [political] strategist" David Ha'ivri—onetime head of the Samaria Regional Council, the pseudo-government of contested Israeli settlements in the northern West Bank—was the man who first introduced him to Papadopoulos. Ha'ivri, like Tawil, says that Tawil and Papadopoulos were engaged in "a business deal involving an oil and gas project," though it is not clear, then, why Tawil urged Papadopoulos to travel from Greece to Tel Aviv to meet with the co-founder of an Israeli cyberintelligence company and the owners of an Arabic-language digital marketing company, or why Prime Minister Netanyahu's office asked Papadopoulos to come to Greece.[124] Ha'ivri will tell the *Daily Caller* that Tawil is also "a part-time consultant for companies that operate in . . . [the] Middle East," but he will offer no more about the Israeli man's activities or interests in the region.[125]

When the *Times of Israel* tracks Tawil down in November 2018 to ask him about his contacts with Papadopoulos, they will find him "in the glittering Gulf city-state of Dubai, where he had come for a conference hosted by the United Arab Emirates' Minister of Tolerance Sheikh Nahayan Mabarak Al Nahayan, with whom Tawil said he is friendly."[126] As of September 2018,

Sheikh Nahayan was involved not in the oil and gas industry but in global telecommunications—as he is "chairman of Warid Telecom International, a regional telecom group based out of Dubai . . . [and] also chairman of Abu Dhabi Group, Union National Bank and United Bank Limited."[127] During the 2016 presidential election, Sheikh Nahayan was the UAE's minister of culture and knowledge development.[128] In the Emiratis' governmental structure, the minister of tolerance and the minister of culture and knowledge are two of just thirty-three cabinet-level positions immediately beneath the president of the UAE—a position held by MBZ's brother, Khalifa bin Zayed Al Nahayan.[129] Sheikh Nahayan's professional background is unrelated to either of his most recent positions in the Emirati government, however; while serving as chancellor of Higher Colleges of Technology in Abu Dhabi from 1988 to 2013, he concurrently acted as the UAE's minister of higher education and scientific research.[130] Tawil admits to being a sometime adviser to world leaders, though he is willing to specify to the *Times of Israel* only the presidents of certain African nations.[131] He does not indicate whether he has ever advised leaders in the country he evidently spends a good deal of time in: the United Arab Emirates.

In the fall of 2017, Elliott Broidy, now the deputy finance chair of the Republican National Committee thanks to Trump, emails George Nader, still an adviser to MBZ, a "detailed report" on a private meeting he has just had with the president.[132] Broidy's report is sent to an encrypted email address used by Nader and is, according to the *New York Times*, sent in response to a request by MBZ that Broidy lobby Trump for the creation of a new "counterterrorism task force" focused on the Middle East.[133] The *Times* reports that by fall 2017 Nader has been trying for months to turn Broidy into an "instrument of influence at the White House for the rulers of Saudi Arabia and the United Arab Emirates."[134] In sum, writes the *Times*, "hundreds of pages of correspondence between the two men reveal an active effort to cultivate President Trump on behalf of the two oil-rich Arab monarchies."[135] In charting Nader and Broidy's three primary ambitions—convincing Trump to fire secretary of state Rex Tillerson, ensuring Trump backs Saudi Arabia and the United Arab Emirates against Iran and Qatar, and orchestrating a private meeting between Trump and MBZ—the *Times* notes that the first two of these ambitions were achieved by the Broidy-Nader partnership. As for the third, it is unknown whether Trump has met secretly with MBZ, though the possibility remains MBZ did so when he attended a Trump Tower meeting in secrecy in December 2016.[136]

Across a number of emails, Nader offers Broidy more than $1 billion in contracts for his private security company, Circinus, in exchange for Broidy's help wooing Trump on behalf of MBZ.[137] Because Nader is offering this money to the Republican National Committee's deputy finance chair, there is a risk from the start that some of the money offered by the Emiratis will end up in Republican Party coffers, either directly or through money laundering—for instance, by Broidy, who is a GOP mega-donor, legally donating to the Republican Party money that he himself has received from MBZ to influence the party's leader. Broidy is already accused by federal prosecutors in court filings of receiving laundered money in a separate case involving 1 Malaysia Development Berhad (1MDB), a Malaysian state-owned fund.[138] In April 2019, shortly after Robert Mueller reports the findings of his Russia investigation to William Barr, Trump's new attorney general—by then facing persistent accusations of "acting like Trump's lawyer" and "trying to protect" Trump—will seek and receive an ethics waiver from the DOJ to oversee the 1MDB case; Barr's former law firm, Kirkland & Ellis, currently represents Goldman Sachs in the 1MDB investigation.[139]

During the 2016 election cycle, Broidy was responsible for raising $108 million for a joint RNC-Trump campaign fund. The August 2016 offer to Trump Jr. by Broidy's partner, Nader—that Nader would do anything he could do, on behalf of MBZ and MBS, to assist the Trump campaign—could therefore have been a promise delivered upon, pre- or post-election, through Broidy's fundraising efforts for the RNC, making the 1MDB investigation a potentially dangerous one not just for Broidy but for Trump and members of his 2016 presidential campaign.[140]

In his emails to Broidy, Nader assures the GOP rainmaker and donor that he is playing a "Pivotal Indispensable Magic Role" in helping both

Saudi Arabia and the UAE.[141] That the special counsel's office will subsequently grant Nader immunity from criminal prosecution—and have him testify multiple times before a federal grand jury—underscores that elements of the secretive efforts Nader made in conjunction with Broidy and MBZ may have amounted to criminal acts, possibly of a sort Broidy has repeatedly been accused of throughout his political career: bribery, a charge not investigated by the special counsel but possibly being considered by other federal jurisdictions that have received evidence from his office.[142] According to the *New York Times*, one of the focuses of Mueller's probe—though this subject does not appear in his report, suggesting any case related to it was referred elsewhere or considered a counterintelligence matter—is whether Nader "funnel[ed] Emirati money to Mr. Trump's political efforts," though it is unclear when Mueller believes any such illegal donations may have been made.[143] What is clear is that Trump's foreign policy aligns with the requests made by MBZ through his agents and intermediaries, and that Nader and Broidy for some reason feel compelled to use code names in their emails, referring to Donald Trump as "Chairman" and to MBZ as "Friend."[144]

In one of the Nader-Broidy emails, first reported on by the *New York Times* in March 2018, Broidy, who by fall 2017 has "hundreds of millions of dollars in contracts with the United Arab Emirates," tells Nader that he "repeatedly pressed Mr. Trump to meet privately with Prince Mohammed [bin Zayed], preferably in an informal setting outside the White House." Broidy also explains to Nader and MBZ that he strongly urged Trump to get behind MBZ's policy agenda in the Middle East.[145] At his fall 2017 private meeting with Trump, moreover, Broidy tells the president to fire Rex Tillerson, which Trump will do (via tweet) in March 2018.[146] Months after the firing, Trump tweets, on December 7, 2018, that Tillerson, the man who had so critiqued the MBS-Kushner relationship—also the former president of Exxon, one of the largest energy companies in the world—"didn't have the mental capacity needed" to be secretary of state.[147] "He was dumb as a rock . . . [and] lazy as hell," Trump will add, suggesting further that he had wanted to get rid of Tillerson from the moment he hired him and "couldn't get rid of him fast enough."[148] The tweet has the effect of erasing

Saudi or Emirati involvement in Tillerson's ouster, as well as the involvement of the by then disgraced former RNC deputy finance chair, Broidy.

Trump takes Broidy's advice with respect not only to Tillerson but also to his administration's continued support for Emirati schemes and adventures abroad. As the New York Times will note in March 2018, "Trump has closely allied himself with the Emiratis, endorsing their strong support for the new heir to the throne in Saudi Arabia [Mohammed bin Salman], as well as their confrontational approaches toward Iran and their neighbor Qatar. In the case of Qatar, which is the host to a major United States military base, Mr. Trump's endorsement of an Emirati- and Saudi-led blockade against that country has put him openly at odds with . . . years of American policy."[149]

When Broidy is confronted with his emails to Nader by the Times, his only response, through a spokesman, is to accuse, without evidence, the nation of Qatar—an enemy of his allies in the UAE—of a "hack . . . sponsored and carried out by registered and unregistered agents of Qatar seeking to punish Mr. Broidy for his strong opposition to state-sponsored terrorism."[150] Neither Broidy nor his spokesman explains which email between him and Nader, in whole or in part, contains content sensitive enough that its revelation could be construed as state-sponsored punishment.[151] In addition to Qatar, Broidy also blames "numerous Washington consultants and former intelligence operatives" for the hack.[152]

By August 2017, just sixty days into his tenure as heir presumptive to the throne of Saudi Arabia, MBS is already thinking with great particularity about which of his enemies he needs to harness and which he needs to torture or kill. According to American intelligence intercepts, he issues instructions to his top associates to lure a noted critic of his regime, Jamal Khashoggi—a Virginia resident with three American-citizen children—to a third country so that he can be kidnapped there and taken back to Saudi Arabia.[153] Under U.S. law (specifically, a 2015 directive to the National Security Act), the receipt of this intercept immediately obligates the Trump administration to warn Khashoggi that he is in danger, as the directive "requires the United States to give 'non-U.S. persons' notice of 'impending threats of intentional killing, serious bodily injury, or kidnapping.'"[154] Khashoggi is given no warning about traveling abroad, however, let alone about the danger of entering Saudi consulates abroad. *Quartz* will note, upon disclosure of these intelligence intercepts, that "the U.S. knew that Khashoggi was a target," while the *Washington Post* will add that "intelligence about Saudi Arabia's earlier plans to detain Khashoggi have raised questions about whether the Trump administration should have warned the journalist that he might be in danger."[155] (The *Post* references "earlier plans" because, as will be revealed in 2018, the Trump administration also acquired advance knowledge of MBS's murderous alternative to his extraordinary rendition plot: according to *Quartz*, "An unnamed National Security Agency official told the . . . [Observer] that US intelligence had learned that Riyadh 'had something unpleasant in store for Khashoggi,' at least a day before Khashoggi went to the embassy in Istanbul," where he was murdered, in early October 2018. "The 'threat warning was communicated to the White House through official intelligence channels' . . . [but] the Office of the Director of National Intelligence has refused to comment on why Khashoggi was not warned.")[156]

In another August 2017 intercept, American intelligence agents hear MBS tell associates—though it is not clear, per the *Wall Street Journal*, if this is a direct quote or a summary of intelligence collected—that if top MBS aide Saud al-Qahtani and others cannot successfully lure Khashoggi to Saudi Arabia, "we could possibly lure him outside Saudi Arabia and make arrangements."[157]

That some of MBS's ire toward Khashoggi stems from his belief that Saudi journalists should be organs of the royal family is almost certain. The *New York Times* reports that "prominent Saudi editors and journalists who have accompanied [MBS] on foreign trips have been given up to $100,000 in cash."[158] According to the *Times*, Saudi journalists living in-country who criticize MBS can see their websites permanently blocked within twenty-four hours, and other "journalists deemed too critical have been quietly silenced through phone calls informing them that they are barred from publishing, and sometimes from traveling abroad."[159] Interestingly, while Khashoggi has already received such a communication from the royal palace, it is because of his criticism of Trump's foreign policy, not MBS's, that he is banned from journalism in Saudi Arabia (see chapter 6).

August 2017 also sees Jared Kushner travel to the Middle East to "build on talks with a budding Sunni Arab coalition of Saudi Arabia, the United Arab Emirates, Egypt and Jordan"—all of the original Red Sea conspirators, except for Bahrain.[160] Kushner and his small entourage of Trump loyalists, including former Trump Organization executive vice president and chief legal officer Jason Greenblatt, will come away from their meetings in the Middle East "hopeful that the new generation of Arab leaders is a potential 'game-changer.'"[161] In reporting on Kushner's multinational tour, the *Washington Post* notes "Trump's unusually close relations with both Israel and the Gulf Arabs."[162] The *Post* notes, too, that Israel and the Sunni Arab Gulf nations are looking for a partner in the Palestinian Authority. It is in this context that the newspaper mentions "Mohammed Dahlan, a Gazan Palestinian now living in the UAE," as a "key intermediary" between the new Israeli-Arab alliance and the Palestinians, adding that "the plan is to provide economic and social support [to Gazans], through Egypt and with Israel's blessing, that can weaken the hard-liners' control" in Gaza.[163] The *Post* concludes its coverage of Kushner's trip by reporting that "beyond the machinations in Gaza is a larger vision for restarting a Palestinian peace process drawing on the alliance of moderate Sunni leaders. Jordan's King Abdullah II and Egypt's President Abdel Fattah el-Sisi already have extensive, friendly relations with Israel. Mohammed bin Zayed, the crown prince and military leader of the UAE, and Saudi Crown Prince Mohammed don't have formal ambassadorial contacts with Israel. But they share a common enemy in Iran."[164]

In September 2017, U.S. intelligence receives more intercepts confirming MBS's intentions with respect to Khashoggi, by now a *Washington Post* journalist. According to the *New York Times*, an intercepted MBS conversation from September includes MBS telling a top aide, Turki Aldakhil, that he will use "a bullet" on Khashoggi if the journalist does not, according to the *Times* report, "return to the kingdom and end his criticism of the Saudi government."[165] The *Times* cites *The Intercept* as "detailed evidence . . . [that]

the crown prince considered killing Mr. Khashoggi long before a team of Saudi operatives strangled him inside the Saudi Consulate in Istanbul and dismembered his body using a bone saw" in October 2018 (see chapter 9). The *Times* reminds its readers that MBS is "a close ally of the Trump White House—especially Jared Kushner, the president's son-in-law and senior adviser."[166]

The September 2017 recording is just one audio file from "years of the crown prince's voice and text communications that the NSA [National Security Agency] routinely intercepted and stored," according to the *Times*, which notes that a late 2018 review by the NSA "and other American spy agencies," which are by then "circulat[ing] intelligence reports [on MBS] to other spy agencies, the White House, and close foreign allies," will result in the CIA "concluding that Prince Mohammed had ordered" Khashoggi's murder.[167]

Indeed, MBS's communications from September 2017, taken in full, reveal that by ninety days into his reign as de facto ruler of Saudi Arabia, the crown prince and other top Saudi officials were growing "increasingly alarmed about Mr. Khashoggi's criticisms of the Saudi government."[168] American intelligence analysts have concluded that, by that September, MBS "had every intention of killing the journalist if he did not return to Saudi Arabia."[169] One tape analyst's review finds MBS opining to Saud al-Qahtani that "Khashoggi had grown too influential . . . and [his] articles and Twitter posts were tarnishing the crown prince's image as a forward-thinking reformer"; when al-Qahtani warns the crown prince to avoid "any move" against Khashoggi because it would be "risky" and could cause "an international uproar," MBS replies, as summarized by the *Times*, that "Saudi Arabia should not care about international reaction to how it handles its own citizens" and that he "did not like half-measures—he never liked them and did not believe in them."[170] Al-Qahtani, who will in late fall 2018 be implicated in Khashoggi's murder, calls Khashoggi in September 2017 to praise his writings about MBS as part of an attempt to lure Khashoggi into a false sense of security—even as he knows MBS's designs on the journalist involve, at a minimum, his arrest and detention.[171]

By fall 2017, Khashoggi is living in the United States, with no plans to return to Saudi Arabia.[172] He has left Saudi Arabia still a nominal supporter of MBS's vision of the kingdom, but the events of October and November 2017 will cause him to realize it is "time to speak" against the new regime in Riyadh.[173] As Khashoggi will later tell *Vanity Fair*, "The people MBS arrested [in October and November 2017] were not radicals. The majority were reformers for women's rights and open society. He arrested them to spread fear."[174] *Vanity Fair* will also speak to an adviser to a Saudi businessman who agrees with Khashoggi's fall 2017 assessment, telling the magazine that by late 2017 Saudi Arabia had become "a bit of a police state."[175]

In early October 2017, as MBS is tightening his grip on Saudi Arabia and just weeks before a surprise visit to Riyadh by Jared Kushner, King Salman, MBS's father, becomes the first ruling monarch in the history of the kingdom to visit Moscow. At the airport in Moscow, bin Salman deplanes via a golden escalator similar to the one Donald Trump descended before announcing his presidential run in June 2015—with the difference that the former's escalator breaks as he is using it, forcing the Saudi king to descend the stairway to an eagerly awaiting Kremlin delegation the old-fashioned way.[176]

King Salman's visit to Russia is hailed as a "turning point in Middle East politics" (the *Guardian*), a "signal[ ] [of] a new era of cooperation with Russia" by the Saudi government (the *Guardian*), a "new qualitative level" for Russian-Saudi relations (Russian foreign minister Sergey Lavrov), "an historical moment" (Lavrov), and a "landmark event" (Putin).[177] While he is in Moscow, MBS's father signs billions of dollars' worth of energy, military, and technological agreements with Putin and announces that in the view of the royal family Russia is now a "friendly country," making clear that one of the things he wants in return is an end to the Syrian conflict that unifies rather than divides that war-torn Arab nation. As part of his own commitment on this score he declines, for the first time, to call for the removal of Syrian president Bashar al-Assad from power, previously a sticking point in Russian-Saudi diplomatic engagements.[178] According to

the *Guardian*, the visit and its accompanying international business transactions signal that while Saudi Arabia has "traditionally seen the United
States as its chief—if not exclusive—foreign policy partner . . . changes inside the Saudi regime . . . have left the kingdom looking to diversify into
a wider set of alliances."[179]

Given that, per the *Guardian*, King Salman's Moscow visit "has been
in the works for months, if not years," and that, as the *Independent* notes,
the trip "comes at the end of several years of [Saudi-Russian] courtship,"
by far the most interesting member of the Saudi delegation to Moscow is
a Maltese professor by the name of Joseph Mifsud.[180] Mifsud is just days
away from being outed by special counsel Robert Mueller as the Kremlin
agent who acted as Trump adviser and self-described Kremlin "intermediary" George Papadopoulos's contact with Putin's government during the
2016 presidential campaign.[181] Mifsud's role as a Kremlin-Trump campaign
conduit had extended from March 2016 until at least September 2016,
meaning that he arrives in Riyadh only a year after his contacts with
Trump national security adviser Papadopoulos—at least the publicly known
ones—have ended.[182] As all of Mifsud's 2016 contacts with Papadopoulos
occurred after both the Saudi-led conspiracy to aid Trump's campaign and
the Saudi-Russian détente had begun, the possibility remains that Mifsud
was working for the Saudis as well as the Kremlin when he made contact with the Trump campaign through Papadopoulos.[183] *BuzzFeed News*
will observe, however, that Mifsud joins King Salman in Moscow as a
guest of the Russian International Affairs Council (RIAC), a "partner"
organization of the Russian Institute for Strategic Studies (RISS)—the
Kremlin think tank that drew up the Russian plan to interfere with the
2016 election in the United States.[184] Mifsud's contact at the RIAC, Ivan
Timofeev, with whom he put Papadopoulos in contact in spring 2016, is a
"sanctions expert," according to Reuters, and, like the RIAC as a whole,
is "close to the Russian Foreign Ministry."[185] Even at the time Mifsud was
representing himself as a Kremlin agent to Papadopoulos in spring 2016,
he may well have also been in contact with powerful royals in Riyadh, as
BuzzFeed News notes that "Mifsud had spoken at . . . events, in both Saudi
Arabia and Russia, organized by RIAC and the King Faisal Center."

BuzzFeed News also notes that during his October 2017 trip to Moscow with the Saudi delegation, Mifsud again met with Timofeev.[186] Asked by the digital media outlet whether he and Mifsud discussed Papadopoulos in Moscow during King Salman's visit, Timofeev will decline to say.[187]

While MBS does not go to Moscow with his father in October 2017, the *Independent* will reveal that, in fact, much of the business of the trip was about him. According to the British media outlet, "King Salman is believed to be in Moscow to shore up international support for his son, Crown Prince Mohammed bin Salman, next in line to the throne."[188] In seeking "Russia's backing for his son," in the words of one RIAC foreign relations expert, the king apparently meets with success—as within a matter of days MBS will purge scores of his domestic enemies using illicit kidnappings and detentions, behavior that could have, had King Salman not paved the way for it in both the United States and Russia, threatened MBS's future rule. The cost Putin demands for supporting MBS appears to be pecuniary: while Saudi Arabia had already pledged $10 billion to Russia from its sovereign wealth fund in 2015—the year the Red Sea Conspiracy was established—by late 2017 only 10 percent of that amount had reached a Russian government "hamstrung by Western sanctions." As the *Independent* notes, during the Saudis' Moscow visit the Russians "made it clear that they hope the Saudi delegation will deliver on investment from the kingdom's sovereign wealth funds."[189] As an Al Jazeera editorial published after King Salman's visit to Moscow opines, "The Russia-Saudi rapprochement of recent months arguably became possible precisely because Russian President Vladimir Putin and MBS speak the same language. Both prefer to use hard power to resolve issues domestically and internationally and both see the world in black and white . . . The Yemen war, the Qatar blockade and, finally, Saudi Arabia's alleged role in recent Lebanese developments [the kidnapping of Lebanon's prime minister], all seem to have been borrowed out of Putin's playbook."[190] The editorial's title asks a prescient question: "Will Mohammed bin Salman be Arabia's Vladimir Putin?"[191]

In 2018, the *Middle East Eye* will quote a Saudi source who calls Putin "a role model [for MBS]. MBS once asked in a gathering, 'How does Putin manage to kidnap his opposition figures and assassinate them in London, and it does not have consequences?'"[192]

Another reason that MBS does not travel to Moscow with his father may be that he has significant plans of his own to attend to at home. In early November, MBS purges his domestic enemies—via arrest and incarceration—with the seeming assistance of a list of Saudi dissidents provided to him by Jared Kushner, now his confidant; Kushner has access, through the President's Daily Brief, to the results of U.S. and international surveillance of prominent Saudis, and is thereby able to provide MBS with a level of insight into the machinations of his enemies that the Saudi crown prince might not otherwise have.[193] The purge ensnares, as itemized by the *New Yorker*, "eleven senior [Saudi] princes, several current or former ministers, the owners of three major television stations, the head of the most important military branch, and one of the wealthiest men in the world, who has been a major shareholder in Citibank, Twentieth Century Fox, Apple, Twitter, and Lyft."[194] The magazine writes that the purge "sends shockwaves of fear through the kingdom." A former U.S. official analogizes MBS's actions this way: "It's the equivalent of waking up to find Warren Buffett and the heads of ABC, CBS, and NBC have been arrested. It has all the appearances of a coup d'état. Saudi Arabia is rapidly becoming another country. The kingdom has never been this unstable."[195]

MBS's November purge follows smaller purges in June—which included MBS placing his cousin and the heir apparent to the Saudi throne, Mohammed bin Nayef, under house arrest—and September, when the Saudi prince "orchestrated the arrest of well-known intellectuals and clerics."[196] That MBS's actions are sanctioned by his father, King Salman, is underscored by the fact that the November action comes just hours after Salman has put his son in charge of an Anti-Corruption Commission.[197] MBS's new position allows him to seize the assets of—and issue blanket travel bans against—individual Saudi citizens.[198]

MBS's arrest of bin Nayef in June 2017, just weeks after Trump rewarded MBS and his family with a presidential visit, had been particularly galling to the U.S. intelligence community. According to the *Washington Post*, "Intelligence fears about the situation in Saudi Arabia rose when Mohammed unseated his cousin and the heir apparent, Mohammed bin Nayef, a longtime U.S. ally against terrorism."[199] Calling bin Nayef "one of the preeminent counterterrorists" in the world, a thirty-plus-year CIA veteran tells the *Post* that bin Nayef "was the closest thing Saudi Arabia had to a genuine hero in this century"—calling gravely into question MBS's insistence, publicly echoed by Trump, that his consolidation of power in the kingdom was born of a commitment to counterterrorism rather than autocratic avarice.[200] Indeed, bin Nayef was considered such an ally to America and such a threat to al-Qaeda that in 2009 he had been injured in an al-Qaeda suicide bombing made notable in part by the bomber's secretion of the explosives in his rectum.[201]

That Trump backs MBS's several purges is borne out not only by his public tweets but also his private actions. The names of those taken by MBS in November hail in substantial part from a list derived from President Trump's classified daily presidential briefing, meaning that they could only have been shared with the Saudis if they were first automatically declassified by Trump.[202] As *The Intercept* notes in a March 2018 investigative report, during a period when he had top-secret clearance (a status he would later briefly lose) Kushner "was known around the White House as one of the most voracious readers of the President's Daily Brief, a highly classified rundown of the latest intelligence intended only for the president and his closest advisers. Kushner . . . was particularly engaged by information about the Middle East. . . . [In the latter half of 2017] the President's Daily Brief contained information on Saudi Arabia's evolving political situation, including a handful of names of royal family members opposed to the crown prince's power grab."[203]

According to high-level government officials familiar with Trump's daily briefings, Kushner made use of the classified intelligence the president had received. In late October 2017, reports *The Intercept*, Kushner "made an unannounced trip to Riyadh, catching some intelligence officials off guard . . . What exactly Kushner and the Saudi royal talked about in Riyadh may be known only to them, but after the meeting, Crown Prince

Mohammed told confidants that Kushner had discussed the names of Saudis disloyal to the crown prince, according to three sources who have been in contact with members of the Saudi and Emirati royal families since the crackdown."[204] A report by David Ignatius of the *Washington Post*, published at the time of Kushner's surprise visit to Saudi Arabia, notes that "the two princes [MBS and Kushner] are said to have stayed up until nearly 4 a.m. several nights, swapping stories and planning strategy."[205]

Much of the information about the clandestine Kushner-MBS summit in October 2017 will come from MBS himself, who in subsequent conversations with confidants will "brag[ ] of receiving classified U.S. intelligence from Jared Kushner and using it as part of a purge of 'corrupt' princes and businessmen."[206] More broadly, MBS will spend time in 2017 and early 2018 "boasting about his close relationship with the president's son-in-law and senior adviser, and the intelligence which he has told his circle Kushner passed to him."[207]

According to the *New York Times*, the domestic purge MBS orders in November 2017 results in at least one death and a number of detainees being tortured—including a Harvard-educated American doctor, Walid Fitaihi, who was "blindfolded, slapped and stripped to his underwear before being bound to a chair and shocked with electricity . . . [an] episode of torture that lasted about an hour."[208] A friend of Fitaihi's will tell the *Times* that the doctor's Saudi torturers "whipped his back so severely that he could not sleep on it for days."[209] A spokesman for MBS's government will say, in response to accusations it tortured the American, that "the kingdom prohibits torture."[210] As of spring 2019, Fitaihi was still imprisoned in the Riyadh Ritz-Carlton without any charges having been announced or trial held, and with no public evidence that the Trump administration is seeking to free him.[211]

Another MBS detainee, according to the *Washington Post*, is a "longtime U.S. ally in the country, billionaire investor Prince Alwaleed bin Talel . . . [who] had publicly attacked Trump as a 'disgrace' to America during the 2016 presidential campaign. Trump followed the crackdown with a public tweet in support of Mohammed's moves."[212] Alwaleed is of course not the only Trump critic MBS targets; as he purges the kingdom in the fall of 2017, he has set in motion a sequence of events that will eventually lead to the gruesome assassination of *Washington Post* journalist Jamal Khashoggi in October 2018 (see chapter 9). The *New York Times* will report in 2019 that MBS's agents also tortured women's rights advocates during the crown prince's late 2017 domestic purge, with the torturers' favorite method of inflicting pain being electrocution.[213]

It is not only the identities of MBS's detainees and torture or murder victims that worry the American intelligence community. It is also that Kushner's "secretive" trip to Riyadh, which preceded MBS's purge by mere days, catches "some intelligence officials . . . off guard," and that the general consensus is that this was intentional on Kushner's part, with "most people in the White House . . . kept out of the loop about the trip and its purpose."[214] After Kushner returns to the United States, "intelligence officials [a]re troubled"—again—"by a lack of information [from Kushner] about the topics [he] discussed" with MBS, with Kushner saying only, euphemistically, that "he and the prince met alone to 'brainstorm' strategies" relating to a "Middle East peace plan." The White House will intimate that other foreign nationals were involved in these meetings with Kushner and MBS as well, but will not say who.[215]

That the "Middle East peace plan" Kushner, MBS, and perhaps some others allegedly discuss in Riyadh in October 2017 is not the Israeli-Palestinian peace plan Kushner has already been tasked with working on by his father-in-law is seemingly confirmed by the fact that, just weeks after Kushner leaves Riyadh, Trump formally recognizes Jerusalem as Israel's capital by announcing he will move the U.S. embassy there. It is a controversial decision that, unsurprisingly, leads to a months-long suspension of diplomatic contact between the Trump administration and the Palestinians on the subject of a Middle East peace deal.[216] Indeed, Kushner evinces no hurry in his peace planning either in October 2017 or at any other time; well over a year after Trump's December 2017 change in U.S. policy on Jerusalem, Kushner will tell an international conference that he refuses to release any Israeli-Palestinian peace plan until after Israel's April 2019 elections, a vote in which Netanyahu ultimately secures reelection (see Epilogue).[217] Kushner instead spends the period from December 2017 to early 2019 in a fashion decidedly not conducive to Israeli-Palestinian peace talks: "pushing to remove the refugee status of millions of Palestinians as part of an apparent effort to shutter the United Nations agency for Palestinian refugees," the United Nations Relief and Works Agency (UNRWA).[218] According to the *Atlantic*, Trump, with Kushner's support, spends 2018 seeking to "cut financial assistance for . . . [UNRWA] out of pique that the Palestinians have not given him the requisite 'appreciation or respect,' as if humanitarian aid, even when it serves U.S. national interests, should be awarded in return for flattery."[219] "It is no surprise, therefore," the magazine adds, "that the Palestinians stopped talking to the administration."[220]

Whether the 2018 freeze in U.S.-Palestinian relations is intentional on Trump and Kushner's part is worth discussion. Certainly, as the *Atlantic* notes, when "dozens of Palestinians in Gaza were killed in clashes with the Israeli Defense Forces [in early 2018], the Trump administration chose neither to express sympathy for the Palestinians killed nor to join international calls for Israeli restraint . . . [Instead] [h]is administration has offered unconstrained support for settlements, with an ambassador who has fought against use of the word 'occupation' and refers to 'Judea and Samaria,' as favored by Israeli settlers, instead of traditional U.S. references to the West Bank."[221] The media outlet calls it a "Kushner fantasy" that "the Arab Gulf states [Saudi Arabia and the UAE], Egypt, and Jordan will help him overcome these major challenges" to working with the Palestinians—thus offering a list of nations almost identical to the list of those with representatives present at the founding of the Red Sea Conspiracy.[222] These nations' leaders share with Israel, however, as the *Atlantic* observes, "a common strategic perspective on Iran and on Islamic extremism . . . [so] they don't prioritize the Palestinian issue as much as previous generations."[223]

Of the source of the intelligence Kushner reportedly gives to MBS in 2017 as part of their discussions of "peace," multiple Saudi sources with knowledge of MBS's boasts to his inner circle describe it as originating "from U.S. wiretaps on conversations between Arab royals in hotels in

London, in major U.S. cities and even on yachts docked close to Monte Carlo . . . information from the daily intelligence briefing provided by the intelligence community to the White House."[224] Kushner therefore either illegally shared classified intelligence with a foreign government or the information was declassified by Trump himself to facilitate its transfer to MBS. An intelligence transmission of this sort—between Trump, his son-in-law, and a foreign leader, with the content of the intelligence arising in part from foreign nationals' hotel stays—would mirror the sort of clandestine, Trump-executed intelligence-gathering operation described by former MI6 Russia desk chief Christopher Steele in the dossier of raw intelligence he compiled in 2015 and 2016. In that document, Steele's MI6-derived sources alleged that "a well-developed conspiracy of co-operation between them [the Trump campaign] and the Russian leadership" was "managed on the Trump side by the Republican candidate's campaign manager, Paul Manafort," and involved the Kremlin "receiving intel from Trump's team on Russian oligarchs and their families in [the] US," a topic "with which Putin and the Kremlin seemed preoccupied"—much like MBS would be, with respect to his own countrymen traveling abroad, in 2017.[225] Steele's dossier will further note that an "intelligence exchange . . . running between" Trump's team and the Kremlin saw Trump's side ably meeting "Putin's priority requirement . . . for intelligence on the activities, business and otherwise, in the United States of leading Russian oligarchs and their families. Trump and his associates duly had obtained and supplied the Kremlin with this information."[226]

Steele's sources' assessment of the Trump family's willingness to pass highly personal information in their possession to foreign autocrats will be echoed by the research that journalist Craig Unger collects for his book *House of Putin, House of Trump*. According to Unger, Trump coordinated with Felix Sater's Bayrock Group, the Trump Organization's scouting outfit for potential Russian clientele, to "indirectly provid[e] Putin with a regular flow of intelligence on what the oligarchs were doing with their money in the United States."[227] According to the *Washington Post*, Putin's aim was "to keep tabs on the billionaires . . . who had made their post–Cold War fortunes on the backs of industries once owned by the state. The oligarchs . . . were stashing their money in foreign real estate, including Trump properties, presumably beyond Putin's reach. Trump, knowingly or otherwise, may have struck a side deal with the Kremlin, Unger argues: He would secretly rat out his customers to Putin, who would allow them to keep buying Trump properties. Trump got rich. Putin got eyes on where the oligarchs had hidden their wealth. Everybody won."[228]

Engaged in what would appear to be a similar operation in late 2017, Trump's son-in-law gives the Saudi crown prince valuable information on the activities of the autocratic Saudi government's wealthiest citizens—an action that suggests either recompense for some past Saudi largesse or a conviction that something Trump wants done by Saudi Arabia could not or would not have been done had Mohammed bin Nayef, the longtime U.S. ally, been left as heir apparent. As reported by the *Daily Mail*, MBS "told members of his circle that the intelligence included information on who was disloyal to him. . . . 'Jared took a list out of names from U.S. eavesdrops of people who were supposedly MBS's enemies,' said one source, characterizing how MBS spoke about the information. 'He took a list out of these people who had been trashing MBS in phone calls, and said 'these are the ones who are your enemies.' MBS was actually bragging about it in Saudi Arabia when it happened, that he and Jared sat up until 4AM discussing things, and Jared brought him this list."[229] A second Saudi source told the *Mail* that Kushner and MBS "sat for several hours together. They literally laid out the future map of the entire region, that's why they stayed up to the early hours of the morning from the afternoon before."[230]

Another disturbing aspect of Kushner's October 2017 trip to Riyadh is the subsequent revelation that during the same week Kushner was in the Saudi capital working on reshaping the geopolitics of the Middle East, another member of the Kushner clan was there as well—working on a business deal. According to the *New York Times*, Jared's brother, Josh, flew out of Riyadh less than twenty-four hours before Jared flew in; Josh had been attending an investor conference at which MBS "promised to spend billions of dollars on a high-tech future for Saudi Arabia." The younger Kushner had "frequently ducked out for more exclusive conversations with

Saudi officials," however.[231] The appearance left by the synchronicity between the Kushner brothers' travel itineraries—that "top aides" to MBS were discussing sizable investments in one Kushner enterprise just hours before receiving classified intelligence from another Kushner to help the crown prince take control of Saudi Arabia—is troubling.[232] What is even more concerning, however, is that, as the *Times* reports, through the entirety of the 2016 presidential campaign Jared Kushner had a financial "interest in his brother's funds" and "ties [to] his brother's company."[233] According to the newspaper, before the election Jared Kushner was "closely involved" in Josh Kushner's firm, Thrive Capital, "having sat on the board and investment committees of Thrive" through the beginning of the Trump administration, and having "received at least $8.2 million in capital gains from various Thrive funds while working in the White House"—meaning that, despite stepping down from Thrive's board in January 2017, Jared Kushner stood to gain financially from any deals his brother did with MBS in the days immediately preceding or following his secret trip to meet with the Saudi crown prince.[234]

Within twelve months of Josh Kushner's meetings with top aides to MBS in Riyadh, Thrive will have raised $1 billion in new funds. It is unclear how much of this came from MBS and his promised "billions" of new investments in American firms.[235] A Thrive spokesman "declined to disclose whether Saudis had invested in any Thrive funds," answering queries from the *Times* instead with a cryptic remark about Thrive having "received no money since the presidential election from any Saudi who had not previously invested in its funds"—inadvertently raising an additional worry for ethics watchdogs in Washington, namely that MBS had been giving money to the younger Kushner during the presidential campaign even as his emissary George Nader was offering money to another member of the Trump family, Don Jr.[236] Asked by the *Times* whether Thrive had in fact continued receiving investments from Saudis who had already invested in Thrive pre-election, Thrive's spokesman "declined to answer."[237]

Josh Kushner's access to top MBS aides like Yasir Al-Rumayyan in Riyadh in October 2017 raises eyebrows in the tech community as well. According to the *Times*, "The Riyadh conference drew Wall Street titans, and some attendees questioned how a relatively small player [Josh Kushner] enjoyed high-level access to Saudi officials."[238] Al-Rumayyan, for instance, is managing director of the kingdom's Public Investment Fund, and his son Faisal began socializing with Josh Kushner in New York after Jared's brother returned there from Riyadh.[239]

That Trump and Kushner agreed to give classified information to MBS to help him solidify his hold on power in Riyadh is seemingly confirmed when, following the crown prince's November 2017 purge, Trump "tell[s] friends that he and Jared had engineered a Saudi coup."[240] "We've put our man on top!" Trump crows.[241] While Kushner's involvement in the intelligence transfer is unsurprising, given that he was at the time a "voracious" reader of the President's Daily Brief, the PDB is in fact "intended only for the president and his closest advisers"; although Kushner is a top adviser to President Trump, it is unclear how much of the classified intelligence included in the PDB is relevant to his official role in the White House.[242] According to a former White House official and a former U.S. intelligence professional familiar with Kushner's habits, Trump's son-in-law is "particularly engaged by information about the Middle East," though whether this interest is born of his role as an adviser to his father-in-law or a personal investment in events in Saudi Arabia is unclear.[243] One indication that Kushner's interest in PDB intelligence on Saudi Arabia is tied to his personal relationship with MBS comes from U.S. intelligence sources— including "a former White House official and two government officials with knowledge of" the PDB—who confirm for *The Intercept* that between June and October 2017, the PDB "contained information on Saudi Arabia's evolving political situation, including a handful of names of royal family members opposed to" MBS deposing bin Nayef.[244] Therefore, when MBS's late fall purge occurs and "the Saudi figures named in the President's Daily Brief [a]re among those rounded up," it suggests that both Trump and Kushner—the former through an intelligence declassification not clearly in the interests of the United States, and the latter through a transmission of intelligence of equally dubious utility to long-term American interests—have focused their respective attentions on putting a Saudi royal they call "our man" on the throne of his kingdom, MBS's qualifications or readiness for that position notwithstanding.[245]

On November 15, 2017, *Salvator Mundi*, a "long-lost Leonardo da Vinci painting of Jesus Christ commissioned by King Louis XII of France more than 500 years ago" (and considered a "male counterpart" to da Vinci's world-famous *Mona Lisa*) sells at auction for $450.3 million, "shattering the world record for any work of art sold at auction."[246] The painting, one of only twenty "great works" ever painted by da Vinci, is termed by Christie's, the auction house that sells it, "a painting of the most iconic figure in the world by the most important artist of all time."[247]

The seller of the painting is Russian oligarch Dmitry Rybolovlev, who has previously bought real estate from Donald Trump under suspicious circumstances, and in the ten days before the 2016 election parked his plane near Trump's (twice) under likewise suspicious circumstances (see chapters 1 and 3); the buyer, through an intermediary, is MBS, on whose yacht *Serene* the da Vinci will later be found.[248]

Immediately after the purchase, however, one of history's most expensive pieces of art—and an arguable pretext for the transfer of nearly half a billion dollars from a Russian associate of Trump's to a Saudi associate of Trump's—is, to all appearances, "lost" by its buyer, with an intended Louvre Abu Dhabi unveiling unceremoniously canceled.[249] Adding to the intrigue is rampant speculation that the painting is, in fact, "far from being a Leonardo," having been painted, rather, "largely . . . by his third-rate imitator, Bernardino Luini"—an allegation that could imply that the sale and purchase of the work are pretextual. If true, this would mean that MBS, through an intermediary, has effectively gifted a Russian oligarch the largest sum ever to change hands at an art auction; such an MBS-Rybolovlev transfer would be suspicious because MBS had previously offered to fund, on Trump's behalf, a pre-election digital disinformation campaign run by Rybolovlev's business associate, Joel Zamel—a commitment that would naturally cause investigators to search for any unexplained transfer of funds between MBS and either

Zamel or anyone (like Rybolovlev) in Zamel's professional milieu.[250] According to *Al-Araby*, "The painting was taken to an unknown location after it was purchased by the crown prince. Art collector and conservator Dianne Dwyer Modestini [restorer of *Salvator Mundi*], who resorted to contacting Louvre Abu Dhabi to ask for the whereabouts of the painting, received no response."[251]

In covering the disappearance of *Salvator Mundi*, *Vanity Fair* will note that not only did MBS's intermediary in the purchase, Saudi Prince Bader bin Abdullah bin Mohammed bin Farhan al-Saud, wildly overpay for the painting, but the seller, Rybolovlev, was shortly thereafter questioned by authorities in Monaco on claims of "corruption and influence peddling."[252] By November 2018, Rybolovlev will be formally charged in Monaco with "trading in passive influence and violation of the secrecy of an investigation"—an accusation involving, of all things, Rybolovlev's original purchase of *Salvator Mundi* for $127 million (an overpayment estimated at $47 million) from Swiss art dealer Yves Bouvier.[253] Rybolovlev's overpayment of Trump for Trump's Florida mansion had been nearly $54 million (see chapter 1).

Writing for *Narativ*, former CBC journalist Zev Shalev will publish an investigative report in January 2019 revealing that federal investigators in the United States are "investigating both the buyer and the seller of the Da Vinci masterpiece as part of the Trump-Russia investigation," as Rybolovlev is said by German media outlet *Der Spiegel* and "Western intelligence officials" to be managing money for Russian deputy premier Yuri Trutnev "in a fiduciary capacity," putting Rybolovlev in a position to be a front man for large-scale Kremlin financial transactions.[254] According to Shalev, given that MBS and MBZ appear to have jointly promised the Trumps money in August 2016 to support Donald Trump's campaign, MBS's transfer of almost half a billion dollars to a Kremlin agent for a painting that might be worth almost nothing is one way to deliver on that promise—and, as with so many of Trump's interactions with Russia, a good way to do so in "plain sight."[255]

Alternatively, given that Psy-Group's Joel Zamel has worked for Rybolovlev in the past, and was at the St. Petersburg International Economic Forum in June 2016 looking for someone to pay him to do secret work on behalf of Trump's campaign—and was, moreover, asking the Saudis and

Emiratis, through George Nader, to be his patrons—there is reason to wonder whether some portion of the money Rybolovlev received from MBS may have passed through the oligarch to Zamel or Psy-Group.[256] A key component of the Psy-Group/Cambridge Analytica deal Zamel signed in mid-December 2016 was a "mutual non-disclosure agreement" that, among other things, prohibited either party from revealing any past or current clients of the other—an unusual rider that seemed to anticipate either future animosity, future litigation, or future investigation by law enforcement.[257]

Within a week of Mueller sending investigators to interview Zamel and members of Psy-Group in 2018, Zamel will "shutter[ ] the entire operation," Zev Shalev notes.[258] Moreover, per Bloomberg, "Psy-Group's decision to shut down appears to have come the same week that Nader testified before the grand jury working with Mueller, according to the timing of that testimony previously reported in the *New York Times*."[259] Originally, George Nader's $2 million post-election payment to Zamel had been pegged to a new Zamel venture, WhiteKnight, and work Zamel theoretically might have done for Nader or Nader's patrons after the election, but a Bloomberg review will find that WhiteKnight did not have a website, had published "little public information" about itself or its products, and in fact was, according to a "person familiar with Psy-Group's operations," simply a "rebranding [of] the firm [Psy-Group] under a different name."[260] According to Bloomberg's source, switching Psy-Group's name to WhiteKnight post-election was already being discussed internally at the firm in 2016, though for what reason is unclear.[261] These machinations only underscore the byzantine processes used by those in Trump's orbit to transfer money to Zamel—a tendency that raises the stakes of (and the attention paid to) the MBS-Rybolovlev transaction.

The most important revelation about the disappearance of *Salvator Mundi* will come in 2018, when it is revealed that MBS did not overpay for the painting by $350 million—Christie's had estimated it might sell for $100 million—merely due to bad luck. Rather, he was bidding against an unusually insistent anonymous party whose aggressive bids raised the painting's price to historic heights. That bidder is revealed, in March

2018, to be MBS's friend, political ally, and geopolitical co-conspirator, MBZ.[262]

A prominent critic of MBS's November 2017 purge in the American media is Jamal Khashoggi.[263] Khashoggi's criticism is well founded, given that, as the *New Yorker* notes, King Salman and his son have, in a very short time, "created a whole new [Saudi] royal family . . . bypass[ing] hundreds (at least) of other princes" who were in line for the Saudi throne.[264] Moreover, with MBS telling confidants that he received significant pre-purge intelligence from Kushner—and even bragging to his Red Sea co-conspirator, MBZ, that Kushner was now "in his pocket" (an allegation he now denies)—the Saudi crown prince has begun, as *The Intercept* notes, "send[ing] a powerful message to [his] allies and enemies that his actions were backed by the U.S. government," an observation whose veracity Trump's celebration of MBS's ascension appears to confirm.[265] Just so, within forty-eight hours of MBS rounding up his enemies—and at least one American—for prolonged detention, torture, and in at least one case death, Trump tweets to his tens of millions of followers that he has "great confidence in King Salman and the Crown Prince of Saudi Arabia, they know exactly what they are doing. Some of those they are harshly treating have been 'milking' their country for years."[266] Trump's words echo the Saudi government's propaganda regarding the purge's necessity.[267] Even so, the odd phrasing of Trump's tweet, in which the word "some" does surprisingly heavy lifting, implies that the president and his primary Middle East adviser, Kushner, are aware that many of those MBS is "treating harshly" have not, in fact, been taking advantage of the Saudi government, but are being rounded up for some other reason—for instance, their opposition to MBS.

In December 2017, it is revealed that MBS has had a man named Ali al-Qahtani tortured to death in the Ritz-Carlton Riyadh. When al-Qahtani's corpse is found, his neck is "twisted unnaturally as though it had been broken," and his body exhibits not only bruises but "burn marks that appear[ ] to be from electric shocks."[268] The *Times* reports that al-Qahtani, a respected Saudi major general, "was not wealthy himself, so his value as a major anti-corruption target is questionable. But he was a top aide to . . . a son of the late King Abdullah . . . and the interrogators may have been pressing the general for information about his boss. The members of King Abdullah's family are seen as rivals of Crown Prince Mohammed and his father, King Salman."[269] When another son of the late king "complain[s] about General Qahtani's treatment to a circle of friends . . . [he] too [is] arrested and locked in the Ritz."[270] Several other MBS detainees are owners and board members of MBC, the Arab world's largest private media company, which MBS had been unsuccessfully trying to buy; during their detention, the businessmen agree to change the valuation and structure of their company to allow for their own imminent ouster.[271] They also, under "order . . . from a senior Saudi official close to Crown Prince Mohammed," cancel six popular and highly lucrative Turkish drama series—a priority for MBS, reports the *Times*, because "the Saudi government is at odds with Turkey over its ties to Qatar, which Saudi Arabia and its allies are boycotting."[272]

At least seventeen other MBS detainees are tortured with sufficient vigor that they require hospitalization, and even those of the hundreds of individuals held by MBS who are released begin "living in fear and uncertainty" thereafter, according to the *New York Times*.[273] Some are issued ankle bracelets to track their movements and to "transmit their conversations" to MBS's agents—mandatory surveillance jewelry that they are told they will be wearing indefinitely.[274] "No one can talk about what happened in the Ritz," an associate of a former detainee tells the *Times*. "In the end, they all have to live in Saudi Arabia."[275]

Within a matter of days of the purge, Trump begins the process of aiding MBS in securing the one thing the crown prince seems to desire above all else: nuclear weapons. According to a November 2017 investigative report by ProPublica, "The Trump administration is holding talks on providing nuclear technology to Saudi Arabia—a move that critics say could upend decades of U.S. policy and lead to an arms race in the Middle East. . . . [C]urrent and former American officials suspect the country's leaders . . . want to keep up with the enrichment capabilities of their rival, Iran."[276] Most troublingly, the Saudis, who in the past "wouldn't commit to certain safeguards against eventually using the technology for weapons," continue to maintain that position—but now, reports ProPublica, Trump "might not insist on the same precautions."[277] While experts agree that the Saudis have a rational basis to want nonmilitary nuclear power, with "growing domestic energy demand" and crude oil being "an expensive and inefficient way to generate electricity," they agree also that nuclear power in the hands of the Saudis is necessarily also "nuclear contingency capability"—the ability to ramp up a nuclear arms program when or if Saudi Arabia's enemy Iran seems close to building a deliverable nuclear bomb.[278]

The two chief proponents of a nuclear deal with Saudi Arabia have long been Thomas Barrack and Michael Flynn. On December 1, ninety-six hours after the ProPublica report is published, Flynn pleads guilty to a federal felony for lying to federal investigators and agrees to cooperate with special counsel Robert Mueller.[279] Days later, Mueller's investigators interview Barrack, asking primarily questions about Paul Manafort and Rick Gates—an investigative decision that would seem to presage Mueller farming out certain other matters involving Barrack and the presidential transition to prosecutors in the Southern District of New York.[280] A second source, however, will tell the Associated Press that Barrack was in fact asked questions on a somewhat broader range of topics, including "financial matters about the campaign, the transition, and Trump's inauguration in January 2017."[281]

Within twenty-four hours of Flynn pleading guilty, Trump publicly declares that he is "not concerned about what Flynn might tell the Special Counsel."[282] In fact, just ten days earlier, on November 22, Trump's personal counsel had called Flynn's counsel to tell him that he needed to know if anything Flynn told the FBI "implicates the president." If so, Trump's attorney John Dowd had said, it would be a "national security issue" that required the president to act to "protect[ ] all our interests."[283]

On December 2, 2017, Trump meets with Elliott Broidy. Broidy informs Trump that his "royal business partners," MBS and MBZ, are "most favorably impressed" by Trump's "leadership."[284] In the days after the meeting, Broidy and George Nader will receive "intelligence contracts good for up to $600 million to be paid over five years by the UAE . . . [with] several other deals, like the creation of an all-Muslim fighting force in the Middle East . . . set to bring their Gulf business initiatives to $1 billion."[285] It is unknown whether the "all-Muslim fighting force" Broidy and Nader are working on is connected to MESA (see chapter 9), though plans for the latter entity—a so-called Arab NATO—suggest a similar description of its affiliated fighting forces.

In private, Nader and Broidy joke about the stupidity of Jared Kushner, with Nader at one point writing Broidy (who he refers to as "my Brother"), "You have to hear in private my Brother what [the] Principals [MBS and MBZ] think of [the] 'Clown prince's' [Kushner's] efforts and his [Middle East peace] plan! Nobody would even waste [a] cup of coffee on him if it wasn't for who he is married to."[286] Though Broidy may call MBS and MBZ his "business partners" in speaking to the president, that he and Nader privately refer to them as "principals"—a legal term for the person an "agent" works on behalf of—suggests an acknowledgment by Broidy that he, like Nader, is a foreign agent. The exchange between Broidy and Nader is also consistent with reporting indicating that MBS had told MBZ he had Kushner "in his pocket" and that Emirati officials had discussed, according to the *Washington Post*, how to "manipulate" Kushner."[287] *Vanity Fair* will even run a headline, in March 2018, contending that MBZ and MBS are currently "feud[ing] over who has more control of Jared Kushner."[288]

In December 2017 or January 2018, MBS's brother Prince Khalid bin Salman invites *Washington Post* journalist Jamal Khashoggi to his office in the Saudi embassy in Washington, and has with Khashoggi what a friend of the journalist will later refer to (quoting Khashoggi) as a "nice chat."[289] NBC News will note in October 2018, after MBS has had Khashoggi brutally murdered, that "both Prince Khalid and Saud bin Abdullah Al Qahtani, a senior royal court adviser who was fired . . . for his role in Khashoggi's killing, had been contacting Khashoggi for at least a year to try to persuade him to return. . . . They said the Saudi officials had told Khashoggi . . . he would be welcomed back warmly to Saudi Arabia and could essentially write his own ticket upon his return. Over the summer [of 2018], Al Qahtani even offered Khashoggi a high-level job in the royal court or in a Saudi think tank."[290]

A major investigative report by *The Intercept* in December 2017 reveals that Erik Prince has secretly been lobbying the Trump administration—along with Iran-Contra scandal figure Oliver North—to create "a global, private spy network that would circumvent official U.S. intelligence agencies . . . as a means of countering 'deep state' enemies in the intelligence community seeking to undermine Donald Trump's presidency."[291] The covert intelligence unit would be "direct-action" and "off the books," reporting exclusively to Trump himself, sharing none of its intelligence with any existing U.S. intelligence agencies.[292] By December 2017, plans for Prince's new intelligence agency are advanced enough that Prince has begun raising money to fund the agency's operations in advance of an order by Trump creating the outfit.[293] Prince's "army of spies" would, according to *The Intercept,* operate around the world with "no official cover" in various countries, including Iran.[294] A complementary military mercenary unit—likewise reporting to Trump exclusively—would, under Prince's plan, act as a "new global rendition unit . . . to capture terrorist suspects around the world . . . [and mount] a propaganda campaign in the Middle East and Europe to combat Islamic extremism and Iran."[295]

Despite the fact that Prince's audacious plan would see Trump operating both a secret army and a secret spy agency in allied European countries—units accountable to no one but Trump himself—*The Intercept* finds that the Prince-North proposal has been "pitched at the White House," including to Vice President Pence.[296] Because the plan calls for secretary of state Mike Pompeo to oversee the operations of the two units on Trump's behalf, the fact that "Pompeo has embraced the plan and lobbied the White House to approve the contract" suggests that Trump has been apprised of the plan as well—as he is the only person above Pompeo in the proposed units' chain of command, and therefore the only official Pompeo would need to successfully lobby to get the plan approved.[297]

In seeking the plan's approval, Prince and North are assisted by John R. Maguire, a Trump transition official now working for intelligence contractor Amyntor Group.[298] Maguire is also a consultant for Prince's Frontier Services Group, though he is most well-known in intelligence circles for having "helped plan the 2003 invasion of Iraq."[299] More recently, Maguire has been propagating the conspiracy theory, in intelligence circles, that "National Security Advisor H. R. McMaster, in coordination with a top official at the National Security Agency, authorized surveillance of Steven [sic] Bannon and Trump family members, including Donald Trump Jr. and Eric Trump."[300] Maguire has also, according to *The Intercept*, been spreading the false and anti-Semitic rumor that McMaster is "us[ing] a burner phone to send information gathered through the surveillance [of the Trumps and Bannon] to a facility in Cyprus owned by George Soros."[301] Perhaps most troubling, Maguire is also known for taking potential donors to the Prince-North plan to the "Tinfoil Room"—a suite at the Trump Hotel in Washington set up to send and receive "secure communications." In the Tinfoil Room, *The Intercept* reports, Maguire tries to convince donors that a cabal of "deep state" plotters is planning a coup of the Trump administration, a treasonous attack that Maguire tells prospective donors throughout 2017 will be executed by the end of 2018.[302]

According to Maguire, his job—and Prince's and North's—is to "protect[ ] the president" by various means, including sending clandestine "intelligence reports" to Mike Pompeo.[303] Both Prince and Maguire, writes *The Intercept*, have also been involved in the planning of unauthorized "snatch operation[s]"—in which private citizens illegally kidnap a foreign national suspected of crimes for extraordinary rendition to the United States. Some of those Prince and Maguire recruit for such operations have previously been involved in a "post-9/11 era CIA assassination program targeting Al Qaeda operatives."[304] According to an associate of Prince's, the men Prince and Maguire are dealing with are "very dark individuals" who are already operating in "Saudi Arabia, Israel, the United Arab Emirates, Egypt, [and] all across North Africa."[305] It is unclear if this is the same outfit capable of conducting "kinetics" that Prince and Nader discuss with Saudi intelligence chief (and suspect in the murder of Jamal Khashoggi) Ahmed al-Assiri when the men meet with him in 2017.

Prince has denied all of the preceding allegations—which, according to a "longtime Prince associate" spoken to by *The Intercept,* is "his exact modus operandi," as he "consistently attempts to ensure plausible deniability of his role in U.S. and foreign government contracts."[306] The associate says that Prince has an international network of "deniable assets" (that is, covert operators) that "has never gone away." "The NOC ["no official cover" operator] network is already there," the associate tells the digital media outlet. "It already exists [and has] for the better part of 15 years now."[307]

The Intercept notes that Prince "revealed part of his strategy in a July 2016 radio interview with Steve Bannon, when he proposed recreating the CIA's Phoenix Program, an assassination ring used in the Vietnam War, to battle the Islamic State."[308] The proposed assassinations would go well beyond ISIS fighters, however: "Prince said in the interview that the program would be used to kill or capture 'the funders of Islamic terror, the wealthy radical Islamist billionaires funding it from the Middle East'"—in other words, anyone MBS or MBZ happens to identify as an enemy of their new anti-Iran alliance.[309] *Just Security,* a media outlet run by national security experts, calls Prince's proposals "alarming" and "dangerous" and a possible prelude to a "private, domestic counterintelligence squad" whose opaque domestic intelligence-gathering functions would make it an outfit the likes of which America has never seen before.[310]

ANNOTATIONS

MBS did not overpay for the painting by $350 million—Christie's had estimated it might sell for $100 million—merely due to bad luck. Rather, he was bidding against an unusually

insistent anonymous party whose aggressive bids raised the painting's price to historic heights.

Oddly, the figure $350 million will recur in the Trump-Russia saga, with former Trump adviser Carter Page—who testifies before Congress that he had no income whatsoever in 2016 or 2017—suddenly coming into exactly $350 million in 2018, according to RD Heritage Group, a U.S. investment company "with oil and gas interests in the Middle East."[311] In 2018, the group will announce that it has received a "$350 million capital commitment by Global Energy Capital . . . an investment management and advisory firm focused on the energy sector primarily in emerging markets. Global Energy Capital was founded by Carter Page . . . a foreign policy advisor to Presidential candidate Donald Trump."[312]

The roughly $350 million profit involved in the sale of *Salvator Mundi* ended up in the pockets of Kremlin agent and onetime Trump business client Dmitry Rybolovlev. According to the Steele dossier, it was Carter Page who negotiated a percentage of the December 2016 sale of a portion of the Kremlin's oil company (Rosneft) being transmitted, possibly through Page himself, to Donald Trump.[313] In the case of RD Heritage—the recipient of $350 million from Page—the company's "main partner in the Middle East is Hadi Al Alawi of the Al Hayat Group, a Bahraini investment company," though Heritage also does business with the state-owned oil companies of Qatar, Kuwait, and Saudi Arabia.[314] Most notable, however, as investigative reporter Scott Stedman discovers in September 2018, is a remark on the company website about an ongoing relationship with the Qatar Investment Authority (QIA)—one of the entities that purchased a substantial stake in Rosneft in December 2016.[315]

While it is not clear what these connections signify, when Stedman brings them to RD Heritage's attention in August 2018, the company immediately scrubs its website of any mention of Carter Page.[316]

CHAPTER 9

1MDB, MESA, THE SAUDI QUARTET, THE TRUMP DOCTRINE, AND THE DEATH OF JAMAL KHASHOGGI

January 2018 to November 2018

As MBS, MBZ, and el-Sisi move to formalize their conspiracy as a Middle East "strategic alliance," the means by which various foreign nations have now established a financial stranglehold over, and crafted a network of debts with, Trump and Kushner becomes clear—a story that ranges from a U.S. tabloid to a Beverly Hills hotel, and from nine-figure loans to the Kushner family to shakedowns in Trump Tower. Against the backdrop of a foreign policy now beholden to foreign interests and hostile to basic democratic principles, the Trump administration commits a shocking transgression: a months-long, Congress-defying campaign to assist MBS in lying about, covering up, and escaping responsibility for the brutal execution of a *Washington Post* journalist.

Emboldened by Donald Trump's election, the same nations whose representatives met on a yacht in the Red Sea to plan the installation of Trump as America's next president will in 2018 take steps to formalize their alliance as the Middle East Strategic Alliance (MESA), functionally an "Arab NATO" in the view of many in the Middle East.[1] First outlined in May 2017, MESA would have included, as originally conceived, all the nations in the Gulf Cooperation Council at the time—Saudi Arabia, the United Arab Emirates, Bahrain, Kuwait, Qatar, and Oman—but dilute significantly the power of the sole member against whom Saudi Arabia and the UAE had expressed animus, Qatar, by adding to the bloc two countries originally part of the Red Sea Conspiracy, Egypt and Jordan.[2]

That MESA is an outgrowth of the late 2015 conspiracy orchestrated by MBZ, MBS, and UAE adviser George Nader is underscored not only by the prospective alliance's plan to have "the United States act[ ] as the guarantor of peace and stability" but also by the two significant changes the original plan for the alliance has undergone by the end of 2017: first, after "[falling] out dramatically with the group which had gathered on the yacht [in 2015]," Jordan may no longer find itself in MESA, according to the *Middle East Eye* and Al Jazeera; and second, Qatar, by December 2017 still the subject of a blockade by Saudi Arabia and the UAE, will, according to Red Sea conspirator Bahrain's foreign minister, Khalid bin Ahmed Al Khalifa, be permitted to join MESA only if it "accept[s] its [MESA's] principles"—seemingly a euphemism for accepting the conditions previously set by Riyadh and Abu Dhabi for ending the ongoing Qatar blockade (see chapter 7).[3] As 2018 begins, the possibility therefore remains that Saudi Arabia and the UAE will get exactly what they began aiming for once it became clear that Jordan was unsupportive of their efforts to isolate Qatar: an anti-Iran, Israel-tolerant Sunni Arab alliance headed by themselves, Bahrain, and Egypt—and supported by an American president willing to appease Russia in ways that will directly benefit the alliance.

Before this can happen, however, MBS and MBZ must conclusively address the Qatar question, which in many respects has become a proxy, too, for the question of Jordan's involvement in MESA. As noted by Al Jazeera in October 2018, "Doubts over MESA have . . . been raised over a protracted dispute between Qatar and four Arab states who launched a blockade against Doha in 2017. Saudi Arabia, the United Arab Emirates, Bahrain, and Egypt cut off travel and trade ties with Qatar in June 2017, accusing it of backing

Iran and supporting terrorism."[4] Since the blockade began, Qatar has vehemently denied the four nations' allegations, ensuring that the "Qatari crisis"
will remain the reason that, as the Middle East Policy Council notes, "there
is much that is unknown about the final composition [of MESA]."[5]

The timing of the Qatar blockade suggests that the longtime U.S. ally
was always unwelcome in the Saudi-led MESA. When news first broke of
the MESA proposal in Riyadh in May 2017—at the Arab Islamic American
Summit, which Trump attended—Qatar was presumed to be a future member.[6] The "Riyadh Declaration" that emerged from the summit "unveiled
plans to establish the Middle East Strategic Alliance with the objective of
establishing peace and security in the region and the world. The process
of establishing the Riyadh-based Alliance with the participation of many
nations will be completed by 2018."[7] Yet it was just days later that Saudi
Arabia, the United Arab Emirates, Bahrain, and Egypt—which, according
to *Foreign Policy*, would soon become known to many in the Middle East as
the "Anti-Qatar Quartet," and by others as the "Saudi Quartet"—"imposed
a historic land, maritime, and air blockade on Qatar" in a move intended
to "permanently ostracize [Saudi Arabia's] rival."[8] In mid-2018, the Dubai-
based *Gulf News* will report that the quartet is, according to Saudi foreign
minister Adel al-Jubeir, willing to "wait for ten to fifteen, twenty, fifty
years" for Qatar to accept its list of demands, with al-Jubeir telling the
Council on Foreign Relations in New York that the four nations' patience
is equal to that of the United States with respect to Cuba (the U.S. has had
an embargo on its Communist neighbor to the south since 1960).[9]

According to *Foreign Policy*, in initiating a blockade on Qatar the quartet's "real goal was to essentially make Qatar a vassal state unable to
carry out any independent foreign policy. To that end, the Saudi camp
initiated a massive public relations effort in Western capitals to increase
diplomatic pressure on Qatar and turn public opinion against it."[10] This
campaign appears to have begun in earnest during a secret meeting in
Riyadh in May 2017 attended by Jared Kushner, Steve Bannon, MBS,
and MBZ (see chapter 8). Because MESA had already been announced as
a Saudi-led alliance by the time of the blockade in mid-2017, the quartet's
actions clearly precluded Qatar from participating in the "Arab NATO"

and, moreover, put the four nations behind the blockade at the forefront of the new organization—with Saudi Arabia and the United Arab Emirates clearly first among equals.

In January 2018, however, Michael Wolff's controversial access-journalism tell-all *Fire and Fury* is released, and its content, an intimate look inside the Trump administration, risks creating a fissure between Trump and the Saudis—a danger Trump may have foreseen, given that he takes the extraordinary step of trying to block the book's publication in court.[11] After the president's effort, which is predictably unsuccessful and (equally predictably) ensures that *Fire and Fury* is an instant *New York Times* bestseller, George Nader emails Elliott Broidy at least twice to "smooth over potential bad feelings created by the book . . . [which] portrayed the president's views of the Saudi prince in an unflattering light."[12] Wolff's book describes MBS as a man with "no education" who "know[s] little," but these views are attributed to the book's author; more problematically, Trump's "foreign policy people" are described as considering MBS, prior to Trump's trip to Riyadh in May 2017, an "opportunist" and "untested," and Trump is quoted by Wolff as cavalierly saying, after his first meeting with MBS in March 2017, "Jared's gotten the Arabs totally on our side. Done deal."[13]

The "deal" to which Trump is referring is one he implies his campaign or transition team has devised, though of course MBS, MBZ, el-Sisi, Putin, and Netanyahu have long since—through their interlocutors, including Birnbaum, Simes, al-Otaiba, Flynn, Barrack, Prince, Nader, Broidy, and others—sold the deal to Kushner, Bannon, Trump Jr., and Trump himself. As Wolff summarizes Trump's understanding of the plan for the Middle East in early 2017, "There are basically four players [in the Middle East] . . . Israel, Egypt, Saudi Arabia, and Iran. The first three can be united against the fourth. And Egypt and Saudi Arabia, [if] given what they want with respect to Iran—and anything else that does not interfere with the United States' interests—will pressure the Palestinians to make a deal."[14] The "anything else" Trump imagines as he begins his presidency in fact, per Wolff, includes a great many things not necessarily in America's interest, including moving the U.S. military command in the Middle East from Qatar to Saudi Arabia and giving the Russians a "free pass" in Ukraine, including a "lifting of sanctions," in return for Putin "giving up on Iran and Syria."[15] While *Fire and Fury*'s emphasis on Trump's hobnobbing with Red Sea conspirators in Riyadh likely causes no offense to MBS on the book's publication (if Trump tells the king of Bahrain he can expect "no strain" in dealing with the Trump administration, or exhibits an odd fervor over el-Sisi's expensive shoes, it makes no difference to MBS, surely), *Fire and Fury* also implies that Trump believes "some members of the Saudi royal family" have provided "support" to "terror groups"—which, while true, MBS takes as a serious slight.[16]

In mid-January, Nader arrives in the United States planning to attend a gala at Trump's Florida home, likely aiming to smooth over any Trump-Saudi tensions in person, but also to strategize with Broidy on how to convince MBS to give a new $650 million contract to Circinus; he is detained at the airport, however, by federal agents acting on the orders of the special counsel's office.[17] Along with getting served a grand jury subpoena, Nader has his phone seized and is quickly brought before Mueller's team for questioning.[18] According to a source close to the Emirati royal family, after Nader is finally allowed to leave the United States to go back to the UAE, MBZ "is keen to know what Mueller asked."[19] Per the source, "George is back in the UAE, though I thought he'd be too scared to go there. The fact that he's gone back there means he's obviously not worried. But MBZ is going to want to see him and know what he told the special counsel."[20] According to the *Daily Mail*, Nader is allowed to leave the United States only "after [MBZ] pull[s] strings with U.S. officials to secure his freedom to move."[21] When Nader returns to the United States in June 2019, he is immediately arrested for possession of child pornography—charges sealed since his departure from the U.S. in January 2018 (see Introduction).

In late February 2018, a bombshell article in the *Washington Post*, full of information taken directly from intelligence reports seen by former U.S. officials, reveals that "officials in at least four countries have privately discussed ways they can manipulate Jared Kushner, the president's son-in-law and senior adviser, by taking advantage of his complex business arrangements, financial difficulties, and lack of foreign policy experience."[22] Two of the countries intercepted discussing such plans are the United Arab

Emirates and Israel, central parties in Saudi Arabia's plan for a reimagined Middle East; Saudi Arabia's MBS has, of course, already bragged that Kushner is "in his pocket."[23] The revelations in the *Post* will appear on their face to be tied to the early-February downgrading of Kushner's security clearance from "top secret" to "secret." According to the *Post*, "H. R. McMaster, President Trump's national security adviser, learned that Kushner had contacts with foreign officials that he did not coordinate through the National Security Council or officially report . . . [and] the issue of foreign officials talking about their meetings with Kushner and their perceptions of his vulnerabilities was a subject raised in McMaster's daily intelligence briefings."[24] U.S. national security officials also express alarm that on many occasions "foreign officials . . . said they wanted to deal only with Kushner directly and not more experienced personnel."[25] McMaster in particular is said to be "taken aback" and "surprised" by Kushner's unreported foreign contacts, considering them "weird" and "unusual" and requiring "an explanation."[26] Trump will "abruptly fire" McMaster just three weeks later.[27]

As the turmoil over Kushner's security clearance comes to a boil in late February and early March 2018, Trump announces that his chief of staff, John Kelly, will make the final determination on whether Kushner will be permitted to hold a top-secret clearance. Trump uses a news conference with Australian prime minister Malcolm Turnbull to assure the public that Kushner's clearance "will be up to General Kelly . . . General Kelly will make that call—I won't make that call. I will let the general . . . make that call."[28] In fact, by the time Trump issues his announcement, Kelly has—unbeknownst to the president—already made his preliminary determination on the issue, downgrading Kushner's security clearance to "interim secret."[29] As the *Washington Post* reports shortly thereafter, Kelly's decision that "the White House will no longer allow some employees with interim security clearances access to top-secret information . . . [is] a move that could threaten Kushner . . . [who] has had a high level of access in the White House and has seen some of the nation's most sensitive secrets."[30] The *Post* adds that the biggest obstacles to Kushner receiving a top-secret clearance are his "repeated amendments . . . to a form detailing his contacts with foreign officials," observing that "not fully disclosing foreign contacts ordinarily would result in a clearance being denied," according to experts on such matters.[31] The newspaper further reports that Kelly's downgrading of Kushner's access resulted from Kelly being "frustrated with Kushner's high level of access without a final clearance" and that not only was Kelly "aware [his] new policies could jeopardize Kushner's ability to carry out his duties in the West Wing" but he had in fact put a "bull's eye" on Kushner.[32]

Despite his public insistence that he will honor Kelly's decision on Kushner no matter what it is, within ninety days of Kelly downgrading Kushner's security clearance Trump will, according to the *New York Times*, "order[ ] his chief of staff to grant his son-in-law and senior adviser, Jared Kushner, a top-secret security clearance . . . overruling concerns flagged by intelligence officials and the White House's top lawyer," Don McGahn.[33] Trump's order, which Kelly follows, contravenes the recommendation of the CIA and "so trouble[s]" Kelly that he will write "a contemporaneous internal memo" documenting that his judgment has been overridden.[34] Within a month of his May 2018 order to Kelly demanding that Kushner's clearance be restored, Trump fires Kelly. Despite the firing, Kelly remains in his job; he decides, according to *Business Insider*, to just "ignore" the president's decision to terminate him.[35] Kelly's reasoning—that Trump has a "short attention span" and will forget (or lose interest in) the fact that he has fired his chief of staff—turns out to be correct, and Kelly retains his position.[36]

Trump's unusual treatment of Kelly over Kushner's security clearance is contemporaneous with a similarly troubling posture toward deputy attorney general Rod Rosenstein on the same issue. On February 9, Rosenstein had "alerted White House Counsel Don McGahn that significant issues would further delay Kushner's security clearance process." While it is unclear how long this information took to get from Rosenstein to Trump, within a matter of weeks of Rosenstein's "alert," Trump had begun discussing firing the deputy attorney general with White House aides, something he had not done previously.[37]

Trump's pattern of behavior on the matter of Kushner's security clearance—firing or attempting to fire anyone who opposes Kushner's having the highest possible clearance, and then dissembling as to how the matter has been handled—will continue in January 2019, when Trump falsely tells the *New York Times* that "he had no role in his son-in-law receiving his [top secret] clearance."[38] The February 2019 revelation that in fact Trump had a significant role in mid-2018 in ordering Kushner's top-secret security clearance restored and made permanent will cause reporters to look at what others in and around the White House were saying on the same subject in 2018—leading to the further discovery that Kushner's attorney Abbe Lowell had falsely told the media in May 2018 that Kushner "went through a standard process" to get his permanent security clearance.[39] Just so, Ivanka Trump's February 2019 claim to ABC News that "the president had no involvement pertaining to my clearance or my husband's clearance, zero," will be proven false on both counts when it is discovered that Trump had ordered Kelly and McGahn to give Ivanka top-secret clearance at the same time he ordered it for his son-in-law.[40]

That Trump regards it as mission-critical that both his daughter and son-in-law have top-secret security clearances underscores the likelihood that husband and wife are familiar not only with each other's financial affairs but diplomatic efforts as well—a probability with especially significant repercussions for Ivanka, whose role in Kushner's secret dealings with foreign leaders remains unexplored by the media. Trump's degree of concern about Kushner's access to the President's Daily Brief and other top-secret intelligence also suggests that the president is broadly aware of the foreign policy maneuvers his son-in-law is undertaking, including the myriad ways in which they sidestep diplomatic protocol and indeed the country's diplomat corps. Trump seems unwilling or unable to seek a "grand bargain" in the Middle East under the watchful eye of career State Department officials—in some cases, even Trump's own staffers and appointees—who might well consider the path Trump and Kushner are treading a dangerous one.

When Trump's overruling of career and appointed White House and intelligence officials on the matter of Jared and Ivanka's security clearances is ultimately revealed, one of his top friends and political allies—former New Jersey governor Chris Christie—will tell media that it is "very,

very difficult" for even Trump's friends to defend his actions.[41] Trump "needs to be held to account for that," Christie adds, asking, "Why not tell the truth about it? Why not just say I did it, and why wouldn't Ivanka do the same?"[42] Speaking broadly of the Trump family's dishonesty in its handling of Ivanka's and Jared's clearances, Christie concludes, "You can't defend that."[43]

Kushner's continued access to top-secret U.S. intelligence maintains his value to MBS as a WhatsApp conversation partner, which ensures Trump's continued value to the Saudis as well. As 2018 wears on, Trump's luxury hotels in Chicago and Manhattan suddenly receive a massive influx of cash from Saudi Arabia. This infusion of capital is critical to Trump, as it comes at the end of a two-year cycle in which receipts at these two key locations in the Trump real estate empire have faltered badly. According to the *Washington Post*, "Revenue at both properties dropped noticeably [between 2015 and 2017] as Trump's political career took off."[44] The drop was 8 percent in Chicago and 14 percent in New York—a startling blow to Trump's income stream over a relatively short period of time. Evidence that Trump has taken notice of this revenue decline comes in an unusual form: his decision to offer a position on his President's Council on Sports, Fitness, and Nutrition to a board member at his New York hotel, a man who, along with Trump's son Don Jr., pushed back strongly against removing Trump's name from the building—a dramatic move then under consideration because of the property's fading prospects.[45] The board member, a New Jersey doctor, was to be given the honor of a position on the president's fitness council alongside six-time Super Bowl–winning pro football coach Bill Belichick, thirteen-time All-Star and five-time World Series champion relief pitcher Mariano Rivera, and six-time *New York Times* bestselling author (and longtime television celebrity) Dr. Mehmet Oz.[46] The board member's response to a press inquiry about his surprising nomination to a high-profile government council features sixty-two exclamation points and the line "Don't write or attempt to reach me again!!"[47]

According to the *Washington Post*, losses at Trump's Manhattan and Chicago hotels were ultimately "cushioned, partly by new customers from overseas. Both hotels noted an influx of visitors from Saudi Arabia," a development that allows Trump's son Eric to announce 2018 as an "incredible year" for Trump's hotels.[48] Eric fails to note that three of fourteen Trump-branded hotels cut ties with Trump—and his name—between Trump's inauguration and October 2018.[49] Moreover, it appears that one reason for Trump Hotels' "incredible" 2018 may have been an especially lucrative onetime event: "a last-minute visit to New York by the Crown Prince of Saudi Arabia" in the first quarter of the year, which the general manager of Trump's Manhattan hotel crows about in a letter to investors.[50] When journalists inquire with the Trump Organization as to whether the Saudi government paid for the block of rooms secured by MBS, they receive no response from the Trumps.[51]

Rentals at Trump's Chicago hotel slump badly in the second quarter of 2018, but a sales and marketing update sent by the hotel to investors in September 2018 reports, as noted by the *Washington Post*, "good news, again, from Saudi Arabia . . . with Saudi-based customers . . . book[ing] 218 nights at Trump Chicago this year [2018]—a 169 percent increase from the same period in 2016."[52]

In early March 2018, the *New York Times* reports that special counsel Robert Mueller has questioned George Nader about his ties to the United Arab Emirates—specifically about whether he assisted the UAE in buying influence with Donald Trump prior to Election Day in 2016.[53] The *Times* describes Nader as "a Lebanese-American businessman [who] has hovered on the fringes of international diplomacy for three decades. He was a back-channel negotiator with Syria during the Clinton administration, reinvented himself as an adviser to the de facto ruler of the United Arab Emirates [Mohammed bin Zayed], and last year [2017] was a frequent visitor to President Trump's White House."[54] Calling Nader a "focus" of the Mueller investigation, the *Times* notes that—despite Nader being a regular sight at the White House post-inauguration—federal investigators' attention is on whether the Emiratis directed money to support Trump during the presidential campaign, a form of collusion that would violate federal law as an illegal campaign donation and could also reveal, if pursued, any covert intelligence-gathering and domestic psy-ops work Joel Zamel's Psy-Group may have done for Trump pre-election on the Emiratis' dime.[55] The *Times* report goes still further, however, noting that "Nader's role in White House policymaking" is also the subject of a federal criminal investigation. Implicit in this revelation is that Mueller is investigating the possibility that Nader, the UAE, or both have attempted to bribe Trump to alter his foreign policy—bribery being a form of "collusion" in lay terms and, more important, both a federal felony and an impeachable offense under the U.S. Constitution.[56] Even worse for Trump, Nader's new status as a cooperating witness for the special counsel's office means, according to the *Times*, that Mueller is likely investigating how money from not just one but "multiple countries" is influencing policymaking at both the White House and elsewhere in Washington "during the Trump era."[57]

The March 3, 2018, revelation that Nader is cooperating with Mueller makes Elliott Broidy—whom Nader used as one of several intermediaries in dealing with Trump, and who is, as of March 2018, still the Trump-appointed deputy finance chair at the Republican National Committee—a potential liability for the president. Less than six weeks later, a sudden event removes Broidy from Trump's political orbit altogether: Broidy is forced to step down from his role at the RNC after it is revealed that he had an affair with a woman, Shera Bechard, who became pregnant, and that Broidy used Trump's attorney, Michael Cohen, to pay her hush money.[58] Cohen, Broidy's co-chair on the Republican National Committee finance committee, is by this time himself under investigation for the hush money pass-through entity he had created for Trump during the presidential campaign—Essential Consultants, LLC—on the grounds of, as later recounted in the Mueller Report, "evidence that it received funds from Russian-backed entities."[59]

It is unclear who told the *Wall Street Journal* about what Elliott Broidy had done and was continuing to do with respect to payoffs to a former mistress. In breaking the story that quickly ends Broidy's tenure with the Republican Party, the *Journal* merely quotes "people familiar with the matter" who have suddenly decided to disclose what they know.[60] It is likewise not clear who, if anyone—besides Broidy, Bechard, and Trump attorney Michael Cohen—knew of the payoffs. Given that the revelation of the payments causes Broidy to stop making them, it would seem Bechard had little to gain from disclosing the arrangement. Indeed, through her attorney Bechard will release the following statement after news breaks of her hush money contract with the top Republican operative: "Ms. Bechard is deeply distressed that someone has revealed information regarding her and Elliott Broidy."[61] As the *Wall Street Journal* will note at the time, "The nondisclosure agreement involving Mr. Broidy [and Bechard] resembles an October 2016 pact in which Mr. Cohen agreed to pay $130,000 to adult-film actress Stephanie Clifford to prevent her from publicly discussing an alleged sexual encounter with Mr. Trump in 2006."[62] Broidy even uses the same fake name ("David Dennison") as Trump did in his contract with Clifford.[63]

In 2018, additional allegations involving the Broidy-Bechard relationship will become public through the release of portions of Bechard's legal filings contesting Broidy's termination of their nondisclosure agreement. According to the filings, the five-year relationship between the married Broidy and the two-time *Playboy* centerfold began in 2013, and early in the relationship Broidy told her he loved her and promised to support her financially.[64] By 2016, he had become "increasingly violent" and demanded that Bechard get liposuction to lose weight.[65] According to Bechard's allegations, Broidy refused to wear a condom and habitually pushed her to drink to excess to make her "more compliant."[66] When Bechard became pregnant, the lawsuit alleges, Broidy demanded she get an abortion and kept her pregnancy a tightly held secret.[67] Finally, Bechard's lawsuit alleges that she was afraid of Broidy, as he owned a gun and had told her in the past that he could "make people disappear."[68]

In March 2018, Abdel Fattah el-Sisi "wins" his "reelection" effort in Egypt, with *Foreign Policy* calling the balloting a "farcical election in which every credible challenger was arrested or intimidated out of the race."[69]

March also sees a visit by MBS to Washington, where he is "feted" by President Trump even as a close Trump ally—David Pecker of AMI, a future Mueller cooperating witness who had spent the 2016 presidential campaign "catching" and "killing" stories that could harm Trump politically—publishes nationwide a large, glossy, ad-free propaganda magazine whose sole purpose is to "sell America on a fellow Trump ally, Saudi Arabia Crown Prince Mohammed bin Salman."[70] The propaganda, which ignores MBS's domestic purges in Riyadh and his sponsorship of war crimes in Yemen, lauds his wealth and his Vision 2030 plan for the future of the kingdom he stands to inherit. At one point it includes a picture of a grinning Donald Trump beside Kacy Grine, a French financial adviser who "acts as an intermediary between . . . [MBS] and Western businesses."[71] Pecker's publication promotes a "new Saudi-led United Arabic Market" that will "build economic relations with Israel."[72]

MBS and the Saudi government will disclaim any knowledge of how the propaganda vehicle came to be, and the White House and the Trump Organization will refuse to comment on the question.[73] The *New York Times* will note, however, that in July 2017 Pecker and Grine went to the White House to visit Trump and Kushner, during which meeting the AMI chairman received "an unofficial seal of approval from the White House . . . [as he was] considering expanding his media and events businesses into Saudi Arabia."[74] According to the *Times*, "Word soon traveled back to Saudi Arabia about the dinner: It signaled Mr. Pecker's powerful status in Washington. Two months later, Pecker was in Saudi Arabia, meeting with Mr. Grine and the crown prince about business opportunities there."[75] When MBS comes to America in March 2018, Pecker and Grine attend multiple events with him, even as his $13.99-per-unit panegyric to MBS is on newsstands across the country "talk[ing] up the relationship between Mr. Trump and the Saudis" and noting, as summarized by the *Times*, that "Mr. Trump 'endorsed the crown prince's high profile anticorruption' crackdown."[76] During his visit to D.C., MBS acquires a $400 million stake in the Hollywood talent agency run by Ari Emanuel, the man who introduced Pecker to Grine.[77]

From Trump's inauguration onward, it is Jared Kushner—not, as during the campaign, Michael Cohen—who acts as Trump's "main conduit" to

Pecker, broadly discussing, according to the *Daily Beast*, "international relations" with the publisher of the *National Enquirer*, as well as "relations with
the Saudi regime" specifically.[78] By the time Pecker publishes his pro-MBS
propaganda in 2018, he has not only been discussing U.S.-Saudi relations
with Kushner for months but also, over the years he has known Kushner,
at various points been "thinking about forging a business relationship"
with Trump's son-in-law, according to the *Daily Beast*.[79]

Following the publication of his glossy MBS propaganda, Pecker becomes concerned that he may be acting as an agent of Saudi Arabia.
Trump's longtime friend is worried on this score not only because of the
magazine he's just published but because AMI has had, per the *Wall Street
Journal*, "plenty of contacts with Saudi Arabia in recent years, including
seeking financial backing from Saudi investors to fund acquisitions"—an
apparent reference to Pecker asking Saudi Arabia to assist the *National
Enquirer* in paying for news stories.[80]

Pecker will ultimately ask the Department of Justice whether AMI—an
entity with significant responsibility for Trump's election as president,
given the stories it purchased and buried for him pre-election—should
register as an agent of the Saudi government.[81] A further reason for Pecker
making the query to the DOJ, though it's unknown if this information
was transmitted to the DOJ at the time, is that, as the Associated Press
will later report, "the Saudi Embassy in Washington got a sneak peek" of
the pro-MBS magazine AMI produced in a print run of 200,000 copies,
"quietly sharing [a digital copy] with Saudi officials . . . almost three weeks
before it was published, despite both parties' insistence that they didn't
coordinate on the magazine."[82] AMI even "reached out to Saudi officials
in the U.S. before publication to seek help with the [magazine's] content."[83]
Image metadata acquired by the Associated Press from two different individuals reveals that shortly after February 19, 2018, AMI sent a pdf of the
magazine to "Saudi officials, including the embassy's military office . . .
it was also passed to Nail al-Jubeir, the former embassy spokesman and
brother of Saudi Foreign Minister Adel al-Jubeir."[84] The latter al-Jubeir
will show up again in American media in February 2019, when he issues
a vague if expansive threat over attempts to hold MBS accountable for the

execution of *Washington Post* journalist Jamal Khashoggi: "Our leadership is a red line," al-Jubeir will announce on Twitter in defense of MBS. "We warn against any attempt to link Khashoggi's crime [*sic*] to our leadership."[85] Al-Jubeir adds, "We will not accept any state to dictate to us what to do."[86]

By 2019, media reports will have revealed that David Pecker's pro-MBS propaganda "included content written by" MBS intermediary Grine, that AMI "also gave [Grine] the whole working draft for advance review, and that he suggested changes, and they implemented changes, and that he provided . . . photographs of MBS."[87] Also revealed will be the fact that Pecker has, sometime since March 2018, entered into an immunity agreement with federal prosecutors, as has Dylan Howard, AMI's chief content officer—who the *New York Times* notes was "known to have a recording device in his office."[88] The *Times* will call Pecker's cooperation deal "another potential blow to the president from a former loyalist."[89]

In a "Statement of Admitted Facts" AMI submits to the Southern District of New York, the organization will admit to acting "in cooperation, consultation, and concert with, and at the request and suggestion of one or more members or agents of a candidate's 2016 presidential campaign, to ensure that a woman did not publicize damaging allegations about that candidate before the 2016 presidential election and thereby influence that election . . . AMI agreed to pay [a] model $150,000—substantially more money than AMI otherwise would have paid to acquire the story—because of Cohen's assurances to Pecker that AMI would ultimately be reimbursed for the payment. . . . AMI's principal purpose in entering into the agreement was to suppress the model's story so as to prevent it from influencing the election."[90] The *Wall Street Journal* thereafter publishes a long exposé on Trump's role in paying his ex-girlfriends for their silence in the run-up to Election Day in 2016, concluding that Trump had a "central role in hush payoffs."[91]

Pecker's DOJ query about his relationship with Saudi Arabia takes on a different cast when the full scope of his pre-election collusion with Trump, including his payment of millions of dollars to hide negative information about Trump from American voters, is considered. Indeed, in August 2018 the Associated Press will reveal that during the general election, AMI "kept a safe containing documents on hush money payments and other damaging stories it killed as part of its cozy relationship with Donald Trump."[92] This means that at a time AMI was seeking—possibly successfully—"financial backing from Saudi investors," it was also, per court papers in the Michael Cohen campaign finance case, "offer[ing] to help [Trump] deal with negative stories about his relationships with women by, among other things, assisting the campaign in identifying such stories so they could be purchased and their publication avoided."[93] Most notably, AMI's assistance of the Trump campaign in this fashion began just seventy-two hours after Saudi emissary Nader had met with Trump's son at Trump Tower on August 3, 2016, to offer assistance to the Trump campaign on behalf of the Saudis; by August 6, AMI had agreed to pay $150,000 to Karen McDougal, a former Trump mistress, for her "life rights" (the right to publish her life story).[94] Just weeks earlier, Pecker's company had flatly refused to purchase McDougal's life rights.[95]

As to whether AMI might have made decisions about whether or not to publish material about then-candidate Trump without contacting him first, Jerry George, a former AMI senior editor, told the *New Yorker* that "in his 25 years at the company, 'we never printed a word about Trump without his approval.'"[96] An unanswered question therefore remains: Did the Saudis pay money to AMI, on Trump's behalf, that AMI had previously been unwilling to expend itself? Whether any such Saudi payments to AMI occurred before the 2016 election or as part of Pecker's expansive and lucrative dealings with the Saudis post-election, if either Trump or Pecker had knowledge that Trump would be receiving outside assistance in paying hush money to his ex-mistresses—or if Trump had been given any such assurance prior to the election, whether or not the payments had yet been made—it is very likely something that has already been discussed in detail among Pecker, Dylan Howard, and federal investigators in the Southern District of New York.

At a news conference with MBS during his March 2018 trip to Washington, Trump brags about how much money he's bringing into the country by selling the Saudis and Emiratis warplanes and other military hardware for their joint campaign in Yemen.[97] The same month, U.S. senators "accuse[ ] the Pentagon of being complicit in the [Saudi-Emirati] coalition's errant bombing" in Yemen, including actions "the United Nations' human rights body determined . . . were likely war crimes."[98] Four-star Army general Joseph Votel tells Congress that the military has no mechanism whatsoever to generate or access information on whether coalition warplanes the U.S. military helps refuel are bombing civilians, but his testimony is immediately contradicted by a State Department adviser, Larry Lewis, who has worked with the Saudi coalition for years and tells senators that the information in question "was readily available from an early stage. At the coalition headquarters in Riyadh, he said, American liaison officers had access to a database that detailed every airstrike: warplane, target, munitions used and a brief description of the attack. American officials frequently emailed him copies of a spreadsheet for his own work."[99] Just 120 days after Votel and Lewis testify about the possibility the United States is participating in war crimes, King Salman, MBS's father, "issue[s] an order lifting 'all military and disciplinary penalties' for Saudi troops fighting in Yemen, an apparent amnesty for possible war crimes," according to the *New York Times*.[100] Nevertheless, Trump's support for MBS's operation in Yemen continues unabated—an operation called a "strategic disaster" and "clumsy" by Daniel Byman, a professor at Georgetown University's Walsh School of Foreign Service, who adds that Saudi and Emirati airstrikes "have shown no sign of defeating the Houthis."[101]

In April 2018, Trump's two eldest sons, Don and Eric, travel to the United Arab Emirates to visit multiple Trump-branded properties there and attend the wedding of a billionaire Emirati business partner of the Trump Organization, Hussain Sajwani.[102] Sajwani has been in business with Trump Sr. since 2005, when he worked with Trump in planning twin Trump-branded towers for Dubai—just a few months after MBZ ascended to his position as the crown prince of Abu Dhabi.[103]

Though the UAE is, at the time of Don and Eric's trip there in April

2018, fully enmeshed in a blockade of Qatar, back at home Trump meets with Qatari emir Tamim bin Hamad Al Thani and—perhaps influenced by recent Qatari largesse in lending large sums of money to his daughter's husband—seems keen to force the UAE and Saudi Arabia to once again embrace their Gulf neighbor.[104] In his remarks in D.C. with the emir, according to an analysis by *Foreign Policy*, Trump appears to "attack[ ] Saudi Arabia, including in reference to terror funding, and acknowledge[ ] Qatar's progress on the matter."[105] Trump's sudden détente with Qatar, after his harsh words for the longtime U.S. ally on Twitter less than a year earlier (see chapter 7), may be explained partly by his administration's view that the Middle East Strategic Alliance cannot proceed until Saudi Arabia and Qatar make peace, and partly by the fact that since the beginning of the Qatar blockade in spring 2017 Qatar has spent $1.5 billion on public relations in the United States.[106] Most important, however, may be Qatar opening its wallet to Trump's family, including, notably, Trump himself. In January 2018, just ninety days before Trump meets with Al Thani, Qatar buys a $6.5 million apartment in Trump World Tower in Manhattan.[107] As the *Guardian* notes at the time, "Qatar's new acquisition at Trump World Tower . . . coincided with an intense lobbying campaign in Washington by the Qatari government amid a regional crisis that has pitted the Gulf monarchy against Saudi Arabia and the United Arab Emirates."[108] The *Guardian* quotes a statement about the sale from the nonpartisan group Citizens for Responsibility and Ethics in Washington, which reads, in part, "This [purchase] plays to the central concern with the president's refusal to divest from his holdings—that he would be susceptible to influence from foreign countries invested in his businesses."[109]

In a May 2018 article published under the headline "The Kushners Are Finally Getting That Sweet, Sweet Qatari Cash," *Vanity Fair* will allege that the Trumps put Qatar "under siege" politically and literally in order to get Brookfield Asset Management, a company with "extensive ties to Qatar"— indeed, a company whose second-largest shareholder is the Qatar Investment Authority—to bail out Kushner Companies from its disastrous 666 Fifth Avenue investment by taking out a "99-year lease" on the property.[110]

Kushner's dealings with Brookfield are problematic from the start, as in

January 2018 Brookfield Property Partners, a subsidiary of Brookfield Asset Management, had purchased a bankrupt nuclear services company, Westinghouse Electric, that was part of IP3's proposed U.S.-Russia nuclear reactor-building consortium.[111] The result is that by the time Kushner Companies receives a large influx of cash from Brookfield in August 2018, Kushner himself is overseeing the very same ACU/IP3 Middle East Marshall Plan that could make Westinghouse Electric fabulously profitable once again. Kushner is therefore in a position to create new wealth through foreign policy in a way that will eventually transfer that wealth back to his family. Moreover, the timing of the two events appears to be related. According to the House Oversight Committee, "In February 2018 it was reported that 'The administration is considering permitting Saudi Arabia to enrich and reprocess uranium as part of a deal that would allow Westinghouse Electric Company and other American companies to build nuclear reactors in the Middle East kingdom.'" Within sixty days, the Kushners are seeking money from the company that owns Westinghouse; it is unknown how or when Brookfield first learned of the Trump administration plans for a nuclear deal with Saudi Arabia.[112]

A third sequence of events seems to close the Kushner-MBS circle over Westinghouse: Between February and April 2018, MBS's entourage for his March trip to the United States spends so much money at Trump International Hotel in Manhattan—in what is called a "last-minute visit to New York"—that the group singlehandedly "'boost[s] the hotel's revenue' by 13 percent 'for the entire quarter.'"[113] The administration's decision on Saudi uranium enrichment, the Kushners' pitch to Brookfield, and MBS's significant assist to a flagging Trump enterprise during a surprise visit to America come together in September 2018 when energy secretary Rick Perry tells reporters that MBS has put the Westinghouse consortium on a "shortlist of potential partners" for nuclear reactor contracts in Saudi Arabia, a development that, per Perry, "keeps U.S. businesses—foremost Westinghouse Electric Company—in the mix for what could ultimately become a market worth tens of billions of dollars."[114]

While the Qatar blockade is still ongoing in April 2018—with Trump's support—the president demonstrates his self-awareness of his leverage with the Qataris during a strange encounter at Mar-a-Lago. Franklin Haney, a wealthy East Tennessee businessman and "longtime Mar-a-Lago member," is dining at the club on a "business trip" when, for no reason Haney is willing to disclose, President Trump comes to his table with "an official with the oil-rich Middle Eastern nation of Qatar."[115] The official, Ahmed al-Rumaihi, is a "top representative" from the very same Qatar Investment Authority Trump's son-in-law Jared Kushner will, in just 120 days, receive more than a billion dollars from. While speaking with Haney at Trump's invitation, al-Rumaihi expresses interest in Haney's "plan to buy an obscure nuclear plant and sell power to the city of Memphis."[116] It is unclear if Haney—who has previously faced (and beaten) forty-two federal charges for campaign finance fraud—has at some prior point told Trump about his business plan, though it is perhaps not coincidental that by April 2018 Haney has given $1 million to Trump's inaugural campaign and $200,000 (over a period of just ninety days) to Trump's attorney Michael Cohen, in the latter case to help him get to Qatari investors.[117] Lest it sound as though Trump introduces Haney first to Cohen and then to the Qataris to simultaneously reward Haney for his donation to Trump's inauguration and enrich his personal attorney at a time when Cohen is under federal investigation, Haney clarifies that Cohen "simply caught wind of his [Haney's] plans to pursue Qatari investment and opportunistically inserted himself into them." Haney goes on to concede, however, that this happened "after Trump introduced the two of them [Haney and Cohen] at Mar-a-Lago."[118] In August 2018, *Mother Jones* will report that a "court filing by a law firm working for al-Rumaihi . . . states that al-Rumaihi currently holds a senior position with the Qatari government. That disclosure raises the question of whether his outreach to influential figures with ties to President Trump, including Steve Bannon and Michael Cohen, may have been part of a Qatari influence campaign."[119]

The Trump-Qatar matter will turn out to be far more complicated than this, however, as al-Rumaihi will later reveal that he attended meetings at Trump Tower during the presidential transition—before the Qatar blockade had begun, and therefore prior to any "influence campaign" related to the Qatari public relations blitz of late 2017 and early 2018.[120] The question becomes, therefore, why Trump appears to have done little or nothing in-volving al-Rumaihi until Cohen receives, per al-Rumaihi, a "$1 million pay-ment in exchange for connecting the Qatar Investment Authority . . . with potential business partners in the United States"—a payment Cohen receives at a time when Trump knows his longtime attorney is or could be under federal investigation over his pre-election activities involving Stormy Dan-iels and Trump Tower Moscow.[121] Was Trump trying to keep his longtime fixer happy by reversing roles and playing fixer for both Cohen and Qatar? Certainly, at the time Trump introduces al-Rumaihi to Haney, Haney's consultant Cohen is under federal investigation in a case that will eventu-ally implicate Trump, as *Vice* notes, in "at least eleven different felonies."[122]

An even more troubling possibility, which leads *Slate* to publish an ar-ticle in May 2018 entitled "Michael Cohen's Meetings with Michael Flynn and a Qatari Diplomat Might Be the Key to Unlocking the Steele Dos-sier," focuses on al-Rumaihi's employment with the QIA and the fact that he is spotted at Trump Tower in December 2016, just as Russia is selling the QIA 20 percent of its state-owned oil company, Rosneft.[123] According to the Steele dossier, it was in December 2016 that Carter Page—already known to have been in Moscow that month meeting with a top Rosneft executive and claiming to speak for Trump—negotiated on Trump's behalf a small piece of the $11.57 billion Rosneft-QIA deal.[124] In 2018, however, it will be revealed that the Kremlin secretly lent the QIA $6 billion of the $11.57 billion it "paid" to Russia—doing so through VTB, the very bank that Elliott Broidy has long worked for as an agent and which told Felix Sater and Michael Cohen it was willing to finance Trump Tower Moscow in the fall of 2015, during the presidential campaign (see chapter 3).[125] The result of these machinations is the apparent confirmation of Steele's raw intelligence, as Trump does indeed secretly negotiate with both of the purchasers involved in the Rosneft deal between fall 2015 and fall 2016, using as his negotiators Carter Page and Michael Cohen. Indeed, in a May 2018 interview with *The Intercept*, al-Rumaihi confesses that Michael Cohen was secretly negotiating American infrastructure policy with him at a series of private meetings in December 2016, with al-Rumaihi dangling $50 billion in investments before the incoming Trump administration and

Cohen pushing him to "do it [invest the money] immediately, to show that Trump was already making America great again by bringing in foreign investment and creating American jobs."[126]

In one meeting with al-Rumaihi, Cohen even seems to suggest the possibility of the Trump Organization receiving illegal kickbacks from any Qatari investment in the United States; Cohen, who will continue to work for the Trump Organization through January 2017, tells al-Rumaihi in December 2016, in the context of a conversation about Trump's new administration, "We can find a steel factory that is about to shut down. You guys [the QIA] can invest. I'll give you some names to appoint as partners. You guys put in the money, we will put in the know-how, and share the profits 50-50. We can perhaps get a federal government 'off-take agreement' for 10 to 15 years." According to *The Intercept*, "Al-Rumaihi surmised that the biggest winners would be the silent 'partners,' who would put in 'know-how,' rather than money and walk away with half the profits."[127]

As troubling as this is, a May 2018 report in *The Intercept* will produce even more complications, revealing that al-Rumaihi is being accused in court not only of having offered a bribe to Steve Bannon to influence Trump administration policy but also of having told Bannon that President-elect Trump's incoming national security advisor, Michael Flynn, had in fact already accepted the Qataris' offer of a bribe.[128] While al-Rumaihi will contest the claim, he acknowledges investing in a basketball league founded by a friend of Steve Bannon, one of the top three officials on the Trump transition team and one heavily involved in Flynn and Kushner's plans for the Middle East and Israel.[129]

All of the above will seem to have positioned al-Rumaihi as a potentially damning witness against Trump, Bannon, Flynn, Broidy, Page, Cohen, and Trump's allies in Russia and the Red Sea Conspiracy governments—until al-Rumaihi's value as a witness is tarnished by sudden allegations from Broidy, who, after months of lobbying Trump on behalf of both the UAE and Saudi Arabia, alleges that al-Rumaihi personally took part "in a scheme to hack Broidy's email and strategically leak information implicating him peddling influence to win business overseas, in particular in the

United Arab Emirates, Qatar's rival."[130] Broidy thereby puts al-Rumaihi at the middle of an international espionage investigation at a time when the Qatari could prove dangerous to the Trump administration and its allies if he cooperates with U.S. intelligence agencies, federal investigators in several Eastern Seaboard jurisdictions, or the special counsel's office. The situation also raises substantially the need for Trump and his allies to discredit America's intelligence agencies, as the details of all of the foregoing are, as all involved are likely aware, probably already known to those agencies. Even Haney's Mar-a-Lago interaction with Trump plays a role: as *Mother Jones* writes, "Haney's account raises questions, in particular whether his hiring of Cohen was related to Trump's intervention. His version of events also raises new questions about Trump's handling of U.S. relations with Qatar and other Gulf states."[131] As the magazine observes of the Qataris' precarious position at the time of the meeting between Haney and al-Rumaihi, "The Qataris had good reason to heed any Trump request to become involved in a specific project. In April 2018 and for much of the prior year, Qatar was aggressively courting Trump and his confidantes, eager to convince the president to drop his support for [the Saudi- and Emirati-led] blockade."[132] *Mother Jones* identifies, therefore, reasons for both Kushner and Trump to support—in a reversal of long-standing U.S. foreign policy toward Qatar—a four-nation blockade against the U.S. ally, even at a time when it hosts within its borders the largest American military installation in the Middle East; the magazine concurrently offers an explanation for why Trump may suddenly have begun praising Qatar for its counter-terrorism efforts in April 2018.[133]

On March 29, 2018, an unusual event occurs involving the ongoing civil war in Syria that will have significant repercussions by the end of the year: Trump tells a crowd in Ohio that he has a plan to withdraw all U.S. forces from Syria "very soon," an idea so at odds with current U.S. foreign policy that it provokes "Pentagon and State Department outcry that the Islamic State . . . [is] not defeated" in Syria.[134] Eleven days later, on April 9, John Bolton becomes Trump's new national security advisor; according to the *Washington Post*, this is "right about the time Trump's [Syria] withdrawal demand [from March 29] was set aside"—suggesting the sudden ascendance of Bolton's view that the United States cannot leave Syria under any circumstances because "the primary enemy in Syria [is] not the Islamic State, but Iran."[135] Bolton would undoubtedly have balked at Trump's March 29 declaration that the United States would be "coming out of Syria" and "very soon."[136] Bolton would have demurred even more forcefully from Trump's same-day amplification of his March 29 remark, in which he emphasized that he wanted all U.S. troops out of Syria "in about a week."[137] Those words had led to "frantic calls from the White House Situation Room . . . pouring in to aides traveling with the president. [Defense secretary Jim] Mattis and Chief of Staff John F. Kelly scrambled to understand what the president was talking about."[138] Bolton would not soon have forgotten either the chaos Trump produced in late March or the efforts required in early April to undo the confusion the president had caused.

Trump's view of the benefits of a precipitous Syria withdrawal does not, in fact, change after March 29—however, his new national security advisor will falsely aver to media and other U.S. officials that it has. Indeed, from early April onward Bolton will hide from national security officials that Trump's plans for Syria remain consistent with the preferences of both the Kremlin and the Saudis and Emiratis, for whom the American military vacating Syria is the ideal scenario: for Russia because it means America has ceded Syria to Kremlin control and influence, and for the Saudis and Emiratis because an American retreat in Syria increases the odds Russia will agree to work with (or at least not against) the United States and the two Sunni Arab nations in their ongoing struggles against Iran elsewhere in the Middle East.

According to the *Post*, the "key moment" in Bolton's dissembling with America's national security apparatus comes at a meeting in September 2018 "that remains shrouded in secrecy. Bolton told senior officials working on Syria policy that Trump, during a no-notes meeting alone with Russian

President Vladimir Putin in Helsinki in July, had insisted that U.S. troops would stay in Syria until Moscow forced out its Iranian allies—an ambitious declaration that could keep [the United States] there for years. With no reason to doubt Bolton's account, officials at the Pentagon and State Department fine-tuned a strategy that made Iran's departure a primary objective of the 2,000-strong U.S. presence" in Syria.[139]

Had Trump in fact delivered such a message to Putin in Helsinki in July 2018, it would have been an iconic moment for the president, with Trump denying the Russian strongman one of his most prized geopolitical ambitions—the removal of the United States from the Syrian combat theater. It will eventually be revealed, however, that Trump made no such statement in Finland; as the *Post* will report in March 2019, Bolton appears to have lied to top national security officials when he told them in mid-2018 that Trump had assented to staying in Syria long-term and was not looking to withdraw troops from the war-torn country.[140] Moreover, "Trump never approved a strategy tying troop withdrawal [in Syria] to Iran's departure [from the country], according to several senior administration officials."[141]

The result of Bolton's deceit is twofold: it hides from both the Pentagon and the State Department for an additional five months that Trump's Syria policy is fully synchronous with the interests of Saudi Arabia, the UAE, and Russia, and it leaves the country's military and diplomatic infrastructure entirely unprepared for Trump's sudden announcement in December 2018 that he plans to immediately withdraw all U.S. forces from Syria. The latter event will lead to the resignation of Trump's secretary of defense, Jim Mattis, who writes to Trump in his resignation letter that although the United States "remains the indispensable nation in the free world, we cannot protect our interests or serve that role effectively without maintaining strong alliances and showing respect to those allies. . . . [W]e must be resolute and unambiguous in our approach to those countries whose strategic interests are increasingly in tension with ours. It is clear that China and Russia, for example, want to shape a world consistent with their authoritarian model—gaining veto authority over other nations' economic, diplomatic, and security decisions—to promote their own interests at the expense of their neighbors, America and our allies. That is why we must use all the tools of American power to provide for the common defense. My views on treating allies with respect and also being clear-eyed about both malign actors and strategic competitors are strongly held and informed by over four decades of immersion in these issues."[142] Mattis's implication is clear: Trump's Syria decision was made more to please the Kremlin and Trump's new allies in the Middle East than to serve America.

In May 2018, Cadre, a real estate company Jared Kushner co-founded and partly owns, seeks "an investment of at least $100 million from a private fund backed by Saudi Arabia and the United Arab Emirates."[143] The private fund, SoftBank Vision Fund, is a $100 billion operation, with approximately $65 billion of its value supplied by the Saudi and Emirati governments.[144] Kushner's stake in Cadre is valued between $25 million and $50 million, according to *Newsweek*.[145] The prospective investment comes less than eighteen months after Kushner Companies "took out four loans from Israel's largest bank, Bank Hapoalim," and not long after Kushner Companies "bought several floors of the former New York Times headquarters building in Manhattan from Lev Leviev, an Israeli businessman and philanthropist" who has also been, according to *Politico*, one of "Putin's closest confidantes" for at least two decades.[146]

In 2017, Trump's surprising firing of the U.S. attorney for the Southern District of New York, Preet Bharara, had paved the way for one of the companies Bharara was then investigating, Prevezon, to pay a fine to the U.S. government and avoid criminal prosecution. Prevezon was at the time represented by self-described Kremlin-linked "informant" Natalia Veselnitskaya—the Russian attorney who will later be revealed as one of the Kremlin agents who met with Donald Trump Jr., Jared Kushner, and Paul Manafort in Trump Tower in June 2016.[147] Prevezon's owner, Israeli citizen Denis Katsyv, is not only the son of a Russian government official but also business partners with Lev Leviev, whose apartments in New York, according to *Haaretz*, "were alleged to have served as a conduit for Prevezon's money laundering."[148] Trump's firing of Bharara thereby leads directly to the exculpation of the business partner of one of Jared Kushner's business associates, not long after Kushner is involved in a $295 million deal with him.[149] Leviev has been connected, too, to Vladimir Putin, especially through his 1999 initiative with Russian billionaire Roman Abramovich—executed at Putin's direct request—to set up a Federation of Jewish Communities in Russia; the head of that entity is now Rabbi Berel Lazar, the same Russian rabbi who attempted to serve as a conduit between Trump, Kushner, and the Kremlin during the 2016 presidential campaign (see chapter 4).[150]

In mid-2018, NBC News reports that Qatari officials have "gathered evidence that the United Arab Emirates has illicit influence over Jared Kushner . . . and other associates," specifically George Nader and Elliott Broidy, as well as substantial new information about "Jared Kushner's [personal financial] business with Emiratis"—but has decided not to share the information with federal investigators for fear it would "burn its own bridges" with Kushner or Trump, a dangerous prospect at a time the tiny nation is still under a blockade by Jared's and the president's top allies in the Middle East, MBS and MBZ.[151] NBC, noting that Trump's and Kushner's friend Tom Barrack has been "the middleman for the Qatari royal family for years," reports that the "dangerous" knowledge gained by the Qataris now constitutes "leverage" it can hold over the Trump administration—a revelation suggesting that the Qataris are now colluding with Trump and Kushner by withholding inculpatory evidence and using it instead for their own geopolitical benefit.[152] According to NBC, the evidence held by the Qataris includes details of previously unknown "secret meetings" involving "Kushner and other Trump associates" and the Emiratis.[153] Some of these meetings appear to have involved both George Nader and Elliott Broidy.[154] The Qataris' decision not to disclose what they have learned to federal law enforcement comes after they have had several "productive" meetings with "top advisers" to Trump.[155] These meetings follow the Qataris hiring not only lobbying firm Mercury Public Affairs—which worked with former Trump campaign manager Paul Manafort—but also Avenue Strategies

Global, the lobbying firm run by Trump's campaign manager before Paul Manafort, Corey Lewandowski.[156]

Prior to the July 16, 2018, Trump-Putin summit in Helsinki, administration officials tell the media that "Syria and Ukraine will be among the topics that Trump and Putin will discuss."[157] Following the event, however, U.S. reporters are not told what the two leaders discussed behind closed doors; Trump had insisted that no one accompany him and Putin into the meeting room besides Trump's interpreter (Marina Gross) and Putin's interpreter.[158] The two presidents meet for two hours—much longer than anticipated—and "several officials" will later say that "they were never able to get a reliable readout" of what happened in the meeting.[159] While Trump does not snatch away Gross's notes at the end of his conversation with Putin—something he had done with another interpreter after his first meeting with the Russian president, in Hamburg in 2017—the only readout given to the media by anyone in the Trump administration, the claim by John Bolton that Trump had stood up to Putin on Syria, will eventually be revealed as false.[160] The *Post* will write in 2019 that "it's still unclear what Trump actually told Putin" in Helsinki.[161] Summarizing Trump's many mysterious meetings with the Russian president, the *New York Times* will write, "The first time they met was in Germany. President Trump took his interpreter's notes afterward and ordered him not to disclose what he heard to anyone. Later that night, at a dinner, Mr. Trump pulled up a seat next to President Vladimir V. Putin to talk without any American witnesses at all. Their third encounter was in Vietnam, when Mr. Trump seemed to take Mr. Putin's word that he had not interfered in American elections. A formal summit meeting followed in Helsinki, Finland, where the two leaders kicked out everyone but the interpreters. Most recently, they chatted in Buenos Aires after Mr. Trump said they would not meet because of Russian aggression."[162] Natasha Bertrand of the *Atlantic* will note, moreover, that "Trump discussed 'adoptions'—sanctions policy—with Putin the night before dictating his son's 'adoptions' statement" [in July 2017], suggesting that Trump's conversation with Putin may have informed his decision to falsely cast his son's June 2016 meeting at Trump Tower with Kremlin agents as a benign conversation about adoptions.[163] More broadly, the *Washington Post* will observe that Trump has long, if often only behind the scenes, "instinctually oppose[d] many of the punitive measures pushed by his Cabinet that have crippled his ability to forge a close relationship with Russian President Vladimir Putin," in one instance shrieking profanities at his top advisers when he believed that they had led him to take a harsher stance on Russian sanctions than he had needed to take.[164]

July 2018 sees the Trump administration moving not only to further shore up its relationship with Moscow but also to mend the budding MESA alliance in the Middle East, whose success materially depends in equal measure on cooperation with—or at least significant allowances from—both the United States and Russia. According to U.S. and Arab officials who speak with Reuters, in July Trump is "quietly pushing ahead with a bid to create a new security and political alliance . . . to counter Iran's expansion in the region."[165] The Trump administration wants Jordan to be included in the alliance, an ambition inconsistent with the post-blockade plans of the Saudi Quartet but consistent with America's long-standing relationship with Jordan, which has been a "strong American ally for decades," according to the Wilson Center.[166] That the White House would be so directly involved in the complex and controversial machinations of Middle East logrolling is surprising, especially when doing so puts the administration in the position of being the central broker of a still-ideational Arab-state organization half a world away. According to Reuters, the White House asks the potential MESA countries to push forward on discussions of the alliance at an October 2018 summit in Washington, specifically asking for "deeper cooperation betwee   n the countries on missile defense, military training, counter-terrorism, and other issues such as strengthening regional economic and diplomatic ties."[167] The White House also reveals that the Saudis first raised the idea of the United States being closely linked to MESA when MBS and his father publicly rolled out the idea of such a regional alliance during Trump's 2017 visit to Riyadh.[168] According to administration officials, "the alliance would put emphasis on Gulf heavyweights Saudi Arabia and the United Arab Emirates working closer together with the Trump administration on confronting Iran," a description that positions MESA more as a formalization of the two Red Sea conspirators' interest in an alliance with Trump than their interest in a new affiliation with peer GCC members such as Kuwait and Oman.[169]

On July 25, 2018, the Trump administration releases to the Egyptian government $195 million in previously frozen military-assistance funds, despite el-Sisi having met none of the benchmarks previously established for the transmission of the money.[170] The benchmarks, which include a cessation of Egyptian aid to North Korea and other more esoteric markers, had been set by former secretary of state Rex Tillerson, who was unceremoniously let go by Trump after intense lobbying by MBS and MBZ through Elliott Broidy.[171] Tillerson's conditions for additional military aid to Egypt had widely been deemed substantially easier to meet than those the Obama administration had established in 2015.[172] Nevertheless, one of Tillerson's conditions—the defeat of a controversial new Egyptian law clamping down on nongovernmental organizations' ability to report human rights abuses to the international community—has by July 2018 not been met, with el-Sisi breaking "his [2017 Oval Office] commitment to President Trump not to pass the law."[173] *Foreign Policy* will note in August 2018 that despite el-Sisi's defiance of Trump, "the Trump administration seem[s] unwilling to hold Sisi accountable."[174] Indeed, the speculation at the time is that by the end of 2018 Trump will free up an additional $195 million in military aid to el-Sisi atop the $195 million he is about to deliver.[175]

In August 2018, the *Wall Street Journal* reports that the Department of Justice is investigating whether a fugitive Malaysian financier, Jho Low—onetime adviser to Malaysia's scandal-ridden 1Malaysia Development Berhad (1MDB), a government-run strategic development company—used tens of millions in laundered money to pay several Americans with close ties to Donald Trump for their legal and lobbying services, including long-time Trump attorney Marc Kasowitz; former New Jersey governor Chris Christie, onetime head of the Trump transition team; Bobby Burchfield, an outside ethics adviser for the Trump Organization; and Elliott Broidy, whom Trump had named deputy finance chair of the Republican National Committee shortly after his inauguration.[176] But the Low investigation has even closer ties to Trump's inner circle than this: in 2009, Low had purchased a Beverly Hills hotel, L'Ermitage, from Thomas Barrack; Low's interlocutors in the purchase were a group of Saudis and Emiratis that included Yousef al-Otaiba, the future Emirati ambassador to the United States and one of Jared Kushner's private Middle East advisers for much of the 2016 presidential campaign.[177]

In 2010, Low's purchase of Barrack's hotel for $44.8 million went through. Sixty days later, Barrack bought almost exactly the same amount of Jared Kushner's debt ($44.9 million) following "a conversation with his [Barrack's] good friend, Donald Trump."[178] The result of the two transactions, just twenty-four months before Trump decided to run for president in 2016—and at a time Trump was still considering entering the 2012 presidential race—will appear to be approximately $45 million in possibly laundered money moving from an international fugitive to Jared Kushner by August 2018, via the intermediary of a Trump friend and with Trump's advice, with the additional ancillary effect of making Kushner extremely indebted to both Barrack and al-Otaiba. That these two men would then become two of Kushner's closest confidants during the 2016 presidential campaign adds an additional troubling dimension to the story, as does the fact that the Kushner debt Barrack purchased was for Kushner's greatest professional failure and obsession: the property at 666 Fifth Avenue.[179]

After the L'Ermitage deal with Barrack, Low partners with a man described as Trump's other "best friend," Howard Lorber.[180] Together, Lorber and Low purchase New York City's Park Lane Hotel in 2013, using money that the DOJ will later say has been laundered. The purchase comes after Trump's decision to run for president, as well as after Low has bought Penthouse 52A at Trump International Hotel and Tower—an apartment previously owned by Trump himself.[181]

Malaysia's former prime minister, Najib Razak, is also implicated in Low's alleged money laundering scheme. Razak stands accused of diverting millions of dollars from SRC International, a subsidiary of 1MDB, to his personal bank accounts. In 2017, Trump adviser and RNC fundraiser Elliott Broidy orchestrated a visit by Razak to the White House; during his trip to the United States, Razak brought sixty guests with him—all of whom stayed at Trump's expensive Washington, D.C., hotel.[182]

As of 2019, Low is being "harbored" in China by the Chinese government, according to the *Wall Street Journal*; it is possible, therefore, that the Chinese are in possession of information—in the person of Low—that can incriminate Trump or one or more of his friends or associates, including Barrack, Broidy, Burchfield, Christie, Kasowitz, and Lorber.[183] The Justice Department is now investigating whether Low donated $100,000 in laundered money to the Broidy-run Trump Victory Committee that supported Trump's 2016 election and is now supporting his 2020 reelection.[184]

In September 2018, top MBS aide Saud al-Qahtani, who has remained in contact with *Washington Post* journalist Jamal Khashoggi for at least a year, calls Khashoggi to "promise[ ] him safety and the prospect of an important job working for [MBS] if [Khashoggi] return[s] home."[185] Khashoggi declines the offer.

Al-Qahtani, MBS's "media adviser" and "right-hand man," is the director of the Saudi royal court's media department, the Center for Studies and Media Affairs at the Royal Court (CSMARC), and in that role he is tasked with "spearhead[ing]" MBS's "zero-tolerance campaign against dissent" and "an effort to repatriate dissidents," according to the *Wall Street Journal*.[186] Al-Qahtani, whom MBS has given "extensive sway over domestic and foreign affairs" for the kingdom, makes Jamal Khashoggi "one of his first targets."[187] During one of his WhatsApp conversations with Khashoggi, al-Qahtani tells him that "the Crown Prince values your role as an editor. He wants you back in Saudi Arabia." Khashoggi's refusal to return to the kingdom leads to his son Salah being banned by MBS from leaving Saudi Arabia.[188]

In August and September 2018, al-Qahtani will, per the *Journal*, be "intimately involved in the kingdom's targeting of Mr. Khashoggi—from efforts to persuade him to return to Saudi Arabia from the U.S., to the planning and execution of the operation that ended with his death in the Saudi consulate in Istanbul on October 2."[189] Though MBS objects when his father, King Salman, fires al-Qahtani shortly after suspicion falls on the crown prince as the seeming mastermind of Khashoggi's fate in Istanbul, around the time of the attack MBS and al-Qahtani texted eleven times and, according to the *Journal*, "the consular official who scheduled [Khashoggi's] meeting [at the Saudi consulate in Istanbul] had been in touch with Mr. Qahtani."[190]

The *Wall Street Journal* calls al-Qahtani "a leading force behind some of [MBS's] most controversial decisions, including the rupture of ties with Qatar . . . [after which] he hunted online for Saudis who expressed sympathy for rival Qatar—asking [his] followers to tag them with a 'Black List' hashtag."[191] In response to queries about his movements and declarations, al-Qahtani once responded, "Do you think I make decisions without guidance? I am an employee and an executor of the orders of the king and the crown prince."[192]

Shortly after his September 2018 call with al-Qahtani, Khashoggi receives a call from MBS's brother, Prince Khaled bin Salman. Bin Salman, knowing Khashoggi is looking to retrieve documents that will allow him to get married, "[tells] Khashoggi he should go to the Saudi consulate in Istanbul to retrieve the documents and [gives] him assurances that it [will] be safe to do so."[193] Between late September and early October, al-Qahtani orders Saudi major general Ahmed al-Assiri, who had been involved in secret meetings with Trump's incoming national security advisor, Michael Flynn, the year before, to assemble a team of assassins to kill Khashoggi.[194]

Al-Assiri, "the deputy chief of Saudi Arabia's intelligence . . . had worked closely with Mr. Qahtani in a previous role as a spokesman for the Saudi-led military coalition fighting in Yemen."[195] Al-Assiri does what al-Qahtani asks him to do, drawing from "Prince Mohammed's top security units in the Royal Guard and in an organization run by Mr. Qahtani, the Center for Studies and Media Affairs at the Royal Court."[196] Five assassins are drawn from the military arm of the CSMARC, and the other ten are taken from MBS's Royal Guard.[197] In issuing his orders to Al-Assiri, reports the *Journal*, al-Qahtani "gave the impression that what he said was what MBS wanted."[198] Once al-Qahtani's team of killers is assembled, it travels from Riyadh to Istanbul on two Gulfstream jets operated by a company MBS owns.[199] Al-Qahtani personally approves the use of the jets.[200]

On October 2, lured by the assurance of safe passage by MBS's brother, Khashoggi visits the Saudi consulate in Istanbul.[201] The next day—while the journalist's whereabouts are unknown, but no foul play is suspected—Khashoggi's assistant submits his latest *Washington Post* column to the newspaper; the column is entitled, "What the Arab World Needs Most Is Free Expression."[202] In this final article of Khashoggi's life, which will be published fifteen days after his death, the *Post* columnist cites a Freedom House report that identifies only four Arab countries as either "free" or "partly free": Tunisia, Jordan, Morocco, and Kuwait. Saudi Arabia, the UAE, Egypt, and Bahrain do not make the list, and therefore are implicitly classified by Khashoggi as "not free." Khashoggi writes that in "not free" countries citizens "are either uninformed or misinformed. They are unable to adequately address, much less publicly discuss, matters that affect the region and their day-to-day lives. A state-run narrative dominates the public psyche."[203] Khashoggi goes on to specifically condemn the Saudi government for issuing to a Saudi writer friend of his "an unwarranted five-year prison sentence for supposed comments contrary to the Saudi establishment." He condemns el-Sisi's government in Egypt for the "seizure of the entire print run of a newspaper, *al-Masry al Youm*." And he condemns both these and the other governments of "not free" Arab nations for "aggressively block[ing] the Internet . . . arrest[ing] local reporters and pressur[ing] advertisers to harm the revenue of specific publications."[204] Perhaps most enraging to MBS and his Red Sea co-conspirators, Khashoggi holds up Qatar—which the Saudi Quartet has now been blockading for months, and to whom the quartet has issued demands about shutting down all of its media outlets—as an "oasis" of press freedom in which the government "continues to support international news coverage."[205] Khashoggi's final printed words in the *Washington Post* decry "nationalist [Arab] governments spreading hate through propaganda."[206]

On October 10, after Khashoggi has been reported missing and is believed dead, Jared Kushner and John Bolton talk to MBS by telephone. The White House does not reveal the content of the conversation.[207] The *Washington Post* later reports that during the call, MBS told Kushner and Bolton that Khashoggi was a "dangerous Islamist" and urged the two men "to preserve the U.S.-Saudi alliance" and not let the death of "a member of the Muslim Brotherhood"—a false claim spread by MBS on many occasions—to interfere with that relationship.[208]

Kushner and Bolton's subsequent refusal to disclose to U.S. media MBS's inculpatory statements—which appear to minimize or even excuse any harm done to Khashoggi, while simultaneously confirming that news is about to emerge regarding Khashoggi's disappearance that could harm the U.S.-Saudi relationship—aids and abets MBS's orchestration of Khashoggi's murder by keeping critical information about the murder from federal law enforcement, American voters, and the international community. Moreover, when Khashoggi is revealed to have died, the official Saudi response calling the journalist's death a "terrible mistake" and "terrible tragedy" would have been undercut by MBS's statements to Kushner and Bolton had they been widely known, further discrediting the Saudis' cover story that the kingdom bore no ill will toward Khashoggi.[209] The same can be said for MBS's subsequent public statement that "the incident that happened is very painful, for all Saudis," as by then MBS had privately told the Trump administration that he in fact believed Khashoggi to be a violent radical.[210] And the same would be true again for statements made publicly by MBS's brother, the man who lured Khashoggi to his death but posthumously called him a "friend" who had given "a great portion of his life to serv[ing] his country."[211]

Whether Kushner secretly has WhatsApp conversations with MBS between Khashoggi's disappearance on October 2 and the MBS-Kushner-Bolton call on October 10—or between October 10 and October 15, when important new details in the Khashoggi case emerge—is unknown, though the *New York Times* will suggest that during this period "Kushner and [MBS] . . . continue[ ] to chat informally," the *Daily Beast* will write that "their first-name-basis exchanges continued after October 2," and the *Washington Post* will note of their communications during this time frame that "Kushner and [MBS] have had private, one-on-one phone calls that were not always set up through normal channels so the conversations could be memorialized."[212] Even the Saudis will admit that, as to private communications between Kushner and MBS, "routine calls do exist from time to time."[213]

In November, however, any confusion on this key point ends, as the *Washington Post* reports that several "people familiar with the matter" say Kushner and MBS spoke "multiple times" between October 2 and October 9.[214] The sources will refuse to say "how many phone calls the crown prince and Kushner have had since Khashoggi's disappearance" beyond saying there was more than one.[215] The *Post* will further report that in the days immediately after Khashoggi's October 2 disappearance, MBS was expressing to many of those he spoke to that he was "puzzled by the high level of concern about Khashoggi" because "he considered [him] part of the Muslim Brotherhood as well as an agent of Qatar."[216] It is unknown whether MBS references Qatar in his private conversations with Kushner during this period, though Trump's son-in-law had repeatedly expressed his support for MBS's blockade against that country, and Trump himself had falsely and publicly attacked Qatar, following the initiation of the Saudi-led blockade, as a state sponsor of terrorism.[217]

On October 11, the day after Kushner and Bolton speak to MBS by phone, a Saudi chemist, Ahmed Abdulaziz Aljanobi, and a toxicologist, Khaled Yahya Al Zharani, arrive in Istanbul to, per *Sabah*, a Turkish daily newspaper, "clean up any leftover evidence" from the Khashoggi murder scene.[218] The Saudis will not allow Turkish investigators into their consulate in Istanbul until October 14.[219]

In early October 2018, Erik Prince is in Afghanistan, pushing his proposal to privatize the war there with the Afghan government. According to the *Washington Post*, the Afghans believe Prince "has the ear—and the potential backing [for a privatization plan]—of the U.S. president."[220] The *Post* adds that "Prince has a willing audience in President Trump, who is known to be frustrated with the cost and slow progress of the [Afghan war] strategy he adopted a year ago."[221]

Meanwhile, in Riyadh, MBS and the Saudi government issue numerous misstatements to the press and others about *Post* journalist Jamal Khashoggi. On October 2, Saudi consulate officials falsely tell Khashoggi's fiancée, when she inquires about his whereabouts after he's been inside the consulate for two hours, that Khashoggi "had already left the building through a backdoor." On October 5, MBS tells Bloomberg News that his understanding is that Khashoggi left the consulate safe and healthy after "a few minutes or one hour." On October 6, Saudi officials open the consulate to the press to "prove" that Khashoggi is not in the building, but do not allow any forensic examination of the property. On October 8, MBS's brother Prince Khalid bin Salman tells Axios that allegations that Khashoggi is missing, detained, or dead are "absolutely false and baseless." On October 10, a Saudi government-owned media outlet calls pictures of an "assassination squad" entering the Saudi consulate on October 2 "misreported news" that is the product of "dubious sources and orchestrated media campaigns." And on October 11, Al Arabiya, a Saudi news outlet, calls the members of al-Qahtani's assassination squad "tourists."[222] As late as October 15—when Trump seems to still credit King Salman's denial of any knowledge of Khashoggi's fate—the Saudis are floating a narrative that "the crown prince approved an interrogation or rendition of Khashoggi back to Saudi Arabia, but the intelligence official [tasked with the job] was incompetent and eagerly sought to prove himself. He then tried to cover up the botched handling of the situation."[223]

Soon, however, major-media reports emerge offering excruciating details as to what actually happened to Khashoggi inside the Saudi consulate—and, critically, who knew about the plan to kill the *Washington Post* journalist beforehand.

(Trigger warning: This section includes descriptions of extreme violence taken from reports by U.S. and Turkish law enforcement.)

By mid-October, the Saudis' lies about Khashoggi's death have unraveled.

The narrative that is ultimately supported by the evidence begins with Khashoggi realizing that something is wrong shortly after entering the Saudi consulate in Istanbul on October 2 to get a marriage license. He is escorted to the consul general's office. The *Washington Post* journalist's sense of wrongness is triggered by seeing there Maher Abdulaziz Mutreb, a "former Saudi diplomat and intelligence official" known to be a "close associate" of MBS who "has often been seen at the crown prince's side," according to Reuters. When Khashoggi asks his escort why Mutreb is there, he is told, "You are coming back [to Saudi Arabia]."[224]

"You can't do that," Khashoggi replies. "People are waiting outside for me."[225]

According to an audiotape of the exchange and a United Nations investigation of the incident, the conversation ends shortly thereafter—after a brief exchange about Khashoggi texting his son—as Khashoggi is grabbed by a group of men and "dragged from the consul-general's office . . . and onto the table of his study next door," at which point "horrendous screams [are] . . . heard by a witness downstairs" at the consulate.[226] The audiotape of the incident recovered from the consulate at this point attributes both "screaming" and "gasping" to Khashoggi.[227] The consul, Mohammed al-Otaibi, vacates his study while one member of the large group of men holding Khashoggi down "injects" the journalist with a "substance" now believed to be a sedative.[228] According to a Turkish source spoken to by the *Middle East Eye*, the London-based Middle East watchdog run by a former *Guardian* editor, "There [is] no attempt to interrogate [Khashoggi].

They had come to kill him."[229] Khashoggi's last recorded words are, "I can't breathe! I can't breathe!"[230]

One of Khashoggi's attackers, according to the *Washington Post*, is Khalid Aedh Alotaibi, a member of the Saudi Royal Guard who had "made several visits to the United States that overlapped or coincided with trips by senior Saudi officials. Earlier [in 2018] . . . , he arrived in the United States three days before Mohammed [MBS] touched down for a nationwide tour"—during which tour MBS met with Trump in the White House.[231] Two other members of the team are among "the crown prince's personal bodyguards."[232]

Also among the fifteen Saudi attackers is Salah Muhammad al-Tubaigy, the head of forensic evidence in the Saudi general security department, as well as president of the Saudi Fellowship of Forensic Pathology and a member of the Saudi Association for Forensic Pathology. Al-Tubaigy had arrived in Istanbul with the fourteen other Saudi agents on a private jet earlier that day.

According to Turkish investigators' account of events, after Khashoggi's last recorded words, "Tubaigy began to cut Khashoggi's body up on a table in the study while he was still alive," a process that required a bone saw and "took seven minutes."[233] According to the audiotape, sounds of a "saw" and "cutting" can be heard at this point.[234] Per the investigators, "As he started to dismember the body, Tubaigy put on earphones and listened to music. He advised other members of the squad to do the same."[235] An audiotape from inside the consulate records al-Tubaigy saying to his co-conspirators, "When I do this job, I listen to music. You should do [that] too. Put your earphones in, and listen to music like me."[236] Once he has put his earphones in, al-Tubaigy uses his bone saw to cut off Khashoggi's fingers.[237] Al-Tubaigy then dismembers Khashoggi; according to the *New York Times*, it is not clear from the audiotape later acquired by Turkish authorities for how long Khashoggi is alive while he is being dismembered.[238] Al-Tubaigy thereafter beheads Khashoggi and throws his limbs into a vat of acid.[239]

Early on in the attack, Consul al-Otaibi briefly objects to the agents' actions—but only on the basis of their venue. "Do this outside," he tells them. "You will put me in trouble."[240] One of the agents replies, "If you want to live when you come back to Arabia, shut up."[241]

After Khashoggi has been executed, Mutreb calls MBS's aide, Saud al-Qahtani, telling al-Qahtani that he should "tell [his] boss" that Khashoggi is dead and that "the thing is done."[242] Around the time al-Qahtani receives this message from Khashoggi's killers, he "and the crown prince exchange[ ] numerous texts," according to the *Washington Post*.[243] Al-Qahtani, who has over a million followers on Twitter, is known as "Lord of the Flies" in Saudi Arabia because he has an online army of "electronic flies" who track, harass, and undermine critics of MBS at al-Qahtani's invitation and direction."[244]

As al-Tubaigy is decapitating and dismembering Khashoggi, one of MBS's assassins, Mustafa al-Madani, puts on the dead man's clothes, along with glasses and a fake beard, and leaves the Saudi consulate by a route he knows will be tracked by video cameras, intending to create a trail of evidence suggesting that Khashoggi has left the building alive.[245] Other Turkish video surveillance units will capture additional members of MBS's assassination squad leaving the consulate with "syringes, electro-shock devices, and a blade similar to a scalpel," according to the *Independent*.[246]

As Khashoggi's doppelganger walks the streets of Istanbul, where he can be tracked by Turkish surveillance stations, Khashoggi's body is removed to the home of the consul, al-Otaibi, where Turkish investigators will later find forensic evidence suggesting that the journalist's remains were injected with a liquid to clot the dead man's blood. The purpose of the injection, investigators say, is to reduce the production of trace evidence during dismemberment. After this, the assassins use chemicals to further dissolve Khashoggi's body; they incinerate what remains in an outdoor oven.[247] It takes MBS's agents three days to burn the body, after which "large quantities of barbeque meat [are] grilled in the oven . . . in order to cover up the cremation."[248]

As information about the gruesome nature of Khashoggi's murder is becoming public—a period of time during which Kushner and MBS are conversing via WhatsApp—Saudi officials falsely claim Khashoggi "left the consulate soon after arriving" and that "video cameras at the consulate were not recording at the time."[249] In the United States, both Trump and his new secretary of state, Mike Pompeo, come out "in support of Saudi officials' denials they know anything about what happened to Khashoggi."[250] Trump tweets that, after speaking to MBS, he can report that the Saudi crown prince "totally denied any knowledge of what took place."[251] Trump adds that "Saudi Arabia has been a great ally to me," even as he asserts, falsely, that he has no financial interests involving the kingdom.[252] The *Hill* immediately criticizes Trump for his deception, noting that "the president, a longtime business mogul, has long-standing and close business ties to the Saudis, with Saudi businessmen spending significant amounts of money at his hotels and properties over decades. One Saudi royal billionaire, Prince Alwaleed bin Talal, purchased Trump's yacht and a stake in New York's Plaza Hotel in the 1990s when Trump was in financial distress."[253]

On October 18, a member of the fifteen-man assassination squad sent by MBS to murder Khashoggi, Mashal Saad al-Bostani—a Saudi Royal Air Force lieutenant—dies in what Turkish newspaper *Yeni Safak* (and a re-reporting in Israel's *Haaretz*) call a "suspicious car accident" in Riyadh.[254]

On October 30, at a time when Robert Mueller's office is likely compiling information about Khashoggi's murder for the counterintelligence component of its investigation, Jacob Wohl, son of Trump surrogate David Wohl, is referred to the FBI by the special counsel's office for possible criminal prosecution. Wohl and another man, Jack Burkman, have allegedly perpetuated a hoax by falsely accusing Robert Mueller of rape.[255]

In an effort to stem criticism of Saudi Arabia's handling of the Khashoggi investigation, Trump issues a statement on October 16, 2018, about the apparent homicide of the *Washington Post* journalist. The statement references Trump's May 2017 arms deal with King Salman and MBS, noting that the Saudis are "investing tremendous amounts of money" in the United States.[256] He adds that Saudi Arabia's support "against Iran" is critical to his foreign policy.[257]

In response to calls for Trump to terminate the 2017 Saudi arms deal as punishment for the Saudis' murder of Khashoggi, Trump tells Fox Business Network, "Aren't we just hurting our own country? Because here's what's going to happen—[they'll] buy [arms] from China, buy them from

Russia. We're not really hurting them, we're hurting ourselves. I don't want to give up a $110 billion order."[258] In fact, just five months earlier U.S. officials had conceded, in response to media inquiries, that "most of the [Trump-Saudi arms] deals have not progressed since Trump's visit [to Riyadh in May 2017]."[259] Moreover, it will be revealed just days after Trump's statement about the Saudis' "$110 billion order" that Trump has significantly inflated the effect of the deal on the U.S. economy, with new U.S. arms sales to Saudi Arabia—should they ever happen—accounting for "fewer than 20,000 U.S. jobs a year" according to the *Guardian*, which is "less than a twentieth of the employment boost Donald Trump has claimed."[260] Noting that the actual value of U.S.-Saudi arms sales to the United States since Trump took office and through 2018 is $14.5 billion—rather than the $110 billion promised by the Saudis in the first stage of their ten-year, $350 billion deal with Trump—a report from the Center for International Policy will declare, as the *Guardian* summarizes, that "Saudi Arabia needs the United States far more than the other way around, and the administration is underplaying its hand" in refusing to "rein in Riyadh in Yemen or punish the [Saudi] monarchy for Khashoggi's murder at the Saudi consulate in Istanbul."[261] The center notes that even the $14.5 billion figure for U.S.-Saudi arms sales—just 13 percent of the value Trump has publicly claimed—represents not "actual signed contracts" but "letters of offer and acceptance," and that in fact Trump is not responsible for even a dollar of the arms sales currently "in the pipeline," as all of them pre-date his presidency.[262] Under the most "generous" possible approach to the numbers, the center writes—including even jobs indirectly related to U.S.-Saudi arms deals—"annual arms deliveries to Saudi Arabia would create 17,500 jobs in any given year," or "a tiny fraction of 1 percent" of the U.S. workforce.[263] The center concludes by noting that even Trump's expressed fear that Saudi Arabia could take its business to Russia or China is false, as "it would take decades for the Kingdom to wean itself from dependence on U.S. equipment, training and support, and [any] new equipment might not be easily interoperable with U.S.-supplied systems."[264]

In late November 2018, ABC News will report that Trump's "$110 billion" figure for the U.S.-Saudi arms deal was not just false but deliberately so: it "was inflated at the direction of Trump's son-in-law and adviser Jared Kushner, according to two U.S. officials and three former White House officials."[265] Per ABC, "Kushner, in a bid to symbolically solidify the new alliance between the Trump administration and Saudi Arabia while claiming a victory on the president's first foreign trip to Riyadh, pushed State and Defense officials to inflate the figure with arms exchanges that were aspirational at best."[266] The State Department and Defense Department had told Kushner that they realistically had only $15 billion in deals they could possibly do with the Saudis—less than 14 percent of the first-stage figure ($110 billion) and approximately 4 percent of the ten-year figure ($350 billion) Trump and Kushner announced to the nation and the world in May 2017 in Riyadh.[267] Trump thereafter cited these inflated figures repeatedly in explaining the necessity of not upsetting the Saudis over any current or future investigation into Jamal Khashoggi's assassination. Trump will similarly exaggerate the number of jobs reasonably attributable to the Saudi arms deal, over time inflating the most generous figure (17,500) to 40,000, then 450,000, then 500,000, then 600,000, and finally "[a] million jobs," according to Daniel Dale of the *Toronto Star*.[268]

In the two weeks after Khashoggi's murder, Turkish law enforcement agents search the Saudi consul general's home multiple times, as well as some of the country's diplomatic vehicles. According to the Associated Press, surveillance videos in the Turkish capital show Saudi diplomatic vehicles traveling to the consul general's residence not long after Khashoggi enters the Saudi consulate in Istanbul.[269] While the Turks also express publicly and privately a desire to search the Saudi consulate itself, the kingdom refuses Turkish investigators access to the building until October 14, twelve days after Khashoggi was last sighted there.[270] Even then, it takes a phone call between President Erdogan and King Salman for Saudi officials to permit Turkish investigators to inspect the consulate's surveillance cameras; many areas of the consulate will remain inaccessible to the Turks by decree of the Saudi king.[271]

Early in the day on October 14, state-linked Saudi media responds to

Trump's implication that Saudi Arabia could face punishment if its government is found to be involved in Khashoggi's death by threatening the United States with the withholding of oil imports.[272] Within a day, Trump has publicly floated a new theory of the Khashoggi case, saying, following his October 15 phone call with King Salman, that "rogue killers" could have been responsible for Khashoggi's death, and noting that "we're going to try getting to the bottom of it very soon"—even though he has mobilized no federal law enforcement resources to do so.[273] Trump repeats Salman's "flat denial" that either he or his son had any knowledge of Khashoggi's death, even as he implies that his "rogue killer" theory was taken from Saudi talking points, remarking shortly after speaking to King Salman that "it sounded to [him]" like the "rogue killer" theory of the Khashoggi case might turn out to be correct.[274]

Early the next morning, on October 16, Trump unexpectedly tweets the following to his tens of millions of Twitter followers: "For the record, I have no financial interests in Saudi Arabia (or Russia, for that matter). Any suggestion that I have is just more FAKE NEWS (of which there is plenty)!"[275] Less than a week earlier, the Trump Organization had released a statement to the press conceding that it had, as previously noted in the Washington Post, "pursued new hotel deals in Saudi Arabia in the past."[276]

Later in the day on October 16, a Turkish official tells the Associated Press that the Turkish government has found "certain evidence" in Saudi Arabia's Istanbul consulate that Khashoggi was murdered there.[277] President Erdogan also reveals to journalists that parts of the Saudi consulate have been recently painted over.[278] President Trump's Twitter response to the news ignores the finding by Turkish officials, noting instead that MBS "told me that he has already started, and will rapidly expand, a full and complete investigation into this matter. Answers will be forthcoming shortly."[279] Trump thereafter tells the Associated Press, in response to the new evidence discovered by Turkish investigators, "Here we go again with 'you're guilty until proven innocent.'"[280]

The next morning, a New York Times investigation reveals that "at least four of the suspects whom Turkish officials have said played a role in

Mr. Khashoggi's disappearance or death have close ties to Crown Prince Mohammed, having traveled with him as members of his security team."[281] The *Times* further discloses that nine of the fifteen men involved in Khashoggi's killing "worked for the Saudi government, military or security services."[282] In response to these reports, Secretary Pompeo "expresse[s] confidence in the promise of the king [King Salman] and crown prince [MBS] to investigate" Khashoggi's death.[283] For his part, Trump will respond by repeating that Saudi Arabia has put in a very large arms order with the United States as a result of his efforts.[284]

By October 17, major-media reports in the United States are accusing Trump and his administration of working with MBS to ensure that the crown prince faces no consequences for Khashoggi's murder, with the *Washington Post* reporting that "the Trump administration and the Saudi royal family are searching for a mutually agreeable explanation for the death of journalist Jamal Khashoggi—one that will avoid implicating Crown Prince Mohammed bin Salman."[285] As Trump and his team hunt for an exit for the administration's top Saudi ally, the *Post* notes that "even one of the president's closest advisers, Rudolph W. Giuliani, said many senior members of the administration concluded more than a week ago that the Saudis had killed Khashoggi," adding that "analysts and officials" had deduced that it was "inconceivable that such a brazen operation . . . could have been pulled off" without coordination with the Saudi government.[286] Giuliani proposes that the only question left is whether it was MBS or a group of his allies who ordered the assassination.[287] Even this, however, is little in doubt by October 17, given the presence of Saudi Arabian Royal Guards among Khashoggi's attackers. As Bruce Reidel, described by the *Washington Post* as "a senior fellow at the Brookings Institution and an expert on Saudi Arabia and the royal family who served more than 30 years in the CIA," tells the *Post*, "As much as the White House is eager to absolve MBS, the rogue [actor] coverup is unraveling before it's even official"; the *Post* bolsters Reidel's analysis by observing that "Mohammed is not considered to be the kind of leader to condone operatives acting outside the chain of command."[288]

Trump dispatches Mike Pompeo overseas, but not to Istanbul—rather, to Riyadh, where the secretary of state meets with King Salman and MBS to discuss "the fate of the journalist [Khashoggi] who wrote critically about the Saudis for the *Washington Post*."[289] The Associated Press describes the meeting between Pompeo, Salman, and MBS as "all smiles and handshakes," even as members of Trump's own party have begun to publicly question the Saudis' denials of complicity in Khashoggi's death.[290] "This guy [MBS] has got to go," says one of Trump's closest allies in the Senate, South Carolina Republican Lindsey Graham. Echoing Trump's now-infamous "Russia, if you're listening . . ." line, Sen. Graham says during an interview on Fox News, "Saudi Arabia, if you're listening, there are a lot of good people you can choose, but MBS has tainted your country and tainted himself."[291] Meanwhile, Trump's attorney general, Jeff Sessions, won't commit DOJ resources to the effort to identify and bring to justice Khashoggi's killers, though he says the possibility of one day doing so is being given "serious evaluation." Sessions offers no criticism of the Saudi investigation, which has publicly called the allegations of Saudi involvement in the journalist's death "baseless" while privately saying, according to the Associated Press, that "the kingdom may acknowledge the writer was killed at the consulate, perhaps as part of a botched interrogation."[292]

The same day Pompeo meets with King Salman and MBS, the United Nations human rights chief, Michelle Bachelet, calls for Saudi Arabia to waive the diplomatic immunity given to consular officials under the 1963 Vienna Convention on Consular Relations; it is this immunity protecting Saudi Arabia's consul general, Mohammed al-Otaibi, from any potential repercussions from Turkish law enforcement.[293] Within a matter of hours of Bachelet's statement, al-Otaibi has left Turkey—without his government either acknowledging his departure from the country or offering any reason for it.[294]

While in Riyadh, Secretary Pompeo assures journalists that the royal family has made a "serious commitment" to holding any involved officials accountable, and parrots MBS's denial that he had any knowledge of Khashoggi's fate.[295] What he does not say is that within hours of him landing in Riyadh, "a previously promised $100 million land[s] in American bank accounts from Saudi Arabia"—money that, as the *New York Times* reports, the Saudis had promised Trump for Syrian reconstruction many months earlier but had never paid.[296] The *Times* writes that the $100 million is "a win for President Trump," even as an American official involved in Syria policy says the timing of the payment "is no coincidence."[297] The *Times* also reports that Saudi Arabia is "planning to blame the killing on rogue elements who did not act on official orders—a scenario that could . . . protect[ ] [Saudi] leaders from culpability. An endorsement of that conclusion by the Trump administration," notes the *Times*, "could help limit damage to Saudi Arabia's international reputation."[298] Consistent with the *Times* reporting, the same day the Trump administration gets the Saudis' long-overdue $100 million payment for Syrian reconstruction efforts, Trump speaks by telephone with MBS, and then uses "his strongest language to date" in defending the crown prince to the Associated Press.[299] He thereafter tweets that "the Crown Prince of Saudi Arabia . . . [has] totally denied any knowledge of what took place in their Turkish Consulate."[300]

The Trump administration, seeking to quell outrage over the kidnapping and execution of a U.S. resident, lights upon a strategy that would, in effect, ease the pressure on MBS by replicating the Saudi crown prince's crime: Trump tries to find a way to offer Pittsburgh resident Fethullah Gulen to the Turks for extradition and execution in exchange for the Turkish government letting MBS off the hook for Khashoggi's murder. Per NBC News, "Trump administration officials . . . asked federal law enforcement agencies to examine legal ways of removing exiled Turkish cleric Fethullah Gulen in an attempt to persuade Erdogan to ease pressure on the Saudi government."[301] The request makes federal law enforcement "furious," according to NBC.[302] The news outlet notes that "the secret effort to resolve one of the leading tensions in U.S.-Turkey relations—Gulen's residency in the U.S.—provides a window into how President Donald Trump is trying to navigate hostility between two key allies after Saudi officials murdered Khashoggi on Oct. 2 . . . [while] preserving Trump's close alliance with Saudi Arabia's controversial de facto leader, Crown Prince

Mohammed bin Salman."[303] NBC reports that it was shortly after Pompeo briefed Trump on his discussions with Erdogan and MBS that the administration reached out to law enforcement and "sent word to Erdogan that [U.S.] officials would re-examine the Gulen issue."[304] The "Gulen issue" had previously been reviewed by federal law enforcement in the summer of 2016, however—in fact, at the request of Michael Flynn, who was at the time both advising candidate Trump on national security matters and secretly a Turkish agent—and it found no evidence admissible in a U.S. court to establish that Gulen had committed acts that would be considered criminal in the United States.[305]

On October 20, Saudi Arabia confesses that Khashoggi was killed in its consulate in Istanbul, though it says his death occurred after a "fight broke out with the people he met there," calling it a "fistfight" and implying that Khashoggi could have been partially responsible for his own demise.[306] Trump declares that the explanation is credible.[307]

The *Washington Post*, Khashoggi's employer, responds immediately to the Saudis' new narrative with a statement that reads, in part, "The government of Saudi Arabia has shamefully and repeatedly offered one lie after another in the nearly three weeks since Jamal Khashoggi disappeared in their Istanbul consulate. Offering no proof, and contrary to all available evidence, they now expect the world to believe that Jamal died in a fight following a discussion. This is not an explanation; it is a coverup. President Trump, Congress, and leaders of the civilized world should demand to see verifiable evidence. The Saudis cannot be allowed to fabricate a face-saving solution to an atrocity that appears to have been directed by the highest levels of their government."[308]

On October 22, Kushner tells the media that the White House is still in the "fact-finding phase" with respect to Khashoggi's death, even as Trump tries to downplay Kushner's relationship with MBS: "They're two young guys. Jared doesn't know him well or anything. They are just two young people. They are the same age. They like each other, I believe," Trump says.[309] On October 23, MBS demands that Khashoggi's son appear before him so that the two can be photographed shaking hands.[310] The same day, Erdogan declares in a televised speech that Khashoggi's death was a "ferocious" and "brutal" pre-planned murder—an allegation the audiotape of the event will subsequently confirm.[311] Forty-eight hours after Erdogan's declaration, Saudi prosecutors announce their agreement with Erdogan on the cause of Khashoggi's death, agreeing that it was a premeditated murder, though the prosecutors do not concede that MBS had any involvement in it.[312]

MBS soon thereafter receives a full-throated public defense from both a member of the Red Sea Conspiracy and an affiliate of the conspiracy: per the *Washington Post*, "Egyptian President Abdel Fatah el-Sisi and Israeli Prime Minister Benjamin Netanyahu reach[ ] out to the Trump administration to express support for the crown prince, arguing that he is an important strategic partner in the region. . . . Israel, Egypt and the United Arab Emirates have united behind the Trump administration's efforts to bring pressure on Iran."[313] Meanwhile, America's long-standing allies in NATO, particularly Germany, Britain, and France, "voice[ ] serious concern about what happened to Khashoggi."[314]

From the moment Khashoggi's disappearance—then his death—becomes an international issue, "Kushner and the prince [keep] calling and texting one another," according to the *Daily Beast*, which notes that these regular communications between the president's son-in-law and the architect of the *Washington Post* journalist's assassination are "first-name-basis exchanges."[315] The *New York Times* notes that such "private, informal conversations" have been occurring "since the early months of the Trump administration."[316] Even after the White House chief of staff mandated that "National Security Council staff members should participate in all calls with foreign leaders," Kushner ignored the directive, the *Times* reports, and "kept chatting" with MBS in "text messages and phone calls."[317]

By mid-November, the CIA has "concluded that Saudi Crown Prince Mohammed bin Salman personally ordered the killing of journalist Jamal Khashoggi," per CNN.[318] Kushner quickly becomes "the prince's most important defender inside the White House," reports the *New York Times*, citing sources familiar with internal White House discussions.[319] The CIA gives a briefing to the Senate on the evidence it has uncovered. Afterward Trump's close ally in the Senate, Lindsey Graham, comments that he entered the briefing believing MBS responsible for Khashoggi's murder, and "left the briefing with high confidence that my initial confidence [was] correct."[320] "There's not a smoking gun," says Graham, "there's a smoking saw."[321]

The Trump administration sanctions seventeen Saudis "for their role in Khashoggi's killing" and revokes the travel visas of twenty-one people in total, but it does not sanction MBS.[322] The Saudis continue to insist MBS "knew nothing of the operation," even as its prosecutors seek the death penalty for five men connected to the crown prince.[323] That the killers of an American resident had travel visas to the United States, and in some cases had previously traveled to America alongside MBS—the man the CIA had determined was responsible for the *Washington Post* journalist's death—will only serve to underscore Trump's January 2017 decision to exempt Saudi Arabia from his purportedly counterterrorism-oriented travel ban, despite the long association of radicalized kingdom citizens with terrorist attacks against American residents.

On November 20, Trump issues an unusual written statement entitled "On Standing with Saudi Arabia." As summarized by *Just Security*, a website run by longtime national security professionals, the themes of the statement are as follows: "The world, and most of its inhabitants, pose an unrelenting threat to Americans, and we are right to be afraid; America derives no benefit from, and has no claim to, a national calling or sense of higher purpose; authoritarian and repressive rulers are America's natural partners, while democratically elected foreign leaders and most of this country's intelligence and law enforcement apparatus are, in their affinity for rule of law, inherently hostile and untrustworthy; and effective statecraft rests upon the pillars of short-term transactionalism, economic mercantilism, and raw coercion."[324] Arguing that the tenets itemized in Trump's statement comprise the "Trump Doctrine," the *Just Security* analysis at first seems unduly contrary. The document it describes, however, indeed conforms to the website's depiction, as Trump's statement begins with "The world is a dangerous place!" and includes such observations as Trump's view that "we may *never* know all of the facts surrounding the murder of Mr. Jamal Khashoggi" but cannot take any action in response to the murder because "in any case, our relationship is with the Kingdom of Saudi Arabia."[325] At another point in the statement, Trump equates the "security and safety of America" with "keeping oil prices at reasonable levels."[326] In all, the official White House statement includes eight exclamation points, a casual reference to the possibility Khashoggi was "an enemy of the state [Saudi Arabia] and a member of the Muslim Brotherhood"—though neither allegation is true—and a conclusion regarding MBS's advance knowledge of the plan to execute Khashoggi that reads, "Maybe he did [know] and maybe he didn't!"[327]

The editorial board of the *Wall Street Journal* will respond to the statement with these words: "We are aware of no President, not even such ruthless pragmatists as Richard Nixon or Lyndon Johnson, who would have written a public statement like this without so much as a grace note about America's abiding values and principles."[328] The board adds that it is "startling to see a U.S. President brag in a statement about a bloodthirsty murder" that he has cut some excellent business deals with the person accused of orchestrating that murder.[329] *Just Security* provides a detailed legal analysis of Trump's statement that concludes that it functions, also, as a statement of the administration's intent to violate the reporting clause of the Global Magnitsky Human Rights Accountability Act of 2016.[330] The analysis by *Just Security* is prescient, as the administration does indeed ignore the Magnitsky Act, producing no written report on MBS's potential human rights violations for Congress as required by law.[331]

Two weeks after the CIA concludes that MBS is responsible for Jamal Khashoggi's assassination, "Trump, MBS, and Ivanka Trump [are] spotted giving each other a warm greeting on the sidelines of the G20 summit in Buenos Aires."[332]

An additional controversy surrounding the Khashoggi assassination arises when the administration prevents CIA director Gina Haspel—who has both heard the audiotape from inside the Saudi consulate in Istanbul and may have seen, too, the text messages between al-Qahtani and MBS—from briefing Congress on the Khashoggi investigation, though her doing so would be customary.[333] Sen. Bob Corker (R-TN) tells the *Washington Post* that he suspects the White House has "clamped down" on intelligence-sharing with Congress—even with him, the chairman of the Senate Foreign Relations Committee—because "the intel is not painting a pretty picture as it relates to Saudi Arabia."[334] In the midst of this White House intransigence, Kirsten Fontenrose, a "top White House official responsible for American policy toward Saudi Arabia," resigns.[335] Her resignation, according to the *Times*, suggests "fractures inside the Trump administration over the response to the brutal killing" of Khashoggi, with Fontenrose having unsuccessfully "pushed for tough measures against the Saudi government," including sanctions.[336]

In late November 2018, the *Guardian* and other media outlets will link the White House's insistence that Haspel not provide the information she has to Congress to the administration's concern that her doing so could lead to a change in U.S. policy in Yemen. As the British media outlet writes, "Trump's faith in the crown prince is treated with profound scepticism by many senators who expected to hear first-hand from Haspel on Wednesday on a brutal killing that appears to have helped sway several senators against continuing military support to Riyadh for the war in Yemen."[337] According to a Senate staffer, the White House's blocking of Haspel's briefing to Congress "is totally unprecedented and should be interpreted as nothing less than the Trump administration trying to silence the intelligence community."[338] Unlike Haspel, neither Bolton—whom Trump sends to brief Congress—nor Trump himself has heard the audiotape of Khashoggi's murder, both of them having publicly refused to do so.[339] Trump tells Fox News that he "doesn't want to hear the tape" because it's a "terrible tape"; in the same interview, he says that MBS "told me he had nothing to do with it . . . will anybody really [ever] know?"[340] According to Turkish president Recep Erdogan, the recording is so brutally horrific that when he plays it for a Saudi intelligence official, the official is so "shocked" he tells Erdogan that the killers "must have done heroin. Only someone who did heroin could have done this."[341]

In mid-December, the United States Senate passes a unanimous resolution that declares MBS "complicit" in Khashoggi's death. It then passes, by a bipartisan vote of 56 to 41, a second resolution calling for an end to U.S. military assistance for the Saudi war in Yemen. The former resolution is immediately decried by MBS's government as "interference in the kingdom's affairs."[342] The *Washington Post* calls the two measures "an unambiguous rejection of Trump's continued defense of Saudi leaders."[343] Khashoggi's murder is clearly a turning point in the Senate's view of the Saudi-Yemeni war, as an earlier, 2018 resolution on ending U.S. support for the war had failed 55–44.[344] As for the House of Representatives, it will not hold a vote to end U.S. support for the war in Yemen until after the Democrats take control of Congress's lower chamber in November 2018; in February 2019, a House resolution similar to the Senate's passes 248–177.[345]

On December 3, Mohammed Dahlan—the former Palestinian Authority security chief and current Emirati adviser and assassination-squad supervisor—angrily responds to a *Yeni Safak* report that claims MBS intended to pin Khashoggi's murder on him. Dahlan accuses the Turkish media outlet of directing "fake news" at MBS, MBZ, and el-Sisi, adding that "these leaders [will] stay in power for five decades"; it is unclear why he singles out the Red Sea Conspiracy's ringleaders.[346] "Rumors [are being] circulated by the Turkish media to sabotage Egypt and Saudi Arabia," Dahlan says to a reporter for *Al Arabiya*, a Saudi television news channel. "Brace yourselves . . . [MBS] will remain in power for the next fifty years unless we witness a divine intervention"—a supernatural event Dahlan makes clear he has no wish to see.[347] Dahlan's statement about MBS having a fifty-year reign is actually an established Emirati rallying cry; notably, the *New Yorker* quotes the Emirati ambassador to the United States, Jared Kushner's pre-election Middle East adviser Yousef al-Otaiba, using identical phrasing in speaking of MBS.[348] According to an American official quoted by the magazine, the "public-relations firms . . . promoting MBS in the United States [are] paid for by Abu Dhabi."[349]

The *Yeni Safak* reporting on Dahlan, which the media outlet reveals is the product of contacts with Egyptian intelligence, is re-reported by news outlets around the Middle East, further angering Dahlan.[350] Dahlan's adamant denials of the *Yeni Safak* story relate in substantial part to a prior claim by the Turkish media outlet in early November that Dahlan, a Gazan exile under Emirati protection, coordinated and dispatched to Istanbul a four-person cleanup and "cover-up" team after Khashoggi's murder. This first *Yeni Safak* report had quickly been re-reported across the Middle East, in Russia, and in Europe, including by major outlets such as the *Middle East Monitor*, *Al Bawaba*, the *Palestine Chronicle*, *Al Araby*, i24 News, *Sputnik*, and *Modern Diplomacy*.[351] While Dahlan denies both *Yeni Safak* reports, in at least one respect the first echoes other reports establishing Dahlan as the coordinator of military and paramilitary teams working on covert and sometimes illicit foreign operations.[352]

In reporting on the December 2018 Senate resolution on MBS, the Associated Press notes the stark difference between the Senate's position on the Saudi crown prince and Trump's: "Trump has been reluctant to condemn the crown prince, despite U.S. intelligence officials concluding that [MBS] must have at least had knowledge of the plot. Trump instead has touted Saudi arms deals worth billions of dollars and has thanked the Saudis for lower oil prices."[353] According to Lindsey Graham, "The current relationship with Saudi Arabia is not working for America."[354] In a separate statement, Graham raises the specter of members of the Trump administration being "in the pocket of Saudi Arabia," declaring that there is "zero chance . . . that this [Khashoggi's murder] happened in such an organized fashion without the crown prince [MBS] being involved. . . . I have great respect for [Secretary of State Mike] Pompeo and [Secretary of Defense Jim] Mattis but if they were in a Dem [sic] administration, I would be all over them for being in the pocket of Saudi Arabia."[355] Graham adds that any administration official—he specifically references Mike Pompeo—who does not believe MBS orchestrated the Khashoggi killing is being "willfully blind" and merely a "good soldier," apparently referencing Pompeo and others' loyalty to Trump.[356]

Corker, the chairman of the Senate Foreign Relations Committee, says in a speech to the Senate, "I absolutely believe [MBS] directed it [Khashoggi's murder]. I believe he monitored it. And I believe he is responsible for it."[357] Referring to the presentation on the Khashoggi killing that CIA director Gina Haspel had given to the Senate the month before, Corker says it was the "most precise presentation I've ever heard in 12 years" in the Senate, adding that a "colleague [had] corrected his comments . . . that a jury would convict bin Salman in 30 minutes . . . [by saying] it would have been '20 minutes.'"[358] Corker may be referring, in part, to the eleven text messages MBS and al-Qahtani sent back and forth that "roughly coincided with the hit team's advance into the Saudi Consulate in Istanbul," a synchronicity that Bruce Riedel, a former CIA official now at the Brookings Institution, will call "the smoking gun, or . . . the smoking phone call" in the Khashoggi case.[359]

Meanwhile, Secretary of State Mike Pompeo is telling the press that "there is no direct reporting connecting the crown prince to the order to murder Jamal Khashoggi."[360] For his part, Trump inaccurately claims, in a statement to the media and the public, that the CIA only has "feelings" about MBS being responsible for Khashoggi's death—a falsehood that will "irk[ ] current and former U.S. intelligence officials," according to the *Wall Street Journal*.[361]

Seventy-two hours before the dual Senate resolutions condemning MBS and the Saudi-led war in Yemen, the White House announces that it has, as paraphrased by *Politico*, "shifted from [the] Khashoggi killing to Israeli-Palestinian peace," with Jared Kushner telling the media, "We're focused now on the broader region."[362] Kushner makes his comment even as *Politico* is reporting that Kushner "has continued to chat informally with [MBS] since Khashoggi's death, and has even advised the young royal on how best to 'weather the storm' of international condemnation bearing down on Riyadh."[363] According to the *Daily Beast*, Kushner's aid and comfort to the mastermind of the Khashoggi assassination "prompt[s] serious concerns among senior American officials"; it will be discovered in June 2019 that the Trump administration's treatment of MBS following Khashoggi's murder in fact went well beyond aid and comfort—with *Politico* reporting that two of the seven times the Trump administration "approved the transfer of nuclear technical expertise to Saudi Arabia" came after "the Saudi-orchestrated murder of Jamal Khashoggi," including one approval on October 18, 2018.[364]

As late as January 2019—a full two months after the CIA concludes that MBS ordered Khashoggi's assassination—Mike Pompeo visits Riyadh to meet with MBS and hold a joint press conference at which the secretary of state declares, while standing beside the Saudi crown prince, that "every single person who has responsibility for the murder of Jamal Khashoggi needs to be held accountable."[365] Pompeo's joint appearance with MBS comes in the middle of a "marathon Middle East tour" that takes him on visits to all four of the Red Sea conspirator nations: Saudi Arabia, Egypt, Bahrain, and the United Arab Emirates.[366] The month before, well after the CIA had made its assessment on MBS's complicity in Khashoggi's execution, Trump had issued a public statement entitled "America First!" that averred that America's interests lay with its business dealings with MBS rather than with any loyalty to U.S. resident Khashoggi. As summarized by CNN, Trump "cited the Kingdom's influence over oil prices and said, 'if we abandon Saudi [sic] it would be a terrible mistake.'" On the matter of MBS's guilt, Trump had written, falsely, that "our intelligence agencies continue to assess all information" but that no conclusion on MBS's responsibility for Khashoggi's death had yet been reached.[367]

In April 2019, the Trump administration will publish a list of sixteen individuals it says had "roles" in the death of Jamal Khashoggi, permanently banning all sixteen from the United States. MBS's name is not on the list.[368] Six and a half weeks later, in late May 2019, Trump will declare a national emergency in order to bypass Congress and sell $8.1 billion in arms and heavy equipment to Saudi Arabia and the UAE—weaponry that includes "surveillance aircraft," "advanced precision kill weapon guidance systems," and "Javelin missiles." The equipment is expected to be used in Yemen, where the Saudi coalition faces accusations of war crimes.[369] According to CNN, the extraordinary move draws "bipartisan condemnation, with lawmakers decrying the precedent it sets, questioning the administration's claims of an emergency, and raising the issue of Saudi Arabia's human rights record and the killing of journalist Jamal Khashoggi"; outrage will only build when it is revealed, in June 2019, that not only will Trump be selling weapons to the Saudis without congressional approval, but some of the weapons—specifically, smart bombs—will be manufactured in Saudi

Arabia, a decision "giving Riyadh unprecedented access to a sensitive [U.S.] weapons technology."[370] It is further revealed, in the same month, that Saudi Arabia has been "significantly escalat[ing] its ballistic missile program . . . threaten[ing] decades of US efforts to limit missile proliferation in the Middle East." Even more troubling is that, as reported by CNN, the Trump administration "did not initially disclose its knowledge of this classified development to key members of Congress."[371]

ANNOTATIONS

Emboldened by Donald Trump's election, the same nations whose representatives met on a yacht in the Red Sea to plan the installation of Trump as America's next president will in 2018 take steps to formalize their alliance as the Middle East Strategic Alliance (MESA), functionally an "Arab NATO" in the view of many in the Middle East.

The comparison is one broadly observed after the announcement of MESA, with the Middle East Policy Council, a D.C. think tank offering analysis and commentary on Middle East politics, noting that the alliance is "modeled after the North Atlantic Treaty Alliance (NATO)."[372] The comparison will also be made by Reuters, the Center for the National Interest, *Haaretz*, Al Jazeera, *Foreign Policy*, and others.[373]

CHAPTER 10

THE SYRIA WITHDRAWAL, THE YEMENI CIVIL WAR, SECRET SUMMITS, AND THE SAUDI NUCLEAR DEAL

December 2018 to March 2019

As Trump threatens to precipitously withdraw U.S. forces from Syria and end U.S. participation in NATO—both outcomes that would greatly please his would-be ally Vladimir Putin—he continues generously funding the Saudis' and Emiratis' ill-conceived military intervention in Yemen, whose human toll has by the end of 2018 become incalculable. Trump increasingly becomes the executor of the designs of his new allies, spreading propaganda for the Kremlin, advocating for the creation of Saudi Arabia's proposed Sunni Arab security alliance, advancing a Saudi nuclear deal after exiting a nuclear deal with Iran while the Iranians were in compliance, and making his phone calls open to Russian intercepts. In Warsaw, Israeli prime minister Benjamin Netanyahu states outright what many have long suspected: that Israel, Saudi Arabia, the UAE, Bahrain, Egypt, and the Trump administration are hoping for a war with Iran.

As 2018 ends, the top priority for both Russia and the Red Sea conspirators is the removal of Syria as a hot-button issue in the region. According to the *Guardian*, Saudi Arabia, the United Arab Emirates, and Egypt want the end of the Syrian civil war and the readmittance to the Arab League of Syria and its president Bashar al-Assad—repeatedly accused of war crimes—to "mark the definitive death of the Arab Spring . . . [and] the hopes of the region's popular revolutions."[1] Per the British news outlet, if MBS and Egypt's Abdel Fattah el-Sisi can stand "shoulder to shoulder" with al-Assad, with all three men in complete control of their respective countries, it will communicate to the world that the transnational push for democracy across the Middle East known as the "Arab Spring" was "crushed by the newest generation of Middle Eastern strongmen."[2]

The first sign of a shift in Saudi, Emirati, and Egyptian attitudes toward the Syrian civil war had come earlier, in 2018, when Bahrain—another Red Sea conspirator—permitted its foreign minister, Khalid bin Ahmed al-Khalifa, to "warmly shak[e] the hand" of the Syrian foreign minister, Walid al-Muallem, on the sidelines of the United Nations general assembly, an event al-Assad revealed in October 2018 signified that Syria had reached "a major understanding" with several Arab states.[3]

The second major sign of a thaw between MBS and al-Assad comes in mid-December 2018, when Sudanese president Omar al-Bashir visits al-Assad in Syria, a move "widely interpreted as a gesture of friendship on behalf of Saudi Arabia."[4] According to the *Guardian*, "For Saudi Arabia and the UAE, re-embracing Syria is a new strategy aimed at pivoting Assad away from Tehran's sphere of influence."[5] In the view of "especially Emirati and Egyptian leaders," the *Guardian* reports, Syria's president is "one of them—an Arab autocrat fighting against what . . . [they] consider subversive [forces]."[6] Meanwhile, "calls in Egyptian and Gulf media for Syria's reinstatement [to the Arab League]" are spreading, as are "rumors about the reopening of the Emirati embassy in Damascus, which observers believe would serve as a backchannel for Saudi diplomatic overtures."[7] Concurrently, Jordan—another nation present at the founding of the Red Sea Conspiracy—"reopen[s] a southern border crossing" to Syria.[8]

Even so, December 2018 is still early days for normalization of the Gulf states' ties to Syria, and there is no indication that any politician in the United States is interested in following suit. The *Guardian* notes that "for the west, Syria is likely to remain a pariah state."[9] According to one top European diplomat speaking in December, "There is no credible, genuine settlement process under way yet in Syria, so fundamentally there's still no incentive for reconciliation with the regime."[10]

In Syria, as elsewhere, Russia's interests once again partially align with those of the Red Sea conspirators and Israel. Indeed, "Israel is working with Russia to reduce tensions in the disputed Golan Heights," reports the *Guardian*.[11] It is clear that if the United States can be convinced in the coming months and years to withdraw its forces from Syria and cede the country back to its autocratic head of state, it will give Russia free rein to continue its military operations in the country without fear of interference from American forces. Just so, Putin can find greater profit in his government's special political and economic relationship with Syria once al-Assad's regime and the nation he leads is brought back into the international community of nations on equal footing with regional peers.

Therefore, the chief problem for Putin, MBS, MBZ, and el-Sisi as December 2018 begins is that there simply has been no serious contemplation in the United States of withdrawing American forces from Syria and thereby opening a path to a political solution to the Syria question—critically, one that involves al-Assad remaining in power. Indeed, such a policy would run directly counter to America's long-standing goals in the region, including both its humanitarian ambitions (with respect to the prevention of future war crimes) and its geopolitical ones, notably the direct and indirect fostering of revolutionary movements seeking the spread of democracy in the Middle East. While Saudi Arabia makes its first public gesture of friendship toward al-Assad in early December 2018, the notion that Saudi policy should lead to any change in American policy in Syria in either the short or medium term is beyond mainstream policy discussion in Washington. One indication of this is that, even as Sudan's al-Bashir and Syria's al-Assad meet, the U.S. State Department is "pressuring both Riyadh and Cairo to hold off on demanding a vote" in the Arab League to readmit Syria, a move that would complicate American military operations there.[12]

All of the foregoing notwithstanding, on December 19, Donald Trump shocks America and the world when CNN reports that "planning is underway for a 'full' and 'rapid' withdrawal of U.S. troops from Syria, [a] decision made by President Trump, [according to] a U.S. defense official."[13] The same day, Trump tweets, "We have defeated ISIS in Syria, my only reason for being there during the Trump presidency."[14] In response, a Pentagon official gives the following statement to CNN: "So when does Russia announce their victory?"[15] The answer turns out to be "within hours," as Putin in the midafternoon of December 19 issues a statement through Russian Foreign Ministry spokeswoman Maria Zakharova lauding Trump's decision as offering "a real prospect for a political solution [in Syria]."[16] The next day Putin adds that "if the U.S. [has] decided to withdraw its [military] contingent, it has done the right thing."[17] Putin may well be responding to news, released the same day, that as part of its Syria withdrawal the United States is "set to close a base in Syria which has drawn the ire of Russia . . . [as] special forces will be withdrawn from the Al-Tanf base near the Syrian border with Jordan," a significant development for the Kremlin because "Russia has frequently condemned the U.S. presence at Al-Tanf. In a response to the U.S. leaving the country, Russian officials specifically noted that de-escalation would now be possible near the base."[18] That Russian Foreign Ministry spokesman Igor Tsarikov had said on December 11 that "there is growing concern [in Moscow] related to the dubious activity of the U.S. and its allies in Syria" might also help explain Trump's announcement—the impetus for which arose, according to GOP sources in Washington, on December 11.[19]

Less than two hours after Russia issues its first statement on Trump's Syria withdrawal, the president takes the unusual step of canceling a meeting with the Republican chairman of the Senate Foreign Relations Committee, Bob Corker of Tennessee—doing so while Corker is waiting in the White House to meet with him.[20] Reports following the snub indicate that Corker was planning to ask Trump about Syria.[21] One report notes that Corker, along with "many senators," was "blindsided . . . by Trump's decision to pull all 2,000 U.S. troops out of Syria as quickly as possible."[22] Notably, Trump cancels his meeting with Corker, the most powerful Republican legislator in the United States on the subject of foreign policy, even though he has no public events on his schedule for the day.[23] During the evening of December 19, Corker says to NBC News, of Trump's decision to withdraw from Syria, "There are significant concerns about what's happened. I've never seen a decision like this since I've been here, in twelve years, where nothing is communicated in advance, and all of a sudden this type of massive decision takes place. It's caught everybody off-guard. I doubt that there's anybody in the Republican caucus in the Senate that just isn't stunned by this precipitous decision that, like, you woke up in the morning and made it."[24] Corker adds that it's a "terrible thing for the nation."[25] As summarized by Atlantic Media journalist Katie Bo Williams, Corker will later note, following a classified call with the secretary of defense, Jim Mattis, that, according to Mattis, "there does not appear to have been any interagency process to the withdrawal decision"—meaning that even the Pentagon was not informed beforehand by the president.[26]

Following Trump's announcement, Mattis quickly resigns as secretary of defense, even as, according to the *Times of Israel*, Trump's claim that ISIS has been defeated is being "largely rejected by defense analysts and officials from around the world"—a circumstance that opens up the question of which intelligence services, if any, have told Trump that ISIS has been eradicated in Syria.[27] Brett McGurk, "the U.S. envoy leading the coalition to defeat ISIS," also, like Mattis, "resign[s] in protest" of Trump's actions.[28] In a last email to his staff, McGurk writes, "I ultimately concluded that I could not carry out these new instructions [from the president] and maintain my integrity at the same time."[29]

At the time of McGurk's resignation, there are 2,000 U.S. soldiers in Syria—and an estimated 2,000 to 8,000 ISIS fighters.[30] If ISIS fighters in neighboring Iraq are counted, the size of the ISIS force increases to 30,000, according to NBC News.[31]

Reaction to Trump's Syria announcement across the Republican Party is exactly as Corker anticipates. On the same day as Trump's declaration, Rep. Adam Kinzinger (R-IL) calls Trump's claim that ISIS has been defeated "simply not true." Trump ally Lindsey Graham calls the decision "a big win for ISIS, Iran, Bashar al-Assad of Syria, and Russia," adding that it will "lead to devastating consequences for our nation, the region, and throughout the world" and that the idea that ISIS is defeated is "fake news." Sen. Marco Rubio (R-FL) labels the decision a "grave error," a "co-lossal mistake," and a "bad decision that will eventually lead to greater risk for the United States." Sen. Ben Sasse (R-NE), calling the announcement a "weak decision," notes that "eight days ago [on December 11] the Admin-istration called a hypothetical pullout [from Syria] 'reckless.' Today, we're leaving. The President's generals have no idea where this weak decision came from. . . . A lot of American allies will be slaughtered if this retreat is implemented."[32]

One place the idea of a Syria withdrawal may have originated is longtime Trump adviser Erik Prince, who, according to *Haaretz*, has been making "the case [to Trump] that the United States should replace its small footprint of 2,000 troops in Syria with mercenaries"—specifically, Prince's mercenaries.[33] Prince is thereby "eyeing a major comeback," *Haaretz* writes, from his tumul-tuous reign as head of the "infamous" company once known as Blackwater, whose private military contractors were accused and convicted of carrying out homicides in Iraq.[34] Prince had previously pitched Trump on the idea of "replacing troops in Afghanistan with private military contractors that would report to a special 'viceroy' for the war who would report directly to the president"; a year later, Trump "vowed to draw down the 7,000 troops from Afghanistan."[35] Prince would likely have made Trump aware, with respect to both Syria and other military theaters, that Vladimir Putin had long since given his approval to a well-known Russian private military com-pany, Wagner Group, "work[ing] and pursu[ing] their interests anywhere in the world" as long as they do not "break Russian law," with the Russian president calling such mercenary companies "an instrument in the pursuit of national interests without the direct participation of the state."[36] Immediately after Mattis resigns over Trump's policy shift on Syria, Blackwater takes out a full-page ad in firearms-enthusiast magazine *Recoil* that implies it will shortly be resuming operations; the ad, written in large white capital letters against a black background, says simply, "WE ARE COMING."[37]

International reaction to Trump's Syria announcement is unambigu-ous. A senior French official tells the Associated Press that France does not "share the assessment" of the situation in Syria that Trump has, and believes if the withdrawal is "made too quickly . . . [it will] affect not only stability in the region, but also the security of the people and the Syrian Democratic Forces."[38] Germany's foreign minister, Heiko Maas, issues a statement saying that "the threat [from ISIS] is not yet over" and "the abrupt change of course by the American side comes as a surprise not only for us."[39] Indeed, it appears Trump has also neglected to tell America's allies in Syria: the Syrian Democratic Forces (SDF) issue a statement declaring that "the war against Islamic State has not ended and the group has not been defeated"; meanwhile, America's Kurdish allies are, according to the Associated Press, "rattled" and "surprise[d]," and see the move "as an abandonment of a loyal ally" after which, one Kurdish journalist tells the AP, "we have every right to be afraid."[40]

Media reaction to Trump's announcement is along the same lines as everyone else's. *Politico* immediately issues a report on Trump's decision calling it "calamitous," "a mistake," "ill-considered," and a move that "will not end well," noting that "ISIS pockets remain in the eastern parts of Syria and there have already been signs that they are regenerating."[41] The digital news outlet observes that the "breach" Trump is leaving may well be filled by "Russia, Iran, and Turkey"—leading it to conclude that Trump is undercutting its commitment to "America's Arab and Israeli partners."[42]

The answer to Sasse's question—what happened between December 11 and December 19 to change Trump's mind about Syria?—may also be the answer to the query from *Politico* about how America's "Arab and Israeli partners" will react to the news that America is leaving Syria. The meeting between Syrian president Bashar al-Assad and Sudanese President Omar al-Bashir—the latter a "key ally for the Saudis and Emiratis" who was once disfavored but is now "welcomed again by Cairo and Riyadh," according to the *Middle East Eye*—occurred on December 16.[43] The London-based Middle East watchdog notes that "Saudi Arabia's role in the [al-Bashir] trip is not to be discounted," adding that the "clear message that Bashir brings [to al-Assad] is that the Arab League is ready to take Syria back and talk to Assad for full restorations of ties. . . . [T]he Saudis and the Arab League . . . want Syria to retake its premier position as the main force in the Levant and push back . . . Iranian and Turkish influence in the region."[44] Trump's decision on withdrawing from Syria therefore comes within seventy-two hours of his most prominent Arab ally and backer, MBS, making his first public acknowledgment, through al-Bashir, that a political rather than military solution in Syria is the best answer—for Saudi Arabia, at least.

There is evidence, however, that MBS is thinking not just about Saudi Arabia and Syria but about Russia as well. The *Middle East Eye* reports, shortly after the al-Bashir visit, that "some Arab states are . . . looking to Russia as being a positive influence in the Middle East, after years of American and European failure in Libya, Iraq, and Yemen. Russia is seen as a success given how it has managed to decisively alter the course of the war in Syria. The message was not lost in Washington [on December 16] that the Sudanese president arrived on a Russian plane."[45] The implication of this observation is that MBS, MBZ, and el-Sisi may not merely be sanguine at the prospect of America ceding Syria to Russian influence and an ongoing Russian military presence, but in fact perhaps would—contrary to what Trump's Republican colleagues are presuming back at home—strongly prefer it.

Israel, another country ostensibly threatened by Trump's decision, is likewise more ambivalent about the announcement than anyone not familiar with the Red Sea Conspiracy might expect. In response to the news that U.S. forces will be abandoning Syria, Israeli prime minister Benjamin Netanyahu, widely but wrongly believed by many in Washington to consider himself betrayed by Trump's announcement, does not decry the move but instead calls Trump to discuss "ways to continue cooperation between Israel and the United States against Iranian aggression."[46] He adds that he is confident Israel has "complete support and backing from the United States."[47] While Trump will dispatch to Israel his national security advisor, John Bolton, in early January, it will not be because the Israelis wish to convince the United States to stay in Syria, but merely to discuss how "swift" the withdrawal will be, as a too-hasty removal of U.S. forces could "enable Iran to expand its influence and presence in Syria."[48] That Netanyahu disputes only the logistics of Trump's stunning gambit in Syria, rather than expressing shock at the bare fact of it, leaves open the possibility that Netanyahu—and perhaps other actors in the region or in

Moscow—had more notice of the administration's dramatic announcement than the Pentagon did. The Associated Press will report that Israel was the first country to learn of Trump's final decision after Turkey (which learned of it on December 14), confirming that Netanyahu might have known about Trump's plan before the Pentagon did, as even on December 19 the Pentagon was indicating that it was caught off guard by the finality and certainty of Trump's declaration.[49]

What is not clear is if Netanyahu is on the same page as his own military commanders with respect to Trump's announcement on Syria. While the *Times of Israel* will report that "top Israeli government officials have publicly refrained from criticizing the move," Israeli intelligence officials tell the *New York Times* that they do indeed feel "betrayed" by Trump's decision.[50] The *Times*, noting that Netanyahu is "a close ally of Mr. Trump's," will observe that the Israeli intelligence officials who spoke to the paper did so "on condition of anonymity," suggesting that they were not cleared by Netanyahu's office to publicly dispute Trump's plan.[51] What they tell the *Times* underscores, however, that Netanyahu's alliance with a U.S. president simultaneously seeking to be allied with the Russians is a perpetual dilemma for Netanyahu's government; per the *Times*, "one [Israeli intelligence] official said the United States was practically evacuating the Middle East, leaving Russia as the sole global power there."[52] Saudi Arabia's designs on becoming a superpower in the Middle East go unmentioned.

MBS's plan for Syria becomes clear in the week after Trump's surprise announcement. By the day after Christmas, the *Guardian* is writing, "For Saudi Arabia and the UAE, re-embracing Syria is a new strategy aimed at pivoting Assad away from Tehran's sphere of influence, fuelled by the promise of normalized trade relations and reconstruction money . . . [as] Riyadh's pockets are much deeper than Tehran's and Moscow's."[53] In ending America's long-standing foreign policy in Syria without so much as a call to the Pentagon—and in doing so in a fashion and on a schedule that aligns with MBS's intricate designs—Trump therefore capitulates to Riyadh and the Kremlin even as the outcry within his own political party wrongly suggests that no one in the Middle East or anywhere else is pleased with his decision.

MBS's Syria policy in December 2018 is a far cry from what it was in December 2017, when Trump, then on a tear about the expense of keeping soldiers in and rebuilding Syria, contacted King Salman to ask the Saudis to contribute more money to the Syrian reconstruction effort. In response, Salman pledged $4 billion—just 1 percent of the amount of money needed to rebuild Syria's devastated infrastructure.[54] By December 2018, however, the Saudis are ready to commit significantly greater resources to the effort. Consequently, though it may appear to American voters that Trump is abandoning Syria to stand firm on his oft-expressed complaint about U.S. military expenditures abroad, his thinking instead appears responsive to the mercurial whims of Riyadh, rather than any avowed principle.

That Trump may have coordinated his capitulation to the Saudis, Emiratis, and Russians with MBS—at a minimum—is indicated by a tweet from Trump just five days after his withdrawal announcement. On Christmas Eve, MBS had given Trump political cover on Syria by indicating that the Saudis would fund Syrian reconstruction, estimated in January 2019 to require a $400 billion investment in total. Trump tweets out, in response to these assurances, "Saudi Arabia has now agreed to spend the necessary money needed to help rebuild Syria, instead of the United States. See? Isn't it nice when immensely wealthy countries help rebuild their neighbors rather than a Great Country, the U.S., that is 5000 miles away[?] Thanks to Saudi A[rabia]!"[55]

What Trump does not reveal is that the Russians are now also planning to move into the Syria-reconstruction business, with the Carnegie Endowment for International Peace making note of "Russia's growing focus on Syria's economic reconstruction," which "Russia wants to benefit from . . . as a foreign capital influx into the Syrian economy could provide vital hard currency for Russian businesses."[56] Trump's announcement that the United States will not participate in the Syrian reconstruction process is therefore a concession to Saudi and Russian interests, which will now dominate a burgeoning subeconomy in the Middle East.[57]

In late December, a new revelation regarding the factors that led to Trump's December 19 Syria decision shifts the focus temporarily from Trump's conversation with Putin in Helsinki and Kushner's conversations with MBS in Riyadh—the latter concurrent to al-Assad reaching a mysterious "major understanding" with the Saudis—to a conversation Trump had with Turkish president Recep Tayyip Erdogan on December 14. According to NBC News, the Trump administration had originally told reporters that during the December 14 call Trump "merely informed Erdogan of his plans to withdraw" from Syria.[58] In fact, the media will learn that Trump agreed to withdraw from Syria after "Erdogan reportedly promised that Turkey would take responsibility for finishing off the Islamic State if the U.S. pulled out of Syria."[59] According to a senior White House official, Erdogan—who had met directly with Vladimir Putin just thirteen days earlier at the G20 summit—said to Trump, "As your friend, I give you my word in this."[60] The *Washington Post* will imply that Trump's conversation with Erdogan on December 14 is, whether planned as such or not, effectively a follow-up to the duo's conversation about Syria at the G20, where in addition to meeting with Putin, Erdogan met with Trump to express "his inability to understand why the United States was still arming and supporting Syrian Kurdish fighters to conduct a ground war against the Islamic State."[61]

Trump had met with Putin at the G20 summit as well. Despite announcing publicly, before the summit, his intention of avoiding the Russian president in Buenos Aires, Trump in fact secretly met with him twice—in both instances meetings at which no note-takers or aides were present and journalists found out only after the fact and by accident, not from the White House.[62] One meeting was a conversation at a "cultural dinner . . . closed to reporters." Another meeting, the next day, was revealed by Putin rather than any U.S. source; according to the Russian president, he and Trump discussed "the situation in Ukraine"—historically, a code word for U.S. sanctions against Russia for Putin's illegal annexation of the Crimean peninsula in early 2014.[63] That Trump, despite his public posturing, had likely always intended to meet with Putin in Buenos Aires is suggested by the Russians' more candid stance on the matter. According to *USA Today*, "Kremlin officials insisted throughout the [first] day [of the G20 that] the two leaders would ultimately meet."[64] Because of how Trump orchestrated his two meetings with Putin, however, no one in the media was in a position to say if the two men had discussed Syria, the Turkish president's G20 meeting with Putin, or anything else that might have informed Trump's thinking on leaving Syria to the Russians and Saudis just thirteen days later. Another meeting in which Putin is involved at the G20 will raise eyebrows as well, as Putin and MBS are caught on videotape high-fiving each other excitedly and, per CNN, exchanging "huge smiles and handshakes."[65]

Other, more esoteric 2018 events—like a threat issued 120 days earlier by one of Turkey's major political parties to "seize [two] Trump Towers" in Istanbul if Trump didn't end sanctions against two top Turkish officials—may also have been on Trump's mind when he capitulated to Erdogan.[66] Certainly, Trump appeared to be unusually solicitous with the Turkish president on December 14. When he suddenly agreed to withdraw U.S. forces in response to Erdogan's promise during their mid-December phone call—saying, according to the *Post*, "You know what? It's yours. I'm leaving"—Erdogan was, according to the Associated Press, so stunned at the speed and finality of Trump's capitulation that, suddenly contradicting himself, he "cautioned Trump against a hasty withdrawal."[67]

White House officials are oddly candid with the media about how "hastily" Trump made his decision to exit Syria—a negative shading of Trump's behavior that would normally serve no purpose to the White House.[68] While it is true, as the Associated Press notes, that Trump's decision was made "without consulting his national security team or allies, and over strong objections from virtually everyone involved in the fight against the Islamic State group . . . [and] stunned his Cabinet, lawmakers and much of the world . . . [in] rejecting the advice of his top aides," the fact remains that Trump's national security advisor, John Bolton, knew of Trump's intention to withdraw from Syria as early as his first day in the White House—April 9, 2018—and hid that fact from national security officials elsewhere in the U.S. government in early September (see chapter 9). Bolton, who was on the Trump-Erdogan phone call, was, according to the Associated Press, "forced to admit [to Trump]" that ISIS retained only "1 percent" of its former territory in Syria, but, having also argued that victory over ISIS had to be "enduring," was purportedly "shocked" when Trump agreed to withdraw U.S. forces.[69] And yet he had been told long before, by the president himself, that Trump was inclined to do just that—and Trump's meetings at the G20 likewise would have seemed to counter any claim that his decision had been a sudden one.

On December 22, Trump appears to concede that he was thinking about more than just the Turkish president's promise to him when he made his decision, tweeting that "other local countries" would be working simultaneously with Turkey to "easily take care of whatever remains" of ISIS, a reference to unnamed nations that by simple process of elimination would seem to include Saudi Arabia and the United Arab Emirates.[70] While messages from the White House are mixed between December 14 and December 22, National Security Council spokesman Garrett Marquis will say that the story of the Trump-Erdogan phone call is false and comes "possibly from unnamed sources in Turkey."[71] Meanwhile, unnamed White House "officials" will say that the Trump-Erdogan call was originally set up so that Trump could "tell Erdogan to back off" from attacking Kurdish forces in northern Syria, as doing so could endanger American forces, but that during the call Trump "ignored the script . . . [and] sided with Erdogan"—a telling of events that has the president deliberately putting American soldiers in harm's way for at least the duration of any Syria pullout.[72]

Whatever the truth may be, the accusations and counteraccusations that surround Trump's decision on Syria leave a cloud of doubt around the possibility of an imminent U.S. withdrawal from the war-torn country— one that obscures not just the time line of Trump's decision on the matter but an itemization of the beneficiaries of his gambit.

In mid-January 2019, Trump again upends U.S. foreign policy in a way certain to please MBS and MBZ when, on January 13, he publicly threatens a country with which they have had hostile relations—Turkey—even though Turkey is a NATO ally. Trump associates his threat with his own inopportune withdrawal of American troops from Syria, tweeting that he will be "starting the long overdue pullout from Syria while hitting the little remaining ISIS territorial caliphate hard . . . will attack [ISIS] again from existing nearby base if it reforms. Will devastate Turkey economically if they hit Kurds."[73] Trump threatening a radical Islamist death cult and a NATO ally in consecutive sentences necessitates secretary of state Mike Pompeo calling Turkish foreign minister Mevlut Cavusoglu to "agree[ ] on the importance of continuing U.S.-Turkish consultations" over Syria.[74] Trump's words further threaten America's comity with its NATO allies, a result Putin is sure to embrace given that, according to the commander of the U.S. Army in Europe, Lt. Gen. Ben Hodges, Putin "wants to destroy" NATO.[75]

The day after Trump's threat against Turkey, the *New York Times* releases a shocking report revealing that Trump repeatedly told top aides throughout 2018 that he was planning to withdraw the United States from NATO, a decision the *Times* notes would be "tantamount to destroying NATO" and, in a single gesture, also gifting Putin one of his chief geopolitical ambitions. "There are few things that President Vladimir V. Putin of Russia desires more than the weakening of NATO, the military alliance . . . that has deterred Soviet and Russian aggression for 70 years," the *Times* writes.[76] The *Times* further notes that Trump's desire to end U.S. participation in NATO "raise[s] new worries among national security officials amid growing concern about Mr. Trump's efforts to keep his meetings with Mr. Putin secret from even his own aides, and an FBI investigation into the administration's Russia ties."[77] Retired admiral James G. Stavridis, former supreme allied commander of NATO, tells the *Times* that "even discussing the idea of leaving NATO" is the "gift of the century for Putin."[78]

December 2018 brings new revelations about Trump's other major military entanglement with Saudi and Emirati interests: the civil war in Yemen, where the Saudis and Emiratis have been staging a violent intervention since March 2015. Beginning in 2015, heavy U.S. tankers have been assisting the two Gulf nations by offering midair refueling of their warplanes. On December 8, the *Atlantic* reveals that while "President Donald Trump repeatedly complains that the United States is paying too much for the defense of its allies, [he] has praised Saudi Arabia for ostensibly taking on Iran in the Yemen war. It turns out, however, that U.S. taxpayers have been footing the bill for a major part of the Saudi-led campaign, possibly to the tune of tens of millions of dollars."[79] By law, Saudi Arabia and the UAE must both be charged for the refueling of their warplanes by American tanker aircraft, in part because to do otherwise is to put the United States in the position of directly funding a foreign war in which it is not engaged by a formal declaration of Congress. Most troubling in the report by the *Atlantic* is that it is not that the Trump administration has forgotten to charge the Saudis and Emiratis altogether, nominally the sort of gross error that might result from a bureaucratic snafu, but that Trump's Department of Defense has in fact charged the Saudis and Emiratis for refueling—but far less than it was supposed to charge them.[80] Moreover, the Trump administration's error is made public only because of a letter sent to the Pentagon by eight Democratic senators.[81]

While the inadvertent funding of the Saudi-Yemeni war by the United States had begun in March 2015 under the Obama administration (the *Atlantic* reports that from March 2015 through March 2016, the Saudis and Emiratis gave America no refueling reimbursement), the fact that it continued for all of 2017 and 2018, Trump's first two years in office, is puzzling given that, as Jeffrey Prescott, Obama's National Security Council senior director for Iran, Iraq, Syria, and the Gulf States, will tell the *Atlantic*, "President Trump has been exceedingly transactional, even threatening to cast aside NATO if our closest allies didn't increase their contributions. That is why it is jarring to see that the Trump administration—save for congressional and public pressure—would continue to refuel Saudi and Emirati aircraft without adequate, if any, reimbursement."[82] Indeed, while the Obama administration's error is explained by the military's habitual use of "third-party arrangements" for refueling (agreements that allow the UAE to be charged the cost of refueling Saudi warplanes under an existing agreement between the U.S. and the UAE signed during the second Bush administration) there is no explanation for the Trump administration's continued undercharging of the Saudis and Emiratis after "third-party arrangements" became illegal in August 2018.[83] Moreover, the undercharging was not caught—or was ignored—as the third-party prohibition was being debated during the fiscal-year appropriations processes in 2017 and 2018.[84]

The seemingly minor Saudi refueling controversy is linked to a much broader one that implicates Trump's historically unusual relationship with the Saudis: whether the Trump administration is, in fact, the only reason the Saudis and Emiratis are able to make war in Yemen at all. In a September 2018 article in the *Atlantic*, the magazine criticizes Trump for a speech he gave to the United Nations General Assembly that month in which he "signaled to Saudi Arabia that he would avoid criticizing its destabilizing actions in the Middle East" in favor of criticizing Iran, exclusively, for its actions in the region.[85] But in fact Trump had gone further, misrepresenting the Saudis' and Emiratis' unilateral military interference in the Yemeni civil war as "pursuing multiple avenues to ending Yemen's horrible, horrific civil war"—when in fact, as the *Atlantic* notes, "Yemen's current conflict escalated dramatically in early 2015, when Saudi Arabia led a coalition of Arab countries to intervene in the war."[86] The magazine goes on to call the war "a humanitarian catastrophe" that has killed so many innocent civilians that the United Nations "stopped counting" in 2016, just a year after MBS decided to go to war, when the number of innocents killed topped 10,000.[87] As of mid-2018, the working estimate from the Armed Conflict Location and Event Data Project puts the total casualties of the Yemeni war, including civilians, at 50,000, though this tracks deaths only from January 2016 (nine months into the Saudi-Emirati intervention) through July 2018.[88] As important, the war had by July 2018 put 22 million people—75 percent of all Yemenis—in need of humanitarian aid.[89]

Unable to stop Trump from supporting the Saudis' and Emiratis' military adventures—or, apparently, Trump's Defense Department from bankrolling their efforts—Congress has, in bipartisan fashion, at least tried to get Trump to "certify that Saudi Arabia and the UAE are taking 'demonstrable actions' to avoid harming civilians and making a 'good faith effort' to reach a political settlement to end the war. Congress required the administration to make this certification a prerequisite for the Pentagon to continue providing military assistance to the coalition."[90] The effort, constituting the very least Congress can do to check Trump's assistance of the Saudis and Emiratis in Yemen, nevertheless has failed, as it has only led to Trump's secretary of state, Mike Pompeo, falsely assuring the bipartisan congressional group in writing that all possible efforts to "minimize civilian casualties and enable deliveries of humanitarian aid to Yemen" are being made, when in fact "virtually every . . . independent assessment of the war, including a recent [United Nations] report . . . allege[s] the [Saudi-Emirati] coalition ha[s] committed war crimes."[91] As the *Atlantic* concludes, "The Saudis and Emiratis have largely ignored international criticism of civilian deaths and appeals for a political settlement—and the Trump administration's latest signal of support shows that strategy is working."[92] On these facts, the conclusion that the Trump administration is knowingly enabling war crimes out of a benighted or simply pretextual belief that the Yemeni civil war is striking a blow against Iran is inescapable.

The evidence that the Houthi rebels the Saudis and Emiratis are fighting in Yemen are a regional danger, or were prompted to enter a civil war in September 2014 because of Iranian influence, is scant. As the *Atlantic* notes, "Beyond recent missile attacks on Saudi Arabia—in retaliation for Saudi air strikes—the Houthis have displayed little regional ambition."[93] Moreover, despite what the Saudis and Trump publicly contend, "several [government] researchers . . . have shown that the Houthis did not receive significant support from Tehran before the Saudi intervention in 2015."[94] There is evidence, therefore, that MBS has generated a proxy war with Iran in Yemen that might otherwise have been a domestic conflict.

Trump's role in the Yemeni civil war has been not only to continue America's policy of broadly supporting the Saudi-led coalition there but also to go above and beyond anything his predecessor had imagined. Per the *Atlantic*, Trump has failed to "us[e] arms deals as leverage for a political settlement [in Yemen]," though he had "the best opportunity to do that that any Western politician could hope for in signing the largest-ever U.S.-Saudi arms deal with King Salman and MBS in May 2017"; he has "shown little interest in . . . forc[ing] the Saudis to take concerns about civilian deaths more seriously"; he has "reversed a decision by the Obama administration to suspend the sale of more than $500 million in laser-guided bombs and other munitions to the Saudi military"; and, when the Houthis retaliated for Saudi aggression in Yemen by firing ballistic missiles into the kingdom in 2017, Trump "escalated U.S. involvement in the war" with no thought to the context for the Houthi counteroffensive. He even went so far as to "secretly dispatch[ ] U.S. special forces to the Saudi-Yemen border to help the Saudi military locate and destroy" Houthi missile installations.[95] In September 2018, Trump's insistence on all but waging open war on Yemen alongside MBS leads the ranking members of the House Armed Services Committee and House Foreign Relations Committee, the House minority whip, and twenty-one other representatives to introduce a resolution invoking the 1973 War Powers Act—demanding that Trump withdraw every one of America's warfighters from the Saudi-Yemeni conflict on the grounds that the engagement has become an illegal war unapproved by Congress.[96] A similar resolution in the U.S. Senate is bipartisan and fails by just six votes.[97]

The only justification the Trump administration has offered for continuing to aid MBS is that America's in-theater training and refueling operations save civilian lives—an argument that flies in the face of hard data confirming that the Saudis and Emiratis are indeed committing war crimes with U.S. assistance.[98] According to an internal U.S. Agency for International Development memo acquired by the *Wall Street Journal*, it is not the case that "continued refueling support will improve [the Saudis' or Emiratis'] approach to civilian casualties or human protections."[99] Moreover, per reporting in *The Intercept*, multiple human rights groups have decried the Saudis' and Emiratis' apparent targeting of civilians. In August 2018, one incident alone saw coalition warplanes bomb a school bus, killing more than forty children with—forensic evidence later revealed—American bombs. The next month, coalition aircraft deliberately attacked the Yemeni port that is "the major conduit for humanitarian aid in Yemen," an action United Nations officials said "could lead to the death of 250,000 people, mainly from mass starvation."[100] According to former assistant secretary of state and current congressman Tom Malinowski, who was interviewed by the *New York Times* in late 2018, the Saudis and Emiratis are "just not willing to listen" to advice from U.S. military personnel on the subject of avoiding the slaughter of innocent civilians. They "were given specific coordinates of targets that should not be struck," Malinowski told the *Times*, "and they continued to strike them."[101] This, despite the fact that in 2017 the Trump administration initiated a $750 million program focused on training the Saudis on how to avoid civilian casualties—money that ought to have given Trump leverage in holding the Saudis to account for civilian deaths, as it could have included benchmarks to measure progress and provisions to withhold new military aid if those benchmarks went unmet.[102] Without such benchmarks, the Saudis and Emiratis have been able to, as Malinowski describes it, exhibit "willful disregard of advice they [a]re getting" regarding airstrike targeting and avoidance of collateral damage.[103]

By December 2018, concern over Trump's support for MBS's Yemeni adventures boils over into a successful Senate vote to end U.S. involvement in the coalition's campaign.[104] The Republican House refuses to take up the legislation, but the bill will pass in bipartisan fashion in February 2019 once the Democrats take control of the lower chamber of Congress.[105] In March 2019, the Senate again passes the bill with bipartisan support—establishing the humanitarian crisis in Yemen, and the systemic cruelties of the Saudis' and Emiratis' military campaign there, as one of the few issues in recent memory that is both of significant moment and the subject of any concurrence whatsoever between the two political parties.[106] Trump immediately vows to veto the measure, which he thereafter does; an attempted Senate override of his veto fails in May 2019.[107]

In March 2019, the first fruits of the new U.S.-Saudi-Russian axis manifest, with the three nations "shocking" delegates "from around the world" during a global climate conference in Poland when they are the only countries to "object[ ] to a statement 'welcoming' the latest scientific report on the impact of manmade climate change."[108] At the three new allies' insistence, the "key" scientific report is not adopted by the conference.[109] The same week, Qatar—an old U.S. ally left out of Trump's new Middle East axis—announces that it may depart OPEC (the Organization of the Petroleum Exporting Countries) due to its treatment at the hands of Saudi Arabia and its Sunni allies in the Gulf.[110] The Associated Press warns that "Qatar's decision . . . throws into question the viability of the [OPEC] cartel."[111]

On January 17, a young Belarussian model, Anastasia Vashukevich, steps off a plane in Moscow and is immediately arrested on prostitution allegations.[112] She has just arrived in the Russian capital from Thailand, where she has been held for months on allegations of soliciting sex.[113] Vashukevich, a former girlfriend of Oleg Deripaska who goes by the name "Nastya Rybka" on social media, is significant to the Trump-Russia investigation inasmuch as her eleven-month detention in Thailand in early 2018 came on the heels of her revelation on social media that she had "16 hours of audio and video proving ties between Russian officials and the Trump campaign that influenced the 2016 U.S. elections."[114] Allegedly, Deripaska orchestrated not only Vashukevich's arrest in Thailand but also—after Russian officials promised her safe passage by plane from Thailand to Belarus following her expulsion from the former country—her detention in Moscow.[115] Whatever Deripaska's involvement in Vashukevich's miseries, the strange saga of her travels in southeast Asia ends only when, according to the Associated Press, the model "give[s] [the recordings] to Deripaska" because, she says, they "relate to him" and she does "not want any more trouble."[116] Following her agreement to transfer the recordings (which the *Washington Post* refers to as "collusion tapes") to the Russian oligarch, she is released from custody.[117] On the day of her arrest in Moscow, a video of her being violently dragged away from a bank of journalists by Russian government agents—journalists she had been about to speak to about the evidence in her possession—goes viral internationally.[118]

Vashukevich's case had drawn international attention because her social media pictures and videos confirmed that she had, as she claimed, both been in close proximity to Deripaska and audiotaped and videotaped him speaking with at least one high-ranking Kremlin official.[119] In February, Vashukevich will say that Russian officials had her flight from Thailand to Minsk (in Belarus) illegally diverted, given that officials in Thailand had deported her to Belarus, not Russia.[120] Meanwhile, international media continue to refer to Deripaska as a central figure in the Trump-Russia scandal, with one outlet, the *Guardian*, suggesting the oligarch may be the "missing link" in the whole affair, given his ties to Paul Manafort and involvement with the Manafort-Kilimnik "Ukraine peace plan."[121]

In February 2019, CNN will reveal that "Saudi Arabia and its coalition partners [in Yemen] have transferred American-made weapons to al Qaeda-linked fighters [and] hardline Salafi [jihadi] militias . . . in violation of their agreements with the United States."[122] The cable news outlet will report, too, that the Saudis and Emiratis have allowed American weapons sold to them by the Trump administration to "[make] their way into the hands of Iranian-backed rebels battling the [Saudi-Emirati] coalition . . . exposing some of America's sensitive military technology to Tehran and potentially endangering the lives of U.S. troops."[123] In light of ongoing revelations regarding clandestine efforts by Trump and his allies to transfer sensitive nuclear technology to the Saudis, the concluding observation in CNN's report seems prescient: "The revelations raise fresh questions about whether the U.S. has lost control over a key ally presiding over one of the most horrific wars of the past decade, and whether Saudi Arabia is responsible enough to be allowed to continue buying the sophisticated arms and fighting hardware."[124] In some cases, CNN found, the Saudis and Emiratis were actually selling American military equipment to dangerous third parties; in other instances, the coalition was simply abandoning it for whoever happened to come across it thereafter.[125] In several instances, pro-Saudi militias have even formed alliances with al-Qaeda, leading to U.S. military equipment moving directly from the U.S. government to the Saudis to al-Qaeda allies.[126] One such pro-Saudi militia, the Abu Abbas brigade—founded by a man, Abu Abbas, the United States declared a terrorist in 2017—not only "enjoys support from the Saudi coalition" but was actively "absorbed into the coalition-supported 35th Brigade of the Yemeni Army."[127] There has also been, per CNN, a documented instance of the Saudis indiscriminately airdropping—for local pickup—U.S. anti-tank missiles in a region of Yemen in which al-Qaeda was operating at the time.[128] The Saudis refused to speak to CNN about its report, while the Emiratis denied having violated any agreements with the United States even after confronted with evidence that equipment signed for by them had ended up in a jihadi camp.[129]

Perhaps unsurprising given the Emiratis' presence there, a ubiquitous figure in the Trump-MBS-MBZ alliance has intermittently appeared in Yemen: Mohammed Dahlan, the security adviser to MBZ who during the

Saudi-Yemeni war is acting as both the Emirati prince's conduit to Putin and his in-theater assassination squad coordinator. While Dahlan has for some time been operating a hit squad in Yemen that uses Israeli spyware, toward the end of 2018 additional focus is placed on the shadowy Gulf-state operator in part because of the murder of Jamal Khashoggi. In late 2018, *Yeni Safak*, a Turkish newspaper, alleges that it was Dahlan's "'cover-up team' from Lebanon" that went to Istanbul shortly after Khashoggi's murder to "help[ ] hide traces" of the gruesome execution.[130] Given Dahlan's past meeting with Trump envoy Erik Prince in the Seychelles in January 2017—a meeting Prince hid from Congress while under oath—the infamous Palestinian's involvement in the highest-profile murder of an American in 2018 would, no matter its extent, be politically prob-lematic for the Trump administration. *Yeni Safak* alleges that Dahlan "dispatched" one of the two crews tasked with covering up Khashoggi's kidnapping, torture, dismemberment, assassination, dissolution, and in-cineration.[131] According to the Turkish media outlet, Dahlan's team spent three nights in Istanbul, and was captured on surveillance footage seized by the Turkish government in the wake of Khashoggi's disappearance.[132] The *Middle East Monitor* not only re-reports the *Yeni Safak* story but notes that Dahlan's team "used fake passports to travel and carried tools and chemicals."[133] The UAE, through its minister of state for foreign affairs, will accuse *Yeni Safak* of making up the story that Dahlan was involved in Khashoggi's murder, an allegation that Dahlan himself also denies—though how convincingly, given his other activities in the Middle East, is another matter.[134]

According to Jordanian news outlet *Al Bawaba*, by November 2018 Dah-lan has earned the nicknames "The Hitman" and "The Strongman" for his years of work on behalf of MBZ.[135] The Jordanian journalists, in re-reporting the *Yeni Safak* article on Dahlan's alleged assassination squad in Istanbul—a significant fact, given Jordan's uneasy alliance with the Saudis and Emiratis (in contrast to Turkey's top-line hostility to both)—further accuse Dahlan of "spying for Israel" and orchestrating assassinations in countries other than Yemen, including Jordan.[136] *Al Bawaba* also closes the circle between two Red Sea conspirators, MBZ and el-Sisi, by accusing Dahlan of being "involved in forming a counter-revolution[ary] movement supported by the UAE to curb the . . . consequences [of the 2011 Egyptian revolution]" in a way that made substantially more likely the nation's 2013 military coup—in which el-Sisi participated as minister of defense—and el-Sisi's subsequent mid-2014 "election" (with 97 percent of the vote) as Egypt's president.[137]

If all of these allegations are true, Dahlan not only was involved in Jamal Khashoggi's murder as an accessory alongside one Red Sea conspirator—MBS—but works for another conspirator (MBZ), helped put a third conspirator into power (el-Sisi), is MBZ's chief conduit to an out-of-region co-conspirator (Putin), and is both accused of spying for, and using the spyware of, a military run by yet another co-conspirator (Netanyahu). Dahlan's meeting in the Seychelles in January 2017—a meeting at least two Trump advisers, Erik Prince and George Nader, attended, with the apparent knowledge of Steve Bannon, Jared Kushner, and Michael Flynn—could thus be seen as a meeting of agents of the Red Sea Conspiracy nations, given that the event was also attended by a top Kremlin agent and the head of the Emirates' security services. That the UAE, Israel, Egypt, and Jordan—with the assent of Saudi Arabia, if history is any guide—also sought to put Dahlan in charge of the Palestinian Authority in spring 2016 only underscores the Palestinian exile's seeming centrality to the Red Sea Conspiracy.[138]

Throughout the atrocities in Yemen and Istanbul, writes the *Atlantic*, "Saudi and Emirati leaders . . . have been emboldened by the Trump administration's unconditional support."[139] The Saudis receiving this level of support for such a brutal course of conduct would be not just improbable but politically impossible were MBS not such close friends with both Jared Kushner and his father-in-law—and would be unlikely to be a political risk worth taking for either Trump or Kushner if they had not received substantial benefit from the Saudis and their allies in turn. As the *Atlantic* concludes, "Trump has shown little sign of pressuring his Saudi and Emirati allies, least of all over Yemen. The only realistic check left is in

Congress, where more voices are asking why the world's most powerful country is helping to perpetuate the world's worst humanitarian crisis."[140]

At the beginning of 2019, Trump makes an unusual statement that suggests, not for the first time, his inexplicably enhanced access to—and susceptibility to—obscure Kremlin talking points. The Russian propaganda Trump publicly parrots, which prompts MSNBC to report that Trump is "curiously well-versed in specific Russian talking points," consists of two false claims the president makes on January 2, 2019: first, that Soviet military involvement in Afghanistan in the 1980s caused the downfall of the Soviet Union; second, that the Soviets' military engagement with Afghanistan was necessitated by the presence of "terrorists" in the latter country.[141] The *Washington Post* will note that the second statement is so beyond the pale in international diplomacy that "the most shameless Soviet propagandist . . . [would] never claim [it]. You can read all Soviet media in the 1980s and never find anything this ridiculous."[142] Moreover, despite the fact that the United States effectively was fighting a proxy war against the Soviet Union in Afghanistan—by way of arming Russia's adversaries, the *muhjahideen*—Trump will say that the Soviets were "right to be there," even though they were fighting U.S. allies.[143] When Trump adds that "a lot of these [former Soviet republics] you're reading about now are no longer part of Russia, because of Afghanistan," the totality of his message becomes clear: Putin is not wrong to want the reconstruction of the Soviet Union through the reacquisition of its "lost" republics, as the only reason these lands broke away from Russia is that a valiant and just Soviet military campaign against terrorists bankrupted the Soviet Union.[144] Trump's account is a staggering and seemingly wholesale endorsement of Putin's geopolitical agenda, and it is made in public and unsolicited.[145] It also has significant implications for the question—an open question, for Trump—of whether the U.S. was right to impose sanctions on Russia after its 2014 annexation of Crimea.

Trump's January 2 statements echo prior instances of Trump or his closest aides expressing undue interest in information seemingly only available on state-controlled Russian media. In February 2017, for instance, Trump's top national security aides had "sought information about Polish incursions in Belarus," a request considered strange at the time because "little evidence of such activities appear[ed] to exist," and indeed, per MSNBC, "the only people in the world at the time saying that there was a real risk Poland might invade Belarus" were Kremlin agents and Kremlin-owned media as part of a Russian "military disinformation campaign." Then, according to MSNBC, "the president brought up something . . . utterly foreign to all American discourse" in the summer of 2018, specifically that Montenegro (a country the size of Connecticut, with a population of under one million) could "start World War III," a canard about the advisability of NATO allowing Montenegro to join its ranks that was once again native, exclusively, to Kremlin military propaganda.[146] Trump publicly and on camera "shov[ing] the prime minister of Montenegro out of [his] way" while walking to a photo op at the 2017 NATO summit in Brussels was therefore seen as a suspiciously aggressive, unpresidential gesture toward the leader of a country that, in the last few years, only Russia had been entangled with in any sort of significant international intrigue, with the Kremlin being accused of attempting to foment a coup in the tiny country.[147] That Trump's needless shove was internationally televised meant, of course, that his symbolic dismissal of the country of Montenegro was broadcast around the world—including in Moscow. Just a few weeks after the incident in Brussels, Trump rejects a U.S. intelligence assessment indicating a recent North Korean intercontinental ballistic missile test on the grounds that Putin had told him "North Korea did not have the capability to launch such missiles."[148] Trump thereafter falsely calls the missile launch—which had indeed occurred—a "hoax."[149]

The circumstance of Trump seeming predisposed to Kremlin talking points and intelligence could be explained in part by the simple fact of Trump's familiarity with each; in a June 2018 statement, Putin insisted that he and Trump "regularly talk over the phone."[150] Reports in the United States, relying on White House readouts of important phone calls, have itemized only eight Trump-Putin phone calls in Trump's first eighteen months in office, however, suggesting that calls may have occurred that were not formally recorded or even acknowledged by Trump to his aides after the fact.[151] While an "administration official" told CNN at the time of Putin's June 2018 statement that "the White House puts out readouts for every call Trump has with Putin ... [as it] would've been a disaster if news leaked of a secret call," this White House claim will be contradicted by a *New York Times* report four months later that reveals that "Mr. Trump typically relies on his cell phones when he does not want a call going through the White House switchboard and logged for senior aides to see," confirming that no one in the White House can be certain that Trump and Putin have spoken only eight times in eighteen months rather than more "regularly" than that, as Putin contends.[152]

On January 9, retired four-star Marine general Anthony Zinni, the former head of U.S. Central Command, leaves his job as a top Middle East envoy for Trump's State Department in what is called by CBS News a "soft resignation."[153] Zinni's departure is notable for two reasons: first, because its proximate cause is "the unwillingness of the regional leaders [behind the Qatar blockade] to agree to a viable mediation effort"—meaning that MBS, MBZ, and el-Sisi are declining to work generatively with the State Department, raising the specter that on the Qatar issue they are instead negotiating directly with Jared Kushner, as they have in the past—and second, more shocking by far, because the Trump administration has asked Zinni to "introduce" the "Middle East Strategic Alliance (MESA) concept ... to regional [Gulf] leaders."[154] The MESA concept, an outgrowth of the Red Sea Conspiracy, had previously been seen as MBS's brainchild, but with Zinni's resignation, it is revealed to be as much the Trump administration's work product as anything developed in Riyadh. Moreover, Zinni's decision to exit the administration includes his own observation that "other members of the administration are carrying [MESA] forward"—another likely reference to Kushner or Kushner's allies within the administration.[155] That Kushner is quite possibly, in cooperation with MBS, one of the chief architects of MESA appears to be confirmed by Zinni's posting at the time of his departure from government service: as CBS notes, Zinni "coordinated with former national security adviser H. R. McMaster and Trump son-in-law and senior adviser Jared Kushner."[156]

After a January 20 television appearance in which he reveals that Trump's negotiation with a Russian businessman and the Kremlin over a prospective Trump Tower Moscow lasted from the fall of 2015 through Election Day 2016, Rudy Giuliani disappears from America's airwaves for nearly two months—with Axios reporting that "Trump did not want him on TV for a while after his last round of interviews."[157] Several months later, Michael Cohen will disclose that Trump had originally "instructed" him to lie to Congress by falsely stating that the Trump Tower Moscow negotiations ended on January 31, 2016, the day before the first Republican primary. This is a lie that would allow Trump to argue, if implausibly, that he had never negotiated with the Kremlin or Russian oligarchs while he was officially a candidate for public office—an apparent, if clumsy, attempt to circumvent accusations of bribery.[158] When Cohen's statement to Congress that the negotiations in fact lasted through the Republican National Convention is contradicted by Giuliani, America learns from Trump's new attorney that Trump had told him that a series of conversations about the Moscow tower "was all going from the day I announced [my candidacy] to the day I won."[159]

Cohen's allegations regarding the Trumps will also include a claim that Ivanka Trump's attorney (Abbe Lowell, who represents Jared Kushner as well) suggested edits to Cohen's congressional testimony about Ivanka's knowledge of the Trump Tower Moscow project that would have made that testimony untrue.[160] In fact, despite Ivanka saying she knew "literally almost nothing" as the Trump Tower Moscow deal was slowly taking shape during the presidential campaign, Cohen will testify to Congress that he briefed her and other family members on the progress of the project on "approximately ten occasions."[161] Moreover, *BuzzFeed News* will report in June 2018 that Ivanka was so involved in the 2015 Trump Tower Moscow negotiations that she put Cohen in touch with Dmitry Klokov, a former Russian government official who "said a meeting between Trump and Putin could expedite a Trump tower in Moscow," and who then offered to set up that meeting.[162] When Cohen ultimately declined Klokov's assistance, he received an email from Ivanka that "questioned [his] refusal to continue communicating with Klokov."[163]

As the special counsel's investigation wears on, current and former federal prosecutors will opine to U.S. media outlets that the lack of any FBI interview with Ivanka is troubling, given that, in addition to what Cohen has alleged, Ivanka was with her father when he crafted a false statement for his son Don to give regarding the June 2016 meeting at Trump Tower; was with Trump in Bedminster, New Jersey, on the day he decided to fire FBI director James Comey; spoke briefly with Kremlin agents at Trump Tower on the day of the infamous June 2016 meeting attended by her brother, her husband, and her father's campaign manager; was instrumental in lobbying Trump to hire Paul Manafort, and played a similar role in Michael Flynn being hired for the presidential transition team over objections and contrary advice from both President Obama and Trump's first transition chief, Chris Christie; and, according to Adam Davidson of the *New Yorker*, oversaw a real estate project through 2016 alongside "the Azerbaijani Mammadov family, who the Trumps knew were likely laundering money for the IRGC [Islamic Revolutionary Guard Corps]."[164] The Associated Press will note, too, that along with her husband, Ivanka aggressively pushed for an urban-renewal "Opportunity Zone" program that would benefit Cadre, a real estate investment firm in which her husband holds a $25 million to $50 million stake.[165] Norm Eisen, a former U.S. ambassador and current board chair of Citizens for Responsibility and Ethics in Washington (CREW), will note in December 2018 that, under 18 U.S.C. 208, if "an employee of the executive branch participates personally and substantially in a particular matter in which, to his knowledge, he has a financial interest," the penalty is "up to five years in jail."[166]

Cohen's revelation that Don Jr. was briefed as extensively as his father and Ivanka on Trump's 2015 and 2016 plans for a Trump Tower Moscow calls into question the accuracy of Trump Jr.'s testimony to Congress, in which he said he "wasn't involved" in the tower deal and "wasn't aware" Cohen had had any dealings with the Kremlin on the subject.[167] Just so, comments made by Giuliani in 2018 to the effect that the Trump Tower Moscow that Trump was planning with Andrey Rozov was "barely more than a notion" with "no plans" behind it will be contradicted when Buzz-Feed News publishes, in January 2019, "hundreds of pages of business documents, emails, text messages, and architectural plans . . . [which] tell a very different story. Trump Tower Moscow was a richly imagined vision of upscale splendor on the banks of the Moscow River."[168]

When a redacted version of the Mueller Report is released in April 2019 (see chapter 11), it will reveal that Giuliani was correct that the Trump Tower Moscow negotiations were still active as of Election Day in 2016. According to testimony by Michael Cohen compiled for the report, as late as November or December 2016 the Trump Organization had the Trump Tower Moscow project on a "list of deals" whose official status with the company was that they had not yet been "closed out."[169] Cohen thereby reveals to the special counsel that from September 2015 through November 2016, "at no time . . . did Trump tell [Cohen] not to pursue the project or that the project should be abandoned."[170] Indeed, according to Cohen, "Trump wanted Trump Tower Moscow to succeed and . . . never discouraged him from working on the project because of the [presidential] campaign."[171] The Mueller Report notes the project would have been "highly lucrative" for Trump, and that Trump "stood to earn substantial sums over the lifetime of the project without assuming significant liabilities or financing commitments"—key points that may explain why, as the report notes, "Trump wanted to be updated on any developments . . . and on several occasions brought the project up with Cohen to ask what was happening on it."[172] In insisting to the special counsel's office that both Ivanka Trump and Donald Trump Jr. were also involved in the secretive Trump-Rozov deal, Cohen tells federal investigators that he not only "provided updates directly to Trump throughout 2015 and 2016" but also coordinated with Ivanka Trump on "design elements" and possible architects for the project, and with Trump Jr. on "his experience in Moscow" and the possibility of him becoming more involved in the project in its early stages.[173]

In February 2019, a White House source leaks to the media nearly every day of Trump's private schedule for the preceding three months. The disclosure reveals that Trump has over that period—at least—been spending at least 60 percent of his "work day" in entirely unstructured "executive time" outside the Oval Office.[174] Trump's public schedule gives the opposite impression to voters, erroneously placing Trump inside the Oval Office from 8:00 to 11:00 a.m. on every day he is in Washington.[175] The discrepancy is significant because, according to six sources with direct knowledge of Trump's habits, Trump has in fact been spending his mornings, among other endeavors, in the executive residence "phoning aides, members of Congress, friends, administration officials and informal advisers."[176] As a senior White House official tells Axios, "He's always calling people, talking to people. He's always up to something."[177] Axios notes that Trump has been, for months if not his entire presidency, hiding from his staff his actual movements—as even the "private schedule sent to staff" on a daily basis excludes meetings Trump "doesn't want most West Wing staff to know about for fear of leaks." Such meetings, estimated at thirty to sixty per month, include, the digital media outlet notes, "calls with heads of state" as well as certain in-person "political meetings."[178] According to Chris Whipple, a "student of presidential schedules" and the author of *The Gatekeepers: How the White House Chiefs of Staff Define Every Presidency*, there is "almost no historical parallel" for President Trump's unstructured, often clandestine daily schedule.[179]

Trump's highly secretive phone use would be less of a concern if it were, like everything else a president does, publicly reviewable through congressional or FOIA oversight. In fact, as the *New York Times* reports in late 2018, Trump has been insisting throughout his presidency on using nonsecure phones unregulated by his aides, the Secret Service, congressional oversight, or any governmental transparency mechanisms. As the *Times* recounts in an October 2018 article entitled "When Trump Phones Friends, the Chinese and the Russians Listen and Learn," Trump regularly uses multiple personal iPhones—it is not clear why he has more than one—to "call[ ] old friends . . . to gossip, gripe, or solicit their latest take on how he is doing," often discussing topics of sufficient gravity that his words provide "invaluable insights" on U.S. domestic and foreign policy to anyone listening in on the line.[180] According to White House officials, during these nonsecure calls to friends and world leaders Trump may well be discussing classified information.

Despite "repeated warnings" from his aides that "Russian spies are routinely eavesdropping on [his iPhone] calls," Trump refuses to cease putting American intelligence and policy at risk—a reckless practice that seems in direct opposition to the supposed paranoia that causes him to hide his schedule and phone habits from even his top aides in the first instance.[181] Indeed, it is unclear why Trump needs these calls to friends, advisers, and world leaders to be outside the conventional call-logging system used at the White House but also—apparently—open to intercept. The *Times* notes that at least one hostile foreign nation has been using its intercepts of Trump's "executive time" iPhone calls to "piece[ ] together a list of the people with whom Mr. Trump regularly speaks in hopes of using them to influence the president."[182] In this way, deliberately or otherwise, Trump is able to speak to individuals around the world without reporting his calls to Congress or other public advocates, while also telegraphing to foreign nations which of his friends and advisers are most deserving of illicit foreign-money largesse and/or can be used to backchannel information to him.

As of 2019, Trump has "two official iPhones that have been altered by the National Security Agency to limit their abilities and vulnerabilities," but a third phone the president insists on using "is no different from hundreds of millions of iPhones in use around the world."[183] "None of [the iPhones]," according to the *New York Times*, "are completely secure . . . calls made from the phones are intercepted as they travel through the cell towers, cables, and switches that make up national and international cell phone networks."[184] Trump's third, "personal" iPhone is consequently as significant a security risk—or perhaps a greater one—than the private, unsecured email server used by former secretary of state Hillary Clinton, the use of which Trump claimed was a federal crime requiring Clinton's imprisonment.[185] Whereas Clinton defended her use of a private email server as a matter of convenience only, according to the *Times* Trump's use of a nonsecure cell phone in the face of warnings from senior White House officials is explained by a deliberate penchant for secrecy—an expressed desire to ensure that even his senior aides don't have knowledge, let alone a record, of his calls.[186] As for his two official phones, Trump has refused to "swap them out" every thirty days as required by White House protocol.[187]

Jared Kushner's unauthorized use of encrypted messaging apps for conversations with foreign leaders, and Ivanka's failure to preserve her email communications in accordance with law, will also come under substantial scrutiny in 2019, with Kushner's WhatsApp practice being called a "recipe for disaster" that puts "highly sensitive government communications . . . at risk of exploitation by foreign governments and hackers," and Ivanka's use of a personal email address for government business widely deemed a violation of federal records laws.[188] Even Trump's deputy national security advisor, K. T. McFarland—one of the top national security officials in the country—will be found to have used a simple AOL email account to discuss with Thomas Barrack the transfer of sensitive nuclear technology to Saudi Arabia.[189] Despite warnings about these and other security risks in the Trump White House, they will continue seemingly unabated, with Kushner still using WhatsApp for conversations he is legally obligated to preserve as late as December 2018.[190]

In February, Kushner family friend Benjamin Netanyahu, the Israeli prime minister, shocks the world by revealing what had heretofore been a secret element of the Red Sea Conspiracy: that "representatives of leading Arab countries . . . are sitting down together with Israel in order to advance the common interest of war with Iran."[191] NBC News reports that Netanyahu's "provocative" and "strident call for Israeli-Arab action against the government in Tehran"—a call translated as "war with Iran" by his own office—"startle[s] Iranians and even the White House" with its directness.[192] NBC goes even further, however, acknowledging that the statement advances an existing perception the world over: "that Israel, its Gulf Arab neighbors, and the United States are interested in using military action to topple the government of Iran."[193] Another comment by Netanyahu in the same venue (an international conference in Warsaw) is equally indelicate, as it sees the Israeli prime minister acknowledging that "representatives of leading Arab countries" and Israel have participated in "many" prior meetings that he would describe as "secret summits."[194] When and where these "secret summits" occurred—and if they involved Israel, Saudi Arabia, the UAE, Egypt, Bahrain, and the United States, as many suspect—Netanyahu does not say, though NBC notes that "communal concerns about Iran have enabled nascent ties between Israel and Sunni Arab states that had been unimaginable for generations. Countries such as Saudi Arabia, the United Arab Emirates, and Bahrain that do not recognize Israel or maintain any formal diplomatic relations have started acknowledging more and more openly their behind-the-scenes ties to Israel and their quiet cooperation on security issues, most notably Iran. President Donald Trump has shared Netanyahu's views about the dangers of Iran."[195] The Associated Press reports that "Saudi Arabia, long rumored to have backdoor ties to Israel, lifted a decades-long ban on the use of its airspace for flights to Israel last spring. The leaders of the small Gulf nation of Bahrain have also expressed willingness to normalize relations. Gulf Arab states have given less voice to their traditional antipathy toward Israel as they have grown increasingly fearful of Iran over its involvement in various regional conflicts and its support for various armed groups. Getting closer to Israel also helps them to curry favor in Washington."[196]

Asked about Netanyahu's comments on a war with Iran, and subsequent claims by the prime minister's office that it mistranslated its own statement, Sen. Angus King (I-ME), a member of three Senate committees relevant to Netanyahu's remarks—the Senate Select Committee on Intelligence, the Senate Committee on Armed Services, and the Senate Energy and Natural Resources Committee—will tell MSNBC, "He [Netanyahu] knew what he meant."[197] Indeed, as the Associated Press notes, the conference in Poland "offers Israeli Prime Minister Benjamin Netanyahu an opportunity to flaunt in public what he has long boasted about happening behind the scenes—his country's improved relations with some Gulf Arab nations . . . [He] has repeatedly stated that Israel has clandestinely developed good relations with several Arab states."[198] Meanwhile, Danny Danon, Israel's United Nations ambassador, goes further than his boss in Warsaw, bragging that "they [Gulf Arab nations] are already cooperating with us. We ask them to recognize us and not to be ashamed for using our technology or our defense systems."[199] One of the instances of cooperation to which Danon may refer is a fall 2018 "security conference" in the United Arab Emirates attended by two of Netanyahu's ministers—a level of Israeli-UAE engagement that once would have been unthinkable.[200] Yoel Guzansky, a senior researcher at Israel's Institute for National Security Studies, tells the Associated Press that "covert meetings [between Israel and Arab nations] already exist, and [their] 'under-the-table' relations are the world's worst-kept secret."[201]

With one of Trump's top international allies having conceded that he is working with Trump's other allies—and has been for some time—to plunge America and countless other nations into a dangerous regional or even global military conflict with Iran, Western media react with predictable shock. "Israeli Prime Minister Benjamin Netanyahu has expressed his desire to go to war with Iran," *Newsweek* reports, noting that Netanyahu plans to "push the initiative forward" by meeting directly with "dozens of foreign envoys, including those from the Arab world."[202] While acknowledging that Netanyahu somewhat weakly attempted to walk back his comments—amending "war with Iran" to "combating Iran"—and that no high-level contacts between Israel and Iran's chief enemy in the region, Saudi Arabia, have been "publicly revealed," *Newsweek* nevertheless notes that "Saudi Arabia has led the charge against Iran, and Israel has often appealed to the kingdom to join forces against the Islamic Republic."[203]

Netanyahu's February 2019 comments are, indeed, only the public blossoming of a story long privately in development. In 2018, the *Washington Times* had written that "a secret alliance between Israel and Saudi Arabia aimed at restraining Iran's imperial desire for a land mass between Tehran and the Mediterranean [is] moving into a new phase. While there aren't formal diplomatic ties between the two countries, military cooperation does exist . . . [and] the Saudi government sent a military delegation to Jerusalem several months ago to discuss Iran's role as a destabilizing force in the region."[204] The *Times* added that Saudi Arabia was considering purchasing an Israeli-designed missile defense system (Iron Dome) as well as other Israeli military technology, a development the newspaper said "bespeaks a newfound respect for Israel and an emerging belief that in any Sunni defense condominium Israel will have a role to play."[205] The *Times* will note, too, that when Trump moved the U.S. embassy from Tel Aviv to Jerusalem in 2018—an act that temporarily halted all peace talks between the Israelis and Palestinians—"neither Saudi Arabia nor Egypt was actively hostile to the address change" beyond a peremptory United Nations vote.[206] The BBC concurred with the *Times* shortly thereafter, noting MBS's historic spring 2018 declaration that "the Israelis have the right to have their own land," and adding that two other nations, Egypt and Jordan—both part of Nader's late 2015 Red Sea meeting—"already have a kind of peace with Israel."[207] As for the UAE, it has participated in at least one secret summit with Netanyahu to address the Iran question, doing so late in President Obama's second term (see chapter 8).

The BBC attributes the thaw in Israeli-Saudi relations to "[MBS's] grand scheme" for Saudi Arabia, observing that Israel "has not missed any opportunity to brief, nudge, and hint at the growing depth of its dialogue with Riyadh. Saudi Arabia has been more reticent. But Prince Salman's comments together with a recent decision to allow Air India flights to and from Tel Aviv to transit Saudi air-space are tangible signs of a shift in Saudi Arabia too."[208] Indeed, as far back as late 2017, when MBS was purging domestic dissidents in the kingdom, NBC News had called the Saudi-Israeli relationship "cozy" and their budding alliance "an open secret."[209] "As . . . [MBS] tries to rally an anti-Iran coalition," NBC had reported, "Israel—with the blessing of the Trump administration—is presenting itself as a willing and able partner."[210] By the time of Netanyahu's February 2019 comments in Warsaw about war with Iran, the *Times of Israel* is even reporting that the "Bahraini Foreign Minister says confronting Tehran [is] more urgent than solving the Palestinian issue," and that the Emiratis' "top diplomat says Israel has [the] right to attack Iranian targets in Syria"—an astounding and historic concession, inasmuch as it gives the Jewish state formal license to kill Muslim hostiles in an Arab country.[211]

The Trump administration's approval of Israel's new alliances and intentions—and perhaps even its warlike rhetoric with respect to Iran—is demonstrated just days after Netanyahu announces his desire for war with the Iranians, as the U.S. military deploys its Terminal High Altitude Area Defense (THAAD) missile defense system in Israel for the first time ever.[212] While ostensibly part of a training exercise, the historic movement of heavy military equipment into Israel on the heels of that nation's prime minister publicly courting war with Iran cannot help but be taken as a sign of increased tensions in the region.

On February 7, Amazon CEO Jeff Bezos—the richest man in the world and a longtime enemy of President Trump, at least in the president's estimation—reveals in an essay for *Medium* that Trump's close friend David Pecker has just tried to blackmail him with intimate texts and seminude pictures of him and his girlfriend, Los Angeles news anchor Lauren Sanchez.[213] According to Bezos's essay, Pecker was "apoplectic" about the investigation by the *Washington Post* (owned by Bezos) into the execution of *Post* journalist Jamal Khashoggi. Writes Bezos, "The Saudi angle seems to hit a particularly sensitive nerve."[214] Bezos adds that Pecker, through an AMI representative, "said they [AMI] had . . . my text messages and photos . . . [and] would publish [them] if we didn't stop our investigation" into MBS's involvement into Khashoggi's death.[215] After Bezos rebuffs the blackmail attempt, Pecker's AMI pushes it further, giving the Amazon CEO a detailed accounting of all the pictures and texts in its possession, once again threatening to publish them if, in addition to ceasing its investigation of MBS's role in Khashoggi's death, the *Washington Post* does not also agree to issue a statement saying that it has "no knowledge or basis for suggesting that AMI's coverage [of the Bezos-Sanchez relationship] was politically motivated or influenced by political forces."[216] Given the allegations of a Pecker-MBS-Trump axis suffusing major media in early 2019, AMI's second missive to Bezos would, if successful at blackmailing the tech executive, protect not only MBS and Pecker but the president as well. Bezos rebuffs this second entreaty also, however.

The next month, March 2019, Bezos's private investigator in the Pecker matter, security specialist Gavin de Becker, writes an article for the *Daily Beast* alleging that Pecker's AMI is "in league with a foreign nation [Saudi

Arabia] that's been actively trying to harm American citizens and companies."[217] De Becker accuses AMI of lying about its primary source for the seminude pictures and intimate texts—which the company claimed came from Sanchez's brother, Michael—revealing that, according to a *Wall Street Journal* investigation, AMI had already "seen text exchanges" between Bezos and Sanchez when it first approached Michael Sanchez.[218] Per de Becker, even though neither Bezos nor de Becker had ever accused AMI of being involved in electronic eavesdropping or hacking, AMI's blackmail letter insisted that Bezos and the *Post* publicly absolve AMI of "any form of electronic eavesdropping or hacking"—an interesting demand, given the next-generation Israeli electronic eavesdropping and hacking equipment, Pegasus 3, that Pecker's friend MBS had acquired in mid-2017.[219] Tellingly, AMI also wanted to be absolved of having "knowledge of such conduct," which insistence seemed to tacitly acknowledge that a third party, for instance the Saudis, might well have engaged in such behavior prior to sending its fruits to Pecker and AMI.[220] The company and its CEO also wanted to be certain that neither de Becker nor Bezos would take any of their findings to law enforcement.[221]

In fact, by March 2019 de Becker had already done just that, along with informing federal law enforcement of his investigation's principal conclusion: "Our investigators and several experts concluded with high confidence that the Saudis had access to Bezos's phone, and gained private information [from it]."[222] In counterintelligence investigations, the designation "high confidence" connotes an assessment based on "high-quality" information.[223] One study of National Intelligence Estimates in the academic journal *Intelligence and National Security* observes that a "high confidence" assessment correlates to an analyst believing "a particular estimate is likely to be correct . . . [and] has a relatively large amount of relatively sound evidence to support [it]."[224] De Becker's evidence includes, per the analyst himself, "a broad array of resources: investigative interviews with current and former AMI executives and sources, extensive discussions with top Middle East experts in the intelligence community, leading cybersecurity experts who have tracked Saudi spyware, discussions with current and former advisers to President Trump, Saudi whistleblowers, people who personally know the Saudi Crown Prince Mohammed bin Salman (also known as MBS), people who work with his close associate Saud al-Qahtani, Saudi dissidents, and other targets of Saudi action, including writer/activist Iyad el-Baghdadi."[225] That MBS has the technology to do what de Becker describes, via his new allies the Israelis, is clear, as is that MBS can "collect vast amounts of previously inaccessible data from smartphones in the air without leaving a trace—including phone calls, texts, [and] emails," and that this capacity for engaging in "extensive surveillance efforts . . . ultimately led to the killing of journalist Jamal Khashoggi," as the *New York Times* had previously reported.[226] That MBS might use such technology to track and kill a personal enemy who is a U.S. resident is harrowing enough; that it might be used to criminally blackmail a Trump enemy using a Trump friend as an intermediary brings the prospect of Trump-Saudi collusion to another level entirely.

Per de Becker, MBS has—in a fashion suspiciously akin to the capabilities possessed and exploited by the Kremlin during the 2016 presidential election—a "cyberarmy" that can use "multi-pronged" digital propaganda campaigns to "attack[ ] people" it is "intent on harming."[227] That MBS emissary George Nader had previously approached Donald Trump Jr. alongside an Israeli man, Joel Zamel, with this very same capability, and had offered the Trumps the use of such technology in the elder Trump's efforts to secure the White House, adds a dimension of intrigue to the Pecker-Bezos affair that will ultimately have to be resolved by the federal law enforcement officers now in possession of the AMI-Bezos case file.

One example of Saudi disinformation quoted by de Becker is particularly troubling, as it suggests MBS's comfort with using a cyberarmy of trolls to spread disinformation about Trump opponents. According to one anti-Semitic message spread on U.S. social media by MBS's trolls (which falsely alleges that Jeff Bezos is Jewish), "We as Saudis will never accept to be attacked by the *Washington Post* in the morning, only to buy products from Amazon and Souq.com [Amazon's Saudi subsidiary] by night! Strange that all three companies are owned by the same Jew who attacks us by day, and sells us products by night! Our weapon is to boycott . . . because the owner of the newspaper is the same as their owner. We're after you—the Jew, worshipper of money, will go bankrupt by the will of God at the hands of Saudi Arabia . . . the owner of Amazon and Souq is the owner of the *Washington Post* is [*sic*] the spiteful Jew who insults us every day."[228]

De Becker concludes his analysis of Pecker and AMI's actions by noting that over time "the Trump/Pecker relationship has metastasized: in effect, the *Enquirer* [published by AMI] became an enforcement arm of the Trump presidential campaign, and presidency, as the U.S. Attorney in the Southern District of New York laid out in its case against [Trump attorney] Michael Cohen, who has pleaded guilty. The U.S. Attorney has done the country a service by levying extensive controls on AMI, David Pecker, and his deputy Dylan Howard, through a nonprosecution agreement that requires them to commit no other crimes for three years, and requires everyone at AMI to attend annual training on federal election laws. I'm guessing that's not how they used to spend their time."[229] De Becker's observation that MBS is trying to infiltrate not only the *Enquirer* and its AMI stablemates but also other American media outlets like *Rolling Stone*, *Variety*, and *National Geographic* is bolstered when the *Wall Street Journal* reveals in February 2019 that MBS is courting Vice Media as another American joint venture partner in his bid to "build an international media empire to combat the kingdom's rivals and remake its image in the West."[230] As with its "glossy magazine" outreach to AMI, Saudi Arabia would begin its proposed partnership with Vice Media with purportedly neutral "documentaries" on MBS's "social reforms in the ultraconservative kingdom."[231] This revelation offers a key counterpoint to MBS's ambitions in initiating his blockade against Qatar, as the blockade was focused on destroying supposedly hostile media outlets (the demands included "shut[ting] down Al Jazeera and its affiliate stations" as well as "all news outlets funded directly and indirectly by Qatar, including *Arabi21*, *Rassd*, *Al Araby Al Jadeed*, *Mekameleen*," and others); meanwhile, MBS's efforts in the United States have been squarely focused on bolstering outlets willing to be supportive of him.[232] Notably, MBS's international campaign—which uses both cyberwarfare and regular military action as well as diplomacy to promote media MBS likes and shutter media he does not—also includes a demand that Qatar orchestrate the closure of the *Middle East Eye*, which is headquartered in London; the *Middle East Eye* is the media outlet that first reported on the Red Sea Conspiracy.[233]

On February 19, House Democrats issue a report alleging that "top White House aides ignored warnings they could be breaking the law as they worked with former U.S. officials and a group called IP3 International to advance a multibillion-dollar plan to build nuclear reactors in the Middle East, including Saudi Arabia."[234] The report accuses Trump of plotting an illegal transfer of U.S. nuclear technology without congressional approval; beyond this, it cites whistleblowers who have reported to Congress "conflicts of interest among top White House advisers that could implicate federal criminal statutes," with the report specifically mentioning former and current Trump advisers Michael Flynn, K. T. McFarland, Derek Harvey, Thomas Barrack, and Rick Gates.[235] NBC News, noting the memo IP3 sent to Flynn seeking Barrack's appointment as steward of the U.S.-Saudi nuclear deal, quotes members of the Trump administration itself expressing deep concern about the plan, with "one senior Trump official saying that the proposal was 'not a business plan,' but rather 'a scheme . . . to make some money. . . . [W]e cannot do this.'"[236] One of the plotters identified by NBC is IP3 co-founder Bud McFarlane, who attended the VIP event orchestrated by Dimitri Simes prior to Trump's Mayflower Hotel speech in April 2016, was long K. T. McFarland's mentor, visited Trump Tower with Michael Flynn during the presidential transition—just ninety-six hours after Sergey Kislyak had met with Flynn and Kushner in the Trump-owned New York City tower—and was one of six Iran-Contra figures convicted during the Reagan administration and then pardoned with the assent of George H. W. Bush's attorney general.[237] The AG who executed Bush's pardon of Bud McFarlane several decades ago happens to also be Trump's current attorney general, William Barr.[238]

Trump appears untroubled by any of these concerns, having met in the White House with "backers of the [IP3] project" and his secretary of energy, Rick Perry, on February 12, with the assembled group finding him "engaged and probing."[239] Reuters adds to this story a key detail: "U.S. reactor builder Westinghouse, owned by Brookfield Asset Management Inc."—a key Kushner Companies lender—"would likely sell nuclear technology to Saudi Arabia in any deal."[240]

On February 21, a story that has dogged Trump since ten days before the 2016 election—that the Kremlin has *kompromat* on him that it can use at will, in addition to the blackmail it has by virtue of knowing that certain statements he has made publicly about his ties to Russia are untrue—returns with vigor, as CNN reports that multiple witnesses have told a bipartisan group of Senate investigators that one man in particular may hold the key to the mystery of Trump *kompromat*: David Geovanis.[241] Geovanis is a Moscow-based American businessman who set up a 1996 trip to Moscow for Trump at a time Trump was looking to develop a Trump-branded tower in Russia. Geovanis subsequently worked for Oleg Deripaska, the Russian oligarch at the center of the Trump-Russia investigation.[242] CNN, in releasing a photo of Geovanis with a scantily clad woman, reports that a "witness has alleged in written testimony, seen by CNN, that Geovanis may be valuable in the mystery of whether Russia has material on Trump that could be personally embarrassing to him."[243] If so, such material may be part of an ongoing FBI and CIA counterintelligence investigation into whether Trump has been compromised by the Kremlin, a Kremlin agent like Deripaska, or any other foreign government—and as such, would not appear (as indeed it does not appear) in the redacted Mueller Report released in April 2019. Notably, another individual on Trump's 1996 trip to Moscow was Howard Lorber, who in February 2019 was revealed as the owner of a blocked phone number Donald Trump Jr. spoke with in the midst of his negotiations with Kremlin agents about meeting them at Trump Tower in June 2016.[244] CNN notes that, having now married a Russian woman and obtained a Russian passport, and having not returned to the United States to visit family since 2017, Geovanis has made a "decision to remain in Moscow [that] means U.S. congressional investigators can't easily find out what he knows," despite at least three congressional witnesses urging members of Congress to speak to him.[245]

On February 26, 2019, while the nation is transfixed by the spectacle of the president's former personal attorney, Michael Cohen, testifying publicly before Congress about Trump having ordered him to violate campaign finance laws in the run-up to the 2016 election, Trump's daughter and son-in-law meet with MBS in Riyadh.[246] The White House statement on the meeting makes no mention of Jamal Khashoggi, the U.S. resident and *Washington Post* journalist whom MBS stands accused of having had kidnapped, dismembered, executed, decapitated, dissolved, and incinerated, but it does discuss, in broad terms, "American-Saudi cooperation and plans to improve conditions in the region through investment."[247] The Kushner-MBS summit, along with a subsequent meeting with Turkey's Erdogan on February 27, thus officially kicks off Kushner's (and Ivanka's) Middle East "tour" to promote a Middle East peace plan—a tour that skips both Israel and the Palestinian territories, the two entities upon which any peace plan would depend, but whose conflict with each other MBS's singular focus on Iran has implicitly sidelined. In meeting with MBS, MBZ, Erdogan, Bahraini king Hamad bin Isa al-Khalifa, and Omani sultan Qaboos bin Said al-Said, Kushner appears to promise $25 billion in investments to the Palestinians and $40 billion to Egypt and Jordan, two of the original Red Sea conspirators, with, as the *Times* reports, "most of that money [coming] from the region's wealthiest states, among them Saudi Arabia."[248] As the *Arab Weekly* notes, after each meeting the White House's official statement on what was discussed is both curiously repetitive and oddly evasive: "they almost all included a variation of this phrase: 'Additionally, they [Kushner and regional leaders] discussed ways to improve the condition of the entire region through economic investment'"—an apparent reference, if a vague one, to Kushner and Flynn's Middle East Marshall Plan.[249]

Later reports will reveal that Kushner and Ivanka's trip to the Middle East was opaque even to those who accompanied them, with the *Daily Beast* reporting that while one senior State Department official was on the trip, "otherwise [it] left American diplomats in the dark . . . [with] embassy staff [in Riyadh] . . . reportedly sidelined from participating in the meetings on the trip, including those with the Royal Court and Crown Prince Mohammed bin Salman."[250] The meetings with MBS are attended only by Kushner, Brian Hook (the State Department's special representative for Iran), and Trump's Middle East envoy Jason Greenblatt.[251] As the *Daily Beast* notes, Hook "is one of several current and former State Department officials under investigation by the Office of the Inspector General for alleged politically motivated personnel decisions"; Greenblatt, the Trump Organization attorney hired into the administration by Kushner and Trump transition team brass in December 2016, is said by *Fortune* to be "a key component of Robert Mueller's ongoing investigation of the president"—not because of any contacts between Greenblatt and the Russians but because Greenblatt, as a Trump Organization executive vice president and in-house attorney for years, has a "knowledge of Trump's business dealings [that] is unparalleled."[252] Kushner thus has with him, as he meets privately with MBS, a man who can understand better than even Kushner how the Trump Organization might benefit from the "economic investment" in the Middle East that the president's son-in-law is proposing. That Greenblatt is able to see clearly these Trump Organization–benefiting angles as they arise may explain, too, why it was he who ended up with the job for which Thomas Barrack had been so eagerly and perhaps avariciously lobbying. Indeed, this may be one reason that House Foreign Affairs Committee chairman Eliot Engel will in March seek "detailed documents from [Kushner's] February trip, including aircraft manifests, clearance records for each person who traveled, invoices and expense reports, and records relating to the State Department's participation in the trip."[253] Congress's interest seems most focused on Hook, as evidenced by the House Foreign Affairs Committee seeking "all emails [Hook] sent or received" relating to the trip, as well as any "handwritten notes" that Hook took during any of the meetings he attended.[254]

It turns out that there is a reason for the Foreign Affairs Committee to be concerned. In March, it will be revealed that the Trump administration "has approved six secret authorizations by companies to sell nuclear power technology and assistance to Saudi Arabia," thereby moving forward with the secret plans for U.S.-Saudi cooperation that former Trump national security advisor Michael Flynn was working on as early as 2015.[255] Reuters notes that the secret authorizations granted by Trump's Energy Department are part of a "quietly pursued . . . wider deal on sharing U.S. nuclear power technology with Saudi Arabia"—a plan that could, consistent with the long-standing multinational "grand bargain" involving the Trumps, Russia, Saudi Arabia, the UAE, Israel, Bahrain, and Egypt, see Russian construction firms acquire contracts to build nuclear power plants in the kingdom.[256] Energy Secretary Rick Perry is revealed to have agreed to keep the authorizations, known as Part 810 authorizations, a secret—at the request of the companies planning to sell nuclear technology to MBS—though "in the past the Energy Department [had] made previous Part 810 authorizations available for the public to read at its headquarters."[257] The Trump administration offers no explanation for this breach of protocol other than to say that the requests contained "proprietary information"; however, Energy Department regulations allow any proprietary information in a Part 810 to be so designated without the whole application becoming secret.[258]

Reaction to the Saudi nuclear deal is unambiguous in the media, with the *Guardian* calling "grotesque" the very idea of "sell[ing] state-of-the-art nuclear technology to Saudi Arabia, potentially enabling Crown Prince Mohammed bin Salman's reckless regime to build nuclear weapons."[259] The British media outlet adds that "the nuclear scheme appears to provide further evidence of attempts to monetize the Trump presidency and of possible conflicts of interest and corruption. . . . The 'nukes-to-Saudi' affair may also help explain why Trump exculpated Salman's regime over its murder of the journalist Jamal Khashoggi, and has ignored Saudi atrocities in Yemen and other abuses. As they say in New York business circles, [Trump] has skin in the game."[260] The *New York Times* concurs, with Nicholas Kristof writing that "of all the harebrained and unscrupulous dealings of the Trump administration in the last two years, one of the most shocking is a Trump plan to sell nuclear reactors to Saudi Arabia that could be used to make nuclear weapons. . . . This is abominable policy tainted by a gargantuan conflict of interest involving Kushner."[261] Kristof adds, "It may be conflicts like these, along with even murkier ones, that led American intelligence officials to refuse a top-secret security clearance for Kushner.... Trump overruled them to grant Kushner the clearance."[262] The columnist's critique of the Trump-MBS relationship also quotes Rep. Brad Sherman (D-CA), who has opined that "a country that can't be trusted with a bone saw shouldn't be trusted with nuclear weapons."[263]

Concern over the Trump administration's clandestine pursuit of a nuclear deal with Saudi Arabia is bipartisan, with Sen. Marco Rubio and Sen. Bob Menendez (D-NJ) initiating an investigation with the Government Account-ability Office (GAO) regarding the existence or parameters of any such deal.[264] Of particular concern, Reuters notes, are statements MBS made to CBS News in 2018 insisting "that the kingdom [of Saudi Arabia] would develop nuclear weapons if its rival Iran did"—a troubling pronouncement, given that MBS's ally Trump withdrew the United States from the Iran nuclear deal at a time when Iran was in compliance with the deal, thereby dramatically increasing the odds that Iran would itself withdraw from the deal and begin developing nuclear weapons.[265] The wire service also notes Saudi Arabia's history of "push[ing] back against agreeing to U.S. standards that would block two paths to potentially making fissile material for nuclear weapons clandestinely: enriching uranium and reprocessing spent fuel."[266]

As Kushner is in Riyadh, Republicans at home are furious with the Trump administration for refusing to send a report to Congress about Jamal Khashoggi's assassination, a violation of the very Magnitsky Act that Kushner, Trump Jr., and Manafort had discussed overturning at their now-infamous June 2016 meeting with Kremlin agents at Trump Tower.[267] To justify this otherwise inexplicable refusal, one of Trump's top allies in the Senate, Jim Risch (R-ID), falsely tells "several of his GOP colleagues that President Donald Trump had complied with the Magnitsky Act by sending Congress a report [via Risch] determining who was responsible for the Saudi journalist's murder," even though, writes *Politico*, "the adminis-tration had already publicly declared that it was going to ignore lawmak-ers' demand."[268] Risch subsequently writes a letter asking the White House to simply give senators a classified briefing on the Khashoggi incident; the letter praises Trump for his "ongoing efforts" to work with Congress and makes no reference to the Magnitsky Act, even as Rubio is complaining to the media that Trump's apparent policy with respect to the act is "that they refuse to follow the law with regard to Magnitsky."[269] Of course, any following of the Magnitsky Act by the Trump administration could signal to the Kremlin, MBS, or other dictators and human rights violators around the world that Trump acknowledges the validity of the act as applicable U.S. law or, still worse, that he supports it. Rubio's anger at Trump's recalcitrance is, per *Politico*, reflective of an incipient "insurgency" of "enraged" Republican senators who—representing a majority of the GOP caucus in the Senate—"after receiving a classified briefing on Khashoggi's murder inside the Saudi Consulate in Istanbul [from the intelligence community], concluded that [MBS] was complicit in the killing. Trump himself has been reluctant to ascribe any blame for Khashoggi's murder to the crown prince, citing the need to maintain a close relationship with Riyadh."[270]

In the wake of revelations that Trump and many of his top allies have been photographed with a former Florida day spa owner who has publicly boasted of selling access to the U.S. government to powerful Chinese nationals, *Mother Jones* reports that the "head of [an] Asian GOP group says he 'wouldn't rule out' [the existence of] illegal foreign donations to Trump" from Chinese sources.[271] The accusation echoes an older one from the Steele dossier, which contends that Trump's "business dealings in China and other emerging markets" are even more legally dubious than his associations with Russia—and include both bribes and kickbacks, the former a constitutionally enumerated impeachable offense.[272]

The Steele dossier becomes relevant again just as it is receiving confirmation on one of its major points of emphasis: a tech firm the dossier implies was exploited by Russian spies during the 2016 campaign was, evidence suggests, used in exactly the way Steele's intelligence indicated.[273] Specifically, the dossier accused Aleksej Gubarev's companies of using "botnets and porn traffic to transmit viruses, plant bugs, steal data and conduct 'altering operations' against the Democratic Party leadership." The *New York Times* notes that "new evidence [has] emerged that indicate[s] that internet service providers owned by Mr. Gubarev appear to have been used to do just that."[274]

The *Atlantic* reports that Manafort, sentenced to seven and a half years in federal prison after convictions in two federal courts, could still face collusion-related charges from federal law enforcement using evidence Robert Mueller gathered about Manafort's coordination with Kremlin agent Konstantin Kilimnik.[275] Just so, the Justice Department has told a federal court that federal prosecutors are still using more than a dozen special counsel's office memos containing information from former Trump national security advisor Michael Flynn for multiple ongoing criminal investigations, leading ABC News to conclude that "much of the legal work that started under the special counsel probe into Russian meddling in the 2016 election could continue long after [Mueller] disbands his team."[276] As Congress continues its own investigations of Russian interference in the 2016 presidential election, one of the top Republicans in Washington, Senate Finance Committee chairman Chuck Grassley (R-IA), publicly torches Trump's Treasury Department for failing to "provide Congress with certain bank records" his committee had previously requested, and indeed for falsely telling Congress that all such records had been proffered when in fact, as revealed in a February 2019 *BuzzFeed News* article about "a Russian-born lobbyist who was at a controversial June 2016 Trump Tower meeting," "'hundreds of thousands of dollars transferred among individuals and entities' mentioned in Grassley's document request to Treasury" were never disclosed even to Senate Republicans.[277]

No explanation is ever provided for the Trump administration withholding these documents from Congress, but the *BuzzFeed News* article to which Grassley refers gives at least one possible explanation: the article alleges that "Soviet military officer turned Washington lobbyist" Rinat Akhmetshin received "suspicious payments totaling half a million dollars before and after" he secretly met with the president's son, son-in-law, and campaign manager at Trump Tower during the heat of the 2016 general election campaign—a meeting both the president and the president's son ultimately lied about in carefully orchestrated statements to the public.[278] For his part, Trump Sr. even lied about his involvement in the writing of the statement that lied about the Trump Tower meeting Akhmetshin attended.[279] As for Akhmetshin, banks had flagged the 2016 payments into his accounts on the "suspicion that they showed Akhmetshin had violated federal lobbying laws . . . by failing to register as a foreign lobbyist" and as "potential evidence of corruption and bribery in the bid to overturn the sanctions law [the Magnitsky Act]"; when this information was turned over to Trump's Treasury Department, it was promptly buried—and stayed buried even after Congress requested it.[280] When *BuzzFeed News* locates Akhmetshin and asks him for a comment, he replies, "Get the fuck out of here, okay?"[281]

In his testimony before the Senate, Akhmetshin said that he went to Trump Tower because he "just happened to be in New York City to see a play" when he received a "last-minute invitation from [self-described Kremlin 'informant' Natalia] Veselnitskaya" to go meet with Trump's son; Akhmetshin told the Senate that he wore a "t-shirt and jeans" to the meeting.[282] Despite Akhmetshin's unusual attire—he was apparently "dressed entirely in pink," according to another meeting attendee—and the fact that, per one eyewitness account, he "did most of the talking" at the Trump Tower meeting, Donald Trump Jr. will testify to Congress that he has no memory of the onetime Soviet military officer being in Trump Tower at all.[283]

Trump Jr.'s contention is an odd one, and not merely because he testifies to Congress that it was Veselnitskaya, not Akhmetshin, who did nearly all the talking during the meeting at Trump Tower. Given Manafort's presence at that meeting, and his subsequent course of negotiations with Konstantin Kilimnik over a sanctions deal authored by a member of the Ukrainian Parliament—a course of negotiations that begins within sixty days of the June 2016 meeting at Trump Tower—it is telling that Akhmetshin will later tell the Senate Judiciary Committee that he himself met with Kilimnik and a member of the Ukrainian Parliament in Washington "probably in 2014." If 2014 is the correct year, it is a point in time soon after Trump decided to run for president; if the year was in fact 2015, it would be after sanctions had been leveled against Russia for its illegal annexation of Crimea.[284] Notably, both Akhmetshin and Kilimnik have been identified as connected to Russian intelligence, indeed the very same unit as the one responsible for election hacking in 2016: the GRU.[285] Though Akhmetshin denies in his congressional testimony having any association with the GRU, the *Guardian* will quote an attorney who has often worked with the Russian-born lobbyist as saying, "He is a former GRU person for sure, but he once said, there is no such thing as 'former.'"[286] The possibility that there was indeed follow-up to the sanctions discussion at Trump Tower in June 2016—and that the follow-up was an ongoing sanctions negotiation conducted by a man, Paul Manafort, who had been present at that June meeting—would fly in the face of repeated claims by Trump Jr. and others in Trump's inner circle that there was, in fact, no such follow-up.[287]

As for the other Russian entity involved in the 2016 election interference, the "troll factory" known as the Internet Research Agency, in January 2019 Robert Mueller will reveal that documents his office provided to the defendants' attorneys in the federal prosecution of the IRA (as part of the "discovery" stage of the case) were later doctored and disseminated online—with the apparent intent to misrepresent the U.S. government's case against more than a dozen Kremlin agents.[288]

The Treasury Department's unwillingness to provide possible evidence of Trump-Russia financial crimes to Congress will come under greater scrutiny when it is revealed that Trump's treasury secretary, Steve Mnuchin—a member of Trump's sixteen-person presidential transition executive committee—struck a $25 million deal in 2017 with Leonard Blavatnik, an "associate" of Oleg Deripaska, the Kremlin-allied Russian oligarch at the heart of the Trump-Russia investigation.[289] "Questions regarding Trump's relationship with Russia include," *Vanity Fair* will write, "why did the president . . . leak confidential information about classified intelligence to Russian envoys? Why did [he] . . . undermine his own U.N. ambassador by telling the Kremlin not to worry about the punishment she promised would be meted out for its actions in Syria? What was up with the president . . . begging for Russia to be allowed back into the G7 after it was kicked out for invading another European country? And . . . [why did] Trump literally sid[e] with Vladimir Putin over his own intelligence agencies? . . . [Now] lawmakers would also like to know why Trump's Treasury Secretary decided to lift sanctions on companies with links to Russian billionaire Oleg Deripaska."[290] The magazine notes that Mnuchin's own response to this last in a litany of critical queries was that lawmakers should simply "trust" the president on Russia.[291]

Mnuchin's dealings with Blavatnik, the Deripaska ally, will come under even further scrutiny from Congress when the Trump administration begins lifting U.S. sanctions "on companies controlled by Deripaska."[292] Deripaska, a man intimately connected to Vladimir Putin and Paul Manafort and also a past employer of Joel Zamel—the Israeli business intelligence expert who visited Trump Tower in August 2016 to offer Trump collusive assistance via a massive online disinformation campaign— formerly employed David Geovanis as well; Geovanis is the man three congressional witnesses have said may know about Russian *kompromat* on Trump (see Chapter 10). As an exposé of Mnuchin's conflicts of interest in the Trump-Russia investigation in *Vanity Fair* details, the treasury secretary's business partner "Blavatnik . . . co-owns Sual Partners with another sanctioned oligarch, Viktor Vekselberg, and Sual 'is a major shareholder' of Rusal, one of Deripaska's sanctioned companies. . . . Blavatnik formerly served on Rusal's board, and . . . one of his companies donated $1 million to Trump's inaugural fund."[293] According to Rep. Jackie Speier (D-CA), Blavatnik "had a clear financial interest in the outcome of the Treasury action" against Deripaska that Mnuchin directly oversaw.[294]

After Mnuchin's Treasury Department lifts sanctions on Deripaska's companies, the largest one, EN+, names Chris Burnham, a former John Bolton assistant and a Trump transition team member alongside Mnuchin, to be on its board of directors.[295] Though the removal of sanctions on three of Deripaska's largest companies had originally been conditioned on his stepping away from them, it will later be revealed, after the sanctions on the company are lifted, that Deripaska has been allowed to retain a majority stake in EN+.[296] In a major investigative report, the *New York Times* will reveal that Deripaska has clearly "benefitted" from the sanctions deal, which is actually governed, the newspaper finds, by a "less punitive" but "binding confidential document . . . [that] the administration negotiated" and that the American public was not intended to see.[297] Per the *Times*, the secret document "shows that the sanctions relief deal will allow Mr. Deripaska to wipe out potentially hundreds of millions of dollars in debt . . . [and] leave allies of Mr. Deripaska and the Kremlin with significant stakes in his companies."[298] Moreover, after Mnuchin declares publicly that Deripaska's children "in no way benefit[ed]" from the Trump administration's sanctions relief, it will be revealed, in April 2019, that in fact Mnuchin and the Treasury Department allowed 10.5 million shares of Deripaska's company (EN+), worth $78 million, to be transferred to a trust fund for his two teenagers.[299] Further controversy is stirred when Deripaska's aluminum company, Rusal, announces, shortly after receiving sanctions relief, that it will be building what media reports call "the largest new aluminum plant built in the U.S. in nearly four decades," and will be building the plant in Kentucky—the home state of Senate majority leader Mitch McConnell.[300] As *Newsweek* will report, "McConnell was among the advocates for lifting sanctions on Rusal."[301]

As outrage over Mnuchin's actions grows, Democrats already upset about other information relevant to the Russia investigation that has been withheld by the Trump administration demand that the administration produce "all documents and communications, regardless of form and classification, that refer or relate to any communications between President Trump and President Putin, including in-person meetings and telephone calls"—and including notes taken by U.S. translators in meetings Trump kept secret from the media and, in some cases, his own aides.[302] The five-page request from the House Intelligence Committee identifies dozens of categories of Trump-Putin communications that have to date remained secret from both Congress and American voters.[303] Committee chairman Adam Schiff tells CBS News that the House Permanent Select Committee on Intelligence is looking "deep" into the "disturbing" Trump Tower Moscow deal in 2015—a deal Schiff says "stood to make him [Trump] more money than he had ever made on any other deal in his life" and involved then-candidate Trump "pursuing help from the Kremlin . . . in the most compromising circumstance I can imagine"—as well as allegations that "Russians have been laundering money through the Trump Organization."[304]

As Schiff is demanding significant additional document production from the White House, the House Judiciary Committee is engaged in a similar exercise with respect to documents from more than eighty individuals and entities whom Republicans had not interviewed or requested materials from when they held Congress.[305] The list of those to whom demands are made—under threat of a subpoena for any nonproduction—includes executives from Cambridge Analytica, WikiLeaks, the Trump Organization, and AMI; aides and advisers from the 2016 Trump campaign; corporate officers from entities that gave suspicious donations to Trump's inaugural committee; White House employees; members of Trump's family, including Eric Trump and Donald Trump Jr.; Trump's attorneys, personal assistants, friends, and spokesmen; and George Nader.[306]

Meanwhile, in the House Financial Services Committee, chairwoman Maxine Waters (D-CA) announces in early March that the one bank that was still willing to lend to the Trump Organization following Trump's string of bankruptcies in the 1990s—Deutsche Bank—has agreed to cooperate with voluminous document requests from Congress that it had previously resisted.[307] Concurrently, the chairman of the House Ways and Means Committee announces that he will move toward demanding that the IRS divulge Trump's tax returns, which in 2016 then-candidate Trump had refused to release on the grounds—since revealed as untrue by his own attorney, Michael Cohen—that he was under audit.[308] And Elijah Cummings (D-MD), chairman of the House Oversight Committee, launches an inquiry into Trump's overruling of government intelligence professionals in granting top-secret security clearance to his daughter and son-in-law after they had each been denied such clearance.[309] In addition to looking at the clearances given to Ivanka Trump and Jared Kushner, Cummings announces his intention to find out why Michael Flynn kept his security clearance after he lied to the FBI about his contacts with a hostile foreign nation, and how Trump adviser Rob Porter maintained his security clearance despite the Trump administration's awareness of "allegations that he had abused two ex-wives."[310] According to Cummings, Congress will "evaluate the extent to which the nation's most highly guarded secrets were provided to officials who should not have had access to them."[311] Outside the purview of the inquiry, for now, is Kushner's reported provision of President's Daily Brief materials to MBS in October 2017 (see chapter 8), and Trump's provision of classified Israeli intelligence to top Kremlin representatives in the Oval Office—at a meeting Trump allowed only Kremlin-controlled media to photograph—in May 2017.[312] Summarizing the new Democratic push for answers on Trump-Russia collusion, Axios observes, "Mueller is just the beginning. House Democrats plan a vast probe of President Trump and Russia—with a heavy focus on money laundering—that will include multiple [congressional] committees and dramatic public hearings, and could last into 2020."[313]

What remains in doubt is whether and when Trump will begin to lose Republican allies. By March 2019, Sen. John Kennedy (R-LA) is calling MBS "the original El Chapo," and Rubio is accusing the Saudi prince of going "full gangster," adding to this slight a demand that the Government Accountability Office look into any actions taken by the Department of Energy, without interagency communication, to initiate the sale of nuclear technology to Saudi Arabia. Even so, it remains unclear how many senators—even among the many said to be enraged at MBS over the Khashoggi killing—will follow Rubio's suit in pressing for answers regarding Saudi Arabia, let alone Russia.[314]

Meanwhile, Trump's legal team appears to back away from earlier claims that no one on Trump's campaign ever colluded with any Russian nationals, which position was itself a retreat from a claim made in 2016 by then-Trump campaign communications director Hope Hicks that "there was no communication between the campaign and any foreign entity during the campaign."[315] Trump attorney Rudy Giuliani tells CNN in an interview that "I never said there was no collusion between the campaign [and Russia]. Or between people in the campaign [and Russia]."[316] In all, the *Washington Post* has identified ten distinct tactical retreats in the Trump team's defenses to accusations of collusion with the Kremlin.[317]

As the new Democratic Congress begins to send out document demands en masse, Trump yet again gives cover to Saudi and Emirati atrocities in Yemen by canceling an Obama-era rule requiring intelligence officials to publish an annual report on American airstrikes in certain countries in and around the Middle East, including Yemen.[318] Even before canceling the legal requirement, the Trump administration had already chosen to ignore it, releasing no report on airstrikes in Yemen in 2018—or, for that matter, in other countries, including Libya, Somalia, and Pakistan.[319] Explaining Trump's decision, the State Department will tell media that the mandatory intelligence reports, which cover CIA-orchestrated strikes, were "redundant" because other U.S. entities besides the CIA publish records of their own airstrikes, and those records, if not the ones required by rule and involving the CIA, are available.[320] In a *Politico* interview, Rachel Stohl, a defense expert at the Stimson Center, asks, "Why [cancel the rule] now? Could this represent a new line of effort or expansion of strikes that we now aren't going to know about?"[321]

On March 14, the House votes 420–0 to make the Mueller report public when it is released to the DOJ. Trump's golfing partner and political ally Lindsey Graham blocks the measure in the Senate, however.[322]

On February 28, Israel's attorney general announces that prime minister Benjamin Netanyahu will be indicted on bribery and breach of trust charges "arising from three separate corruption investigations," making Netanyahu the first sitting Israeli prime minister to ever face indictment on such allegations.[323] Just days later, a "leak" from Israel's Shin Bet intelligence service (a government entity under Netanyahu's leadership) reveals that "Iranians" have infiltrated the cell phone of Netanyahu's opponent in the upcoming Israeli presidential elections, Benny Gantz.[324] While noting that "Israel's Iran hacking scandal could ensure Netanyahu's election"—as it suggests Gantz is weak on national security—*Haaretz*, a major Israeli media outlet, adds, cryptically, that "it is also possible that other players with an interest in [Gantz] could have [hacked him], masquerading behind an 'Iranian signature.'"[325] Given that MBS has recently purchased state-of-the-art Pegasus 3 phone-hacking software from Israeli spyware firm NSO, a firm founded and run by former Israeli intelligence agents, and that MBZ has recently been caught using NSO software to target the phone of a prominent human rights activist, the fears expressed in *Haaretz* of a non-Iranian intervention in the Israeli election are worth consideration.[326] Nor is NSO disconnected from Netanyahu's biggest booster in the United States, President Trump. In 2016, while he was advising Trump, Michael Flynn was also a paid adviser for both NSO Group's parent company, Francisco Partners, and an NSO offshoot, OSY Technologies.[327]

Trump's willingness to publicly insert himself into the Israeli elections is evidenced when, just days before the April 9 vote, he invites Netanyahu to the White House to announce that the United States now recognizes Israeli sovereignty over the Golan Heights—a major public relations boost for the Likud politician at perhaps the most fraught moment of his political career, as he is trailing Gantz in the polls with only days left before the election.[328] The Associated Press calls this and other Trump-Netanyahu overtures part of "an unspoken [Trump administration] endorsement of Netanyahu, and in Israel, having close ties with whoever occupies the White House is seen as a major asset."[329]

By comparison to Trump and his allies in Saudi Arabia and the UAE, who are seeking an alliance with Netanyahu, the Iranians are far more likely to support Gantz than Netanyahu, given the latter's recent declaration that he favors war with Tehran; the Iranians are therefore far less likely to threaten the election chances of the "Blue and White" party's candidate (Gantz) by publicly exposing him to blackmail.[330] Days before the election, the Associated Press reports that a mysterious "network of social media bots," including "hundreds of fake accounts," are "frequently and exclusively" supporting Netanyahu and attacking Gantz—even, in an echo of the 2016 general election in the United States, "inciting hate speech."[331] The country from which these bots and fake accounts originate is unknown.

On April 9, Netanyahu defeats Gantz in the race for Israeli's presidency, a development the Associated Press reports means that Netanyahu will "press ahead with a hardline agenda that will likely eliminate the last hopes of a two-state solution with the Palestinians."[332] Netanyahu's reelection also ensures that all six of the world leaders who endorse a "grand bargain" in the Middle East—MBS, MBZ, el-Sisi, Trump, Putin, and Netanyahu—remain in power in their respective countries.

In 2019, the world will see new revelations regarding the scope of Putin's international election meddling. In Italy, *L'Espresso* reports, as summarized by *Mother Jones*, that "Deputy Prime Minister Matteo Salvini of the hard-right Lega Nord party . . . sought [in 2018] a 3 million euro funding commitment from Kremlin-linked entities to finance his political campaign . . . [with] the money to flow to Lega Nord covertly, tucked behind an ordinary-seeming oil export deal between Italian and Russian companies."[333] In England, Channel 4 News reveals that "in the heated months in the run-up to the 'Brexit' referendum"—a referendum whose passage Putin strongly favored—"millionaire Brexit backer Arron Banks eagerly pursued a multibillion-pound gold deal brought to him by a Russian oligarch with links to the Kremlin"; by June, the European Union, along with the Parliament of the United Kingdom, the governing body most immediately and profoundly affected by "Brexit," will announce that "Russia conducted a 'continued and sustained' disinformation campaign against Europe's recent parliamentary elections."[334] And in the United States, the *Washington Post* cites a recent report by the French Ministry of Foreign Affairs establishing that "Russia is responsible for 80 percent of disinformation activities in Europe."[335] Meanwhile, CNBC reveals that Putin's top lieutenant, Dmitry Peskov, has managed to place his daughter as an intern at the European Union—a particularly troubling development given the Kremlin's commitment to breaking up the EU and its past interference with the union's elections.[336] Indeed, as far back as 2016 the BBC had aired a report accusing Putin of "using hybrid warfare"—that is, the BBC explains, "any form of [international] aggression short of open invasion"—to "destabilize the EU."[337]

In the spring of 2019, new attention is focused on Trump's connections to China—first detailed as problematic and potentially collusive in the Steele dossier—as a Chinese woman with a suspicious thumb drive looking to meet with Trump gains access to Mar-a-Lago, and numerous individuals close to Trump are found to have been in contact with a second Chinese woman, Cindy Yang, who bragged online about selling access to the president.[338] In the first instance, the woman who breaches security at the president's country club, Yujing Zhang, is found to have two Chinese passports, a self-executing malware application, nine USB drives, five SIM cards, $7,500 in $100 bills, and a "signal detector to detect hidden cameras."[339] Most troublingly, Zhang presents "an invitation to Mar-a-Lago managers . . . [that] is the same as an invitation posted on the website of Cindy Yang, the Florida spa founder who was allegedly selling access to Trump events at Mar-a-Lago" to Chinese nationals.[340] Federal agents tell a court that they "believe she [Zhang] may be a Chinese intelligence agent and an 'extreme' flight risk."[341] Yang, the spa owner, is at the time a potential witness in a "human trafficking investigation" as the former owner of several spas that were shut down by federal investigators for allegedly selling illicit sexual services; the investigation, notes the *Miami Herald*, had by the time of Zhang's arrest "shutter[ed] ten massage parlors and result[ed] in charges against more than 300 men"—including one well-known businessman who is a close friend of the president, New England Patriots president Robert Kraft.[342] Of Kraft, the *Miami Herald* writes, "Only in Florida could a billionaire's massage parlor pit stop unmask a possible spy ring."[343]

In the days following Kraft's arrest, pictures will emerge online of Yang posing with Trump himself, as well as numerous Trump friends, family, and allies, including Rep. Matt Gaetz (R-FL), Kellyanne Conway, Melania Trump, Florida's Republican governor Ron DeSantis, Florida's Republican senator Rick Scott, Donald Trump Jr., Eric Trump, Sarah Palin, Fox News host Jesse Watters, pro-Trump Twitter personality Dan Bongino, actor Jon Voight, and former Trump administration adviser Sebastian Gorka.[344]

In April, the *Palm Beach Post* reports that there is "no trace of the money raised" from Trump's Asian Pacific American Presidential Inaugural Gala. Corporate donors for the event included, per the *Post*, "an embattled Saipan-based casino later raided by the FBI . . . [and] a Guam-based shipyard and a handful of Pacific Island hotel operators, all of which benefited from a foreign labor bill signed into law by Trump" in early 2018.[345]

Congressional Democrats quickly call for criminal and counterintelligence investigations of Yang's online claims that she has successfully sold access to Trump.[346] An April 5, 2019, *Miami Herald* story will carry the startling headline, "Cindy Yang Helped Chinese Tech Stars Get $50K Photos with Trump. Who Paid?"[347] By law, notes the newspaper, "Selling tickets to campaign fundraisers without disclosing the buyer to the Federal Election Commission is illegal. Selling tickets to foreign nationals, who are banned from donating to American political causes, would be an additional violation of U.S. law."[348]

Meanwhile, U.S. media begins covering Erik Prince's new overseas venture, the Hong Kong–based Frontier Services Group (FSG), which in early 2019—just weeks after Prince has stepped down as chairman, while retaining a 9 percent stake and deputy chairman position within the business—holds a "signing ceremony to build a training center in far western China, where the Chinese government has detained as many as a million Uighur Muslims in political camps."[349] Prince had reportedly secured, by 2014, support for FSG from China's CITIC investment conglomerate, an entity holding assets of nearly $1 trillion.[350] Tellingly, one of the chief investors in Prince's FSG is, according to *Fast Company*, "Abu Dhabi's Crown Prince Court"—in other words, MBZ.[351]

In a March 2019 interview with Al Jazeera, Prince denies participating in the construction in China of what the media outlet calls "basically concentration camps," falsely saying that FSG has only contracted with the Chinese for "construction services" when, as Al Jazeera notes, the company's own press release, which names Prince multiple times, advertises the creation of "training facilities" for the camps' guards.[352] In fact, as *BuzzFeed News* first reported in 2017, Prince "is setting up a private army for China," a project similar to the one he had already executed in the United Arab Emirates and has been seeking to undertake in Afghanistan, he has also proposed such as project—with an idea for an "army of spies" controlled by Trump—in America itself.[353]

When a March 2019 ProPublica report reveals that Elliott Broidy's California offices were raided by federal agents in the summer of 2018—on suspicion of Broidy having committed "conspiracy, money laundering, and violations of the law governing covert lobbying on behalf of foreign officials"—the Trump-China connection once again enters the news, as it is Trump whom Broidy has primarily directed his bribery efforts at, if anyone, and China, along with Saudi Arabia and the UAE, is noted by ProPublica as one of the foreign nations with whom Broidy is suspected of covertly dealing.[354] One particularly telling email exchange between Nader and Broidy revealed as a result of the raid sees the former praising the latter for "how well you handle Chairman"—since revealed as a code name for Trump.[355]

That the Broidy case is in the Northern District of California under-scores that cases involving Trump and collusion—in this case, collusive behavior undergirding potential bribery and money laundering charges—persist even after the termination of the special counsel's investigation in D.C. in March. Indeed, the total number of federal and state entities still investigating Trump, his family, his aides, and his business associates after the end of the special counsel's probe is twenty.[356]

Additional evidence that investigations into possible money laundering by Trump and his business will continue beyond the completion of the special counsel's work appears in early April, when two congressional com-mittees not only subpoena Deutsche Bank for Trump's banking records but also issue subpoenas to eight other banks for information related to Russian money laundering.[357]

ANNOTATIONS

The same week, Qatar—an old U.S. ally left out of Trump's new Middle East axis—announces that it may depart OPEC (the Organization of the Petroleum Exporting Countries) due to its treatment at the hands of Saudi Arabia and its Sunni allies in the Gulf.

February 2019 sees the nation of Qatar trying to clean up the historical record with respect to Jared Kushner's blockade-enabled shakedown of the Qatar Investment Authority in 2017 and 2018. Reuters reports that the Qatari government now claims it "unwittingly helped bail out a New York skyscraper owned by the family of Jared Kushner," as it was unaware that Brookfield Asset Management's subsidiary Brookfield Property Partners, a company in which it heavily invests, "struck a deal last year [2018] that rescued the Kushner Companies' 666 Fifth Avenue tower in Manhattan from financial straits."[358] Doha's claim—that it didn't know what Brookfield was doing because it owned nearly a tenth of Brookfield rather than being its exclusive owner—doesn't track with common governance practices in the international financial sector, however; the Qataris would have been unlikely to miss a transfer of more than a billion dollars from a fund with an $87 billion value, especially as the recipient was a desperately underwater property owner sitting on a virtually worthless property.[359] Moreover, the Qataris' hire of a former Trump campaign staffer, Stuart Jolly—during the same month as their announcement regarding the Brookfield-Kushner deal—underscores that they understand very well the association between favorable economic treatment from the Trump campaign and proximity to those Trump cares about.[360] In 2016, Jolly oversaw Trump's field campaign in thirty states, and said, upon transitioning from campaign work to involvement with lobbying-adjacent super PACs, "I think I can be effective [helping Trump] from the outside."[361]

> According to White House officials, during these nonsecure calls to friends and world leaders Trump may well be discussing classified information. Despite "repeated warnings" from his aides that "Russian spies are routinely eavesdropping on [his iPhone] calls," Trump refuses to cease putting American intelligence and policy at risk—a reckless practice that seems in direct opposition to the supposed paranoia that causes him to hide his schedule and phone habits from top aides in the first instance.

In February 2019, *Time* publishes a report revealing that Trump's disregard for the advice of his intelligence advisers goes far beyond anything Americans had supposed. Speaking for the first time about Trump's conduct during two years' worth of closed-door intelligence briefings, intelligence officials reveal to *Time* that Trump has adopted a position of "willful ignorance" toward intelligence assessments that do not align with his personal preferences, forcing officials into "futile attempts to keep his attention by using visual aids, confining some briefing points to two or three sentences, and repeating his name and title as frequently as possible."[362] Even more troubling, Trump—whose positions on geopolitics often seem to be drawn directly from the mouths of foreign adversaries like Vladimir Putin or Mohammed bin Salman—is, according to his briefers, prone to "angry reactions when he is given information that contradicts positions he has taken or beliefs he holds." Intelligence officers have even been "warned," though it is not clear by whom, that they must "avoid giving the President intelligence assessments that contradict stances he has taken in public."[363]

To the extent these admonitions are acknowledged and acceded to, they permit Trump to receive foreign policy talking points directly from world leaders such as Putin and MBS and then accurately say that he has received no intelligence assessments from his own briefers to contradict them. It can therefore be presumed that, at least on certain hot-button issues, America's foreign policy is the product not of independent assessments by the American intelligence community but the whims and self-interest of America's staunchest strategic competitors and even its enemies. Trump's recalcitrance on intelligence matters has "existed since the beginning of Trump's presidency, intelligence officials say," and may explain why, during one 85-day period of assessment between 2018 and 2019, Trump skipped his President's Daily Brief—the most significant regular intelligence briefing any president receives—on 68 of the 85 days.[364] While NBC observes that presidents often do not receive a face-to-face PDB every day, it also reports that Trump "does not regularly read" the written intelligence briefings sent to him daily whether or not he receives a live PDB.[365] In this respect he is entirely unlike his predecessors, per NBC.[366]

In February 2019, when Trump's intelligence chiefs offer him a report on Russia's continued efforts at interfering with American elections—a report that both Trump and Putin disagree with—and when they offer, too, a positive assessment of Iran's compliance with the nuclear treaty it signed with President Obama (an assessment disagreed with by both Trump and his allies in Saudi Arabia, the United Arab Emirates, and Israel), Trump tweets that his intelligence chiefs are "extremely passive," "naive," "wrong," and need to "go back to school."[367]

There is also evidence that Trump is assessing America's strategic interests through the lens of his own personal enrichment. According to *Time*, during one briefing on the British Indian Ocean territory of Diego Garcia, "home to an important airbase and a U.S. Naval Support Facility . . . central to America's ability to project power in the region, including in the war in Afghanistan," the only questions Trump asked of his briefers were, "Are the people nice, and are the beaches good?"[368] An official familiar with the briefing tells *Time* that "some of us wondered if he was thinking about . . . security issues . . . [or] thinking like a real estate developer."[369]

One of the plotters identified by NBC is IP3 co-founder Bud McFarlane, who attended the VIP event orchestrated by Dimitri Simes prior to Trump's Mayflower Hotel speech in April 2016.

Another connection between Trump and McFarlane is a now widely seen photograph of McFarlane entering Trump's April 2016 Mayflower Hotel foreign policy speech alongside Sergey Kislyak. A video of the event shows the men as they return from the twenty-four-person VIP event that Trump held before the speech. McFarlane is, in both the photograph and video, carrying what appears to be a ceremonial Arabian sword—though it is unclear whether the sword is a gift that was given to him, a gift he has been asked to give to someone else, or is present at Trump's first major foreign policy speech for some other, unknown reason.[370]

CHAPTER 11

THE MUELLER REPORT

April 2019 to June 2019

In April 2019, the DOJ releases a redacted version of special counsel Robert Mueller's final report. The report is missing any counterintelligence findings from federal law enforcement, all grand jury testimony compiled by the special counsel's office, and all information about the fourteen criminal investigations referred to other jurisdictions by Mueller and his team. The report does, however, provide overwhelming evidence that the Trump campaign colluded with Kremlin agents, even as it notes that it cannot establish beyond a reasonable doubt that the campaign conspired with the IRA or GRU in particular. A thousand former federal prosecutors of both parties opine in a public letter that the report proves that Trump obstructed justice—an impeachable offense.

On April 18, 2019, a redacted version of special counsel Robert Mueller's final report (the "Mueller Report") is released to the public. All told, the Department of Justice has made 946 redactions from Mueller's 448-page document, totaling approximately 8 percent of the report, according to CNN.[1] Because most of the redactions are in the report's first volume, a 198-page document that focuses on the possibility of a pre-election Trump-IRA or Trump-GRU conspiracy to commit computer crimes or defraud the United States—and because even the redactions in the second, obstruction-of-justice-focused volume of the report appear to be those items most relevant to the "conspiracy" question—approximately 15 percent of the information needed to understand the results of the special counsel's conspiracy probe has been elided from the report. A separate analysis of the report by the *Wall Street Journal* concludes that 12 percent of the report has been redacted, meaning that nearly 20 percent of the material relevant to the special counsel's conspiracy investigation has been removed.[2] The report contains no counterintelligence findings, quotations from grand jury testimony, or evidence critical to ongoing federal investigations; it lacks, too, any information that President Trump's attorney general, William Barr, deemed overly embarrassing to parties not charged with any crime.[3] Though Federal Rule of Criminal Procedure 6(e) allows Barr to seek a court order to release all grand jury transcripts from the special counsel's investigation, he declines to do so, implying under oath in May 2019 testimony before Congress that he believes—erroneously—that Rule 6(e) is a prohibition against publishing grand jury materials under any and all circumstances.[4]

Prior to the release of the Mueller Report, Barr had issued a four-page letter summarizing his view of the report's conclusions and declaring that, in his estimation, President Trump had not committed obstruction of justice; he relies in part on his legal opinion that there can be no obstruction of justice without an underlying crime. It will later be revealed that Mueller sent a letter to the Department of Justice in response to Barr's prefatory letter, complaining that the attorney general's summary had failed to "capture the context, nature, and substance" of the special counsel office's "work and conclusions," and that the result of Barr's errors was "public confusion about critical aspects of the results of [the] investigation."[5] Mueller adds that Barr's actions "threaten[ ] to undermine a central purpose for which the Department appointed the Special Counsel: to assure full public confidence in the outcome of the [conspiracy and obstruction] investigations."[6] The near-universal opinion of legal scholars in reaction to Barr's claim that obstruction cannot be charged without an underlying crime is that, as a matter of long-standing legal precedent, the attorney general is incorrect.[7]

Despite the report explicitly distinguishing between "conspiracy," the narrow statutory offense the special counsel's office investigated, and "collusion," a lay term with broad implications that Mueller did not consider in his nearly two years of work, Barr will falsely declare at a press conference after the report's release that the report found "no collusion" between Trump or his campaign and Russian nationals. "As [Trump] said from the beginning, there was, in fact, no collusion," Barr declares.[8] As discussed earlier (see Introduction), "collusion" is a term under whose umbrella many criminal statutes may be considered to reside, including a number outside the purview of the special counsel's investigation, such as bribery, aiding and abetting, solicitation of foreign campaign donations, and money laundering.[9]

Volume 1 of the Mueller Report addresses a narrow question: whether the special counsel's office found proof beyond a reasonable doubt of any of four pre-election crimes, specifically conspiracy to commit computer crimes, conspiracy to defraud the United States, criminal violations of the Foreign Agents Registration Act (FARA), or a criminal violation of the ban on foreign campaign donations (though this last assessment is applied by the special counsel only to the June 9, 2016, meeting at Trump Tower between Paul Manafort, Donald Trump Jr., Jared Kushner, and several individuals connected to the Russian government).[10] The volume does not consider other federal criminal statutes undergirded by "collusive" contact between Americans and foreign nationals. Nor does it apply any standard of proof besides the highest standard in U.S. law, "beyond a reasonable doubt"; as the report includes no counterintelligence findings, it does not apply the much lower "preponderance of the evidence" standard—the standard relevant to the identification of compromised persons and the redress of ongoing national security threats—to any of the events considered by the report.[11] As noted by Fordham law professor Jed Shugerman in the *New York Times*, "preponderance of the evidence" is likewise the appropriate standard of proof for a noncriminal proceeding like impeachment, whose ultimate penalty is merely loss of employment and authority rather than loss of liberty.[12]

On the first page of the report, the special counsel's office announces that its investigation "established that the Russian government perceived it would benefit from a Trump presidency and worked to secure that outcome, and that the [Trump] Campaign expected it would benefit electorally from information stolen and released through Russian efforts."[13] The report adds that the "investigation established that several individuals affiliated with the Trump Campaign lied to the [special counsel's] Office, and to Congress, about their interactions with Russian-affiliated individuals and related matters. Those lies materially impaired the investigation of Russian election interference."[14] Explaining in detail the nature of the "material impairment" caused by Trump campaign deception, the report notes that "the investigation did not always yield admissible information or testimony, or a complete picture of the activities undertaken by subjects of the investigation . . . [because] [s]ome individuals invoked their Fifth Amendment right against compelled self-incrimination and were not, in the Office's judgment, appropriate candidates for grants of immunity. The Office limited its pursuit of other witnesses and information . . . in light of Department of Justice policies. Some of the information obtained via court process, moreover, was presumptively covered by legal privilege and was screened from investigators . . . [and] [e]ven when individuals testified or agreed to be interviewed, they sometimes provided information that was false or incomplete . . . [a]nd the Office faced practical limits on its ability to access relevant evidence as well—numerous witnesses and subjects lived abroad, and documents were held outside the United States. Further, the Office learned that some of the individuals we interviewed or whose conduct we investigated—including some associated with the Trump Campaign—deleted relevant communications or communicated during the relevant period using applications that feature encryption or that do not provide for long-term retention of data or communications records. In such cases, the Office was not able to corroborate witness statements through contemporaneous communications or fully question witnesses about statements that appeared inconsistent with other known facts. Accordingly, while this report embodies factual and legal determinations that the Office believes to be accurate and complete to the greatest extent possible, given these identified gaps, the Office cannot rule out the possibility that the unavailable information would shed additional light on (or cast in a new light) the events described in the report."[15] According to CNN, the report identifies a minimum of seventy-seven lies told by Trump campaign aides, advisers, and associates, many on matters the truth of which the special counsel's office was never able to ascertain. Other possible lies or half-truths—including the hundreds of instances in which Trump, his campaign staff, or transition officials told Congress or the special counsel they "couldn't recall" a fact investigators might have expected a witness to recall—had to be left "as is" in the report.[16]

The special counsel's office notes that it "did not . . . investigate every public report of a contact between the Trump Campaign and Russian-affiliated individuals and entities."[17] An appendix to the report lists fourteen federal criminal cases that have been referred to other federal jurisdictions and prosecutors for further consideration and possible prosecution; only two of these referred cases are revealed to the public, however, with summaries of the rest being redacted in their entirety.[18] Given the narrow scope of the main inquiry, it is unsurprising that "the Office periodically identified evidence of potential criminal activity that was outside the scope of the Special Counsel's authority . . . [which] the Office referred . . . to appropriate law enforcement authorities."[19] As of summer 2019, it is therefore unknown whether any of these referred but unnamed cases involve non-conspiracy "collusive" activity connected to the Trump campaign, transition, or administration.

One indication of the limited scope of the report is that in its 448 pages, MBZ's name appears only four times, Thomas Barrack's name just twice, and Michael Flynn Jr.'s and Abdel Fattah el-Sisi's names but once each. Other names, like Bijan Kian or Ekim Alptekin, appear only in appendices. Among the many names relevant to Trump and his inner circle's acts of international collusion that appear nowhere in the body of the Mueller Report are Elliott Broidy, Mohammed bin Salman (MBS), Mohammed bin Nayef, Joel Zamel, Yousef al-Otaiba, Jon Iadonisi, Jamal Khashoggi, Mohammed Dahlan, Ahmed al-Assiri, Saud al-Qahtani, Alexander Rovt, George Birnbaum, Eli Groner, Benjamin Netanyahu, Dmitry Rybolovlev, Alexander Nix, Mark Turnbull, Jho Low, Howard Lorber, David Pecker, Hamad bin Jassim bin Jaber Al Thani (HBJ), Franklin Haney, Viktor Vekselberg, Curt Weldon, Andrii Artemenko, Dana Rohrabacher, Nastya Rybka (Anastasia Vashukevich), Prince Salman bin Hamad (the crown prince of Bahrain), Alexander Torshin, Maria Butina, Lisa Korbatov, Matthew Whitaker, Randy

Credico, Hussain Sajwani, Ahmed al-Rumaihi, and King Salman of Saudi Arabia. Indeed, the kingdom of Saudi Arabia is mentioned only once in the report—a passing reference to a flight President Trump took that departed from Riyadh.

The special counsel's office acknowledges that during the course of its nearly two-year investigation into the 2016 Trump campaign it "identif[ied] foreign intelligence and counterintelligence information relevant to the FBI's broader national security mission . . . not all of which is contained in this Volume."[20] Consequently, the report does not reveal whether, under the preponderance of the evidence ("more likely than not") standard used in counterintelligence cases to determine the likelihood of an individual posing a national security threat, Donald Trump or any individuals still in the White House as of the summer of 2019—for instance, Jared Kushner—present a danger to the United States by virtue of having been compromised, for any reason and in any fashion, by a foreign power or entity.[21] Finally, the report notes that it discovered evidence that "other Russian entities" besides the two government actors whose possible role in a Trump-Russia conspiracy it considered—the IRA and the GRU—"engaged in active measures operations targeting the United States" during the 2016 presidential campaign, and that this evidence has been "shared . . . with other offices in the Department of Justice and FBI" for further review.[22]

These numerous and significant investigative limitations and obstacles noted, the special counsel's office reports that it has not established beyond a reasonable doubt that the Trump campaign engaged in a before-the-fact conspiracy with either the Internet Research Agency or Russian military intelligence. These two specific allegations had, notwithstanding the report's emphasis on them, been largely absent from major-media discourse in the two years preceding the report's release. One reason for the special counsel's particular focus on these two possible crimes is that it limited itself to "the framework of conspiracy law" and to interactions between Trump, his aides, his allies, his advisers, and his associates with Russian government entities rather than with Russian nationals generally (or with nationals of other countries, whether in government service or not).[23]

While not finding sufficient evidence—in the evidence available to the special counsel's office—to establish a criminal conspiracy beyond a reasonable doubt, the report does identify "a series of contacts between Trump Campaign officials and individuals with ties to the Russian government . . . [these] contacts consisted of business connections, offers of assistance to the Campaign, invitations for candidate Trump and Putin to meet in person, invitations for Campaign officials and representatives of the Russian government to meet, and [meetings on] policy positions seeking improved U.S.-Russian relations."[24] The report finds, too, that in June 2016, as the revelation of Russian hacking was becoming public, "the Campaign anticipated receiving information from Russia that could assist candidate Trump's electoral prospects," specifically in the form of "official documents and information that would incriminate" Clinton.[25] Weeks later, shortly after WikiLeaks posted thousands of emails stolen from the DNC on its website, and just after "public reporting that U.S. intelligence agencies had 'high confidence' that the Russian government was behind the theft of emails and documents from the DNC," candidate Trump publicly asked the Russian government to conduct further hacks to locate and publish any Clinton emails it could find. By July 31, 2016, these events, coupled with two more of great significance—Papadopoulos telling an Australian diplomat the Trump campaign knew the Kremlin had Clinton emails, and months of intelligence from seven allied intelligence agencies revealing previously unknown "contacts between Trump's inner circle and Russians"—had led to an FBI investigation into "potential coordination between the Russian government and individuals associated with the Trump Campaign."[26] The nations whose intelligence agencies the FBI relied upon in opening an investigation of the Trump campaign are France, the United Kingdom, the Netherlands, Australia, Germany, Estonia, and Poland.[27]

Despite its narrow legal scope, the report implies that, while it did not find pre-election violations of conspiracy law in the Trump-Russia contacts it identified, it cannot say the same of the notion of "two parties [the Trump campaign and the Kremlin] taking actions that were informed by or responsive to the other's actions or interests."[28] Consequently, the report is silent as to the commission, by members of the Trump campaign, of felonies that do not require a "tacit or express agreement"—which the federal conspiracy statute does—but instead can be violated when "two parties tak[e] actions . . . informed by or responsive to the other's actions or interests," such as in the federal bribery and aiding and abetting statutes.[29]

As to allegations that Trump sought to thwart, through deceitful words and clandestine actions, any federal investigation of his, his family's, and his associates' pre-election ties to the Kremlin and Kremlin agents—as well as encouraging deceit, secrecy, and malfeasance by his subordinates— the Mueller Report concludes that "the evidence does point to a range of . . . possible personal motives animating the president's conduct . . . [including] uncertainty about whether certain events . . . could be seen as criminal activity by the President, his campaign, or his family."[30] It adds that the special counsel considered not only "whether the President had a motive [to obstruct justice] related to Russia-related matters that an FBI field investigation could uncover" but also whether Trump was afraid of "other conduct that could come to light as a result of the FBI's Russian-interference investigation," including, but not limited to, revelations regarding pre-election "campaign-finance offenses"—a category that would include not only hush-money payments made to former mistresses but payments made illegally to Trump, or on Trump's behalf, by foreign nations during the 2016 presidential campaign or presidential transition.[31] Mueller concludes that "the evidence does indicate that a thorough FBI investigation would uncover facts about the campaign and the President personally that the President could have understood to be crimes or that would give rise to personal and political concerns."[32] The special counsel's reference to "a thorough FBI investigation" seems to acknowledge that the Mueller Report is not, in itself, that investigation. As to other possible offenses Trump may have believed could be revealed as a result of the Russia investigation, Mueller notes that Trump felt the investigation was specifically hindering his ability to execute his preferred foreign policy in three locations around the world: Russia, China, and the Middle East.[33]

The Middle East may well have been of particular concern to the president during the week the special counsel was appointed. Trump's references, in conversations with aides, to losing some of his "authority with foreign leaders" because of his status as the subject of a federal criminal investigation would likely have included the two foreign leaders he was scheduled to meet in Riyadh just forty-eight hours after Mueller's appointment: King Salman of Saudi Arabia and his son, Mohammed bin Salman.[34] Mueller notes that Trump, during the period of time reviewed by the special counsel's office, was also "particularly" concerned about the state of his relationship with Vladimir Putin, an observation seemingly confirmed by Trump having told Sergey Lavrov and Sergey Kislyak in the Oval Office the day after he fired FBI director James Comey that "I just fired the head of the FBI. He was crazy, a real nut job. I faced great pressure because of Russia. That's taken off. . . . I'm not under investigation."[35] Notably, the Oval Office meeting with Lavrov and Kislyak—which Trump and Putin had agreed upon during a May 2 phone call—was officially confirmed by the White House and the Kremlin on the very day Trump decided to fire Comey.[36]

The decision to terminate Comey's employment had led White House counsel Don McGahn's chief of staff, Annie Donaldson, to write in her early May 2017 notes, "Is this the beginning of the end?"—a statement she later explained to Mueller as referring to the end of Trump's presidency.[37] Donaldson's concern may have been caused in part by the fact that Trump had previously told McGahn that a president has the "authority to terminate [an FBI director] without cause," which the White House counsel's office may have read as a confession that Trump did not believe he had any legally permissible cause to fire Comey.[38] Trump's advisers, including Steve Bannon, had previously told the president that he "could not fire Comey" because he had waited too long to do so to credibly claim that Comey's performance during the Obama administration was the cause of his dismissal.[39]

As to whether Trump's conduct in this and other episodes in which he sought to thwart the investigation of his campaign, transition, and administration constitutes felony obstruction or felony witness tampering, the report concludes that while both statutes are fully applicable to presidential conduct—a legal premise to which the president's counsel had strenuously objected—it will nevertheless "not . . . make a traditional prosecutorial judgment" on the grounds that there are constitutional remedies other than indictment when a president misbehaves.[40] However, the report underscores that it "does not exonerate" Trump of allegations of obstruction and witness tampering, and that, while acts that aim to corruptly interfere with ongoing federal investigations need not successfully cause interference to be criminal, "the President's efforts to influence the [Russia] investigation were mostly unsuccessful . . . largely because the persons who surrounded the President declined to carry out orders or accede to his requests"—an observation suggesting that the natural effect of Trump's orders and requests would indeed have been significant interference with the special counsel's investigation had they been carried out.[41]

The report emphasizes that one of the obstacles Mueller faced in investigating Trump-Russia ties was the president himself. After the special counsel's office submitted written questions for Trump—the president having broken his promise to speak to the office face-to-face just a year after making that promise in the White House Rose Garden—Mueller records that he "informed [Trump's] counsel of the insufficiency of [the president's] responses," noting both that some were "incomplete or imprecise" and that "the President stated on more than 30 occasions that he 'does not recall' or 'remember' or have an 'independent recollection' of [the] information called for."[42] Mueller further opines that the president "declined" to either answer follow-up questions, have his recollection "refresh[ed]" by investigators, or let investigators "clarify the extent or nature of his lack of recollection."[43] This refusal stood even when the special counsel informed the president, who had consistently declared his innocence as to all allegations involving Russia and obstruction of justice, that his written answers were on the whole "inadequate."[44]

Writing on the president's "inadequate" responses to its interrogatories, the special counsel's office observes that "In his written answers, the President did not provide details about the timing and substance of his discussions with Cohen about the [Trump Tower Moscow] project and gave no indication that he had decided to no longer pursue the project. After Cohen pleaded guilty, the President publicly stated that he had personally made the decision to abandon the project. The President then declined to clarify the seeming discrepancy to our Office or to answer additional questions."[45] One of the most important questions the special counsel asked Trump was whether he had participated in a money-for-policy quid pro quo with the Kremlin: "Did you intend to communicate . . . at any . . . time during the campaign a willingness to lift sanctions and/or recognize Russia's annexation of Crimea if you were elected? What consideration did you give to lifting sanctions and/or recognizing Russia's annexation if you were elected? Describe who you spoke with about this topic, when, the substance of the discussion(s)."[46] Trump refused to offer any answers to these questions at all, one of the few cases in which he did not even attempt a reply.[47]

In his written answers to the special counsel's interrogatories, Trump also denies any knowledge of pre-election conversations his family or any-one connected to his campaign may have had establishing a quid pro quo with nations other than Russia—for instance, Saudi Arabia, the UAE, or Israel—telling the special counsel, "I have no recollection of being told during the campaign that any foreign government or foreign leader had provided, wished to provide, or offered to provide tangible support to my campaign."[48] By his answer, Trump expresses that not only did his son Don conceal from him any information about his June 9, 2016, Trump Tower meeting with Kremlin agents for the entirety of the 2016 campaign, but that Don took the same tack with respect to his meeting with Nader, Prince, Miller, and Zamel at Trump Tower on August 3, 2016.

Trump offers the same response with respect to whether his friend and longtime adviser Roger Stone ever told him, during any of their numerous phone calls during the campaign, about the critical information he had received regarding the timing of WikiLeaks' release of stolen Democratic materials: "I have no recollection of being told that WikiLeaks possessed or might possess emails related to John Podesta before the[ir] release. . . . I do not recall being told during the campaign that Roger Stone or anyone associated with my campaign had discussions with [WikiLeaks, Guccifer 2.0, or DCLeaks] . . . regarding the content or timing of release of hacked emails."[49] In fact, Trump told Mueller he had "no recollection of any of the specifics of any conversations I had with Mr. Stone between June 1,

2015, and November 8, 2016. I do not recall discussing WikiLeaks with him, nor do I recall being aware of Mr. Stone having discussed WikiLeaks with individuals associated with my campaign."[50] Trump's answer to another question indicates that, just as he claimed his son had never told him about his June 9 or August 3 meetings at Trump Tower, Don Jr. also had withheld from his father—despite discussing it with other members of the campaign—his September 2016 contacts with WikiLeaks, with Trump telling Mueller, "I do not recall being aware during the campaign of any communications between [Stone, Don Jr., Manafort, or Gates] . . . and anyone I understood to be a representative of WikiLeaks."[51]

Michael Cohen's voluminous testimony to the contrary, Trump tells Mueller—under penalty of a federal felony—that he "do[es] not recall being aware at the time of any communications between Mr. Cohen or Felix Sater and any Russian government official regarding the [Trump-Rozov] Letter of Intent."[52] Just so, despite his years-long relationship with the Agalarov family, whose patriarch has received one of the highest civilian honors the Kremlin can bestow—and indeed received it directly from Putin's hand—Trump tells the special counsel that he has "no meaningful relationship with people in power in Russia."[53] Nor was Trump, by his own account, in any way advised by Paul Manafort on issues relating to either Ukraine or Russia, despite Manafort's expertise on these topics being a key part of the job application he sent to Trump in late February 2016, and Trump and Manafort having stayed in contact for months while Manafort was discussing Ukraine and sanctions relief with a former Russian intelligence agent: "I do not remember Mr. Manafort communicating to me any particular positions Ukraine or Russia would want the United States to support."[54] Trump's insistence that he never spoke to Manafort about either Ukraine or Russia, contradicted by major-media reporting, would leave open, if true, the question of why Trump was so concerned by the possibility of Manafort "flip[ping]" on him in the Russia investigation.[55]

Despite eighteen of his family members and closest political aides and associates having direct pre-election contact with Russian nationals—Manafort, Flynn, Gates, Trump Jr., Kushner, Papadopoulos, Page, Sessions, Gordon, Stone, Caputo, Prince, Cohen, Hicks, Sater, (Avi) Berkowitz, social media director Dan Scavino, and even his daughter Ivanka—Trump tells the special counsel that he "do[es] not recall being told during the campaign of efforts by Russian officials to meet with me or with senior members of my campaign."[56] At least one of these individuals, Cohen, has made public statements, as well as statements to the special counsel, contradicting Trump's account, while others have offered accounts of varying improbability about having kept all their pre-election contacts with Russian nationals from the GOP presidential candidate.

Trump's inability to recall any information of substance about his conversations with key advisers during the presidential campaign mirrors his son's inability to recall many of his own conversations during the campaign. In his testimony before the Senate Judiciary Committee, Trump Jr. told the senators he "couldn't remember" or "didn't know" the answer to a question 186 times.[57]

Apropos of this litany of accounts of Trump being kept in the dark by members of his inner circle, the Mueller Report details the president's habit of communicating the fact that he is "pleased" with a Russia-probe witness's public statements or testimony either directly, through counsel, or on social media; in the narrative of events outlined by the report, both Michael Cohen and Jared Kushner receive such a message from the president.[58] In the case of Cohen's congressional testimony, the report further details how Trump's personal counsel ensured that additional "communications with Russia and more communications with candidate Trump" would be elided from Cohen's sworn statement.[59] According to Cohen, Trump's attorney told him to "stay on message and not contradict the president" by "keeping Trump out of the narrative," and that Cohen listing in his statement all his contacts with Russia on Trump's behalf—as requested by Congress—would unacceptably "muddy the water."[60] Cohen told Mueller that he consequently lied to Congress, a federal felony, because "it was what he was expected to do" by Trump and his legal team.[61] Moreover, Cohen's joint defense agreement with Trump's legal team allowed the team to unilaterally remove from Cohen's draft of his statement sentences such as "The [Trump Tower Moscow] building project led me to make limited contacts with Russian government officials," even as sentences that were manifestly untrue—such as Cohen's claim he could "not recall any response to any email to [Putin lieutenant Dmitry Peskov], nor any other contacts by me with Mr. Peskov or other Russian government officials"—were left untouched by Trump's lawyers.[62] This conduct mirrors Trump's removal of potentially inculpatory evidence from his son Don's statement about his June 9, 2016, meeting with Kremlin agents in Trump Tower. In that instance, candidate Trump personally "delet[ed] a line [in the statement] that acknowledged that the [June 9] meeting was with 'an individual who [Trump Jr.] was told might have information helpful to the campaign.'"[63]

Among the Trump team's interferences with Cohen's congressional testimony, perhaps most startling was its insistence that Cohen not reveal to Congress that Trump "told Cohen to reach out to Putin's office" about "a meeting between Trump and Putin in New York during the 2015 United Nations General Assembly," as well asking him to hide the additional fact that, after his 2015 directive to Cohen to connect him with Putin, Trump "asked him multiple times for updates on the proposed meeting."[64] The private meeting Trump sought with Putin would have occurred while Trump was being aided by a Kremlin intermediary, Felix Sater, in negotiations to build a tower in Moscow that could net Trump—whose total net worth in 2015 was $4.5 billion, per *Forbes*—more than $1 billion in revenue. The idea of effectuating such a deal during a presidential election was so unprecedented and deeply problematic that Putin's office had to scold Trump through his attorney, telling Cohen that "it would not follow proper protocol for Putin to meet with Trump."[65] Putin would instead meet with Trump's top national security advisor, Michael Flynn, in Moscow ninety days later.

According to Cohen, Trump was also responsible for his removing from his congressional testimony a May 2016 discussion he had with Trump about whether Trump would travel to Russia during the presidential campaign to complete negotiations over his $1 billion Russian tower, a trip Trump told Cohen he would take—regardless, apparently, of any effect on his presidential campaign—if the tower deal was "lock[ed] and load[ed]" for him by Cohen. "Cohen recalled discussing the invitation to the St. Petersburg economic forum with candidate Trump and saying that Putin or Russian prime minister Dmitry Medvedev might be there," according to the report.[66]

As recounted by the special counsel's office, throughout Cohen's interactions with Trump's attorneys he was told that he would be "protected" by Trump, and Trump would "[have] his back," but only if he "stayed on message" and never "went rogue"—in other words, never contradicted the "script" or "talking points" Cohen said he had "developed with President-Elect Trump and others" to put reporters off the scent of the Trump Tower Moscow project.[67] According to Mueller's summary of Cohen's statements to the special counsel's office, Trump "knew [the talking points] were untrue."[68] According to the report, "During the summer of 2016, Cohen recalled that candidate Trump publicly claimed that he had nothing to do with Russia and then shortly afterwards privately checked with Cohen about the status of the Trump Tower Moscow project."[69] All told, Cohen briefed Trump on the project six times between February and June 2016—after numerous briefings from the fall of 2015 through January 2016—with some of those briefings being initiated by Trump and some involving Cohen updating Trump on his contacts with the Kremlin.[70]

The report presents Trump as someone who angrily denies—even in private conversation—having done things he knows he has done. For instance, in February 2018, according to the Mueller Report, Trump told Rob Porter that a *New York Times* story about him wanting to fire Mueller was "bullshit" when his actions and words in other contexts confirm that he knew the *Times* story was true.[71] At another point, the report recounts Trump calling White House counsel Don McGahn a "lying bastard" for accurately memorializing Trump's conduct in notes he produced as part of his professional work product.[72] Despite Trump's subsequent protestations in public and in private, the Mueller Report details how he did indeed "discuss[ ] 'knocking out Mueller'" from the Russia probe by means of what his own advisers termed "silly," "not real," and "ridiculous" accusations of a conflict of interest.[73]

The report underscores, moreover, that Trump took many of his actions in the face of strenuous opposition and contrary advice by both his top advisers and his legal team. After a Trump-Comey phone call in April 2017,

Donaldson wrote in her notes that the "[president] Called Comey—[on the] Day we told him not to?"[74] The next month, McGahn explicitly told Trump any attempt to "knock[ ] out Mueller" would be "another fact used to claim obstruction of justice" by the president; nevertheless, Trump persisted in his clandestine efforts to engineer Mueller's ouster.[75] The month after that, "the President made . . . calls to McGahn [about firing Mueller for alleged conflicts of interest] after McGahn had specifically told the President that the White House Counsel's Office—and McGahn himself—could not be involved in pressing conflicts claims and the President should consult with his personal counsel if he wished to raise conflicts."[76] This pattern of behavior results in a report that finds that Trump on multiple occasions acted "against the advice of White House advisers" who had told him that his planned actions "could be perceived as improper interference in an ongoing investigation"—in other words, obstruction of justice.[77] In establishing Trump's state of mind following such admonitions, Mueller notes that in at least one instance Trump engaged in problematic behavior "even though he knew [attorneys from the White House counsel's office] had advised against" it.[78] Deputy director of the National Security Agency Richard Ledgett, a recipient of one of Trump's inappropriate, advised-against phone calls, called the resultant conversation "the most unusual thing that he had experienced in 40 years of government service."[79]

In all, the report paints the picture of a man surrounded by two types of aides, allies, and associates: those who will maintain under any circumstances that they have never transmitted inculpatory information to Trump or received any such information from him, and those who have given or received such information and will reveal it, but only under subpoena and even then only after great effort has been expended by law enforcement. Meanwhile, Trump himself is cast as a man who—even in his private dealings—fluidly underwrites his self-narrative with a lifetime of venal instincts and is perpetually rewriting his own actions, once they are completed, to eliminate from his personal history any hint of malfeasance. Taken as a whole, the report suggests that if at any time Trump had knowledge of the Red Sea Conspiracy he quite possibly could have eliminated it from his memory, and if at any time any of his aides, allies, or associates had any such knowledge they might well either deny transmitting it to their boss or, if in legal extremis, grudgingly acknowledge doing so and provide only the barest fraction of the inculpatory information in their possession. The need for the public to see a detailed counterintelligence report on the pre- and post-election actions of Trump and his inner circle in the areas of Russian and Middle Eastern affairs—a report that would, presumably, have access to methods of intelligence-gathering able to circumvent both idiosyncratic memory loss and misguided loyalty—is underscored by the contents of the Mueller Report.

Just so, the report explicitly commends its evidence to Congress for further consideration, stating that "Congress may apply the obstruction laws to the President's corrupt exercise of the powers of office"—one of the report's several unambiguous references to the process of impeachment.[80] The special counsel's office declares that its refusal to make a "traditional prosecution or declination decision" is based in part on its fear of "preempt[ing] constitutional processes for addressing presidential misconduct," another apparent reference to impeachment, given that a subsequent footnote raises the possibility of a president being "removed from office . . . by impeachment" as a means of redressing presidential malfeasance without a DOJ prosecution.[81] The self-declared purpose of the report's obstruction investigation is, therefore, to "preserve the evidence" relating to that federal offense.[82] "If we had confidence after a thorough investigation of the facts that the President clearly did not commit obstruction of justice, we would so state," the report observes, notably declining to make any such statement.[83]

The report's declared inability to establish beyond a reasonable doubt "that the President was involved in an underlying crime related to Russian election interference" leaves untouched the question of whether Trump in 2015, 2016, or 2017 either established a money-for-policy quid pro quo with Russian or Middle Eastern individuals—of which quid pro quo Russian election interference would have been merely a symptom rather than the cause—or, alternatively or in addition, aided and abetted Russian, Saudi, Emirati, or Israeli election interference by promising policy rewards, sanctions relief, or future payment to foreign nationals he knew were already in the midst of such illicit activities.[84]

THE POINT OF RETURN

Summer 2019

There may be those who read the many intertwining narratives in this book and wonder whether a man with as much wealth as Donald Trump would sacrifice America's foreign policy, our rule of law, our democratic processes, and our standing in the world on the altar of some additional real estate business in, or investments from, Moscow, Riyadh, Abu Dhabi, Cairo, Tel Aviv, Doha, and the former Soviet republics—even if this prospective new business could, by the end of the 2020s, bring in tens of billions of dollars to the Trump Organization's coffers. Surely the price of a man's integrity and a nation's safety and security is higher than an eleven-figure sum? Surely no man who is a father, a husband, a longtime public presence in American life—and, in the bargain, a billionaire—would risk nuclear war in the Middle East just to earn a little more coin?

Consider, in answer to this question, the following anecdote. In 1990, a "hip, satirical, bomb-throwing magazine," *Spy*, concocted a prank to lure fabulously wealthy celebrities into publicly revealing their greed.[1] The plan: send a "refund" check for a "miniscule" amount of money, under the cover of a shell corporation, to a small group of extremely rich individuals, and see if they cash it; if they do, send them a check for half that amount and again wait to see if they cash it; and then proceed from there until the ruse discloses which already-rich person in America or beyond our shores is so venal that they would cash even a virtually worthless check.[2] *Spy* learned that twenty-six of its fifty-eight targets would cash a check for $1.11; that thirteen of *those* people would cash checks for half that amount, 64 cents; and that two billionaires in the world would actually go so far as to cash a check for just *thirteen cents*. The first of those two people was a billionaire

Saudi arms dealer and international "fixer" who had been implicated in the Iran-Contra scandal and lived a life of such "infamy," "influence peddling," and "spectacular scandals" that he was ultimately on the receiving end of an indictment for racketeering.[3] Imagine, if you can, someone so hedonistic that the band Queen felt it had to write a song about him; that's the first man *Spy* caught in its trap.[4]

The other was Donald Trump.

So what would a man like that do for $50 billion and the chance to rule autocratically over one of human history's richest and most esteemed nations?

Just as Trump's self-admitted greed has become legendary, so too has his deceitfulness. A representative anecdote: Trump is a onetime real estate developer who always took great pride in his prowess as a builder, but who also repeatedly added nonexistent stories to his buildings whenever he talked about them. He didn't merely add one or two floors, either; in Vancouver, Trump added six imaginary stories to a sixty-three-story tower so that it could better be marketed as one of the tallest in that Canadian city.[5] In his hometown, New York City, Trump outdid himself, adding a full ten stories to Trump Tower in order to claim that a fifty-eight-story building was actually sixty-eight stories.[6] This is a man who, in 1989, used the death of a good friend of his in a helicopter crash as a way of getting good press for himself, lying to the media and saying he'd been planning to be on the ill-fated helicopter on the day it went down. It was a lie, of course, but as he said to the roomful of people, several of them friends of the deceased, who watched him during the call with the media that set up the hoax, "You're going to hate me for this, but I just can't resist. I can get some publicity out of this."[7]

Donald Trump couldn't resist thirteen cents. He couldn't resist despoiling the memory of a friend who died tragically. He couldn't resist "cheat[ing] on [Melania] throughout their relationship, including when she was pregnant and soon after Barron's birth," according to *Business Insider*. He couldn't resist leaking classified intelligence to Kremlin agents in the Oval Office in May 2017, a violation of his sworn duty as president so grave that, in June 2019, the *New York Times* reveals that "Pentagon and intelligence officials [have] described broad hesitation to go into detail with Mr. Trump about [cyber] operations against Russia for concern over his reaction—and the possibility that he might countermand it or discuss it with foreign officials." Trump couldn't resist the prospect of illegally receiving stolen Clinton emails from Kremlin hackers during the 2016 election, nor, apparently, would he be able to resist committing the federal crime of illegal solicitation of foreign campaign donations even today: the *New York Times*, recounting an interview with Trump by ABC News' George Stephanopoulos, reports that Trump still proudly believes "there would be nothing wrong with accepting incriminating information about an election opponent from Russia or other foreign governments" and would see "no reason to call the F.B.I. if it were to happen again."[8] And more broadly, Trump couldn't resist telling 10,000 lies in his first 825 days as president of the United States, an average of twelve lies a day—and those are just the ones the *Washington Post* happened to catch.[9] The *Post* has more recently conducted a major investigative report revealing Trump's decades-long career of wildly inflating his assets and his wealth.[10] The *New York Times* has likewise uncovered evidence that Trump's business successes in the 1980s and 1990s were a mirage: he wasn't just losing money throughout much of those two decades, the *Times* found, but was losing more money than anyone in America.[11] He lied about that, too; he probably just couldn't resist.

The question, of course, has never been about what Donald Trump can or cannot resist. Rather, it has always been about what a society that values the rule of law is willing to tolerate. And more recently—since November 8, 2016—the question has been an even more dire one: What happens to a nation when it not only tolerates the worst excesses and degradations of the human condition but *celebrates* them? What happens when a once-great nation makes of its very worst instincts and proclivities a shudderingly grotesque political and cultural idol? The question is rhetorical, of course, as the answer is what lies before America every day of every week: not just what cable and network news reveal, or what digital and print newspapers disclose, but the story of what is happening that is plainly visible if we merely look for it. This book has sought for it in existing major-media reporting, not just from the scores of reliable outlets in America but from those of the United Kingdom, the Netherlands, Israel, Qatar, Turkey, Canada, and many other nations. Told in these pages are not just news stories revealed in the past few days or months or years but even some that date back decades. The archive of information on Trump and his allies around the world is broad and deep and still too little known.

What we find when we train this sort of lens on a man like Donald Trump is that his desire to rule has always been co-extensive with his desire to accumulate. Indeed, the fact that, as president, Trump now wants to combine diplomacy with business—even if it threatens America's national security—is clear. In March 2019, Trump actually complained, according to the *New York Times*, "that his generals and intelligence agencies don't consider business and economics in their intelligence analyses."[12] This same perverse attitude was even more vigorously in evidence pre-election, though it took until 2018 for Trump himself to ably summarize it, as he did in telling a press gaggle in November of that year that his ethos as a presidential candidate was this: to make as much money as he could while running, because, as he explained, "There was a good chance that I wouldn't have won [the election], in which case I would have gotten back into the [real estate] business, and why should I lose lots of opportunities?"[13] This was a man, remember, who had run for president in part on the idea that he loved America so much he was willing to forgo new wealth to serve it. Like so much else he said, that turned out to be untrue.

Now in the Oval Office, with overwhelming support from a political party he has shattered and rebuilt in his own image, the world Trump and his allies at home and abroad seek to create is a crueler, more dangerous, and more autocratic world than most Americans had ever thought to see a U.S. president endorse. In mid-April 2019, the Egyptian parliament amended Egypt's constitution to allow its strongman president, Abdel Fattah el-Sisi, to stay in power until 2030—plunging Egypt into autocratic rule for years to come—and Trump lauded el-Sisi, indeed everything from his "97 percent" election victory to his designer shoes.[14] More than this, Trump now seeks to declare el-Sisi's enemies, the Muslim Brotherhood, a terrorist organization, a move the United States has long resisted because it will wrongly classify even nonmilitants as dangerous radicals.[15] As the *New York Times* has explained, in describing the turmoil surrounding Trump's policy reversal, "The Pentagon, career national security staff, government lawyers and diplomatic officials have voiced legal and policy objections, and have been scrambling to find a more limited step that would satisfy the White House. As a matter of law, officials have argued that the criteria for designating a terrorist organization are not a good fit for the Muslim Brotherhood, which is less a coherent body than a loose-knit movement with chapters in different countries. . . . Several political parties in places like Tunisia and Jordan consider themselves Muslim Brotherhood or have ties to it, but eschew violent extremism."[16] The result of Trump's ill-conceived classification decision is that thousands of peaceful Muslims may now be wrongly characterized as violent killers and hence be subject to drone strikes—though we should, by now, expect nothing less from a president who celebrates his "bromance" with Kim Jong Un, the North Korean dictator who obliterates the bodies of his enemies (while they are still alive) with flamethrowers, wild dogs, mortars, and anti-aircraft guns.[17]

Just a few days after the Egyptian parliament gave el-Sisi a clear path to stay in power through 2030, Trump issued the second veto of his presidency, blocking Congress's attempt to end U.S. support for the devastating Saudi-led war in Yemen. The result of Trump's veto is that America will continue to provide assistance to a war effort that has indiscriminately killed thousands of civilians.[18] More recently, Trump has invoked his "emergency powers" to send new missiles and other heavy military equipment to Saudi Arabia—though he knows, as we all do, that these weapons will shortly be carelessly used in areas with large civilian populations, especially now that King Salman, MBS's father, has publicly absolved his entire army of war crimes with a preemptive royal decree.[19]

Now reports come from Palestine that the Saudis are trying to bribe Mahmoud Abbas into accepting Trump and Kushner's cobbled-together "peace deal" by paying the Palestinian president $10 billion—a gambit that underscores how little Trump's new Sunni allies are committed to justice for the Palestinian people, whom they have long professed to care for.[20] According to the *Jerusalem Post*, King Salman asked Abbas before making his offer, "What is the annual budget of your entourage?" to which Abbas replied, "I'm not a prince to have my own entourage."[21] King Salman's insulting query underscores not just the slick venality behind what now passes for a peace process in Israel and the Occupied Territories, but a way of seeing fellow humans that stands as Trump's clearest kinship with the world's despots. Trump is, after all, a man who withheld billions in disaster relief from storm-torn Puerto Rico because he felt the Americans on that island had shown him insufficient gratitude.[22]

In Libya—originally intended as a Red Sea Conspiracy nation, until it became clear that MBS could determine the course of its future without much input from its people—Trump, according to the *New York Times*, in 2019 "abruptly reversed American policy" by "issuing a statement endors[ing] a militia leader [Khalifa Hifter] who [was] battling to control Tripoli and depose the United Nations–backed government."[23] In addition to putting American rhetoric on the opposite side of the United Nations in a key geopolitical and military conflict, Trump's about-face once again saw him "publicly endorsing an aspiring strongman" whose "regional sponsors" were, unsurprisingly, Saudi Arabia, the United Arab Emirates, and Egypt.[24] The *Washington Post* notes that the conflict in Libya is "yet another civil war" fueled by "Saudi Arabia's reckless prince," adding, in reference to Saudi Arabia, the UAE, and Egypt, that "these Arab governments and Russia have deliberately sabotaged an international effort that had the support of the European Union, the African Union and the United States." The *Post* attaches Hifter's recent resurgence to a visit to Saudi Arabia, "where he was promised [by MBS and King Salman] millions of dollars in aid to pay for the [new military] operation" he was then planning.[25] Hifter, like MBS, has been credibly accused of war crimes by American and international media.[26]

In Iran, Trump continues his march toward war by ending the U.S. policy of offering sanctions waivers to countries that import Iranian oil—a decision sure to increase tensions in the Middle East and render an already economically devastated Iran even more isolated, desperate, and dangerous; more recently, Trump's secretary of state, Mike Pompeo, was heard telling members of Congress that "the 2001 AUMF [Authorization for Use of Military Force] might authorize [a] war on Iran."[27] Trump's decision on the sanctions waivers, like his ultimate decision on whether or not to go to war with Iran, stands to greatly enrich his allies MBS and MBZ—a fact Trump even alluded to in his announcement of the administration's decision on the waivers.[28]

Meanwhile, as Saudi Arabia faces the prospect of a gradual decline in oil revenues in the coming decades, Trump is aiding its turn to nuclear energy instead of the more obvious solution: solar power. As the *Bulletin of the Atomic Scientists* observes, "For sun-baked Saudi Arabia, the economical and obvious switch [from oil] is to solar energy, which also doesn't result in carbon emissions and can be used to reduce domestic consumption of oil and gas. The limited efforts in installing solar power capacity on the part of the Saudi government suggest that climate action and economics may not be the driving motivations for its extensive nuclear energy plan. Indeed, members of the Saudi regime have, on other occasions, made it clear that their interests in nuclear energy derive from the idea that it would help them acquire the capability to make nuclear weapons and match Iran, whose regional status is seen to have risen as a result of its uranium enrichment program."[29]

Trump's coddling of Saudi Arabia's foolish nuclear enterprise exponentially increases the odds of a cataclysmic nuclear war in the Middle East, as events in the late spring of 2019 have confirmed. In May, Iran declared it would pull out of parts of the nuclear deal it signed with the Obama administration in 2015—a deal the Trump administration had pulled out of in May 2018—including its uranium-enrichment restrictions, unless Europe moved quickly to counteract the devastating effects of Trump's newly imposed sanctions.[30] Days later, the United Arab Emirates and Saudi Arabia issued public allegations of Iranian sabotage of Saudi oil tankers; the allegations made reference to holes in tanker hulls, but there were no reports of casualties, no photographs of any damage, no details on the alleged weapon used to produce the holes, no claims of any oil spillage, and no claims of responsibility from Iran or a proxy authorized to speak for Iran.[31] The Saudis' and Emiratis' report of Iranian sabotage came just days after the two nations had communicated to U.S. intelligence that an Iranian attack might be imminent, an allegation that led Trump's administration to credulously move bombers and a heavily armed carrier group into a forward position in the Persian Gulf; meanwhile, the British deputy commander of coalition forces in Iraq and Syria was announcing that he had seen "no increased threat" from Iranian-backed forces in either country. For its part, Iran quickly denied any ill intent in the Gulf, and asserted that the Saudi and Emirati allegations were part of a "conspiracy" to provoke the United States into a war with Tehran.[32] These events led "national security experts [to] warn [that] the two countries [the United States and Iran] may be headed toward a military confrontation."[33]

While the Iranians have often not been good-faith actors in the Middle East, and have rarely given their Sunni neighbors or the United States much reason to trust their medium-term geopolitical designs, that President Trump withdrew from the Iran nuclear deal at a time when Iran was in compliance with it—and that he did so at the behest of men like MBS, MBZ, el-Sisi, and Netanyahu, who have proven themselves to be as faithless to rule of law as they are dangerous—doubly damages America's credibility as a good-faith broker in the many conflicts of the Middle East. As already noted, Trump's chief Israeli ally, Netanyahu, has implied publicly that he, Saudi Arabia, the UAE, and other allies (with many reasonably presuming he means allies in the White House) want a "war" with Iran.[34] It is difficult, therefore, to see in the events of early 2019 anything but a Trump administration–encouraged escalation of regional tensions that would have remained quelled had the United States not unilaterally backed out of its commitment to the Iranian nuclear deal.[35] This sense of a commitment dishonored and a hard-won reputation for honest brokerage sullied was only reinforced when, on May 13, 2019, the *New York Times* reported that the Trump administration was "review[ing] military plans against Iran," thus echoing Netanyahu and further raising the prospect of hostilities between the United States and Tehran breaking out prior to the 2020 presidential election.[36]

At home, Trump has installed a new attorney general, William Barr, whose recent holding that a president cannot obstruct justice was in early May disputed by more than one thousand former federal prosecutors of both political parties, who collectively declared that the evidence from the Mueller Report that Barr said did not rise to the level of obstruction of justice in fact provably did so.[37] Even the famously taciturn and retiring special counsel, Robert Mueller, could not help but angrily conclude, in a letter he must have been certain would become public, that Barr had done a disservice to the work of the special counsel's office through the DOJ's misrepresentations of its substance and context.[38] The Speaker of the House, Nancy Pelosi, has gone so far as to call Barr's April 2019 testimony before Congress on the subject of the Mueller Report a perjury in violation of the federal criminal code.[39] Many Americans—including many Americans who are attorneys—would agree with her. That Trump has now given Barr unprecedented oversight over the U.S. intelligence community, with the ability to declassify classified documents at will, can therefore cause nothing but concern to Americans who believe in the rule of law.[40] *Slate* has called Trump's move to give Barr broad new powers a "threat to national security," and doubtless many Americans—including many Americans who are national security experts—would agree with that assessment as well.[41]

Meanwhile, the increasingly unpredictable and idiosyncratically empowered Barr is seeing his conflicts of interest mount, with his son-in-law currently working in the White House counsel's office advising the president on the very investigations his father-in-law is overseeing, and his daughter working at the Financial Crimes Enforcement Network (Fin-CEN), the very agency that increasingly is at the center of what *Vanity Fair* calls "Russian intrigues" involving the Trump administration—including the pre-election referrals to the Treasury Department and the Federal Reserve that Trump adviser Dimitri Simes made on behalf of Kremlin agents Alexander Torshin and Maria Butina.[42] According to *Newsweek*, Barr even has conflicts of interest involving the Russians, with the magazine noting that "Barr's previous employers are connected to key subjects in the [special counsel's] probe . . . [and] his financial ties to companies linked to aspects of the Russia investigation raise questions about whether he should—like his predecessor, Jeff Sessions—recuse himself."[43] The media outlet references, in particular, a "public financial disclosure report [in which Barr] admits to working for a law firm that represented Russia's Alfa Bank and for a company whose co-founders allegedly have long-standing business ties to Russia. What's more, he received dividends from Vector Group, a holding company with deep financial ties to Russia. . . . [Vector's] president, Howard Lorber, brought Trump to Moscow in the 1990s to seek investment projects there. The trip is widely seen as the first of many attempts to establish a Trump Tower in Moscow."[44] In the midst of his conversations with Emin Agalarov about Kremlin agents coming to Trump Tower to offer incriminating information about Hillary Clinton, the man Donald Trump Jr. called wasn't his father or his sister, but Howard Lorber.[45]

These conflicts now sit atop other, more personal reasons one might imagine William Barr voluntarily accepting recusal from not just the Russia investigation but the counterintelligence probes and fourteen pending federal investigations that grew out of the work now formally completed by the special counsel's office. As *Vanity Fair* notes in February 2019, "Last June, [Barr] sent an unsolicited 20-page memo to the Justice Department calling the inquiry into potential obstruction of justice by Trump 'fatally misconceived' and Mueller's actions 'grossly irresponsible,' and insisting 'Mueller should not be permitted to demand that the President submit to interrogation about alleged obstruction.'"[46] It is clear, given how Trump has selected his appointees in the past—former acting attorney general Matt Whitaker being one example—that Barr's memo served as a job application of sorts for the new AG, and ultimately was critical to netting him Trump's nomination for the job; the likely collateral effect of writing such a memo to this president could not have been lost on as seasoned a D.C. operative as Barr. Nor could Barr have failed to appreciate the concern another recent move of his would cause ethicists the nation over: his receipt of an ethics waiver to oversee yet another scandal that could threaten the political future of the man who nominated him as attorney general, the 1MDB case involving allegations of potential criminal misconduct against Jho Low—allegations that could, in time, draw into their web Trump associates Barrack, Lorber, and Broidy.[47]

William Barr's evident hostility to conventional legal judgments and processes is of course mirrored by similar traits in appointees and advisers found throughout the Trump administration, which in spring 2019 began opposing all House subpoenas intended to further Democrats' investigative oversight, regardless of their purpose, scope, or target.[48] It is mirrored, too, in revelations about former deputy attorney general Rod Rosenstein, who despite overseeing a federal investigation that found substantial evidence that the president of the United States had run afoul of the law nevertheless secretly assured the president that he was "on his team" and that he could "land the plane" for Trump with respect to the special counsel's Russia investigation.[49] Indeed, Rosenstein was privately assuring Trump that he was not a "target" of the Mueller investigation even when he knew the president was exactly that with respect to at least the question of obstruction; Rosenstein's were a clandestine set of promises to Trump that seemed to presage his idiosyncratic and ahistorical conclusion, shared with and aided and abetted by Barr, that obstruction cannot be charged without an underlying crime. And yet, just days after the Mueller Report's publication, the DOJ did precisely what both Barr and Rosenstein had publicly claimed it could not do with Trump: in an unrelated investigation, it charged an American citizen with obstruction without identifying any underlying crime.[50] That in Trump's case the underlying crimes obscured by Trump's obstruction had in fact already been identified by the special counsel, the Southern District of New York, the Eastern District of Virginia, and the U.S. attorney's office in D.C.—cases involving Russian hacking, Russian disinformation, Trump's own campaign finance crimes, the financial and obstructive crimes of Trump's campaign manager and deputy campaign manager, and the crimes of two Trump national security advisers—was of no moment to Barr or Rosenstein.

In the face of such unusual legal and administrative wrangling, even Mueller eventually felt compelled to speak out, giving a ten-minute statement to the press on May 29, 2019, in which he underscored that the chief reason the special counsel's office did not reach a final conclusion on obstruction with respect to President Trump was that "under longstanding Department policy, a president cannot be charged with a federal crime while he is in office . . . [e]ven if the charge is kept under seal and hidden from the public. . . . Charging the president with a crime was therefore not an option we could consider." On the other hand, Mueller noted, the DOJ opinion precluding the indictment of a sitting president "explicitly permits the investigation of a sitting president because it is important to preserve evidence while memories are fresh and documents available . . . [and] says that the Constitution requires a process other than the criminal justice system to formally accuse a sitting president of wrongdoing."[51] That the special counsel was referring to impeachment was lost on no one.

Perhaps it is little surprise, then, with this degradation of moral reasoning at the highest levels of American government, that Trump's current and former inner circle has begun to make its own controversial views and ambitions, many of an international scale, better known. According to The Intercept, Erik Prince and Steve Bannon are now business partners, selling arms directly to the Emiratis—this time an updated version of Prince's original idea for a militarized crop duster, with "Israeli-made avionics and surveillance software for geo-locating targets on the ground."[52] It is unclear whether Prince will face consequences for Congress's recent perjury referral to the DOJ; The Intercept opines that, "given his wealth and political ties, it may be that the Department of Justice will never have the political fortitude to thoroughly investigate Prince for defense brokering and trafficking violations, or to challenge his questionable ties to China's intelligence service . . . [but] the FBI is currently probing Prince's work at Frontier Services Group, with a team assigned from the Washington field office. It is unclear whether the investigation is a continuation of the 2016 probe or stems from the Mueller investigation."[53] Certainly, Prince's current relationship with Bannon casts doubt on the possibility, raised implicitly by the Mueller Report, that Bannon had betrayed Prince, or vice versa, with the contradictory testimonies they gave to the special counsel's office. The evidence suggests that, more probably, the two men have worked in tandem on U.S. foreign policy issues even as they have, in their federal interrogatories, implied that their actions on the campaign and during the transition were not coordinated.

At a Time 100 gala in April 2019, Jared Kushner minimized the massive disinformation campaign the Kremlin deployed during the 2016 general election, describing a coordinated assault on America's information architecture that infected as many as 135 million U.S. voters as nothing more than "a couple Facebook ads"; he made no mention of the fact, revealed in the *Independent,* that the Trump administration has been running through the State Department a taxpayer-funded anti-Iran troll factory nearly identical to the Kremlin's Internet Research Agency—with the difference that Trump's trolls also "target[ ] American citizens critical of the administration's hardline Iran policy and accuse[ ] [U.S.] critics of being loyal to the Tehran regime."[54] Kushner's recalcitrance in recognizing the awesome influence of Russian (or American) psy-ops in this decade, and the continued danger these operations pose in 2020 and beyond, may be connected to the fact that, increasingly, Americans are also being subjected to psy-ops coordinated by Kushner's autocratic friend, MBS. Indeed, after the release of the Mueller Report, thousands upon thousands of Twitter bots descended upon unsuspecting Americans with the message that the report revealed a massive deep-state "hoax"—Twitter bots that were ultimately traced to pro-MBS forces within Saudi Arabia.[55] That the Saudis increasingly have the hacking capabilities they do because of dangerous Israeli technology sold to them by private Israeli companies with the blessing of Netanyahu's government (expressly because that government wants the Saudis as allies in future campaigns, political and otherwise, against Iran) only underscores how complicated America's foreign policy debates will become in the years ahead.

As America engages with these new and increasingly fraught assessments of our geopolitical position, MBS is in Riyadh beheading his own citizens by the dozens—including, recently, an incoming freshman at Western Michigan University—and torturing others before executing them, including a young man who was ultimately beheaded for sending WhatsApp messages about an anti-MBS protest when he was sixteen.[56] Yet MBS is the sort of scoundrel beside whom America's foreign policy now sleeps.

In exchange for all of the above concessions of our national dignity and foundational values, America has gotten nothing more than a "peace plan devised by Jared Kushner that wholly depends upon—of all things—the creation of new 'desalination plants' in Gaza."[57] According to investigative journalist Vicky Ward, author of *Kushner Inc.,* under Kushner's grand plan the Saudis and Emiratis would "provide economic assistance to the Palestinians . . . [and build] an oil pipeline from Saudi Arabia to Gaza, where refineries and a shipping terminal" would then be built, along with the new desalination plants to spur employment.[58] *New York Magazine* calls the "alleged" plan "preposterous," noting that it asks Jordan to "give territory to the Palestinian authority," and in return, per Ward's book, "Jordan would get land from Saudi Arabia, and that country would get back two Red Sea islands it gave Egypt to administer in 1950."[59] All told, *New York Magazine* concludes, the plan "would involve no less than five countries (plus Palestine) coordinating to give aid or renegotiate boundaries in the most politically convoluted region on the planet . . . [while] not requir[ing] the Netanyahu government—a close ally of Kushner's—to make any significant concessions."[60] In the balance, the magazine observes, the plan would create "inefficient" desalination plants that produce "1.5 times more unusable brine than potable water."[61] Has America thrown over its principles and its foreign policy—not to mention the decades-long hope of a two-state solution in Israel and the Occupied Territories—for a few strategically ludicrous and likely purposeless desalination plants in Gaza?

Even as America's newly amateurish foreign policy descends into meltdown, the matter of whether Trump or anyone tied to him poses a national security threat to the U.S. by a preponderance of the evidence due to their communications with Kremlin agents or other foreign nationals remains unresolved. It is unclear, indeed, whether America even understands the dangers that such a widespread compromising of our nation's governmental apparatuses would pose. In a 2019 filing in the Maria Butina case, the Department of Justice opined about "Russia's broader scheme to acquire information and establish relationships and communication channels that can be exploited to the Russian Federation's benefit. . . . Acquiring information valuable to a foreign power does not necessarily involve collecting classified documents or engaging in cloak-and-dagger activities. Something as basic as the identification of people who have the ability to influence policy in a foreign power's favor is extremely attractive to those powers. The identification could form the basis of other forms of intelligence operations, or targeting, in the future."[62] According to the DOJ, "Such channels bypass open channels of diplomacy and can be used to win concessions or influence positions that contradict declared official policies articulated by governments. . . . [These channels and identifications are] of substantial intelligence value to the Russian government, and Russian intelligence services will be able to use this information for years to come in their efforts to spot and assess Americans who may be susceptible to recruitment as foreign intelligence assets."[63]

By this metric, the third Russian election-interference operation—one that American media never identifies as such—was a coordinated effort to infiltrate the Republicans' 2016 presidential campaign in the hope of future Kremlin-friendly policy victories. That that effort was wildly successful during both the pre-election, transition, and post-election periods is now clear. And indeed, this particular threat continues, as the Trump administration periodically drops sanctions on new Russian individuals and companies and promotes within its ranks men and women whose ties to Russian interests either have never been explored or have been ignored. As of May 2019, the Trump administration was considering making Monica Crowley the spokeswoman for Steve Mnuchin's Treasury Department, even though Crowley has in the past lobbied on behalf of Victor Pinchuk, a Soviet-born Ukrainian businessman whom *Mother Jones* describes as a man "whose large payments . . . to prominent Americans, including Donald Trump, and apparent promotion of pro-Russian interests drew scrutiny from special counsel Robert Mueller."[64] Crowley has also worked with Pinchuk on a "peace deal" for the Ukraine—with "peace deal" a euphemism for, as we have learned from the many covert Kremlin operations described in the Mueller Report, Putin's duplicitous efforts to achieve his primary policy goal: sanctions relief.[65]

Trump has also brought potential witnesses against him in future criminal or congressional proceedings into his fold. For instance, despite claims by former Trump communications adviser Michael Caputo that Richard Nixon's son-in-law Ed Cox and Trump were at loggerheads about Trump's political future in 2013 and 2014—when the evidence suggests that in fact Cox, who is closely connected to both Dimitri Simes's CNI and Carter Page, ultimately facilitated Trump's run—in May 2019 Trump will effectively confirm Cox's importance to his political operation by bringing him aboard his reelection campaign via the Trump Victory Committee.[66]

As the *Hill* reports, "The role with Trump's reelection effort provides a soft landing spot for Cox."[67] Indeed, the Trump Victory Committee has a history of welcoming individuals whose testimony could be damaging to Trump, including, most notably, Elliott Broidy, the committee's longtime director.[68] On a broader scale, Trump has sought to reward those with whom his team colluded by, per *Politico* and congressional Democrats, "violating a law requiring a report on human rights abuses in Russia"; specifically, Trump's administration is now five months late in delivering a report required by the Magnitsky Act and other Russian sanctions regimes and, moreover, is "misleading Congress about the reason for the delay."[69]

Despite all of these conflagrations at home and abroad, the House Permanent Select Committee on Intelligence has still not received a comprehensive briefing on the ongoing counterintelligence investigation into the Trump campaign, transition, and administration.[70] The result is a 2020 American electorate not fully informed on who it can trust to advance America's interests rather than those of our enemies.

Trump's venality, penchant for deception, and disregard for American values and the nation's security interests in dealings abroad can persist for only so long without severely destabilizing America's rule of law, its democratic principles, and, finally, its abiding self-identity. Already we are seeing historic erosion in the American spirit—one that can be traced to a leader whose first principles are fundamentally not in line with those of the nation he leads. Most troubling—not just in Trump himself and his inner circle but also in his enablers in Washington—is a celebration of willful ignorance incompatible with American greatness. Sen. Angus King summarizes Trump's attitude toward receiving intelligence from American intelligence agencies, which are among the world's best, in this way: "Don't tell me information I don't want to hear."[71] Just so, Trump's most ardent supporters inside and outside the Beltway can now regularly be found on social media and elsewhere referring to the backbone of American journalism as "fake news" worthy of little more than a sneer. Encompassed in this preposterous moniker are such television outlets as CNN, MSNBC, and the broadcast networks; in print, the *New York Times* and the *Washington Post*; and online, the digital editions of both these outlets and Pulitzer Prize–winning newcomers such as *BuzzFeed News*. Once-valued standards of conduct are everywhere being diminished; for instance, it was recently revealed that the Trump administration hid from Congress emoluments-clause-violative leases to foreign governments at Trump-branded properties, including a luxury apartment now occupied by Saudi government officials.[72] A Trump appointee to the Department of Housing and Urban Development announced publicly—on social media, no less—that she "honestly doesn't care" about abiding by the federal Hatch Act preventing political activity by government employees. It's not clear why she would, either, given that it is hardly ever enforced or even gesturally attended to: not when the White House press secretary is repeatedly accused of violating it; not when top Trump adviser Kellyanne Conway repeatedly violates it, taunting her critics with lines like, "Let me know when the jail sentence starts"; and not when members of the New York field office of the FBI routinely leaked intimate details of the ongoing Clinton email investigation to conservative media in October 2016.[73] Even the universal conclusion of America's highly regarded intelligence agencies that the Russians interfered with the 2016 presidential election is a subject for public mockery by the president and his allies. During an early May 2019 phone call with Putin, Trump and the Russian president commiserated about Mueller's Russia investigation being predicated on a "hoax"—a shared assessment that Trump immediately thereafter merrily outlined to American media.[74] In view of this dangerous accord between two men whose mutual admiration has never been sufficiently explained or investigated, it is increasingly difficult to retain our faith in those deeply held American values that once distinguished us so readily from the world's autocracies.

In view of all the foregoing, it appears that former FBI director James Comey was right when he wrote in the *New York Times* that "Mr. Trump eats your soul in small bites."[75] He neglected to add that the same can be said of the very soul of our nation, and that while the spirit of a dynamic and historically progressive people can be replenished, it is not, finally, inexhaustible. At some point America crosses a proverbial point of no return, beyond which a great nation risks being consumed by animuses, false equivalencies, and perversions of revered institutions that are incompatible with the complex fabric of our history and culture. I fear that a time is approaching when, as Americans and as America, we will be rendered permanently unrecognizable to ourselves and to anyone else in the world.

At the end of December 2018, the United States for the first time in its history became one of the five most dangerous nations in the world for journalists.[76] We cross this dark threshold at a time when the nation's journalistic ecosystem simultaneously produces too much quality investigative reporting for even the nation's best analysts to synthesize; too little accountability for corporate journalism that places profits above ethics; too many stories where commitment to evenhandedness masks an unwillingness to render conventional journalistic and even moral judgments about truth and falsehood, integrity and moral degradation; and too little attention for innovations in the journalistic enterprise that might allow the profession to survive, even if generatively transformed, amid the bewildering transfigurations of a digitized and increasingly virtual (if too rarely virtuous) world.

Recently, one of Trump's attorneys and closest campaign advisers, Rudy Giuliani, announced on national television that receiving stolen material from a hostile foreign power during a presidential election is hereafter, as his view was summarized by NBC News, "fair game"—a new doctrine of political corruption that former acting attorney general Sally Yates told NBC is "shocking" and a "devolution" of American patriotism.[77] The FBI has begun sounding the alarm about a 2020 Russian election-interference operation it calls a "significant counterintelligence threat," though there is little evidence the Trump administration takes this threat seriously.[78] The chance that Americans will have little faith in the integrity of our future national elections is now higher than it has ever been—not merely because of cyberintrusions and social media disinformation, but also because of the rise of doctored multimedia "supercuts" and "deep fakes"—all of which promise disastrous consequences for both the spirit and the level of engagement of America's electorate. The *New Yorker* quotes Tamir Pardo, the director of Israel's chief spy agency Mossad from 2011 to 2016, as saying of the Russian election-interference operation in 2016—which appears to have received significant assists from Israeli, Saudi, and Emirati entities—"It was the biggest Russian win ever. Without shooting one bullet, American society was torn apart."[79] Yet U.S. media still spends more time dissecting Trump's tweets than seeking to curate the hundreds of major-media investigative reports from around the world that confirm that it is Trump who is, piece by piece, dissecting our nation's foreign policy and domestic institutions.

Trump's influence on the national psyche is so powerful that the violence of his language and his psychology has transformed into actual violence in the spaces to which he sends his words and ideations. Indeed, U.S. counties that hosted a Trump rally in 2016 saw a 226 percent increase in hate crimes in the ensuing twelve months.[80] It's no wonder, writes Tamir Pardo, that when Russia considered its anti-Western geopolitical ambitions, it "took a look at the political map in Washington, 'and thought, which candidate would we like to have sitting in the White House? Who will help us achieve our goals? And they chose him [Trump]. From that moment, they deployed a system [of bots] for the length of the elections, and ran him for president.'"[81] It makes sense that Putin's Kremlin would reach this conclusion—and that MBS would, and MBZ, and Benjamin Netanyahu—not merely because the evidence tells us they did but because Trump shares with these men a certain sort of contempt for legal process and conventional civics, and an avarice for ever-greater authority over others. In time, a man of such a mind-set decides these goals can best be achieved by doing violence to humankind's most prized values.

There are signs that a change is coming, however.

According to the *Atlantic*, "dozens" of federal whistleblowers—"a small army" of them—have now contacted Congress about malfeasance in the Trump administration.[82] With Julian Assange now in custody in the United Kingdom for bail-jumping, there remains a possibility that he can be extradited to the United States and questioned, under the threat of pending indictments in the Eastern District of Virginia—including one under the Espionage Act—about his contacts with the Trump campaign, the Kremlin, or cutouts acting as agents for either.[83] Assange has extradition-related hearings scheduled in London for May 30 and June 12, but the presiding magistrate in his case says the extradition issue will likely not be resolved for "many months."[84] George Nader has signed a cooperation agreement with the FBI that is so favorable to him, the *New Yorker* reports, that a Nader representative told the magazine, "Someone who has this kind of immunity has no incentive to lie"; this offers some hope that Nader, especially after his recent arrest on new child pornography charges, will be fully transparent with U.S. intelligence agents about what he did, and for whom, from 2014 onward.[85] Andrew Miller, a longtime Roger Stone associate who fought a special counsel's office grand jury subpoena for months, has now agreed to testify, raising the prospects of a successful prosecution of Stone this fall—and the possibility of a Stone cooperation agreement that will see the GOP political operative finally giving the lie to certain of Trump's statements about what he knew about WikiLeaks and when, and from whom.[86] Cindy Yang, the now-infamous Florida massage parlor owner, has conceded in a legal filing that she was selling Chinese nationals access to Trump's home in Florida, suggesting the possibility of future revelations about Trump-Chinese collusion involving Trump not just selling access but possibly cutting deals to ensure favorable treatment for his and his family's brands abroad. Indeed, the Chinese government approved sixteen Ivanka Trump trademarks just forty-eight hours before Election Day in 2016.[87]

Meanwhile, at least fourteen ongoing federal criminal investigations involving evidence uncovered by the special counsel's office—and witnesses in federal cooperation agreements in a position to reveal new counterintelligence threats resulting from Trump campaign collusion and possible criminal conduct—offer hope that the full story of the Trump campaign, transition, and administration can eventually be brought to light. For instance, as reported by the *Daily Beast*, "Rick Gates, the former campaign aide to Donald Trump, is cooperating with Special Counsel Robert Mueller's probe into whether individuals from the Middle East worked with the Trump campaign to influence the election, according to two individuals with first-hand knowledge of the investigation."[88] The digital media outlet adds that the repeated delays in Gates's federal sentencing hearing are due to ongoing investigations with which Gates is involved, and that "one of the ongoing investigations is into possible Middle Eastern election influence."[89] New evidence suggests that it may have been George Birnbaum, Benjamin Netanyahu's longtime adviser, who acted as the Trump campaign's most consequential intermediary to Zamel's Psy-Group, rather than Rick Gates, a possibility that would even more powerfully expand the Trump-Russia scandal to include the Israeli government as well as Saudi and Emirati agents; meanwhile, *Politico* reports that Senate investigators have found a witness—a British security consultant named Walter Soriano—who may be able to establish significant links between Oleg Deripaska, Viktor Vekselberg, Wikistrat, and Psy-Group.[90] Specifically, Soriano may be able to more closely tie Joel Zamel to his former employer Deripaska.[91]

On the document-production front, Congress has had recent successes in its efforts to get Trump financial documents from Deutsche Bank and Trump's accountant, Mazars.[92] And the doggedness of American journalists is likely to, in time, rescue forgotten stories from the domestic and international news archive and reconnect them with today's latest news developments. For instance, in March 2018 a *Business Insider* article revealed that Trump was offered a $2 billion deal by an old Emirati business partner days before his 2017 inauguration—and that while he "rejected" the offer, the Trump Organization's concurrent dealings abroad raise questions about why Trump found this offer particularly politically dangerous. It is stories like these that deserve new life as America turns its attention to pre-election and transition-period Trump-Saudi and Trump-Emirati collusion, especially as it intersects with Trump-Russia collusion and Benjamin Netanyahu's evident support for Trump's presidential candidacy.[93]

And yet, particularly in the absence of any Republican appetite for holding Trump accountable for his actions—other than the presently isolated support for impeachment from Rep. Justin Amash (R-MI)—it may be too late for America to conclusively shift back toward equal justice for all and honorable bipartisan governance in Washington.[94] So much described in this book has already progressed to what appears, at first blush, to be points of no return. In April 2019, Bloomberg published a satellite photo of Saudi Arabia's nearly completed first-ever nuclear reactor (at King Abdulaziz City for Science and Technology in Riyadh), a construction that marks the beginning of the Saudi-Iranian arms race and its attendant "risk[ ] of the [Saudi] kingdom using [nuclear] technology without signing up to the international rules governing the industry." In Egypt, el-Sisi's power is now unchallenged and absolute. The Emiratis have developed a complex ecosystem of assassination squads operating across the Middle East. Benjamin Netanyahu won reelection in Israel (notwithstanding that he was thereafter unable to form a coalition government, and will have to stand for reelection again in September 2019). And Trump is planning to send 10,000 more troops to the Middle East, in what could presage U.S. preparations for a military conflict with Iran.[95] There are also other indications that things are worse behind the scenes than Americans realize, and perhaps more such things than U.S. journalism can readily uncover in the short term. In late April 2019, for instance, Americans discovered that former secretary of defense Jim Mattis had to routinely ignore directives from the White House—an astounding, perhaps even unprecedented recourse for a respected lifelong soldier atop the country's military infrastructure—in order to save the world from further bloodshed in Iran, North Korea, and Syria.[96] This is news that should send a chill down the spine of the world.

That America will eventually learn the full story of what was done in 2015 and 2016, in locations around the world, to secure the election of Donald Trump as U.S. president is certain. Whether that discovery will come in a year, a decade, or a century remains unclear. Fortunately, there is evidence that, before formally ending his investigation, Mueller was looking with great intensity at the "grand bargain" this book describes— and clearly, from his report, he was willing to contribute his findings to other federal investigations and to counterintelligence probes that remain ongoing and will, presumably, report their results to someone eventually. Alongside these efforts, there is every indication that the president's legal strategy, which comprises simply ignoring congressional subpoenas and urging all the administration's allies to do the same, will not hold water before either the lower courts of the nation or the Supreme Court. The combination of business-record revelations and counterintelligence findings these separate developments could portend may well make all that this book has disclosed merely the opening chapter of the sorriest story of corruption and treachery this country has ever known. If this account has done anything to signpost that glimmer of light somewhere down the road—to remind us that America's story remains one of inquisitiveness, courage, and renewal—then it has done all it can.

ACKNOWLEDGMENTS

Any work of curatorial journalism is necessarily a celebration of journalism. While the very fact of curatorial journalism confirms that not all journalism is reportage, and not every journalist participates in the common activities of a reporter—accessing spaces, developing sources, perceiving what others miss, and using institutional resources to disseminate what sources relay and senses detect—curatorial journalism does use existing reportage as its unit of measure, rather than primary sources. To fully encompass the stories it pursues, it therefore relies just as much as conventional journalistic practice does on journalists, journalistic institutions, and the journalistic ethos on which both journalists and journalistic institutions depend.

That being the case, this book would not have been possible without the courageous and tireless contributions of both hardworking journalists and the ever-embattled journalistic organizations that support them. Even more than a curator, curatorial journalism requires investigative reporters of every mode and method and the media institutions around the world that give them resources and encouragement. *Proof of Conspiracy* was, in this sense, a team effort whose team I will never have the pleasure of meeting in full, as it includes superlative journalists from the *New York Times*, the *Washington Post*, the *Wall Street Journal*, the *New Yorker*, the *Atlantic*, *Mother Jones*, *Newsweek*, *Time*, *Politico*, *Just Security*, *The Intercept*, *BuzzFeed News*, ProPublica, Vox, the Associated Press, Reuters, McClatchy DC, Bloomberg, ABC News, CBS News, NBC News, CNN, MSNBC, NPR, the *Guardian*, the *Independent*, *Le Monde*, Al Jazeera, *Al-Monitor*, the *Middle East Eye*, the *Lebanon Daily Star*, the *Times of Israel*, the *Jerusalem Post*, *Haaretz*, and the scores of other outlets in the United States and around the world whose employees made telling this decade- and continent-spanning story possible. I wish I could name and thank each journalist upon whose work this book relies; instead, I commend to readers the online endnotes to this text, which will direct you to the best conventional reportage yet done on the most important political story of this century—certainly in the United States, and perhaps anywhere in the world.

Fortunately, many members of the team behind *Proof of Conspiracy* are well known to me—their endurance, their insight, their good humor, and their many erudite contributions. As ever, the foremost of all these team members is my wife, whose energies produced this book as much as my own or anyone else's. Without my wife's support across many difficult months, and without her wisdom and love across many years, this book would not exist. Whatever of me is in the world, including this book, runs through her. That is true now, and it will always be true.

My family and friends, as ever, abide me, for which grace—and for all they are in themselves—they have my love.

My agent, Jeff Silberman, is the kind of friend, adviser, and advocate an author dreams of finding sometime during the course of a long writing career. I am fortunate beyond deserving that we found each other so early in the Trump administration and, more broadly, in my life as a nonfiction author. Jeff has been a constant and trusted companion throughout every stage of the writing of this book.

The team at St. Martin's Press did yeoman's work to get this book to readers on an ambitious schedule; their stalwart commitment to this story being told is what made its telling possible. My deepest thanks to Michael Flamini, Rebecca Lang, Martin Quinn, Hannah Phillips, Jonathan Hollingsworth, Rafal Gibek, Thomas Mis, Steven Seighman, Paul Hochman, and Gwen Hawkes. I owe a great debt, as well, to the four eagle-eyed fact-checkers who scoured this book for untold hours: Liz Mazucci, Ivan Solotaroff, Kristina Rebelo, and Keith Schneider. And the inimitable Robert Petkoff has earned not just my thanks but my deep wonder and admiration for performing the audiobook edition of *Proof of Conspiracy*—as I know that it, like *Proof of Collusion*, which he also performed, is a book (length-wise, grammatically, and semantically) that would test any performer's patience.

My thanks go out as well to those in the media who looked past the unusual method and format of *Proof of Collusion* and *Proof of Conspiracy* to see that these texts want only what we all do: for our democracy to survive the dark deeds—some done in darkness, some in broad daylight—these two books detail. I'd like to offer special thanks, therefore, to the journalists and others working in media without whom these books would not have found an audience or this author a voice: Virginia Heffernan, Scott Carter, Mary Knowles, Bill Maher, John Fugelsang, Shane Singh, Dean Obeidallah, Chelsea Braun, Mark Siegel, Aaron Gell, Andy Fitch, Christoph Scheuermann, Michael Bloch, Nat Johnson, John Vause, Alex Blasdel, Dimi Reider, Laura Davis, and the many others I have not named whose faith in curatorial journalism specifically and in innovation and investigation more broadly has been an inspiration. These generous folks—like the others working in media at the news organizations I've mentioned—are champions of the people who stand in the breach between America and those who would end it.

I would be remiss if I did not thank the readers of this book and its predecessor; your patience with the idiosyncrasies of each has been, I hope, rewarded. I am inspired by your curiosity, commitment, and engagement. America will need the full measure of these qualities from all its citizens in the months and years ahead.

Finally, my thanks to Natalie Mehring, Victoria Legrand, and Alex Scally for their art. It smoothed many a rough path I encountered on the way to this book's publication, and reminded me, when I needed it, that beauty survives small men.

INDEX